Computational Methods and Applications for Numerical Analysis

Computational Methods and Applications for Numerical Analysis

Editors

Fajie Wang
Ji Lin

MDPI • Basel • Beijing • Wuhan • Barcelona • Belgrade • Manchester • Tokyo • Cluj • Tianjin

Editors
Fajie Wang
Qingdao University
Qingdao, China

Ji Lin
Hohai University
Nanjing, China

Editorial Office
MDPI
St. Alban-Anlage 66
4052 Basel, Switzerland

This is a reprint of articles from the Special Issue published online in the open access journal *Mathematics* (ISSN 2227-7390) (available at: https://www.mdpi.com/journal/mathematics/special_issues/Computational_Methods_Applications_Numerical_Analysis).

For citation purposes, cite each article independently as indicated on the article page online and as indicated below:

LastName, A.A.; LastName, B.B.; LastName, C.C. Article Title. *Journal Name* **Year**, *Volume Number*, Page Range.

ISBN 978-3-0365-8284-9 (Hbk)
ISBN 978-3-0365-8285-6 (PDF)

Contents

About the Editors

Fajie Wang

Fajie Wang is a professor at the College of Mechanical and Electrical Engineering, Qingdao University, China. He was awarded a DAAD—K.C. Wong Postdoctoral Fellowship, and is a member of the Academic Committee of the International Conference on Building Energy, Environment, and Sustainable Development.

His research activities include computational mechanics, machine learning, optimum structural design, and fractal and fractional modeling. More than 80 of his papers with more than 1400 citations (Google Scholar) have been published in international journals, such as *Computer Methods in Applied Mechanics and Engineering, International Journal for Numerical Methods in Engineering, International Journal of Heat and Mass Transfer*, etc. Among them, eight papers have been selected as ESI highly cited papers and four papers have been the ESI hot papers. He has conducted more than 10 national and provincial projects.

Ji Lin

Ji Lin has been a professor at the College of Mechanics and Materials, Hohai University, China, since 2020. He completed his bachelor's degree in Mathematics in 2009 and received his Ph.D. in Engineering Mechanics from Hohai University, China, in 2014. Currently, he is severing as a member or on the committee of several provincial and international scientific societies.

Prof. Lin's research activities include computational mechanics, computational mathematics, software development, etc. His overall research output has culminated in more than 100 publications and one book in internationally respected journals which have been cited more than 1900 times by researchers. Among them, seven papers have been selected as ESI highly cited papers. He is the PI of two projects funded by the NSFC and has conducted more than 15 provincial projects.

Preface to "Computational Methods and Applications for Numerical Analysis"

The rapid development in computer technology has provided the direction for utilizing computational methods to solve complex engineering problems through numerical analysis. With their immense computing power and storage capabilities, computers have made it possible to perform numerical computations and simulations with high accuracy and reliability. The development of computational methods for numerical analysis can be traced back to the early 20th century. Over time, as computer hardware and software have advanced, researchers have devised more high-performance computing techniques to enhance the accuracy and reliability of computations. The most commonly used numerical algorithms include the finite element method, the boundary element method, meshless methods, and the neural network algorithm, among others.

The applications of computational methods and numerical analysis encompass a wide range of disciplines and fields. Numerical analysis has extensive applications in science and engineering. It enables the simulation and analysis of complex systems, including structural mechanics, fluid dynamics, acoustic wave propagation, electromagnetic fields, etc. Furthermore, it is significant in computer science and artificial intelligence, such as in image processing, pattern recognition, machine learning, and neural network construction, and it facilitates the solving of complex optimization problems, the training of neural networks, and autonomous decision-making. By utilizing numerical computations, researchers and practitioners can address complex mathematical problems, simulate and predict various phenomena, optimize system designs, and provide decision support. The broad scope of numerical analysis highlights its indispensable role in furthering scientific knowledge and technological advancements.

The present book contains the 20 articles accepted for publication to the Special Issue "Computational Methods and Applications for Numerical Analysis" of the MDPI "Mathematics" journal. The 20 articles, which appear in the present book in the order that they were published in, Volumes 10 (2022) and 11 (2023) of the journal, involve the theory, algorithms, programming, software, numerical simulation, and/or novel applications of computational methods to solve problems in engineering, science, and other disciplines related to computations. These topics include finite element methods, finite difference methods, meshless/meshfree methods, physics-informed neural networks, interpolation, approximation, optimization, numerical methods for ordinary/partial differential equations, etc. Their applications include crack propagation, acoustic analysis, elastodynamic analysis, free vibration analysis, structure and topology optimization, fractional equations, the eigenvalue problem, inverse problems, etc.

Numerical analysis is an increasingly important link between pure mathematics and its application in science and technology. It is hoped that the book will be interesting and useful for those working in the area of numerical analysis, as well as for those with a proper mathematical background and willing to become familiar with novel applications of computational techniques, which have rapidly developed nowadays.

As a Guest Editor of the Special Issue, I have had the privilege of working with and contributing to the MDPI "Mathematics" journal, and it has been a valuable experience. Furthermore, I am grateful to the authors of the papers for their outstanding research work, to the reviewers for their valuable comments toward the improvement of the submitted works, and to the administrative staff of the MDPI publications for the support to complete this project.

Fajie Wang and Ji Lin
Editors

mathematics

MDPI

Article

A Simple, Accurate and Semi-Analytical Meshless Method for Solving Laplace and Helmholtz Equations in Complex Two-Dimensional Geometries

Xingxing Yue, Buwen Jiang, Xiaoxuan Xue and Chao Yang *

College of Materials Science and Engineering, Qingdao University, Qingdao 266071, China; qdxxy90@qdu.edu.cn (X.Y.); Buwen_Jiang_qdu@163.com (B.J.); Xiaoxuan_Xue_qdu@163.com (X.X.)
* Correspondence: yangchao@qdu.edu.cn

Abstract: A localized virtual boundary element–meshless collocation method (LVBE-MCM) is proposed to solve Laplace and Helmholtz equations in complex two-dimensional (2D) geometries. "Localized" refers to employing the moving least square method to locally approximate the physical quantities of the computational domain after introducing the traditional virtual boundary element method. The LVBE-MCM is a semi-analytical and domain-type meshless collocation method that is based on the fundamental solution of the governing equation, which is different from the traditional virtual boundary element method. When it comes to 2D problems, the LVBE-MCM only needs to calculate the numerical integration on the circular virtual boundary. It avoids the evaluation of singular/strong singular/hypersingular integrals seen in the boundary element method. Compared to the difficulty of selecting the virtual boundary and evaluating singular integrals, the LVBE-MCM is simple and straightforward. Numerical experiments, including irregular and doubly connected domains, demonstrate that the LVBE-MCM is accurate, stable, and convergent for solving both Laplace and Helmholtz equations.

Keywords: localized meshless collocation method; virtual boundary element; fundamental solution; Laplace equations; Helmholtz equations

MSC: 35J05; 35J25; 65N35

Citation: Yue, X.; Jiang, B.; Xue, X.; Yang, C. A Simple, Accurate and Semi-Analytical Meshless Method for Solving Laplace and Helmholtz Equations in Complex Two-Dimensional Geometries. *Mathematics* **2022**, *10*, 833. https://doi.org/10.3390/math10050833

Academic Editor: Whye-Teong Ang

Received: 26 January 2022
Accepted: 3 March 2022
Published: 5 March 2022

1. Introduction

The boundary element method (BEM) [1,2] is a well-known numerical method that has become an alternative to domain methods such as the finite element method (FEM) [3,4] for the simulation of certain physical problems. The core of this method is to accurately solve singular integrals, especially nearly singular, strongly singular, and hypersingular integrals, among others. Substantial efforts have been devoted to developing and applying efficient estimation techniques for such integrals. Lutz [5] proposed a special Gaussian-type numerical integral to calculate the singular and nearly singular integrals. Johnston and Elliott [6] proposed a sinh transformation to evaluate nearly singular integrals. Niu and Zhou [7,8] suggested that the asymptotic expansion of the kernel function with respect to the local co-ordinates should be employed to address singular integrals. Besides these methods, there are other techniques that can be used to deal with various singular integrals. Although they were proven to be the effective strategies, these methods are often time consuming, tedious, and expensive.

In recent years, the virtual boundary element method (VBEM) [9–13] has been proposed to overcome the above shortcomings. The VBEM introduces the virtual boundary to avoid the calculation of singular integrals and inherits the semi-analytical and high-accuracy features of the BEM. Sun and Yao [14] used the VBEM to successfully solve thin plate elastic obstacle problems. Yao et al. [10,15] used the VBEM to simulate magnetoelectroelastic and piezoelectric problems. Yang et al. [16] and Liu et al. [17] resolved three-dimensional inverse heat conduction problems using the VBEM. As a boundary-type scheme with global discretization, however, the VBEM encounters challenges when simulating large-scale and/or high-dimensional problems.

More recently, the localization of boundary-type meshless methods have received considerable attention, and various localized meshless methods [18–23] have been proposed to solve mathematical and mechanical problems, such as the generalized finite difference method (GFDM) [24,25], the localized method of fundamental solutions (LMFS) [26,27], the local knot method (LKM) [28,29], and the localized singular boundary method (LSBM) [30,31]. Unlike traditional boundary-type methods, these methods are not only simple, accurate, and easy-to-program, but also suitable for large-scale simulations in complicated domains. On the other hand, boundary-type meshless methods encounter many difficult issues. Similar to the fundamental solution method, the VBEM uses fundamental solutions as the basis functions and requires a virtual boundary outside of the physical domain to avoid source singularity. The selection of this artificial boundary is still a well-known tricky issue in spite of the great deal of effort that has been made to address this problem [32,33], especially in terms of complex geometries.

Motivated by the above works using localized methods, we establish a localized numerical framework for the VBEM in this paper, which we called the localized virtual boundary element–meshless collocation method (LVBE-MCM). The accuracy and effectiveness of the LVBE-MCM was verified via its ability to solve Laplace and Helmholtz equations in complex 2D domains. In the traditional VBEM, it is difficult to determine the position and shape of virtual boundaries in the complex domain because these boundaries have a certain impact on the calculation accuracy. On the contrary, the LVBE-MCM only uses the circular virtual boundary during the local approximation, and it is insensitive to the location of the boundary. Furthermore, the resulting LVBE-MCM system is sparse and can thus be easily solved using an ordinary computer. This also means that the method has certain application prospects for solving large-scale problems.

The rest of the paper is organized as follows: In Section 2, the considered problem is briefly introduced. Section 3 describes the detailed numerical procedure for the LVBE-MCM. Section 4 develops an augmented moving least squares approximation using the fundamental solutions. In Section 5, two numerical examples are provided to confirm the effectiveness and applicability of the proposed method. The conclusions are summarized in Section 6.

2. Preliminaries

Let $\Omega \in R^2$ be an open bounded domain surrounded by the boundary $\Gamma = \partial\Omega$, which is assumed to be piecewise smooth, and consider the following boundary value problem:

$$Lu(x) = 0,\ x \in \Omega, \tag{1}$$

$$u(x) = f(x),\ x \in \Gamma_D, \tag{2}$$

$$\frac{\partial u(x)}{\partial \mathrm{n}} = g(x),\ x \in \Gamma_N, \tag{3}$$

$$\alpha u(x) + \beta \frac{\partial u(x)}{\partial \mathrm{n}} = h(x),\ x \in \Gamma_R, \tag{4}$$

where L is the Laplace ($L = \nabla^2$) or Helmholtz ($L = \nabla^2 + \lambda^2$) operator, λ is the wave number, n is the unit outward normal vector, α and β are constants, and $f(x)$, $g(x)$, $h(x)$ are the provided smooth functions on the boundaries. Here, Γ_D, Γ_N, and Γ_R represent the Dirichlet, Neumann, and Robin boundaries, respectively.

The fundamental solutions for the Laplace and Helmholtz operators are determined by [34]

$$u^*(r) = -\frac{1}{2\pi}\ln(r), \text{ for Laplace operator} \quad (5)$$

$$u^*(r) = \frac{\mathrm{i}}{4}H_0^{(1)}(\lambda r), \text{ for Helmholtz operator} \quad (6)$$

where r denotes the Euclidean distance between the field point and the source point, and $H_0^{(1)}$ is a zero-order Hankel function of the first kind.

3. Localized Virtual Boundary Element–Meshless Collocation Method

First of all, the $N = n_i + n_{b1} + n_{b2} + n_{b3}$ discrete nodes $x^{(i)}$, $i = 1,2,\ldots,N$ are placed over the computational domain Ω, where n_i is the number of nodes inside the domain, and n_{b1}, n_{b2}, and n_{b3} indicate the number of nodes along the Dirichlet, Neumann, and Robin boundary, respectively. Considering an arbitrary node $x^{(i)}$, which is also known as the central node, its m supporting nodes $x_j^{(i)}$, $j = 1,2,\ldots,m$ can be determined based on the nearest nodes. At the same time, the local supporting domain Ω_s covering m+1 nodes can also be determined, and its virtual boundary $\Gamma^{(i)}$ can be specified at a certain distance from the boundary of the supporting domain. For 2D problems, this boundary is a circle. Figure 1 shows the schematic diagram of the LVBE-MCM.

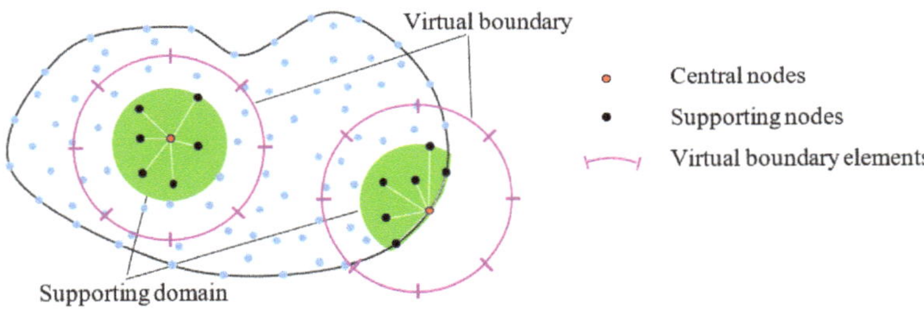

Figure 1. Schematic diagram of the LVBE-MCM for the 2D problem.

In the present study, the virtual boundary is discretized by M exact geometrical elements, and the physical quantity is approximated by the constant element. Using $x_0^{(i)}$ to represent $x^{(i)}$, the unknowns at nodes $x_j^{(i)}$, $j = 0,1,\ldots,m$ are expressed as

$$u\left(x_j^{(i)}\right) = \int_{\Gamma^{(i)}} u^*(x_j^{(i)},\xi)\varphi^{(i)}(\xi)d\Gamma_s^{(i)} = \sum_{k=1}^{M}\varphi_k^{(i)}\int_{\Gamma_k^{(i)}} u^*(x_j^{(i)},\xi)d\Gamma_k^{(i)},\ x_j^{(i)} \in \Omega_s^{(i)},\ j = 0,1,\ldots,m, \quad (7)$$

where $u^*(x_j^{(i)},\xi)$ is the fundamental solution of the governing equation, and $\varphi(\xi)$ is the distribution density function associated with the virtual boundary $\Gamma^{(i)}$. Equation (7) can be rewritten in the following matrix form:

$$u^{(i)} = G^{(i)}\varphi^{(i)}. \quad (8)$$

For the above local approximation, the moving least squares (MLS) can be employed to obtain the unknown coefficient vector $\varphi^{(i)} = \left[\varphi_1^{(i)},\varphi_2^{(i)},\ldots,\varphi_M^{(i)}\right]$, resulting in

$$\varphi^{(i)} = H^{(i)}u^{(i)}. \quad (9)$$

Replacing $x_j^{(i)}$ in Equation (7) with $x^{(i)}$, the following formula is yielded:

$$u\left(x^{(i)}\right) = \sum_{k=1}^{M} \varphi_k^{(i)} \int_{\Gamma_k^{(i)}} u^*(x^{(i)}, \xi) d\Gamma_k^{(i)} = E^{(i)} \varphi^{(i)}. \tag{10}$$

Then, substituting Equation (9) into Equation (10), we obtain

$$u\left(x^{(i)}\right) = E^{(i)} H^{(i)} u^{(i)} = F^{(i)} u^{(i)}. \tag{11}$$

If $x^{(i)}$ is a node on the boundary, the normal derivative can be calculated by

$$\frac{\partial u(x^{(i)})}{\partial n} = N^{(i)} \varphi^{(i)} = N^{(i)} H^{(i)} u^{(i)} = C^{(i)} u^{(i)}, \tag{12}$$

where $N^{(i)} = n_1 \sigma_1^{(i)} + \ldots + n_d \sigma_d^{(i)}$, and

$$\sigma_l^{(i)} = \left[\int_{\Gamma_1^{(i)}} \frac{\partial u^*(x^{(i)}, \xi)}{\partial x_l^{(i)}} d\Gamma_1^{(i)}, \int_{\Gamma_2^{(i)}} \frac{\partial u^*(x^{(i)}, \xi)}{\partial x_l^{(i)}} d\Gamma_2^{(i)}, \ldots, \int_{\Gamma_M^{(i)}} \frac{\partial u^*(x^{(i)}, \xi)}{\partial x_l^{(i)}} d\Gamma_M^{(i)} \right], \ l = 1, \ldots, d. \tag{13}$$

In the above equations, $n_1, \ldots, n_d$ denote the components of the vector n, and $x_1^{(i)}, \ldots, x_d^{(i)}$ denote the coordinate components of the node $x^{(i)}$.

Taking all of the nodes $x^{(i)}$, $i = 1, 2, \ldots, N$ and the boundary data provided in Equations (2)–(4) into account, the following overdetermined equations can be obtained:

$$\begin{cases} u_i - F^{(i)} u^{(i)} = 0, \ i \in \{1, 2, \ldots, n_i\} \\ u_i = f_i, \ i \in \{n_i + 1, \ldots, n_i + n_{b1}\} \\ E^{(i)} u^{(i)} = g_i, \ i \in \{n_i + n_{b1} + 1, \ldots, n_i + n_{b1} + n_{b2}\} \\ \alpha u_i + E^{(i)} u^{(i)} = 0, \ i \in \{n_i + n_{b1} + n_{b2} + 1, \ldots, N\} \end{cases} \text{or } Au = b, \tag{14}$$

where $u = \left[u(x^{(1)}), \ u(x^{(2)}), \ \ldots, \ u(x^{(N)})\right]^T$, $b_{N \times 1}$ is a vector composed of zero elements and boundary data, and $A_{N \times N}$ is a sparse matrix. Equation (14) is a well-conditioned system, and in this work, it is solved by MATLAB routine "$A \backslash b$".

4. Augmented Moving Least Squares Approximation

The moving least squares approximation is a widely used technique in various meshless/meshfree methods. In this study, the fundamental solutions are introduced into the traditional moving least squares method, and we then developed the augmented moving least squares approximation, which is similar to the one outlined in [35]. According to its basic idea, the vector $\alpha^{(i)}$ is deduced by minimizing the following functional equation:

$$Ju^{(i)} = \left(G^{(i)} \varphi^{(i)} - u^{(i)}\right)^{\mathrm{T}} \omega^{(i)} \left(G^{(i)} \varphi^{(i)} - u^{(i)}\right), \tag{15}$$

where $\omega^{(i)} = diag\left(w_0^{(i)}, w_1^{(i)}, \ldots, w_m^{(i)}\right)$, and

$$\omega_j^{(i)} = 1 - 6\left(d_j / d_{\max}\right)^2 + 8\left(d_j / d_{\max}\right)^3 - 3\left(d_j / d_{\max}\right)^4, \tag{16}$$

in Equation (16), $d_j = \|x_j^{(i)} - x^{(i)}\|_2$ and $d_{\max} = \max\limits_{j=0,1,\ldots,m} (d_j)$.

Hence, we have

$$\frac{\partial J u^{(i)}}{\partial \varphi^{(i)}} = 2\left[G^{(i)}\right]^T \omega^{(i)} G^{(i)} \varphi^{(i)} - 2\left[G^{(i)}\right]^T \omega^{(i)} u^{(i)} = 0. \tag{17}$$

By calculating and reorganizing Equation (17), we can obtain a system equation in matrix form:

$$P^{(i)}\varphi^{(i)} = Q^{(i)}u^{(i)}, \tag{18}$$

where $P^{(i)} = \left[G^{(i)}\right]^T \omega^{(i)} G^{(i)}$, and $Q^{(i)} = \left[G^{(i)}\right]^T \omega^{(i)}$. Solving Equation (18) yields $\varphi^{(i)} = \left[P^{(i)}\right]^{-1} Q^{(i)}u^{(i)}$; hence, $H^{(i)}$ in Equation (9) is equal to $\left[P^{(i)}\right]^{-1} Q^{(i)}$. It should be pointed out that we used MATLAB's mldivide (matrix left divide) function ($P^{(i)} \backslash Q^{(i)}$) to obtain $H^{(i)}$ instead of the matrix inversion.

5. Numerical Examples

Two numerical examples are provided to demonstrate the effectiveness and accuracy of the proposed method. To evaluate the numerical errors, we adopt the maximum absolute error (MAE) and the root-mean-square error (RMSE), which are defined as follows:

$$\text{MAE} = \max_{1 \le j \le n_i} \left| u_n(x_j) - u_e(x_j) \right|, \tag{19}$$

$$\text{RMSE} = \sqrt{\frac{1}{n_i} \sum_{j=1}^{n_i} \left(u_n(x_j) - u_e(x_j) \right)^2}, \tag{20}$$

where u_n and u_e represent the numerical and analytical solution at node x_j, respectively. All computations were performed using MATLAB 2018b on a desktop PC (Intel® Core TMi7-6700 CPU at 3.4 GHz, 16G RAM, and Hard Disk-500G).

Example 1. *Consider a Laplace equation on an irregular domain with mixed boundary conditions. The geometry and boundary conditions are shown in Figure 2. For the Robin boundary condition, $\alpha = 1$ and $\beta = 5$. The analytical solution is obtained by*

$$u(x_1, x_2) = \cos(x_1)\cosh(x_2) + \sin(x_1)\sinh(x_2) + e^{x_1}\cos(x_2) + e^{x_2}\sin(x_1) + {x_1}^2 - {x_2}^2 + 2x_1 + 3x_2 + 1. \tag{21}$$

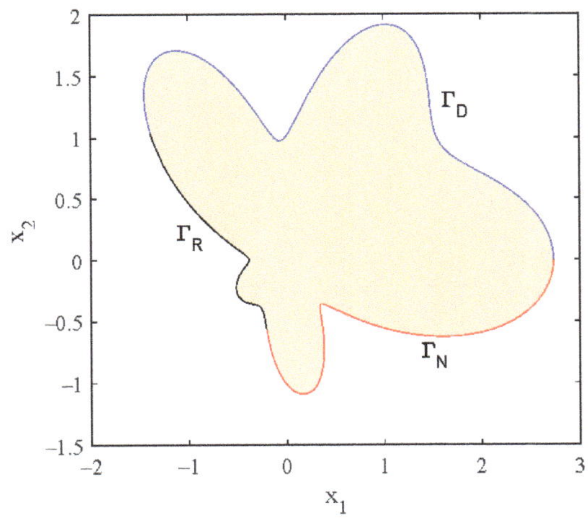

Figure 2. Computational domain and boundary conditions for Example 1.

First of all, N = 6784 nodes are chosen, and 8 Gaussian points are used. It can be seen from Figure 3 that the numerical error first decreases and then increases as the number of virtual elements increases, meaning that high computational accuracy has been achieved. Then, M = 15 is fixed. From Figure 4, we can observe that the number of Gaussian points has little effect on the calculation accuracy, and therefore, fewer Gaussian points can be used in the calculation.

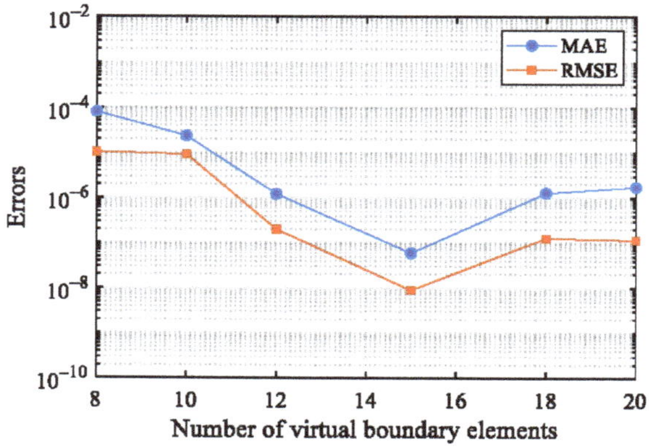

Figure 3. Error curves with respect to the number of virtual elements.

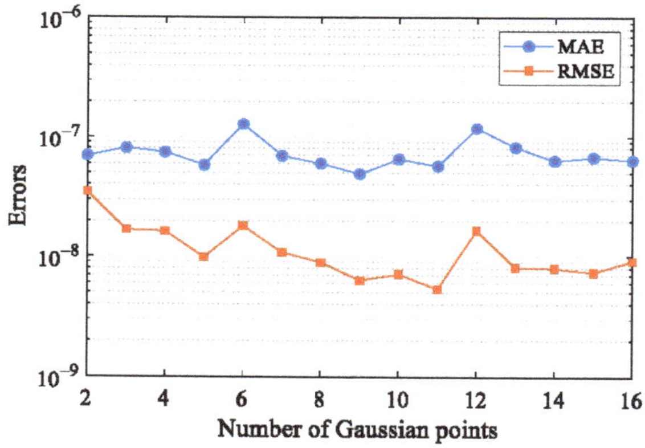

Figure 4. Error curves with respect to the number of Gaussian points.

The LMFS and GFDM are recently developed meshless approaches that are very similar to the present LVBE-MCM. In Table 1, these two methods are compared to the proposed approach. It can be observed that all methods are convergent. Although the LMFS and LVBE-MCM have similar numerical accuracy, the latter is slightly better than the former.

Table 1. The RMSEs derived from the LVBE-MCM, LMFS, and GFDM under different numbers of total nodes.

N	448	765	1211	2592	4475	6784
LVBE-MCM	5.3674×10^{-7}	3.7938×10^{-7}	2.7616×10^{-7}	1.2551×10^{-7}	3.4856×10^{-8}	8.9528×10^{-9}
LMFS	1.4072×10^{-6}	4.7048×10^{-7}	4.3495×10^{-7}	1.3170×10^{-7}	1.4663×10^{-7}	9.8769×10^{-8}
GFDM	2.6038×10^{-3}	4.2642×10^{-5}	3.3704×10^{-5}	1.6361×10^{-5}	4.1832×10^{-7}	1.3909×10^{-7}

Example 2. *A Helmholtz equation on a doubly connected domain (see Figure 5) is considered. The boundary conditions are specified by the analytical solution* $u(x_1, x_2) = \cos(x_1/2 + \sqrt{3}x_2/2)$ *with* $\lambda = 1$.

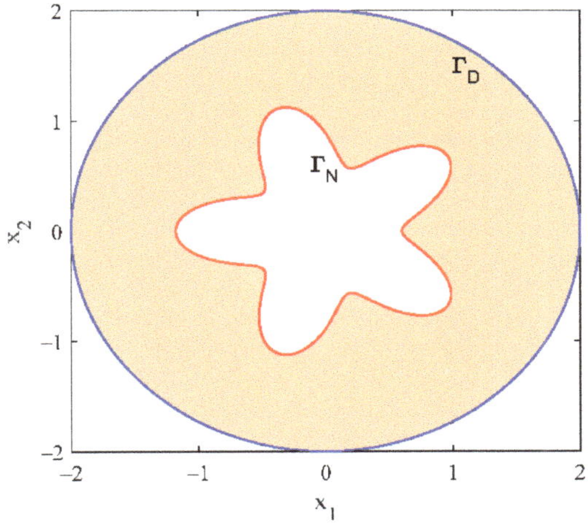

Figure 5. Computational domain and boundary conditions for Example 2.

The profiles of the exact solution and absolute error in the computational domain under $N = 1840$ and $M = 15$ are shown in Figure 6. The maximum absolute error and the root-mean-square error are 3.3238×10^{-8} and 6.4048×10^{-9}, respectively. This indicates the high-accuracy of the proposed method. Furthermore, it can be observed from Table 2 that the LVBE-MCM has higher numerical accuracy than the LMFS when the same number of sources and elements is adopted.

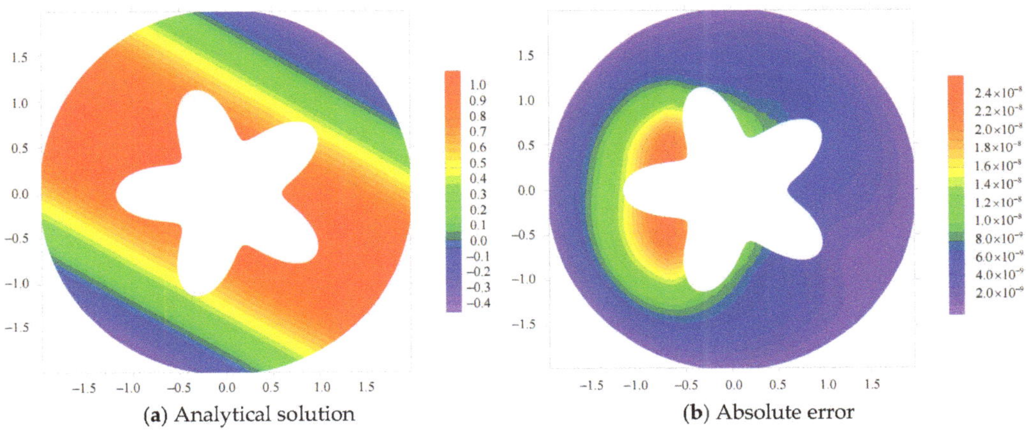

Figure 6. Profiles of the (**a**) exact solution and (**b**) absolute error.

Table 2. The RMSEs derived from the LVBE-MCM and LMFS under different elements or sources.

M	10	15	20	25	30	35
LVBE-MCM	3.6573×10^{-6}	6.4048×10^{-9}	1.1714×10^{-8}	5.7849×10^{-8}	5.1474×10^{-8}	4.8111×10^{-8}
LMFS	1.4772×10^{-5}	1.3537×10^{-8}	3.5835×10^{-8}	7.4075×10^{-8}	6.5249×10^{-8}	6.7892×10^{-8}

6. Conclusions

The localized virtual boundary element–meshless collocation method (LVBE-MCM) was proposed as a novel domain-type meshless method that could be used to solve Laplace and Helmholtz equations in complex 2D geometries. In this work, the traditional virtual boundary element method with a global approximation was modified to a local approximation approach by introducing the moving least square method and local approximation theory. Numerical integrations are only required on the circular virtual boundary; thus, the exact geometry elements are convenient to use. The proposed LVBE-MCM avoids the need to evaluate the singular/strong singular/hypersingular integral in the boundary element method and has a higher calculation accuracy than the LMFS.

Two examples involving irregular geometries and doubly connected domains were investigated in detail. The numerical results indicate that the LVBE-MCM is accurate and effective for solving Laplace and Helmholtz equations in complex two-dimensional geometries. The number of Gaussian points has a little effect on the calculation accuracy, and therefore, fewer Gaussian points can be used in the calculation. Moreover, the scheme is convergent with respect to increasing the number of total nodes. It is worth noting that the proposed method can be directly extended to other partial differential equations with known fundamental solutions, such as diffusion equations, Stokes equations, and biharmonic equations.

It should also be pointed out that this paper investigates the accuracy and convergence of the LVBE-MCM numerically. Unlike the difference method and Taylor expansion, it is not an easy work to formally prove the convergence and stability of the LVBE-MCM since there are few related assumptions and theorems on approximation techniques that use the fundamental solution and the augmented moving least squares scheme. Consequently, a theoretical analysis of the LVBE-MCM will be the key issue in our subsequent work.

Author Contributions: Conceptualization, X.Y.; methodology, C.Y.; software, B.J. and X.X.; investigation, B.J. and X.X.; writing—original draft preparation, X.Y.; writing—review and editing, C.Y. and X.Y.; visualization, B.J. and X.X.; supervision, X.Y. All authors have read and agreed to the published version of the manuscript.

Funding: This research was funded by the Scientific Research Starting Foundation of Qingdao University (No. DC2100000881).

Institutional Review Board Statement: Not applicable.

Informed Consent Statement: Not applicable.

Data Availability Statement: Not applicable.

Conflicts of Interest: The authors declare no conflict of interest.

References

1. Liu, Y.J.; Mukherjee, S.; Nishimura, N.; Schanz, M.; Ye, W.; Sutradhar, A.; Pan, E.; Dumont, N.A.; Frangi, A.; Saez, A. Recent Advances and Emerging Applications of the Boundary Element Method. *Appl. Mech. Rev.* **2011**, *64*, 030802. [CrossRef]
2. Beer, G.; Smith, I.; Duenser, C. *The Boundary Element Method with Programming: For Engineers and Scientists*; Springer: Vienna, Austria, 2008.
3. Chai, Y.; Li, W.; Liu, Z. Analysis of transient wave propagation dynamics using the enriched finite element method with interpolation cover functions. *Appl. Math. Comput.* **2022**, *412*, 126564. [CrossRef]
4. Li, W.; Zhang, Q.; Gui, Q.; Chai, Y. A Coupled FE-Meshfree Triangular Element for Acoustic Radiation Problems. *Int. J. Comput. Methods* **2021**, *18*, 2041002. [CrossRef]
5. Lutz, E. Exact Gaussian quadrature methods for near-singular integrals in the boundary element method. *Eng. Anal. Bound. Elements* **1992**, *9*, 233–245. [CrossRef]
6. Johnston, P.R.; Elliott, D. A sinh transformation for evaluating nearly singular boundary element integrals. *Int. J. Numer. Methods Eng.* **2005**, *62*, 564–578. [CrossRef]
7. Zhou, H.; Niu, Z.; Cheng, C.; Guan, Z. Analytical integral algorithm applied to boundary layer effect and thin body effect in BEM for anisotropic potential problems. *Comput. Struct.* **2008**, *86*, 1656–1671. [CrossRef]
8. Niu, Z.; Cheng, C.; Zhou, H.; Hu, Z. Analytic formulations for calculating nearly singular integrals in two-dimensional BEM. *Eng. Anal. Bound. Elements* **2007**, *31*, 949–964. [CrossRef]

9. Cascio, M.L.; Milazzo, A.; Benedetti, I. A hybrid virtual–boundary element formulation for heterogeneous materials. *Int. J. Mech. Sci.* **2021**, *199*, 106404. [CrossRef]
10. Yao, W.; Wang, H. Virtual boundary element integral method for 2-D piezoelectric media. *Finite Elem. Anal. Des.* **2005**, *41*, 875–891.
11. Lee, C. Stability characteristics of the virtual boundary method in three-dimensional applications. *J. Comput. Phys.* **2003**, *184*, 559–591. [CrossRef]
12. Saiki, E.; Biringen, S. Numerical Simulation of a Cylinder in Uniform Flow: Application of a Virtual Boundary Method. *J. Comput. Phys.* **1996**, *123*, 450–465. [CrossRef]
13. Desiderio, L.; Falletta, S.; Scuderi, L. A Virtual Element Method coupled with a Boundary Integral Non Reflecting condition for 2D exterior Helmholtz problems. *Comput. Math. Appl.* **2021**, *84*, 296–313. [CrossRef]
14. Huanchun, S.; Weian, Y. Virtual boundary element-linear complementary equations for solving the elastic obstacle problems of thin plate. *Finite Elements Anal. Des.* **1997**, *27*, 153–161. [CrossRef]
15. Li, X.-C.; Yao, W.-A. Virtual boundary element-integral collocation method for the plane magnetoelectroelastic solids. *Eng. Anal. Bound. Elem.* **2006**, *30*, 709–717. [CrossRef]
16. Yang, D.; Yue, X.; Yang, Q. Virtual boundary element method in conjunction with conjugate gradient algorithm for three-dimensional inverse heat conduction problems. *Numer. Heat Transf. Part B Fundam.* **2017**, *72*, 421–430. [CrossRef]
17. Liu, X.; Shao, G.; Yue, X.; Yang, Q.; Su, J. A Virtual Boundary Element Method for Three-Dimensional Inverse Heat Conduction Problems in Orthotropic Media. *Comput. Model. Eng. Sci.* **2018**, *117*, 189–211. [CrossRef]
18. Wang, X.; Wang, J.; Wang, X.; Yu, C. A Pseudo-Spectral Fourier Collocation Method for Inhomogeneous Elliptical Inclusions with Partial Differential Equations. *Mathematics* **2022**, *10*, 296. [CrossRef]
19. Li, X.; Dong, H. An element-free Galerkin method for the obstacle problem. *Appl. Math. Lett.* **2021**, *112*, 106724. [CrossRef]
20. Xi, Q.; Fu, Z.; Zhang, C.; Yin, D. An efficient localized Trefftz-based collocation scheme for heat conduction analysis in two kinds of heterogeneous materials under temperature loading. *Comput. Struct.* **2021**, *255*, 106619. [CrossRef]
21. Qu, W.; Gao, H.; Gu, Y. Integrating Krylov deferred correction and generalized finite difference methods for dynamic sim-ulations of wave propagation phenomena in long-time intervals. *Adv. Appl. Math. Mech.* **2021**, *13*, 1398–1417.
22. Li, X.; Li, S. A fast element-free Galerkin method for the fractional diffusion-wave equation. *Appl. Math. Lett.* **2021**, *122*, 107529. [CrossRef]
23. Wang, F.; Zhao, Q.; Chen, Z.; Fan, C.-M. Localized Chebyshev collocation method for solving elliptic partial differential equations in arbitrary 2D domains. *Appl. Math. Comput.* **2021**, *397*, 125903. [CrossRef]
24. Qu, W.; He, H. A GFDM with supplementary nodes for thin elastic plate bending analysis under dynamic loading. *Appl. Math. Lett.* **2022**, *124*, 107664. [CrossRef]
25. Benito, J.; Ureña, F.; Gavete, L. Solving parabolic and hyperbolic equations by the generalized finite difference method. *J. Comput. Appl. Math.* **2007**, *209*, 208–233. [CrossRef]
26. Wang, F.J.; Fan, C.M.; Zhang, C.Z.; Lin, J. A Localized Space-Time Method of Fundamental Solutions for Diffusion and Convection-Diffusion Problems. *Adv. Appl. Math. Mech.* **2020**, *12*, 940–958. [CrossRef]
27. Gu, Y.; Fan, C.-M.; Fu, Z. Localized Method of Fundamental Solutions for Three-Dimensional Elasticity Problems: Theory. *Adv. Appl. Math. Mech.* **2021**, *13*, 1520–1534.
28. Wang, F.; Wang, C.; Chen, Z. Local knot method for 2D and 3D convection–diffusion–reaction equations in arbitrary domains. *Appl. Math. Lett.* **2020**, *105*, 106308. [CrossRef]
29. Yue, X.; Wang, F.; Li, P.-W.; Fan, C.-M. Local non-singular knot method for large-scale computation of acoustic problems in complicated geometries. *Comput. Math. Appl.* **2021**, *84*, 128–143. [CrossRef]
30. Wang, F.; Chen, Z.; Li, P.-W.; Fan, C.-M. Localized singular boundary method for solving Laplace and Helmholtz equations in arbitrary 2D domains. *Eng. Anal. Bound. Elem.* **2021**, *129*, 82–92. [CrossRef]
31. Lin, J.; Qiu, L.; Wang, F. Localized singular boundary method for the simulation of large-scale problems of elliptic operators in complex geometries. *Comput. Math. Appl.* **2022**, *105*, 94–106. [CrossRef]
32. Chen, C.S.; Karageorghis, A.; Li, Y. On choosing the location of the sources in the MFS. *Numer. Algorithms* **2016**, *72*, 107–130. [CrossRef]
33. Wang, F.; Liu, C.-S.; Qu, W. Optimal sources in the MFS by minimizing a new merit function: Energy gap functional. *Appl. Math. Lett.* **2018**, *86*, 229–235. [CrossRef]
34. Wang, F.; Fan, C.-M.; Hua, Q.; Gu, Y. Localized MFS for the inverse Cauchy problems of two-dimensional Laplace and bi-harmonic equations. *Appl. Math. Comput.* **2020**, *364*, 124658.
35. Wang, F.; Qu, W.; Li, X. Augmented moving least squares approximation using fundamental solutions. *Eng. Anal. Bound. Elem.* **2020**, *115*, 10–20. [CrossRef]

mathematics

MDPI

Article

Reliability-Based Topology Optimization of Thermo-Elastic Structures with Stress Constraint

Liang Zhang [1], Qinghai Zhao [1,2,*] and Jianliang Chen [1]

[1] School of Mechanical and Electrical Engineering, Qingdao University, Qingdao 266071, China; 2020025584@qdu.edu.cn (L.Z.); 2020020438@qdu.edu.cn (J.C.)
[2] National Engineering Research Center for Intelligent Electrical Vehicle Power System, Qingdao University, Qingdao 266071, China
* Correspondence: zhaoqh@qdu.edu.cn

Abstract: Traditional topology optimization of thermo-elastic structures is based on deterministic conditions, without considering the influence of uncertainty factors. To address the impact uncertainty on structural strength, a reliability-based topology optimization of thermo-elastic structure with stress constraint is proposed. The probabilistic uncertainty quantities are associated with the structural material property, mechanical loads and the thermal stress coefficient with the topology optimization formulation considering volume minimization and stress constraint. The relaxation stress method combined with normalized p-norm function is adopted to condense whole element stresses into the global stress measurement that approximates the maximum stress. The adjoint variable method is utilized to derive the sensitivity of the stress constraint and the optimization problem is solved by the method of moving asymptote (MMA). Finally, several numerical examples are presented to demonstrate the effectiveness and validity of the proposed approach. Compared with the deterministic design, the reliability design has distinct topological configurations and the optimized structures maintain a higher reliability level.

Keywords: thermo-elastic structure; topology optimization; reliability analysis; stress constraint

MSC: 65K10

Citation: Zhang, L.; Zhao, Q.; Chen, J. Reliability-Based Topology Optimization of Thermo-Elastic Structures with Stress Constraint. *Mathematics* **2022**, *10*, 1091. https://doi.org/10.3390/math10071091

Academic Editors: Fajie Wang, Ji Lin and Armin Fügenschuh

Received: 4 March 2022
Accepted: 24 March 2022
Published: 28 March 2022

1. Introduction

Various mechanical parts, such as turbines, rockets and battery systems, are subjected to both thermal and mechanical loads because of the working environment with coupled temperature and structural fields. In this scenario, it is necessary for the thermo-elastic design to consider the temperature factor's impact on structural strength to prevent structural failure [1].

In recent years, topology optimization methods are widely used in thermo-elastic structure design, including the variable density method, the homogenization method, the evolutionary optimization method, the level set method, etc. Rodrigue et al. [2] first proposed the topology optimization of thermo-elastic structures by the homogenization method. Du et al. [3] performed the topology optimization of thermal-driven compliant mechanisms by the variable density method. Li et al. [4] conducted a study on the optimal design of thermo-elastic structures under the non-uniform temperature field based on the evolutionary optimization method. Deng et al. [5] used the level set method to derive the topological sensitivity information for the thermo-elastic structures. Most of the studies in the above-mentioned literature are based on the compliance minimization, while the strength is an essential design criterion in engineering practice. Recently, it has been stated in Ref. [6] that the topology optimization model of compliance minimization is not suitable for thermo-elastic topology optimization, because when the temperature load is comparable to the mechanical load, compliance minimization cannot obtain an optimal structure with reasonable strength. More researches have illustrated that simple reinforcement techniques cannot sufficiently solve the problem of thermo-elastic structural strength failure caused by destructive stress [7]. Therefore, stress-based topology optimization design is necessary and has been gradually emerged.

Topology optimization related with stress constraint is the most challenging research field. This is mainly due to the following three problems: (i) the singularity problem, (ii) the local nature of stresses, and (iii) the highly nonlinear behavior of stress constraints [8]. According to the relevant literature, there are some efficient approaches to deal with the above-mentioned problems. Regarding the singular phenomenon, the commonly used methods include ε-relaxation techniques [9,10], qp-relaxation techniques [11,12], etc. For the local nature of stress, local stress constraints are transformed into global stress constraint by using aggregation function, including the p-norm [13,14] and KS-function [15]. In addition to the above numerical problems, the third challenge is the highly nonlinear stress behavior wherein stress distribution is highly sensitive to even subtle topological variations, particularly at critical regions with high stress concentration [16]. This feature is reflected in the tendency of the optimization iterations to have repeated oscillations. To stabilize the convergence, a density filtering method and suitable optimization solution algorithm were adopted by Le et al. [17]. Recently, Deaton et al. [18] investigated the topology optimization problem of thermo-elastic structures under stress constraint. However, the above studies on topology optimization considering stress constraint are based on deterministic topology optimization (DTO). In practical engineering, the material properties and the mechanical loads are often uncertain due to the differences of the internal conditions and the time-varying nature of the external environment. These uncertainties maybe affect the reliability of the structural performance and even lead to failure [19–21]. Thus, reliability-based topology optimization (RBTO) is becoming more and more prominent.

According to the different mathematical tools used to describe the properties of uncertainty, uncertainty can be divided into stochastic uncertainty and epistemic uncertainty. The former describes the inherent variability in the physical system or working environment, also known as objective uncertainty, and usually uses probabilistic methods to model random variables or stochastic processes, while the latter is mainly due to subjective knowledge limitations or incomplete information. The resulting, also known as subjective uncertainty, can be modeled by non-probabilistic methods such as fuzzy analysis [22]. Therefore, reliability topology optimization considering uncertainty conditions is mainly divided into probabilistic and non-probabilistic types. At present, the research on reliability topology optimization design with random variables as a probability distribution is relatively mature. Kharmanda et al. [23] first combined structural reliability analysis with deterministic topology optimization and established an effective reliability flowchart for structural strain energy minimization. Jung et al. [24] investigated the reliability topology optimization for the three-dimensional geometric nonlinear structure design. Zhao et al. [25] studied the multi-material topology optimization problem with reliability constraints considering the effects of incomplete measurement of structures, inaccurate information, and insufficient cognition on structures. For practical engineering applications, Silva et al. [26] adopted a single-loop topology optimization mathematical model of components and systems and applied it to the design of automotive control arms, and the results showed that the method has good practicality and efficiency.

To the author's knowledge, this is the first attempt to reliability-based topology optimization of thermo-elastic structure with stress constraint. The material property, thermal stress coefficient and mechanical loads are chosen as uncertainty variables with the probability distributions. Based on probability theory, the structural topology optimization design method considering stress constraint is combined with the existing reliability structural topology optimization model [27]. A reliability-based topology optimization design method for thermo-elastic structures under global stress constraint is proposed. The RBTO and the DTO design are compared to verify the effectiveness and feasibility of the proposed method.

2. Finite Element Formulation of Thermo-Elastic Structure

Figure 1 illustrates the generalized design domain Ω for the thermo-elastic structure problem, which consists of the predefined design domain containing the fixed displacement boundary Γ_d, surface mechanical load F^m applied on the boundary Γ_f, and the uniform temperature variation $\Delta T(x, y)$. In addition, the isotropic material is considered and the design domain is discretized into quadrilateral elements and eight-node hexahedral elements in 2D and 3D problems, respectively.

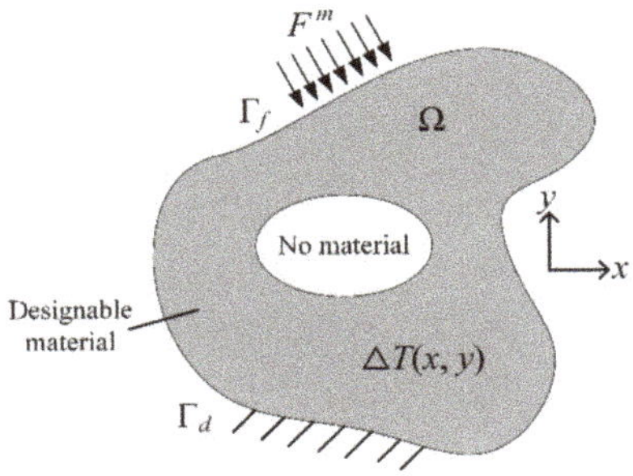

Figure 1. Generalized design domain of thermo-elastic structure.

For the thermo-elastic structure coupled with temperature and mechanical loads, the static equilibrium equations can usually be expressed as

$$\boldsymbol{K}(\boldsymbol{\rho})\boldsymbol{U}(\boldsymbol{\rho}) = \boldsymbol{F}^m + \boldsymbol{F}^{th}(\boldsymbol{\rho}) \quad (1)$$

where $\boldsymbol{\rho}$ is the density variable vector, $\boldsymbol{K}(\boldsymbol{\rho})$ is the structural global stiffness matrix, $\boldsymbol{U}(\boldsymbol{\rho})$ is the structural nodal displacement vector, $\boldsymbol{F}^m$ is the mechanical load vector, and $\boldsymbol{F}^{th}(\boldsymbol{\rho})$ is the temperature load vector due to thermal strain. The stiffness matrix $\boldsymbol{K}(\boldsymbol{\rho})$ is assembled by

$$\boldsymbol{K}(\boldsymbol{\rho}) = \sum_{e=1}^{N_e} \int_{\Omega_e} \boldsymbol{B}_e^{\mathrm{T}} \boldsymbol{D}_e(\rho_e) \boldsymbol{B}_e h d\Omega_e \quad (2)$$

where N_e is the total element number, Ω_e represents the element domain, h is the thickness of the planar element, $\boldsymbol{B}_e$ is the element strain-displacement matrix, $\boldsymbol{D}_e(\rho_e)$ is the material elasticity matrix of element e [28]. Adopting the SIMP material interpolation method, $\boldsymbol{D}_e(\rho_e)$ can be expressed as a function of the material elastic modulus, defined by

$$\boldsymbol{D}_e(\rho_e) = E(\rho_e)\boldsymbol{D}_0 = {\rho_e}^{\alpha} E_0 \boldsymbol{D}_0 \quad (3)$$

where $E(\rho_e)$ is the elastic modulus of element e, α is the elastic modulus penalty factor, E_0 is the elastic modulus of the solid material, $\boldsymbol{D}_0$ is the coefficient matrix for an element with unit elastic modulus.

The temperature load $\boldsymbol{F}^{th}(\boldsymbol{\rho})$ can be assembled by accumulating the element temperature load, defined as

$$\boldsymbol{F}^{th}(\boldsymbol{\rho}) = \sum_{e=1}^{N_e} E(\rho_e) \int_{\Omega_e} {\boldsymbol{B}_e}^{\mathrm{T}} \boldsymbol{D}_0 {\boldsymbol{\varepsilon}_e}^{th}(\rho_e) d\Omega_e \quad (4)$$

where

$${\boldsymbol{\varepsilon}_e}^{th}(\rho_e) = \gamma(\rho_e)\Delta T \boldsymbol{\phi} \quad (5)$$

where ${\boldsymbol{\varepsilon}_e}^{th}(\rho_e)$ is the thermal strain vector for the element, $\gamma(\rho_e)$ is the material thermal expansion coefficient, ΔT is the amount of uniform variation of the temperature, $\boldsymbol{\phi}$ is defined as $[1, 1, 0]^{\mathrm{T}}$ in 2D problems and $[1, 1, 1, 0, 0, 0]^{\mathrm{T}}$ in 3D problems. Substituting Equation (6) into Equation (5) yields

It is noted that $E(\rho_e)$ and $\gamma(\rho_e)$ are both concerned with the element density variables. Hence, by using the thermal stress coefficient (TSC) [29], the parameters are combined into the single thermal stress coefficient, defined as

$$\delta(\rho_e) = E(\rho_e)\gamma\rho_e) = {\rho_e}^k E_0\gamma_0 = {\rho_e}^k\delta_0 \quad (6)$$

where γ_0 is the expansion coefficient of the solid material, k is the thermal stress penalty factor, δ_0 is the thermal stress coefficient of the solid material.

Substituting Equations (5) and (6) into Equation (4), $\boldsymbol{F}^{th}(\boldsymbol{\rho})$ can be expressed as

$$\boldsymbol{F}^{th}(\boldsymbol{\rho}) = \sum_{e=1}^{N_e}\delta(\rho_e)\Delta T\int_{\Omega_e}{\boldsymbol{B}_e}^{\mathrm{T}}\boldsymbol{D}_0\boldsymbol{\phi}d\Omega_e \quad (7)$$

3. Deterministic Topology Optimization of Thermo-Elastic Structure

3.1. Mathematical Model of Deterministic Topology Optimization

With regard to the deterministic topology optimization of the thermo-elastic structure problem, the volume minimization and stress constraint are considered to satisfy the static strength failure and lightweight design. The deterministic topology optimization of the thermo-elastic structure can be established as

$$\begin{cases} find\ \ \boldsymbol{\rho} \\ min\ V(\boldsymbol{\rho}) = \sum\limits_{e=1}^{N_e}\rho_e v_e \\ s.t.\boldsymbol{K}(\boldsymbol{\rho})\boldsymbol{U}(\boldsymbol{\rho}) = \boldsymbol{F}^m + \boldsymbol{F}^{th}(\boldsymbol{\rho}) \\ \quad \sigma_e^{VM}(\boldsymbol{\rho}) \le \sigma_s \qquad (e = 1, 2, \ldots, N_e) \\ \quad 0 < \rho_{min} \le \rho_e \le 1(e = 1, 2, \ldots, N_e) \end{cases} \quad (8)$$

where $\boldsymbol{\rho}$ is the density variable vector, $V(\boldsymbol{\rho})$ is the overall structural volume, v_e is the element volume, ${\sigma_e}^{VM}(\boldsymbol{\rho})$ is the von Mises stress of each element, σ_s is the material yield strength, and ρ_{min} is the lower limit of the design variable.

3.2. Global Stress Constraint

The topological optimization of the stress-constrained structure appears as a singular solution phenomenon, i.e., the density of the element tends to zero, yet the stress of the element is a non-zero value. To solve the singular solution phenomenon, based on the SIMP material interpolation model, the stress relaxation method is used to penalize the element stresses in the form of

$$\sigma_e(\boldsymbol{\rho}) = \rho_e^q\sigma_{e0} \quad (9)$$

where $\boldsymbol{\sigma}_e(\boldsymbol{\rho})$ is the interpolated element stress, q is the intensity penalty factor, and $\boldsymbol{\sigma}_{e0}$ is the stress vector at the center of the eth element, defined as

$$\sigma_{e0} = E_0(\boldsymbol{D}_0\boldsymbol{B}_e\boldsymbol{U}_e - \boldsymbol{D}_0\gamma_0\boldsymbol{\phi}\Delta T) \quad (10)$$

where $\boldsymbol{U}_e$ is the nodal displacement vector of the element. The element stress vector $\boldsymbol{\sigma}_{e0}$ in 2D and 3D problems is respectively expressed as

For 2D problems,

$$\sigma_{e0} = \left[\sigma_{ex}, \sigma_{ey}, \tau_{exy}\right] \quad (11)$$

For 3D problems,

$$\sigma_{e0} = \left[\sigma_{ex}, \sigma_{ey}, \sigma_{ez}, \tau_{exy}, \tau_{eyz}, \tau_{ezx}\right] \quad (12)$$

where σ_{ex}, σ_{ey} and σ_{ez} are the stress components in the x, y and z directions of element e, respectively. τ_{exy}, τ_{eyz}, and τ_{ezx} are the shear stress components on the xy, yz, and zx planes of the element e, respectively.

The fourth strength theorem is used as the failure criterion of the material, the von Mises stress ${\sigma_e}^{VM}$ of the element can be obtained from the three components of the element stress vector, expressed as

$$\sigma_e^{VM} = \sqrt{\sigma_e^{\mathrm{T}}\boldsymbol{M}\sigma_e} \quad (13)$$

The Stress coefficient matrix $\boldsymbol{M}$, in 2D and 3D problems are respectively expressed as

For 2D problems,

$$\text{For 2D problems, } \boldsymbol{M} = \begin{bmatrix} 1 & -1/2 & 0 \\ -1/2 & 1 & 0 \\ 0 & 0 & 3 \end{bmatrix} \tag{14}$$

For 3D problems,

$$\boldsymbol{M} = \begin{bmatrix} 1 & -1/2 & -1/2 & 0 & 0 & 0 \\ -1/2 & 1 & -1/2 & 0 & 0 & 0 \\ -1/2 & -1/2 & 1 & 0 & 0 & 0 \\ 0 & 0 & 0 & 3 & 0 & 0 \\ 0 & 0 & 0 & 0 & 3 & 0 \\ 0 & 0 & 0 & 0 & 0 & 3 \end{bmatrix} \tag{15}$$

In order to reduce the problem of computational burden caused by numerous local stress constraints, the p-norm function is adopted to construct the global stress constraint, denoted as

$$\sigma^{PN} = \left(\sum_{e=1}^{N_e} \left(\frac{\sigma_e^{VM}}{\sigma_s} \right)^p \right)^{\frac{1}{p}} \tag{16}$$

where p is the aggregation parameter. Note that p tends to infinity, and σ^{PN} is equivalent to $max({\sigma_e}^{VM}/\sigma_s)$. The stress constraint is equivalent to the global stress constraint, defined as

$$\sigma^{PN} \leq 1 \tag{17}$$

However, when p enlarges, the degree of nonlinearity of the aggregation function increases that leads to oscillation convergence in the optimization process. Otherwise, with smaller p, the aggregation function cannot capture the maximum of the stress [30]. To overcome this defect, a revised coefficient is introduced into the constraint equation, expressed as

$$\overline{\sigma}^{PN} = c\sigma^{PN} \leq 1 \tag{18}$$

where c is the revised coefficient, and before each optimization process, is defined as

$$c = \frac{max\left(\sigma_e^{VM}\right)}{\sigma_s \cdot \sigma^{PN}} \tag{19}$$

4. Reliability-Based Topology Optimization of Thermo-Elastic Structure

4.1. Reliability-Based Topology Optimization Problem Description

Reliability is an important property reflecting the degree of structural safety [31]. The reliability-based optimization design measures the uncertainty of the structure by the failure probability or reliability index. While pursuing the optimal structural performance, it reduces the probability of the structure failure under the influence of uncertain factors, thereby improving the safety of the structure. Reliability-based topology optimization is a combination of reliability analysis and deterministic topology optimization design, aiming to integrate the problem of structural optimization and reliability constraint. The RBTO is slightly different from the traditional reliability structure optimization, and the variables are mainly divided into deterministic variables and random variables. The deterministic variables are used to characterize the physical density $\boldsymbol{\rho}$ (in the case of the variable density method), which are the design variable for topology optimization. And the random variables $\boldsymbol{Y}$, which are used to characterize the structural uncertainty factor, are continuous variables. This paper mainly studies random uncertain variables, such as the material properties of structures, loads, etc., which are suitable for using probability theory to describe their distribution characteristics [32]. In order to facilitate the calculation, it is generally necessary to standardize the non-normally distributed random variables into mutually independent standard normal random variables $\boldsymbol{u}$.

4.2. Mathematical Model of Reliability-Based Topology Optimization

Based on the above description of the random variables, a mathematical model for reliability-based topology optimization of thermo-elastic structure is established. Considering a general RBTO formulation, the stress constraint of Equation (8) is simply transformed into a probabilistic constraint, as follows

$$\begin{cases} find \;\; \boldsymbol{\rho} \\ min \; V(\boldsymbol{\rho}) = \sum\limits_{e=1}^{N_e} \rho_e v_e \\ s.t. \;\; P_r[G(\boldsymbol{\rho},\boldsymbol{Y}) \leq 0] = P_f \leq P_f^* \\ \quad P_f = \int_{G\leq 0} f_Y(\boldsymbol{y}) dy_1 \cdots dy_n \\ \quad 0 < \rho_{min} \leq \rho_e \leq 1 (e = 1, 2, \ldots, N_e) \end{cases} \tag{20}$$

This optimization model is expressed as finding the optimized structural configuration, i.e., minimizing the overall structural volume under the reliability stress constraint. $\boldsymbol{Y}$ is a vector of random variables, G is a limit state function, $f_Y(\boldsymbol{y})$ is the joint probability density function of $\boldsymbol{Y}$, P_r is the probability sign, P_f is the failure probability, obtained by multidimensional integration, and P_f^* is the value of the permissible failure probability. In reliability analysis, the limit state is defined as G ($\boldsymbol{\rho}$, $\boldsymbol{Y}$) = 0, the failure state and the safety state are G ($\boldsymbol{\rho}$, $\boldsymbol{Y}$) < 0 and G ($\boldsymbol{\rho}$, $\boldsymbol{Y}$) > 0, respectively.

In practical engineering, it is difficult to solve the multidimensional integral to obtain the exact probability density distribution. Therefore, approximate analytical methods are generally used to calculate the failure probability, such as the first order second moment method [33] and the first order reliability method [34]. The first order reliability method is selected in this paper to approximate the failure probability.

According to the stress intensity interference theory [35,36], this paper characterizes the limit state function, G, in terms of the load-bearing capacity of the structure, denoted as

$$G(\boldsymbol{\rho}, \boldsymbol{Y}) = R - S = \sigma_s - \sigma_e^{VM}(\boldsymbol{\rho}, \boldsymbol{Y}) \tag{21}$$

where R denotes the structural resistance and S denotes the load variable. In this paper, we consider the possibility that the random variables may cause the von Mises stress somewhere in the structure to exceed the yield strength limit of the material, thus causing the structure to fail. So here R is denoted as the yield strength σ_s of the material and S is denoted as the von Mises stress $\sigma_e{}^{VM}(\boldsymbol{\rho}, \boldsymbol{Y})$ of element. $G > 0$, the structure is reliable, $G < 0$, the structure fails, and G = 0, the structure is in the limit state.

If both R and S obey normal distribution, their mean and variance are φ_R, φ_S and σ_R, σ_S, respectively. Then G also obeys normal distribution, and let its mean and variance be φ_G and σ_G, respectively. Therefore, the failure probability can be expressed as

$$P_f = P_r[\sigma_s - \sigma_e^{VM}(\boldsymbol{\rho}, \boldsymbol{Y}) \leq 0] = \Phi\left(\frac{\varphi_S - \varphi_R}{\left(\sigma_R^2 + \sigma_S^2\right)^{1/2}}\right) = \Phi\left(-\frac{\varphi_G}{\sigma_G}\right) \tag{22}$$

where Φ is the standard cumulative distribution function.

Introducing the reliability index β, let be

$$\beta = \frac{\varphi_G}{\sigma_G} \tag{23}$$

Using the first order reliability method, the calculation of the probability of failure is converted into a measurable reliability index β, which is specifically expressed as the minimum distance from the origin to the limit state function in the normalized space ($\boldsymbol{u}$ space) with the most probable point (MPP) being searched, as shown in Figure 2. According to the corresponding relationship of the failure probability and the reliability index in the first order reliability method, the failure probability constraint can be transformed into the following reliability index constraint

$$\begin{cases} P_f = \Phi(-\beta) \\ P_f^* = \Phi(-\beta^*) \\ P_f \leq P_f^* \Rightarrow \beta \geq \beta^* \end{cases} \tag{24}$$

where β^* is the target reliability index, and the intersection point $\boldsymbol{u}^*$ is the design point, also known as the most probable failure point (MPP). The random variable $\boldsymbol{Y}$ needs to be normalized into an independent standard normal random variable $\boldsymbol{u}$, expressed as $\boldsymbol{u} = \mathrm{T}(\boldsymbol{Y})$, or $\boldsymbol{Y} = \mathrm{T}^{-1}(\boldsymbol{u})$. In the standard normal space, $\boldsymbol{u}$ is given by the following expression, defined as

$$\boldsymbol{u} = \frac{\boldsymbol{Y} - \boldsymbol{\varphi_y}}{\sigma_y} \tag{25}$$

where $\boldsymbol{\varphi_y}$ and σ_y are the vector of mean values and the standard deviations associated with $\boldsymbol{Y}$, respectively.

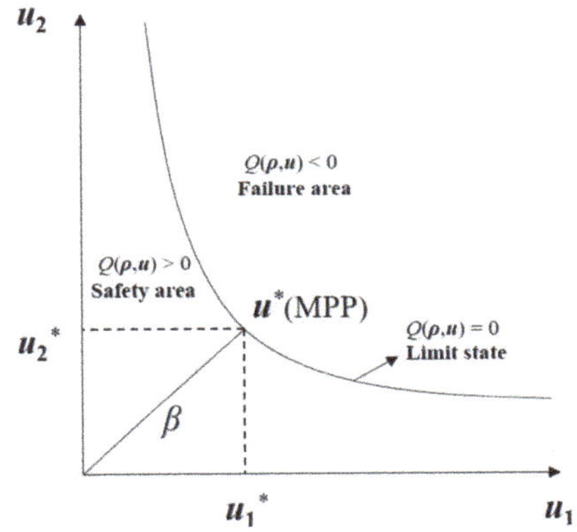

Figure 2. Geometric description of reliability index in standard normal space.

After the above transformation, in the standard normal space, the limit state function is then transformed into

$$G(\rho, Y) = G\left(\left(\rho, T^{-1}(\boldsymbol{u})\right) = Q(\rho, \boldsymbol{u})\right. \tag{26}$$

4.3. Reliability-Based Topology Optimization for Thermo-Elastic Structures

The design variables and random variables in the reliability-based topology optimization are respectively assigned into deterministic topology optimization and reliability analysis and are independent of each other, which leads to the reliability-based topology optimization computation intensively and makes it difficult to converge [37]. Therefore, the proposed predecessor-decoupling hybrid method is adopted that decomposed the RBTO problem into two successively independent design processes that the deterministic topology optimization and reliability analysis.

In the reliability analysis, the MPP point $\boldsymbol{u}^*$ is obtained by solving the following mathematical model according to the geometric meaning of the reliability index β in Figure 2.

$$\begin{cases} \min\limits_{u} \|\boldsymbol{u}\| = \beta = \sqrt{\Sigma u_i^2} \\ s.t. \beta(\boldsymbol{u}) \geq \beta^* \end{cases} \tag{27}$$

The sensitivity of the reliability index concerning the normal random variable can be expressed as

$$\frac{\partial \beta}{\partial u_i} = \frac{1}{2}\left(\sum u_i^2\right)^{-1/2} 2u_i = \frac{u_i}{\beta} \tag{28}$$

The sensitivity of the objective function with respect to the chosen means of random variables can simply be calculated using the classical finite difference approach, written as

$$\frac{\partial V}{\partial \varphi_{y_i}} = \frac{\Delta V}{\Delta \varphi_{y_i}} = \frac{V(\varphi_{y_i} + \Delta \varphi_{y_i}) - V(\varphi_{y_i})}{\Delta \varphi_{y_i}} \tag{29}$$

where φ_{yi} and σ_{yi} are the mean value and standard deviation of the random variable y_i, respectively.

According to the above sensitivity calculation result, the revised random variable $\boldsymbol{y}^*$ through Rosenblatt inverse transform, is defined as

$$\begin{cases} y_i^* = \varphi_{y_i} + u_i^* \sigma_{y_i}, & \frac{\partial V}{\partial \varphi_{y_i}} \geq 0 \\ y_i^* = \varphi_{y_i} - u_i^* \sigma_{y_i}, & \frac{\partial V}{\partial \varphi_{y_i}} \leq 0 \end{cases} \tag{30}$$

5. Sensitivity Analysis

The sensitivity of the structural volume respect to the element density can be obtained by the direct differentiation method, defined by

$$\frac{\partial V(\boldsymbol{\rho})}{\partial \rho_e} = v_0 \tag{31}$$

The sensitivity information of the stress relative to the element density is obtained by the adjoint variable method. The Lagrangian function C of the stress is constructed by introducing the Lagrangian product factor as

$$C = \overline{\sigma}^{PN} - \boldsymbol{\lambda}^{\mathrm{T}}\left(\boldsymbol{K}(\boldsymbol{\rho})\boldsymbol{U} - \boldsymbol{F}^{m} - \boldsymbol{F}^{th}(\boldsymbol{\rho})\right) \tag{32}$$

The sensitivity of the Lagrangian function with respect to the element density is derived as

$$\frac{\partial C}{\partial \rho_e} = \frac{\partial \overline{\sigma}^{PN}}{\partial \rho_e} - \boldsymbol{\lambda}^{\mathrm{T}}\left(\frac{\partial \boldsymbol{K}(\boldsymbol{\rho})}{\partial \rho_e}\boldsymbol{U} + \boldsymbol{K}(\boldsymbol{\rho})\frac{\partial \boldsymbol{U}}{\partial \rho_e} - \frac{\partial \boldsymbol{F}^{m}}{\partial \rho_e} - \frac{\partial \boldsymbol{F}^{th}(\boldsymbol{\rho})}{\partial \rho_e}\right) \tag{33}$$

According to the chain rule, it is easy to obtain the sensitivity corresponding the element density ρ_e as

$$\frac{\partial \overline{\sigma}^{PN}}{\partial \rho_e} = \sum_{i=1}^{N_e} c \frac{\partial \sigma^{PN}}{\partial \sigma_e^{VM}} \left(\frac{\partial \sigma_e^{VM}}{\partial \sigma_e}\right)^{\mathrm{T}} \frac{\partial \sigma_e}{\partial \rho_e} \tag{34}$$

From the above equation, the sensitivity information for solving the global stress can be obtained by combining the derivative of the p-norm function with respect to the von Mises stress, the derivative of the von Mises stress with respect to the stress component, and the derivative of the stress component with respect to the design variable. This sensitivity information is performed separately.

5.1. Derivative of the p-Norm Function with Respect to the Von Mises Stress

Taking the expression of Equation (16), the derivative information of the p-norm function to the von Mises stress of each element can be obtained as

$$\frac{\partial \sigma^{PN}}{\partial \sigma_e^{VM}} = \left(\sum_{e=1}^{N_e} \left(\frac{\sigma_e^{VM}}{\sigma_s}\right)^p\right)^{\frac{1}{p}-1} \left(\frac{\sigma_e^{VM}}{\sigma_s}\right)^{p-1} \frac{1}{\sigma_s} \tag{35}$$

5.2. Derivative of the Von Mises Stress with Respect to the Stress Component

For planar and spatial structural problems, the derivatives of element stress with respect to the stress components are respectively described as

For 2D problems,

$$\begin{cases} \frac{\partial \sigma_e^{VM}}{\partial \sigma_{ex}} = \frac{1}{2\sigma_e^{VM}}\left(2\sigma_{ex} - \sigma_{ey}\right) \\ \frac{\partial \sigma_e^{VM}}{\partial \sigma_{ey}} = \frac{1}{2\sigma_e^{VM}}\left(2\sigma_{ey} - \sigma_{ex}\right) \\ \frac{\partial \sigma_e^{VM}}{\partial \tau_{exy}} = \frac{3\tau_{exy}}{\sigma_e^{VM}} \end{cases} \tag{36}$$

For 3D problems,

$$\begin{cases} \frac{\partial \sigma_e^{VM}}{\partial \sigma_{ex}} = \frac{1}{2\sigma_e^{VM}}\left(2\sigma_{ex} - \sigma_{ey} - \sigma_{ez}\right) \\ \frac{\partial \sigma_e^{VM}}{\partial \sigma_{ey}} = \frac{1}{2\sigma_e^{VM}}\left(2\sigma_{ey} - \sigma_{ex} - \sigma_{ez}\right) \\ \frac{\partial \sigma_e^{VM}}{\partial \sigma_{ez}} = \frac{1}{2\sigma_e^{VM}}\left(2\sigma_{ez} - \sigma_{ex} - \sigma_{ey}\right) \\ \frac{\partial \sigma_e^{VM}}{\partial \tau_{exy}} = \frac{3\tau_{exy}}{\sigma_e^{VM}} \\ \frac{\partial \sigma_e^{VM}}{\partial \tau_{exz}} = \frac{3\tau_{exz}}{\sigma_e^{VM}} \\ \frac{\partial \sigma_e^{VM}}{\partial \tau_{ezx}} = \frac{3\tau_{ezx}}{\sigma_e^{VM}} \end{cases} \tag{37}$$

5.3. Derivative of Stress Components with Respect to Design Variable

The derivative of the element stress component with respect to the density variable is obtained as

$$\frac{\partial \boldsymbol{\sigma}_e}{\partial \rho_e} = q\rho_e^{q-1}E_0(\boldsymbol{D}_0\boldsymbol{B}_e\boldsymbol{U}_e - \boldsymbol{D}_0\gamma_0\boldsymbol{\phi}\Delta T) + \rho_e^q E_0 \boldsymbol{D}_0\boldsymbol{B}_e \frac{\partial \boldsymbol{U}_e}{\partial \boldsymbol{U}}\frac{\partial \boldsymbol{U}_e}{\partial \rho_e} \tag{38}$$

Considering the loading independence, the derivative of the mechanical load $\boldsymbol{F}^m$ on the element density can be ignored, and combining Equation (35) with Equation (34) and substituting it into Equation (33), we can obtain

$$\begin{aligned} \frac{\partial C}{\partial \rho_e} = & \sum_{e=1}^{N_e} c\frac{\partial \sigma^{PN}}{\partial \sigma_e^{VM}}\left(\frac{\partial \sigma_e^{VM}}{\partial \sigma_e}\right)^{\mathrm{T}} q\rho_e^{q-1}E_0(\boldsymbol{D}_0\boldsymbol{B}_e\boldsymbol{U}_e - \boldsymbol{D}_0\gamma_0\boldsymbol{\phi}\Delta T) \\ & -\boldsymbol{\lambda}^T\left(\frac{\partial \boldsymbol{K}(\boldsymbol{\rho})}{\partial \rho_e}\boldsymbol{U} - \frac{\partial \boldsymbol{F}^{th}(\boldsymbol{\rho})}{\partial \rho_e}\right) \\ & +\left[\sum_{e=1}^{N_e} c\frac{\partial \sigma^{PN}}{\partial \sigma_e^{VM}}\left(\frac{\partial \sigma_e^{VM}}{\partial \sigma_e}\right)^{\mathrm{T}} \rho_e^q E_0\boldsymbol{D}_0\boldsymbol{B}_e\frac{\partial \boldsymbol{U}_e}{\partial \boldsymbol{U}} - \boldsymbol{\lambda}^{\mathrm{T}}\boldsymbol{K}(\boldsymbol{\rho})\right]\frac{\partial \boldsymbol{U}_e}{\partial \rho_e} \end{aligned} \tag{39}$$

In order to eliminate the unknown displacement sensitivity term, let the term containing $\partial \boldsymbol{U}/\partial \rho_e$ be zero, then the adjoint vector equation is established as

$$\boldsymbol{K}(\boldsymbol{\rho})\boldsymbol{\lambda} = \sum_{e=1}^{N_e} c\frac{\partial \sigma^{PN}}{\partial \sigma_e^{VM}}\rho_e^q E_0\left(\frac{\partial \boldsymbol{U}_e}{\partial \boldsymbol{U}}\right)^{\mathrm{T}}\boldsymbol{B}_e^T\boldsymbol{D}_0^T\left(\frac{\partial \sigma_e^{VM}}{\partial \sigma_e}\right) \tag{40}$$

Then the corresponding sensitivity is

$$\begin{aligned} \frac{\partial C}{\partial \rho_e} = & \sum_{e=1}^{N_e} c\frac{\partial \sigma^{PN}}{\partial \sigma_e^{VM}}\left(\frac{\partial \sigma_e^{VM}}{\partial \sigma_e}\right)^{\mathrm{T}} q\rho_e^{q-1}E_0 q\rho_e^{q-1}E_0(\boldsymbol{D}_0\boldsymbol{B}_e\boldsymbol{U}_e - \boldsymbol{D}_0\gamma_0\boldsymbol{\phi}\Delta T) \\ & -\boldsymbol{\lambda}^T\left(\frac{\partial \boldsymbol{K}(\boldsymbol{\rho})}{\partial \rho_e}\boldsymbol{U} - \frac{\partial \boldsymbol{F}^{th}(\boldsymbol{\rho})}{\partial \rho_e}\right) \end{aligned} \tag{41}$$

Combining Equation (4) information, the derivation of Equations (2) and (7) can respectively obtain the sensitivity of stiffness matrix $\boldsymbol{K}(\boldsymbol{\rho})$ and temperature load vector $\boldsymbol{F}^{th}(\boldsymbol{\rho})$, defined as

$$\frac{\partial \boldsymbol{K}(\boldsymbol{\rho})}{\partial \rho_e} = \sum_{e=1}^{N_e} \alpha\rho_e^{\alpha-1}E_0\int_{\Omega_e}\boldsymbol{B}_e^{\mathrm{T}}\boldsymbol{D}_0\boldsymbol{B}_e h d\Omega_e \tag{42}$$

$$\frac{\partial \boldsymbol{F}^{th}(\boldsymbol{\rho})}{\partial \rho_e} = \sum_{e=1}^{N_e} k\rho_e^{k-1}\delta_0 \Delta T \int_{\Omega_e} \boldsymbol{B}_e^T \boldsymbol{D}_0 \boldsymbol{\phi} d\Omega_e \tag{43}$$

6. Density Filtering

In order to avoid the phenomenon of checkerboard and intermediate elements in the topology optimization results, the density filtering technology [38] is used to suppress the problems that are defined as

$$\rho_e = \frac{1}{\sum_{i \in N_e} H_{ei}} \sum_{i \in N_e} H_{ei} x_i \tag{44}$$

where ρ_e is the element density, which is used to calculate the volume and stiffness matrix of the element, x_i is the design variable of the element, N_e is the number of all elements whose distance from the center of element e is less than the filter radius r_{min}, and H_{ei} is the linear distance function, namely

$$H_{ei} = max(0, r_{min} - \Delta(e, i)) \tag{45}$$

where $\Delta(e, i)$ is the distance between the centers of element e and element i.

The difference between the design variable x and the physical density $\boldsymbol{\rho}$ can be noted here. The finite element model is parameterized using the density variable ρ_e contained in $\boldsymbol{\rho}$. The density variable is now calculated by applying a density filter to the design variable x. For sensitivity consistency, the following chain rule is used, where g is the objective or constraint function

$$\frac{\partial g}{\partial x_j} = \sum_{e \in N_j} \frac{\partial g}{\partial \rho_e} \frac{\partial \rho_e}{\partial x_j} = \sum_{e \in N_j} \frac{1}{\sum_{i \in N_e} H_{ei}} H_{je} \frac{\partial g}{\partial \rho_e} \tag{46}$$

The method of moving asymptote (MMA) [39] is used to solve the reliability-based stress-constrained topology optimization problem for thermo-elastic structures. Due to the highly nonlinear behavior of the stress constraint, the optimization process is prone to iterative oscillations and even non-convergence. To avoid non-convergence, then an external move limit m is imposed on the MMA algorithm to limit the maximum absolute value of the difference between the design variables updated during the current iteration and the previous iteration step.

In summary, the design of the reliability topology optimization of thermo-elastic structures considering the stress constraint based on the hybrid precursor-decoupling format is decoupled into two parts executed in separate sequences: the precursor reliability analysis and the deterministic topology optimization. The specific process is: first, according to the geometric meaning of the reliability index in the primary reliability method, seek the design point that satisfies the target reliability index; then, according to the sensitivity information of the random variable, modify the random variable and convert it into a deterministic parameter; finally, the deterministic topology optimization design is carried out. The specific optimization flowchart is shown in Figure 3.

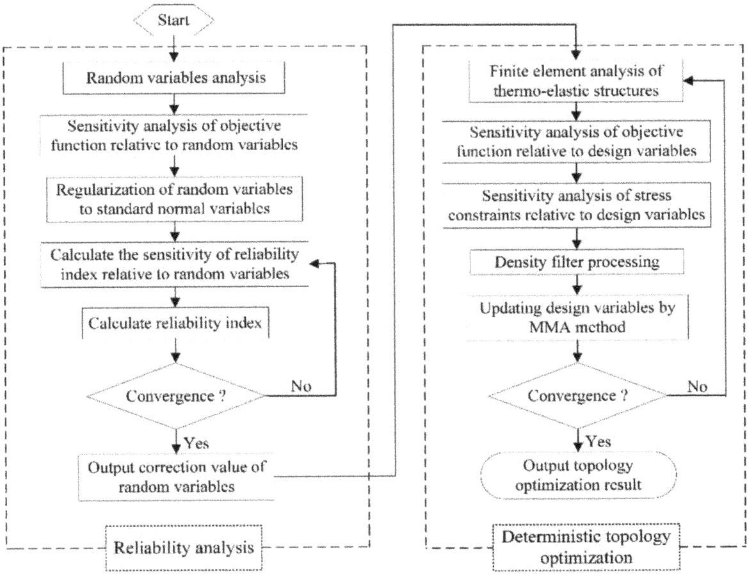

Figure 3. Flowchart of reliability topology optimization in hybrid format.

7. Numerical Examples

In this section, three numerical examples of reliability-based stress-constrained topology optimization of thermo-elastic structures are selected to verify the effectiveness of the proposed method. The selected materials are chosen with the Young's modulus E = 2.1 × 10^5 MPa, Poisson's ratio $\mu = 0.3$, thermal expansion coefficient $\gamma_0 = 12.1 \times 10^{-6}/°C$. The p-norm penalization factor is $p = 8$. The penalty factors are defined as $\alpha = 3$, $k = 3$, and $q = 0.8$. The initial element density values are taken as 1. The corresponding initial design domain volume is V_0, and the ratio V/V_0 of the optimized structure volume to the initial structure volume is used as the objective function, and the temperature field is uniformly varying.

7.1. 2D L-Shaped Beam Structure

The design domain of the L-shaped beam structure is illustrated in Figure 4. The design domain has dimensions of 120 mm × 120 mm with a thickness of 1 mm and is discretized into 14,400 quadrilateral elements. The top end of the L-shaped beam structure is clamped and the mechanical load F^m is applied to the upper right end of the structure, which is uniformly distributed over six adjacent nodes to avoid stress concentration. The stress constraint value for the structure is 235 MPa, and the amount of temperature change ΔT = 10 °C.

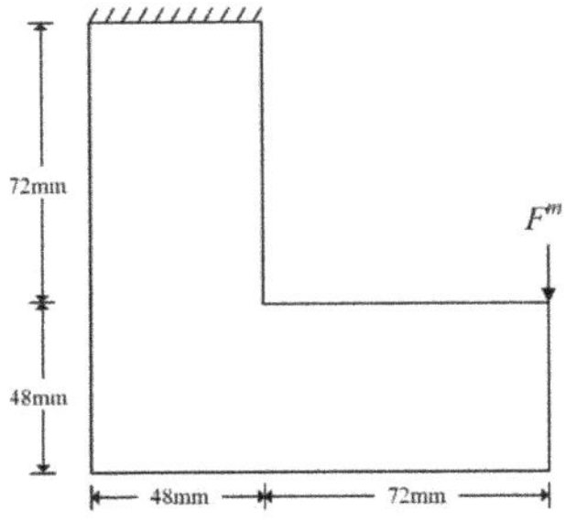

Figure 4. Design domain of L-shaped beam.

For the reliability analysis, the random variables are chosen as $\mathbf{Y} = (F^m, E, \delta_0)^{\mathrm{T}}$, and assume that they obey normal probabilistic distribution. The mean value of mechanical load, Young's modulus and thermal stress coefficient are $\varphi_F{}^m = 280$ N, $\varphi_E = 2.1 \times 10^5$ MPa and $\varphi_{\delta 0} = 2.541$ MPa/°C, respectively. The variance is set to 5% of the mean value and the permitted reliability index is set to 3.0.

The detailed evolution of the deterministic and reliable structures and the von Mises stress distribution are shown in Figures 5 and 6, respectively, and the initial structural maximum on the von Mises stress value is 246.82 MPa. The optimized deterministic and reliable topological configurations and von Mises stress distributions are shown in Figures 7 and 8, respectively. The corresponding topology optimization results are shown in Table 1, and the reliability indexes are calculated using the Monte Carlo simulation method, where u_1, u_2, and u_3 correspond to the standard normalized variable values of the random variables F^m, E, and δ_0, respectively.

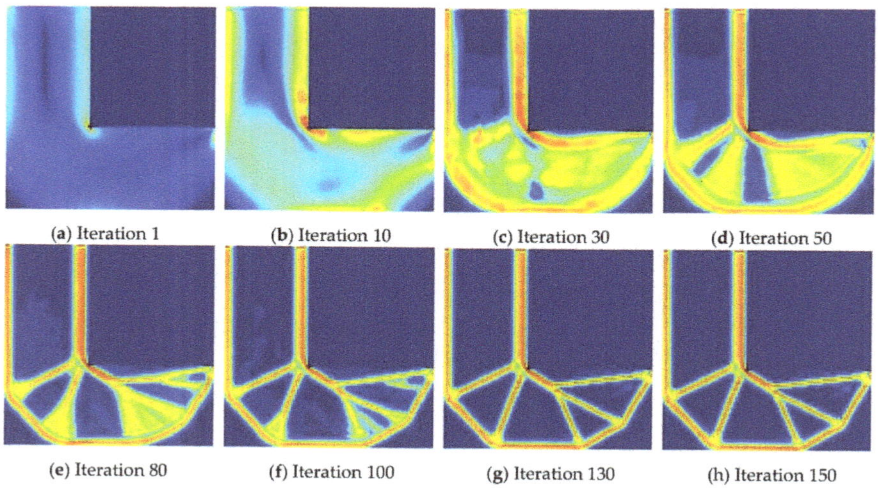

Figure 5. Structural evolution for deterministic topology optimization with stress distribution (**a**–**h**).

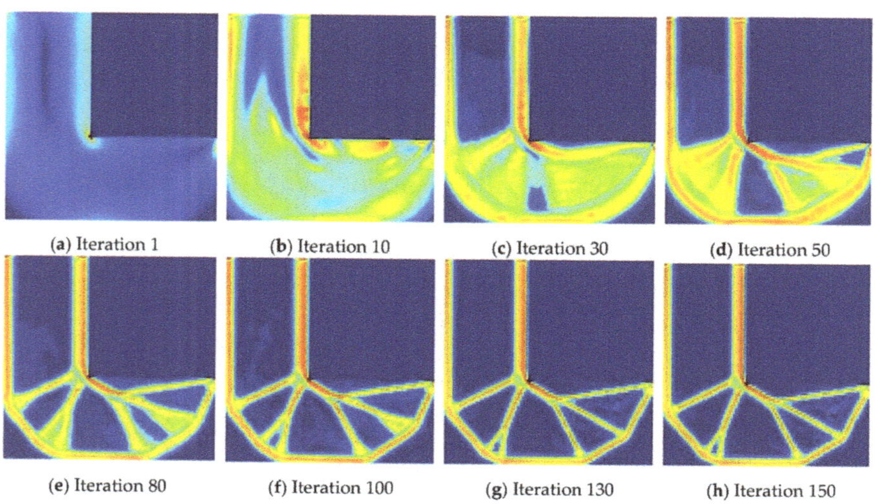

Figure 6. Structural evolution for reliability topology optimization with stress distribution (**a**–**h**).

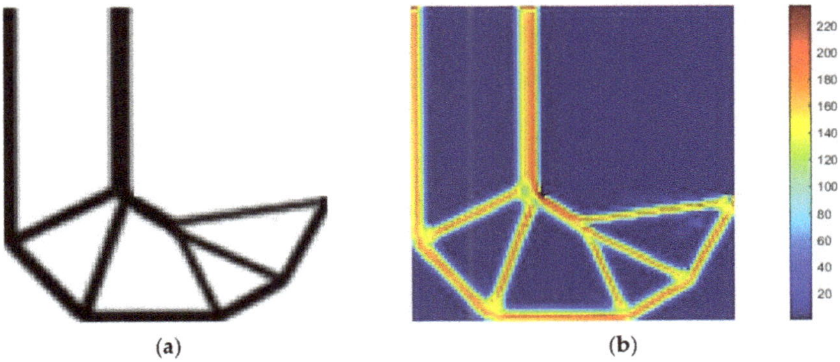

Figure 7. Deterministic topology optimization result of L-beam structure (14,400 elements): (**a**) Topological structure; (**b**) Von Mises stress distribution.

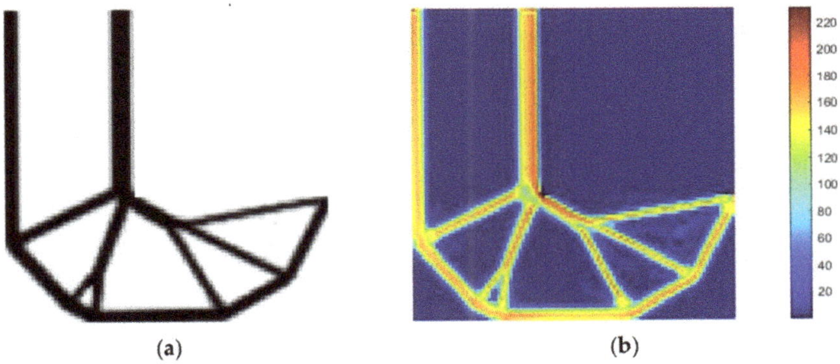

Figure 8. Reliability topology optimization result of L-beam structure (14,400 elements): (**a**) Topological structure; (**b**) Von Mises stress distribution.

Table 1. Comparison of topology optimization design results.

Approach	Volume Fraction (%)	Reliability Index (β)	Computing Time (s)	Max Von Mises Stress (MPa)	MPP (u_1, u_2, u_3)
DTO	19.8	1.7759×10^{-5}	371.63	234.95	-
RBTO	24.3	2.9745	395.49	234.60	(1.7321, 1.7321, 1.7321)

In addition, in order to illustrate that the number of elements in the divided design domain has no obvious effect on the optimized topology, the design domain shown in Figure 4 is discretized into 6400 quadrilateral elements, where the mechanical load F^m does not change, and is applied to the upper right end of the structure and uniformly distributed over four adjacent nodes. The optimized deterministic and reliable topologies and von Mises stress distributions are shown in Figures 9 and 10, respectively.

By observing Figures 5 and 6 and Table 1, it can be seen that the right-angle corner of the initial structure is the stress concentration area, and the maximum von Mises stress exceeds the material strength. The structure after deterministic and reliable topology optimization not only reduces the maximum von Mises stress, but also meets the strength requirements of the material, and the original stress concentration corner evolves into a rounded structure, which alleviates the stress concentration phenomenon.

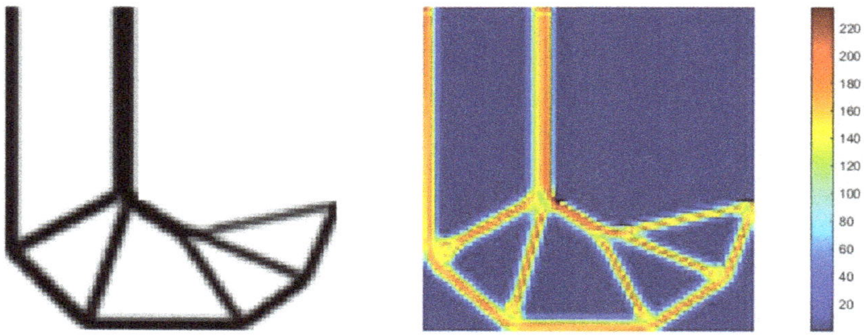

(a) (b)

Figure 9. Deterministic topology optimization result of L-beam structure (6400 elements): (**a**) Topological structure; (**b**) Von Mises stress distribution.

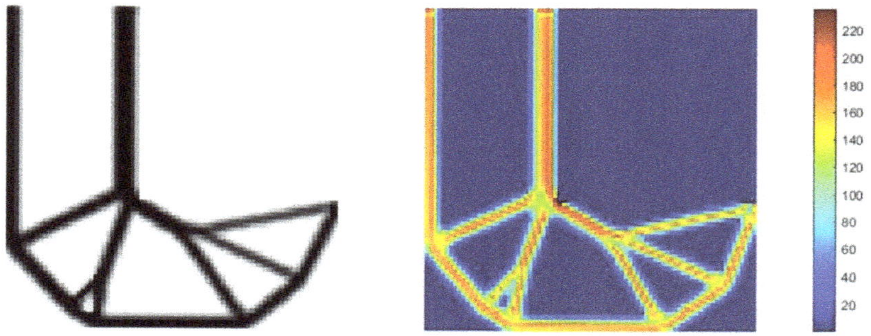

(a) (b)

Figure 10. Reliability topology optimization result of L-beam structure (6400 elements): (**a**) Topological structure; (**b**) Von Mises stress distribution.

The results for DTO and RBTO show very different optimal topologies, where DTO is less reliable and therefore allows less margin for performance fluctuations and an increased probability of structural failure when parameter variations that are considered as random variables are considered. The topology obtained from RBTO uses about 4% more material than DTO to make the structure meet the target reliability index. We also find that RBTO obtains a slightly lower computational efficiency due to the need to solve the MPP in the reliability analysis. In terms of the respective stress distribution, the RBTO presents a more uniform stress distribution in the structure compared to the DTO, and the structure is subjected to a smaller maximum von Mises stress value. Finally, comparing the topological configurations in Figures 7 and 8 with Figures 9 and 10, respectively, it can be seen that the deterministic and reliable topological configurations under different numbers of elements are relatively similar, which indicates that the number of elements does not have a significant effect on the topological configuration, that is, the proposed method is mesh independence.

The volume fraction and maximum von Mises stress iteration curves for the DTO and RBTO processes shown in Figures 7 and 8 are shown in Figure 11. The results show that the iterative oscillation of the maximum von Mises stress during optimization is caused by the highly nonlinear behavior of the stress constraint. Compared with DTO, the fluctuation degree of the maximum von Mises stress in the iterative process of RBTO is reduced, and the iterative process is more stable. The above analysis can show that the proposed method is feasible and effective.

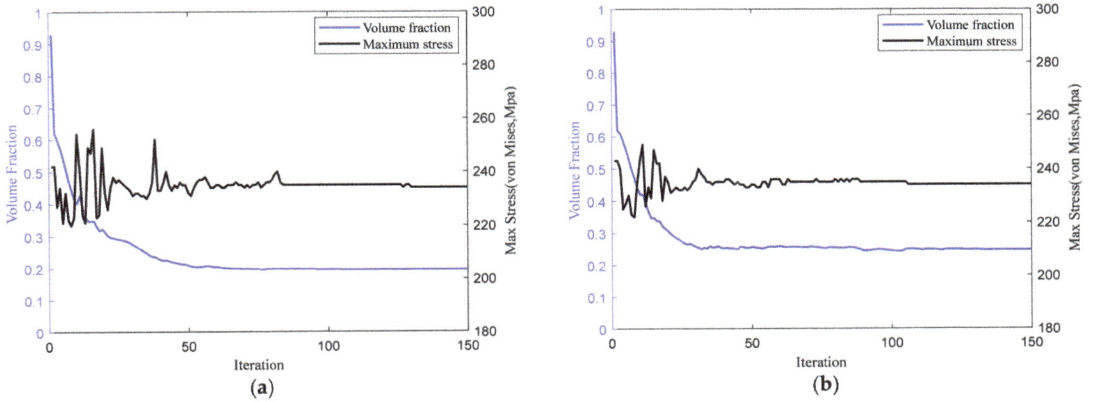

Figure 11. Volume fraction and maximum von Mises stress iteration curves of (**a**) DTO and (**b**) RBTO.

7.2. 2D T-Shaped Beam Structure

The design domain of the T-beam structure is shown in Figure 12. The design domain is 160 mm × 100 mm in structural dimensions and 1 mm in thickness, which is discretized into 16,000 four-node elements. The left and right sides of the structure are solidly supported, and the mechanical loads $F_x{}^m$ and $F_y{}^m$ are applied to the upper right end of the structure, which are uniformly distributed to the five adjacent nodes horizontally. The stress constraint value for the structure is 235 MPa.

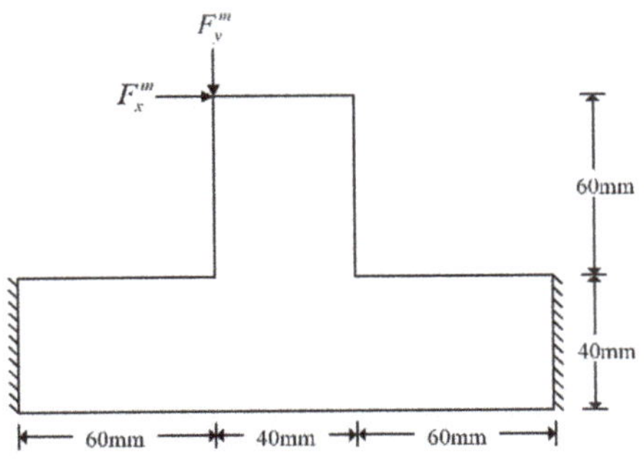

Figure 12. Design domain of T-shaped beam.

For the reliability analysis, the random variables are chosen as $\boldsymbol{Y} = (F_x{}^m, F_y{}^m, E, \delta_0)^{\mathrm{T}}$, and assume that they obey normal probabilistic distribution. The mean value of mechanical loads, Young's modulus and thermal stress coefficient are $\varphi_{Fx}{}^m$ = 350 N, $\varphi_{Fy}{}^m$ = 300 N, $\varphi_E = 2.1 \times 10^5$ MPa and $\varphi_{\delta 0}$ = 2.541 MPa/°C, respectively. The variance is set to 10% of the mean value.

The initial stress distribution of the structure is shown in Figure 13, and the maximum von Mises stress value is 315.04 MPa. In order to consider the effect of different temperature variations ΔT on the topology optimization results, when the temperature variations ΔT are set to 20 °C and 30 °C, the DTO and RBTO topologies and von Mises stress distributions obtained are shown in Figures 14 and 15, respectively. The corresponding topology optimization results are shown in Table 2, and the reliability indexes are calculated using the Monte Carlo simulation method, where u_1, u_2, u_3 and u_4 correspond to the standard normalized variable values of the random variables $F_x{}^m$, $F_y{}^m$, E and δ_0, respectively.

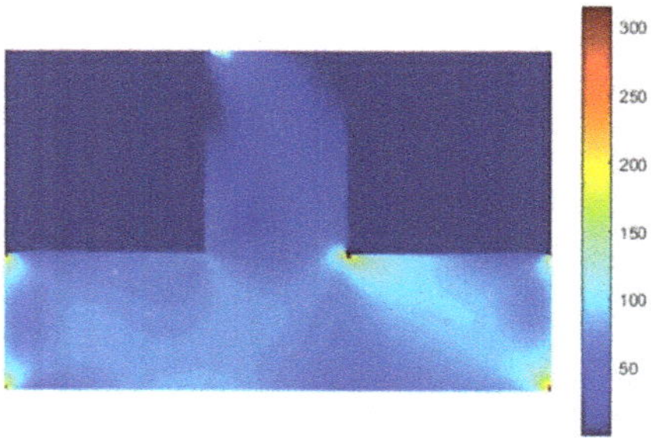

Figure 13. Initial structural stress distribution.

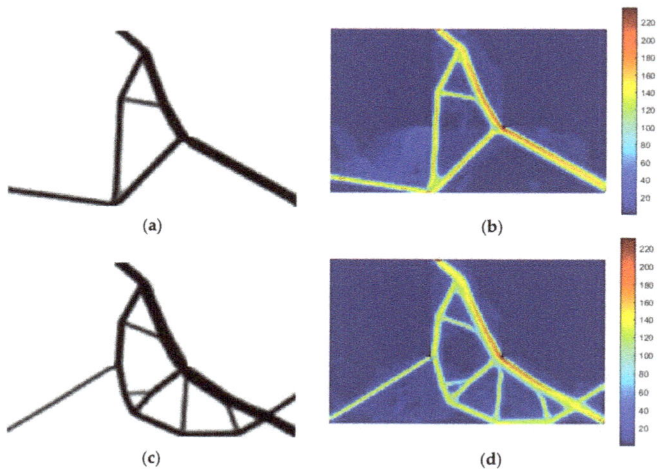

Figure 14. Topology optimization results of T-beam (ΔT = 20 °C): (**a**) DTO topological structure (**b**) DTO Von Mises stress distribution; (**c**) RBTO topological structure; (**d**) RBTO Von Mises stress distribution.

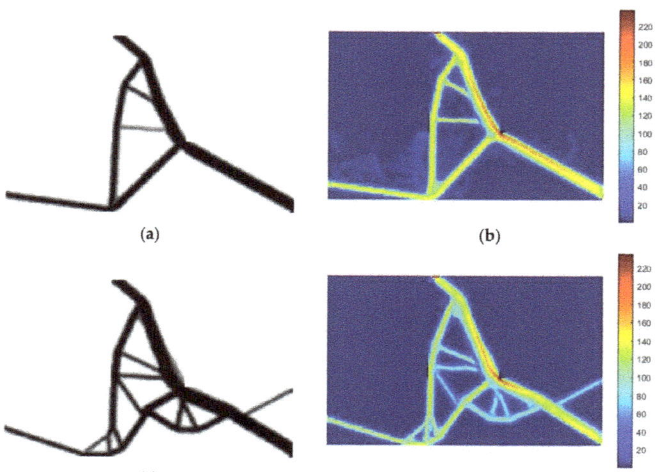

Figure 15. Topology optimization results of T-beam (ΔT = 30 °C): (**a**) DTO topological structure; (**b**) DTO Von Mises stress distribution; (**c**) RBTO topological structure; (**d**) RBTO Von Mises stress distribution.

Table 2. Comparison of topology optimization design results.

ΔT (°C)	Approach	Volume Fraction (%)	Reliability Index (β)	Computing Time (s)	Max Von Mises Stress (MPa)	MPP (u_1, u_2, u_3, u_4)
20	DTO	10.2	2.0201×10^{-5}	354.02	234.96	-
	RBTO	13.5	3.9722	428.21	234.72	(2.000, 2.000, 2.000, 2.000)
30	DTO	11.2	2.5426×10^{-5}	359.37	234.85	-
	RBTO	14.4	3.9764	435.19	234.53	(2.000, 2.000, 2.000, 2.000)

By comparing the above optimization results with the initial structure, it can be seen that the right-angle part of the original structure evolves into a slightly rounded shape, which relieves the stress concentration, the stress distribution of the structure is uniform, and the design results of both DTO and RBTO meet the stress constraint requirements.

Comparing the reliability indicators of DTO and RBTO results in Table 2, we can see that the reliability level of the DTO results is close to 0, so the probability of structural failure is higher. The reliability index of RBTO results has been improved compared with that of the DTO results, but the target reliability has not been achieved precisely, and it also reflects that the proposed method can effectively improve the reliability of the structure, but the computational accuracy is still slightly inadequate. Compared with DTO, the structures obtained by RBTO are both significantly different, and the reliability of the structure is improved, and the overall stress distribution of the structures is more uniform.

A comparative analysis of the optimization results of the structures in Table 2 shows that the topologies of both DTO and RBTO are slightly different for different temperature variations ΔT. This is mainly due to the fact that as the temperature variation ΔT increases, the temperature load enlarges and more material needs to be filled to bring the structures to the allowed reliability index, which leads to a slight increase in volume.

The volume fraction and maximum von Mises stress iteration curves for the DTO and RBTO at different temperature variations ΔT are shown in Figure 16, respectively. Compared with DTO, RBTO has less fluctuation of the maximum von Mises stress during the iterative process. It can be demonstrated that it is necessary and effective to incorporate the reliability analysis into the stress-constrained topology optimization of a thermo-elastic problem considering the uncertainties of mechanical loads, the thermal stress coefficient, and the material's property.

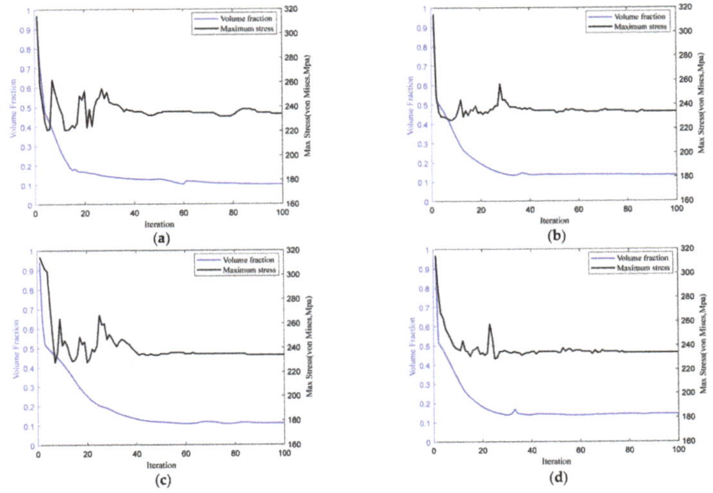

Figure 16. Volume fraction and maximum von Mises stress iteration curves of (**a**) DTO (ΔT = 20 °C) and (**b**) RBTO (ΔT = 20 °C); (**c**) DTO (ΔT = 30 °C) and (**d**) RBTO (ΔT = 30 °C).

7.3. 3D L-Shaped Beam Structure

In this section, we extend the previous 2D L-bracket example to a 3D design problem. The design domain of the 3D L-beam structure is shown in Figure 17. The design domain size is 50 mm × 50 mm and the thickness is 4 mm. The domain is discrete into 10,000 eight-node hexahedral elements. The upper left of the structure is fixed. The mechanical load F^m is applied vertically downward on the right side of the structure. The stress constraint value for the structure is 235 MPa and the amount of temperature change $\Delta T = 30\ ^\circ\text{C}$.

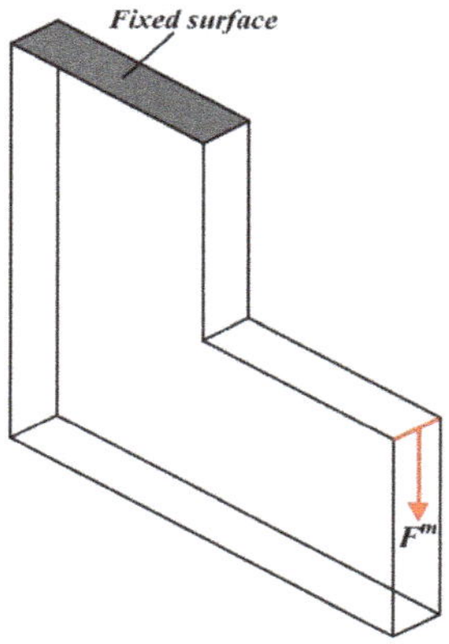

Figure 17. 3D L-beam design domain.

For the reliability analysis, the random variables are chosen as $\boldsymbol{Y} = (F^m, E, \delta_0)^{\mathrm{T}}$ and assume that they obey normal probabilistic distributions. The mean values of mechanical load, Young's modulus and thermal stress coefficient are $\varphi_F{}^m = 67$ N, $\varphi_E = 2.1 \times 10^5$ MPa and $\varphi_{\delta 0} = 2.541$ MPa/°C, respectively. The variance is set to 7% of the mean value, and the permissible reliability index is set to 5.0.

The initial structural stress distribution is shown in Figure 18 and the maximum von Mises stress value is 273.81 MPa. The deterministic and reliable topologies and von Mises stress distributions are shown in Figures 19 and 20, respectively. The corresponding topology optimization results are shown in Table 3, and the reliability indexes are calculated using the Monte Carlo simulation method, where u_1, u_2, and u_3 correspond to the standard normalized variable values of the random variables F^m, E, and δ_0, respectively.

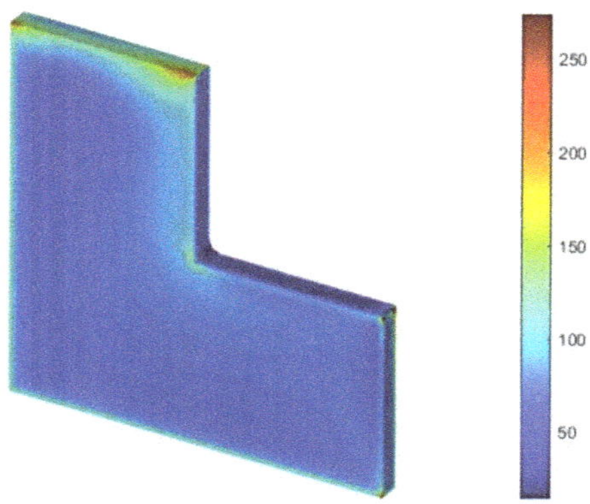

Figure 18. Initial structural stress distribution.

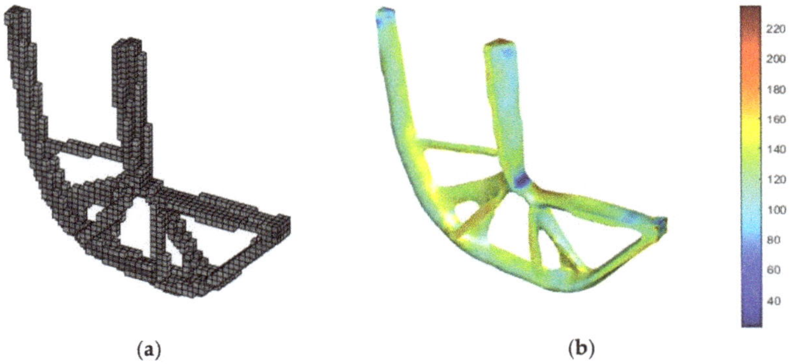

Figure 19. Deterministic topology optimization results for 3D L-shaped beam: (**a**) Topological structure; (**b**) Von Mises stress distribution.

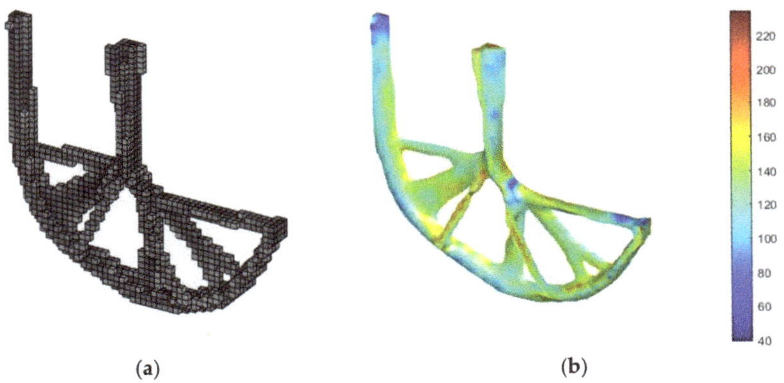

Figure 20. Reliability topology optimization results for 3D L-shaped beam: (**a**) Topological structure; (**b**) Von Mises stress distribution.

Table 3. Comparison of topology optimization design results.

Approach	Volume Fraction (%)	Reliability Index (β)	Computing Time (s)	Max Von Mises Stress (MPa)	MPP (u_1, u_2, u_3)
DTO	12.8	4.2818×10^{-5}	326.02	234.93	-
RBTO	15.7	4.9864	383.62	234.65	(2.8868, 2.8868, 2.8868)

From the above optimization results, it can be seen that the DTO and RBTO optimal configurations also achieve the maximum von Mises stress constraint.

The analysis of the DTO and RBTO results show that the DTO result has a lower reliability level and a higher probability of structural failure. Similar to the 2D L-shaped problem, the structure obtained by RBTO has a significant difference compared to the DTO result, mainly in the filling of the lower part of the structure with bar material that increases the structural volume. In terms of stress distribution, the structure obtained by RBTO has more uniform stress distribution than that obtained by DTO, and the structure is more reliable and stable.

The volume fraction and maximum von Mises stress iteration curves of DTO and RBTO are shown in Figure 21, respectively. This 3D example proves that the reliability-based stress-constrained topology optimization method for thermo-elastic structures proposed in this paper is also applicable to the 3D structures problem, which has practical significance and application prospects for solving the uncertainty problem of thermo-elastic structures.

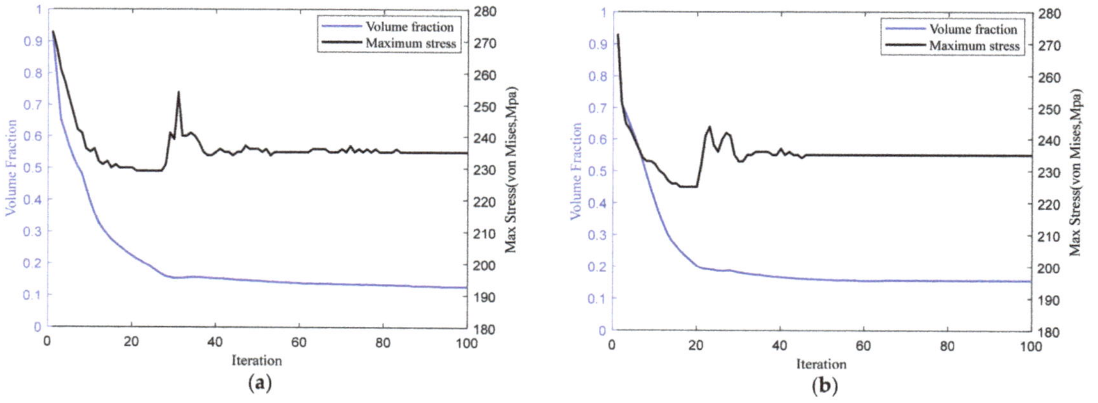

Figure 21. Volume fraction and maximum von Mises stress iteration curves of (**a**) DTO and (**b**) RBTO.

8. Conclusions

In this paper, the reliability analysis is integrated into SIMP-based topology optimization to solve the uncertainty problem in the stress-constraint topology optimization of thermo-elastic structures. The thermo-elastic topology optimization model based on global stress constraint considering the combined effect of temperature and mechanical load is established. The material property, the mechanical load and thermal stress coefficient are considered as uncertainty variables. Combining the deterministic topology optimization with the reliability hybrid method, the following conclusions can be drawn.

The structures after DTO and RBTO can satisfy the stress constraints, and the stress concentration phenomenon is alleviated. They differ in that the optimal topology obtained by the proposed RBTO method is more reliable than that obtained by the DTO method, and the RBTO exhibits significantly different topologies.

The corresponding DTO and RBTO results are also distinct for different temperature variations. It is also noted that as the temperature change increases, more material needs to be filled to meet the stress constraint and to reach the allowable reliability requirement.

The feasibility and effectiveness of the proposed method is verified by the 3D numerical example. It is shown that it is necessary to consider the uncertainty of the mechanical loads and material properties, thermal stress coefficients, and to incorporate the reliability concept into topology optimization.

In addition, the results of the above numerical examples show that the RBTO method in the predecessor-decoupling hybrid format used in this paper does not consider the influence of the functional function in the reliability analysis, so the calculation accuracy is slightly deficient. Therefore, further development of this work can try to introduce different reliability topology optimization methods for thermo-elastic structures with non-uniform temperature distribution for discussion to reduce the limitations.

Author Contributions: Formal analysis, L.Z.; funding acquisition, Q.Z.; supervision, Q.Z. and J.C.; data curation, L.Z.; writing—original draft preparation, L.Z.; writing—review and editing, Q.Z. and J.C. All authors have read and agreed to the published version of the manuscript.

Funding: The work described in this paper was supported by the National Natural Science Foundation of China (52175236).

Institutional Review Board Statement: Not applicable.

Informed Consent Statement: Not applicable.

Data Availability Statement: Not applicable.

Acknowledgments: The authors are thankful for Krister Svanberg for MMA program made freely available for research purposes and the anonymous reviewers for their helpful and constructive comments.

Conflicts of Interest: The authors declare that they have no conflict of interest.

References

1. Pedersen, P.; Pedersen, N.L. Interpolation/penalization applied for strength design of 3D thermo-elastic structures. *Struct. Multidiscip. Optim.* **2012**, *45*, 773–786. [CrossRef]
2. Rodrigues, H.; Fernandes, P. A material based model for topology optimization of thermo-elastic structures. *Int. J. Numer. Methods Eng.* **1995**, *38*, 1951–1965. [CrossRef]
3. Du, Y.X.; Luo, Z.; Tian, Q.H.; Chen, L.P. Topology optimization for thermo-mechanical compliant actuators using mesh-free methods. *Eng. Optim.* **2009**, *41*, 753–772. [CrossRef]
4. Li, Q.; Steven, G.P.; Xie, Y.M. Thermo-elastic topology optimization for problems with varying temperature fields. *J. Therm. Stress.* **2001**, *24*, 347–366. [CrossRef]
5. Deng, J.D.; Yan, J.; Cheng, G.D. Multi-objective concurrent topology optimization of thermo-elastic structures composed of homogeneous porous material. *Struct. Multidiscip. Optim.* **2013**, *47*, 583–597. [CrossRef]
6. Deaton, J.D.; Grandhi, R.V. Stiffening of restrained thermal structures via topology optimization. *Struct. Multidiscip. Optim.* **2013**, *48*, 731–745. [CrossRef]
7. Haney, M.A.; Grandhi, R.V. Consequences of material addition for a beam strip in a thermal environment. *AIAA J.* **2009**, *47*, 1026–1034. [CrossRef]
8. Le, C.; Norato, J.; Bruns, T.; Ha, C.; Tortoreli, D. Stress-based topology optimization for continua. *Struct. Multidiscip. Optim.* **2010**, *41*, 605–620. [CrossRef]
9. Cheng, G.D.; Guo, X. ε-relaxed approach in structural topology optimization. *Struct. Optim.* **1997**, *13*, 258–266. [CrossRef]
10. Wang, X.; Wang, J.; Wang, X.; Yu, C.J. A pseudo-spectral fourier collocation method for inhomogeneous elliptical inclusions with partial differential equations. *Mathematics* **2022**, *10*, 296. [CrossRef]
11. Bruggi, M.; Venini, P. A mixed FEM approach to stress-constrained topology optimization. *Int. J. Numer. Methods Eng.* **2008**, *73*, 1693–1714. [CrossRef]
12. Gao, J.; Xue, H.; Gao, L.; Luo, Z. Topology optimization for auxetic metamaterials based on isogeometric analysis. *Comput. Meth. Appl. Mech. Eng.* **2019**, *352*, 211–236. [CrossRef]
13. Chen, Z.; Long, K.; Wen, P.; Nouman, S. Fatigue-resistance topology optimization of continuum structure by penalizing the cumulative fatigue damage. *Adv. Eng. Softw.* **2020**, *150*, 102924. [CrossRef]
14. Yue, X.X.; Wang, F.J.; Hua, Q.S.; Qiu, X.Y. A novel space–time meshless method for nonhomogeneous convection–diffusion equations with variable coefficients. *Appl. Math. Lett.* **2019**, *92*, 144–150. [CrossRef]
15. Yang, R.J.; Chen, C.J. Stress-based topology optimization. *Struct. Multidiscip. Optim.* **1996**, *12*, 98–105. [CrossRef]
16. Guo, X.; Zhang, S.W.; Wang, M.Y.; Wei, P. Stress-related topology optimization via level set approach. *Comput. Meth. Appl. Mech. Eng.* **2011**, *200*, 3439–3452. [CrossRef]
17. Zhang, W.S.; Guo, X.; Wang, M.Y.; Wei, P. Optimal topology design of continuum structures with stress concentration alleviation via level set method. *Int. J. Numer. Methods Eng.* **2013**, *93*, 942–959. [CrossRef]
18. Deaton, J.D.; Grandhi, R.V. Stress-based design of thermal structures via topology optimization. *Struct. Multidiscip. Optim.* **2016**, *53*, 253–270. [CrossRef]
19. Liu, J.; Qing, Q.; Deng, Y.; Wen, G.; Yin, H. Fatigue reliability study on T-welded component considering load shedding. *Fatigue Fract. Eng. Mater. Struct.* **2015**, *38*, 780–788. [CrossRef]
20. Li, X.Q.; Zhao, Q.H.; Zhang, H.X.; Zhang, T.Z.; Chen, J.L. Robust topology optimization of periodic multi-Material functionally graded structures under loading uncertainties. *CMES-Comput. Model. Eng. Sci.* **2021**, *127*, 683–704. [CrossRef]
21. Glowacz, A. Fault diagnosis of electric impact drills using thermal imaging. *Measurement* **2021**, *171*, 108815. [CrossRef]
22. Rabcan, J.; Levashenko, V.; Zaitseva, E.; Kvassay, M.; Subbotin, S. Non-destructive diagnostic of aircraft engine blades by fuzzy decision tree. *Eng. Struct.* **2019**, *197*, 109396. [CrossRef]
23. Kharbanda, G.; Olhoff, N.; Mohamed, A.; Lemaire, M. Reliability-based topology optimization. *Struct. Multidiscip. Optim.* **2004**, *26*, 295–307. [CrossRef]
24. Jung, H.S.; Cho, S. Reliability-based topology optimization of geometrically nonlinear structures with loading and material uncertainties. *Finite Elem. Anal. Des.* **2004**, *41*, 311–331. [CrossRef]
25. Zhao, Q.H.; Zhang, H.X.; Zhang, T.Z.; Hua, Q.S.; Yuan, L.; Wang, W.Y. An efficient strategy for non-probabilistic reliability-based multi-material topology optimization with evidence theory. *Acta Mech. Solida Sin.* **2019**, *32*, 803–821. [CrossRef]
26. Silva, M.; Tortorelli, D.A.; Norato, J.A.; Ha, C.; Bae, H.-R. Component and system reliability-based topology optimization using a single-loop method. *Struct. Multidiscip. Optim.* **2010**, *41*, 87–106. [CrossRef]
27. Zhao, Q.H.; Chen, X.K.; Ma, Z.D.; Lin, Y. A Comparison of deterministic, reliability-based topology optimization under uncertainties. *Acta Mech. Solida Sin.* **2016**, *29*, 31–45. [CrossRef]
28. Wang, C.; Wang, F.J.; Gong, Y. Analysis of 2D heat conduction in nonlinear functionally graded materials using a local semi-analytical meshless method. *AIMS Math.* **2021**, *6*, 12599–12618. [CrossRef]

29. Gao, T.; Zhang, W.H. Topology optimization involving thermo-elastic stress loads. *Struct. Multidiscip. Optim.* **2010**, *42*, 725–738. [CrossRef]
30. Aoues, Y.; Chateauneuf, A. Benchmark study of numerical methods for reliability-based design optimization. *Struct. Multidiscip. Optim.* **2010**, *41*, 277–294. [CrossRef]
31. Niccolai, A.; Caputo, D.; Chieco, L.; Grimaccia, F.; Mussetta, M. Machine learning-based detection technique for NDT in industrial manufacturing. *Mathematics* **2021**, *9*, 1251. [CrossRef]
32. Wang, F.J.; Zhao, Q.H.; Chen, Z.T.; Fan, C.M. Localized Chebyshev collocation method for solving elliptic partial differential equations in arbitrary 2D domains. *Appl. Math. Comput.* **2021**, *397*, 125903. [CrossRef]
33. Lee, S.H.; Chen, W. A comparative study of uncertainty propagation methods for black-box-type problems. *Struct. Multidiscip. Optim.* **2009**, *37*, 239–253. [CrossRef]
34. Hasofer, A.M.; Lind, N.C. Exact and invariant second moment code format. *J. Eng. Mech.* **1974**, *100*, 111–121. [CrossRef]
35. Maute, K.; Frangopol, D.M. Reliability-based design of MEMS mechanisms by topology optimization. *Comput. Struct.* **2003**, *81*, 813–824. [CrossRef]
36. Wang, L.; Xia, H.J.; Zhang, X.Y.; Lv, Z. Non-probabilistic reliability-based topology optimization of continuum structures considering local stiffness and strength failure. *Comput. Meth. Appl. Mech. Eng.* **2019**, *346*, 788–809. [CrossRef]
37. Xiao, M.; Zhang, J.H.; Gao, L. A system active learning Kriging method for system reliability-based design optimization with a multiple response model. *Reliab. Eng. Syst. Saf.* **2020**, *19*, 106935. [CrossRef]
38. Bruns, T.E.; Tortorelli, D.A. Topology optimization of non-linear structures and compliant mechanisms. *Comput. Meth. Appl. Mech. Eng.* **2001**, *190*, 3443–3459. [CrossRef]
39. Svanberg, K. The method of moving asymptotes-a new method for structural optimization. *Int. J. Numer. Methods Eng.* **1987**, *24*, 359–373. [CrossRef]

mathematics

Article

A Simplified Radial Basis Function Method with Exterior Fictitious Sources for Elliptic Boundary Value Problems

Chih-Yu Liu [1] and Cheng-Yu Ku [2,*]

1 Graduate Institute of Applied Geology, National Central University, Taoyuan 320317, Taiwan; liu20452003@ncu.edu.tw
2 School of Engineering, National Taiwan Ocean University, Keelung 20224, Taiwan
* Correspondence: chkst26@mail.ntou.edu.tw

Abstract: In this article, we propose a simplified radial basis function (RBF) method with exterior fictitious sources for solving elliptic boundary value problems (BVPs). Three simplified RBFs, including Gaussian, multiquadric (MQ), and inverse multiquadric (IMQ) without the shape parameter, are adopted in this study. With the consideration of many exterior fictitious sources outside the domain, the radial distance of the RBF is always greater than zero, such that we can remove the shape parameter from RBFs. Additionally, simplified Gaussian, MQ, and IMQ RBFs and their derivatives in the governing equation are always smooth and nonsingular. Comparative analysis is conducted for three different collocation types, including conventional uniform centers, randomly fictitious centers, and exterior fictitious sources. Numerical examples of elliptic BVPs in two and three dimensions are carried out. The results demonstrate that the proposed simplified RBFs with exterior fictitious sources can significantly improve the accuracy, especially for the Laplace equation. Furthermore, the proposed simplified RBFs exhibit the simplicity of solving elliptic BVPs without finding the optimum shape parameter.

Keywords: radial basis function; the shape parameter; multiquadric; inverse multiquadric; Gaussian

MSC: 65D12

Citation: Liu, C.-Y.; Ku, C.-Y. A Simplified Radial Basis Function Method with Exterior Fictitious Sources for Elliptic Boundary Value Problems. *Mathematics* **2022**, *10*, 1622. https://doi.org/10.3390/math10101622

Academic Editors: Fajie Wang and Ji Lin

Received: 13 April 2022
Accepted: 7 May 2022
Published: 10 May 2022

1. Introduction

Meshfree methods have been applied to solve problems with complicated and irregular geometry because of the advantages of their meshfree characteristics [1–4]. With the capability to deal with different kinds of partial differential equations (PDEs), the radial basis function collocation method (RBFCM) is one of the prominent methods for solving PDEs, where the variables are expressed by the function approximation [5–8]. Proposed by Hardy in 1971 [9], the multiquadric (MQ) radial basis function (RBF) was used for scattered data interpolation. The first attempt to extend the MQ RBF to the solution of PDEs was presented by Kansa in the early 1990s [10]. In addition to the MQ RBF, several RBFs have been presented, such as the inverse multiquadric (IMQ), Gaussian, and polyharmonic spline (PS) functions [11–14]. Among them, PS and MQ RBFs have received more attention for interpolation due to their high accuracy [15–17]. These RBFs are usually categorized into piecewise and infinite smooth functions. For example, the PS is piecewise smooth. On the other hand, the MQ is infinite smooth. In order to remain smooth, the shape parameter is introduced in the MQ [18]. Many RBF methods often contain the shape parameter, which has been proven to have a significant influence on the accuracy of RBF interpolation [19–21].

In the Kansa method, the centers are uniformly scattered within the domain, where the positions of the interior and center points are exactly the same [22]. The centers are often regarded as fictitious sources, which are randomly scattered within the domain [23]. On the other hand, the fictitious sources can also be simultaneously scattered within and outside the closure of the domain [24]. Recently, Ku et al. proposed the MQ RBF without the shape parameter using fictitious sources collocated outside the domain [25]. Because the fictitious sources are situated on the exterior domain, the radial distance always has a non-zero value, such that the RBFs and their derivatives are always smooth and globally infinitely differentiable [26]. The fictitious sources used for the collocation method have received significant attention due to their superior properties and wide utilization for solving PDEs. Accordingly, the accuracy of different RBFs when using fictitious sources in the collocation method to solve PDEs is of significant interest and needs to be investigated.

Identification of the shape parameter is often very challenging and tedious in the original RBFs when solving partial differential equations. In this study, we attempt to remove the shape parameter in conventional RBFs to solve partial differential equations. We propose three simplified Gaussian, MQ, and IMQ RBFs without using the shape parameter. The simplified RBFs have the advantages of a simple mathematical expression, high precision, and easy implementation. Furthermore, we demonstrate that the simplified RBFs, with the consideration of many exterior fictitious sources outside the domain, can achieve highly accurate results to solve elliptic boundary value problems.

In this article, the accuracy of three RBFs in the collocation method for solving stationary convention diffusion equations is investigated. Three RBFs, including the Gaussian, MQ, and IMQ, are adopted. Additionally, three different collocation types are considered in the collocation method. Accuracy analysis of the collocation types of each RBF is carried out. Numerical solutions are approximated by utilizing the RBFs to solve the elliptic boundary value equations. Comparisons of the accuracy of three RBFs are made. The remainder of this article is organized as follows: in Section 2, the mathematical formulations, including the governing equation, the RBFs, the discretization of the governing equation, and the location of fictitious sources, are introduced. Section 3 describes the convergence analysis conducted to evaluate the robustness and effectiveness of the three RBFs in the collocation method. Three different collocation types are considered in the collocation method. Accuracy analysis of the three collocation types of each RBF is also carried out. In Section 4, several investigations of the elliptic boundary value problems are conducted to examine the robustness of the RBFs. Finally, the conclusions of this study are presented in Section 5.

2. Methodology

2.1. Elliptic Boundary Value Problems

The equation of the elliptic boundary value problem is expressed as follows:

$$\nabla^2 u(\mathbf{x}) + \mathbf{A} \cdot \nabla u(\mathbf{x}) + B(\mathbf{x}) u(\mathbf{x}) = f(\mathbf{x}), \tag{1}$$

$$u(\mathbf{x}) = g(\mathbf{x}) \text{ on } \partial\Omega, \tag{2}$$

where ∇ defines the gradient operator; $u(\mathbf{x})$ denotes the variable of interest, which is usually the concentration; $\mathbf{x}$ is the Cartesian coordinate, defined as $\mathbf{x} = (x, y, z)$; $\mathbf{A}$ is the velocity, defined as $A = (A_x, A_y, A_z)$; $B(\mathbf{x})$ is the given function; $f(\mathbf{x})$ is the given function value; $g(\mathbf{x})$ defines the given boundary conditions; and Ω is the domain with the boundary $\partial\Omega$.

2.2. Simplified Radial Basis Functions

Three simplified Gaussian, MQ, and IMQ RBFs without the shape parameter are proposed for solving elliptic boundary value problems, as listed in Table 1. The simplified RBF simply removes the shape parameter from its original one. For example, the simplified Gaussian RBF can be expressed as:

$$\phi_{Gaussian\_S}(r) = e^{-\left(\frac{r}{R}\right)^2}, \tag{3}$$

where $\phi_{Gaussian\_S}(r)$ denotes the simplified Gaussian RBF; r denotes the radial distance, $r = |\mathbf{x} - \mathbf{x}^s|$; $\mathbf{x}$ denotes the interior point; $\mathbf{x}^s$ denotes the source point, defined as $\mathbf{x}^s = (x^s, y^s, z^s)$;

and R denotes the characteristic length, which is the maximum radial distance. We can easily obtain the simplified MQ RBF as follows:

$$\phi_{MQ\_S}(r) = r, \tag{4}$$

where $\phi_{MQ\_S}(r)$ denotes the simplified MQ RBF. Similarly, the simplified IMQ RBF is expressed as:

$$\phi_{IMQ\_S}(r) = \frac{1}{r}, \tag{5}$$

where $\phi_{IMQ\_S}(r)$ denotes the simplified IMQ RBF. In this study, three simplified MQ, IMQ, and Gaussian RBFs are developed without assigning any shape parameter. Table 1 lists a comparison of the original RBFs and the simplified RBFs. From Table 1, the original Gaussian, MQ, and IMQ RBFs in the RBFCM are defined by the shape parameter. The accuracy of these RBFs is strongly affected by the shape parameter. Accordingly, optimization techniques are required to determine the optimal shape parameter for these RBFs [19–21]. As for the proposed simplified RBFs, it is clear that the shape parameter has been completely eliminated in the RBFs.

Table 1. RBFs adopted in this study.

Type of RBFs	Original RBFs	Simplified RBFs
Gaussian	$\phi_{Gaussian}(r) = e^{-\left(\frac{r}{c}\right)^2}$	$\phi_{Gaussian\_S}(r) = e^{-\left(\frac{r}{R}\right)^2}$
Multiquadric (MQ)	$\phi_{MQ}(r) = \sqrt{r^2 + c^2}$	$\phi_{MQ\_S}(r) = r$
Inverse multiquadric (IMQ)	$\phi_{IMQ}(r) = \frac{1}{\sqrt{r^2+c^2}}$	$\phi_{IMQ\_S}(r) = \frac{1}{r}$

Notation: c denotes the shape parameter.

2.3. Discretization

Utilizing the RBFCM, the unknown can be approximated as:

$$u(\mathbf{x}) = \sum_{j=1}^{M} \lambda_j \phi(r_j), \tag{6}$$

where M denotes the total number of source points; λ_j denotes the coefficient to be solved; $\phi(r_j)$ denotes the RBF; r_j denotes the radial distance at the jth source point, defined as $r_j = \left|\mathbf{x} - \mathbf{x}_j^s\right|$; and $\mathbf{x}_j^s$ denotes the jth source point, defined as $\mathbf{x}_j^s = (x_j^s, y_j^s, z_j^s)$.

2.3.1. Discretization in Two Dimensions

The two-dimensional elliptic boundary value equation is expressed as:

$$\frac{\partial^2 u(x,y)}{\partial x^2} + \frac{\partial^2 u(x,y)}{\partial y^2} + A_x \frac{\partial u(x,y)}{\partial x} + A_y \frac{\partial u(x,y)}{\partial y} + B(x,y)u(x,y) = f(x,y). \tag{7}$$

Utilizing the simplified Gaussian RBF, the derivative of Equation (7) with respect to x is as follows:

$$\frac{\partial \phi(r_j)}{\partial x} = -\frac{2A_x(x - x_j^s)}{R^2} e^{-\left(\frac{r_j}{R}\right)^2}. \tag{8}$$

Taking the derivative of Equation (7) with respect to y also gives:

$$\frac{\partial \phi(r_j)}{\partial y} = -\frac{2A_y(y - y_j^s)}{R^2} e^{-\left(\frac{r_j}{R}\right)^2}. \tag{9}$$

Again, the derivative of Equation (8) with respect to x is as follows:

$$\frac{\partial\phi^2(r_j)}{\partial x^2} = \frac{4(x-x_j^s)^2}{R^4}e^{-(\frac{r_j}{R})^2} - \frac{2}{R^2}e^{-(\frac{r_j}{R})^2}. \tag{10}$$

Similarly, we take the derivative of Equation (9) with respect to y:

$$\frac{\partial\phi^2(r_j)}{\partial y^2} = \frac{4(y-y_j^s)^2}{R^4}e^{-(\frac{r_j}{R})^2} - \frac{2}{R^2}e^{-(\frac{r_j}{R})^2}. \tag{11}$$

Substituting the aforementioned Equations (8)–(11) into Equation (7), the approximation of the two-dimensional governing equation is as follows:

$$\sum_{j=1}^{M}\lambda_j\frac{4}{R^2}e^{-(\frac{r_j}{R})^2}[(\frac{r_j}{R})^2-1] - \sum_{j=1}^{M}\lambda_j\frac{2}{R^2}e^{-(\frac{r_j}{R})^2}[A_x(x-x_j^s)+A_y(y-y_j^s)] + B(\mathbf{x})\sum_{j=1}^{M}\lambda_j e^{-(\frac{r_j}{R})^2} = f(x,y). \tag{12}$$

Equation (12) describes the discretization of the governing equation in two dimensions using the simplified Gaussian RBF. In the same way, we substitute the simplified MQ RBF into Equation (7):

$$\sum_{j=1}^{M}\lambda_j\frac{1}{r_j} + \sum_{j=1}^{M}\lambda_j\frac{A_x(x-x_j^s)+A_y(y-y_j^s)}{r_j} + B(\mathbf{x})\sum_{j=1}^{M}\lambda_j r_j = f(x,y). \tag{13}$$

Substituting the simplified IMQ RBF into Equation (7) also obtains:

$$\sum_{j=1}^{M}\lambda_j\frac{1}{r_j^3} - \sum_{j=1}^{M}\lambda_j\frac{A_x(x-x_j^s)+A_y(y-y_j^s)}{r_j^3} + B(\mathbf{x})\sum_{j=1}^{M}\lambda_j\frac{1}{r_j} = f(x,y). \tag{14}$$

Equations (13) and (14) describe the discretization of the governing equation in two dimensions using the simplified MQ and IMQ RBFs, respectively.

2.3.2. Discretization in Three Dimensions

The three-dimensional elliptic boundary value equation is:

$$\begin{array}{l} \frac{\partial^2 u(x,y,z)}{\partial x^2} + \frac{\partial^2 u(x,y,z)}{\partial y^2} + \frac{\partial^2 u(x,y,z)}{\partial z^2} \\ +A_x\frac{\partial u(x,y,z)}{\partial x} + A_y\frac{\partial u(x,y,z)}{\partial y} + A_z\frac{\partial u(x,y,z)}{\partial z} \\ +B(x,y,z)u(x,y,z) = f(x,y,z) \end{array}. \tag{15}$$

Considering the three-dimensional problem depicted in Equation (15), the derivative of the simplified Gaussian RBF interpolation is as follows:

$$\begin{array}{l} \sum\limits_{j=1}^{M}\lambda_j\frac{(4r_j^2-6R^2)}{R^4}e^{-(\frac{r_j}{R})^2} - \sum\limits_{j=1}^{M}\lambda_j\frac{2}{R^2}e^{-(\frac{r_j}{R})^2}[A_x(x-x_j^s)+A_y(y-y_j^s)+A_z(z-z_j^s)] \\ +B(\mathbf{x})\sum\limits_{j=1}^{M}\lambda_j e^{-(\frac{r_j}{R})^2} = f(x,y,z). \end{array} \tag{16}$$

Using the same perspective, we obtain the derivative of Equation (15) by the simplified MQ RBF as:

$$\sum_{j=1}^{M}\lambda_j\frac{2}{r_j} + \sum_{j=1}^{M}\lambda_j\frac{A_x(x-x_j^s)+A_y(y-y_j^s)+A_z(z-z_j^s)}{r_j} + B(\mathbf{x})\sum_{j=1}^{M}\lambda_j r_j = f(x,y,z). \tag{17}$$

Identifying the derivative of Equation (15) with the simplified IMQ interpolation results in the following equation:

$$-\sum_{j=1}^{M}\lambda_j\frac{A_x(x-x_j^s)+A_y(y-y_j^s)+A_z(z-z_j^s)}{r_j^3}+B(\mathbf{x})\sum_{j=1}^{M}\lambda_j\frac{1}{r_j}=f(x,y,z). \quad (18)$$

From the above equations, the shape parameter has been eliminated from the original Gaussian, MQ, and IMQ RBFs. Considering the boundary conditions, the following system of linear equations is finally acquired:

$$\begin{bmatrix}[\mathbf{A}_L]_{N_i\times M}\\ [\mathbf{A}_B]_{N_b\times M}\end{bmatrix}[\boldsymbol{\alpha}]=\begin{bmatrix}[\mathbf{f}]_{N_i\times 1}\\ [\mathbf{g}]_{N_b\times 1}\end{bmatrix}, \quad (19)$$

where $\mathbf{A}_L$ is an $N_i \times M$ matrix for the interior points; $\mathbf{A}_B$ is an $N_b \times M$ matrix for the boundary points; $\boldsymbol{\alpha}$ is an $M \times 1$ vector of undetermined coefficients containing the unknown coefficients; $\mathbf{f}$ is an $N_i \times 1$ vector of the function values for the interior points, written as $\mathbf{f} = [f_1, f_2, \ldots, f_{N_i}]$; $\mathbf{g}$ is an $N_b \times 1$ vector of boundary data, written as $\mathbf{g} = [g_1, g_2, \ldots, g_{N_b}]$; N_i is the number of interior points; and N_b is the number of boundary points. Once the unknown coefficients are determined, we can collocate the validation points uniformly placed inside the domain to obtain the computed results.

To investigate the effectiveness and accuracy of the simplified RBFs in the collocation method, this study adopts the root mean square error (RMSE) as follows:

$$\mathrm{RMSE}=\sqrt{\sum_{i=1}^{N_T}|u_A(\mathbf{x}_i)-u_N(\mathbf{x}_i)|^2/N_T}, \quad (20)$$

where N_T denotes the number of validation points, $\mathbf{x}_i$ denotes the ith validation point, and $u_A(\mathbf{x}_i)$ and $u_N(\mathbf{x}_i)$ are the analytical and numerical solutions evaluated at the ith validation point, respectively.

2.4. Location of Fictitious Sources

In the conventional RBF method, the interior, center, and boundary points must be placed where the positions of the interior and center points usually coincide at the same place. In this study, the center points in the conventional RBFs are regarded as the fictitious sources, where three different collocation types for locating the fictitious sources are considered in the collocation method as depicted in Figure 1. The implementation of the three different collocation types for solving the elliptic boundary value problems are described as follows.

2.4.1. Type A: Uniform Centers

In type A, the source points are uniformly scattered within the domain. Figure 1a,d illustrate the location of the fictitious sources for the two-dimensional and three-dimensional domains, respectively. In Figure 1a, the two-dimensional amoeba-like object is adopted. The boundary shape is defined as follows:

$$\begin{aligned}&\partial\Omega=\{(x,y)|x=\rho(\theta)\cos\theta,\ y=\rho(\theta)\sin\theta\},\\&\rho(\theta)=0.5\left[e^{\sin(\theta)}\sin^2(2\theta)+e^{\cos(\theta)}\cos^2(2\theta)\right],\ 0\le\theta\le2\pi\end{aligned}. \quad (21)$$

The fictitious sources are uniformly scattered within the two-dimensional amoeba-like domain, as depicted in Figure 1a. The interior, sources, and boundary points are placed such that the positions of the interior and fictitious sources are identical.

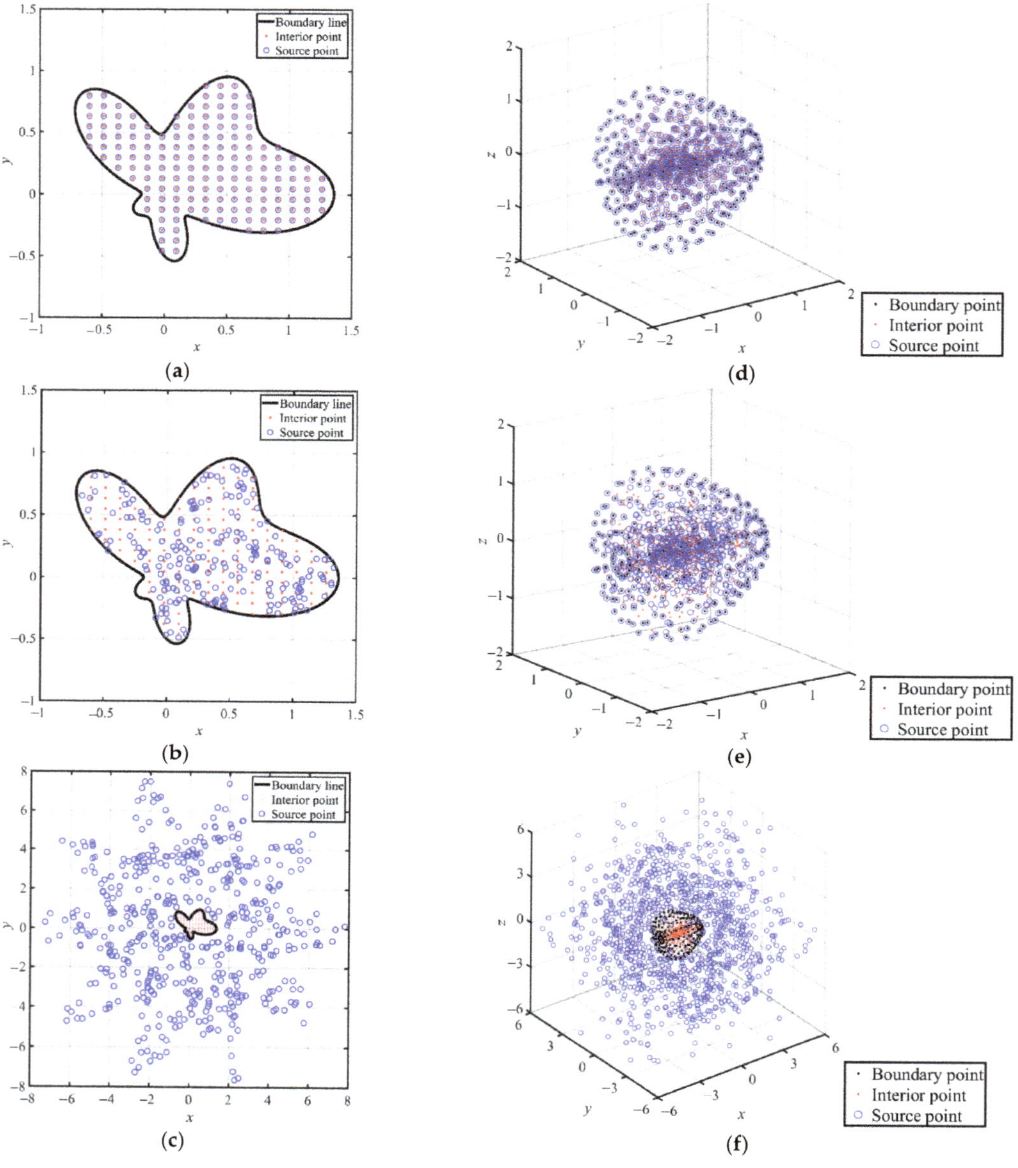

Figure 1. Location of the fictitious sources for the two-dimensional and three-dimensional domain. (**a**) A two-dimensional domain: Type A. (**b**) A two-dimensional domain: Type B. (**c**) A two-dimensional domain: Type C. (**d**) A three-dimensional domain: Type A. (**e**) A three-dimensional domain: Type B. (**f**) A three-dimensional domain: Type C.

Considering the three-dimensional object, the boundary shape is given by the spherical parametric equation as follows:

$$\begin{aligned} \partial\Omega &= \{(x, y, z) | x = \rho(\theta)\cos\theta\cos\varphi,\ y = \rho(\theta)\cos\theta\sin\varphi,\ z = \rho(\theta)\sin\theta\}, \\ \rho(\theta) &= 0.25 \times [2 + \cos(\theta)][\cos(3\varphi) + \sqrt{8 - \sin^2(3\varphi)}]^{1/3}. \end{aligned} \quad (22)$$

Figure 1d illustrates the location of the fictitious sources for three-dimensional domains. Similarly, the positions of the interior and source points are collocated exactly at the same place [23] in Figure 1d.

2.4.2. Type B: Randomly Fictitious Centers

In type B, the boundary shapes in two and three dimensions are exactly the same as those in type A. However, the source points are regarded as the fictitious centers, which are randomly scattered within the domain [24], as depicted in Figure 1b,e.

2.4.3. Type C: Exterior Fictitious Sources

In type C, the fictitious sources are randomly collocated in the exterior domain, as shown in Figure 1c,f. In Figure 1c, the two-dimensional amoeba-like object is adopted. The fictitious sources are randomly scattered within the range between the domain boundary and the fictitious boundary, as depicted in Figure 1c. The boundary shape of the problem domain is defined as Equation (21). The fictitious boundary is defined by the following parametric equation:

$$\partial\Omega^s = \left\{ (x_j^s, y_j^s) \middle| x_j^s = \eta\rho_j^s(\theta_j^s)\cos\theta_j^s,\ y_j^s = \eta\rho_j^s(\theta_j^s)\sin\theta_j^s \right\}, \quad (23)$$

where $\partial\Omega^s$ denotes the fictitious boundary; x_j^s denotes the x-coordinate of the jth source point; y_j^s denotes the y-coordinate of the jth source point; η denotes the dilation factor, which is used to adjust the size of the fictitious boundary; θ_j^s denotes the angle of the fictitious sources; and ρ_j^s denotes the radius of the fictitious sources, defined as $\rho_j^s(\theta_j^s) = 2 \times [\sqrt[1/3]{\cos(10\theta_j^s) + \sqrt{2 - \sin^2(10\theta_j^s)}}],\ 0 \le \theta_j^s \le 2\pi$.

Considering a three-dimensional object, the boundary shape is given by the spherical parametric equation as shown in Equation (22). The fictitious sources are randomly scattered within the three-dimensional space between the domain boundary and the fictitious boundary, as depicted in Figure 1f. The boundary shape of the problem domain is defined as Equation (22). The three-dimensional fictitious boundary is defined by the following parametric equations:

$$\partial\Omega^s = \left\{ (x_j^s, y_j^s, z_j^s) \middle| x_j^s = \rho_j^s(\theta_j^s)\cos\theta_j^s\cos\varphi_j^s,\ y_j^s = \rho_j^s(\theta_j^s)\cos\theta_j^s\sin\varphi_j^s,\ z_j^s = \rho_j^s(\theta_j^s)\sin\theta_j^s \right\}, \quad (24)$$

where z_j^s denotes the z-coordinate of the jth source point; ρ_j^s represents the radius of the fictitious sources, defined as $\rho_j^s(\theta_j^s) = \eta \times \left\{0.51 + [\frac{1}{28}\sin(10\varphi_j^s)\sin(9\theta_j^s)]\right\},\ 0 \le \theta_j^s \le 2\pi$; θ_j^s is the polar angle used to describe the location of the fictitious sources in cylindrical coordinates; and φ_j^s is the azimuth angle of the fictitious sources.

The fictitious sources are randomly collocated in the exterior domain, as shown in Figure 1c,f. Since the radial distance for RBFs remains greater than zero, the shape parameter for the original Gaussian, MQ, and IMQ RBFs can be completely eliminated. The three simplified Gaussian, MQ, and IMQ RBFs with exterior fictitious sources (type C) are utilized to solve elliptic boundary value problems.

3. Validation of the Methodology

3.1. Example 1

To investigate the accuracy, a comparison of the three collocation types is performed. The Laplace equation in two dimensions is described as Equation (1), where $\mathbf{A} = 0$, $\mathbf{B} = 0$, and $f(\mathbf{x}) = 0$. The domain boundary is defined as Equation (21). Boundary data for the boundary conditions are assigned to the boundaries by adopting the following exact solution:

$$u(x, y) = \sin(x)e^y + \cos(y)e^x. \tag{25}$$

Three simplified RBFs, including Gaussian, MQ, and IMQ, are adopted to solve this problem. Three collocation types for locating the sources are considered. In type A, the fictitious sources are uniformly scattered within the domain, as depicted in Figure 1a. The interior, sources, and boundary points are placed such that the positions of the interior and fictitious sources are identical. In type B, the fictitious sources are randomly scattered within the domain, as depicted in Figure 1b. In type C, the fictitious sources are simultaneously scattered outside the closure of the domain, as depicted in Figure 1c. The location of the exterior fictitious sources is defined as Equation (23). A total of 164 interior points, 315 source points, and 200 boundary points are used. The dilation factor is 3.

For comparison purposes, the original Gaussian, MQ, and IMQ RBFs with various shape parameters for type A and type B are also considered in the analysis. Particularly, for type C, the above RBFs without a shape parameter are utilized. The RMSE is used to examine the accuracy of the computed results. Comparisons of the accuracy for the three RBFs are then conducted.

3.1.1. The Gaussian RBF

The Gaussian RBF with three different collocation types with various shape parameters is first investigated, as shown in Figure 2a. From Figure 2a, it appears that the simplified Gaussian RBF without the shape parameter utilizing the exterior fictitious sources of type C provides the most accurate solution. The results obtained demonstrate that the RMSE of the simplified Gaussian RBF without a shape parameter for type C is in the order of 10^{-12}. It seems that the simplified Gaussian RBFs utilizing the exterior fictitious sources of type C have the best accuracy among those Gaussian RBFs for type A and type B even when different values of the shape parameter are considered.

3.1.2. The MQ RBF

The MQ RBF with various shape parameters for type A and type B is considered. For type C, the simplified MQ RBF is utilized. Figure 2b illustrates the accuracy of the MQ RBFs for the three collocation types. According to Figure 2b, the RMSE of the MQ RBF in type A and type B are in the order of 10^{-2} to 10^{-7} as the shape parameter ranges from 0.2 to 5. However, the RMSE of the simplified MQ RBF in type C is 10^{-13}. It was found that the RMSE of the simplified MQ RBF without a shape parameter in type C has the best accuracy among the MQ RBFs for type A and type B for different values of the shape parameter.

3.1.3. The IMQ RBF

The IMQ RBF is analyzed by adopting the same perspective. Figure 2c illustrates the accuracy of the IMQ RBF for the three collocation types. Similar to the results obtained in Figure 2b, we also found that the simplified IMQ RBF for type C acquires more accurate results than the other IMQ RBFs for type A and type B with the best shape parameter, as illustrated in Figure 2c. It is obvious that the simplified IMQ RBFs without a shape parameter that utilize the exterior fictitious sources of type C provide the most accurate solution.

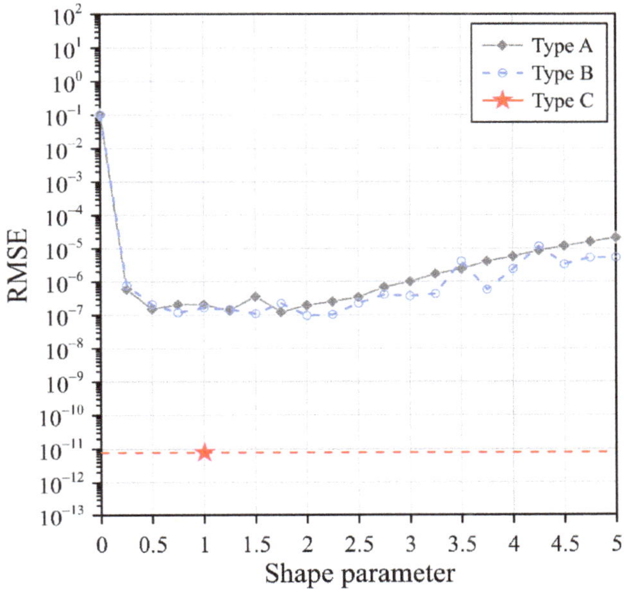

(**a**)

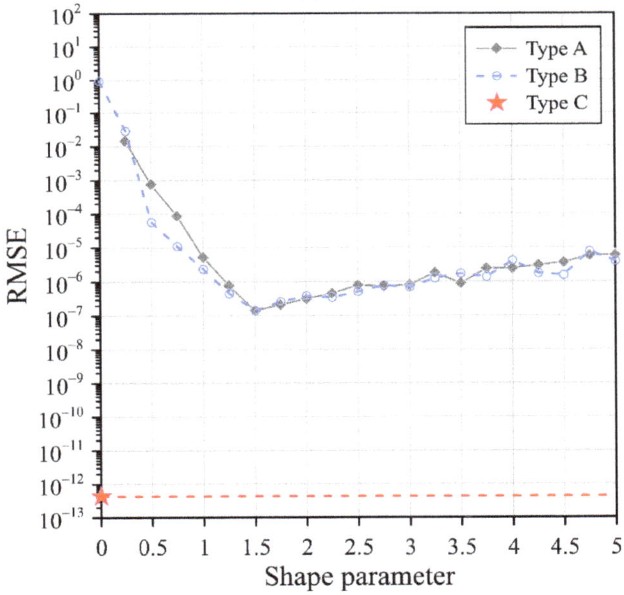

(**b**)

Figure 2. *Cont.*

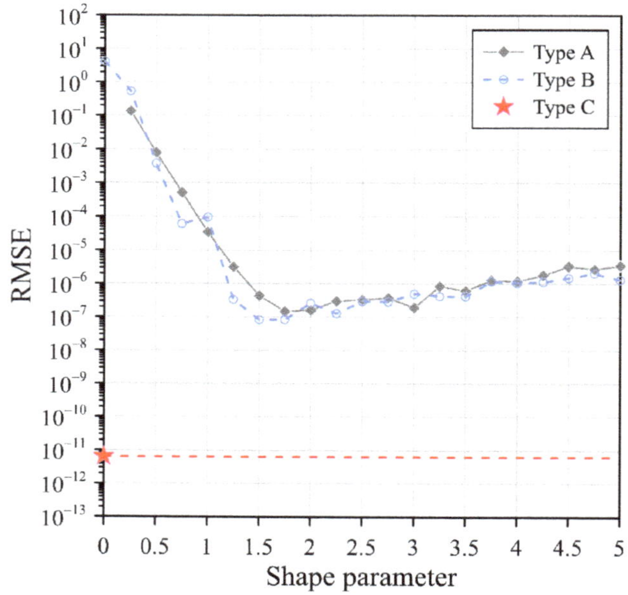

(c)

Figure 2. The RMSE of the three RBFs with three different collocation types: (**a**) Gaussian RBF, (**b**) MQ RBF, and (**c**) IMQ RBF.

Table 2 lists the results of the RMSE using the three RBFs with the three different collocation types. The processor used was an AMD Ryzen 7 5800X 8-Core @ 3.80 GHz. As depicted in Table 2, all the simplified Gaussian, MQ, and IMQ RBFs utilizing the exterior fictitious sources of type C provided more accurate results than the other two fictitious source collocation types, even when the best shape parameter was adopted. The simplified Gaussian, MQ, and IMQ RBFs utilizing the exterior fictitious sources of type C provided the most accurate results, with an RMSE of the order of 10^{-12}, 10^{-13}, and 10^{-12}, respectively. From the results, we also demonstrated that the above simplified RBFs with exterior fictitious sources can be used to solve this two-dimensional Laplace problem with very high accuracy. From Table 2, the comparison of the computing time also illustrates the efficiency of the proposed method.

Table 2. Comparison of the results for example 1.

RBF	RMSE		
	Type A	**Type B**	**Type C (η=3)**
Gaussian	1.24×10^{-7} ($c = 1.75$) ($t = 5.84$ s)	9.73×10^{-8} ($c = 2.0$) ($t = 4.62$ s)	7.87×10^{-12} ($c = 1$) ($t = 8.11$ s)
MQ	1.42×10^{-7} ($c = 1.5$) ($t = 5.78$ s)	1.46×10^{-7} ($c = 1.75$) ($t = 5.75$ s)	4.35×10^{-13} ($c = 0$) ($t = 7.96$ s)
IMQ	1.47×10^{-7} ($c = 1.5$) ($t = 6.12$ s)	8.46×10^{-8} ($c = 1.5$) ($t = 6.28$ s)	6.37×10^{-12} ($c = 0$) ($t = 8.51$ s)

Notation: c denotes the shape parameter; t denotes the computing time.

To further clarify the possible influences of the positions of the exterior fictitious sources for type C on the accuracy, a sensitivity analysis was further conducted. Three RBFs considering the MQ, IMQ, and Gaussian RBFs were adopted to solve the two-dimensional Laplace problem. The MQ, IMQ, and Gaussian RBFs without the shape parameter were used.

In this example, the values of the dilation factor ranged from 0.5 to 5. A plot of the RMSE versus the dilation factor is depicted in Figure 3. From Figure 3, the RMSE of the MQ, IMQ, and Gaussian RBFs utilizing the exterior fictitious sources for type C fluctuates between 10^{-11} and 10^{-13} while the dilation factor ranges from 2.5 to 5. The results obtained show that the dilation factor has low sensitivity regarding the numerical accuracy while the dilation factor is greater than 2.5. Accordingly, the following numerical implementations of type C were solved using $\eta = 3$.

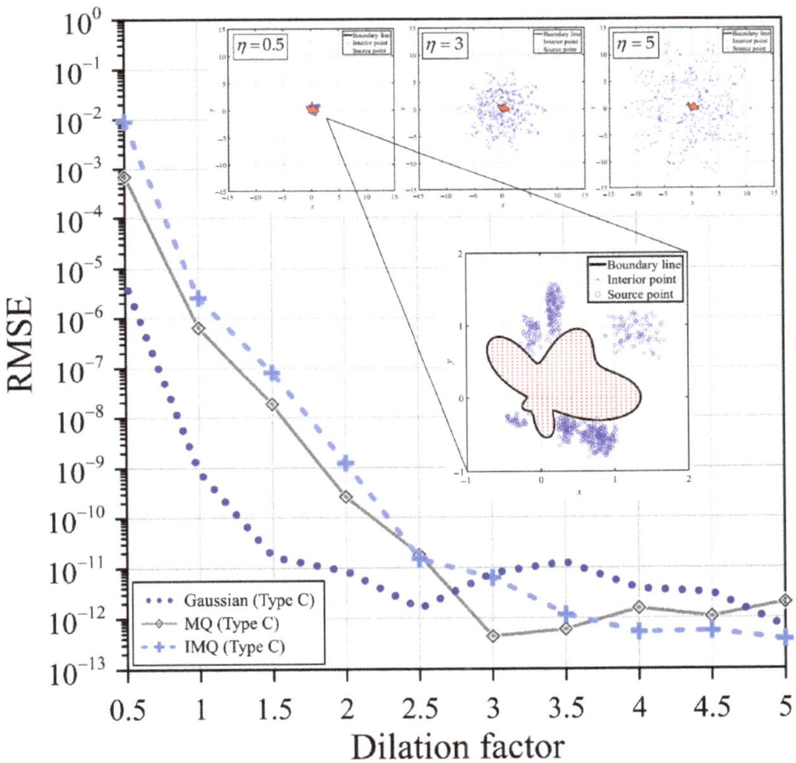

Figure 3. RMSE versus the dilation factor.

3.2. *Example 2*

A three-dimensional problem is enclosed by a sophisticated irregular domain boundary, as shown in Figure 4a. The governing equation in three dimensions is expressed as Equation (1), where **A**, **B**, and $f(\mathbf{x})$ are 0. The object boundary is given by the spherical parametric equation as follows:

$$\begin{aligned} &\partial\Omega = \{(x,y,z)|x = \rho(\theta)\cos\theta\cos\varphi,\ y = \rho(\theta)\cos\theta\sin\varphi,\ z = \rho(\theta)\sin\theta\}, \\ &\rho(\theta) = \left[\cos(2\theta) + \sqrt{1.5 - \sin^2(2\theta)}\right]^{1/2}. \end{aligned} \tag{26}$$

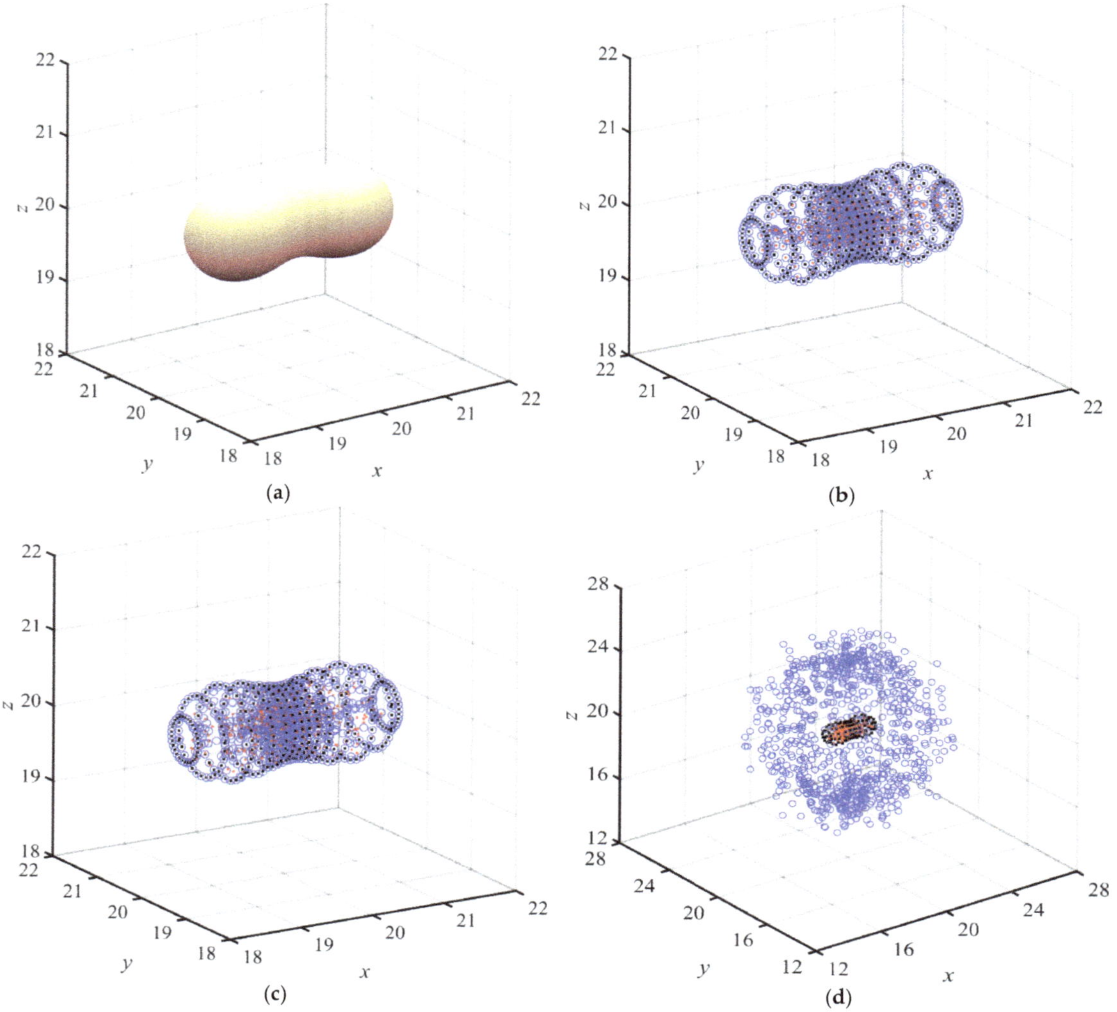

Figure 4. Problem domain and location of the fictitious sources for example 2. (**a**) Problem domain. (**b**) Type A. (**c**) Type B. (**d**) Type C (blue and red circles denote the source and interior points, respectively).

The Dirichlet data are imposed using the following exact solution for this three-dimensional problem as:

$$u(x, y, z) = \frac{1}{\sqrt{x^2 y^2 z^2}}. \tag{27}$$

The Gaussian, MQ, and IMQ RBFs were utilized in the analysis. Additionally, three collocation types were considered. As depicted in Figure 4b–d, there were 2461 source points, 1600 interior points, and 861 boundary points.

Figure 5 illustrates the RMSE of the Gaussian, MQ, and IMQ RBFs with three different collocation types. The RMSE of the simplified Gaussian, MQ, and IMQ RBFs (type C) was 10^{-14}, 10^{-15}, and 10^{-13}, respectively. It is significant that excellent agreement was achieved, and highly accurate results were acquired using the simplified RBFs. From these results, it is demonstrated that the simplified RBFs with exterior fictitious sources can be used to solve the three-dimensional stationary Laplace equation with very high accuracy.

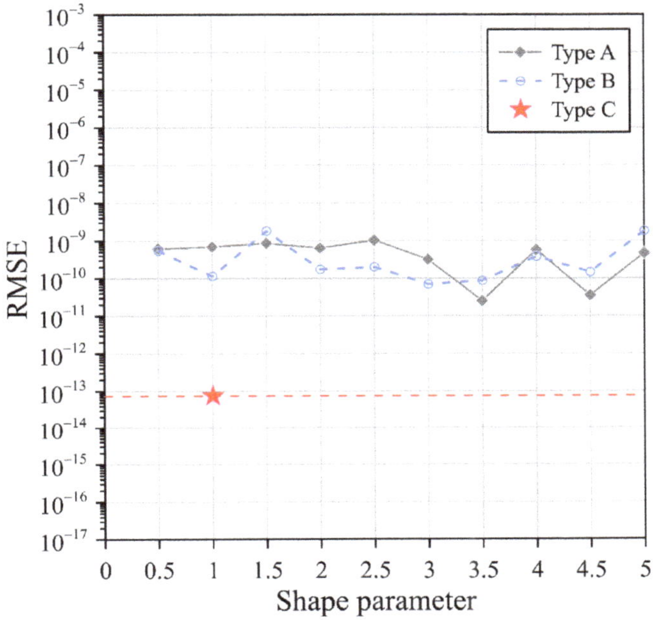

(**a**)

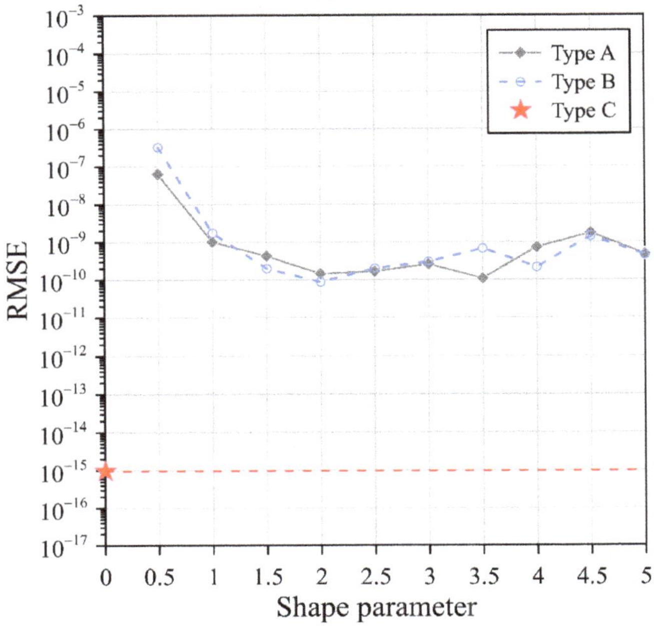

(**b**)

Figure 5. *Cont.*

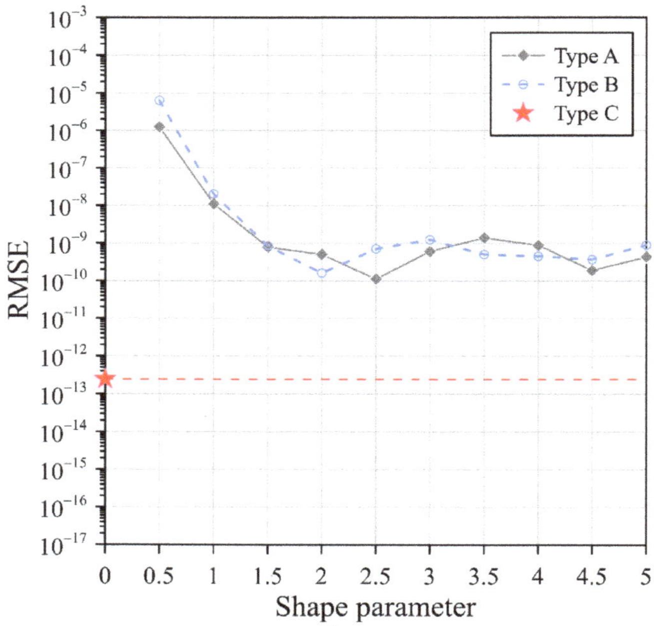

(c)

Figure 5. RMSEs of three RBFs using three different collocation types: (**a**) Gaussian RBF, (**b**) MQ RBF, and (**c**) IMQ RBF.

4. Application Examples

4.1. Application Example 1

The governing equation for the first application example is depicted in Equation (1), where $\mathbf{A} = 0$, $\mathbf{B} = 0$, and $f(\mathbf{x}) = -\lfloor x\cos(y) + y\sin(x)\rfloor$. The boundary is defined as follows:

$$\partial\Omega = \{(x,y)|x = \rho(\theta)\cos\theta,\ y = \rho(\theta)\sin\theta\}, \rho(\theta) = 0.5 \times [0.5 + [1 + 0.5\sin(12\theta)]],\ 0 \le \theta \le 2\pi. \quad (28)$$

The Dirichlet data are assigned from the analytical solution:

$$u(x,y) = y\sin(x) + x\cos(y). \quad (29)$$

Three RBFs, including the Gaussian, MQ, and IMQ, were used in the collocation method. Three collocation types for locating the sources as illustrated in Figure 6 were considered in the above RBFs to solve this problem. There were 342 source points, 151 interior points, and 200 boundary points. In type A, the fictitious sources are uniformly scattered within the domain, as depicted in Figure 6a. The interior, sources, and boundary points are placed such that the positions of the interior and fictitious sources are identical. In type B, the fictitious sources are randomly scattered within the domain, as depicted in Figure 6b. In type C, the fictitious sources are randomly scattered outside the closure of the domain, as depicted in Figure 6c. The collocation of the exterior fictitious sources is defined by the following parametric equations:

$$\partial\Omega^s = \left\{(x_j^s, y_j^s)\middle|x_j^s = \eta\rho_j^s(\theta_j^s)\cos\theta_j^s,\ y_j^s = \eta\rho_j^s(\theta_j^s)\sin\theta_j^s\right\}, \quad (30)$$

where $\rho_j^s(\theta_j^s) = 2 \times [\sqrt[1/3]{\cos(10\theta_j^s) + \sqrt{2 - \sin^2(10\theta_j^s)}}]$, $0 \le \theta_j^s \le 2\pi$. In this example, the dilation factor for type C is 3.

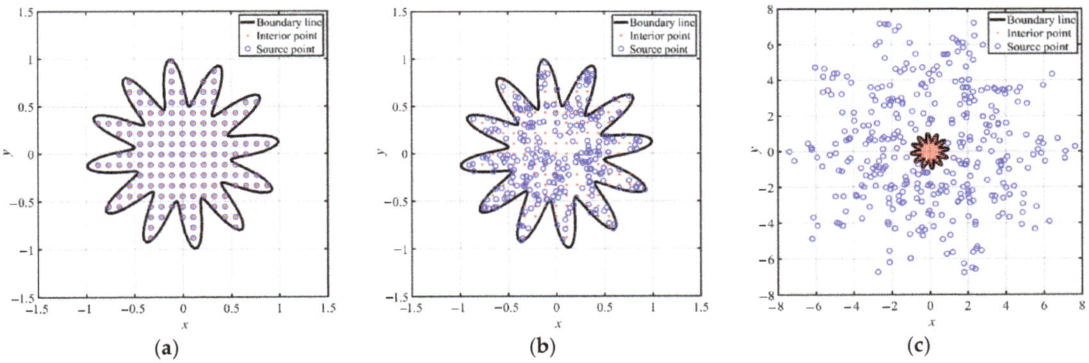

Figure 6. Collocation points for application example 1. (**a**) Type A. (**b**) Type B. (**c**) Type C.

The Gaussian, MQ, and IMQ RBFs with various shape parameters for type A and type B were considered. For type C, the above RBFs without a shape parameter were utilized. The accuracy of the Gaussian, MQ, and IMQ RBFs for the three collocation types are illustrated in Figure 7. According to Figure 7a, the Gaussian RBF utilizing the exterior fictitious sources for type C obtained more accurate results, where the RMSE of the Gaussian RBF without a shape parameter in type C reached the order of 10^{-13}. Figure 7b demonstrates the RMSE of the MQ RBF for the three collocation types. According to Figure 7b, the RMSE of the MQ RBF in type A and type B was in the order of 10^{-2} to 10^{-7} as the shape parameter ranged from 0 to 5. The RMSE of the MQ RBF without a shape parameter in type C was in the order of 10^{-10}. The IMQ RBFs was analyzed by adopting the same perspective. The RMSE values of the IMQ for the three collocation types are illustrated in Figure 7c. Similar to the results obtained in Figure 7b, we also found the IMQ without the shape parameter for type C reached the order of 10^{-8}. From the results, it is significant that the Gaussian RBF without the shape parameter for type C showed a high-accuracy performance.

Table 3 presents a comparison of the results for the application example 1. For type A and type B, the Gaussian, MQ, and IMQ RBFs with the optimal shape parameter were utilized. For type C, the above RBFs without a shape parameter were adopted. As depicted in Table 3, all the RBFs, including the Gaussian, MQ, and IMQ RBFs, utilizing the fictitious sources of type C provided more accurate results than the other two source collocation types even with the optimum shape parameter. From the results, it is clear that numerical solutions with a very high accuracy can be obtained by utilizing the proposed simplified Gaussian, MQ, and IMQ RBFs with exterior fictitious sources.

4.2. Application Example 2

The governing equation for the second application example is expressed as Equation (1) [25], where $\mathbf{A} = 0$, $\mathbf{B} = -\lambda^2$, $f(\mathbf{x}) = 0$, and $\lambda^2 = 3$. The object boundary is defined as:

$$\partial\Omega = \{(x,y)|x = \rho(\theta)\cos\theta,\ y = \rho(\theta)\sin\theta\},\ \rho(\theta) = 0.5[\sqrt{\cos(3\theta) + \sqrt{3 + \sin^4(3\theta)}}],\ 0 \le \theta \le 2\pi. \quad (31)$$

The Dirichlet data are assigned to the boundaries utilizing the exact solution as follows:

$$u(x,y) = e^{\frac{\sqrt{2}\lambda(x-y)}{2}}. \quad (32)$$

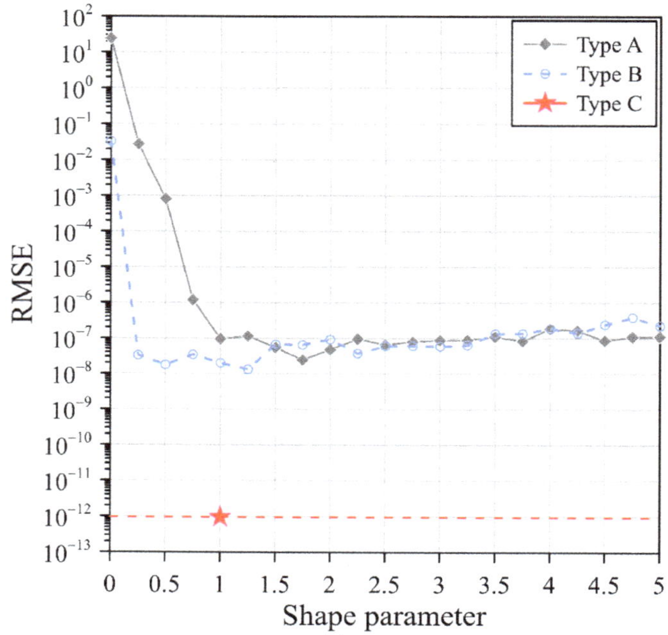

(a)

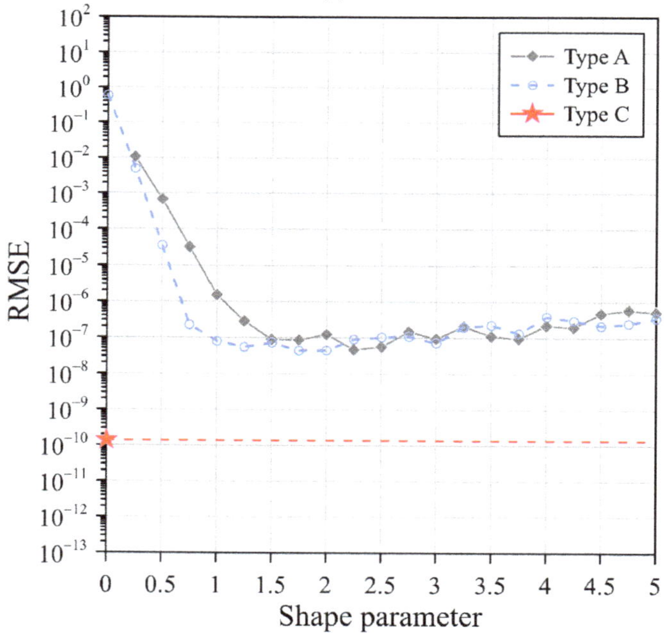

(b)

Figure 7. *Cont.*

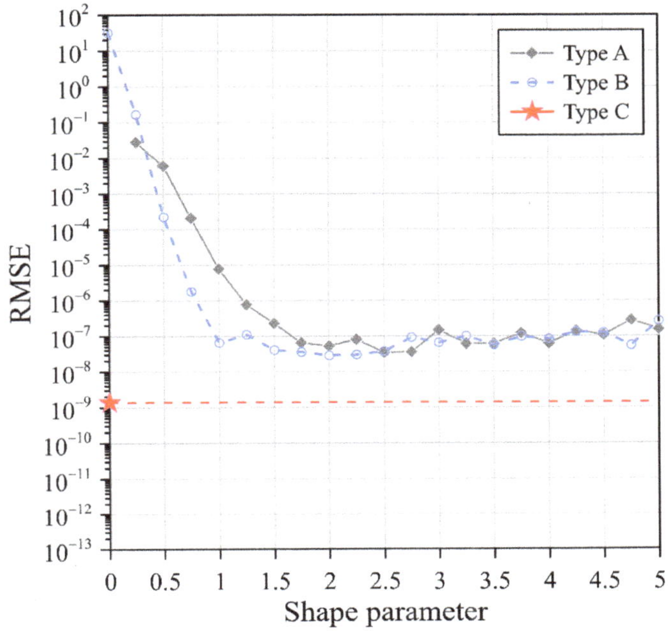

(c)

Figure 7. RMSEs of three RBFs with three different collocation types: (**a**) Gaussian RBF, (**b**) MQ RBF, and (**c**) IMQ RBF.

Table 3. Comparison of the results for the application example 1.

RBF	RMSE		
	Type A	**Type B**	**Type C (η=3)**
Gaussian	2.45×10^{-8} ($c = 1.75$) (t = 3.82 s)	1.33×10^{-8} ($c = 1.25$) (t = 7.02 s)	9.50×10^{-13} ($c = 1$) (t = 8.81 s)
MQ	4.61×10^{-8} ($c = 2.25$) (t = 3.80 s)	4.41×10^{-8} ($c = 1.75$) (t = 6.90 s)	1.39×10^{-10} ($c = 0$) (t = 8.77 s)
IMQ	3.38×10^{-8} ($c = 2.5$) (t = 3.80 s)	2.85×10^{-8} ($c = 2.0$) (t = 6.99 s)	1.37×10^{-9} ($c = 0$) (t = 8.83 s)

Three RBFs, including the Gaussian, MQ, and IMQ, are were in the collocation method. Three collocation types for locating the sources, as illustrated in Figure 8, were considered in the above RBFs to solve this problem. There were 355 source points, 210 interior points, and 200 boundary points. In type A, the fictitious sources are uniformly scattered within the domain, as depicted in Figure 8a. The interior, sources, and boundary points are placed such that the positions of the interior and fictitious sources are identical. In type B, the fictitious sources are randomly scattered within the domain, as depicted in Figure 8b. In type C, the fictitious sources are randomly scattered outside the closure of the domain, as depicted in Figure 8c. The collocation of the exterior fictitious sources is defined by the following parametric equations:

$$\partial\Omega^s = \left\{ (x_j^s, y_j^s) \middle| x_j^s = \eta\rho_j^s(\theta_j^s)\cos\theta_j^s,\ y_j^s = \eta\rho_j^s(\theta_j^s)\sin\theta_j^s \right\}. \tag{33}$$

where $\rho_j^s(\theta_j^s) = 2 \times [\sqrt[1/3]{\cos(10\theta_j^s) + \sqrt{2 - \sin^2(10\theta_j^s)}}]$, $0 \le \theta_j^s \le 2\pi$. In this example, the dilation factor for type C is 3.

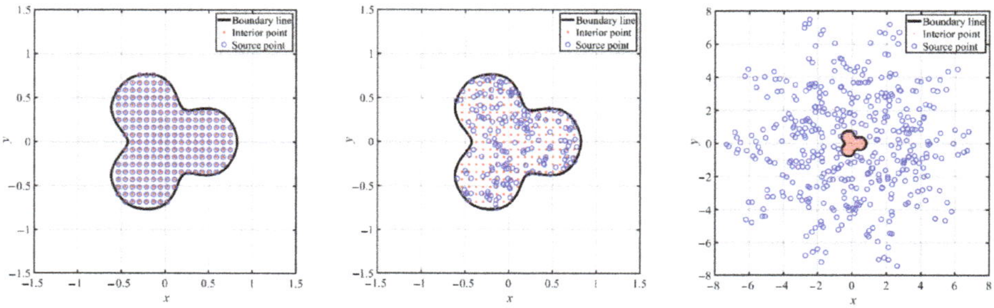

(a) (b) (c)

Figure 8. Collocation points of the three types in the application example 2. (**a**) Type A. (**b**) Type B. (**c**) Type C.

Figure 9a demonstrates the RMSE of the Gaussian RBF for the three collocation types. From Figure 9a, the RMSE of the Gaussian RBF in type A and type B was in the order of 10^{-1} to 10^{-6} as the shape parameter ranged from 0.5 to 5. However, the RMSE of the Gaussian RBF without a shape parameter in type C reached the order of 10^{-11}. The MQ and IMQ RBFs were analyzed by adopting the same perspective. The RMSE of the MQ and IMQ RBFs for the three collocation types are illustrated in Figure 9b,c, respectively. Similar to the results shown in Figure 9a, we also found that the MQ and IMQ RBFs without the shape parameter for type C reached the order of 10^{-9} and 10^{-8}, respectively.

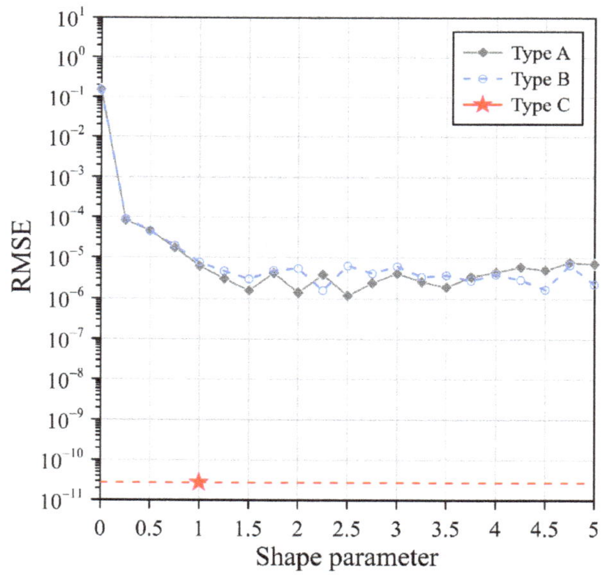

(a)

Figure 9. *Cont.*

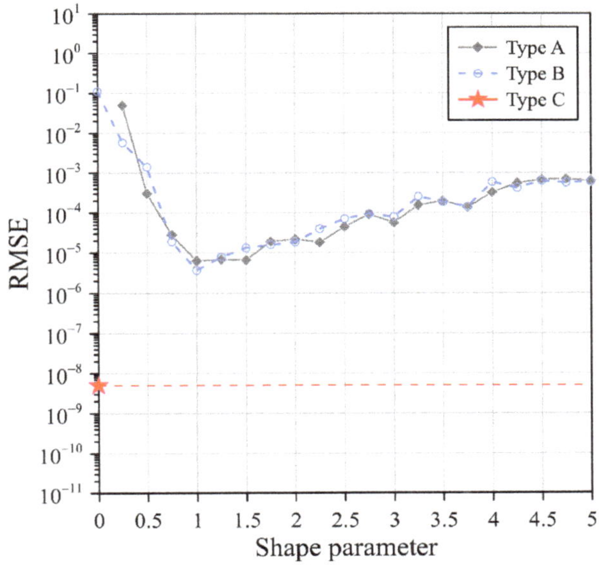

(b)

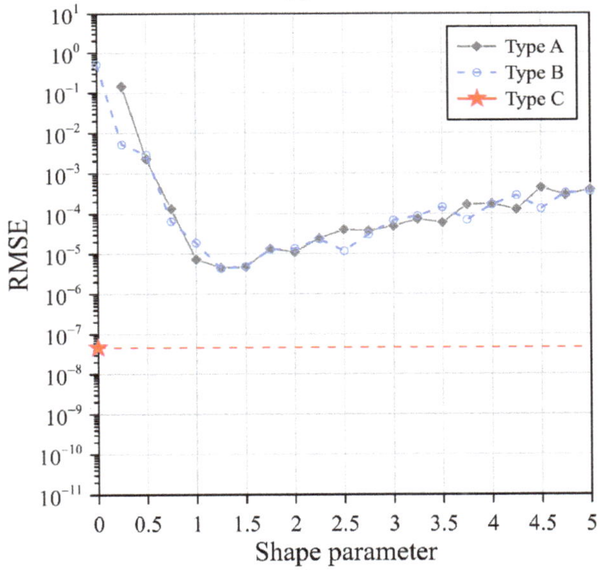

(c)

Figure 9. RMSEs of RBFs with three different collocation types: (**a**) Gaussian RBF, (**b**) MQ RBF, and (**c**) IMQ RBF.

Table 4 presents a comparison of the results for the application example 2. For type A and type B, the Gaussian, MQ, and IMQ RBFs with the optimal shape parameter were utilized. For type C, the above RBFs without a shape parameter were adopted. As depicted in Table 4, all the RBFs, including the Gaussian, MQ, and IMQ RBFs utilizing the fictitious sources of type C, provided more accurate results than the other two source collocation types, even when the best shape parameter was adopted. The obtained results demonstrate that numerical solutions with a very high accuracy can be obtained by utilizing the proposed simplified Gaussian, MQ, and IMQ RBFs with exterior fictitious sources.

Table 4. Comparison of the results for the application example 2.

RBF	RMSE		
	Type A	Type B	Type C (η=3)
Gaussian	1.18×10^{-6} ($c = 2.50$) (t = 7.24 s)	1.61×10^{-6} ($c = 2.25$) (t = 9.47 s)	2.76×10^{-11} ($c = 1$) (t = 12.57 s)
MQ	6.28×10^{-6} ($c = 1$) (t = 7.28 s)	3.70×10^{-6} ($c = 1$) (t = 10.34 s)	5.04×10^{-9} ($c = 0$) (t = 13.01 s)
IMQ	4.54×10^{-6} ($c = 1.25$) (t = 7.24 s)	4.32×10^{-6} ($c = 1.25$) (t = 11.67 s)	4.59×10^{-8} ($c = 0$) (t = 12.67 s)

4.3. Application Example 3

The three-dimensional problem is enclosed by a sophisticated irregular domain boundary, as shown in Figure 10a. The three-dimensional elliptic boundary value problems is expressed as Equation (1), where $A_x = A_y = 1$, $A_z = B = 0$, and $f(x, y, z) = 2z\cos(x)\sinh(y)$. The object boundary is given by the spherical parametric equation as Equation (22). The Dirichlet data are imposed using the following exact solution for this three-dimensional problem as:

$$u(x, y, z) = z\cos(x)\cosh(y) + z\sin(x)\sinh(y). \quad (34)$$

Three RBFs, including the Gaussian, MQ, and IMQ, were used in the collocation method. Three collocation types for locating the sources were considered in the above RBFs to solve this three-dimensional problem. There were 2500 source points, 1600 interior points, and 861 boundary points. The three collocation types of this three-dimensional problem are illustrated in Figure 1. In type A, the fictitious sources are uniformly scattered within the domain, as depicted in Figure 1d. The interior, sources, and boundary points are placed such that the positions of the interior and fictitious sources are identical. In type B, the fictitious sources are randomly scattered within the domain, as depicted in Figure 1e. In type C, the fictitious sources are randomly scattered outside the closure of the domain, as depicted in Figure 1f.

Figure 10 illustrates the RMSE of the Gaussian, MQ, and IMQ RBFs with the three different collocation types. From Figure 10, it appears that the RMSE of the above RBFs for type A and type B fluctuated between 10^{-2} to 10^{-6} as the shape parameter ranged from 0.5 to 5. However, the RMSE of the simplified Gaussian, MQ, and IMQ RBFs (type C) without a shape parameter reached the order of 10^{-8}, 10^{-8}, and 10^{-10}, respectively.

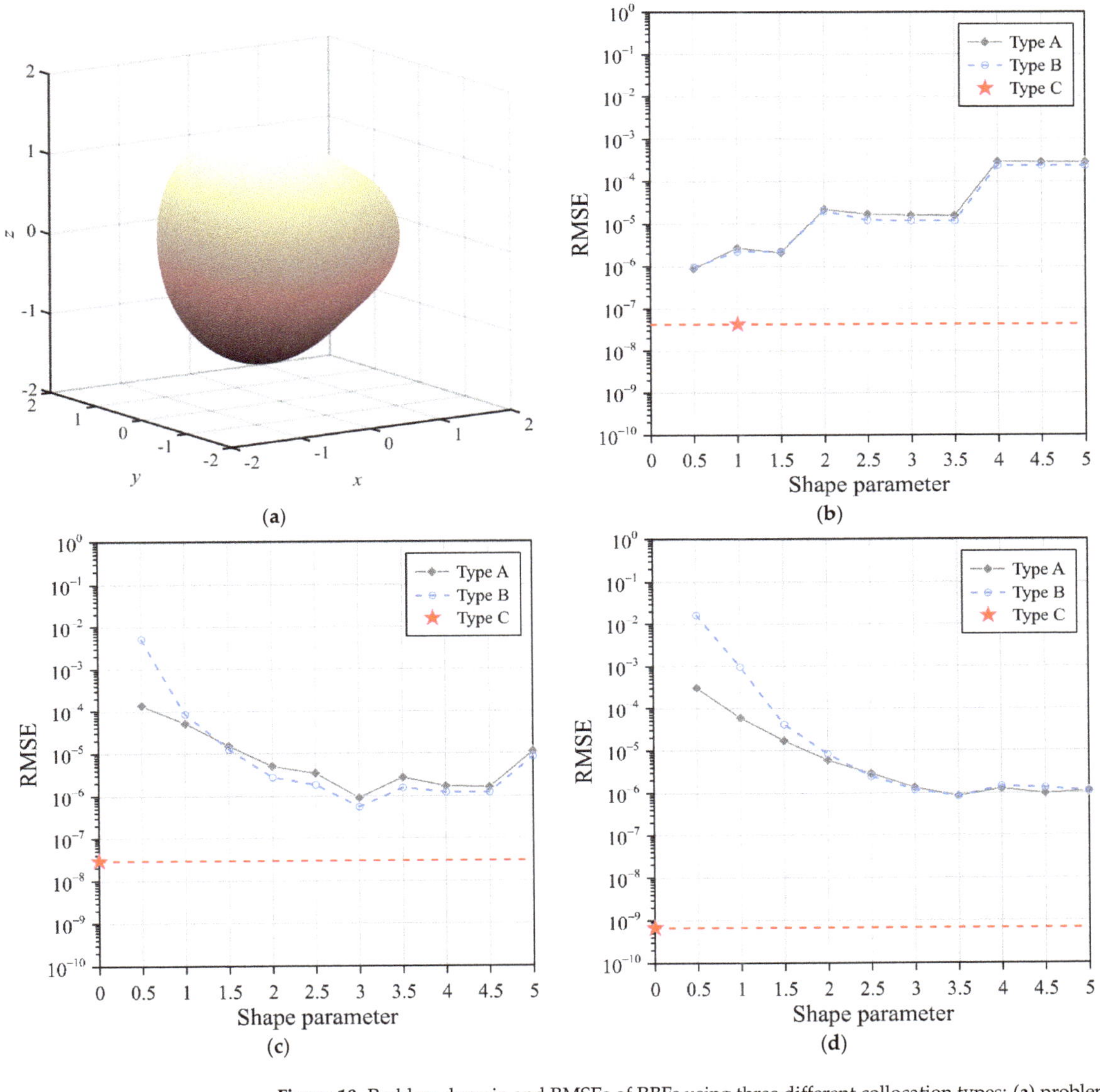

Figure 10. Problem domain and RMSEs of RBFs using three different collocation types: (**a**) problem domain, (**b**) Gaussian RBF, (**c**) MQ RBF, and (**d**) IMQ RBF.

5. Conclusions

In this study, a novel concept of using exterior fictitious sources to solve elliptic boundary value problems with the simplified radial basis function method was proposed. The concept of the proposed approach was addressed in detail. The significant findings are concluded as follows.

(1) In this study, we demonstrated that the simplified RBFs, which consider many exterior fictitious sources outside the domain, can achieve accurate results to solve elliptic boundary value problems. The obtained results demonstrate that the simplified RBFs obtain a better accuracy than the original RBFs with the optimum shape parameter when solving elliptic boundary value problems.

(2) Identification of the shape parameter is often very challenging and tedious in the original RBFs when solving partial differential equations. In this study, we proposed three simplified Gaussian, MQ, and IMQ RBFs without the shape parameter. The simplified RBFs have the advantages of a simple mathematical expression, high precision, and easy implementation.
(3) With the consideration of many exterior fictitious sources outside the domain, we found that the radial distance is always greater than zero. The simplified Gaussian, MQ, and IMQ RBFs and their derivatives in the governing equation are always smooth and nonsingular.
(4) Comparative analysis was conducted on the three different collocation types considering conventional uniform centers, randomly fictitious centers, and exterior fictitious sources. It was found that the exterior fictitious sources proposed in this study significantly improved the accuracy when solving problems.
(5) Numerical examples, including elliptic BVPs in two and three dimensions, were carried out. The simplified radial basis function method with exterior fictitious sources can be applied to three-dimensional problems with ease and high accuracy.
(6) In this study, we attempted to remove the shape parameter in conventional RBFs to solve partial differential equations. We achieved a promising result for three simplified Gaussian, MQ, and IMQ RBFs, especially for solving Laplace-type equations in two and three dimensions. Further studies to investigate the characteristics of the proposed method to solve different kinds of PDEs are suggested.

Author Contributions: Designing the study, C.-Y.K. and C.-Y.L.; formulation, C.-Y.L.; performing the analysis, C.-Y.L.; writing and editing, C.-Y.K. and C.-Y.L. All authors have read and agreed to the published version of the manuscript.

Funding: This research received no external funding.

Institutional Review Board Statement: Not applicable.

Informed Consent Statement: Not applicable.

Data Availability Statement: Research data are available on request.

Conflicts of Interest: The authors declare no conflict of interest.

References

1. Sanyasiraju, Y.V.S.S.; Chandhini, G. A note on two upwind strategies for RBF-based grid-free schemes to solve steady convection–diffusion equations. *Int. J. Numer. Methods Fluids* **2009**, *61*, 1053–1062. [CrossRef]
2. Stevens, D.; Power, H.; Lees, M.; Morvan, H. The use of PDE centres in the local RBF Hermitian method for 3D convective-diffusion problems. *J. Comput. Phys.* **2009**, *228*, 4606–4624. [CrossRef]
3. Wang, F.; Wang, C.; Chen, Z. Local knot method for 2D and 3D convection–diffusion–reaction equations in arbitrary domains. *Appl. Math. Lett.* **2020**, *105*, 106308. [CrossRef]
4. Gu, Y. Meshfree methods and their comparisons. *Int. J. Comput. Methods* **2005**, *2*, 477–515. [CrossRef]
5. Grabski, J.K. On the sources placement in the method of fundamental solutions for time-dependent heat conduction problems. *Comput. Math. Appl.* **2021**, *88*, 33–51. [CrossRef]
6. Ku, C.Y.; Liu, C.Y.; Xiao, J.E.; Hsu, S.M.; Yeih, W. A collocation method with space–time radial polynomials for inverse heat conduction problems. *Eng. Anal. Bound. Elem.* **2020**, *122*, 117–131. [CrossRef]
7. Cheng, A.H.-D. Particular solutions of Laplacian, Helmholtz-type, and polyharmonic operators involving higher order radial basis functions. *Eng. Anal. Bound. Elem.* **2000**, *24*, 531–538. [CrossRef]
8. Hu, H.Y.; Li, Z.C.; Cheng, A.H.-D. Radial basis collocation methods for elliptic boundary value problems. *Comput. Math. Appl.* **2005**, *50*, 289–320. [CrossRef]
9. Hardy, R.L. Multiquadric equations of topography and other irregular surfaces. *J. Geophys. Res.* **1971**, *76*, 1905–1915. [CrossRef]
10. Kansa, E.J. Multiquadrics—A scattered data approximation scheme with applications to computational fluid-dynamics. II Solutions to parabolic, hyperbolic and elliptic partial-differential equations. *Comput. Math. Appl.* **1990**, *19*, 147–161. [CrossRef]
11. Beatson, R.K.; Light, W.A. Fast evaluation of radial basis functions: Methods for two-dimensional polyharmonic splines. *IMA J. Numer. Anal.* **1997**, *17*, 343–372. [CrossRef]
12. Santos, L.G.C.; Manzanares-Filho, N.; Menon, G.J.; Abreu, E. Comparing RBF-FD approximations based on stabilized Gaussians and on polyharmonic splines with polynomials. *Int. J. Numer. Methods Eng.* **2018**, *115*, 462–500. [CrossRef]

13. Soleymani, F.; Barfeie, M.; Haghani, F.K. Inverse multiquadric RBF for computing the weights of FD method: Application to American options. *Commun. Nonlinear Sci. Numer. Simul.* **2018**, *64*, 74–88. [CrossRef]
14. Liu, G. An overview on meshfree methods: For computational solid mechanics. *Int. J. Comput. Methods* **2016**, *13*, 1630001. [CrossRef]
15. Uddin, M. RBF-PS scheme for solving the equal width equation. *Appl. Math. Comput.* **2013**, *222*, 619–631. [CrossRef]
16. Liu, C.S.; Chang, C.W. An energy regularization of the MQ-RBF method for solving the Cauchy problems of diffusion-convection-reaction equations. *Commun. Nonlinear Sci. Numer. Simul.* **2019**, *67*, 375–390. [CrossRef]
17. Ku, C.Y.; Hong, L.D.; Liu, C.Y.; Xiao, J.E. Space–time polyharmonic radial polynomial basis functions for modeling saturated and unsaturated flows. *Eng. Comput.* **2021**, 1–14. [CrossRef]
18. Fornberg, B.; Wright, G. Stable computation of multiquadric interpolants for all values of the shape parameter. *Comput. Math. Appl.* **2004**, *48*, 853–867. [CrossRef]
19. Chen, W.; Hong, Y.; Lin, J. The sample solution approach for determination of the optimal shape parameter in the Multiquadric function of the Kansa method. *Comput. Math. Appl.* **2018**, *75*, 2942–2954. [CrossRef]
20. Cavoretto, R.; De Rossi, A. Adaptive procedures for meshfree RBF unsymmetric and symmetric collocation methods. *Appl. Math. Comput.* **2020**, *382*, 125354. [CrossRef]
21. Issa, K.; Humbali, K.M.; Biazar, J. An algorithm for choosing best shape parameter for numerical solution of partial differential equation via inverse multiquadric radial basis function. *Open J. Math. Sci.* **2020**, *4*, 147–157. [CrossRef]
22. Zhang, J.; Wang, F.Z.; Hou, E.R. The conical radial basis function for partial differential equations. *J. Math.* **2020**, *2020*, 6664071. [CrossRef]
23. Katsiamis, A.; Karageorghis, A. Kansa radial basis function method with fictitious centres for solving nonlinear boundary value problems. *Eng. Anal. Bound. Elem.* **2020**, *119*, 293–301. [CrossRef]
24. Liu, C.Y.; Ku, C.Y.; Hong, L.D.; Hsu, S.M. Infinitely smooth polyharmonic RBF collocation method for numerical solution of elliptic PDEs. *Mathematics* **2021**, *9*, 1535. [CrossRef]
25. Ku, C.Y.; Liu, C.Y.; Xiao, J.E.; Hsu, S.M. Multiquadrics without the shape parameter for solving partial differential equations. *Symmetry* **2020**, *12*, 1813. [CrossRef]
26. Yue, X.; Jiang, B.; Xue, X.; Yang, C. A Simple, Accurate and Semi-Analytical Meshless Method for Solving Laplace and Helmholtz Equations in Complex Two-Dimensional Geometries. *Mathematics* **2022**, *10*, 833. [CrossRef]

mathematics

MDPI

Article

epSFEM: A Julia-Based Software Package of Parallel Incremental Smoothed Finite Element Method (S-FEM) for Elastic-Plastic Problems

Meijun Zhou [1], Jiayu Qin [1,*], Zenan Huo [1], Fabio Giampaolo [2] and Gang Mei [1,*]

[1] School of Engineering and Technology, China University of Geosciences (Beijing), Beijing 100083, China; meijun.zhou@cugb.edu.cn (M.Z.); zenan.huo@email.cugb.edu.cn (Z.H.)

[2] Consorzio Interuniversitario Nazionale per l'Informatica (CINI), 80100 Naples, Italy; fabio.giampaolo@consorzio-cini.it

* Correspondence: jiayu.qin@cugb.edu.cn (J.Q.); gang.mei@cugb.edu.cn (G.M.)

Abstract: In this paper, a parallel Smoothed Finite Element Method (S-FEM) package epSFEM using incremental theory to solve elastoplastic problems is developed by employing the Julia language on a multicore CPU. The S-FEM, a new numerical method combining the Finite Element Method (FEM) and strain smoothing technique, was proposed by Liu G.R. in recent years. The S-FEM model is softer than the FEM model for identical grid structures, has lower sensitivity to mesh distortion, and usually produces more accurate solutions and a higher convergence speed. Julia, as an efficient, user-friendly and open-source programming language, balances computational performance, programming difficulty and code readability. We validate the performance of the epSFEM with two sets of benchmark tests. The benchmark results indicate that (1) the calculation accuracy of epSFEM is higher than that of the FEM when employing the same mesh model; (2) the commercial FEM software requires 10,619 s to calculate an elastoplastic model consisting of approximately 2.45 million triangular elements, while in comparison, epSFEM requires only 5876.3 s for the same computational model; and (3) epSFEM executed in parallel on a 24-core CPU is approximately 10.6 times faster than the corresponding serial version.

Keywords: elastic-plastic problems; incremental theory; Smoothed Finite Element Method (S-FEM); Julia language; parallel programming

MSC: 35-04

Citation: Zhou, M.; Qin, J.; Huo, Z.; Giampaolo, F.; Mei, G. epSFEM: A Julia-Based Software Package of Parallel Incremental Smoothed Finite Element Method (S-FEM) for Elastic-Plastic Problems. *Mathematics* **2022**, *10*, 2024. https://doi.org/10.3390/math10122024

Academic Editors: Fajie Wang and Ji Lin

Received: 12 May 2022
Accepted: 9 June 2022
Published: 11 June 2022

1. Introduction

Currently, numerical methods are the most important tools for solving various scientific and engineering problems [1]. For example, the Finite Element Method (FEM), one of the most successful numerical methods, has been widely employed in different scientific and engineering fields because of its mathematically rigorous proof and satisfactory efficiency [2–4]. However, the shortcomings and deficiencies of FEM are becoming increasingly significant [2,5–8]. (1) The FEM applies the problem domain of finite degrees of freedom to the problem domain of infinite degrees of freedom, which makes the system stiffness matrix "too rigid". (2) The conventional FEM has high requirements for mesh quality and cannot deal with distorted meshes. (3) When the conventional FEM uses simple and low-order elements to calculate large and complex structures, the calculation accuracy is often unsatisfactory, while when higher-order elements with higher accuracy are used, the computational cost is quite expensive.

To cope with the above deficiencies of FEM or decrease the computational cost of generating meshes, meshfree methods have emerged, such as Radial Point Interpolation Method (RPIM), Element Free Galerkin (EFG) and Meshless Local Petrov–Galerkin

(MLPG) [2,5,9,10]. The mesh-free methods can be used to analyze crack problems and large deformation problems because mesh-free methods employ a group of scattered nodes in the discrete problem domain, avoiding the requirement for continuity of the problem domain. However, the more complex computational process of mesh-free methods leads to the desire to achieve higher computational accuracy, which is not only computationally time-consuming but also inefficient [7].

In recent years, the Smoothed Finite Element Method (S-FEM), a new numerical method combining the FEM and strain smoothing technique was proposed by Liu G.R. et al. [7,11]. The system stiffness matrix of S-FEM model is softer than the FEM model for identical grid structures, has lower sensitivity to mesh distortion, and usually produces more accurate solutions and a higher convergence speed [7]. Due to the above characteristics, S-FEM is frequently used in the fields of material mechanics [12,13], dynamics [14,15], fracture mechanics [16], plate and shell mechanics [17], fluid structure interaction [18], acoustics [19], heat transfer [20] and biomechanics [21].

Typical S-FEM models include cell-based S-FEM (CS-FEM) [15,22], node-based S-FEM (NS-FEM) [23,24], edge-based S-FEM (ES-FEM) [14,16] for 2D and 3D problems and face-based S-FEM (FS-FEM) [25] for 3D problems. In addition, there are hybrid and modified types of S-FEM. For example, Chen et al. [26] proposed an edge-based smoothed extended finite element method, ESm-XFEM, for the analysis of linear elastic fracture mechanics. An improved ES-FEM method, bES-FEM, was proposed by Nguyen-Xuan et al. [27]. bES-FEM can be applied to almost incompressible and incompressible problems. Xu et al. [28] proposed a hybrid smoothed finite element method (H-SFEM) for solving solid mechanics problems by combining FEM and NS-FEM based on triangular meshes. Zeng et al. [29] proposed a beta finite element method (βFEM) based on the smooth strain technique applied to the modeling of crystalline materials.

Compared with FEM, the calculation of the S-FEM has the following two differences. First, we need to construct the smoothing domains and modify or reconstruct the strain field in the S-FEM. Moreover, because the smoothing domain may involve a portion of adjacent elements, the memory requirements for S-FEM will be larger [7]. The two differences mentioned above may lead to a higher computational cost for the S-FEM than the FEM for the same grid structure. However, given the calculation cost, the results calculated by the S-FEM model are more accurate than the FEM, and thus, achieve higher efficiency. To make S-FEM more applicable to large-scale engineering problems, parallel strategies of multicore CPUs and/or multicore GPUs are usually used to improve and optimize the computational power of S-FEM.

Currently, there are many software packages developed for utilizing FEM to solve various scientific and engineering problems, while the development of software and library packages for the S-FEM is still in progress [30]. Current S-FEM software packages are mostly implemented in C++ and Fortran. However, static languages such as Fortran and C/C++ have more complex language structures, are more difficult to learn, and require high programming skills. Although high-level dynamic languages, such as MATLAB and Python, are easy to learn, highly visual and interactive, the computing speed of dynamic language is slow and there are expensive licensing fees associated with the use of commercial software such as MATLAB. Julia is an efficient, user-friendly, open-source programming language, developed by MIT in 2009 [31]. Furthermore, it balances the problems of computing performance, programming difficulty and code legibility [32].

Many researchers have used the Julia language to develop software packages related to numerical computation. For example, Frondelius et al. [33] designed an FEM structure by using the Julia language, which enables large-scale FEM models to be processed by using distributed simple programming models across a cluster of computers. Sinaie et al. [34] implemented the Material Point Method (MPM) in the Julia language. In the large strain solid mechanics simulation, only Julia's built-in characteristics are used, which has better performance than the MPM code based on MATLAB. Zenan Huo et al. [35] implemented a package of S-FEM for linear elastic static problems by using Julia language. Pawar et al. [36] developed a one-dimensional solver for the Euler equation, and an arakawa spectral solver and pseudo-spectral solver for the two-dimensional incompressible Navier–Stokes equation for the analysis of computational fluid dynamics using the Julia language. Heitzinger et al. [37] used the Julia language to implement numerical stochastic homogeneity of elliptic problems and discussed the advantages of using Julia to solve multiscale problems involving partial differential equations. Kemmer et al. [38] designed a finite element and boundary element solver using Julia to calculate the electrostatic potential of proteins in structural solvents. Fairbrother et al. [39] developed a package for Gaussian processes, GaussianProcesses.jl, using the Julia language. GaussianProcesses.jl takes advantage of the inherent computational benefits of the Julia language, including multiple assignments and just-in-time compilation, to generate fast, flexible and user-friendly packages for Gaussian processes.

In this paper, a parallel incremental S-FEM software package epSFEM for elastic-plastic problems is designed and implemented by utilizing the Julia language on a multi-core CPU. Distributed parallelism and partitioned parallelism are used for the assembly of the stiffness matrix, allowing multiple cells to be assembled simultaneously, avoiding excessive for loops and saving computation time. The system of equations is solved using the PARDISO [40] parallel sparse matrix solver. epSFEM applies to more common and complex elastic-plastic mechanical problems in practical engineering. Moreover, epSFEM adopts an incremental theory suitable for most load cases to solve elastic-plastic problems, and the calculation results are more reliable and accurate.

The contributions of this paper can be summarized as follows:

(1) A parallel S-FEM package epSFEM using incremental theory to solve elastic-plastic problems is developed by Julia language.

(2) The computational efficiency of epSFEM is improved by using distributed and partitioned parallel strategy on a multi-core CPU.

(3) epSFEM features a clear structure and legible code and can be easily extended.

The rest of this paper is organized as follows. The theory related to S-FEM and Julia language are presented in Section 2. The detailed implementation steps of the software package epSFEM are described in Section 3. Two sets of numerical examples are used to assess the correctness of the epSFEM and to evaluate its efficiency in Section 4. The performance, strengths and weaknesses of the epSFEM and the future direction of work are discussed in Section 5. Section 6 presents the main conclusions.

2. Background

In this section, the theoretical basis of the S-FEM and parallelization strategy of the Julia language on a multicore CPU are introduced.

2.1. *Smoothed Finite Element Method (S-FEM)*

2.1.1. Overview of the S-FEM

The S-FEM is the implementation of the FEM by employing the strain smoothing technique to modify or reconstruct the strain field such that more accurate or special performance solutions can be obtained. NS-FEM, for example, has an upper bound solution to the model because of its weak super-convergence, insensitivity to mesh deformation and an overly soft system stiffness matrix. In the ES-FEM and FS-FEM models, there are no unphysical modes, so both methods give good results for dynamic and static problems. In the S-FEM, the most important goal is the modification of the compatible strain field or reconstruction of the strain field only from the displacement field [11]. To guarantee the stable and convergent properties of the established S-FEM model, this strain modification or reconstruction needs to be conducted in an appropriate way to obtain special characteristics. Strain modification or reconstruction can be implemented within the element, but it is generally conducted across the element to obtain more information from adjacent elements. Different modification or reconstruction methods correspond to separate S-FEMs, that is, CS-FEM, NS-FEM, ES-FEM and FS-FEM.

For two-dimensional static problems, ultra accurate numerical solutions can be obtained using ES-FEM, and the calculation results of ES-FEM based on T3 elements are even more accurate than traditional FEM with Q4 elements (same number of nodes) [11,14]. Therefore, the ES-FEM is employed to solve the two-dimensional elastic-plastic problem in this paper, and the implementation steps are introduced as follows.

2.1.2. Workflow of the ES-FEM

The ES-FEM calculation process is similar to that of the FEM, except that the ES-FEM needs to construct a smoothing domain on the basis of the FEM model and modify or reconstruct the strain field. As shown in Figure 1, many techniques designed for FEM can be adapted for ES-FEM. In short, the difference between the ES-FEM and FEM is that all calculations of the FEM are based on elements, while all calculations of the ES-FEM are conducted on smoothing domains.

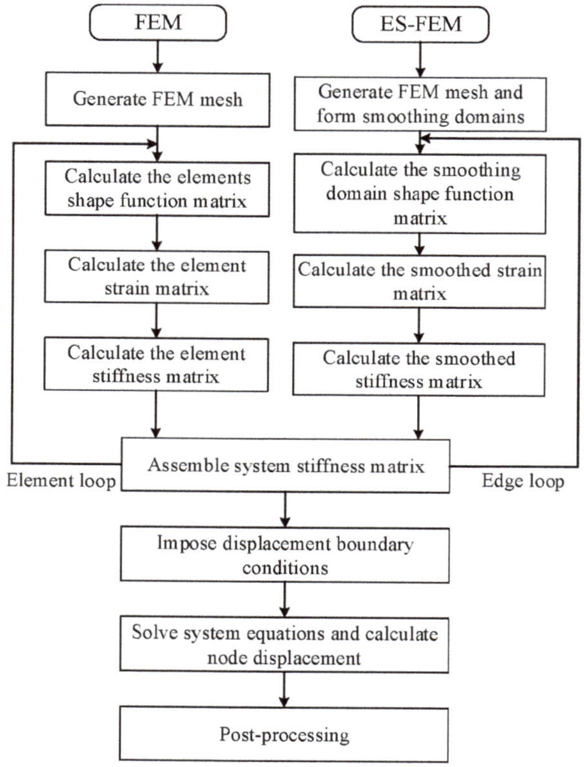

Figure 1. Flow chart of the FEM and ES-FEM.

The two-dimensional solid mechanics problem with problem domain Ω and boundary $\Gamma = \Gamma_u \cup \Gamma_t$ are considered, where Γ_u is the essential boundary where displacement conditions are prescribed and Γ_t is the natural or force boundary.

The calculation procedure of ES-FEM is as follows [7,11,14]:

(1) Discretization of the problem domains and construction of the smoothing domains

In the ES-FEM, general polygonal elements are used to divide the problem domain, mainly T3 elements suitable for solving two-dimensional problems. When the T3 element is used, the meshing can be the same as the standard FEM, such as the widely used Delaunay triangulation method.

As shown in Figure 2, on the basis of the polygonal element mesh, the smoothing domain is constructed. The problem domain is divided into N_e polygonal elements, including N_{eg} edges. The edge-based smoothing domain is composed of two nodes connecting one edge and the centroid of its adjacent elements. The two nodes A and B connecting edge AB and centroid D of the triangle element form the smoothing domain (ABD), see Figure 2. The construction of the smoothing domain, such as the discrete problem domain, must follow the principle of no gap and no overlap, that is, $\Omega = \Omega_1^s \cup \Omega_2^s \cup \ldots \cup \Omega_{N_e}^s$, $\Omega_i^s \cap \Omega_j^s = \emptyset$, and $i \neq j$.

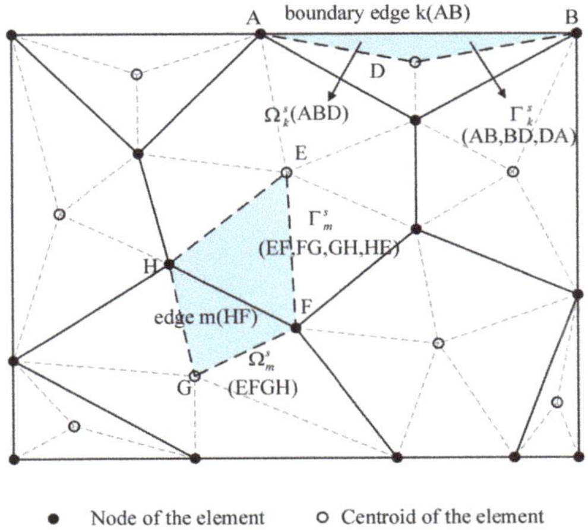

Figure 2. Polygon element mesh and the edge-based smoothing domain in ES-FEM.

(2) Creation of the displacement field

The generalized displacement field $\tilde{\mathbf{u}}$ at any point in the triangular element is approximated as:

$$\tilde{\mathbf{u}} = \sum_{i=1}^{N_n} \mathbf{N}_i(\mathbf{x})\tilde{\mathbf{d}}_i \tag{1}$$

where N_n is the number of smoothing domain nodes, $\tilde{\mathbf{d}}_i$ is the nodal displacement at node i, and $\mathbf{N}_i(\mathbf{x})$ is the shape function:

$$\mathbf{N}_i(\mathbf{x}) = \begin{bmatrix} N_i(x) & & \\ & \ddots & \\ & & N_i(x) \end{bmatrix}_{n \times n} \tag{2}$$

where n is the degree of freedom of the smoothing domain nodes.

The Gauss integration point interpolation distribution of the ES-FEM shape function is illustrated in Figure 3. As shown in Figure 3, the commonly used linear triangular elements are employed to divide the mesh. Here, the shape function values at the Gauss integral point are calculated in two cases: boundary edge and internal edge. The results are shown in Tables 1 and 2.

(3) Construction of the smoothed strain field

For triangular, quadrilateral and polygonal elements, strain smoothing techniques can be used to construct the strain field directly from the boundary integrals of the shape function without the need for coordinate mapping.

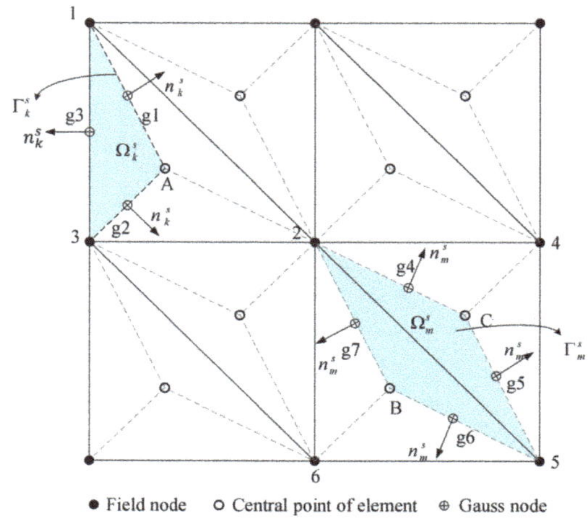

Figure 3. Illustration of the interpolation distribution of the Gaussian integration points of the ES-FEM shape function.

Table 1. The shape function entries at different points on the boundary of the smoothing domain connected to the outer edge 1–2 in Figure 3.

Node Number	1	2	3	Node Attributes
1	1.0	0.0	0.0	Field node
2	0.0	1.0	0.0	Field node
3	0.0	0.0	1.0	Field node
A	1/3	1/3	1/3	Centroid of element
g1	1/2	1/2	0.0	Gauss point
g2	1/6	4/6	1/6	Gauss point
g3	4/6	1/6	1/6	Gauss point

Table 2. The shape function entries at different points on the internal smoothing domain connected with the inner edges 3–5 in Figure 3.

Node Number	3	4	5	6	Node Attributes
3	1.0	0.0	0.0	0.0	Field node
4	0.0	1.0	0.0	0.0	Field node
5	0.0	0.0	1.0	0.0	Field node
6	0.0	0.0	0.0	1.0	Field node
B	1/3	1/3	1/3	0.0	Centroid of element
C	1/3	0.0	1/3	1/3	Centroid of element
g4	4/6	1/6	1/6	0.0	Gauss point
g5	1/6	1/6	4/6	0.0	Gauss point
g6	1/6	0.0	4/6	1/6	Gauss point
g7	4/6	0.0	1/6	1/6	Gauss point

In the ES-FEM, the smoothed strain $\bar{\varepsilon}$ is computed as follows:

$$\bar{\varepsilon} = \int_{\Omega_k^s} \tilde{\varepsilon}(\mathbf{x})\Phi(x)d\Omega \tag{3}$$

where $\tilde{\varepsilon}(\mathbf{x}) = \mathbf{L_d u}$ is the strain that satisfies the compatibility condition in the traditional FEM, $\Phi(x)$ is the smoothing function, and Ω_k^s is the smoothing domain, which can be defined as follows:

$$\Phi(x) = \begin{cases} \frac{1}{A_k^s}, x \in \Omega_k^s \\ 0, x \notin \Omega_k^s \end{cases} \tag{4}$$

where A_k^s is the area of the smoothing domain.

Combining the Gaussian divergence theorem, the domain integral is transformed into the edge integral to obtain the following smoothed strain calculation equation:

$$\bar{\varepsilon} = \int_{\Omega_k^s} \tilde{\varepsilon}(\mathbf{x}) d\Omega = \int_{\Omega_k^s} \mathbf{L_d} \tilde{\mathbf{u}}(\mathbf{x}) d\Omega = (1/A_k^s) \int_{\Gamma_k^s} \mathbf{L_n}(\mathbf{x}) \tilde{\mathbf{u}}(\mathbf{x}) d\Gamma, x \in \Omega_k^s \tag{5}$$

where $\mathbf{L_d}$ is the partial differential matrix operator, $\mathbf{L_n}$ is the outward unit normal vector and Γ_k^s is the boundary of the edge-based smoothing domain.

$$\mathbf{L_n}(\mathbf{x}) = \begin{bmatrix} n_x & 0 \\ 0 & n_y \\ n_y & n_x \end{bmatrix} \tag{6}$$

where n_x and n_y are the x-axis and y-axis components of the normal vector outside the unit, respectively.

Similar to the FEM, the smoothed strain field is divided into:

$$\bar{\varepsilon}(\mathbf{x}) = \sum_I^{N_n} \bar{\mathbf{B}}_\mathbf{I}(\mathbf{x_k}) \mathbf{d_I} \tag{7}$$

where $\mathbf{B_I}$ is the smoothed strain matrix:

$$\bar{\mathbf{B}}_\mathbf{I}(\mathbf{x_k}) = \begin{bmatrix} \bar{b}_{Ix}(x_k) & 0 \\ 0 & \bar{b}_{Iy}(x_k) \\ \bar{b}_{Iy}(x_k) & \bar{b}_{Ix}(x_k) \end{bmatrix} \tag{8}$$

where $\bar{b}_{Ix}(x_k)$ and $\bar{b}_{Iy}(x_k)$ is defined as shown in Equation (9). The boundary integral method is used to solve the smoothed strain matrix. This method is applicable to any polygonal geometry in the smoothing domain.

$$\begin{cases} \bar{b}_{Ix} = (1/A_k^s) \int_{\Gamma_k^s} n_x N_I(x) d\Gamma = (1/A_k^s) \sum_{i=1}^{N_I} n_{i,x} N_I(x_i^G) l_i \\ \bar{b}_{Iy} = (1/A_k^s) \int_{\Gamma_k^s} n_y N_I(x) d\Gamma = (1/A_k^s) \sum_{i=1}^{N_I} n_{i,y} N_I(x_i^G) l_i \end{cases} \tag{9}$$

where N_I is the number of segments of Γ_k^s, $n_{i,x}$ and $n_{i,y}$ are the outer normal vectors of the Ith integration segment, x_i^G is the midpoint of each segment of the boundary, that is, the Gauss integration point, and $N_I(x_i^G)$ is the shape function value at the Gauss integration point.

(4) Establishment system of equations

The smoothed Galerkin weak form is utilized to establish the system equation in the ES-FEM. During this process, only a simple summation calculation of the relevant parameters of the smoothing domain is required.

The linear system of equations of ES-FEM is:

$$\bar{\mathbf{K}}^{\mathbf{ES-FEM}} \bar{\mathbf{d}} = \tilde{\mathbf{f}} \tag{10}$$

where $\bar{\mathbf{d}}$ is the displacement vector of all nodes in the S-FEM and $\tilde{\mathbf{f}}$ is the vector of all loads. $\bar{\mathbf{K}}^{\mathbf{ES-FEM}}$ is the system stiffness matrix of the ES-FEM and defined as Equation (11):

$$\bar{\mathbf{K}}_{\mathbf{IJ}}^{\mathbf{ES-FEM}} = \sum_{k=1}^{N_{eg}} \int_{\Omega_k^s} \bar{\mathbf{B}}_\mathbf{I}^\mathbf{T} \mathbf{c} \bar{\mathbf{B}}_\mathbf{J} d\Omega = \sum_{k=1}^{N_{eg}} \bar{\mathbf{B}}_\mathbf{I}^\mathbf{T} \mathbf{c} \bar{\mathbf{B}}_\mathbf{J} A_k^s \tag{11}$$

where **c** is the matrix of elasticity coefficients.

(5) Imposition of the boundary conditions

In the ES-FEM, the application process of displacement boundary conditions is similar to that of the FEM because the shape function used in the S-FEM has the same delta property as the FEM. The main methods include the direct method, set "1", multiple large numbers, Lagrange multiplier and penalty function. The force boundary conditions are added directly to the corresponding nodes.

(6) Postprocessing

The weighted average rule is used to obtain the equivalent nodal stress in the smoothing domain, and the shape function interpolation technique is used to obtain the continuous stress field in the problem domain. The process is similar to the FEM. Finally, the accuracy of the results is assessed in relation to the actual problem.

2.2. *The Julia Language*

Julia, officially released in 2012, is a flexible dynamic language for scientific and numerical computation [41]. To solve large-scale numerical computation problems, parallel computing is considered essential. There are useful built-in features in Julia that make it easier for developers to design efficient parallel code. Three of the parallel strategies, that is, coroutine, multithreaded and distributed computing, are dependent on a multicore CPU. Developers can select the appropriate parallelism method for their needs. Parallel computing on many-core GPUs can be conducted by using specific packages or utilizing the built-in function of Julia and parallel arrays [1].

In this paper, parallelism on a multicore CPU is applied to effectively improve the calculation and assembly efficiency of the global stiffness matrix. In the Julia language, distributed computing based on a multicore CPU first redistributes tasks according to the number of CPU cores of the computer and then dynamically allocates computing tasks to each process so that multiple processes can be calculated at the same time, thus improving the computing efficiency. In the parallel computing of Julia language, "SharedArray" is used to reduce memory usage and improve computational efficiency. Moreover, when a "SharedArray" is employed, multiple processes are allowed to operate on the same array in the meantime [42,43].

3. The Implementation of Package epSFEM

3.1. *Overview*

A parallel S-FEM package using incremental theory to solve elastic-plastic problems is developed on a multicore CPU. This package contains the following three components:

Preprocessing: The preprocessing includes mesh generation and the construction of smoothing domains based on the mesh. After the preprocessing is completed, the model details of constructing the smoothing domain can be obtained, and stored in sparate five files: nodes, elements, internal edges, external edges and the centroids of mesh elements.

Solver: The solver uses incremental S-FEM to solve the elastoplastic problems, which is the main part of the whole software package. It is mainly categorized into: (1) assembly of the elastic stiffness matrix and (2) incremental loading and semismooth Newton method iterations to solve the system of equations. The calculation procedure of the incremental loading and semismooth Newton method iterations of the solver is illustrated in Figure 4.

Postprocessing: ParaView [44] is utilized to visualize the numerical calculation results. The WriteVTK.jl package in Julia is used to write the "vtu" format file needed for ParaView visualization.

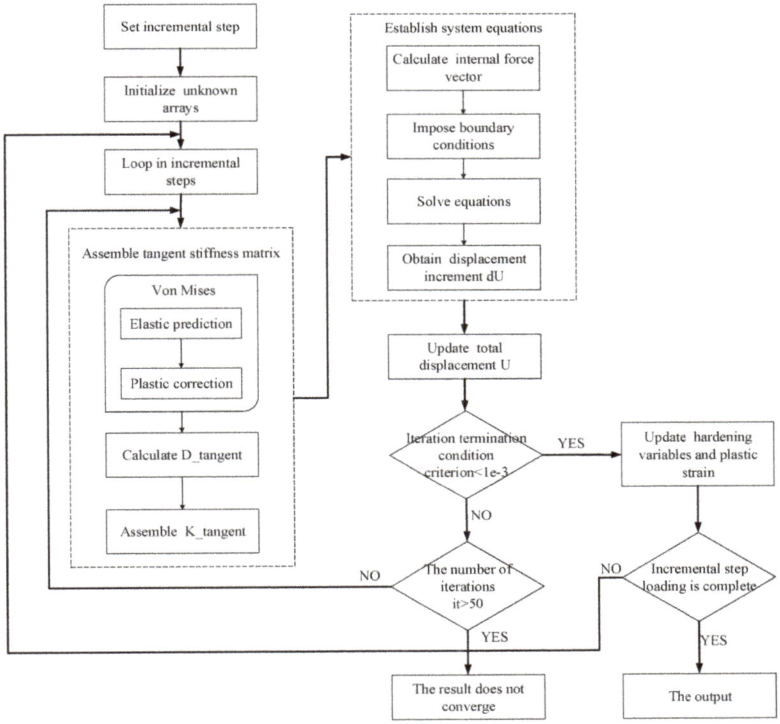

Figure 4. Illustration of the calculation procedure of incremental loading and semismooth Newton method iterations.

3.2. Preprocessing

3.2.1. Mesh Generation

Mesh generation is the first step of the numerical analysis, which also affects the accuracy and efficiency of the numerical analysis. Currently, there are many mature mesh generation algorithms and software. The focus of this paper is on the solver section, so a simple direct generation method is used to generate the mesh and then divide the smoothing domain on this basis. Because T3 elements have good adaptability and are most used in science and engineering practice, we choose T3 elements to divide the problem domain.

3.2.2. Construction of the Smoothing Domain

Constructing the smoothing domain based on the meshing of the problem domain is one of the key tasks of the S-FEM. According to the methods of constructing the smoothing domain and storing model information in Refs. [35,45], the smoothing domain of the mesh is constructed, and the model information after dividing the smoothing domain is output. To get the best performance out of the Julia language, the following calculations can be looped in the unit of column, and the model information is stored based on the column. In this paper, we address the mesh details by integrating the features of ES-FEM and Julia parallel computation and then utilize five matrices to save the mesh details in an appropriate way; see Figure 5.

The "Node" matrix stores the x and y coordinates of the mesh nodes. The "Centroid" matrix stores the x and y coordinates of the center of the cell. The node numbers corresponding to the mesh cells are stored in the "Element". The three node numbers of the triangular cells are stored in the three rows of "Element" in a counterclockwise order, and the number of columns is the number of mesh cells.

In the ES-FEM, the smoothing domain is constructed by using edges as the basis. We divide all the edges of the model into two categories: the outer edges are saved in the "Edge_out" matrix, and the inner edges are saved in the "Edge_in" matrix. For the matrix "Edge_out", the two node numbers of the outer edge are stored in the first two rows, the serial number of the triangle is appended to the third row, and the rest point of the triangle is appended to the fourth row. Because one inner edge belongs to two triangles, the first two rows store the node numbers of the inner edges, the third and fourth rows of "Edge_in" are the serial numbers of neighboring triangles and the last two rows are the numbers of the other points in the triangle.

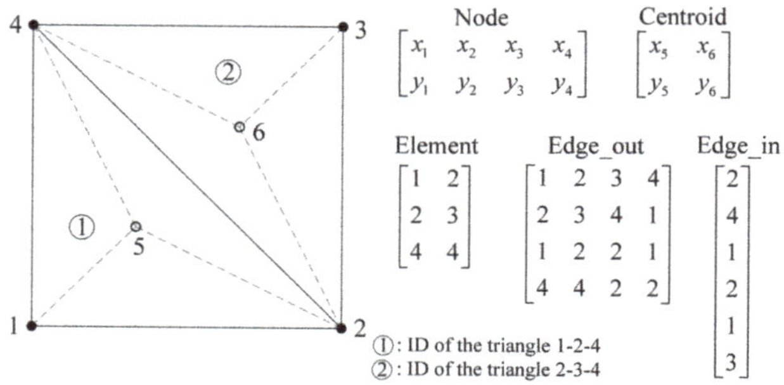

Figure 5. Illustration of the matrices "Node", "Centroid", "Element", "Edge_out" and "Edge_in", using two adjacent triangles as examples.

3.3. *Solver*

The incremental S-FEM is utilized to address the elastoplastic problem, choosing the implicit constitutive integration algorithm of the linear kinematic hardening Von Mises constitutive model and the corresponding consistent tangent modulus. First, the elastic predicted stress is calculated according to the strain of the equilibrium iteration, and then the modified stress is calculated according to a certain direction to make the stress return to the updated yield surface [46,47]. The nonlinear equations are solved by employing the semismooth Newton method.

The solution process is composed of two major procedures: (1) assembly of the elastic stiffness matrix and (2) incremental loading and semismooth Newton method iterations. The second procedure is composed of multiple incremental step cyclic calculations. Each incremental step can be divided into three steps: (1) assembly of tangent stiffness matrix, (2) solving of equations and (3) updating of hardening variables and plastic strain. According to the characteristics of parallel computing, the calculation of the latter step cannot be dependent on the previous step, so when assembling the elastic stiffness matrix, the tangent stiffness matrix can be calculated in parallel to improve efficiency. Distributed computing is used in Julia to calculate the elastic stiffness matrix and the tangent stiffness matrix for multiple elements in parallel. When solving the overall nonlinear system equations, we utilize the semismooth Newton method for each iteration. For the set of equations in each iteration, a parallel sparse equation solver, PARDISO, is used [40]. The detailed procedure of the solver in epSFEM will be presented in the subsequent sections.

3.3.1. Assembly of Elastic Stiffness Matrix

After the model is preprocessed, it needs to be assembled with an elastic stiffness matrix first. In epSFEM, we calculate the stiffness matrix of the associated smoothing domain by dividing the outer edge and the inner edge, and the calculation process is basically the same. Taking the internal edge as an example:

(1) The areas of the two triangle elements that share the inner edge is attached are computed. This process is conducted by procedure "area.jl" according to Equations (12)–(16):

$$a = \sqrt{(x_1 - x_2)^2 + (y_1 - y_2)^2} \quad (12)$$

$$b = \sqrt{(x_2 - x_3)^2 + (y_2 - y_3)^2} \quad (13)$$

$$c = \sqrt{(x_3 - x_1)^2 + (y_3 - y_1)^2} \quad (14)$$

$$p = (a + b + c)/2 \quad (15)$$

$$A = \sqrt{(p(p-a)(p-b)(p-c)} \quad (16)$$

where xi and yi is the coordinate of the node i.

(2) The length of each edge of the smoothing domain is calculated in Equation (17). For the smoothing domain of the inner side, there are four edges. This process is realized in the file "lp.jl":

$$lp = \sqrt{(x_1 - x_2)^2 + (y_1 - y_2)^2} \quad (17)$$

(3) The normal outward vector $v1$ is calculated for each side of the smoothing domain. This is performed in "vectorin.jl", according to Equations (18)–(20):

$$y = y_2 - y_1 \quad (18)$$

$$x = x_1 - x_2 \quad (19)$$

$$v1 = \left[\frac{y}{\sqrt{(y^2 + x^2)}} \frac{x}{\sqrt{(y^2 + x^2)}} \right] \quad (20)$$

(4) Assembly of the global elastic stiffness matrix and the global smoothed strain matrix. First, the stiffness matrix of the smoothing domain element is computed and then assembled according to the smooth domain nodes. Due to the large number of zero elements in the matrix, to reduce the memory occupation, the matrix is stored in a sparse form. There are three common ways to construct sparse arrays: Compressed Sparse Row (CSR), Compressed Sparse Column (CSC) and COOrdinate (COO).

First, the COO format is used to construct the global elastic stiffness matrix, since the multi-dimensional arrays in Julia are stored according to column-based sequence. Then, for the convenience of solving the subsequent system equations, we replace it with the CSC format. To construct a sparse array according to COO format, we first need to construct three one-dimensional arrays, that is, IK_elast, JK_elast and VK_elast.

IK_elast, JK_elast and VK_elast denote the row number, column number and value of each entry in the global stiffness matrix according to the order of each row. Since the sparse functions can accumulate the entries at the same position automatically, the magnitudes of IK_elast, JK_elast and VK_elast can be predetermined.

The assembly method of the global smoothed strain matrix is basically the same as the stiffness matrix, except that when it is assembled, the rows are carried out according to the elements, and the columns are carried out according to the nodes. Three one-dimensional arrays, IB, JB and VB, are constructed in advance.

For parallel computing, the six arrays of IK_elast, JK_elast, VK_elast, IB, JB and VB need to be converted to "SharedArrays" in advance, and the elastic stiffness matrix is assembled in parallel using the "@distributed" macro in Julia. Because the stiffness matrix calculation of each element has no data dependence, there will be no data interference when performing parallel computing.

The number of processes needs to be added using the function "addprocs" before all parallel computing starts. In the parallel elastic stiffness matrix assembly, we use the "@distributed" macro to automatically allocate tasks to each process according to the number of processes and the total number of tasks for parallel computing of the loop. The total number of tasks currently is equal to the total number of smoothing domains. The "@distributed" macro is executed asynchronously on the loop; it will generate independent tasks on all available processes and return immediately without waiting for the computing to complete. To wait for the computing task to complete, the "@sync" macro must be used before the call. The procedure of assembling the elastic stiffness matrix for the internal edges by distributed parallel computation is illustrated in Algorithm 1. After the global stiffness matrix and the global smoothed strain matrix are assembled, the "Sparse" function is used to convert them into the CSC format.

Algorithm 1 Parallel calculation and assembly of the elastic stiffness matrix

```
Input: Node, Centroid, Element, Edge_in, shear, bulk
Output: K_elast, B
Set the number of CPU cores for the Julia program.
Set IK_elast, JK_elast, VK_elast, IB, JB and VB to SharedArrays.
@sync @distributed begin
for every internal edge do
    Compute the area of the interior quadrilateral.
    Compute the side lengths of the interior quadrilateral.
    Compute the normal unit vectors of the four sides of the interior quadrilateral.
    Compute the smoothed strain matrix of an interior quadrilateral.
    Compute the stiffness matrix of an interior quadrilateral.
    Compute the elastic coefficient matrix.
    Assemble global stiffness matrix and smoothed strain matrix.
end for
end
K_elast = sparse (IK_elast, JK_elast, VK_elast)
B = sparse (IB, JB, VB)
```

3.3.2. Assembly of the Tangent Stiffness Matrix

The tangent stiffness matrix of the model needs to be calculated when solving the elastic-plastic problem using incremental theory. Equation (21) is used instead of Equation (22) to calculate the global tangent stiffness matrix. Among them, elastic stiffness matrix $\mathbf{K}_{\mathbf{elast}}$, smoothed strain matrix $\mathbf{B}$ and elastic matrix $\mathbf{D}_{\mathbf{elast}}$ can be obtained in advance at the stage of assembling the elastic stiffness matrix; only elastoplastic matrix $\mathbf{D}_{\mathbf{tangent}}$ depends on the plastic model, and must be partially reorganized or modified in each Newton iteration. When most portions of the model are in the elastic stage, $\mathbf{D}_{\mathbf{tangent}} - \mathbf{D}_{\mathbf{elast}}$ is more sparse than $\mathbf{D}_{\mathbf{tangent}}$ [48,49].

$$\mathbf{K}_{\mathbf{tangent}} = \mathbf{K}_{\mathbf{elast}} + \mathbf{B}^{\mathbf{T}}(\mathbf{D}_{\mathbf{tangent}} - \mathbf{D}_{\mathbf{elast}})\mathbf{B} \tag{21}$$

$$\mathbf{K}_{\mathbf{tangent}} = \mathbf{B}^{\mathbf{T}}\mathbf{D}_{\mathbf{tangent}}\mathbf{B} \tag{22}$$

$\mathbf{D}_{\mathbf{tangent}}$ is calculated by the constitutive integral. The implicit discrete method is used to solve the constitutive integral, that is, elastic prediction and plastic correction. For the constitutive relation, the linear kinematic hardening Von Mises model is employed.

The steps to calculate the tangent stiffness matrix are as follows:

(1) Calculation of the smoothed strain field. Since the global smoothed strain matrix $\mathbf{B}$ has been calculated and assembled in the stage of assembling the elastic stiffness matrix, the smoothed strain field ε can be acquired according to the strain coordination Equation $\varepsilon = \mathbf{Bu}$.

(2) The implicit Von Mises constitutive integral algorithm is used to obtain the stress **S** and tangent operator **DS** of the model, by procedure "constitutive_problem1.jl". The formula, according to [48–51], is:

$$T_k(\varepsilon_k) = \begin{cases} \sigma_k^{tr}, \left|\mathbf{s}_k^{tr}\right| \leq Y, \\ \sigma_k^{tr} - \frac{2G}{2G+a}(\left|\mathbf{s}_k^{tr}\right| - Y)\mathbf{n}_k^{tr}, \left|\mathbf{s}_k^{tr}\right| > Y \end{cases} \tag{23}$$

where $T_k(\varepsilon_k)$ represents the stress–strain operator, $\sigma_k^{tr} = C(\varepsilon_k - \varepsilon_{k-1}^p)$, $\mathbf{s}_k^{tr} = \mathrm{I}_D\sigma_k^{tr} - \beta_{k-1}$, $\mathbf{n}_k^{tr} = \frac{\mathbf{s}_k^{tr}}{\left|\mathbf{s}_k^{tr}\right|}$, a is the hardening parameters and Y is the yield stress.

$$T_k^0(\varepsilon_k) = \begin{cases} C, \left|\mathbf{s}_k^{tr}\right| \leq Y, \\ C - \frac{4G^2}{2G+a}\mathrm{I}_D + \frac{4G^2}{2G+a}\frac{Y}{\left|\mathbf{s}_k^{tr}\right|}(\mathrm{I}_D - \mathbf{n}_k^{tr} \otimes \mathbf{n}_k^{tr}), \left|\mathbf{s}_k^{tr}\right| > Y \end{cases} \tag{24}$$

where $T_k^0(\varepsilon_k)$ is the derivative of the stress–strain operator, $C = K\mathrm{I} \otimes \mathrm{I} + 2G\mathrm{I}_D$, $\mathrm{I} \otimes \mathrm{I}$ is the unit second-order tensor, $\mathrm{I}_D = \mathrm{I} - \frac{\mathrm{I} \otimes \mathrm{I}}{3}$, $K = E/3(1-2\mu)$ is the bulk modulus and $G = E/2(1+\mu)$ is the shear modulus.

The modification of hardening variable β_k and plastic strain ε_k^p is:

$$\beta_k = \begin{cases} \beta_{k-1}, \left|\mathbf{s}_k^{tr}\right| \leq Y, \\ \beta_{k-1} + \frac{a}{2G+a}(\left|\mathbf{s}_k^{tr}\right| - Y)\mathbf{n}_k^{tr}, \left|\mathbf{s}_k^{tr}\right| > Y \end{cases} \tag{25}$$

$$\varepsilon_k^p = \begin{cases} \varepsilon_{k-1}^p, \left|\mathbf{s}_k^{tr}\right| \leq Y, \\ \varepsilon_{k-1}^p + \frac{1}{2G+a}(\left|\mathbf{s}_k^{tr}\right| - Y)\mathbf{n}_k^{tr}, \left|\mathbf{s}_k^{tr}\right| > Y \end{cases} \tag{26}$$

where β_{k-1} hardening tensor from the previous incremental step and ε_{k-1}^p plastic strain tensor from the previous incremental step.

To check whether plastic correction is needed, the array CRIT of $1 \times s\_n\_e$ is defined representing the yield criterion, that is, $\left|\mathbf{s}_k^{tr}\right| - Y$, and the corresponding logical array IND_p of $1 \times s\_n\_e$ with the smoothing domain of plastic behavior, where *s_n_e* represents the total number of smoothing domains. The parallel implementation of the implicit Von Mises constitutive integral is shown in Algorithm 2.

In the parallel computing of constitutive integrals, all processes can access the underlying data. To avoid conflicts, we first construct a "myrange" function to assign tasks to each process according to the number of CPU cores added. Then, the main computing process is defined as a kernel function "assembly_tangent", and a wrapper "shared_constructive" is defined to encapsulate the kernel function. Finally, the function "constitutive_problem" is constructed to call the packaged kernel function for partition parallel computing. The "constitutive_problem" function minimizes the communication between the processes so that each process can continue to compute the allocated part for a period of time, and improve the efficiency of parallelism. The "@async" macro is used to wrap arbitrary expressions into tasks. For any content within its scope, Julia will start to run this task and then continue to execute the next code in the script without waiting for the current task to complete before executing it. The "@sync" macro means that the next task will not be executed until the dynamic closure defined by the macro "@async" is completed.

(3) Calculation of the global tangent stiffness matrix. First, the sparse elastoplastic matrix $\mathbf{D_{tangent}}$ is constructed according to the tangent operator **DS** obtained by the constitutive integral and then the global tangent stiffness matrix is calculated according to Equation (21).

Algorithm 2 Parallel implementation of implicit Von Mises constitutive integral algorithm

Input: E, Ep_prev, Hard_prev, shear, bulk, a, Y, S, DS, IND_p
Output: S, DS, IND_p

Set the number of CPU cores for the Julia program.
Set E, Ep_prev, Hard_prev, S, DS, IND_p to ShareArray.
Assign the number of tasks for each process according to the number of processes.
for number of tasks in each process **do**
  Check whether the smoothing domain yields according to the yield criterion.
  Elastic prediction of stress tensor.
  Calculate the consistent tangent operator.
  Plastic correction of the stress tensor.
  Plastic correction of the consistent tangent operator.
end for
Parallel computing using "remotecall" in Julia language.

3.3.3. Solution of System of Equations

In this process, the internal force of the model is calculated by using the stress obtained from the constitutive relationship and the smoothed strain matrix. Then, the displacement boundary conditions are applied by the direct method; that is, the corresponding rows and columns with displacement boundary conditions of "0" are deleted. A logical array Q is designed, which sets the displacement boundary condition of "0" to "0" and the rest to "1". Then, the stiffness matrix, displacement and force are calculated with a logical array index. After that, the Pardiso.jl package is added and the "MKLPardisoSolver" solver in the package is used to solve the system of equations. Finally, the node displacement increment "**dU**" of one Newton iteration in an incremental step can be obtained.

In this paper, the semismooth Newton method is employed to solve nonlinear system of equations and check whether iteration is convergent according to Algorithm 3. "MKLPardisoSolver" is the solver in the Pardiso.jl package, Q is the logical array corresponding to the displacement boundary conditions, **f** is the external force vector, **F** is the internal force vector, the subscript k represents the kth incremental step and the superscript it represents the it-th iteration step, and $\|\mathbf{U}\|_e^2 = \mathbf{U}^{\mathrm{T}}\mathbf{K}_{\mathbf{elast}}\mathbf{U}$. In each Newton iteration, the tangent stiffness matrix $\mathbf{K}_{\mathbf{tangent}}$ is used to solve the linear problem, which corresponds to the system of linear equations:

$$\mathbf{K}_k^{it}\mathbf{dU}^{it} = \mathbf{f}_k - \mathbf{F}_k \tag{27}$$

Algorithm 3 Newton iteration terminates judgment

initialization $\mathbf{U}_k^0 = \mathbf{U}_k$
for $it = 1, 2, 3 \ldots$ **do**
  $ps = MKLPardisoSolver()$
  $\mathbf{dU}^{it}[Q] = solve(ps, \mathbf{K}_k{}^{it}[Q1, Q1], (\mathbf{f}_k - \mathbf{F}_k{}^{it}))$
  $\mathbf{U}_k^{it} = \mathbf{U}_k^{it-1} + \mathbf{dU}^{it}$
  $\|\mathbf{dU}^{it}\|_e / (\|\mathbf{U}_k^{it-1}\|_e + \|\mathbf{U}_k^{it}\|_e) \leq criterion$
end for
set $\mathbf{U}_k = \mathbf{U}_k^{it}$

3.3.4. Update of Hardening Variable and Plastic Strain

After each incremental step is calculated, the hardening variable and plastic strain need to be updated by using Equations (25) and (26). Based on the implicit constitutive integration algorithm of Algorithm 2, the modification of the hardening variable and plastic strain is added. The parallel strategy in this part is consistent with Algorithm 2.

3.4. Postprocessing

After the execution of the solver, the widely used visualization software ParaView is used to visualize the numerical computational results. The relevant package WriteVTK.jl in Julia can write VTK XML files and use ParaView to visualize multidimensional datasets [44]. The VTK format files support include straight line (.vtr), structured mesh (.vts), image data (.vti), unstructured mesh (.vtu) and polygon data (.vtp) [52].

An unstructured mesh "vtu" format file is designed. Its implementation steps are as follows: (1) we need to define a cell type, which is defined in this paper as "VTKCell-Types.VTK_TRIANGLE", representing the linear triangular element; (2) the "MeshCell" function is used to define the mesh model and obtain an array containing all mesh cells; (3) to generate a "vtu" format file, we need to initialize the file with mesh nodes and element information and then add node displacement data and other information to the file; (4) we can save the file as a "vtu" format file.

4. Validation and Evaluation of epSFEM

In this section, two sets of benchmark tests are performed on a powerful computational platform to evaluate the correctness and efficiency of epSFEM. The details of the workstation computer used are shown in Table 3.

Table 3. Specifications of the workstation computer for performing the benchmark tests.

Specifications	Details
CPU	Intel Xeon Gold 5118 CPU
CPU Cores	24
CPU Frequency	2.30 GHz
CPU RAM	128 GB
OS	Windows 10 professional
IDE	Visual studio Code
Julia	Version 1.5.2

4.1. Validation of the Accuracy of epSFEM

To validate the correctness of epSFEM, we use the model shown in Figure 6a to perform elastoplastic analysis and compare its calculation accuracy with traditional finite element software. In this example, a symmetric displacement boundary condition is set up on the left and bottom of the computational model. The traction force of $F_t = 200$ N/m acts on the top of the model along the normal direction, and the traction force is added in increments through the cyclic load shown in Figure 6b. The elastic parameters are: $E = 206{,}900$ (Young's modulus) and $\mu = 0.29$ (Poisson's ratio). The parameters related to plastic materials are specified as follows: $a = 1000$, $Y = 450\sqrt{(2/3)}$. The mesh computational model with 150 triangular elements is illustrated in Figure 7a, and the computational model after constructing the smoothing domain is shown in Figure 7b.

To demonstrate the accuracy of the calculation, the displacement calculation of the model in Figure 6a is conducted, and comparisons are made in the three following cases.

(1) epSFEM is employed to calculate the displacement of a mesh model, which includes 341 nodes and 600 triangular elements (T3 elements); see Figure 8a.

(2) According to Ref. [49], the conventional FEM is used to calculate the displacement of a mesh model, which includes 341 nodes and 600 triangular elements (T3 elements); see Figure 8b.

(3) According to Ref. [49], the conventional FEM is employed to calculate the displacement of a highly accurate mesh model that includes 231,681 nodes and 76,800 eight-node quadrilateral elements (Q8 elements).

The displacements of the top node of the model calculated by the above three methods are compared in Figure 9. As shown in Figure 9, the displacement calculated by epSFEM has higher accuracy than FEM-T3 and slightly lower accuracy than FEM-Q8. Hence, the correctness of epSFEM is proven.

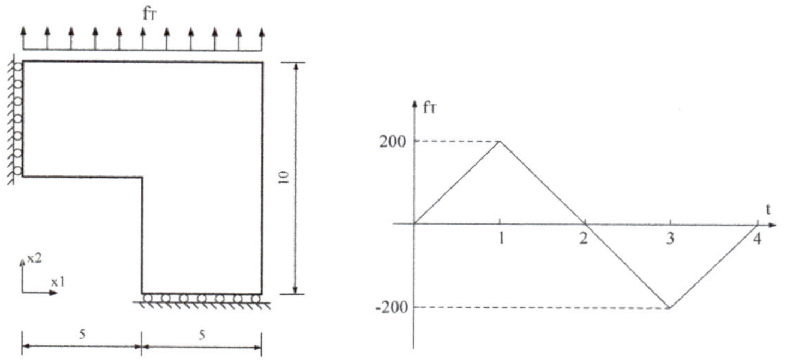

(a) (b)

Figure 6. (**a**) Simplified 2D geometry of the elastic-plastic problem and (**b**) history of the traction force.

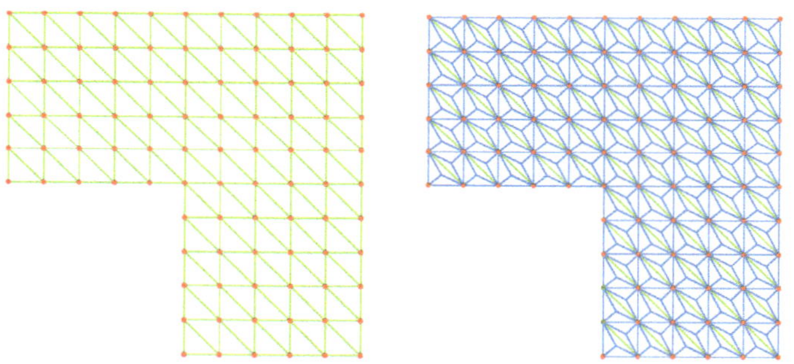

(a) (b)

Figure 7. (**a**) A mesh computational model with 150 triangular elements and (**b**) a computational model after constructing the smoothing domain.

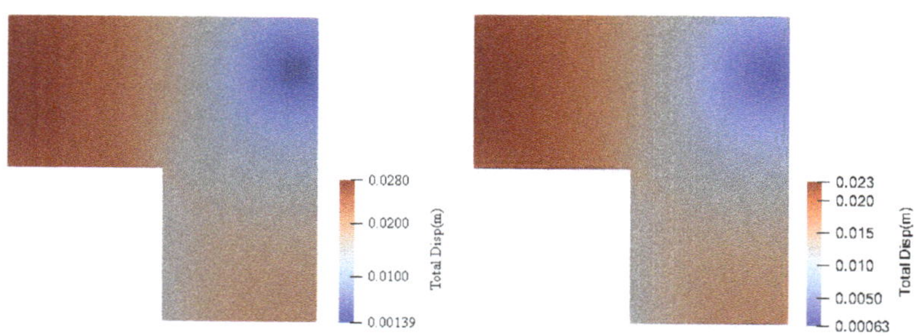

(a) (b)

Figure 8. (**a**) The contour of displacement calculated using epSFEM and (**b**) the contour of displacement calculated using FEM-T3.

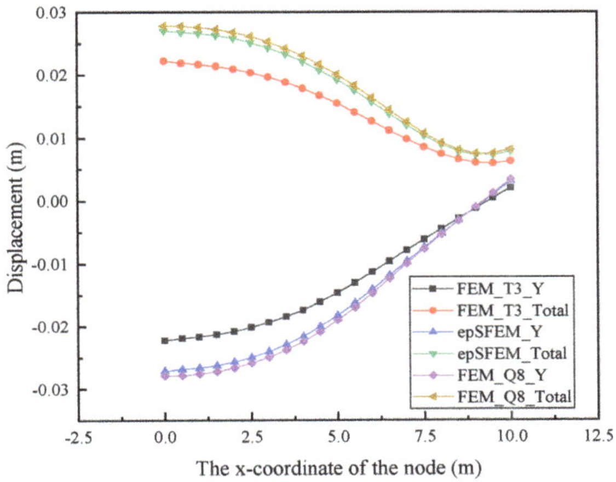

Figure 9. Comparison curves of node displacements at the top of the model calculated by different methods.

4.2. Evaluation of the Efficiency of epSFEM

To better analyze the computing efficiency of epSFEM, the computational efficiency of the serial and parallel versions of the epSFEM are recorded and compared. Five mesh models were created based on the same size model, shown in Figure 6a. Detailed information on the mesh is shown in Table 4.

Table 4. Details of the used five mesh models.

Mesh Models (T3)	Number of Nodes	Number of Elements
1	173,761	345,600
2	308,481	614,400
3	609,301	1,215,000
4	909,701	1,815,000
5	1,231,361	2,457,600

In epSFEM, the calculation procedure can be composed of two steps: (1) assembly of the elastic stiffness matrix and (2) incremental loading and semismooth Newton method iterations. In this paper, we focus on the solution of elastic-plastic problems, so the time consumption is predominantly in the second step, which is composed of multiple incremental cyclic loading steps. Each of the incremental steps can be composed of three stages: (1) assembly of tangent stiffness matrix, (2) solving of system of equations and (3) updating of hardening variables and plastic strain. Since the Pardiso.jl package is employed to solve equations in serial and parallel code, the efficiency of solving equations in serial and parallel ways are not discussed. For the assembly of the elastic stiffness matrix, its time consumption accounts for a small proportion in the whole elastic-plastic analysis, which is not discussed in this paper. The parallel method of the hardening variable and plastic strain update part is consistent with the parallel method of tangent stiffness matrix assembly. Therefore, we mainly evaluate the computing efficiency of assembling the tangent stiffness matrix in this paper.

As shown in Figure 10, the time to compute the parallelizable section of the tangent stiffness matrix in the serial and parallel versions for five different scale mesh models is compared. As shown in Figure 10, it takes only approximately 335 s to compute a mesh model, including 2.45 million elements on the parallel version, while it takes approximately

3537.6 s to compute the same model on the serial version. On the 24-core CPU, the parallel speedup can reach 10.6.

To reflect the computational efficiency of epSFEM, we also made a comparison between commercial software and epSFEM in terms of the time required to calculate the five scale models, as shown in Table 4. The total time required for the solver computing is recorded for comparison. As shown in Figure 11, for a model containing 2.45 million elements, ABAQUS requires 10,619 s to compute, while the parallel version of epSFEM needs only 5876.3 s to complete the computation. The parallel version of epSFEM is approximately 1.8 times faster than ABAQUS.

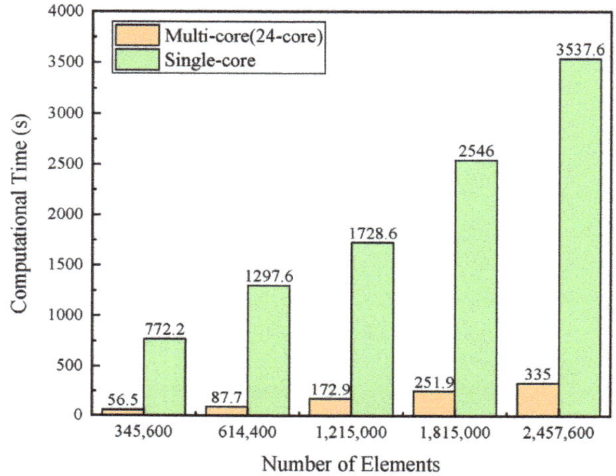

Figure 10. Comparison of serial and parallel epSFEM computing time of the parallelizable section of the tangent stiffness matrix.

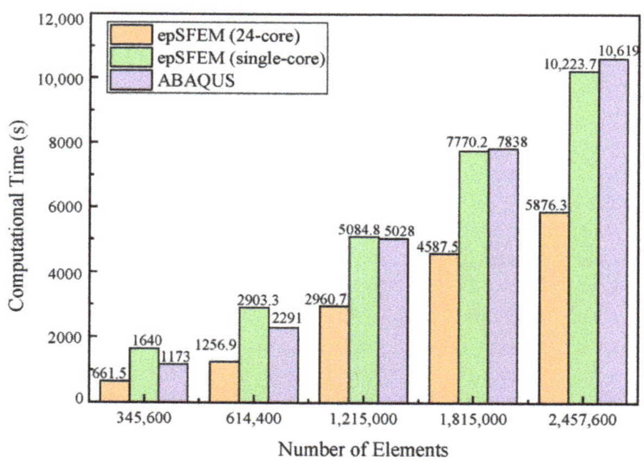

Figure 11. Comparison of the computation time of serial and parallel epSFEM and ABAQUS solvers for elastic-plastic problems.

ABAQUS was also used to calculate the displacements for a mesh model with 341 nodes and 600 triangular cells and to compare the displacements obtained by ABAQUS with those obtained by epSFEM_T3 and FEM_Q8 in Section 4.1. Using the displacement solution of FEM_Q8 as the reference solution, it can be seen that the displacement calculation accuracy of epSFEM is higher than that of ABAQUS; see Figure 12. It can be seen from the above results that the calculation time of epSFEM is shorter than that of ABAQUS when calculating the same mesh model, and the calculation accuracy of epSFEM is higher than that of ABAQUS, so the calculation efficiency of epSFEM is higher than that of ABAQUS.

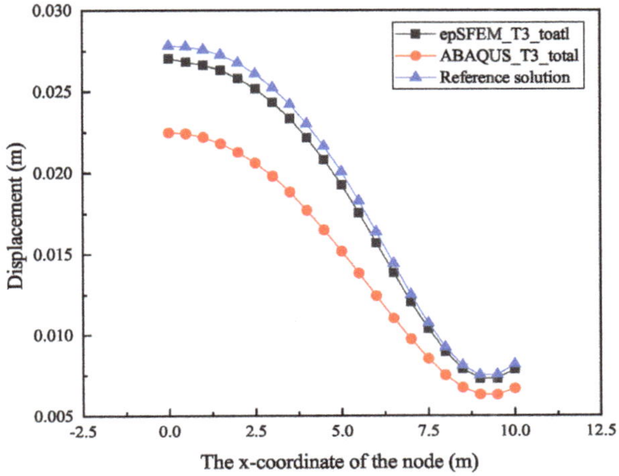

Figure 12. Comparison curves of node displacements at the top of the model calculated with ABAQUS and epsFEM.

5. Discussion

In this section, the capability, strengths and weaknesses of the epSFEM software package, as well as the future direction of work, are discussed.

5.1. Comprehensive Evaluation of epSFEM

5.1.1. Computational Accuracy

The accuracy of the calculation is the first guarantee for whether a software package can be used. To verify the correctness of the epSFEM calculation, a numerical example is used in Section 4.1. As listed in Table 5, the total displacement results of the six nodes at the top $y = 10$ m of the model are selected for comparison. Taking the displacements of FEM-Q8 as the baseline and comparing the displacements of epSFEM-T3 and FEM-T3 with them, it can be shown that the displacements of epSFEM-T3 are significantly closer to the baseline. The result difference is expressed by relative error. As seen in Table 5, for the node displacement at $x = 0$ and $y = 10$ m, the error of FEM-T3 compared with FEM-Q8 is 25.24%, while the error of epSFEM-T3 compared with FEM-Q8 is only 2.96%. This is because the S-FEM is based on the smoothing domain calculation that optimizes the system stiffness matrix and enables the displacements to be closer to the reference values.

Table 5. Validation of the accuracy of the epSFEM by comparison of calculated displacements.

Position	Method			Relative Error	
	FEM-T3	epSFEM-T3	FEM-Q8	FEM-T3	epSFEM-T3
0.0 m	0.02223 m	0.02704 m	0.02784 m	25.24%	2.96%
2.0 m	0.02095 m	0.02583 m	0.02680 m	27.92%	3.76%
4.0 m	0.01787 m	0.02217 m	0.02423 m	35.59%	9.29%
6.0 m	0.01267 m	0.01572 m	0.01640 m	29.44%	4.33%
8.0 m	0.00744 m	0.00896 m	0.00924 m	24.19%	3.13%
10.0 m	0.00626 m	0.00788 m	0.00819 m	30.83%	3.93%

5.1.2. Computational Efficiency

In this paper, the efficiency of computation is contrasted in two aspects: parallel speedup of parallelizable code and solver computation time; see Figures 10 and 11.

In this paper, we recorded the time required to compute the parallelizable portion of the tangent stiffness matrix, that is, constitutive integral algorithm, for seven different size mesh models using serial and parallel epSFEM. As shown in Table 6, the parallel speedup is 10.2 for the computing model with 38,400 elements, increases to 14.8 for the computing model with 0.6 million elements and decreases to 10.0 for the computational model with 1.2 million elements, after which the parallel speedup increases slightly with the increase of the computational model size and basically stabilizes.

Table 6. The parallel speedup of the parallelizable section of the tangential stiffness matrix.

Number of Nodes	Number of Elements	Computing Time (s)		
		Single-Core	**Multi-Core (24-Core)**	**Parallel Speedup**
19,521	38,400	69.7	6.83	10.2
77,441	153,600	283.3	23.5	12.05
173,761	345,600	772.2	56.5	13.7
308,481	614,400	1297.6	87.7	14.8
609,301	1,215,000	1728.6	172.9	10.0
909,701	1,815,000	2546	251.9	10.1
1,231,361	2,457,600	3537.6	335	10.6

The reasons why the parallel speedup shows a pattern of increasing then decreasing and finally converging as the mesh scale increases are analyzed are as follows: (1) Parallel computing includes the time to allocate tasks; the amount of computation allocated to each process cannot be exactly the same, and there is the problem of load imbalance for each process, so the parallel speedup cannot reach the ideal parallel speedup. (2) When the mesh scale is small, such as 38,400 to 614,400, the total computation time increases as the mesh scale increases, the percentage of assigned tasks in the total time decreased, and the parallel speedup increases. (3) When the mesh scale increases to 1.2 million, the performance of the code decreases due to the larger memory allocation required and the increased garbage collection time during the code run. In the benchmark tests of this paper, the above effects do not have a significant impact on the overall performance of epSFEM as the scale continues to increase. On the contrary, it tends to a steady state.

TimerOutputs.jl package is used to test the time consumption and memory allocation in each part of the calculation process and generate the formatted table to output [53]. As listed in Table 7, the allocation of time and memory for each part of the parallel epSFEM solver when the number of elements is 600,000. Table 7 shows that the time proportion of the elastic stiffness matrix is very small, which is only 0.07% when the number of elements is 600,000. Therefore, we focus on the time and memory consumption of each part of the incremental loading and the semismooth Newton iteration, which is the plastic section in Table 7. Figure 13 presents the time occupancy of the tangent stiffness matrix assembly, solving equations, hardening variables and plastic strain updating when calculating the model with 2.45 million elements using the serial and parallel versions of epSFEM. Because the hardening variable and plastic strain only need to be updated once for each incremental step, the time proportion is the smallest. The tangent stiffness matrix assembly and solving equations need to be calculated not only for each incremental step, but also for each iteration, so the time proportion is longer. As shown in Figure 13, the proportion of time spent solving the equations in parallel computing is considerably larger than in serial computing, accounting for approximately 80%.

Table 7. Time and memory allocation of each part of the parallel epSFEM solver when the number of elements is 600,000.

Tot /% Measured		Time			Allocation		
			1256.9 s/100%			337.83 GiB/100%	
Section	ncalls	Time	%tot	avg	alloc	%tot	avg
solver	1	1256.9 s	100%	1256.9 s	337.83 GiB	100%	337.83 GiB
elastic	1	0.9 s	0.07%	0.9 s	1.83 GiB	0.54%	1.83 GiB
plastic	1	1256 s	99.93%	1256 s	336 GiB	99.46%	336 GiB
solving	132	946 s	75.3%	7.16 s	62.6 GiB	18.53%	486 MiB
assembly	132	246 s	19.6%	1.86 s	256 GiB	75.78%	1.94 GiB
constitutive	132	87.7 s	6.98%	664 ms	62.0 MiB	0.02%	481 KiB
K_tangent	132	150.1 s	11.95%	1.14 s	252 GiB	74.6%	1.91 GiB
hardening and strain	40	33.0 s	2.62%	824 ms	1.03 GiB	0.3%	26.3 MiB

In summary, epSFEM combines the features of incremental theory and the parallel strategy of the Julia language to achieve a parallel and efficient incremental S-FEM for solving the elastoplastic problem. Although epSFEM can take full advantage of multicore processors, it still requires a considerable amount of time to solve linear system equations for large sparse matrices. Moreover, due to the use of incremental theory, the calculation of the latter incremental step depends on the previous incremental step, and multiple incremental steps cannot be calculated in parallel, which also limits the computational efficiency of the code.

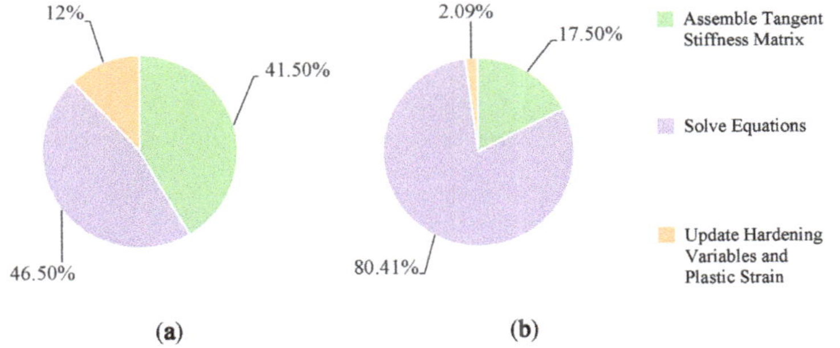

Figure 13. The proportion of time in each part of the epSFEM solver when calculating the model with 2.45 million elements using (**a**) the serial version of epSFEM and (**b**) the parallel version of epSFEM.

5.2. Comparison with Other S-FEM Programs

Compared with the S-FEM packages implemented with C++, epSFEM code is more readable and convenient for further development, and has lower requirements for programming ability. In contrast with the S-FEM packages implemented by MATLAB, epSFEM does not require the payment of licensing fees for the Julia language; additionally, the computational efficiency of the Julia language is higher than that of MATLAB. Moreover, epSFEM has a clear structure and modular implementation, and each calculation step is highly customized and has the characteristics of high efficiency and simplicity.

The epSFEM is suitable to more common and complex elastoplastic mechanical problems in practical engineering and has a wider range of applications than the elastic S-FEM package implemented using the Julia language. In contrast with the elastic-plastic S-FEM package with total strain theory realized by the Julia language, epSFEM uses incremental theory suitable for most loading situations to solve elastic-plastic problems, and the calculation results are more reliable and accurate.

5.3. Outlook and Future Work

epSFEM is an incremental ES-FEM to solve two-dimensional elastoplastic problems. The next step is to expand it to an incremental FS-FEM to solve three-dimensional elastoplastic problems. Currently, the S-FEM has been commonly utilized in material mechanics and biomechanics, but it is still less applied in the field of geotechnical mechanics [54,55]. We plan to extend epSFEM to use the Mohr-Coulomb criterion combined with the strength reduction method to analyze the deformation and failure of slopes. With the maturity of artificial intelligence technology such as machine learning and deep learning, mechanical analysis and numerical simulation methods can be well integrated with machine learning, which provides a new direction for computational mechanics [56–59]. In the future, the authors wish is to use machine learning combined with epSFEM to solve partial differential Equations (PDEs), or study parameter inversion.

6. Conclusions

In this paper, a parallel incremental S-FEM package epSFEM for elastic-plastic problems has been designed and implemented by the Julia language on a multicore CPU. epSFEM has a clear structure and legible code and can be easily developed further. epSFEM utilizes incremental S-FEM to solve elastic-plastic mechanics problems for complex load cases more common in practical engineering, and the calculation results are more accurate and reliable. A partitioned parallel strategy was designed to improve the computational efficiency of epSFEM. This strategy can avoid conflicts when accessing the underlying data in parallel computing. To demonstrate the correctness of epSFEM and assess its efficiency, two sets of benchmark tests were performed in this paper. The results indicated that (1) when calculating the same mesh model, the calculation accuracy of epSFEM is higher than that of the traditional FEM; (2) it requires only 5876.3 s to calculate an elastoplastic model, consisting of approximately 2.45 million T3 elements using the parallel epSFEM software package, while it needs 10,619 s to calculate the same model using the commercial FEM software ABAQUS; (3) on a 24-core CPU, the parallel execution of epSFEM is approximately 10 times faster than the corresponding serial version.

Author Contributions: Conceptualization, M.Z., J.Q. and G.M.; methodology, M.Z. and J.Q.; software, M.Z. and Z.H.; validation, M.Z. and G.M.; formal analysis, J.Q., Z.H. and F.G.; investigation, J.Q., Z.H. and F.G.; resources, M.Z.; data curation, M.Z.; writing—original draft preparation, M.Z. and G.M.; writing—review and editing, M.Z. and G.M.; visualization, M.Z.; supervision, J.Q. and G.M.; project administration, G.M.; funding acquisition, G.M. All authors have read and agreed to the published version of the manuscript.

Funding: This research was jointly supported by the Fundamental Research Funds for China Central Universities (Grant Numbers: 2652018091) and the National Natural Science Foundation of China (Grant Numbers: 11602235).

Institutional Review Board Statement: Not applicable

Informed Consent Statement: Not applicable

Data Availability Statement: Not applicable

Acknowledgments: The authors would like to thank the editor and the reviewers for their valuable comments.

Conflicts of Interest: The authors declare no conflict of interest.

Abbreviations

COO	COOrdinate
CPU	Central Processing Unit
CSC	Compressed Sparse Column
CS-FEM	Cell-based Smoothed Finite Element Method
CSR	Compressed Sparse Row
EFG	Element Free Galerkin
ES-FEM	Edge-based Smoothed Finite Element Method
FEM	Finite Element Method
FS-FEM	Face-based Smoothed Finite Element Method
GPU	Graphics Processing Unit
MLPG	Meshless Local Petrov-Galerkin
MPM	Material Point Method
NS-FEM	Node-based Smoothed Finite Element Method
PDEs	Partial Differential Equations
RPIM	Radial Point Interpolation Method
S-FEM	Smoothed Finite Element Method

References

1. Xiao, L.; Mei, G.; Xi, N.; Piccialli, F. Julia Language in Computational Mechanics: A New Competitor. *Arch. Comput. Methods Eng.* **2021**, *29*, 1713–1726. [CrossRef]
2. Xu, N.; Mei, G.; Qin, J.; Li, Y.; Xu, L. GeoMFree^{3D}: A package of meshfree local Radial Point Interpolation Method (RPIM) for geomechanics. *Comput. Math. Appl.* **2021**, *81*, 113–132. [CrossRef]
3. Vizjak, J.; Bekovic, M.; Jesenik, M.; Hamler, A. Development of a Magnetic Fluid Heating FEM Simulation Model with Coupled Steady State Magnetic and Transient Thermal Calculation. *Mathematics* **2021**, *9*, 2561. [CrossRef]
4. Li, Y.C.; Dang, S.N.; Li, W.; Chai, Y.B. Free and Forced Vibration Analysis of Two-Dimensional Linear Elastic Solids Using the Finite Element Methods Enriched by Interpolation Cover Functions. *Mathematics* **2022**, *10*, 456. [CrossRef]
5. Liu, G.R. *Meshfree Methods: Moving Beyond the Finite Element Method*, 2nd ed.; CRC Press: Boca Raton, FL, USA, 2009.
6. Liu, G.R. An Overview on Meshfree Methods: For Computational Solid Mechanics. *Int. J. Comput. Methods* **2016**, *13*, 1630001. [CrossRef]
7. Zeng, W.; Liu, G.R. Smoothed Finite Element Methods (S-FEM): An Overview and Recent Developments. *Arch. Comput. Methods Eng.* **2018**, *25*, 397–435. [CrossRef]
8. Liu, G.R.; Zhang, G.Y. *Smoothed Point Interpolation Methods: G Space Theory and Weakened Weak Forms*; World Scientific: Singapore, 2013.
9. Ding, R.; Shen, Q.; Yao, Y. The element-free Galerkin method for the dynamic Signorini contact problems with friction in elastic materials. *Appl. Math. Comput.* **2022**, *415*, 126696. [CrossRef]
10. Liu, Z.; Wei, G.; Qin, S.; Wang, Z. The elastoplastic analysis of functionally graded materials using a meshfree RRKPM. *Appl. Math. Comput.* **2022**, *413*, 126651. [CrossRef]
11. Liu, G.R.; Trung, N.T. *Smoothed Finite Element Methods*; CRC Press: Boca Raton, FL, USA, 2016.
12. Cui, X.Y.; Liu, G.R.; Li, G.Y.; Zhang, G.Y.; Sun, G.Y. Analysis of elastic-plastic problems using edge-based smoothed finite element method. *Int. J. Press. Vessel. Pip.* **2009**, *86*, 711–718. [CrossRef]
13. Cazes, F.; Meschke, G. An edge-based smoothed finite element method for 3D analysis ofsolid mechanics problems. *Int. J. Numer. Methods Eng.* **2013**, *94*, 715–739. [CrossRef]
14. Liu, G.R.; Nguyen-Thoi, T.; Lam, K.Y. An edge-based smoothed finite element method (ES-FEM) for static, free and forced vibration analyses of solids. *J. Sound Vib.* **2009**, *320*, 1100–1130. [CrossRef]
15. Nguyen-Thoi, T.; Phung-Van, P.; Rabczuk, T.; Nguyen-Xuan, H.; Le-Van, C. Free and forced vibration analysis using the n-sided polygonal cell-based smoothed finite element method (nCS-FEM). *Int. J. Comput. Methods* **2013**, *10*, 1340008. [CrossRef]
16. Tian, F.; Tang, X.; Xu, T.; Li, L. An adaptive edge-based smoothed finite element method (ES-FEM) for phase-field modeling of fractures at large deformations. *Comput. Methods Appl. Mech. Eng.* **2020**, *372*, 113376. [CrossRef]
17. Cui, X.Y.; Liu, G.R.; Li, G.Y.; Zhao, X.; Nguyen, T.T.; Sun, G.Y. A smoothed finite element method (SFEM) for linear and geometrically nonlinear analysis of plates and shells. *Comput. Model. Eng. Sci.* **2008**, *28*, 109–125.
18. Zhang, Z.Q.; Liu, G.R.; Khoo, B.C. Immersed smoothed finite element method for two dimensional fluid–structure interaction problems. *Int. J. Numer. Methods Eng.* **2012**, *90*, 1292–1320. [CrossRef]
19. He, Z.C.; Liu, G.R.; Zhong, Z.H.; Zhang, G.Y.; Cheng, A.G. Coupled analysis of 3D structural-acoustic problems using the edge-based smoothed finite element method/finite element method. *Finite Elem. Anal. Des.* **2010**, *46*, 1114–1121. [CrossRef]
20. Li, E.; Zhang, Z.; He, Z.C.; Xu, X.; Liu, G.R.; Li, Q. Smoothed finite element method with exact solutions in heat transfer problems. *Int. J. Heat Mass Transf.* **2014**, *78*, 1219–1231. [CrossRef]
21. Jiang, C.; Zhang, Z.Q.; Liu, G.R.; Han, X.; Zeng, W. An edge-based/node-based selective smoothed finite element method using tetrahedrons for cardiovascular tissues. *Eng. Anal. Bound. Elem.* **2015**, *59*, 62–77. [CrossRef]

22. Lee, K.; Lim, J.H.; Sohn, D.; Im, S. A three-dimensional cell-based smoothed finite element method for elasto-plasticity. *J. Mech. Sci. Technol.* **2015**, *29*, 611–623. [CrossRef]
23. Liu, G.R.; Nguyen-Thoi, T.; Nguyen-Xuan, H.; Lam, K.Y. A node-based smoothed finite element method (NS-FEM) for upper bound solutions to solid mechanics problems. *Comput. Struct.* **2009**, *87*, 14–26. [CrossRef]
24. Li, Y.; Liu, G. A novel node-based smoothed finite element method with linear strain fields for static, free and forced vibration analyses of solids. *Appl. Math. Comput.* **2019**, *352*, 30–58. [CrossRef]
25. Nguyen-Thoi, T.; Liu, G.R.; Lam, K.Y.; Zhang, G.Y. A face-based smoothed finite element method (FS-FEM) for 3D linear and geometrically non-linear solid mechanics problems using 4-node tetrahedral elements. *Int. J. Numer. Methods Eng.* **2009**, *78*, 324–353. [CrossRef]
26. Chen, L.; Rabczuk, T.; Bordas, S.P.A.; Liu, G.R.; Zeng, K.Y.; Kerfriden, P. Extended finite element method with edge-based strain smoothing (ESm-XFEM) for linear elastic crack growth. *Comput. Methods Appl. Mech. Eng.* **2012**, *209*, 250–265. [CrossRef]
27. Nguyen-Xuan, H.; Liu, G.R. An edge-based smoothed finite element method softened with a bubble function (bES-FEM) for solid mechanics problems. *Comput. Struct.* **2013**, *128*, 14–30. [CrossRef]
28. Xu, X.; Gu, Y.; Liu, G. A Hybrid smoothed finite element method (H-SFEM) to solid mechanics problems. *Int. J. Comput. Methods* **2013**, *10*, 1340011. [CrossRef]
29. Zeng, W.; Liu, G.R.; Li, D.; Dong, X.W. A smoothing technique based beta finite element method (beta FEM) for crystal plasticity modeling. *Comput. Struct.* **2016**, *162*, 48–67. [CrossRef]
30. Dudzinski, M.; Rozgič, M.; Stiemer, M. oFEM: An object oriented finite element package for Matlab. *Appl. Math. Comput.* **2018**, *334*, 117–140. [CrossRef]
31. Gao, K.; Mei, G.; Piccialli, F.; Cuomo, S.; Tu, J.; Huo, Z. Julia language in machine learning: Algorithms, applications, and open issues. *Comput. Sci. Rev.* **2020**, *37*, 100254. [CrossRef]
32. Bezanson, J.; Edelman, A.; Karpinski, S.; Shah, V.B. Julia: A Fresh Approach to Numerical Computing. *SIAM Rev.* **2017**, *59*, 65–98. [CrossRef]
33. Frondelius, T.; Aho, J. JuliaFEM-open source solver for both industrial and academia usage. *Raken. Mek.* **2017**, *50*, 229–233. [CrossRef]
34. Sinaie, S.; Nguyen, V.P.; Nguyen, C.T.; Bordas, S. Programming the material point method in Julia. *Adv. Eng. Softw.* **2017**, *105*, 17–29. [CrossRef]
35. Huo, Z.; Mei, G.; Xu, N. juSFEM: A Julia-based open-source package of parallel Smoothed Finite Element Method (S-FEM) for elastic problems. *Comput. Math. Appl.* **2021**, *81*, 459–477. [CrossRef]
36. Pawar, S.; San, O. CFD Julia: A Learning Module Structuring an Introductory Course on Computational Fluid Dynamics. *Fluids* **2019**, *4*, 159. [CrossRef]
37. Heitzinger, C.; Tulzer, G. Julia and the numerical homogenization of PDEs. In Proceedings of the 1st Workshop on High Performance Technical Computing Dynamic Languages, New Orleans, LA, USA, 17 November 2014; pp. 36–40. [CrossRef]
38. Kemmer, T.; Rjasanow, S.; Hildebrandt, A. NESSie.jl–Efficient and intuitive finite element and boundary element methods for nonlocal protein electrostatics in the Julia language. *J. Comput. Sci.* **2018**, *28*, 193–203. [CrossRef]
39. Fairbrother, J.; Nemeth, C.; Rischard, M.; Brea, J.; Pinder, T. GaussianProcesses.jl: A Nonparametric Bayes Package for the Julia Language. *J. Stat. Softw.* **2022**, *102*, 1–36. [CrossRef]
40. Pardiso.jl. 2021. Available online: https://github.com/JuliaSparse/Pardiso.jl (accessed on 10 February 2021).
41. The Julia Programming Language. 2021. Available online: https://julialang.org/ (accessed on 5 January 2021).
42. Huo, Z.; Mei, G.; Casolla, G.; Giampaolo, F. Designing an efficient parallel spectral clustering algorithm on multi-core processors in Julia. *J. Parallel Distrib. Comput.* **2020**, *138*, 211–221. [CrossRef]
43. Julia 1.6 Documentation. 2021. Available online: https://docs.julialang.org/en/v1/ (accessed on 10 May 2021).
44. Paraview. 2019. Available online: https://www.paraview.org/ (accessed on 28 May 2021).
45. Li, Y.; Yue, J.H.; Niu, R.P.; Liu, G.R. Automatic mesh generation for 3D smoothed finite element method (S-FEM) based on the weaken-weak formulation. *Adv. Eng. Softw.* **2016**, *99*, 111–120. [CrossRef]
46. Dodds, R.H., Jr. Numerical techniques for plasticity computations in finite element analysis. *Comput. Struct.* **1987**, *26*, 767–779. [CrossRef]
47. Blaheta, R. Convergence of Newton-type methods in incremental return mapping analysis of elasto-plastic problems. *Comput. Methods Appl. Mech. Eng.* **1997**, *147*, 167–185. [CrossRef]
48. De, Souza Neto, E.A.; Peri, D.; Owen, D.R.J. *Computational Methods for Plasticity*; Wiley: Hoboken, NJ, USA, 2008.
49. Čermák, M.; Sysala, S.; Valdman, J. Efficient and flexible MATLAB implementation of 2D and 3D elastoplastic problems. *Appl. Math. Comput.* **2019**, *355*, 595–614. [CrossRef]
50. Carstensen, C.; Klose, R. Elastoviscoplastic finite element analysis in 100 lines of Matlab. *J. Numer. Math.* **2002**, *10*, 157–192. [CrossRef]
51. Sysala; S. Properties and simplifications of constitutive time-discretized elastoplastic operators. *ZAMM-J. Appl. Math. Mech./Z. fÃ¼r Angew. Math. Und Mech.* **2014**, *94*, 233–255. [CrossRef]
52. WriteVTK.jl. 2021. Available online: https://github.com/jipolanco/WriteVTK.jl (accessed on 10 June 2021).
53. TimerOutputs.jl. 2021. Available online: https://github.com/KristofferC/TimerOutputs.jl (accessed on 10 August 2021).

54. Ma, Z.; Mei, G. Deep learning for geological hazards analysis: Data, models, applications, and opportunities. *Earth-Sci. Rev.* **2021**, *223*, 103858. [CrossRef]
55. Mei, G.; Xu, N.; Qin, J.; Wang, B.; Qi, P. A Survey of Internet of Things (IoT) for Geohazard Prevention: Applications, Technologies, and Challenges. *IEEE Internet Things J.* **2020**, *7*, 4371–4386. [CrossRef]
56. Rudy, S.; Alla, A.; Brunton, S.; Kutz, J. Data-driven identification of parametric partial differential equations. *SIAM J. Appl. Dyn. Syst.* **2019**, *18*, 643–660. [CrossRef]
57. Raissi, M.; Perdikaris, P.; Karniadakis, G. Physics-informed neural networks: A deep learning framework for solving forward and inverse problems involving nonlinear partial differential equations. *J. Comput. Phys.* **2019**, *378*, 686–707. [CrossRef]
58. Haghighat, E.; Raissi, M.; Moure, A.; Gomez, H.; Juanes, R. A physics-informed deep learning framework for inversion and surrogate modeling in solid mechanics. *Comput. Methods Appl. Mech. Eng.* **2021**, *379*, 113741. [CrossRef]
59. Jacobs, B.; Celik, T. Unsupervised document image binarization using a system of nonlinear partial differential equations. *Appl. Math. Comput.* **2022**, *418*, 126806. [CrossRef]

mathematics

MDPI

Article

Solving Inverse Conductivity Problems in Doubly Connected Domains by the Homogenization Functions of Two Parameters

Jun Lu [1,*], Lianpeng Shi [2], Chein-Shan Liu [3,*] and C. S. Chen [4]

1 Nanjing Hydraulic Research Institute, Nanjing 210029, China
2 College of Mechanics and Materials, Hohai University, Nanjing 210098, China; shilianpeng123@126.com
3 Center of Excellence for Ocean Engineering, National Taiwan Ocean University, Keelung 20224, Taiwan
4 Department of Mathematics, University of Southern Mississippi, Hattiesburg, MS 39406, USA; cschen.math@gmail.com
* Correspondence: lujun@nhri.cn (J.L.); csliu@ntou.edu.tw (C.-S.L.)

Abstract: In the paper, we make the first attempt to derive a family of two-parameter homogenization functions in the doubly connected domain, which is then applied as the bases of trial solutions for the inverse conductivity problems. The expansion coefficients are obtained by imposing an extra boundary condition on the inner boundary, which results in a linear system for the interpolation of the solution in a weighted Sobolev space. Then, we retrieve the spatial- or temperature-dependent conductivity function by solving a linear system, which is obtained from the collocation method applied to the nonlinear elliptic equation after inserting the solution. Although the required data are quite economical, very accurate solutions of the space-dependent and temperature-dependent conductivity functions, the Robin coefficient function and also the source function are available. It is significant that the nonlinear inverse problems can be solved directly without iterations and solving nonlinear equations. The proposed method can achieve accurate results with high efficiency even for large noise being imposed on the input data.

Keywords: nonlinear elliptic equation; doubly connected domain; inverse problems; two-parameter homogenization functions

MSC: 65N21; 65N35

Citation: Lu, J.; Shi, L.; Liu, C.-S.; Chen, C.S. Solving Inverse Conductivity Problems in Doubly Connected Domains by the Homogenization Functions of Two Parameters. *Mathematics* **2022**, *10*, 2256. https://doi.org/10.3390/math10132256

Academic Editor: Yury Shestopalov

Received: 7 April 2022
Accepted: 24 June 2022
Published: 27 June 2022

1. Introduction

In recent decades, a large number of inverse problems of the nonlinear elliptic-type partial differential equation (PDE) have been well investigated, involving the inverse source problem, inverse conductivity problem as well as inverse Robin problem, which arise in several branches of applications in science and engineering. Analytical solutions to inverse problems are difficult to obtain since some information is missing, such as the boundary conditions or sources compared with the forward problems. Therefore, many numerical approaches have been developed to resolve inverse problems [1]. In the linear elliptic type PDEs, for identifying unknown sources, the regularization methods were advocated in [2,3]. Klose [4] solved an inverse source problem based on the radiative transfer equation arising in optical molecular imaging. In Ref. [5], Hon et al. applied Green's function for the inverse source identification. Then Li et al. [6] proposed the modified regularization method on the Poisson equation for determining an unknown source. Ahmadabadi and co-workers proposed the method of fundamental solutions for the inverse space-dependent heat source problems by using a new transformation [7]. The source function for a seawater intrusion problem in an unconfined aquifer has been studied by Slimani [8]. The inverse source problems were examined by Alahyane et al. [9] using the regularized optimal control method. Some new regularization methods were proposed for inverse source problems governed by fractional PDEs [10,11]. Nguyen [12] investigated the inverse source problems of the fractional diffusion equations based on the Tikhonov regularization method. Recently,

Liu [13] have proposed a new procedure of boundary functions, which preserves the energy identity to identify the sources of 2D elliptic-type nonlinear PDEs. However, the methods proposed in [13] required extra boundary conditions of source function on a rectangle. We will extend the work to any 2D nonlinear elliptic equation without using extra boundary data of the source function in the doubly connected domain.

On the other hand, linear and nonlinear inverse conductivity problems have been studied by many authors. Kwon considered the anisotropic inverse conductivity and scattering problems [14]. The inverse problem of time-dependent thermal conductivity was studied by Huntul and Lesnic by recasting the original problems into the nonlinear least-squares minimization [15]. Isakov and Sever provided an integral equation method for inverse conductivity problems using the linearization method [16]. Based on Calderón's linearization method, a new direct algorithm was suggested for the anisotropic conductivities [17]. Liu et al. [18] constructed two-parameter homogenization functions for solving the bending problem of a thin plate in a rectangular domain where the boundary conditions can be exactly satisfied. Using the Lie-group iterative method, Liu and Atluri [19] solved the linear Calderón inverse problem in a rectangular domain, where the unknown conductivity function is effectively recovered. The linear and nonlinear inverse conductivity problems have also been studied by meshless methods, such as the meshless local Petrov-Galerkin method [20], the singular boundary method [21], and the local radial point interpolation method [22], the method of fundamental solutions [23], etc.

In this paper, based on the previous work in [18,19], we focus on the construction of two-parameter 2D homogenization functions in a doubly connected domain, and take linear equations to identify the space-dependent and temperature-dependent conductivity functions, the Robin coefficient function and also the source function in the 2D nonlinear elliptic equations. The derived homogenization functions are used as the bases. The undetermined expansion coefficients are solved by imposing the extra boundary conditions. In this way, the nonlinear inverse problems can be solved directly with high accuracy and efficiency even when twenty percent of noise is added to the known data.

We arrange the rest of this paper as follows. Section 2 describes some nonlinear inverse problems in a doubly connected domain of a 2D nonlinear elliptic equation, which includes the recovery of conductivity functions $\alpha(x,y)$ and $\alpha(u)$, the inverse Robin problem and the inverse source problem. In Section 3, we develop the homogenization functions with two parameters. In Section 4, the two-parameter homogenization functions act as the bases for the solution. In Section 5, the space-dependent conductivities of inverse problems are considered. In Section 6, we solve the temperature-dependent conductivity inverse problems. The inverse Robin problem and one example are given in Section 7, and the inverse source problem is solved in Section 8, where two examples are given. Section 9 makes the conclusions.

2. Nonlinear Inverse Problems

For this part, we briefly sketch the problems to be considered that desire the retrieval of unknown functions in the doubly connected domains.

2.1. Space-Dependent Inverse Conductivity Problem

First a space-dependent conductivity function $\alpha(x,y)$ is to be recovered from

$$\nabla \cdot [\alpha(x,y)\nabla u(x,y)] = Q(u,u_x,u_y) + S(x,y),\ \ (x,y) \in \Omega \subset \mathbb{R}^2, \tag{1}$$

$$u(x,y) = h_1(x,y),\ \ (x,y) \in \Gamma_o, \tag{2}$$

$$u_n(x,y) = g(x,y),\ \ (x,y) \in \Gamma_o, \tag{3}$$

where n is an outward unit normal on Γ_o. Besides an unknown conductivity function $\alpha(x,y)$ and the unknown solution $u(x,y)$, other functions are given.

Ω is a doubly connected domain with boundary $\Gamma = \Gamma_o \cup \Gamma_i$, where $\Gamma_o \cap \Gamma_i = \varnothing$. While $\Gamma_o := \{(r,\theta)|r = \rho_o(\theta), 0 \leq \theta \leq 2\pi\}$ denotes an outer boundary, $\Gamma_i := \{(r,\theta)|r = \rho_i(\theta),$

$0 \leq \theta \leq 2\pi\}$ is an inner boundary. $0 < \rho_i(\theta) < \rho_o(\theta)$ are, respectively, the radius functions of inner boundary and outer boundary. In order to recover $\alpha(x, y)$, we over-specify

$$u(x,y) = h_2(x,y), \ \ (x,y) \in \Gamma_i, \tag{4}$$

where $h_2(x, y)$ is a given function. In Figure 1, we sketch the inverse conductivity problem.

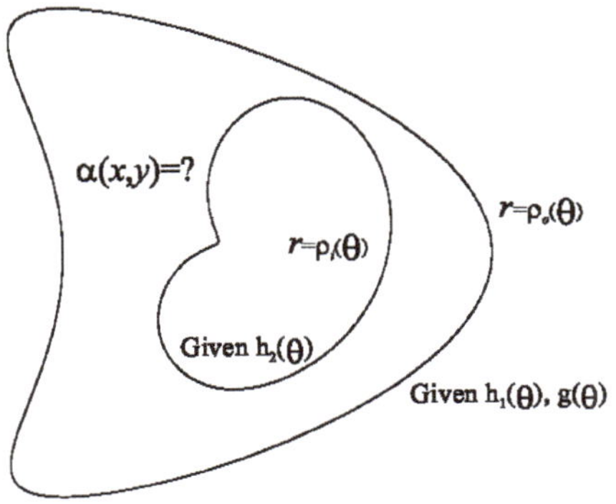

Figure 1. A schematic plot to show a doubly connected domain and for identification.

In the polar coordinates (r, θ), Equation (1) is recast to

$$\alpha\left[u_{rr} + \frac{1}{r}u_r + \frac{1}{r^2}u_{\theta\theta}\right] + \alpha_r u_r + \frac{1}{r^2}\alpha_\theta u_\theta = Q(u, u_r, u_\theta) + S(r, \theta). \tag{5}$$

Equation (5) is a first-order PDE for the function $\alpha(r, \theta) = \alpha(x, y)$ with respect to r and θ, where u_r, u_θ, u_{rr} and $u_{\theta\theta}$ are the coefficient functions. It is a nontrivial task to determine α even with the known u prescribed inside the Ω unless the boundary information of α on Γ is given in advance. Indeed, the inverse conductivity problem, which is considered in this paper, becomes more difficult and troublesome since the information of u is not given inside the solution domain, and only the boundary information is given according to Equations (2)–(4).

2.2. Temperature-Dependent Inverse Conductivity Problem

Secondly, we attempt to retrieve $\alpha(u)$ in

$$\left[u_{rr} + \frac{1}{r}u_r + \frac{1}{r^2}u_{\theta\theta}\right]\alpha(u) + \alpha'(u)u_r^2 + \frac{1}{r^2}\alpha'(u)u_\theta^2 = Q(u, u_r, u_\theta) + S(r, \theta), \tag{6}$$

when S and Q are given.

The temperature-dependent inverse conductivity problem is to determine the unknown conductivity function $\alpha(u)$ considering the above governing equation along with the information from Equations (2)–(4). The problem becomes harder for the reason that Equation (6) is nonlinear for u and linear ODE for $\alpha(u)$ with respect to u.

2.3. Inverse Robin Problem to Determine $\gamma(\theta)$

In the inner boundary, which is an inaccessible part of the boundary Γ, we cannot directly detect the transfer coefficient $\gamma(\theta)$ in

$$u_n(x,y) + \gamma(\theta)u(x,y) = h_3(x,y), \ \ (x,y) \in \Gamma_i. \tag{7}$$

When the information of $u(x, y)$ and $u_n(x, y)$ on Γ_i is unknown, $h_3(x, y)$ is given. Taken into the consideration of Equations (1)–(3), the unknown Robin coefficient $\gamma(\theta)$ will be recovered, which is known as the inverse Robin problem.

2.4. Inverse Problem for $S(x,y)$

When the function $u(x,y)$ is known in advance, we can recover $S(x,y)$ by

$$S(x,y) = \nabla \cdot [\alpha(x,y)\nabla u(x,y)] - Q(u,u_x,u_y), \tag{8}$$

where $\alpha(x,y)$ and $Q(u,u_x,u_y)$ are given functions. We will show that $S(x,y)$ is recoverable from Equations (2)–(4) and (8), without solving nonlinear equations.

3. Two-Parameter Basis Functions

First, we demonstrate the basic idea of homogenization function by starting from a 2D boundary value problem (BVP):

$$\mathcal{L}[u(x,y)] = S(x,y), \ \ (x,y) \in (0,a) \times (0,b), \tag{9}$$

$$u(0,y) = h_1(y), \ \ u(a,y) = h_2(y), \ \ u(x,0) = h_3(x), \ \ u(x,b) = h_4(x), \tag{10}$$

where $\mathcal{L}$ is a second-order linear differential operator. Let

$$B^0(x,y) = h_1(y)\left(1 - \frac{x}{a}\right) + \frac{x}{a}h_2(y), \tag{11}$$

and then,

$$B^0(0,y) = h_1(y), \ \ B^0(a,y) = h_2(y) \tag{12}$$

are apparent.

Upon letting

$$B(x,y) = B^0(x,y) + \left(1 - \frac{y}{b}\right)[h_3(x) - B^0(x,0)] + \frac{y}{b}[h_4(x) - B^0(x,b)], \tag{13}$$

and according to the following compatibility conditions:

$$\begin{aligned} &h_3(0) = B^0(0,0) = h_1(0), \ \ h_4(0) = B^0(0,b) = h_1(b), \\ &h_3(a) = B^0(a,0) = h_2(0), \ \ h_4(a) = B^0(a,b) = h_2(b), \end{aligned} \tag{14}$$

it is easy to verify

$$B(0,y) = h_1(y), \ \ B(a,y) = h_2(y), \ \ B(x,0) = h_3(x), \ \ B(x,b) = h_4(x). \tag{15}$$

Therefore, we can produce the 2D homogenization function for the 2D BVP:

$$\begin{aligned} B(x,y) = &\left(1 - \frac{x}{a}\right)\left[h_1(y) - \left(1 - \frac{y}{b}\right)h_3(0) - \frac{y}{b}h_4(0)\right] \\ &+ \frac{x}{a}\left[h_2(y) - \left(1 - \frac{y}{b}\right)h_3(a) - \frac{y}{b}h_4(a)\right] + \left(1 - \frac{y}{b}\right)h_3(x) + \frac{y}{b}h_4(x). \end{aligned} \tag{16}$$

Due to $B(x,y)$, we can transform the original 2D BVP with non-homogeneous boundary conditions to one with homogeneous boundary conditions:

$$\mathcal{L}[v(x,y)] = S(x,y) - \mathcal{L}[B(x,y)], \ \ (x,y) \in (0,a) \times (0,b), \tag{17}$$

$$v(0,y) = v(a,y) = v(x,0) = v(x,b) = 0, \tag{18}$$

with the help of the variable transformation from $u(x,y)$ to $v(x,y) = u(x,y) - B(x,y)$. Obviously, Equations (17) and (18) are more easy to tackle than Equations (9) and (10). As an extension of $B(x,y)$ to a two-parameter family, we have

$$B(x,y,j,k) = \left[1-\left(\frac{x}{a}\right)^j\right]\left[h_1(y) - \left[1-\left(\frac{y}{b}\right)^k\right]h_3(0) - \frac{y}{b}h_4(0)\right]$$
$$+\left(\frac{x}{a}\right)^j\left[h_2(y) - \left(1-\left(\frac{y}{b}\right)^k\right)h_3(a) - \left(\frac{y}{b}\right)^k h_4(a)\right] + \left(1-\left(\frac{y}{b}\right)^k\right)h_3(x) + \left(\frac{y}{b}\right)^k h_4(x). \tag{19}$$

$B(x,y,j,k)$ is indeed a family of 2D polynomials, which are complete bases and satisfy the boundary conditions automatically,

$$B(0,y,j,k) = h_1(y),\ B(a,y,j,k) = h_2(y),\ B(x,0,j,k) = h_3(x),\ B(x,b,j,k) = h_4(x). \tag{20}$$

A function is a so-called homogenization function if it satisfies the boundary conditions on the boundary of a domain. Since the solution $u(x,y)$ must satisfy the prescribed boundary conditions, it is a member of homogenization functions.

Continuously, the two-parameter homogenization functions are constructed for developing the present method to solve the inverse problems of Equations (1)–(4).

Definition 1. *$B^0(r,\theta) \in C^2(\Omega)$, with $\Gamma_o = \{(r,\theta)|r = \rho_o(\theta), 0 \le \theta \le 2\pi\}$, is a homogenization function, if the following conditions:*

$$B^0(\rho_o,\theta) = h_1(\theta),\ B^0_n(\rho_o,\theta) = g(\theta) \tag{21}$$

are fulfilled. $h_1(\theta)$ and $g(\theta)$ read as $h_1(\rho_o(\theta)\cos\theta, \rho_o(\theta)\sin\theta)$ and $g(\rho_o(\theta)\cos\theta, \rho_o(\theta)\sin\theta)$, respectively, and B^0_n signifying the normal derivative of $B^0(r,\theta)$ on Γ_o is given by

$$B^0_n(\rho_o,\theta) = \eta(\theta)\left[\frac{\partial B^0(\rho_o,\theta)}{\partial \rho_o} - \frac{\rho_o'}{\rho_o^2}\frac{\partial B^0(\rho_o,\theta)}{\partial \theta}\right], \tag{22}$$

where

$$\eta(\theta) = \frac{\rho_o(\theta)}{\sqrt{\rho_o^2(\theta) + \rho_o'(\theta)^2}}. \tag{23}$$

The following homogenization function has been derived [18]:

$$B^0(r,\theta) = h_1(\theta) + [r - \rho_o(\theta)]\frac{\partial u(\rho_o,\theta)}{\partial \rho_o}, \tag{24}$$

$$B^0(\rho_o,\theta) = h_1(\theta),\ B^0_n(\rho_o,\theta) = g(\theta). \tag{25}$$

Theorem 1. *For the given Cauchy data $h_1(\theta)$ and $g(\theta)$ on Γ_o, there exist homogenization functions $B(j,k,r,\theta)$ in Ω, satisfying Equation (21):*

$$B(j,k,r,\theta) = \left[\frac{2r}{\rho_o} - \frac{r^2}{\rho_o^2}\right]^j h_1(\theta) + \left[\frac{r^k}{k\rho_o^{k-1}} - \frac{\rho_o}{k}\right]\frac{\partial u(\rho_o,\theta)}{\partial \rho_o}, \tag{26}$$

where $j+1, k \in \mathbb{N}$ are parameters.

Proof. By Equation (26), $B(j,k,\rho_o,\theta) = h_1(\theta)$ satisfies the first equation in Equation (21). Next, we consider the second equation in Equation (21), for which we need to prove

$$\frac{\partial B(j,k,\rho_o,\theta)}{\partial \rho_o} = \frac{\partial u(\rho_o,\theta)}{\partial \rho_o},\ \frac{\partial B(j,k,\rho_o,\theta)}{\partial \theta} = \frac{\partial u(\rho_o,\theta)}{\partial \theta}. \tag{27}$$

It is obvious that

$$\left[\frac{2r}{\rho_o}-\frac{r^2}{\rho_o^2}\right]^j\Bigg|_{r=\rho_o}=1,\quad \frac{\partial}{\partial r}\left[\frac{2r}{\rho_o}-\frac{r^2}{\rho_o^2}\right]^j\Bigg|_{r=\rho_o}=0, \tag{28}$$

$$\frac{\partial}{\partial\theta}\left[\frac{2r}{\rho_o}-\frac{r^2}{\rho_o^2}\right]^j\Bigg|_{r=\rho_o}=j\left[\frac{2r}{\rho_o}-\frac{r^2}{\rho_o^2}\right]^{j-1}\left[\frac{-2r\rho_o'}{\rho_o^2}+\frac{2r^2\rho_o'}{\rho_o^3}\right]\Bigg|_{r=\rho_o}=0, \tag{29}$$

$$\left[\frac{r^k}{k\rho_o^{k-1}}-\frac{\rho_o}{k}\right]\Bigg|_{r=\rho_o}=0,\quad \frac{\partial}{\partial r}\left[\frac{r^k}{k\rho_o^{k-1}}-\frac{\rho_o}{k}\right]\Bigg|_{r=\rho_o}=1, \tag{30}$$

$$\frac{\partial}{\partial\theta}\left[\frac{r^k}{k\rho_o^{k-1}}-\frac{\rho_o}{k}\right]\Bigg|_{r=\rho_o}=\left[\frac{r^k}{k}(1-k)\rho_o^{-k}\rho_o'-\frac{\rho_o'}{k}\right]\Bigg|_{r=\rho_o}=-\rho_o'. \tag{31}$$

It follows from Equations (26), (28) and (30) that the first part in Equation (27) holds when $B(j,k,r,\theta)$ is differentiated to r, and we take $r=\rho_o(\theta)$ on Γ_o.

The second part in Equation (27) is proven below. It follows from Equation (2) that

$$h_1'(\theta)=\frac{\partial u(\rho_o,\theta)}{\partial\rho_o}\rho_o'(\theta)+\frac{\partial u(\rho_o,\theta)}{\partial\theta}. \tag{32}$$

From Equations (26) and (28)–(32), it follows that

$$\begin{aligned}\frac{\partial B(j,k,\rho_o,\theta)}{\partial\theta}&=h_1'(\theta)-\rho_o'(\theta)\frac{\partial u(\rho_o,\theta)}{\partial\rho_o}\\&=\frac{\partial u(\rho_o,\theta)}{\partial\rho_o}\rho_o'(\theta)+\frac{\partial u(\rho_o,\theta)}{\partial\theta}-\rho_o'(\theta)\frac{\partial u(\rho_o,\theta)}{\partial\rho_o}=\frac{\partial u(\rho_o,\theta)}{\partial\theta}.\end{aligned} \tag{33}$$

Due to Equation (27),

$$\begin{aligned}B_n(j,k,\rho_o,\theta)&=\eta(\theta)\left[\frac{\partial B(j,k,\rho_o,\theta)}{\partial\rho_o}-\frac{\rho_o'}{\rho_o^2}\frac{\partial B(j,k,\rho_o,\theta)}{\partial\theta}\right]\\&=\eta(\theta)\left[\frac{\partial u(\rho_o,\theta)(\rho_o,\theta)}{\partial\rho_o}-\frac{\rho_o'}{\rho_o^2}\frac{\partial u(\rho_o,\theta)}{\partial\theta}\right]=g(\theta)=u_n(x,y),\ (x,y)\in\Gamma_o,\end{aligned} \tag{34}$$

thus we prove

$$B(j,k,\rho_o,\theta)=h_1(\theta),\ B_n(j,k,\rho_o,\theta)=g(\theta), \tag{35}$$

which ends the proof of this theorem. □

In Theorem 1, the numbers (j,k) are parameters, and then $B(j,k,r,\theta)$ is a two-parameter function. In addition to Theorem 1, we also have the following result for another two-parameter function $E(j,k,r,\theta)$.

Theorem 2. *On Γ_o given the Cauchy data $h_1(\theta)$ and $g(\theta)$, the two-parameter function $E(j,k,r,\theta)\in C^2(\Omega)$ satisfies Equation (21):*

$$E(j,k,r,\theta)=B^0(r,\theta)+[r-\rho_o(\theta)]^2x^{j-k}y^k=B^0(r,\theta)+[r-\rho_o(\theta)]^2r^j(\cos\theta)^{j-k}(\sin\theta)^k, \tag{36}$$

where $j+1,k\in\mathbb{N}$ are parameters and B^0 was defined by Equation (24).

Proof. Let

$$E^0(r,\theta):=[r-\rho_o(\theta)]^2.$$

When $r=\rho_o(\theta)$, it is obvious that

$$E^0(r,\theta)=[r-\rho_o(\theta)]^2=0,\ E_n^0(r,\theta)=2[r-\rho_o(\theta)][r-\rho_o(\theta)]_n=0. \tag{37}$$

Inserting $r = \rho_o(\theta)$ into Equation (36) and using Equations (24), (25) and (37), it follows that

$$E(j,k,\rho_o,\theta) = h_1(\theta).$$

Taking the normal derivative of Equation (36) on Γ_o and using Equations (24), (25) and (37), we have

$$E_n(j,k,\rho,\theta) = B_n^0(\rho_o,\theta) + E_n^0(r,\theta)r^j(\cos\theta)^{j-k}(\sin\theta)^k + E^0(r,\theta)[r^j(\cos\theta)^{j-k}(\sin\theta)^k]_n$$
$$= B_n^0(\rho_o,\theta) = g(\theta), \text{ when } r = \rho_o(\theta).$$

This completes the proof. □

4. A Novel Two-Parameter Homogenization Function Method

Since the set $E(j,k,r,\theta)$ is generated from the Pascal polynomials $x^{j-k}y^k$, it is a complete basis for the problem. By the same token, $B(j,k,r,\theta)$ is a complete basis. All the homogenization functions consist of a weighted Sobolev space denoted as $\mathcal{B} := \{v(x,y) \in C^2(\Omega) | v(x,y) = h_1(x,y),\ v_n(x,y) = g(x,y),\ (x,y) \in \Gamma_o\}$, which is a weighted space, because for any two functions $v_1(x,y), v_2(x,y) \in \mathcal{B}$ with a weighted linear combination $w_1v_1(x,y) + w_2v_2(x,y) \in \mathcal{B}$ where $w_1 + w_2 = 1$. The Sobolev norm

$$\|v(x,y)\|^2 := \int_0^{2\pi} [v^2(\rho_o\cos\theta,\rho_o\sin\theta) + v_n^2(\rho_o\cos\theta,\rho_o\sin\theta)]d\theta \tag{38}$$

is defined in the space $\mathcal{B}$. More importantly, the approximate solution $u(x,y) \in \mathcal{B}$.

In terms of the bases $B(j,k,x,y)$, $u(x,y)$ can be expanded by

$$u(x,y) \approx \sum_{j=0}^{m-1}\sum_{k=1}^{m} a_{jk}B(j,k,x,y), \tag{39}$$

where a_{jk} satisfies

$$\sum_{j=0}^{m-1}\sum_{k=1}^{m} a_{jk} = 1, \tag{40}$$

and guarantees conditions (2) and (3) being satisfied by $u(x,y)$. The number of the coefficients a_{jk} is $n_1 = m^2$.

As shown in Equation (4), we suppose that there are N data of $u(x,y)$ on the inner boundary Γ_i available, and then we can solve a linear system, including Equation (40), to determine a_{jk}:

$$\sum_{j=0}^{m-1}\sum_{k=1}^{m} a_{jk}B(j,k,x_q,y_q) = h_2(x_q,y_q), \tag{41}$$

where $\theta_q = 2q\pi/N$, $x_q = \rho_i(\theta_q)\cos\theta_q$ and $y_q = \rho_i(\theta_q)\sin\theta_q$.

5. Numerical Procedure to Determine $\alpha(x,y)$

5.1. Numerical Algorithm

Next, when $u(x,y)$ is obtained from Equation (39), we recover $\alpha(x,y)$ by supposing

$$\alpha(x,y) = \sum_{i=0}^{m_0}\sum_{j=0}^{i} b_{ij}x^{i-j}y^j = \sum_{i=0}^{m_0}\sum_{j=0}^{i} b_{ij}r^i(\cos\theta)^{i-j}(\sin\theta)^j, \tag{42}$$

where b_{ij} are $n := (m_0+1)(m_0+2)/2$ unknown weighted parameters to be determined by the proposed numerical algorithm. In order to solve this problem, $m_1 \times m_2$ points of (x,y) inside the solution domain Ω are collocated by

$$x_{pq} = r_p \cos\theta_q,\ y_{pq} = r_p \sin\theta_q,$$
$$\theta_q = 2q\pi/m_1,\ r_p = \rho_i(\theta_q) + p[\rho_o(\theta_q) - \rho_i(\theta_q)]/(m_2+1),\ q = 1,\dots,m_1,\ p = 1,\dots,m_2. \tag{43}$$

Since $u(x,y)$ can be approximated by Equation (39), we have

$$u(x_{pq}, y_{pq}) = \sum_{j=0}^{m-1}\sum_{k=1}^{m} a_{jk} B(j,k,x_{pq},y_{pq}). \tag{44}$$

Then, inserting Equation (42) into Equation (5) and collocating at point (x_{pq}, y_{pq}), the following linear system can be obtained:

$$\Delta u(x_{pq},y_{pq}) \sum_{i=0}^{m_0}\sum_{j=0}^{i} b_{ij} x_{pq}^{i-j} y_{pq}^{j} + u_r(x_{pq},y_{pq}) \sum_{i=0}^{m_0}\sum_{j=0}^{i} i b_{ij} r_p^{i-1} (\cos\theta_q)^{i-j} (\sin\theta_q)^{j}$$
$$+ \frac{1}{r_p^2} u_\theta(x_{pq},y_{pq}) \sum_{i=0}^{m_0}\sum_{j=0}^{i} b_{ij} r_p^{i} [j(\cos\theta_q)^{i-j+1}(\sin\theta_q)^{j-1} - (i-j)(\cos\theta_q)^{i-j-1}(\sin\theta_q)^{j+1}]$$
$$= Q(u(x_{pq},y_{pq}), u_r(x_{pq},y_{pq}), u_\theta(x_{pq},y_{pq})) + S(r_p,\theta_q),\ q = 1,\dots,m_1,\ p = 1,\dots,m_2, \tag{45}$$

from which we can determine b_{ij} easily, and, correspondingly, the $\alpha(x,y)$ can be determined from Equation (42).

Therefore, the proposed algorithm for recovering $\alpha(x,y)$ consists of two linear systems of equations, Equations (41) and (45). We impose the data by a noise:

$$\hat{h}_1(\theta_j) = h_1(\theta_j) + sR(j),\ \hat{g}(\theta_j) = g(\theta_j) + sR(j), \tag{46}$$

where $R(j)$ are random numbers between $[-1,1]$, which are used to check the stability of the numerical solution.

To evaluate the accuracy, we consider the maximum error (ME) and a relative error defined by

$$\mathrm{ME}(\alpha) := \max |\alpha_n(x_{pq},y_{pq}) - \alpha(x_{pq},y_{pq})|, \tag{47}$$

$$e(\alpha) = \sqrt{\frac{\sum_{q=1}^{N_1}\sum_{p=1}^{N_2}[\alpha_n(x_{pq},y_{pq}) - \alpha(x_{pq},y_{pq})]^2}{\sum_{q=1}^{N_1}\sum_{p=1}^{N_2}\alpha^2(x_{pq},y_{pq})}}, \tag{48}$$

upon comparing the numerical solution of α_n to the exact one α at $N_1 \times N_2$ grid points (x_i, y_j) inside the domain with

$$x_{pq} = r_p \cos\theta_q,\ y_{pq} = r_p \sin\theta_q,$$
$$\theta_q = 2q\pi/N_1,\ r_p = \rho_i(\theta_q) + p[\rho_o(\theta_q) - \rho_i(\theta_q)]/(N_2+1),\ q = 1,\dots,N_1,\ p = 1,\dots,N_2. \tag{49}$$

We take $N_1 = 50$ and $N_2 = 10$ in all computations.

We must emphasize that all the linear systems we consider are over-determined, which means that the number of linear equations is much larger than the number of unknown coefficients. Therefore, we apply the conjugate gradient method (CGM) to solve the corresponding normal linear system, whose solution is unique in the sense of least squares.

5.2. Example 1

For Equation (5) with $Q = 0$, we consider

$$u = r^2 + r\cos\theta = x^2 + y^2 + x,\ \alpha = 10 + r^2 + r^4\cos^2\theta = 10 + (x^2+y^2)(x^2+1). \tag{50}$$

The outer boundary of the domain Ω is an ellipse:

$$\rho_o(\theta) = \frac{ab}{\sqrt{b^2 + (a^2 - b^2)\sin^2\theta}}, \tag{51}$$

where we take $a = 1.5$ and $b = 0.5$, and the inner boundary is $\rho_i = 0.2$.

With $m = 2$, $N = 40$, $m_0 = 4$, $m_1 = 30$, $m_2 = 10$ and a noise $s = 5\%$ added into the given data, Figure 2a reveals that the maximum absolute error of u is 2.11×10^{-2}, which is much smaller than $\max(u) = 3.29$. The maximum absolute error of coefficient $\alpha(x, y)$ denoted as ME(α) is 0.18, which is quite a lot smaller than $\max(\alpha) = 15.56$. The value $e(\alpha) = 3.8 \times 10^{-3}$ is smaller than 7.65×10^{-2} from previous studies. For this problem the dimension of the normal matrix of the first linear system of (41) and (40) is $n_1 \times n_1 = 4 \times 4$, and the condition number is small with COND = 570.046. The dimension of the normal matrix of the second linear system (45) is $n \times n = 15 \times 15$, and the condition number is COND = 41,996.23. They show that these two linear systems are stable.

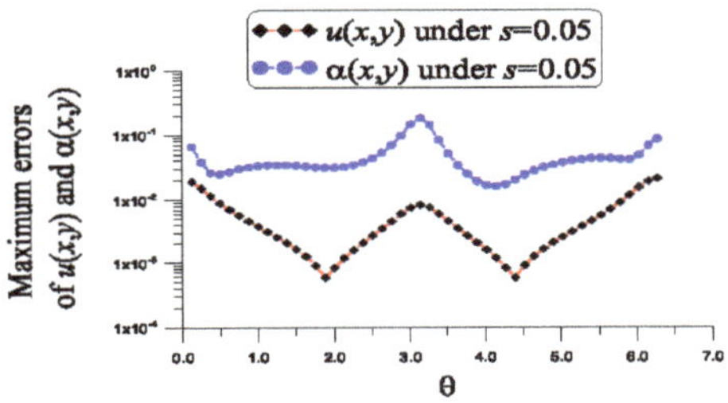

(a)

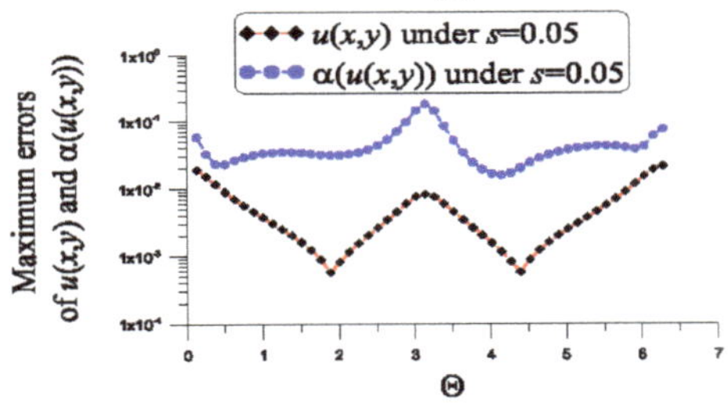

(b)

Figure 2. For example 1, showing the errors in the numerical recovery of u and α under a noise $s = 0.05$, (**a**) $Q = 0$ and (**b**) $Q = u^2$.

The convergence rate is a central issue in numerical methods and algorithms. In Table 1, we consider a different mesh parameter $m_1 \times m_2$ used in the collocation method to influence the convergence rate as reflected in ME(α) and $e(\alpha)$. It can be seen that more collocated points lead to a more accurate solution of α.

Table 1. For example 1, the influence of mesh parameter $m_1 \times m_2$ on ME(α) and $e(\alpha)$.

$m_1 \times m_2$	5×5	7×5	10×10	10×5	30×10
ME(α)	7.7369	1.8430	0.4017	0.2147	0.18364
$e(\alpha)$	1.46×10^{-1}	2.34×10^{-2}	1.83×10^{-2}	5.15×10^{-2}	3.79×10^{-3}

Although for a nonlinear elliptic equation:

$$\alpha\left[u_{rr} + \frac{1}{r}u_r + \frac{1}{r^2}u_{\theta\theta}\right] + \alpha_r u_r + \frac{1}{r^2}\alpha_\theta u_\theta = u^2(r,\theta) + S(r,\theta), \tag{52}$$

where the exact value of $S(r,\theta)$ can be obtained by inserting Equation (50) into the above equation, as shown in Figure 2b, the ME of u is 2.11×10^{-2}, the ME of $\alpha(x,y)$ is 0.18 and $e(\alpha)=3.74\times10^{-3}$. For the nonlinear problem, we have the same condition numbers because the parameters used are the same.

5.3. Example 2

Consider

$$\alpha\left[u_{rr}+\frac{1}{r}u_r+\frac{1}{r^2}u_{\theta\theta}\right]+\alpha_r u_r+\frac{1}{r^2}\alpha_\theta u_\theta=\sin u(r,\theta)+u^2(r,\theta)+S(r,\theta), \tag{53}$$

$$u=r^2+r\cos\theta=x^2+y^2+x,\ \ \alpha=20+r^2\sin(2\theta)=20+2xy. \tag{54}$$

For this problem, the outer boundary is given by Equation (51) with $a=4$ and $b=3.5$, and

$$\rho_i(\theta)=1.5+\cos\theta \tag{55}$$

is the inner boundary. Feeding Equation (54) into Equation (53), $S(r,\theta)$ can be obtained.

With $m=2$, $N=50$, $m_0=2$, $m_1=10$, $m_2=10$ and a noise $s=20\%$, as shown in Figure 3, the ME of u is 1.44×10^{-2}, which is much smaller than $\max(u)=18.79$. The ME of $\alpha(x,y)$ is 2.47, which is much smaller than $\max(\alpha)=32.96$. The value $e(\alpha)=3.85\times10^{-2}$ is small. For this problem the dimension of the normal matrix of the first linear system (41) and (40) is $n_1\times n_1=4\times4$, and the condition number is small with COND = 1844.258. The dimension of the normal matrix of the second linear system (45) is $n\times n=6\times6$, and the condition number is COND = 1013.03. They show that these two linear systems are stable.

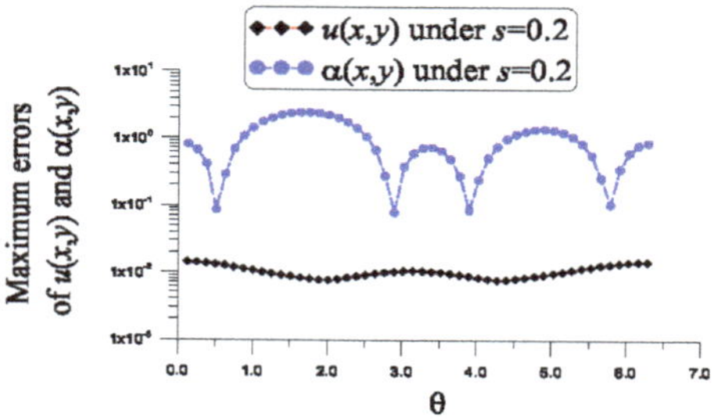

Figure 3. For example 2, showing the errors in the numerical recovery of u and α under a noise $s=0.2$ with $Q=u^2+\sin u$.

6. Numerical Algorithm to Determine $\alpha(u)$

6.1. Numerical Algorithm

From the last section, we have already recovered the coefficients preceding $\alpha(u)$ and $u_r^2+u_\theta^2/r^2$ preceding $\alpha'(u)$ in Equation (6), if Q and S are prescribed in advance. Indeed $u(x,y)$ can be derived from Equation (39). In this case, Δu before $\alpha(u)$, and $u_r^2+u_\theta^2/r^2$ before $\alpha'(u)$ can be obtained numerically from Equation (39).

Suppose that

$$\alpha(u)=\sum_{i=0}^{m_0}c_i u^i, \tag{56}$$

where c_i are under-determined weighted parameters to be determined.

Similar to Equation (43) in the last section, we arrange $m_1\times m_2$ points of (x,y) inside the solution domain. Then, inserting Equation (56) into Equation (6) and collocating (x_{pq},y_{pq}), we come to

$$\sum_{i=0}^{m_0} c_i u^i(x_{pq}, y_{pq})\Delta u(x_{pq}, y_{pq}) + \sum_{i=0}^{m_0} c_i i u^{i-1}(x_{pq}, y_{pq})[u_r^2(x_{pq}, y_{pq}) + u_\theta^2(x_{pq}, y_{pq})/r_p^2]$$
$$= Q(u(x_{pq}, y_{pq}), u_r(x_{pq}, y_{pq}), u_\theta(x_{pq}, y_{pq})) + S(x_{pq}, y_{pq}),\ p = 1, \ldots, m_2,\ q = 1, \ldots, m_1. \quad (57)$$

from which we can obtain c_i, and then, $\alpha(u)$ is recovered from Equation (56).

It should be noted here that that even for the highly nonlinear inverse problems for coefficient $\alpha(u)$, solving nonlinear equations is not needed.

6.2. Example 3

For a quadratic nonlinear Poisson equation:

$$\Delta u\alpha(u) + \alpha'(u)u_r^2 + \frac{1}{r^2}\alpha'(u)u_\theta^2 + u^2 = S(r, \theta), \quad (58)$$
$$u = r^2 = x^2 + y^2, \quad (59)$$

$\alpha(u) = 10 + u^2 + u$ is to be recovered. The outer boundary is Equation (51) with $a = 3.5$ and $b = 2.5$, and $\rho_i = 1$ is a unit circle.

With $m = 2$, $N = 40$, $m_0 = 2$, $m_1 = 20$, $m_2 = 5$ and $s = 5\%$, as shown in Figure 4a, the ME of u is 5.68×10^{-3}, which is much smaller than $\max(u) = 10.7$. The ME of $\alpha(u)$ is 0.082, which is much smaller than $\max(\alpha) = 135.43$. The value $e(\alpha) = 6.03 \times 10^{-4}$ is quite small. Figure 4b compares the numerical and exact $\alpha(u)$ in the range of $u \leq 11$. These two curves almost coincide.

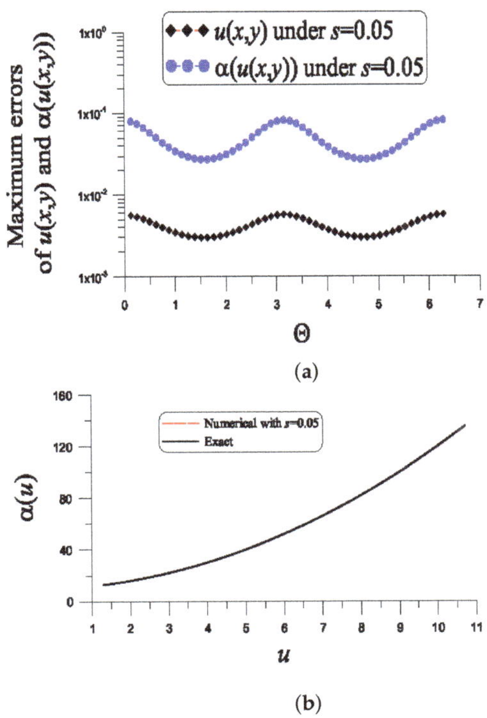

Figure 4. For example 3, showing **(a)** the errors in the numerical recovery of u and α and **(b)** the numerical recovery of α under a noise $s = 0.05$.

For this problem, the dimension of the normal matrix of the first linear system (41) and (40) is $n_1 \times n_1 = 4 \times 4$, and the condition number is very small with COND = 33.959. The dimension of the normal matrix of the second linear system (57) is $n \times n = 3 \times 3$, and the condition number is COND = 177,571.79. They show that these two linear systems are stable.

6.3. Example 4

For a quadratic and cubic nonlinear Poisson equation:

$$\Delta u \alpha(u) + \alpha'(u) u_r^2 + \frac{1}{r^2} \alpha'(u) u_\theta^2 + u^2 + u^3 = S(r, \theta), \tag{60}$$

$$u = r^2 = x^2 + y^2, \tag{61}$$

$\alpha(u) = 10 + u^2 + \sin u$ is to be recovered. The boundaries of Ω are given by

$$\rho_o(\theta) = 3\sqrt{\cos(2\theta) + \sqrt{1.5 - \sin^2(2\theta)}}, \tag{62}$$

$$\rho_i(\theta) = \exp(\sin\theta)\sin^2(2\theta) + \exp(\cos\theta)\cos^2(2\theta). \tag{63}$$

With $m = 2$, $N = 40$, $m_0 = 3$, $m_1 = 15$, $m_2 = 10$ and $s = 5\%$, as shown in Figure 5a, the ME of u is 2.78×10^{-2}, which is much smaller than $\max(u) = 18.6$. The ME of $\alpha(u)$ is 2.23, which is much smaller than $\max(\alpha) = 356.45$. The value $e(\alpha) = 9.35 \times 10^{-3}$ is quite small. Figure 5b compares the numerical and exact $\alpha(u)$ in the range of $u \le 19$. These two curves almost coincide.

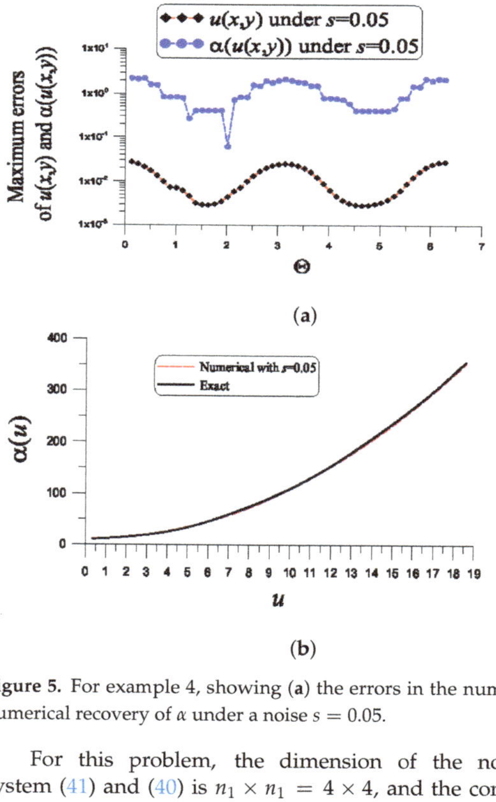

Figure 5. For example 4, showing (**a**) the errors in the numerical recovery of u and α and (**b**) the numerical recovery of α under a noise $s = 0.05$.

For this problem, the dimension of the normal matrix of the first linear system (41) and (40) is $n_1 \times n_1 = 4 \times 4$, and the condition number is very small with

COND = 6.3185. The dimension of the normal matrix of the second linear system (57) is $n \times n = 4 \times 4$, and the condition number is COND = 2.15×10^8.

To reduce the condition number for the second linear system (57), we choose $m_0 = 2$, $m_1 = 10$ and $m_2 = 10$, such that the dimension of the normal matrix reduces to $n \times n = 3 \times 3$, and the condition number reduces to COND = 297,651.317. Meanwhile, ME(α) and $e(\alpha)$ are slightly increased to 2.38 and 1.08×10^{-2}, respectively.

7. Numerical Method to Detect $\gamma(\theta)$

7.1. Numerical Method

Now, we detect $\gamma(\theta)$ by using the data in Equations (2) and (3). Basically, we need to solve Equations (1)–(3) in Ω. For this purpose, we take

$$u(x,y) = \sum_{j=0}^{m} \sum_{k=0}^{j} a_{jk} E(j,k,x,y), \tag{64}$$

where the number of a_{jk}, $j,k = 1,\ldots,m$ is $n_1 = (m+1)(m+2)/2$, which are to be determined. Instead of $B(j,k,x,y)$ used in Equation (39), we employ $E(j,k,x,y)$ from Equation (36) as the bases of $u(x,y)$. The reason is that the order of r^{j+2} in $E(j,k,x,y)$ is much lower than the order of r^{2j} in $B(j,k,x,y)$.

Like Equation (43), we arrange $m_1 \times m_2$ points of (x,y) and collocating which comes to:

$$\begin{aligned}
&\alpha(x_{pq},y_{pq}) \sum_{j=0}^{m} \sum_{k=0}^{j} a_{jk} \Delta E(j,k,x_{pq},y_{pq}) + \alpha_x(x_{pq},y_{pq}) \sum_{j=0}^{m} \sum_{k=0}^{j} a_{jk} E_x(j,k,x_{pq},y_{pq}) \\
&+\alpha_y(x_{pq},y_{pq}) \sum_{j=0}^{m} \sum_{k=0}^{j} a_{jk} E_y(j,k,x_{pq},y_{pq}) \\
&= Q\left(\sum_{j=0}^{m} \sum_{k=0}^{j} a_{jk} E(j,k,x_{pq},y_{pq}), \sum_{j=0}^{m} \sum_{k=0}^{j} a_{jk} E_x(j,k,x_{pq},y_{pq}), \sum_{j=0}^{m} \sum_{k=0}^{j} a_{jk} E_y(j,k,x_{pq},y_{pq}) \right) \\
&+S(x_{pq},y_{pq}),\ p = 1,\ldots,m_2,\ q = 1,\ldots,m_1.
\end{aligned} \tag{65}$$

from which we can compute a_{jk}, and then $u(x,y)$ is obtained from Equation (64), which is inserted in Equation (7) to find $\gamma(\theta)$ along the inner boundary Γ_i.

7.2. Example 5

We give a solution of a linear diffusion-convection equation:

$$\alpha \Delta u(x,y) + \alpha_x u_x(x,y) + \alpha_y u_y(x,y) = S(x,y), \tag{66}$$

$$u = x^2 + y^2 + x, \tag{67}$$

where $\alpha = 1 + x^2 + y^2$, which is defined in a domain Ω by Equation (51) with $a = 2.5$ and $b = 1.5$ and by

$$\rho_i(\theta) = 1.3 + 0.1 \cos\theta. \tag{68}$$

With $m = 2$, $m_1 = 20$, $m_2 = 20$ and $s = 20\%$, as shown in Figure 6a, the ME of u is 4.58×10^{-3}, which is much smaller than $\max(u) = 8.16$. Figure 6b compares the numerical and exact $\gamma(\theta)$, of which these two curves almost coincide with the ME being 1.28×10^{-2}. For this problem, we merely solve the linear system (65) and (40), whose dimension of the normal matrix is $n_1 \times n_1 = 6 \times 6$, and the condition number is small with COND = 446.16.

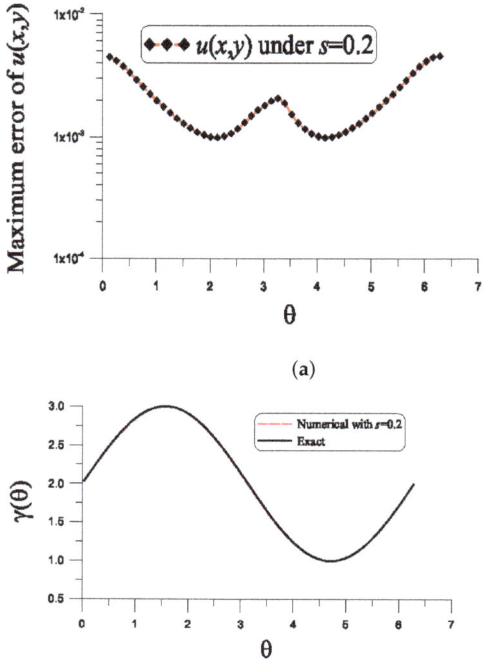

(a)

(b)

Figure 6. For example 5, showing (**a**) the error in the numerical recovery of u and (**b**) comparing the numerical recovery of γ under a noise $s = 0.2$.

8. Numerical Method to Recover $S(x, y)$

The numerical method to recover $S(x, y)$ is very simple, which is obtained by merely inserting the numerical solution of $u(r, \theta)$ in Equation (39) into the following equation:

$$S(r,\theta) = \alpha \left[u_{rr} + \frac{1}{r} u_r + \frac{1}{r^2} u_{\theta\theta} \right] + \alpha_r u_r + \frac{1}{r^2} \alpha_\theta u_\theta - Q(u(r,\theta), u_r(r,\theta), u_\theta(r,\theta)), \tag{69}$$

where $\alpha(r, \theta)$ and $Q(u(r,\theta), u_r(r,\theta), u_\theta(r,\theta))$ are given functions.

8.1. Example 6

For Equation (69) with $Q = u^2$, we consider

$$u = r^2 + r\cos\theta = x^2 + y^2 + x, \;\; \alpha = 10 + r^2 + r^4 \cos^2\theta = 10 + (x^2 + y^2)(x^2 + 1), \tag{70}$$

with $a = 1.5$ and $b = 0.5$ in Equation (51), and we take $\rho_i = 0.2$.

In this case, we have $m = 2$, $N = 30$ and a noise $s = 5\%$ added into the given data, as shown in Figure 7a, the maximum absolute error of u is 1.35×10^{-2}, which is much smaller than $\max(u) = 3.29$. The maximum absolute error of $S(x, y)$, denoted as $\text{ME}(S)$, is 1.22, which is much more accurate than $\max S = 101.5$. The value $e(S) = 5.2 \times 10^{-3}$ is small. For this problem, we merely solve the linear system (41) and (40), whose dimension of the normal matrix is $n_1 \times n_1 = 4 \times 4$, and the condition number is small with COND = 476.623.

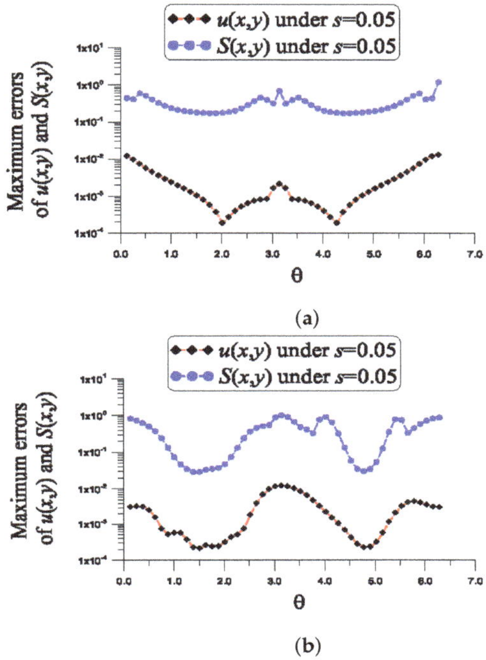

Figure 7. Showing the errors in the numerical recovery of u and S under a noise $s = 0.05$, (**a**) example 6 and (**b**) example 7.

In Table 2, we consider different mesh parameters N used in the collocation method for $u(x, y)$ to influence the convergence rate as reflected in ME(S) and $e(S)$. It can be seen that more collocated points lead to a more accurate solution of S.

Table 2. For example 6, the influence of mesh parameter N on ME(S) and $e(S)$.

N	5	10	20	25	30
ME(S)	57.34	43.59	45.93	37.06	1.22
$e(S)$	1.18×10^{-1}	9.55×10^{-2}	8.70×10^{-2}	6.52×10^{-2}	5.24×10^{-3}

8.2. Example 7

For Equation (69) with $Q = u^2 + \cos u$, we consider

$$u = r^2 = x^2 + y^2, \ \ \alpha = 10 + r^2 + r^4 \cos^2 \theta = 10 + (x^2 + y^2)(x^2 + 1). \tag{71}$$

The outer and inner boundaries are given by Equations (62) and (63), respectively.

For this example, we have $m = 2$, $N = 20$ and a noise $s = 5\%$, as shown in Figure 7b, the maximum absolute error of u is 2.03×10^{-2}, which is more accurate than $\max(u) = 18.62$. The ME of $S(x, y)$ is 1.04, which is much smaller than $\max S = 4001.42$. The value $e(S) = 2.99 \times 10^{-4}$ is quite small. The dimension of the normal matrix of the linear system (41) and (40) is $n_1 \times n_1 = 4 \times 4$, and the condition number is small with COND = 19.858.

In Table 3, we consider different mesh parameters of N used in the collocation method for $u(x, y)$ to influence the convergence rate as reflected in ME(S) and $e(S)$. It can be seen that more collocated points lead to a more accurate solution of S and even for a small $N = 3$ the accuracy is good.

Table 3. For example 7, the influence of mesh parameter N on ME(S) and $e(S)$.

N	3	8	14	18	20
ME(S)	12.09	10.98	8.98	8.51	1.04
$e(S)$	3.70×10^{-3}	2.87×10^{-3}	2.57×10^{-3}	2.17×10^{-3}	2.99×10^{-4}

9. Conclusions

In the paper, we have constructed a category of two-parameter homogenization functions in the 2D doubly connected domain for automatically satisfying the outer Dirichlet and Neumann boundary conditions of the nonlinear elliptic equation. A new numerical method was developed for solving the inverse problems through the technique of two-parameter homogenization functions, which include the recovery of the space-dependent and temperature-dependent conductivity functions and also the source function. We first determine $u(x,y)$ in terms of the bases and then a linear system to satisfy the inner boundary condition by the method of collocation is solved. Back-substituting the solution into the nonlinear elliptic equation, we recovered the unknown space-dependent and temperature-dependent conductivity functions by collocating points inside the domain and solving the derived linear equations. The basis $B(j,k,x,y)$ has good behavior used in the interpolation for $u(x,y)$ in a weighted Sobolev space, such that we can recover $u(x,y)$ very well; hence, after the back substitution of $u(x,y)$ into the governing equation, the source function was directly recovered with high accuracy. It maintains the same advantages of accuracy and efficiency for solving the inverse conductivity problems and inverse Robin problems, even for large noise.

Author Contributions: Conceptualization, C.-S.L.; Investigation, L.S.; Methodology, J.L.; Writing—review & editing, C.S.C. All authors have read and agreed to the published version of the manuscript.

Funding: This research was funded by the National Key Research and Development Program (Nos. 2021YFB2600700, 2021YFC3090100), the National Natural Science Foundation of China (No. 52171272), and Key Special Projects of the Science and Technology Help Economy 2020 (No. 1).

Conflicts of Interest: The authors declare no conflict of interest.

References

1. Tuan, N.H.; Khoa, V.A.; Tran, T. On an inverse boundary value problem of a nonlinear elliptic equation in three dimensions. *J. Math. Anal. Appl.* **2015**, *426*, 1232–1261. [CrossRef]
2. Farcas, A.; Elliott, L.; Ingham, D.B.; Lesnic, D.; Mera, N.S. A dual reciprocity boundary element method for the regularized numerical solution of the inverse source problem associated to the Poisson equation. *Inv. Prob. Sci. Eng.* **2003**, *11*, 123–139. [CrossRef]
3. Jin, B.T.; Marin, L. The method of fundamental solutions for inverse source problems associated with the steady-state heat conduction. *Int. J. Numer. Meth. Eng.* **2007**, *69*, 1570–1589. [CrossRef]
4. Klose, A.D.; Ntziachristos, V.; Hielscher, A.H. The inverse source problem based on the radiative transfer equation in optical molecular imaging. *J. Comput. Phys.* **2005**, 202, 323–345. [CrossRef]
5. Hon, Y.C.; Li, M.; Melnikov, Y.A. Inverse source identification by Green's function. *Eng. Anal. Bound. Elem.* **2010**, *34*, 352–358. [CrossRef]
6. Li, X.X.; Guo, H.Z.; Wan, S.M.; Yang, F. Inverse source identification by the modified regularization method on Poisson equation. *J. Appl. Math.* **2012**, *2012, 971952*. [CrossRef]
7. Ahmadabadi, M.N.; Arab, M.; Ghaini, F. The method of fundamental solutions for the inverse space-dependent heat source problem. *Eng. Anal. Bound. Elem.* **2009**, *33*, 1231–1235. [CrossRef]
8. Slimani, S.; Medarhri, I.; Najib, K.; Zine, A. Identification of the source function for a seawater intrusion problem in unconfined aquifer. *Numer. Algor.* **2020**, *84*, 1565–1587. [CrossRef]
9. Alahyane, M.; Boutaayamou, I.; Chrifi, A.; Echarroudi, Y.; Ouakrim, Y. Numerical study of inverse source problem for internal degenerate parabolic equation. *Int. J. Comput. Meth.* **2020**, *18*, 2050032. [CrossRef]
10. Djennadi, S.; Shawagfeh, N.; Arqub, O.A. A fractional Tikhonov regularization method for an inverse backward and source problems in the time-space fractional diffusion equations. *Chaos Solitons Fractals* **2021**, *150*, 111127. [CrossRef]
11. Ma, Y.K.; Prakash, P.; Deiveegan, A. Generalized Tikhonov methods for an inverse source problem of the time-fractional diffusion equation. *Chaos Solitons Fractals* **2018**, *108*, 39–48. [CrossRef]

12. Nguyen, H.T.; Le, D.L. Regularized solution of an inverse source problem for a time fractional diffusion equation. *Appl. Math.* **2016**, *40*, 8244–8264. [CrossRef]
13. Liu, C.-S. An energetic boundary functional method for solving the inverse source problems of 2D nonlinear elliptic equations. *Eng. Anal. Bound. Elem.* **2020**, *118*, 204–215. [CrossRef]
14. Kwon, K. Identification of anisotropic anomalous region in inverse problems. *Inverse Probl.* **2004**, *20*, 1117–1136. [CrossRef]
15. Huntul, M.J.; Lesnic, D. An inverse problem of finding the time-dependent thermal conductivity from boundary data. *Int. Commun. Heat Mass Transf.* **2017**, *85*, 147–154. [CrossRef]
16. Isakov, V.; Sever, A. Numerical implementation of an integral equation method for the inverse conductivity problem. *Inverse Probl.* **1996**, *12*, 939–951. [CrossRef]
17. Murthy, R.; Lin, Y.H.; Shin, K.; Mueller, J.L. A direct reconstruction algorithm for the anisotropic inverse conductivity problem based on Calderón method in the plane. *Inverse Probl.* **2020**, *12*, 125008. [CrossRef]
18. Liu, C.-S.; Qiu, L.; Lin, J. Simulating thin plate bending problems by a family of two-parameter homogenization functions. *Appl. Math. Model.* **2020**, *79*, 284–299. [CrossRef]
19. Liu, C.-S.; Atluri, S.N. An iterative and adaptive Lie-group method for solving the Calderón inverse problem. *Comput. Model. Eng. Sci.* **2010**, *64*, 299–326.
20. Sladek, J.; Sladek, V.; Hon, Y.C. Inverse heat conduction problems by meshless local Petrov–Galerkin method. *Eng. Anal. Boundary Elem.* **2006**, *30*, 650–661. [CrossRef]
21. Gu, Y.; Chen, W.; Zhang, C.; He, X. A meshless singular boundary method for three-dimensional inverse heat conduction problems in general anisotropic media. *Int. J. Heat Mass Transf.* **2015**, *84*, 91–102. [CrossRef]
22. Shivanian, E.; Khodabandehlo, H.R. Application of meshless local radial point interpolation (MLRPI) on a one-dimensional inverse heat conduction problem. *Ain Shams Eng. J.* **2016**, *7*, 993–1000. [CrossRef]
23. Sun, Y.; He, S. A meshless method based on the method of fundamental solution for three-dimensional inverse heat conduction problems. *Int. J. Heat Mass Transf.* **2017**, *108*, 945–960. [CrossRef]

mathematics MDPI

Article

Failure Transition and Validity of Brazilian Disc Test under Different Loading Configurations: A Numerical Study

Peng Xiao [1], Guoyan Zhao [1] and Huanxin Liu [2,3,*]

[1] School of Resources and Safety Engineering, Central South University, Changsha 410083, China; xiaopengaizhanghuimin@csu.edu.cn (P.X.); gyzhao@csu.edu.cn (G.Z.)
[2] Deep Mining Laboratory, Shandong Gold Group, Yantai 264000, China
[3] Shandong Province Key Laboratory of Deep Earth and Deep Sea Intelligent Mining, Shandong Gold Group, Yantai 264000, China
* Correspondence: liuhuanxin@sd-gold.com

Abstract: The Brazilian disc test is a popular tensile strength test method for engineering materials. The fracture behavior of specimens in the Brazilian disc test is closely related to the validity of the test results. In this paper, the fracture process of granite discs under different loading configurations is simulated by using a coupled finite–discrete element method. The results show that the maximum tensile stress value is located within 18 mm (0.7 times the disc radius) of the vertical range of the disc center under different loading configurations. In small diameter rods loading, the invalid tensile strength is obtained because the crack initiation and plastic strain is at the end of the disc. The crack initiation points of flat platen loading and curved jaws loading are all within the center of the disc, and the valid tensile strength can be obtained. The tensile strength test results under different loading configurations show that the error of small diameter rods loading is 13%, while the errors of flat platen loading and curved jaws loading are both 1%. The curved jaws loading is the most suitable for measuring the tensile strength of brittle materials such as rock, followed by flat platen loading. The small diameter rods loading is not recommended for the Brazilian test.

Keywords: Brazilian disc test; numerical simulation; crack evolution; failure mode; indirect tensile strength

MSC: 65Z05

Citation: Xiao, P.; Zhao, G.; Liu, H. Failure Transition and Validity of Brazilian Disc Test under Different Loading Configurations: A Numerical Study. *Mathematics* **2022**, *10*, 2681. https://doi.org/10.3390/math10152681

Academic Editor: Andrey Amosov

Received: 23 June 2022
Accepted: 27 July 2022
Published: 29 July 2022

1. Introduction

The tensile strength of brittle materials such as rock is far less than the compressive strength. The initiation and development of a tensile crack is an important factor leading to brittle materials failure [1–5]. The brittle materials fail in tension under the uniaxial tension or Brazilian test [6–8]. In addition, the macroscopic shear cracks of brittle materials under uniaxial compression or dynamic impact are mainly caused by the development of internal tensile micro-cracks [9–12]. In order to measure the tensile strength of brittle materials, the Brazilian test was put forward by Carneiro and Akazawa [13,14]. At present, the Brazilian disc test is still a popular tensile strength test method because its specimen preparation and test procedures are much more convenient than the uniaxial tensile test [15–19].

The loading configuration for the Brazilian disc test were originally flat loading platens. In the Brazilian tensile test with flat loading platens, Hudson, Swab et al. observed that the crack initiation point and the maximum tensile strain of the Brazilian disc are frequently away from the center of the disc under flat platen loading [20,21]. It may lead to the invalid estimation of tensile strength because it does not accord with the assumptions of the Brazilian disc test and the Griffith criterion. As a supplement, the Brazilian tests with different loading configurations were proposed in the past. In addition to flat platen loading, the other two popular configurations are a small diameter rod and curved jaw loading. The small diameter rod loading can make the disc have a relatively complete splitting failure along the loading direction [22]. The curved jaw loading can reduce the shear stress concentration at the end of the disc [23].

Among the tensile strength test values, the tensile strength obtained by small diameter loading rod is the smallest, the tensile strength obtained by flat platen loading is the second, and the tensile strength obtained by curved jaw loading is the largest [24,25]. It should be noted that the tensile strength of the small diameter loading rod is significantly lower than that of the other two kinds of loading, and the tensile strength of curved jaw loading is only slightly higher than that of flat platen loading. According to the basic assumption of the Brazilian disc test recommended by ISRM, the crack initiation point must be at the location of maximum tensile stress [26]. That is, the valid tensile strength can be calculated only when the tensile failure occurs first at the position of maximum tensile stress under the peak load. In the Brazilian disc test under different loading configurations, the analytical solution and numerical simulation results show that the maximum tensile stress appears in a certain range of the center of the disc in the loading direction [27–30]. Yanagidani et al. observed that the crack originated in the center of the disc under flat platen loading through the strain gages as a crack detector [31]. Through numerical simulation and digital image correlation technology, Li and Stirling et al. [15,24,32] found that the maximum tensile strain occurs far away from the center of disc under small diameter rod loading and flat platen loading, even at the end of the disc, and the maximum tensile strain appears in the center of disc under curved jaw loading. There are still some debates about the validity of the Brazilian disc test under different loading configurations.

The tensile strength of materials is an important parameter for engineering stability analysis and is often obtained through Brazilian tests. Considering that the Brazilian tests of three loading configurations are widely used, some loading configurations may lead to an invalid tensile strength value of brittle materials. In general, the existing studies mainly evaluate the validity of the Brazilian test by the maximum tensile stress distribution and the crack initiation point. Few studies have considered the development of the damage zone or plastic strain in the disc. Some studies have shown that cracks originate in the fracture process zone (damage zone), which is an important basis for judging the initiation and propagation of cracks [33–35]. In this research, a coupled finite−discrete element method (FDEM) is used to study the crack propagation, stress field, and damage (plastic) zone of Brazilian discs under three loading configurations. The validity of three loading configurations is evaluated and some new insights into the Brazilian disc test are presented. This is helpful for testers to select the appropriate loading configuration to obtain an effective tensile strength value of brittle materials.

2. Numerical Method and Model

2.1. FDEM Method

The coupled finite–discrete element method (FDEM) can realize the real simulation of material failure process by combining finite and discrete elements and introducing the principle of fracture mechanics. The unique feature of the method is to simulate the transition from continuous state to discontinuous state by explicitly simulating the fracturing and crushing process [36]. A hybrid code ELFEN has been increasingly used to simulate the fracture process of brittle materials under laboratory tests [37–40], which is also the code used in this research. The code can simulate the fracture initiation, propagation, and penetration of brittle material under increasing strain. If the failure criterion of intact model (initially expressed as finite element domain) is satisfied, cracks will occur, and the model will become discrete element. As shown in Figure 1, the code allows new fractures to pass through the existing grid element, and the insertion of discrete fractures can be intra−element fracturing and inter−element fracturing. As shown in Figure 1b, using the intra−element fracturing method with small grid size, a single small fracture can be inserted according to the appropriate fracture stress direction, thereby obtaining a more real fracture propagation behavior. Some studies show that this method successfully simulates the fracture process of rock under static and dynamic loading [41–43].

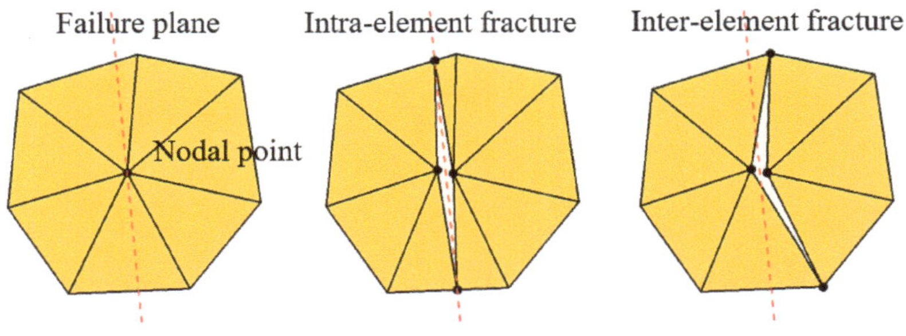

Figure 1. The crack insertion procedure: (**a**) failure plane, (**b**) intra−element fracture, (**c**) inter−element fracture.

The ELFEN formula assumes that the new crack in the quasi−brittle material model is related to tensile deformation. The model under compressive load will expand in the orthogonal direction of the loading direction due to the Poisson effect, and the crack originates on the loading path and expands along the loading direction. Cai believes that the formation of typical shear bands observed in compression tests is actually a secondary process of interaction polymerization of extension cracks [12].

The Mohr–Coulomb with Rankine tensile yield criterion is used to judge the failure of Brazilian discs under different loading configurations. The model includes five material parameters: cohesion (c), friction angle (φ), expansion angle (ψ), tensile strength (σ_t), and fracture energy (G_f). Compared with the traditional Mohr–Coulomb criterion, the modified criterion can better describe the shear and tensile failure of the material, as shown in Figure 2.

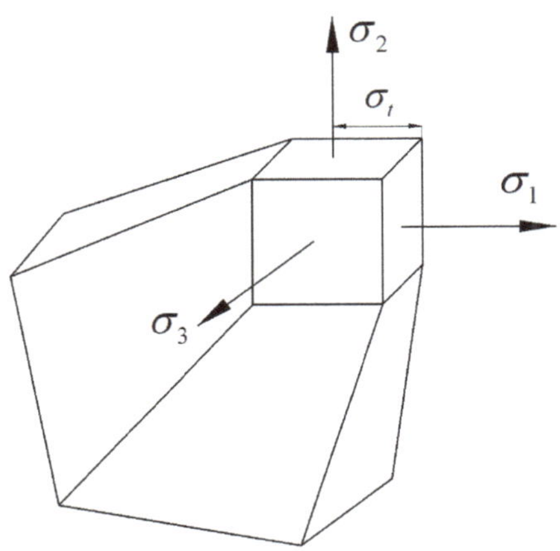

Figure 2. Mohr–Coulomb with Rankine tensile yield surface.

The Mohr–Coulomb with Rankine tensile yield criterion combines the Mohr–Coulomb yield criterion and the Rankine tensile yield criterion. The Mohr–Coulomb yield criterion is used to judge shear failure and is described by:

$$\tau = c - \sigma_n \tan \varphi \tag{1}$$

where τ is the shear stress, c is the cohesion, σ_n is the normal pressure, and φ is the friction angle. The Rankine tensile yield criterion is used to judge tensile failure and is described by:

$$\sigma_i - \sigma_t = 0 \quad i = 1, 2, 3 \tag{2}$$

where σ_i is the principal stress and σ_t is the tensile strength. The cohesion of model decreases after plastic strain occurs, and the tensile strength is softened by the decrease in cohesion, as shown in Equation (3). This ensures that there is always normal stress on the failure shear surface.

$$\sigma_t \le c(1 - \sin\varphi)/\cos\varphi \tag{3}$$

The stress–strain relationship of the discrete crack model is shown in Figure 3, which includes an elastic part and a softening (plastic) part [44], and damage begins after peak intensity. The cracks can be introduced in a direction perpendicular to the principal strain and are assumed to rotate upon further loading to maintain this orthogonal relationship.

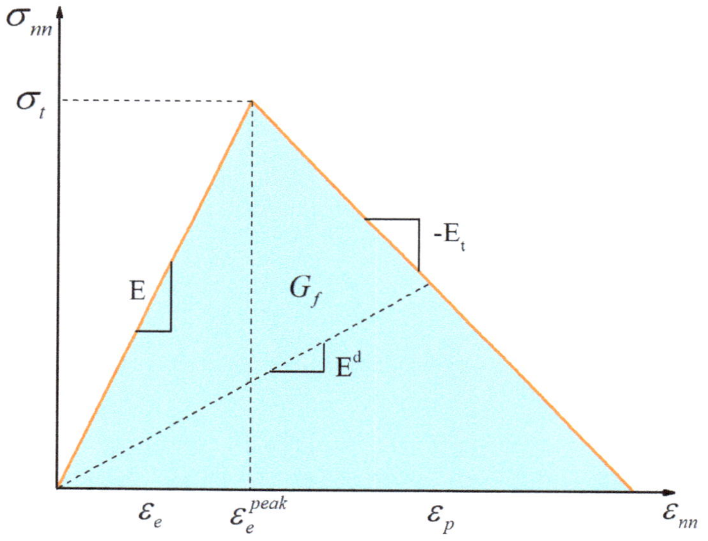

Figure 3. The stress–strain curve of discrete crack model.

In the post–peak region, the rotational crack formulation shows the anisotropic damage evolution by decreasing the elastic modulus in the direction of major principal stress, and is formulated as:

$$\sigma_{nn} = E^d \varepsilon_{nn} = (1 - \omega) E \varepsilon_{nn} \tag{4}$$

where n-s is the local coordinate related to the principal stress, E^d is the elastic damage secant modulus, E is the Young's modulus, and ω is the damage parameter. The scalar damage evolution of the linear strain softening curve is defined by:

$$\omega = \frac{\psi(\varepsilon) - 1}{\psi(\varepsilon)} \tag{5}$$

where $\psi(\varepsilon)$ is a function of strain described by [45]:

$$\begin{array}{lll} \text{For } \varepsilon \le \frac{\sigma_t}{E} & \psi(\varepsilon) = 1 & \omega = 0 \\ \text{For } \frac{\sigma_t}{E} < \varepsilon \le \frac{\sigma_t}{E} + \frac{\sigma_t}{E_t} & \psi(\varepsilon) = \frac{E^2 \varepsilon}{E_t \sigma_t + E \sigma_t - E_t E \varepsilon} & 0 < \omega < 1 \\ \text{For } \varepsilon > \frac{\sigma_t}{E} + \frac{\sigma_t}{E_t} & \psi(\varepsilon) \to \infty & \omega = 1 \end{array} \tag{6}$$

where E_t is the tangential softening modulus. The fracture energy G_f is an important parameter for fracture development. It refers to the energy required to generate continuous cracks per unit area, which is defined as:

$$G_f = \int \sigma du = \int \sigma \varepsilon(s) ds \tag{7}$$

where σ is the tensile stress and u is the tensile displacement. The fracture energy is related to the stress intensity factor (K_{IC}) and elastic modulus (E):

$$G_f = \frac{K_{IC}^2}{E} \tag{8}$$

The localized bandwidth l_c of the linear slope softening model is integrated to obtain:

$$E_t = -\frac{\sigma_t^2 l_c}{2G_f} \tag{9}$$

2.2. Numerical Model

The three loading configurations commonly used in Brazilian testing are small diameter rod, flat plate, and curved jaw. As shown in Figure 4, three Brazilian disc models with different loading configurations are built: small diameter loading rods (Type I), flat loading platens (Type II), and curved loading jaws (Type III). The diameter of Brazilian discs is 50 mm and the thickness is 25 mm. The two rods of Type I test are 2 mm in diameter. The loading speed is set to 0.5 mm/s and the corresponding strain rate is 0.01, which can be regarded as quasi−static loading.

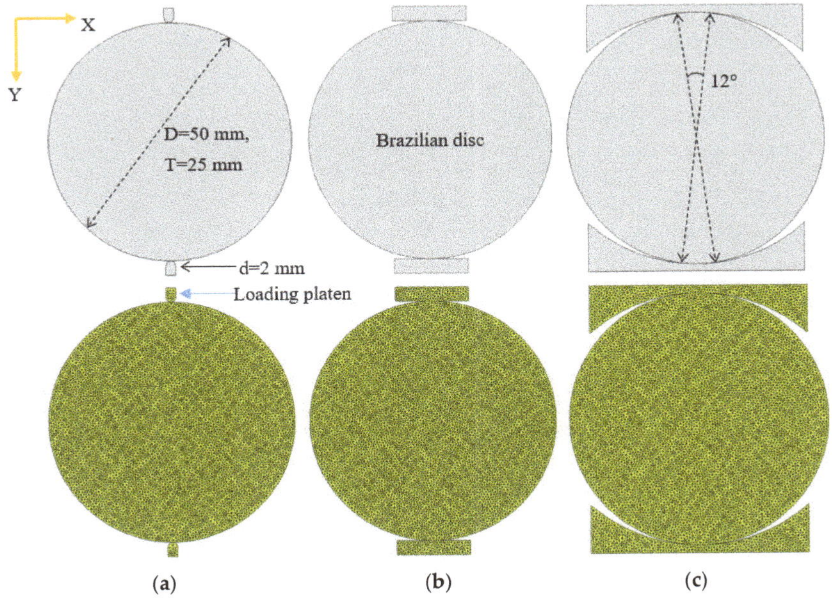

Figure 4. Three Brazilian disc models and meshes under different loading configurations. (**a**) small diameter loading rods (Type I), (**b**) flat loading platens (Type II), and (**c**) curved loading jaws (Type III). Note: The loading rod of Type I is composed of a small semicircle and a small rectangle. The semicircle part contacts the disc to transmit the load, and the upper right corner of the rectangle is used to record the load–displacement data.

The mechanical parameters of a granite are selected as the parameters of the Brazilian disc and the mechanical parameters of loading platen and granite disc are shown in Table 1. The material properties of the granite disc come from Li's research [24,46]. The failure energy of hard and brittle materials are the range of 0.01 N/mm to 0.3 N/mm [47], and 0.05 N/mm is used as the failure energy of granite in this study. The normal penalty is generally 1.0 times the elastic modulus, and the tangential penalty is 0.1 times the normal penalty. The friction refers to the friction between the disc and loading plate. The element size of model is 0.5 mm, and the diameter of disc is 100 times the element size, which ensures that the element size can obtain accurate crack propagation. The influence of the mesh size is shown in Appendix A.

Table 1. Material properties adopted in Brazilian test.

Name	Granite Disc	Loading Platen
Young's modulus (E, GPa)	43.2	211.00
Poisson's ratio (ν)	0.23	0.29
Shear modulus (G, GPa)	17.5	-
Density (ρ, Ns^2/mm^4)	2.8×10^9	7.84×10^9
Cohesion (c, MPa)	50	-
Friction angle (φ)	34°	-
Tensile strength (σ_t, MPa)	12.0	-
Fracture energy (G_f, N/mm)	0.05	-
	Discrete contact parameters	
Normal penalty (P_n, N/mm^2)	43,200	211,000
Tangential penalty (P_t, N/mm^2)	4320	21,100
Friction (γ)	0.1	0.1
Mesh size (mm)	0.5	0.5
Contact type	Node–Edge	Node–Edge

3. Results

3.1. Load Versus Displacement Curve

The load and displacement are recorded through the loading plate. The horizontal direction is the X direction and the vertical direction is the Y direction. Figure 5 is the load–displacement curve for the Type I Brazilian disc testing. The peak load and peak displacement are 20.7 kN and 0.189 mm, respectively. The load–displacement curve before the peak value is approximately a straight line, and the vertical stress at the contact part between the rod and disc is much greater than that at other positions. Due to the small contact area between the rod and the disc, there is a large local compression stress concentration. When the macro crack almost penetrates the disc after the peak load, there is a certain vertical stress on both sides of the crack, and the vertical stress in other areas is very small.

Figure 6 is the load–displacement curve for the Type II Brazilian disc testing. The peak load and peak displacement are 23.8 kN and 0.126 mm, respectively. The load–displacement curve of the Type II test is similar to that of Type I. The stress concentration of the disc before the peak load under the Type II test is less than that of Type I. After the peak load, the vertical stress distribution of the disc is more evenly distributed on both sides of the crack. There are some arc–shaped stress zones around the vertical main crack, and the value of the arc–shaped stress zone decreases from the center to the circumference. The crack inside the disc is consistent with the loading direction and the occurrence of a straight crack is related to the spreading of stress propagation.

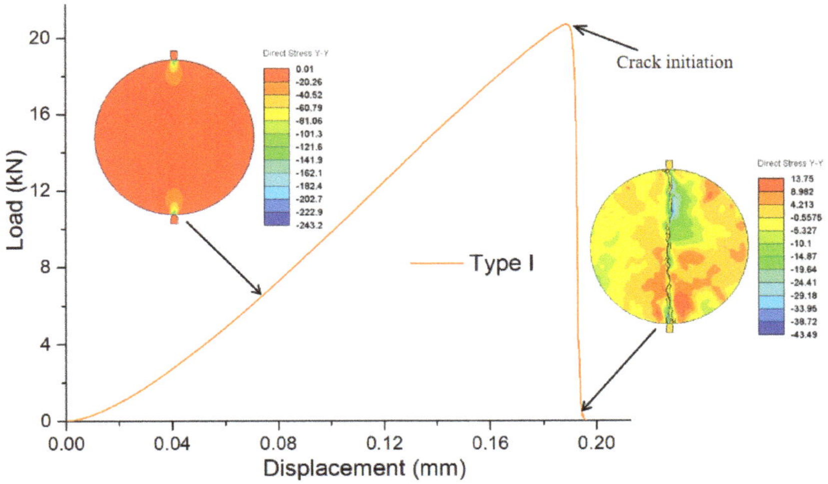

Figure 5. Load−displacement curves for the Type I Brazilian disc testing.

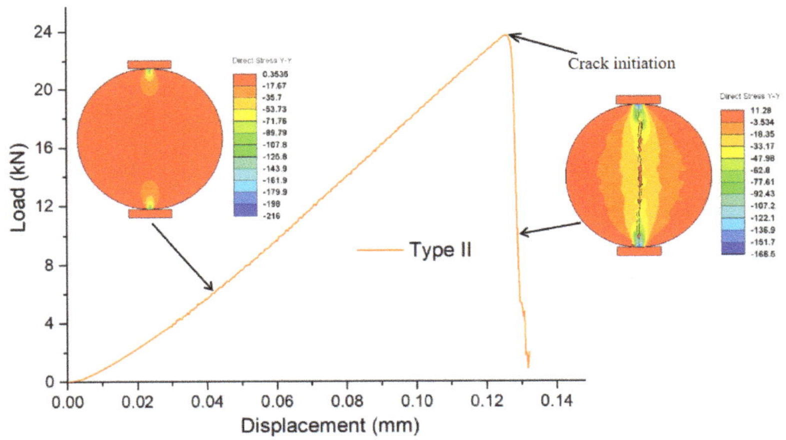

Figure 6. Load–displacement curves for the Type II Brazilian disc testing.

Figure 7 is the load–displacement curve for the Type III Brazilian disc testing. The peak load and peak displacement are 24.1 kN and 0.103 mm, respectively. The load–displacement curve of the Type III test before peak value is similar to that of Type II and Type I. After the crack penetrates the disc, the disc still has a certain bearing capacity, due to the contact area being larger than the Type II and Type I test. The stress concentration of the disc before the peak load of the Type III test is less than that of Type II and Type I, and the vertical stress distribution of the disc is more uniform in the whole loading stage. A more dense arc−shaped stress zone appears around the vertical main crack.

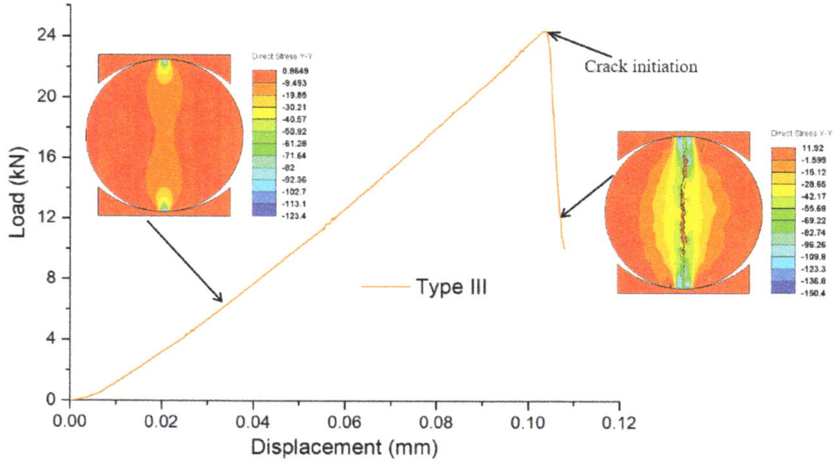

Figure 7. Load–displacement curves for the Type III Brazilian disc testing.

3.2. Fracture Process

In order to express the whole fracture process of the disc, the crack propagation process is divided into four parts: crack initiation, crack propagation, crack penetration, and final failure. Figure 8 is the fracture process for the Type I Brazilian disc testing. The crack of the Type I test starts at the end of the disc, then develops towards the center of the disc, and finally penetrates the disc. The disc is finally divided into two halves by the main crack. Although the final failure mode is good under Type I testing, the crack initiation point is located at the end of the disc due to the high degree of compressive stress concentration. It was also found by the digital image correlation method in Li's physical test of five types of rocks [24].

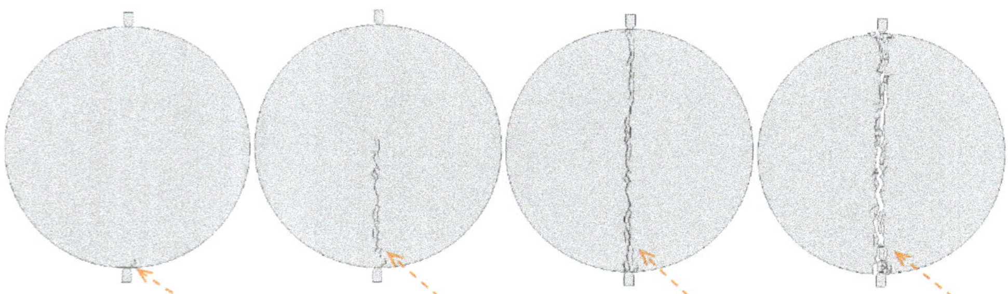

Figure 8. Failure process for the Type I Brazilian disc testing.

Figure 9 is the fracture process for the Type II Brazilian disc testing. The crack in the Type II test starts from the center of the disc, then develops to both ends of the disc, and finally penetrates the disc. The disc was eventually divided into two halves, and the damage degree of the end of the disc is greater than that of the center. Although the end failure of the disc is serious under the Type II testing, the crack initiation point is close to the center of the disc, which is consistent with the hypothesis of the Brazilian disc test.

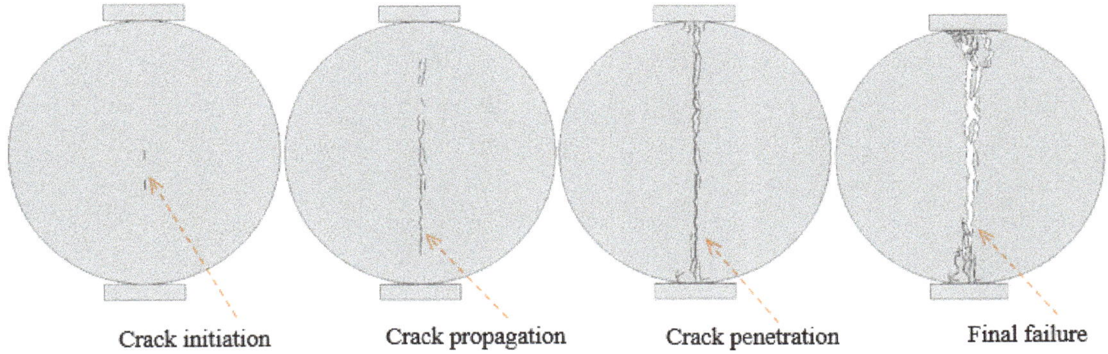

Figure 9. Failure process for the Type II Brazilian disc testing.

Figure 10 is the fracture process for the Type III Brazilian disc testing. The crack in the Type III test starts from the center of the disc and then develops to both ends of the disc. When the main crack penetrates the disc, the secondary cracks are generated on both sides of the main crack. The disc is finally divided into two parts, accompanied by obvious secondary cracks. Although four secondary cracks appeared at the end of the disc under Type III testing, the starting point of the main crack was close to the center of the disc, which was also consistent with the hypothesis of the Brazilian disc test.

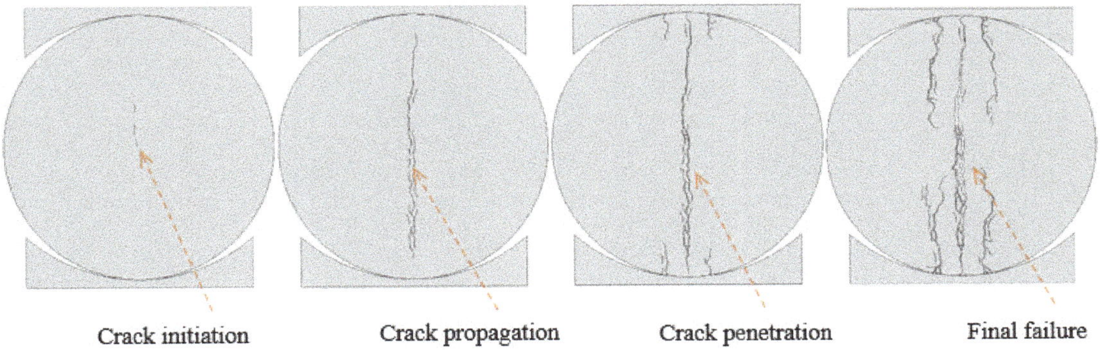

Figure 10. Failure process for the Type III Brazilian disc testing.

3.3. Stress Distribution in Central Line

As shown in Figure 11, a horizontal stress monitoring line is arranged in the center of the Brazilian disc. Figure 12 is the horizontal stress X-X distribution in the monitoring line for Type I testing under an external load of 10 kN. It shows that the horizontal stress distribution within the range of less than 20 mm from the center is relatively uniform, and the horizontal tensile stress is approximately 5.08 MPa. When the distance from the center is more than 20 mm, the horizontal stress changes rapidly from tensile stress to compressive stress with a large value. When the distance from the center is 24.5 mm, the horizontal compressive stress reaches 90 MPa.

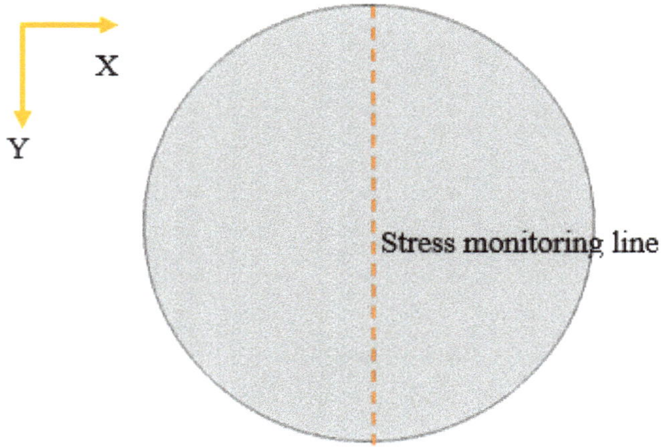

Figure 11. Location of stress monitoring line in Brazilian disc.

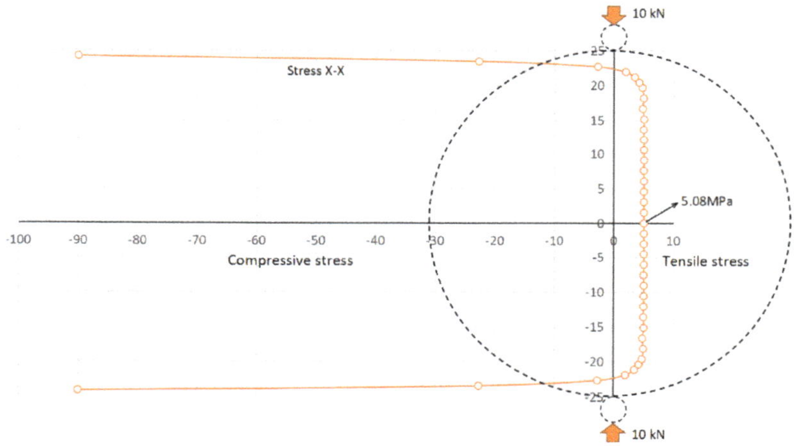

Figure 12. The stress X−X distribution in the monitoring line for Type I testing under external load of 10 kN.

Figure 13 is the horizontal stress X-X distribution in the monitoring line for Type II testing under an external load of 10 kN. It shows that the horizontal stress is approximately a tensile stress of 5.02 MPa within the range of less than 18 mm from the center. When the distance from the center is more than 18 mm, the horizontal stress changes rapidly from tensile stress to compressive stress with a large value. When the distance from the center is 24.5 mm, the horizontal compressive stress reaches 78 MPa.

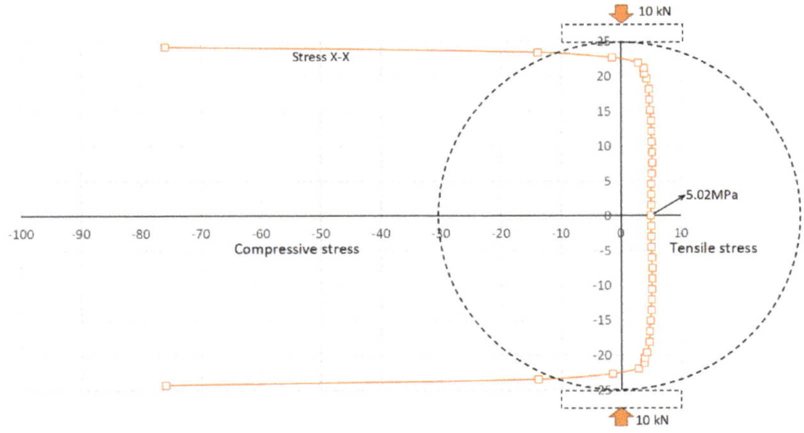

Figure 13. The stress X−X distribution in the monitoring line for Type II testing under external load of 10 kN.

Figure 14 is the horizontal stress X-X distribution in the monitoring line for Type III testing under an external load of 10 kN. It shows that the horizontal stress is approximately a tensile stress of 4.96 MPa within the range of less than 18 mm from the center. When the distance from the center is more than 18 mm, the horizontal stress changes rapidly from tensile stress to compressive stress with a large value. When the distance from the center is 24.5 mm, the horizontal compressive stress reaches 77 MPa.

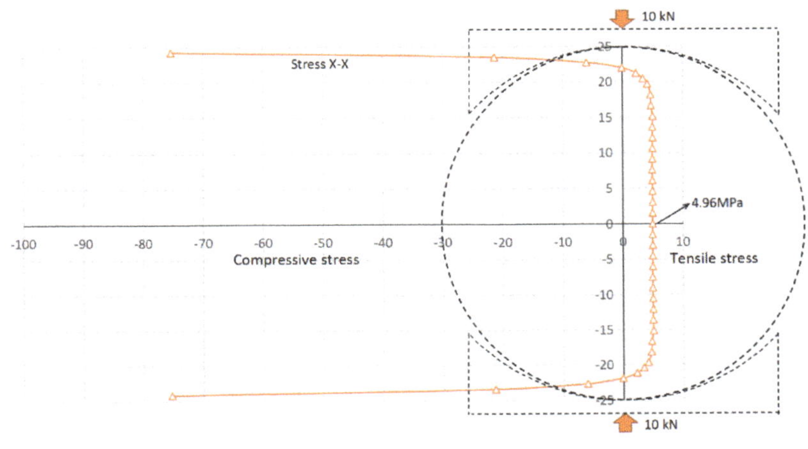

Figure 14. The stress X−X distribution in the monitoring line for Type III testing under external load of 10 kN.

Comparing Figures 12–14, it can be seen that under the same load, the stress concentration on the stress monitoring line of the Type I test is the most obvious. The stress concentration of Type II and Type III tests decrease in turn, which can also be seen from Figures 5–7. Under the same external load, the difference of the maximum tensile stress within 18 mm (0.7 times the disc radius) of the center for the three Types of tests is small, and the difference is mainly reflected in the compressive stress at the end of the disc. Type III testing is beneficial for reducing stress concentrations at the ends of the disc, which is conducive to the initiation of cracks in the center of the disc.

3.4. Evolution of Fracture Process Zone

The plastic strain law in the model has been described in Figure 3. The strain generated after the peak elastic strain is defined as the plastic strain, which is used to characterize the fracture process zone before fracture. Figure 15 is the plastic strain evolution with load for the Type I loading. When the external load is 6.8 kN, two plastic zones appear in the contact part between the disc and the rod. When the external load is 20.6 kN, the plastic strain at the end of the disc is approximately 0.2%, which indicates that the damage at the end is obvious. As the loading progresses, the crack initiates from the plastic zone at the bottom of the disc. At 19.2 kN, after the peak load, the plastic zone develops rapidly to the center of the disc, and the crack develops rapidly in the plastic zone. Finally, the plastic zone continues to develop rapidly throughout the disc, resulting in a rapid decrease in the load−carrying capacity of the disc.

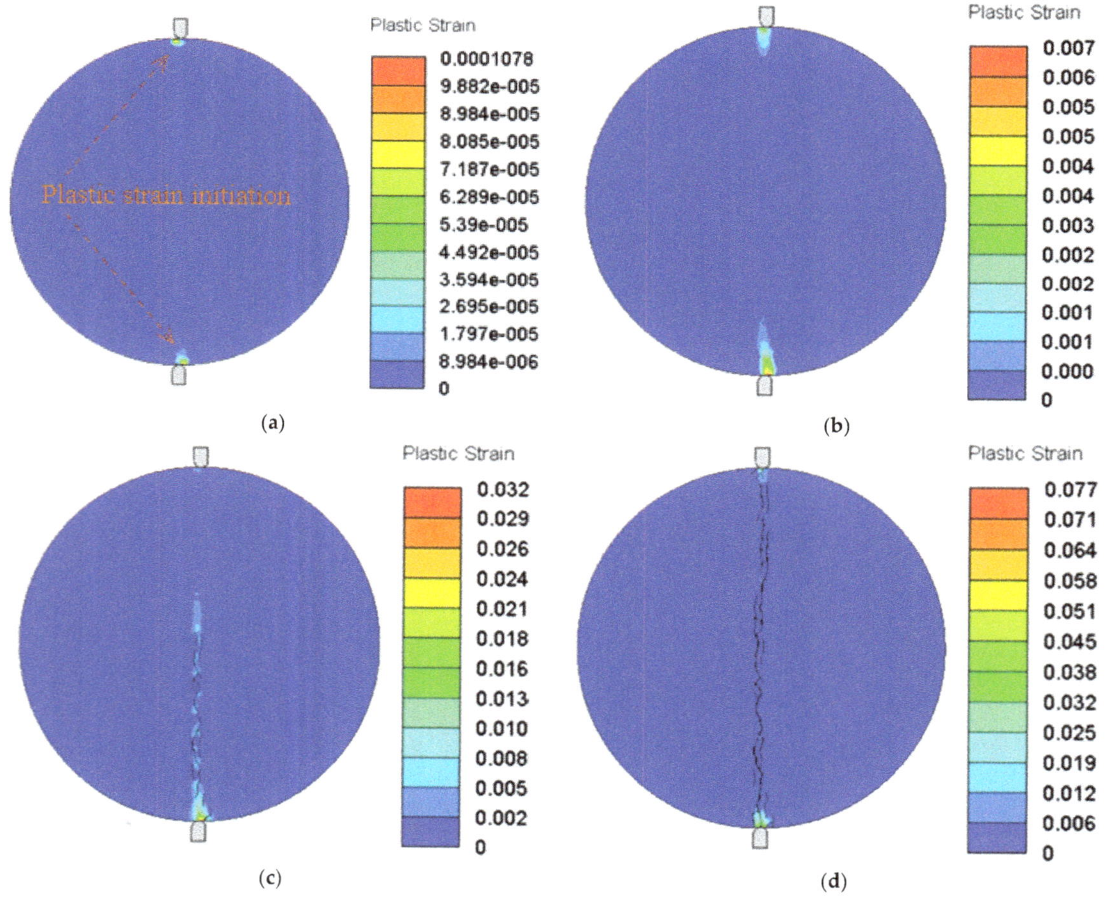

Figure 15. The plastic strain evolution with load for the Type I testing: (**a**) 6.8 kN, (**b**) 20.6 kN, (**c**) 19.2 kN (post−peak), (**d**) 4.2 kN (post−peak).

Figure 16 is the plastic strain evolution with load for the Type II loading. When the external load is 17.5 kN, the plastic zone appears in the contact part between the disc and the flat platen. When the external load is 22.0 kN, the plastic zone develops rapidly in the center of the disc. As the loading progresses, the crack initiates from the center of the plastic zone of the disc. At 20.0 kN, after the peak load, the plastic zone continues to develop rapidly throughout the disc and a crack develops rapidly in the plastic zone. At 7.7 kN, after the peak load, two triangular plastic zones are formed at the end of the disc, which is the cause of shear failure at the end of the disc under Type II loading.

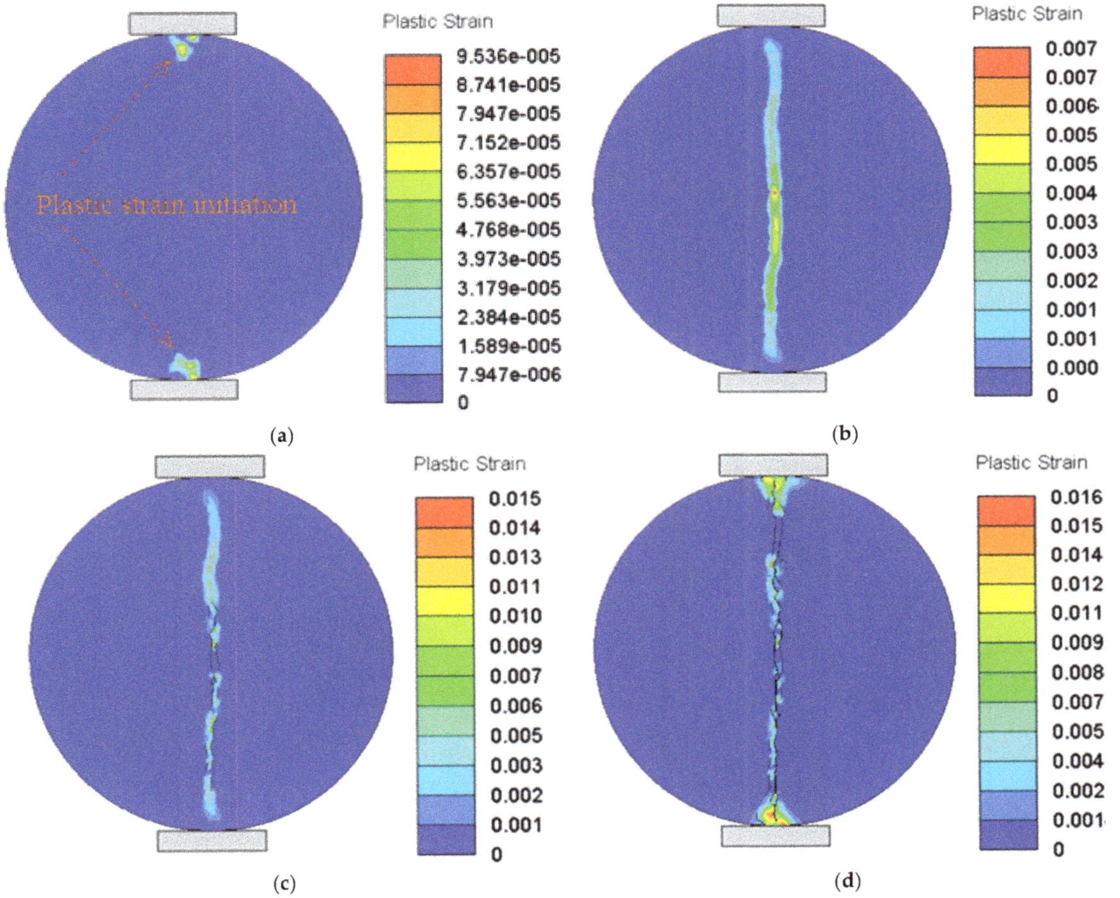

Figure 16. The plastic strain evolution with load for the Type II testing: (**a**) 17.5 kN, (**b**) 22.0 kN, (**c**) 20.0 kN (post−peak), (**d**) 7.7 kN (post−peak).

Figure 17 is the plastic strain evolution with load for the Type III loading. When the external load is 23.6 kN, a plastic zone appears in the center of the disc. When the external load is 23.9 kN, the plastic zone develops rapidly in the center of disc towards both ends of the disc. As the loading progresses, the crack initiates from the center of the plastic zone. At 11.4 kN, after the peak load, the crack developed rapidly in the plastic zone and penetrated the disc, and the secondary plastic zones and cracks were produced at the end of the disc.

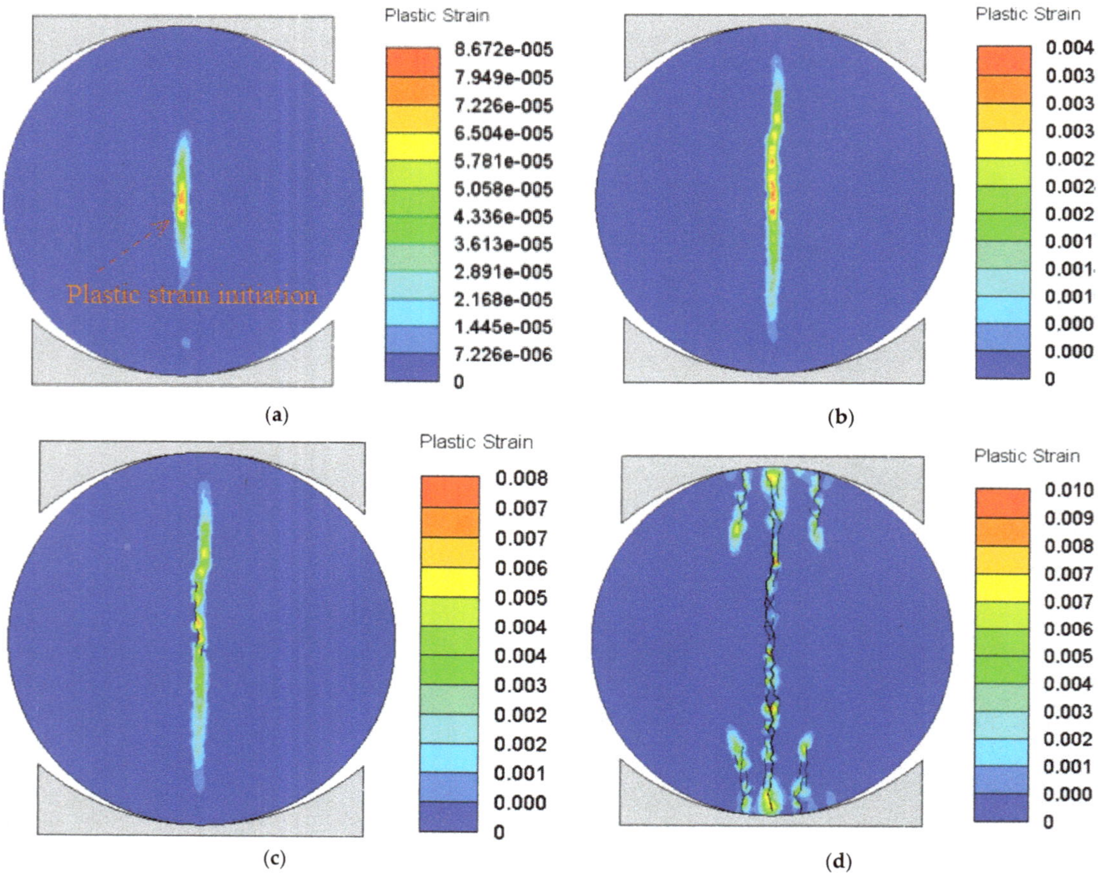

Figure 17. The plastic strain evolution with load for the Type III testing: (**a**) 23.6 kN, (**b**) 23.9 kN, (**c**) 22.6 kN (post−peak), (**d**) 11.4 kN (post−peak).

4. Discussion

4.1. Failure Mode Transition

Figures 18 and 19 are the failure mode transitions of the Brazilian disc test with different loading configurations. It can be seen that the Brazilian disc under the Type I test mainly suffered tensile failure and a small shear failure at the end. The Brazilian disc under the Type II test mainly suffered tensile failure and an obvious conical shear failure zone at the end. The Brazilian disc under the Type III test mainly suffered tensile failure, and obvious secondary cracks are associated on both sides of the main tensile crack.

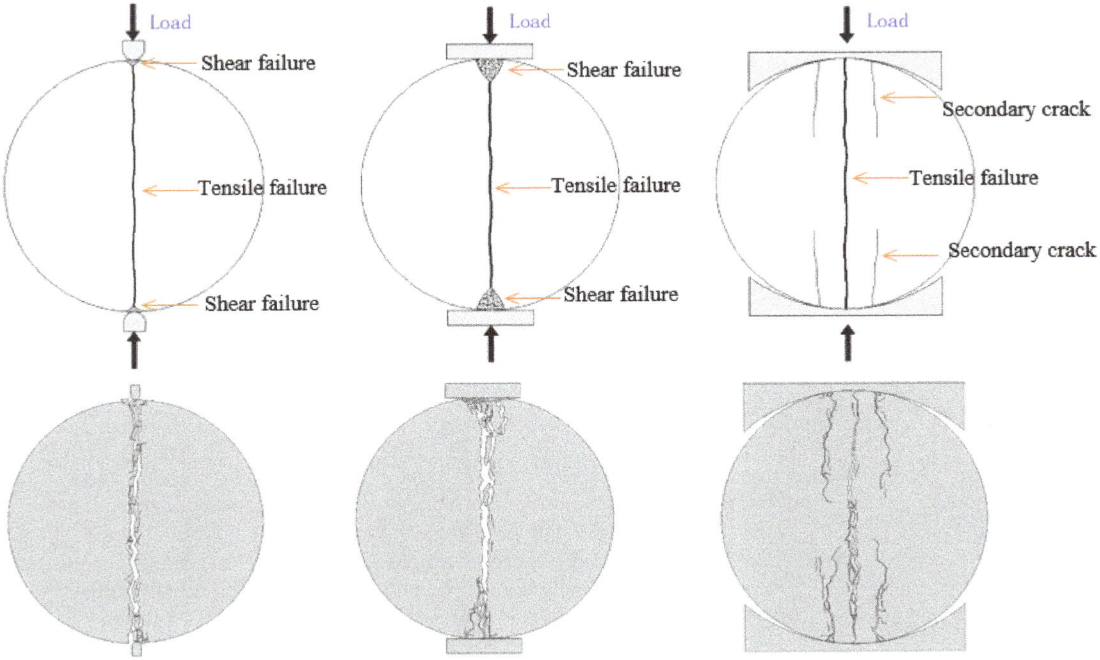

Figure 18. The failure mode transition of Brazilian disc test with different loading configurations.

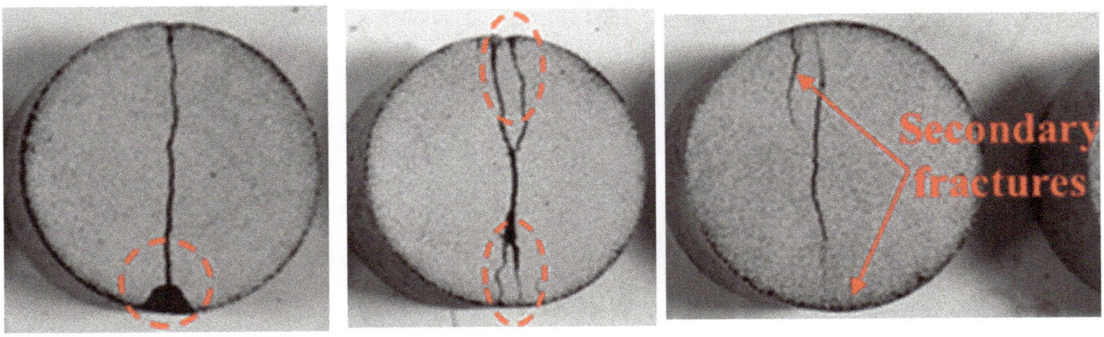

Figure 19. The failure mode of disc with different loading configurations in physical test [24].

It is worth noting that although the disc of Type I testing has a relatively good splitting failure, the crack is initiated at the end of the disc, which does not meet the assumptions of the Brazilian disc test. The shear conical failure zone at the end of the disc under the Type II test occurs after the peak load and does not affect the magnitude of the peak load; that is, it does not affect the validity of the tensile strength. The secondary cracks at the end of the disc under the Type III test also occurred after the peak load and did not affect the magnitude of the peak load and the validity of the tensile strength.

4.2. Validity of Tensile Strength

The tensile strength for Type I and Type II testing can be calculated according to Equation (10), and the tensile strength for Type III testing can be calculated according to Equation (11) [27]. The 2α is the angle of the circular arc of the contact area between the curved jaw and the disc, which is 12° in this model. The calculation results are shown in Table 2. It can be seen that the error of tensile strength for Type I is 13%, while the errors of tensile strength for Type II and Type III are both 1%. It shows that the Type I test is not suitable for testing the tensile strength, while the Type II and Type III tests are suitable for testing the tensile strength.

$$\sigma_t = \frac{2P}{\pi D t} \tag{10}$$

$$\sigma_t = \frac{2P}{\pi D t}\left(\frac{\sin 2\alpha}{\alpha} - 1\right) \tag{11}$$

Table 2. The tensile strength and error of three loading types.

Loading Type	*P*/kN	*α*/°	Tested Tensile Strength/MPa	Actual Tensile Strength/MPa	Error
Type I	20.7	0	10.5		13%
Type II	23.8	0	12.1	12.0	1%
Type III	24.1	6	12.1		1%

5. Conclusions

The main conclusions were obtained as follows:

(1) The Brazilian disc under the Type I test mainly suffered tensile failure and small shear failure at the end. The Brazilian disc under the Type II test mainly suffered tensile failure and an obvious conical shear failure zone at the end. The Brazilian disc under the Type III test mainly suffered tensile failure, and obvious secondary cracks are associated on both sides of the main tensile crack.

(2) The maximum tensile stress value is located within 18mm (0.7 times the disc radius) of the center of the disc under different loading configurations. Therefore, the Brazilian disc test is valid only where the crack initiation point is within 18 mm of the vertical range of the disc center, which means that the crack initiation is located in the area of maximum tensile stress.

(3) In the Type I test, the invalid tensile strength is obtained because the crack initiation and plastic strain point is at the end of the disc. The crack initiation points of the Type II and Type III tests are all within the center of the disc, and the valid tensile strength can be obtained. The tensile strength test results under different loading configurations show that the error of the Type I test is 13%, while the errors of the Type II and Type III tests are both 1%.

(4) The plastic strain of the Type III test is also initiated at the center of the disc, and the plastic strain of the Type II test is initiated at the end of the disc. It can be considered that the Type III test is better than the Type II. In summary, the curved jaws loading (Type III) is the most suitable for measuring the tensile strength of brittle materials such as rock, followed by the flat platens loading (Type II). The small diameter rods loading (Type I) testing is not suitable for testing the tensile strength of materials.

Author Contributions: Conceptualization, P.X.; methodology, P.X.; software, P.X.; validation, P.X., G.Z. and H.L.; formal analysis, H.L. funding acquisition, G.Z. All authors have read and agreed to the published version of the manuscript.

Funding: This research was funded by the State Key Research Development Program of China (No. 2018YFC0604606).

Institutional Review Board Statement: Not applicable.

Informed Consent Statement: Not applicable.

Data Availability Statement: The data presented in this study are available on request from the corresponding author.

Conflicts of Interest: The authors declare no conflict of interest.

Appendix A

The influence of mesh size on the loading curve for the Brazilian testing is shown in Figures A1–A3. It can be seen that the mesh size has little effect on the loading curve. Considering that a smaller mesh size is conducive to obtain a more accurate damage zone and crack propagation, a mesh size of 0.5 mm is set to analyze the fracture process of Brazilian discs under different loading configurations.

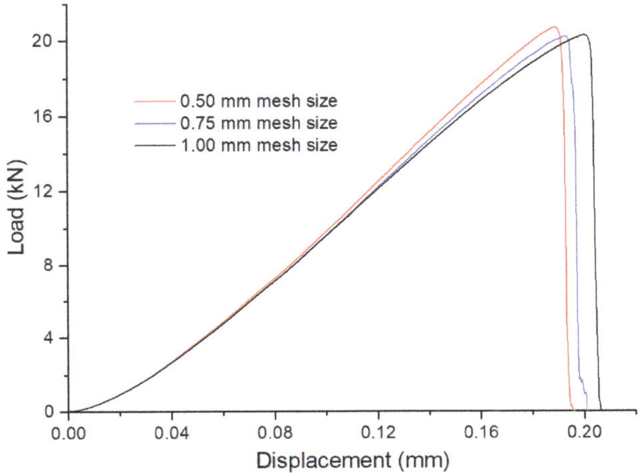

Figure A1. The influence of mesh size on the loading curve for the Type I Brazilian testing.

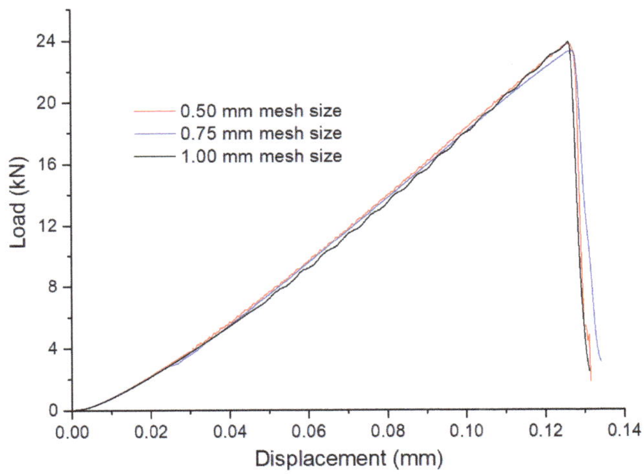

Figure A2. The influence of mesh size on the loading curve for the Type II Brazilian testing.

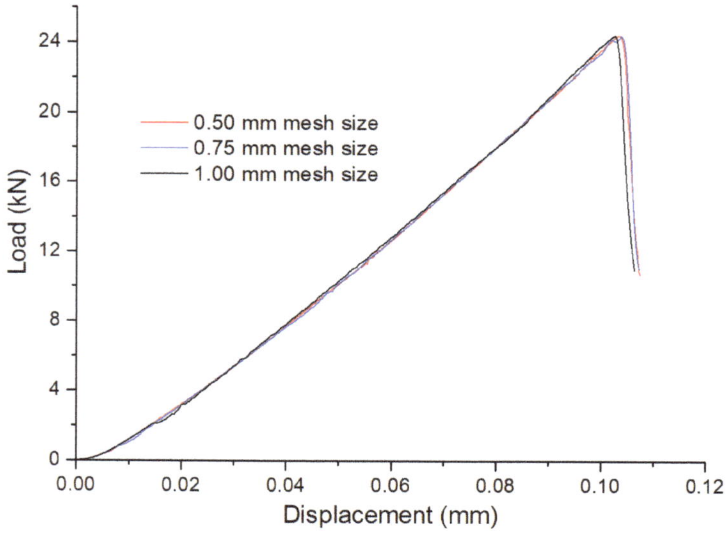

Figure A3. The influence of mesh size on the loading curve for the Type III Brazilian testing.

References

1. Dan, D.Q.; Konietzky, H.; Herbst, M. Brazilian tensile strength tests on some anisotropic rocks. *Int. J. Rock Mech. Min. Sci.* **2013**, *58*, 1–7. [CrossRef]
2. Zhou, J.; Zhang, L.Q.; Yang, D.X.; Braun, A.; Han, Z.H. Investigation of the Quasi-Brittle Failure of Alashan Granite Viewed from Laboratory Experiments and Grain-Based Discrete Element Modeling. *Materials* **2017**, *10*, 835. [CrossRef]
3. Zhu, Q.Q.; Li, D.Y.; Han, Z.Y.; Li, X.B.; Zhou, Z.L. Mechanical properties and fracture evolution of sandstone specimens containing different inclusions under uniaxial compression. *Int. J. Rock Mech. Min. Sci.* **2019**, *115*, 33–47. [CrossRef]
4. Tao, R.; Sharifzadeh, M.; Zhang, Y.; Feng, X.-T. Analysis of Mafic rocks Microstructure damage and failure Process under Compression Test Using Quantitative Scanning Electron Microscopy and Digital Images Processing. *Eng. Fract. Mech.* **2020**, *231*, 107019. [CrossRef]
5. Xiao, P.; Li, D.; Zhao, G.; Liu, H. New criterion for the spalling failure of deep rock engineering based on energy release. *Int. J. Rock Mech. Min. Sci.* **2021**, *148*, 1–12. [CrossRef]
6. Li, D.; Li, X.; Li, C.C. Experimental Studies of Mechanical Properties of Two Rocks Under Direct Compression and Tension. *Chin. J. Rock Mech. Eng.* **2010**, *29*, 624–632.
7. Erarslan, N.; Liang, Z.Z.; Williams, D.J. Experimental and Numerical Studies on Determination of Indirect Tensile Strength of Rocks. *Rock Mech. Rock Eng.* **2012**, *45*, 739–751. [CrossRef]
8. Hashiba, K.; Fukui, K. Effect of Water on the Deformation and Failure of Rock in Uniaxial Tension. *Rock Mech. Rock Eng.* **2015**, *48*, 1751–1761. [CrossRef]
9. Li, H.B.; Zhao, J.; Li, T.J. Micromechanical modelling of the mechanical properties of a granite under dynamic uniaxial compressive loads. *Int. J. Rock Mech. Min. Sci.* **2000**, *37*, 923–935. [CrossRef]
10. Wong, L.N.Y.; Einstein, H.H. Crack Coalescence in Molded Gypsum and Carrara Marble: Part 2-Microscopic Observations and Interpretation. *Rock Mech. Rock Eng.* **2009**, *42*, 513–545. [CrossRef]
11. Xiao, P.; Li, D.; Zhao, G.; Zhu, Q.; Liu, H.; Zhang, C. Mechanical properties and failure behavior of rock with different flaw inclinations under coupled static and dynamic loads. *J. Cent. South Univ.* **2020**, *27*, 2945–2958. [CrossRef]
12. Cai, M. Influence of intermediate principal stress on rock fracturing and strength near excavation boundaries-Insight from numerical modeling. *Int. J. Rock Mech. Min. Sci.* **2008**, *45*, 763–772. [CrossRef]
13. Carneiro, F. A new method to determine the tensile strength of concrete. In Proceedings of the 5th Meeting of the Brazilian Association for Technical Rules ("Associacao Brasileire de Normas Tecnicas—ABNT"), Brazil, September 1943.
14. Akazawa, T. New test method for evaluating internal stress due to compression of concrete: The splitting tension test. *J. Jpn. Soc. Civ. Eng.* **1943**, *29*, 777–787.
15. Li, D.; Wong, L.N.Y. The Brazilian Disc Test for Rock Mechanics Applications: Review and New Insights. *Rock Mech. Rock Eng.* **2013**, *46*, 269–287. [CrossRef]
16. Yu, Y.; Zhang, J.X.; Zhang, J.C. A modified Brazilian disk tension test. *Int. J. Rock Mech. Min. Sci.* **2009**, *46*, 421–425. [CrossRef]
17. Erarslan, N.; Williams, D.J. Experimental, numerical and analytical studies on tensile strength of rocks. *Int. J. Rock Mech. Min. Sci.* **2012**, *49*, 21–30. [CrossRef]

18. Komurlu, E.; Kesimal, A. Evaluation of Indirect Tensile Strength of Rocks Using Different Types of Jaws. *Rock Mech. Rock Eng.* **2015**, *48*, 1723–1730. [CrossRef]
19. Aliabadian, Z.; Zhao, G.F.; Russell, A.R. Crack development in transversely isotropic sandstone discs subjected to Brazilian tests observed using digital image correlation. *Int. J. Rock Mech. Min. Sci.* **2019**, *119*, 211–221. [CrossRef]
20. Hudson, J.; Brown, E.; Rummel, F. The controlled failure of rock discs and rings loaded in diametral compression. *Int. J. Rock Mech. Min. Sci. Geomech. Abstr.* **1972**, *9*, 241–248. [CrossRef]
21. Swab, J.J.; Yu, J.; Gamble, R.; Kilczewski, S. Analysis of the diametral compression method for determining the tensile strength of transparent magnesium aluminate spinel. *Int. J. Fract.* **2011**, *172*, 187–192. [CrossRef]
22. *GB/T 50266-99*; National Standards Compilation Group of People's Republic of China. Standard for Tests Method of Engineering Rock Masses. China Plan Press: Beijing, China, 1999.
23. Mellor, M.; Hawkes, I. Measurement of tensile strength by diametral compression of discs and annuli. *Eng. Geol.* **1971**, *5*, 173–225. [CrossRef]
24. Li, D.; Li, B.; Han, Z.; Zhu, Q. Evaluation on Rock Tensile Failure of the Brazilian Discs under Different Loading Configurations by Digital Image Correlation. *Appl. Sci.* **2020**, *10*, 5513. [CrossRef]
25. Sgambitterra, E.; Lamuta, C.; Candamano, S.; Pagnotta, L. Brazilian disk test and digital image correlation: A methodology for the mechanical characterization of brittle materials. *Mater. Struct.* **2018**, *51*, 19. [CrossRef]
26. ISRM. Suggested methods for determining tensile strength of rock materials. *Int. J. Rock Mech. Min. Sci. Geomech. Abstr.* **1978**, *15*, 99–103. [CrossRef]
27. Hondros, G. The evaluation of Poisson's ratio and the modulus of materials of a low tensile resistance by the Brazilian (indirect tensile) test with particular reference to concrete. *Aust. J. Appl. Sci.* **1959**, *10*, 243–268.
28. Yu, Y.; Yin, J.M.; Zhong, Z.W. Shape effects in the Brazilian tensile strength test and a 3D FEM correction. *Int. J. Rock Mech. Min. Sci.* **2006**, *43*, 623–627. [CrossRef]
29. Markides, C.F.; Pazis, D.N.; Kourkoulis, S.K. Closed full-field solutions for stresses and displacements in the Brazilian disk under distributed radial load. *Int. J. Rock Mech. Min. Sci.* **2010**, *47*, 227–237. [CrossRef]
30. Markides, C.F.; Kourkoulis, S.K. The Stress Field in a Standardized Brazilian Disc: The Influence of the Loading Type Acting on the Actual Contact Length. *Rock Mech. Rock Eng.* **2012**, *45*, 145–158. [CrossRef]
31. Yanagidani, T.; Sano, O.; Terada, M.; Ito, I. The observation of cracks propagating in diametrically-compressed rock discs. *Int. J. Rock Mech. Min. Sci. Geomech. Abstr.* **1978**, *15*, 225–235. [CrossRef]
32. Stirling, R.A.; Simpson, D.J.; Davie, C.T. The application of digital image correlation to Brazilian testing of sandstone. *Int. J. Rock Mech. Min. Sci.* **2013**, *60*, 1–11. [CrossRef]
33. Wei, M.; Dai, F.; Xu, N.; Zhao, T.; Xia, K.W. Experimental and numerical study on the fracture process zone and fracture toughness determination for ISRM-suggested semi-circular bend rock specimen. *Eng. Fract. Mech.* **2016**, *154*, 43–56. [CrossRef]
34. Nallathambi, P.; Karihaloo, B. Determination of the specimen size independent fracture toughness of plain concrete. *Mag. Concr. Res.* **1986**, *38*, 67–76. [CrossRef]
35. Xu, S.; Reinhardt, H. Determination of double-K criterion for crack propagation in quasi-brittle materials, Part I: Experimental investigation of crack propagation. *Int. J. Fract.* **1999**, *98*, 111–149. [CrossRef]
36. Mahabadi, O.K.; Cottrell, B.E.; Grasselli, G. An Example of Realistic Modelling of Rock Dynamics Problems: FEM/DEM Simulation of Dynamic Brazilian Test on Barre Granite. *Rock Mech. Rock Eng.* **2010**, *43*, 707–716. [CrossRef]
37. Feng, F.; Li, X.; Luo, L.; Zhao, X.; Chen, S.; Jiang, N.; Huang, W.; Wang, Y. Rockburst response in hard rock owing to excavation unloading of twin tunnels at great depth. *Bull. Eng. Geol. Environ.* **2021**, *80*, 7613–7631. [CrossRef]
38. Cai, M.; Kaiser, P.K. Numerical simulation of the Brazilian test and the tensile strength of anisotropic rocks and rocks with pre-existing cracks. *Int. J. Rock Mech. Min. Sci.* **2004**, *41*, 450–451. [CrossRef]
39. Hamdi, P.; Stead, D.; Elmo, D. Damage characterization during laboratory strength testing: A 3D-finite-discrete element approach. *Comput. Geotech.* **2014**, *60*, 33–46. [CrossRef]
40. Mitelman, A.; Elmo, D. Analysis of tunnel support design to withstand spalling induced by blasting. *Tunn. Undergr. Space Technol.* **2016**, *51*, 354–361. [CrossRef]
41. Li, X.; Feng, F.; Li, D. Numerical simulation of rock failure under static and dynamic loading by splitting test of circular ring. *Eng. Fract. Mech.* **2018**, *188*, 184–201. [CrossRef]
42. Feng, F.; Li, X.; Rostami, J.; Li, D. Modeling hard rock failure induced by structural planes around deep circular tunnels. *Eng. Fract. Mech.* **2019**, *205*, 152–174. [CrossRef]
43. Xiao, P.; Li, D.; Zhao, G.; Liu, M. Experimental and Numerical Analysis of Mode I Fracture Process of Rock by Semi-Circular Bend Specimen. *Mathematics* **2021**, *9*, 1769. [CrossRef]
44. Rockfield. *ELFEN Explicit/Implicit Manual, V.R.S.L.*; Rockfield: West Glamorgan, UK, 2013.
45. Cai, M. Fracture Initiation and Propagation in a Brazilian Disc with a Plane Interface: A Numerical Study. *Rock Mech. Rock Eng.* **2013**, *46*, 289–302. [CrossRef]
46. Li, D.; Li, B.; Han, Z.; Zhu, Q.; Liu, M. Evaluation of Bi-modular Behavior of Rocks Subjected to Uniaxial Compression and Brazilian Tensile Testing. *Rock Mech. Rock Eng.* **2021**, *54*, 3961–3975. [CrossRef]
47. Klerck, P.A. The Finite Element Modelling of Discrete Fracture in Quasi-Brittle Materials. Ph.D. Thesis, University of Wales Swansea, Wales Swansea, UK, 2000.

mathematics

MDPI

Article

Simultaneous Design of the Host Structure and the Polarisation Profile of Piezoelectric Sensors Applied to Cylindrical Shell Structures

David Ruiz [1], Sergio Horta Muñoz [2,*] and Reyes García-Contreras [2]

[1] OMEVA Research Group, Escuela de Ingeniería Industrial y Aeroespacial de Toledo, Universidad de Castilla-La Mancha, Av. Carlos III, Campus Fábrica de Armas, 45004 Toledo, Spain; david.ruiz@uclm.es

[2] Instituto de Investigación Aplicada a la Industria Aeronáutica, Escuela de Ingeniería Industrial y Aeroespacial de Toledo, Universidad de Castilla-La Mancha, Av. Carlos III, Campus Fábrica de Armas, 45004 Toledo, Spain; mariareyes.garcia@uclm.es

* Correspondence: sergio.horta@uclm.es

Abstract: Piezoelectric actuators and sensors are applied in many fields in order to produce forces or displacements with the aim of sensing, manipulating or measurement, among other functions. This study presents the numerical methodology to optimize the static response of a thick-shell structure consisting of piezoelectric sensors, based on the maximisation of the electric charge while controlling the amount of piezoelectric and material required. Two characteristic functions are involved, determining the topology of the sensor and the polarisation profile. Constraints over the reaction force are included in the optimisation problem in order to avoid singularities. The topology optimisation method is used to obtain the optimal results, where regularisation techniques (density filtering and projection) are used to avoid hinges. The minimum length scale can be controlled by the use of three different projections. As the main novelty, a displacement-controlled scheme is proposed in order to generate a robust algorithm for future studies including non-linearities.

Keywords: topology optimisation; piezoelectric actuator; shell; finite element method

MSC: 74P15

Citation: Ruiz, D.; Horta Muñoz, S.; García-Contreras, R. Simultaneous Design of the Host Structure and the Polarisation Profile of Piezoelectric Sensors Applied to Cylindrical Shell Structures. *Mathematics* **2022**, *10*, 2753. https://doi.org/10.3390/math10152753

Academic Editors: Fajie Wang and Ji Lin

Received: 14 July 2022
Accepted: 29 July 2022
Published: 3 August 2022

1. Introduction

The topology optimisation method is a conceptual tool which allows us to increase the capabilities of different types of devices. The classical mechanical problem is the minimisation of the compliance or the weight of a structure, but in the last years this method has been used in different fields of science such as electronics, propagation of waves and optics, among others. This paper is focused on the improvement of the response of piezoelectric sensors, with the objective of reducing the size of the device to increase the range of applications.

The application of piezoelectric sensors and actuators has experienced significant development in recent years. Piezoelectric sensors are devices that produce a small voltage when they are deformed, while piezoelectric actuators take advantage of the ability to generate a displacement when voltage is applied. This effect is generally used in situations that require the application of large forces in an ultra-precise way [1], as well as to generate systems capable of developing handling functions at a microscopic level [2–4].

One of the common applications is the placement of piezoelectric patches on structures subjected to vibrations, so that it is possible to monitor the state of vibrational states and control undesirable vibrations, generating so-called smart structures [5–11]. In these structures, the location of the piezoelectric elements is critical, due to the need to adjust the positioning so that their effect is maximised, reducing the cost of the material to be used. In addition, another critical design factor in structural elements is usually weight, so it is of interest to minimize the volume of material used in the host structure, while maintaining certain levels of rigidity [12,13]. Another application associated with the maximisation of electrical load obtained by piezoelectric sensors is energy harvesting systems. This has also significantly grown in recent years [14] considering that they can be used as a way for recovering waste energy from many surfaces, not only in industry, but also in our daily lives. A particular example of their applicability is the shock absorbers of vehicles which are cylindrical elements that are subjected to vibration loads during service [15].

In addition, the use of cylindrical shells is increasingly widespread in engineering applications, mainly in sectors such as civil, chemical, aerospace and naval transportation [8]. In these sectors, the structural analysis of shell elements such as pressurised tanks, aircraft fuselage, fuel tanks or fluid pipes are commonly found in literature [16,17]. These structures have characteristics such as high rigidity and lightweight, which leads to their application in loading conditions resulting in high level of stresses. It is interesting to use piezoelectric elements for the purpose of Structural Health Monitoring (SHM), or to modify the shape of the structure to improve its structural response [18,19] or aerodynamics [20]. There are numerous works that seek to analyse the response of shell-type structures with piezoelectric layers from the analytical, numerical and experimental points of view [21–23]. For instance, Yue et al. [9] experimentally measured the capacity for sensing and vibration control with piezoelectric patches in a paraboloidal shell structure, which can be implemented in structonic systems typical of aerospace sector. Similarly, Li et al. [8] theoretically estimated and experimentally validated the effect of the orientation of diagonal piezoelectric sensors in a cylindrical shell excited by piezoelectric actuators. It is also worth mentioning in this field the work of Varelis and Saravanos [24], in which the ability to predict the non-linear electromechanical response of laminated piezoelectric shell under buckling and elastic instability is analytically demonstrated. In this work, a commonly used iterative technique is maintained, i.e., Newton–Raphson, therefore the Cylindrical Arc-Length method was applied in order to overcome the snap-through points.

Previous works [13,25,26] have shown that the implementation of topological optimisation on numerical models based on the Finite Element Method (FEM) allows, simultaneously, an optimizing host structure and a polarisation profile of the electrodes. These works were carried out on different geometries in the form of flat plates and one-dimensional beams. A similar work, applied in this case to curved shell-type structures, was carried out by Donoso et al. [27], but limited to the design of the polarisation profile.

Nevertheless, none of the previously mentioned studies apply topological optimisation to the simultaneous design of the support structure and the polarisation profile in shell elements. The present work develops the numerical modelling that allows this optimal design, maximizing the electric energy produced and allowing the application of restrictions on the volume of material, in order to achieve a light and low-cost structure. In addition, regularisation techniques [28–30] are used in order to avoid the appearance of hinges. Unlike previous works by the authors [13,25,26], a control scheme based on the application of displacement was specifically developed, in contrast to the usual approach of the compliance optimisation problem which takes the applied force as a reference. This control scheme may avoid a lack of convergence when snap-through issues arise [31,32].

The work is divided as follows. Section 2 describes the mathematical formulation of the electric charge and the mechanical elastic response of the shell. The mathematical formulation of the optimisation problem is presented in Section 3. Numerical results are found in Section 4. Finally, the conclusions of the work are shown in Section 5.

2. Formulation of the Problem

2.1. Governing Equations

The computation of the electric charge q, which represents the capacity of the piezoelectric sensor, is obtained following Equation (1) [33]. This equation is simplified considering the negligible effect of the piezoelectric layer on the stiffness of the structure and the piezoelectric isotropy ($e_{31} = e_{32}$) of the sensor [27].

$$q = e_{31} \int_{\Omega} \chi_p(x_1, x_2)[\varepsilon_{11} + \varepsilon_{22}]\mathrm{d}\Omega = e_{31} \int_{\Omega} \chi_p(x_1, x_2)\left[\frac{\partial u}{\partial x_1} + \frac{\partial v}{\partial x_2} + x_3\left(\frac{\partial \phi_2}{\partial x_1} - \frac{\partial \phi_1}{\partial x_2}\right)\right]\mathrm{d}\Omega, \tag{1}$$

where (u, v) are the translational in-plane displacements, (ϕ_1, ϕ_2) the rotation over the x_1 and x_2-axis, respectively, Ω is the design domain and e_{31} is the piezoelectric constant, i.e., a material property. $\chi_p \in \{-1, 0, 1\}$ is a characteristic function that represents the polarity of the surface electrode, ε_{11} and ε_{22} are the in-plane normal strains.

The displacements and rotations are calculated by solving the equilibrium equation:

$$\begin{cases} -\mathrm{div}(\mathbf{E_s}(\chi_s) : \boldsymbol{\varepsilon}) &= f_v, \quad \text{in } \Omega \\ (\mathbf{E_s}(\chi_s) : \boldsymbol{\varepsilon}) \cdot \mathbf{n} &= f_s, \quad \text{in } \Gamma_f \end{cases},$$

subject to the boundary conditions:

$$\begin{cases} u, v, w &= 0, \quad \text{in } \Gamma_c \\ u &= u_{in} \quad \text{in } \Gamma_u \\ v &= v_{in} \quad \text{in } \Gamma_v \\ w &= w_{in} \quad \text{in } \Gamma_w \end{cases},$$

with w the vertical displacement, $\mathbf{E_s}$ the stiffness tensor, $\boldsymbol{\varepsilon}$ the infinitesimal strain tensor, f_v and f_s the volumetric and surface forces, respectively. Γ_f and Γ_c represent the boundary of Ω where forces are imposed and displacements are constraint, respectively, $\mathbf{n}$ the normal vector of the boundary and u_{in}, v_{in} and w_{in} the displacements imposed in Γ_u, Γ_v and Γ_w. $\chi_s \in \{0, 1\}$ represents the host structural variable that defines void or solid, respectively.

2.2. Finite Element Model

Flat thick-shell formulation is developed based on Reissner-Mindlin plate theory for a bidimensional finite element consisting of four nodes with six degrees of freedom (DOF), three displacements u, v and w, and three rotations ϕ_1, ϕ_2 and ϕ_3 [34,35], described with regard to an element local coordinate system (x_1, x_2, x_3). Displacement and rotations are defined independently and therefore they are interpolated separately. The interpolation of in-plane displacements, associated to membrane behaviour, is shown in Equation (2).

$$\begin{bmatrix} \tilde{u} \\ \tilde{v} \end{bmatrix} = \mathbf{N_m} \begin{bmatrix} u_i \\ v_i \end{bmatrix}, \tag{2}$$

where $\tilde{u}$, $\tilde{v}$ are the element interpolated displacements, $\mathbf{N_m}$ is the shape functions matrix for a quadrinodal membrane element and subscript $i \in \{1, 2, 3, 4\}$ refers to the specific node. The bending DOFs, representing the out-of-plane displacements and rotations, are interpolated applying bending shape functions as shown in Equation (3).

$$\begin{bmatrix} \tilde{w} \\ \tilde{\phi_1} \\ \tilde{\phi_2} \end{bmatrix} = \mathbf{N_b} \begin{bmatrix} w_i \\ \phi_{1i} \\ \phi_{2i} \end{bmatrix}, \tag{3}$$

with $\mathbf{N_b}$ being the bending shape functions matrix.

The stiffness matrix in local element coordinates is obtained by concatenating the membrane matrix (defined in Equation (4)), corresponding to the two in-plane translational displacements (u and v), while the bending terms (Equation (5)) are obtained from the thick-plane element, which consists of three DOFs (w, ϕ_1 and ϕ_2). The sixth DOF, ϕ_3, is assigned an arbitrary stiffness, much lower than the rest of components, taking into consideration that this rotation does not contribute to strain energy [34]. Nevertheless, this DOF is required for consistency of matrices when transforming to the global coordinate system. The integration in the domain of the element (Ω^e) is reduced to an integration in the area (A), described in the x_1 and x_2 directions. This integration is performed numerically using a reduced integration scheme based on Gaussian Quadrature to avoid shear locking.

$$\mathbf{K_m} = \int_{\Omega^e} \mathbf{B_m}^T \mathbf{C_m} \mathbf{B_m} \, \mathrm{d}\Omega^e = \int_A \left(\int_0^h \mathrm{d}x_3 \right) \mathbf{B_m}^T \mathbf{C_m} \mathbf{B_m} \, \mathrm{d}A = h \int_A \mathbf{B_m}^T \mathbf{C_m} \mathbf{B_m} \, \mathrm{d}A \tag{4}$$

$$\mathbf{K_b} = \int_A \mathbf{B}_b^T \frac{h^3}{12} \mathbf{C}_b \mathbf{B}_b \, \mathrm{d}A + \int_A \mathbf{B}_s^T hk \mathbf{C}_s \mathbf{B}_s \, \mathrm{d}A, \tag{5}$$

where $\mathbf{B}$ is the derivative of the shape functions, $\mathbf{C}$ the material stiffness tensor, particularised in this study for a linear isotropic elastic material and h is the thickness of the element (dimension in x_3-direction). The subscripts b, m and s represent bending, membrane and shear, respectively. Finally, k represents the stiffness associated with the drilling DOF (ϕ_3), the value of which is about one-thousandth of the smallest diagonal element of the element matrix stiffness, following recommendations in the literature [34]. More information about the definition of these parameters could be found in finite element reference books [34,35].

Additionally, with the aim of computing the electric charge generated by the piezoelectric elements, it is necessary to compute the sum of strains in each element. This is defined in local coordinates in Equation (6), which can be related to the discretised problem by means of the derivative of shape functions.

$$\begin{bmatrix} \tilde{\varepsilon}_{11} \\ \tilde{\varepsilon}_{22} \\ \tilde{\varepsilon}_{12} \end{bmatrix} = \begin{bmatrix} \dfrac{\partial \tilde{u}}{\partial x_1} \\ \dfrac{\partial \tilde{v}}{\partial x_2} \\ \dfrac{\partial \tilde{u}}{\partial x_2} + \dfrac{\partial \tilde{v}}{\partial x_1} \end{bmatrix} - x_3 \begin{bmatrix} -\dfrac{\partial \tilde{\phi}_2}{\partial x_1} \\ \dfrac{\partial \tilde{\phi}_1}{\partial x_2} \\ \dfrac{\partial \tilde{\phi}_1}{\partial x_1} - \dfrac{\partial \tilde{\phi}_2}{\partial x_2} \end{bmatrix} = \mathbf{B_m} \begin{bmatrix} u_i \\ v_i \end{bmatrix} - x_3 \mathbf{B_b} \begin{bmatrix} w_i \\ \phi_{1i} \\ \phi_{2i} \end{bmatrix}. \tag{6}$$

As the geometry to be modelled is not coplanar, the elements have different local orientations, therefore it is necessary to compute the global stiffness matrix in global coordinates, which are called xyz. The rotation could be performed by means of a transformation matrix defined by the direction cosines relating to both coordinate systems.

3. Topology Optimisation Problem and Sensitivity Analysis

In this work we aim to maximize the electric charge produced in a cylindrical-type structure submitted to a static deformation. The expression for the discretised objective function is:

$$q = \mathbf{F}^T(\rho_p, \rho_s)\mathbf{U} = \sum_e^{n_{el}} \rho_{pe} \rho_{se}^3 \mathbf{B}_e^T \mathbf{U}_e, \tag{7}$$

where n_{el} is the number of finite elements, $\mathbf{B}_e$ is the discretisation of the strain displacement matrix, $\mathbf{U}_e$ is the vector with the displacement of the element e. The variable ρ_{pe} defines the sign of the polarisation profile, while the role of the relaxed variable ρ_{se} is to penalize the electric charge generated by void elements [36]. The piezoelectric property e_{31} has been removed from the objective function, since a constant does not affect the optimal design. The constraint over the maximum volume fraction is included in the problem, as this usually improves the convergence of the optimisation algorithm. The global stiffness of the structure is controlled by adding two constraints over the reaction forces in the structure. This ensures that the point where the displacement is imposed is connected with the boundary conditions. Finally, taking into account Equation (7), the formulation of the discretised problem is stated as follows:

$$\max_{\rho_s, \rho_p} : \quad q$$

subject to:

$$\begin{cases} \tilde{\boldsymbol{\rho}}_s &= \mathbf{H}(\boldsymbol{\rho}_s) \\ \hat{\boldsymbol{\rho}}_s &= \mathbf{P}(\tilde{\boldsymbol{\rho}}_s) \\ \mathbf{K}(\hat{\boldsymbol{\rho}}_s)\mathbf{U} &= \mathbf{R} \\ \mathbf{L}_u^T\mathbf{U} &= u_{in} \\ \mathbf{v}^T(\hat{\boldsymbol{\rho}}_s) &\leq V_0 \mid \Omega \mid \\ \mathbf{L}_r^T\mathbf{R} &\leq r_{max} \\ \mathbf{L}_r^T\mathbf{R} &\geq r_{min} \end{cases},$$

where $\mathbf{L}_r$ is a vector of zeros with the value 1 in the constrained degrees of freedom, $\mathbf{R}$ is the reaction force vector, $\tilde{\boldsymbol{\rho}}_s$ is the filtered structural density, $\hat{\boldsymbol{\rho}}_s$ is the projected density [37], $\mathbf{L}_u$ is a vector of zeros with the value 1 in the degree of freedom where the displacement is imposed, u_{in} is the fixed displacement, $\mathbf{v}$ is a vector containing the measure of the elements, V_0 is the maximum volume fraction, $\mid \Omega \mid$ is the measure of the design domain, finally, r_{max} and r_{min} are the maximum and minimum reaction force allowed, respectively, used to avoid singular solutions.

The well-known Solid Isotropic Material with Penalisation (SIMP) method [28] is used to penalize intermediate densities. The expression for a smoothed threshold projection [29] based on the hyperbolic tangent function is:

$$\hat{\rho}_{se} = \frac{\tanh(\beta\eta) + \tanh(\beta(\tilde{\rho}_{se} - \eta))}{\tanh(\beta\eta) + \tanh(\beta(1 - \eta))}, \tag{8}$$

where $\eta \in [0, 1]$ and β are tuning parameters that define the threshold and the sharpness of the function, respectively. The filtered densities of Equation (8) are projected to 0 or 1 depending if these value are smaller or bigger than the threshold η. The filtered densities $\tilde{\boldsymbol{\rho}}$ are expressed as [30]:

$$\tilde{\rho}_{se} = \frac{\sum_j^{n_{el}} d_e(\mathbf{x}_j)\rho_{sj}}{\sum_j^{n_{el}} d_e(\mathbf{x}_j)},$$

where $\mathbf{x}_j$ is the barycentre of the j-th element, and the weighting function $d_e(\mathbf{x}_j)$ is given by the cone-shape function:

$$d_e(\mathbf{x}_j) = \max\{R_f - ||\mathbf{x}_j - \mathbf{x}_e||, 0\},$$

where R_f is the filter radius.

The use of the filtering technique together with the projection method ensures a mesh-independent 0–1 design. As shown in [25], the polarisation variable $\boldsymbol{\rho}_p$ does not need any kind of regularisation.

3.1. Robust Formulation

This section presents the robust formulation of the problem, which was introduced in [29]. This consists of the use of three different projections called erode, intermediate and dilate and from now on, the projection will be represented with the superscript (m) for each projection ((e), (i) and (d), respectively). The implementation of this approach ensures a minimum length scale in both void and solid regions, hence avoiding the appearance of hinges.

The robust topology optimisation problem is written in terms of a min-max problem, which is not differentiable. The problem is then reformulated using the so-called bound formulation:

$$\max_{\boldsymbol{\rho}_s, \boldsymbol{\rho}_p} : \quad \alpha \tag{9}$$

subject to:

$$\left\{\begin{array}{rcl} q^{(m)} & \geq & \alpha \\ \tilde{\boldsymbol{\rho}}_s & = & \mathbf{H}(\boldsymbol{\rho}_s) \\ \hat{\boldsymbol{\rho}}_s^{(m)} & = & \mathbf{P}^{(m)}(\tilde{\boldsymbol{\rho}}_s) \\ \mathbf{K}(\hat{\boldsymbol{\rho}}_s^{(m)})\mathbf{U}^{(m)} & = & \mathbf{R}^{(m)} \\ \mathbf{L}_u^T\mathbf{U}^{(m)} & = & u_{in} \\ \mathbf{v}^T\hat{\boldsymbol{\rho}}_s^{(d)} & \leq & V_0^* \mid \Omega \mid \\ \mathbf{L}_r^T\mathbf{R}^{(m)} & \leq & r_{max} \\ \mathbf{L}_r^T\mathbf{R}^{(m)} & \geq & r_{min} \\ m & \equiv & \{e,i,d\}, \end{array}\right. \tag{10}$$

where α is an additional bound variable, superscript (m) represents the projection and $V_0^* = \dfrac{V_0}{V^{(i)}}V^{(d)}$ is the maximum volume fraction allowed for the dilate projection. This value is updated every 20 iterations. This formulation solves the non-differentiability issue with the max–min function. It is important to remark that the equilibrium equation and the constraints of the reaction forces must be computed for each projection.

3.2. Computation of Sensitivities

The optimisation problem is solved using the Method of the Moving Asymptotes (MMA) [38]. This algorithm needs the partial derivatives with respect to the variables $\boldsymbol{\rho}_s$ and $\boldsymbol{\rho}_p$.

The derivatives of the elastic problem equations (the equilibrium equations and the constraints) are straightforward, and they are not included in this work for the sake of brevity. The derivative of the function q with respect to $\boldsymbol{\rho}_s$ is computed using the chain rule:

$$\frac{\partial q}{\partial \rho_{se}} = \frac{\partial q}{\partial \hat{\rho}_{se}}\frac{\partial \hat{\rho}_{se}}{\partial \tilde{\rho}_{se}}\frac{\partial \tilde{\rho}_{se}}{\partial \rho_{se}},$$

with:

$$\frac{\partial q}{\partial \hat{\rho}_{se}} = \left(\frac{\partial \mathbf{F}^T}{\partial \hat{\rho}_{se}}\mathbf{U} + \mathbf{F}^T\frac{\partial \mathbf{U}}{\partial \hat{\rho}_{se}}\right).$$

Note that the adjoint method can be used to circumvent the computational cost of computing the derivative of the displacement vector $\mathbf{U}$. The derivatives of q with respect to $\boldsymbol{\rho}_p$ is:

$$\frac{\partial q}{\partial \rho_{pe}} = \frac{\partial \mathbf{F}^T}{\partial \rho_{pe}}\mathbf{U}.$$

In practice, it is convenient to work with normalised parameters in order to avoid computations with numbers with different magnitude order. The electrical charge is normalised with the electrical charge generated by the homogeneous design.

A summary of the process is shown in Algorithm 1.

Algorithm 1: Algorithm and computational implementation

Set : material properties, geometry and BC's
Set : Optimisation parameters
Define : initialisation ρ_p and ρ_s
Compute: reference charge q_{ref}
Set : Optimisation method tolerance *tol*
While $e > tol$
  Filtering and projection $\rho_s \rightarrow \tilde{\rho}_s \rightarrow \hat{\rho}_s$;
  Assembly of global matrix $\mathbf{K}(\hat{\rho}_s)$ and vector $\mathbf{F}(\hat{\rho}_s, \rho_p)$;
  Get vector **U**;
  Compute objective function $c = q$;
  Compute constraints;
  Calculate derivatives;
  Update variables with MMA (ρ_s^*, ρ_p^*);
  Define convergence variable $e = ||(\rho_s^*, \rho_p^*) - (\rho_s, \rho_p)||$;
end

4. Numerical Examples

Commercial software Matlab R2020b has been used to solve the finite element models and the optimisation problem proposed in this work. The results obtained, in terms of force, displacement, stress and strain fields, have been validated by means of the comparison with a commercial FEM software, i.e., Abaqus 2019 [39].

4.1. First Example

The domain Ω is defined as a semicylindrical shell. The dimensions are $L_x = 1$ m and $L_y = 1$ m with a global thickness of $t = 0.01$ m. The Young's modulus of the material is set to $E = 1$ Pa and the Poisson's ratio to $\nu = 0.3$.

The proposed structure is discretised in 60×60 elements. The scheme of the structure and its boundary conditions are shown in Figure 1. The displacements and rotations over the red lines are fixed to zero (clamped), while vertical displacement is imposed at the coordinates $(x, y, z) = (0, 0.5, 0.5)$ m with a value of $u_{in} = 0.15$ mm.

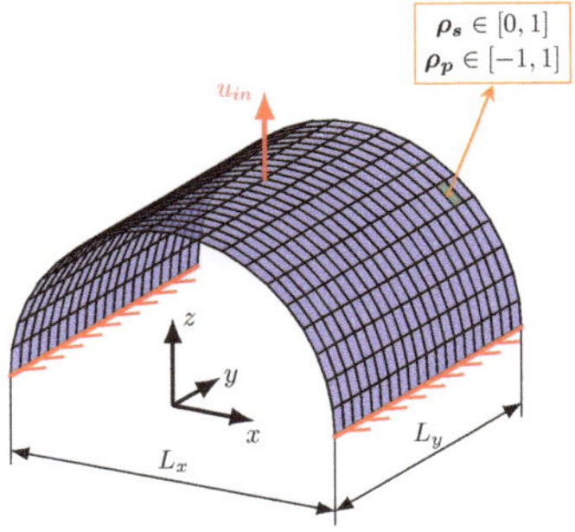

Figure 1. Dimensions and boundary conditions.

This case study is focused in obtaining the optimal electrode profile ρ_p that will be used as initialisation in the rest of the examples. Since the host structure ρ_s is fixed, it makes no sense to add constraints over the reaction force.

The result of the optimisation process is shown in Figure 2. The structure variable ρ_s is represented in Figure 2 (left), with the black colour showing solid areas. The electrode profile appears at the centre, where blue and pink mean electrodes of different polarity. The whole structure including electrodes is depicted in Figure 2 (right).

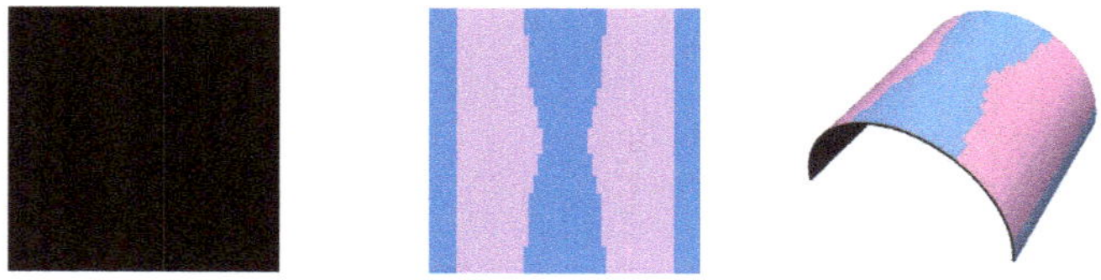

Figure 2. Structure layout ρ_s (**left**), electrode profile ρ_p (**centre**) and 3D design (**right**) for the first example.

The reference value used to compare the results is the cost generated by the homogeneous design $\rho_s = 1$ and $\rho_p = 1$. The cost excluding the piezoelectric constant e_{31}, is $\frac{c_{ref}}{e_{31}} = 0.721\ \text{m}^2$. For the rest of examples, the objective function is the non-dimensional parameter defined as: $\lambda = \frac{c}{c_{ref}}$.

The value of the objective function for this first example is $\lambda_1 = 31.92$, showing the importance of the optimisation process. This value is larger than the reference, since the homogeneous electrode $\rho_p = 1$ is far from being a good design. The polarisation profile in Figure 2 shows that approximately half of the surface shell is subjected to strain with the opposite sign, and then most of the electrical charge produced by the positive polarity is cancelled with charge generated by the negative electrode.

The result of the optimisation process shows that the electrode profile obtained for each finite element is related to its curvature. This example clearly demonstrates that the optimisation of only one variable, the electrode—polarisation ρ_p—increases the electric charge generated by the sensor.

4.2. Second Example

The volume fraction is fixed to $V_0 = 0.5$ and the reaction force to $r = -3 \times 10^{-9}$ N. The values of r_{min} and r_{max} are computed by subtracting and adding a small value $\epsilon = r/100$. Concerning the tuning parameters of the filter and the projections, the filter radius is set to $R_f = 0.1$ m, the smoothness of the projection to $\beta = 1$ at the beginning of the iterative process, and it doubles the value every 40 iterations up to $\beta = 8$. The thresholds for the three projections are $\eta_e = 0.7$, $\eta_i = 0.5$ and $\eta_d = 0.3$, for the erode, intermediate and dilate projection, respectively.

The variable ρ_s is initialised with a homogeneous design according to the volume constraint, and ρ_p with the optimised polarity profile of the previous example. The optimal design is shown in Figure 3 (right).

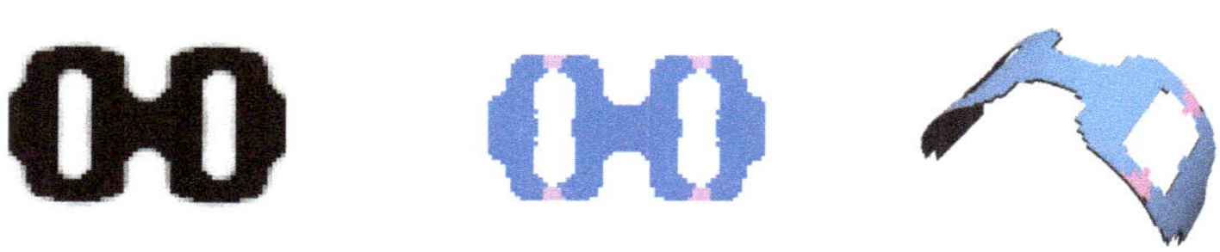

Figure 3. Structure layout ρ_s (**left**), electrode profile ρ_p (**centre**) and 3D design (**right**) for the second example.

The value of the objective function for the optimum design is $\lambda_2 = 20.91$. This result surpasses the reference charge, however, this value is smaller than λ_1. This is due to the maximum volume fraction imposed. The smaller the volume fraction is, the bigger the displacements are since the structure is less stiff, but the region Ω is also smaller. It is very convenient to use this constraint as this improves the convergence of the topology optimisation problem, as well as this can be used to control the amount of material if we have in mind the fabrication cost, the weight or the size of the structure.

The structural variable ρ_s depicted in Figure 3 (left) shows that the whole structure is continuous, in the way that the point of application of the mechanical force is connected with the clamped edges. The robust scheme is working properly, which is corroborated by the absence of hinges.

4.3. Third Example

For this case study, the value of constraint over the reaction force is fixed to $r = -4 \times 10^{-9}$ N, while the rest of parameters do not change. This variation of the reaction force increases the structure stiffness, since the imposed displacement is the same as in the previous example. The results are shown in Figure 4.

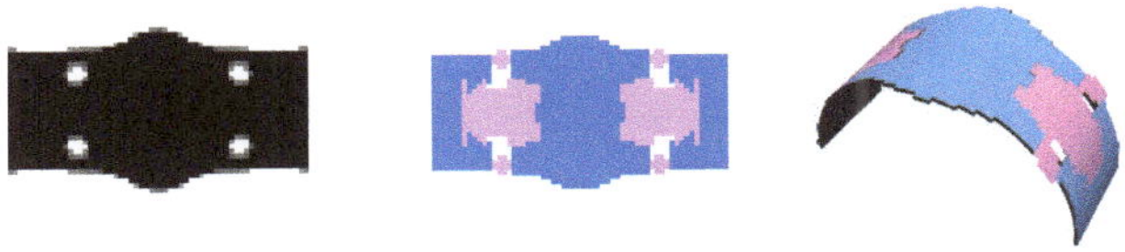

Figure 4. Structure layout ρ_s (**left**), electrode profile ρ_p (**centre**) and 3D design (**right**) for the third example.

The value of the objective function for the optimum design is $\lambda_3 = 60.44$. With this method, the stiffness of the structure can be modelled by imposing a different constraint r. This parameter can be adapted to the function of the application, since this is part of the input data.

In this last example the structure layout ρ_s is stiffer than in the previous case. This is due to the reaction force, which is 25% higher than in the second example. This parameter can be fixed depending on the proposed application of the sensor.

4.4. Validation of the Results

The finite element problem has been solved by using an ad hoc script developed with the software Matlab. In order to validate the results obtained, the displacement field (the control variable in the optimisation problem) has been checked with Abaqus in the reference design (first example).

For the reference example, the deformed structure is shown in Figure 5, where the displacement has been scaled in order to better observe the deformed structure. It can be visually verified that the deformation obtained with both softwares is similar.

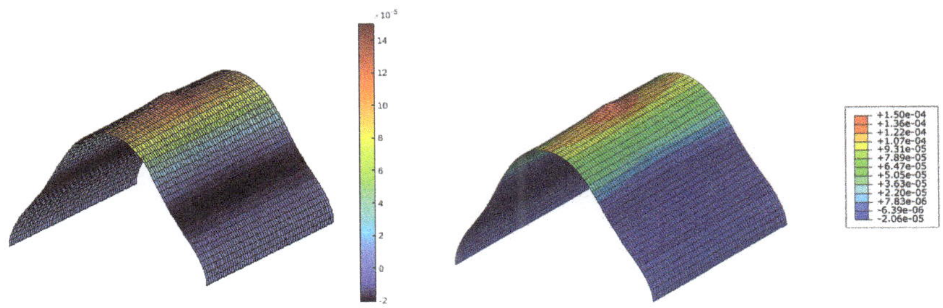

Figure 5. Deformation of the structure obtained with Matlab (**left**) and Abaqus (**right**).

Additionally, to corroborate that the finite element method has been correctly implemented, the vertical displacement of the midline (arc with coordinate $y = L_y/2$ following Figure 1) of the sensor is compared. To avoid a high relative error, the infinity norm has been used to compare the difference between both softwares:

$$||\tilde{\mathbf{w}}_M - \tilde{\mathbf{w}}_A||_\infty = 2.3740 \times 10^{-6} \text{ m},$$

where $\tilde{\mathbf{w}}$ represents the vertical displacement computed at the midline, and subscripts M and A stand for Matlab and Abaqus, respectively.

The vertical reaction forces computed at the node where the displacement is imposed are $\tilde{r}_M = 7.477 \times 10^{-9}$ N and $\tilde{r}_A = 7.551 \times 10^{-9}$ N. With a difference of $\approx$1% we can consider the results obtained with Matlab valid.

5. Conclusions

In this work, a systematic procedure to maximize the electric charge generated by a semi-cylindrical piezoelectric sensor is presented. The objective function is computed in terms of two variables related through the deformation of the structure, the topology of the sensor and the polarisation profile of the electrode. The main novelty presented in this paper is the simultaneous optimisation of both variables.

The advantage of solving an optimisation problem is shown in several optimal designs, showing that the electric charge of the device has been improved for different volume fractions and values of the reaction force. The well-known issue of the appearance of hinges is overcome by implementing a robust scheme with three different projections. This regularisation also allows us to control the minimum length scale.

The shell modelled in this work is subjected to small displacements and small strains, but a control scheme based on the application of displacement (instead of controlling the applied force) is implemented with the objective of modelling a geometrically non-linear problem in the future.

In order to validate the mechanical response of the structure, the displacement field of the shell is computed with two different commercial softwares—Matlab and Abaqus.

Author Contributions: Conceptualisation, D.R.; investigation, D.R. and S.H.M.; writing—original draft preparation, D.R. and S.H.M.; writing—review and editing, D.R., S.H.M. and R.G.-C.; supervision, R.G.-C.; funding acquisition, D.R., S.H.M. and R.G.-C. All authors have read and agreed to the published version of the manuscript.

Funding: This project has been funded through grant PID2020-116207GB-I00 from the Spanish Ministerio de Ciencia e Innovación and SBPLY/19/180501/000110 from Junta de Castilla-La Mancha. In addition, the authors also acknowledge the financial support provided by the University of Castilla-La Mancha and the ERDF under the grants 2018/11744 and 2020/3771.

Institutional Review Board Statement: Not applicable.

Informed Consent Statement: Not applicable.

Data Availability Statement: Not applicable.

Conflicts of Interest: The authors declare no conflict of interest.

References

1. Zhang, P. Sensors and actuators. In *Advanced Industrial Control Technology*; Zhang, P., Ed.; William Andrew Publishing: Oxford, UK, 2010; Chapter 3, pp. 73–116.
2. Manzaneque, T.; Ruiz-Díez, V.; Hernando-García, J.; Ababneh, A.; Al-Omari, A.; Kucera, M.; Bittner, A.; Schmid, U.; Seidel, H.; Sánchez-Rojas, J. Piezoelectric in-plane microplate resonators based on contour and flexure-actuated modes. *Microsyst. Technol.* **2014**, *20*, 691–699. [CrossRef]
3. Toledo, J.; Ruiz-Díez, V.; Diaz-Molina, A.; Ruiz, D.; Donoso, A.; Bellido, J.C.; Wistrela, E.; Kucera, M.; Schmid, U.; Hernando-García, J.; et al. Design and Characterisation of In-Plane Piezoelectric Microactuators. *Actuators* **2017**, *6*, 19. [CrossRef]
4. Toledo, J.; Ruiz-Díez, V.; Hernando-García, J.; Sánchez-Rojas, J.L. Piezoelectric Actuators for Tactile and Elasticity Sensing. *Actuators* **2020**, *9*, 21. [CrossRef]

5. Kim, S.J.; Hwang, J.S.; Mok, J.; Koh, H.M. Active vibration control of composite shell structure using modal sensor/actuator system. In Proceedings of the Smart Structures and Materials 2001: Smart Structures and Integrated Systems, Newport Beach, CA, USA, 5–8 March 2001; Davis, L.P., Ed.; International Society for Optics and Photonics, SPIE: Bellingham, WA, USA, 2001; Volume 4327, pp. 688–697.
6. Kumar, R.; Mishra, B.K.; Jain, S.C. Thermally induced vibration control of cylindrical shell using piezoelectric sensor and actuator. *Int. J. Adv. Manuf. Technol.* **2008**, *38*, 551–562. [CrossRef]
7. Kucuk, I.; Yildirim, K.; Adali, S. Optimal piezoelectric control of a plate subject to time-dependent boundary moments and forcing function for vibration damping. *Comput. Math. Appl.* **2015**, *69*, 291–303. [CrossRef]
8. Li, H.; Zhang, X.; Tzou, H. Diagonal piezoelectric sensors on cylindrical shells. *J. Sound Vib.* **2017**, *400*, 201–212. [CrossRef]
9. Yue, H.; Lu, Y.; Deng, Z.; Tzou, H. Modal sensing and control of paraboloidal shell structronic system. *Mech. Syst. Signal Process.* **2018**, *100*, 647–661. [CrossRef]
10. Rahman, N.; Alam, M.; Junaid, M. Active vibration control of composite shallow shells: An integrated approach. *J. Mech. Eng. Sci.* **2018**, *12*, 3354–3369. [CrossRef]
11. Jamshidi, R.; Jafari, A. Conical shell vibration control with distributed piezoelectric sensor and actuator layer. *Compos. Struct.* **2021**, *256*, 113107. [CrossRef]
12. Bendsøe, M.P.; Sigmund, O. *Extensions and Applications*; Springer: Berlin/Heidelberg, Germany, 2004; pp. 71–158.
13. Ruiz, D.; Díaz-Molina, A.; Sigmund, O.; Donoso, A.; Bellido, J.C.; Sánchez-Rojas, J.L. Optimal design of robust piezoelectric unimorph microgrippers. *Appl. Math. Modell.* **2018**, *55*, 1–12. [CrossRef]
14. Lv, X.; Ji, Y.; Zhao, H.; Zhang, J.; Zhang, G.; Zhang, L. Research Review of a Vehicle Energy-Regenerative Suspension System. *Energies* **2020**, *13*, 441. [CrossRef]
15. Zhao, Z.; Wang, T.; Zhang, B.; Shi, J. Energy Harvesting from Vehicle Suspension System by Piezoelectric Harvester. *Math. Probl. Eng.* **2019**, *2019*, 1086983. [CrossRef]
16. Pietraszkiewicz, W.; Witkowski, W. (Eds.) *Shell Structures: Theory and Applications*; CRC Press: Boca Raton, FL, USA, 2017; Volume 4.
17. Zamani Nejad, M.; Jabbari, M.; Hadi, A. A review of functionally graded thick cylindrical and conical shells. *J. Comput. Appl. Mech.* **2017**, *48*, 357–370.
18. Schultz, M.; Hyer, M. Snap-through of unsymmetric cross-ply laminates using piezoceramic actuators. *J. Intell. Mater. Syst. Struct.* **2003**, *14*, 795–814. [CrossRef]
19. Schultz, M.R.; Hyer, M.W.; Brett Williams, R.; Keats Wilkie, W.; Inman, D.J. Snap-through of unsymmetric laminates using piezocomposite actuators. *Compos. Sci. Technol.* **2006**, *66*, 2442–2448. [CrossRef]
20. Ozaki, T.; Hamaguchi, K. Electro-Aero-Mechanical Model of Piezoelectric Direct-Driven Flapping-Wing Actuator. *Appl. Sci.* **2018**, *8*, 1699. [CrossRef]
21. Bernadou, M.; Haenel, C. Modelisation and numerical approximation of piezoelectric thin shells: Part I: The continuous problems. *Comput. Methods Appl. Mech. Eng.* **2003**, *192*, 4003–4043. [CrossRef]
22. Bernadou, M.; Haenel, C. Modelisation and numerical approximation of piezoelectric thin shells: Part II: Approximation by finite element methods and numerical experiments. *Comput. Methods Appl. Mech. Eng.* **2003**, *192*, 4045–4073. [CrossRef]
23. Bernadou, M.; Haenel, C. Modelisation and numerical approximation of piezoelectric thin shells: Part III: From the patches to the active structures. *Comput. Methods Appl. Mech. Eng.* **2003**, *192*, 4075–4107. [CrossRef]
24. Varelis, D.; Saravanos, D.A. Coupled nonlinear mechanics for the electromechanical response of multi-stable piezoelectric shallow shells with piezoelectric films. *Aerosp. Sci. Technol.* **2021**, *109*, 106444. [CrossRef]
25. Donoso, A.; Bellido, J.C. Systematic design of distributed piezoelectric modal sensors/actuators for rectangular plates by optimizing the polarisation profile. *Struct. Multidiscip. Optim.* **2009**, *38*, 347–356. [CrossRef]
26. Ruiz, D.; Horta Muñoz, S. Optimal design of electrode polarisation in piezoelectric unimorph beams to induce traveling waves. *Appl. Math. Modell.* **2021**, *99*, 1–13. [CrossRef]
27. Donoso, A.; Bellido, J.C.; Chacón, J.M. Numerical and analytical method for the design of piezoelectric modal sensors/actuators for shell-type structures. *Int. J. Numer. Methods Eng.* **2010**, *81*, 1700–1712. [CrossRef]
28. Bendsøe, M.P.; Sigmund, O. Material interpolation schemes in topology optimisation. *Arch. Appl. Mech.* **1999**, *69*, 635–654.
29. Wang, F.; Lazarov, B.S.; Sigmund, O. On projection methods, convergence and robust formulations in topology optimisation. *Struct. Multidiscip. Optim.* **2011**, *43*, 767–784. [CrossRef]
30. Bourdin, B. Filters in topology optimisation. *Int. J. Numer. Methods Eng.* **2001**, *50*, 2143–2158. [CrossRef]
31. Sekimoto, T.; Noguchi, H. Homologous Topology Optimisation in Large Displacement and Buckling Problems. *Jpn. Soc. Mech. Eng. Int. J. Ser. A* **2001**, *44*, 616–622.
32. Al-Aukaily, A.; Scott, M.H. Sensitivity Analysis for Displacement-Controlled Finite-Element Analyses. *J. Struct. Eng.* **2018**, *144*, 04017222. [CrossRef]
33. Lee, C.K.; Moon, F.C. Modal Sensors/Actuators. *J. Appl. Mech.* **1990**, *57*, 434–441. [CrossRef]
34. Neto, M.A.; Amaro, A.; Roseiro, L.; Cirne, J.; Leal, R. *Engineering Computation of Structures: The Finite Element Method*; Springer: Cham, Switzerland, 2015.
35. Benito Muñoz, J.J.; Álvarez Cabal, R.; Ureña Prieto, F.; Salete Casino, E.; Aranda Ortega, E. *Introducción al Método de los Elementos Finitos*; UNED: Madrid, Spain, 2016.

36. Ruiz, D.; Bellido, J.C.; Donoso, A.; Sánchez-Rojas, J.L. Design of in-plane piezoelectric sensors for static response by simultaneously optimizing the host structure and the electrode profile. *Struct. Multidiscip. Optim.* **2013**, *48*, 1023–1026. [CrossRef]
37. Guest, J.K.; Prévost, J.H.; Belytschko, T. Achieving minimum length scale in topology optimisation using nodal design variables and projection functions. *Int. J. Numer. Methods Eng.* **2004**, *61*, 238–254. [CrossRef]
38. Svanberg, K. The method of moving asymptotes-a new method for structural optimisation. *Int. J. Numer. Meth. Eng.* **1987**, *24*, 359–373. [CrossRef]
39. Dassault Systèmes. *Abaqus 2019 Documentation*; Dassault Systèmes: Vèlizy-Villacoublay, France, 2019.

mathematics

MDPI

Article

A Novel Divisional Bisection Method for the Symmetric Tridiagonal Eigenvalue Problem

Wei Chu [1], Yao Zhao [1,2] and Hua Yuan [1,2,*]

1 School of Naval Architecture and Ocean Engineering, Huazhong University of Sciences and Technology, Wuhan 430074, China
2 Hubei Key Laboratory of Naval Architecture and Ocean Engineering Hydrodynamics (HUST), Wuhan 430074, China
* Correspondence: yuanhua@hust.edu.cn; Tel.: +86-027-8754-3258

Abstract: The embarrassingly parallel nature of the Bisection Algorithm makes it easy and efficient to program on a parallel computer, but with an expensive time cost when all symmetric tridiagonal eigenvalues are wanted. In addition, few methods can calculate a single eigenvalue in parallel for now, especially in a specific order. This paper solves the issue with a new approach that can parallelize the Bisection iteration. Some pseudocodes and numerical results are presented. It shows our algorithm reduces the time cost by more than 35–70% compared to the Bisection algorithm while maintaining its accuracy and flexibility.

Keywords: symmetric tridiagonal matrix; eigenvalue solver; matrix division; parallel algorithm

MSC: 65F15

Citation: Chu, W.; Zhao, Y.; Yuan, W. A Novel Divisional Bisection Method for the Symmetric Tridiagonal Eigenvalue Problem. *Mathematics* **2022**, *10*, 2782. https://doi.org/10.3390/math10152782

Academic Editors: Fajie Wang and Ji Lin

Received: 10 July 2022
Accepted: 4 August 2022
Published: 5 August 2022

1. Introduction

The symmetric tridiagonal matrices often arise as primary data in many computational quantum physical [1,2], mathematical [3–5], dynamical [6,7], computational quantum chemical [8,9], signal processing [10], or even medical [11] problems and hence are important. The current software reduces the generalized and the standard symmetric eigenproblems to a symmetric tridiagonal eigenproblem as a common practice [10,12,13]. What is more interesting is that the opposite path is also productive. Marques [14] computes the SVD of a bidiagonal matrix through the eigenpairs of an associated symmetric tridiagonal matrix. In this paper, we focus on symmetric eigenvalue solving.

People desire a parallel algorithm of good performance and flexibility, especially today as CPU cores and massively parallel technology have skyrocketed. We noticed that in many application scenes of eigenvalue computation, for example, in dynamics, it is often necessary to solve only the first few orders of eigenvalues of a large matrix. The desire for the largest eigenvalue is also common in practice [15–17]. However, the current QR, MRRR (Multiple Relatively Robust Representations), DC (Divided and Conquer), and Bisection algorithms do not seem to perform sufficient parallel operations if the number of CPU cores (say, 40) is significantly larger than the number of eigenvalues (say, 1) to be solved.

The most popular algorithm at present for a symmetric eigenproblem is the QR algorithm because of its stability and computational efficiency [18–20]. When only eigenvalues are desired, all square roots can be eliminated in the QR transformation. This was first observed by Ortega and Kaiser in 1963 [21] and a fast, stable algorithm was developed by Pal, Walker, and Kahan (PWK) in 1969 [22]. However, the parallelization of the QR algorithm is a problem, in this case, requiring more than a straightforward transcription of serial code to parallel code. Many researchers have made attempts, such as blocking the given matrix [23], look-ahead strategies [24], load-balancing schemes [25], pipelining of iterations [20,26], or dimensional analysis [27]. However, few seem adequate for the symmetric tridiagonal matrices because most of those attempts are for dense matrices. One more essential trouble is that the QR algorithm is unsuitable for computing one or several selected eigenvalues. The MRRR algorithm [28] has a similar disadvantage as it is based on the DQDS algorithm [29,30] to compute the eigenvalues. In detail, both QR and DQDS algorithms use a designed shift, for example, Wilkinson's shift, to obtain a high-order asymptotic convergence rate. As a consequence, the order of eigenvalue convergence is not manageable.

The DC algorithm [31] is easily parallelizable and has developed well in recent years [32,33]. However, efficient parallel implementations are not straightforward to program, and the decision to switch from task to data parallelism depends on the characteristics of the underlying machine. Its space complexity is also an obvious shortcoming. In fact, even the "dstedc" routine corresponding to the DC algorithm in LAPACK calls "dsterf" when only eigenvalues are computed, i.e., the PWK version of the QR algorithm. The DC algorithm also does not support the computation of eigenvalues of a specific order or within a particular interval, let alone parallelization.

The Bisection method [34] calculates eigenvalues in any order or interval with a variable precision, which is suitable and handy for the mixed precision calculation [35]. Its embarrassingly parallel nature and high accuracy make it implemented in current software libraries for distributed memory computers. In addition, the Bisection method has a parallelizing efficiency of 1 (unless the number of computational cores is larger than the matrix dimension, which is rare) and little communication cost, which makes it highly advantageous in massively parallel computations. However, parallel Bisection can only be implemented if the number of unsolved eigenvalues is no less than the number of CPU cores. In addition, the computational efficiency of the Bisection method disconcerts.

We briefly summarize here: QR, DC, and MRRR algorithms are only available for obtaining all the eigenvalues. The Bisection method has excellent accuracy and flexibility but with limited efficiency when computing all the eigenvalues. All existing methods fail to calculate a single eigenvalue in parallel. Therefore, this paper has two goals: (1) to give a new Bisection method that can perform parallel operations with any number of threads when computing one specific eigenvalue; (2) to improve the efficiency of the Bisection method when calculating a major set of or all eigenvalues.

Section 2 presents some theorems, lemmas, corollaries, and equations. They are demonstrated for the design of Algorithms 4 and 5 and the accuracy analyses in Section 5. The big view of our method for one specific eigenvalue is dividing the matrix for parallel computing and merging them for the final result, with an insignificant time cost in the merging process. For the Bisection method to retain its ability to compute eigenvalues of any order, our strategy is to make the underlying iteration loop parallelizable. Instead of counting Sturm sequences iteratively, Algorithm 4 (provided in Section 3) distributes the task into the submatrices, which can be fulfilled independently. To merge these submatrices, in Section 2, we give a special determinant Formula (2) (with our new proof inspired by Maxwell's reciprocity theorem), Corollary 1, and Theorem 3.

We give Algorithm 5 in Section 4 as a modified Bisection method for all the eigenvalues. To reduce the number of iterations, the key is called a faster root-finder, which has less than 20% time cost of the traditional Bisection iteration process. However, it can only work when an isolating interval, i.e., an interval within only one eigenvalue, is obtained. Theorem 3 provides an excellent approach to such an interval, and the calculation is executed by dividing and merging. To accelerate convergence, we prove Theorem 4 in Section 4 and utilize the deflation property in Algorithm 5.

In Section 5, we analyze the accuracy and present the numerical experiments. Section 5.2 shows the accuracy results and Section 5.3 shows the efficiency result. In Section 5.3, diversified computing tasks are discussed and the feasibility is analyzed. The results show that the new Divisional Bisection method can substantially improve the efficiency of the Bisection algorithm while maintaining its accuracy and flexibility.

2. Dividing the Matrix

The sequential principal minors of an ST (Symmetric Tridiagonal) matrix form a Sturm Chain, which is the key to the Bisection algorithm. We denote the ith sequential principal minor of a matrix A by $A_{1:i}$, which is similar to the conventions in Matlab. The submatrix of A in rows i through j will be denoted by $A_{i:j}$; A is determinant by $det(A)$. We denote the characteristic polynomial $det(A - uI)$ by $C_{1:n}$, $C_{1:n}(u)$, or $C^A_{1:n}(u)$ if necessary.

Let A be an $n \times n$ unreduced ST matrix (all ST matrices discussed in this paper are unreduced), λ_i be its ith eigenvalue, v_i be its ith eigenvector and v_{ij} be the jth component of v_i. Then, we have the iterative formulae of the ST determinants from [34] as

$$\begin{aligned} q_0 = 1, q_1 = a_1 - u, q_i = a_i - u - b_{i-1}^2 / q_{i-1}, \\ p_0 = 1, p_1 = a_n - u, p_i = a_{n+1-i} - u - b_{n+1-i}^2 / p_{i-1}, \end{aligned} \tag{1}$$

where $q_i = C_i / C_{i-1}$ and $p_i = C_{n-i+1} / C_{n-i+2}$.

The Bisection method counts Sturm sequences by q or p. The number of eigenvalues that are less than u is equal to the number of negative q values, while the number of $\lambda_i > u$ is equal to the non-negative q's. The neighboring C_i and q_i have the following theorem from [12].

Theorem 1 (Root Separation Theorem).
C_i has only simple roots, which are separated strictly by the roots of C_{i-1}, for $i = 2, \ldots, n$.

From Theorem 1, we have the following corollary.

Corollary 1. *The signs of C_{i-1} and C_i in the intervals separated by their roots can be expressed as*

$$\begin{aligned} +s_1 - s_2 + s_3 - \ldots \\ +\lambda_1 - \lambda_2 + \lambda_3 - \lambda_4 + \ldots \end{aligned}$$

where $s_k (k = 1, \ldots, i-1)$ denotes the kth root of $C_i - 1$ and $\lambda_k (k = 1, \ldots, i)$ denotes the kth root of C_i.

Proof. As $C(u) = \prod_{i=1}^n (\lambda_i - u)$, we have

$$Sign(C(u)) = \begin{cases} 1, & u \to -\infty \\ (-1)^n. & u \to +\infty \end{cases}$$

Considering that C_i has only simple roots (Theorem 1), the result shows. □

We stress Theorem 1 and Corollary 1 here because they are not only the basis for the following Theorems 2 and 3 but also support our subsequent algorithms and analyses. When merging the submatrices, we use Corollary 1 and the signs of C_i values to decide the global ζ in Algorithm 4. The accuracy of original iterations in Algorithm 5 is analyzed through Theorem 1 and Corollary 1, which guarantee that the original results can be checked and fixed with an acceptable iteration number (this process is carried by Algorithm 7). See more details in Sections 3 and 5.

Recall that our task is to count Sturm sequences in submatrices; then, it is convenient to calculate q values and p values from both ends of A. A specific determinant formula shows the connection between $det(A)$ and $det(A_{1:k})$ and $det(A_{k+1:n})$ or q_i and p_i, which is from [36]. Here, we present a new proof inspired by Maxwell's reciprocity theorem.

According to Maxwell's reciprocity theorem, the output at j caused by input at any point i in a linear system is equal to the output at i caused by equal input at j. If we consider the ST matrix A to be a dynamical system, the following lemma holds.

Lemma 1. *For an invertible symmetry matrix A, if $Ax = e_i$ and $Ay = e_j$ then $x_j = y_i$, where x and y are both column vectors.*

Proof. It can be easily established by symmetry. □

Theorem 2 (Determinant Formula).
Let a be the diagonal of an unreduced ST matrix A and b be the sub-diagonal, we have

$$\begin{aligned} C_{1:n} &= det(A - uI) \\ &= -b_{k-1}^2 C_{1:k-2}C_{k+1:n} + (a_k - u)C_{1:k-1}C_{k+1:n} - b_k^2 C_{1:k-1}C_{k+2:n} \\ &= C_{1:k-1}C_{k+1:n}(C_{1:k}/C_{1:k-1} - b_k^2 C_{k+2:n}/C_{k+1:n}) \\ &= C_{1:k-1}C_{k+1:n}(C_{k:n}/C_{k+1:n} - b_{k-1}^2 C_{1:k-2}/C_{1:k-1}). \end{aligned} \tag{2}$$

Proof. Let:

$$\begin{aligned} x &= [1, C_{1:1}/-b_1, \ldots, C_{1:n-1}/(\prod_{t=1}^{n-1} -b_t)]^T; \\ y &= [C_{2:n}/(\prod_{t=1}^{n-1} -b_t), \ldots, C_{n:n}/-b_{n-1}, 1]^T, \end{aligned} \tag{3}$$

substitute them into (1), then we have

$$\begin{aligned} (A - uI)x &= [0, \ldots, 0, F_1]^T; \\ (A - uI)y &= [F_1, 0, \ldots, 0]^T; \\ F_1 &= C_{1:n}/\prod_{i=1}^{n-1}(-b_i) \end{aligned} \tag{4}$$

when uniting (1) and (3).

Construct a vector z so that

$$\begin{aligned} z_{1:k} &= x_{1:k}; \\ z_{k:n} &= \eta \times y_{k:n}; \\ (A - uI)z &= [0, \ldots, F_2, \ldots, 0]^T, \end{aligned} \tag{5}$$

where η is a nonzero scalar.

As $z_k = x_k$, we have

$$\eta = \frac{C_{1:k-1}/(\prod_{t=1}^{k-1} -b_t)}{C_{k+1:n}/(\prod_{t=k}^{n-1} -b_t)}.$$

According to Lemma 1,

$$\frac{x_k}{F_1} = \frac{z_n}{F_2}. \tag{6}$$

Unite (4)–(6); then, the result shows. □

Remark 1. *(2) can also be expressed as*

$$C_{1:n} = C_{1:k-1}C_{k+1:n}(q_k - b_k^2/p_{n-k}).$$

In addition, although u should not be an eigenvalue of A in Lemma 1, (2) also holds for all λ_i valuesof A. To prove this, we need to check the existence of x and y first, as $A - \lambda_i I$ is a singular matrix. We have $F_1 = 0$ in (4), which means x and y are both eigenvectors. Consider the eigenvectors-from-eigenvalues formula (see [37])

$$v_{ij}^2 \prod_{k=1;k\neq i}^{n} (\lambda_i - \lambda_k) = \prod_{k=1}^{n-1}(\lambda_i - \lambda_k(A_{\ominus j})), \tag{7}$$

where $A_{\ominus j}$ denotes the $n-1 \times n-1$ minor formed from A by deleting the jth row and column of A. As A is symmetric and tridiagonal, (7) can be expressed as

$$v_{ij}^2 \prod_{k=1;k\neq i}^{n} (\lambda_k - \lambda_i) = C_{1:j-1}(\lambda_i)C_{j+1:n}(\lambda_i). \tag{8}$$

Let $i = n$, from (8) we have

$$v_{nj}^2 \prod_{k=1}^{n-1}(\lambda_k - \lambda_n) = C_{1:n-1}(\lambda_n).$$

Consider Theorem 1; then, it shows that the eigenvector of an ST matrix has no zero components at both ends. So, existence is guaranteed. Then, the result can be easily verified by the continuous prolongation theorem.

Remark 2. *The determinant formula is introduced in [36] (page 518, Equation (5)), which gives a form of a general tridiagonal matrix, not having to be symmetric. (2) is the specific form for symmetry. Nevertheless, we insist on presenting this different proof here because some intermediate products of the derivation process consist of the basis of Theorem 4, which is one key technology to accelerate Algorithm 5. See more details in Section 4.*

Theorem 3 (Interlacing Property). *If $C_{1:k-1}$ and $C_{k:n}$ do not have a common root, the roots of $C_{1:k-1}C_{k:n}$ (i.e., the eigenvalues of $A_{\ominus k}$) separate the eigenvalues of A strictly; if not, the common roots are some eigenvalues of A and the others still separate strictly. In addition, Corollary 1 also holds for $C_{1:k-1}C_{k:n}$ and $C_{1:n}$.*

Proof. According to [12,38], we have

$$\lambda_1 \leq s_1 \leq \lambda_2 \leq s_2 \leq \cdots \leq s_{n-1} \leq \lambda_n \tag{9}$$

where $s_i (i = 1, \ldots, n-1)$ denotes the ith eigenvalue of $A_{\ominus k}$.

If $C_{1:k-1}$ and $C_{k:n}$ have a common root, it can be easily seen from (2) that $C_{1:n} = 0$; if not, we have $C_{1:n} \neq 0$ similarly.

So, the equal signs hold if and only if $C_{1:k-1}$ and $C_{k:n}$ have a common root. □

With Theorem 2 and 3, we now divide the unreduced ST matrix A into $A_{1:k-1}$ and $A_{k+1:n}$, and we count the negative Sturm sequences of a tentative eigenvalue u independently. In $A_{1:k-1}$, ζ_1 is the number of negative q_i values ($i = 1, \ldots, k-1$) and ζ_2 is the negative p_i values ($i = 1, \ldots, n-k$) in $A_{k+1:n}$. Let $\zeta = \zeta_1 + \zeta_2$; apparently, it is equal to the number of eigenvalues of $A_{\ominus k}$ that are less than u. Thus, the sign of $C_{1:k-1}C_{k:n}$ is $(-1)^{\zeta}$. According to Theorem 3, this also means $u \in (\lambda_\zeta, \lambda_{\zeta+2})$. Theorem 2 shows the connection between the sign of $C_{1:k-1}C_{k:n}$ and the sign of $C_{1:n}$. Thus, the final ζ, which is either equal to the previous $\zeta_1 + \zeta_2$ or $\zeta_1 + \zeta_2 + 1$, can be concluded with a cheap merging calculation. See more details in the next section.

3. Computing One ST Eigenvalue

We now consider more details of the Divisional Bisection method. First, we introduce Algorithm 1 for computing q_i, ζ and $C_{1:n}$ in an unreduced $n \times n$ ST matrix A according to [34], and the simplified variant Algorithm 2, for the determinant only.

Algorithm 1: Bisection Iteration

Input :a, b^2, n
// a is the diagonal of A, b is the sub-diagonal and n is the size
Output:$\zeta, q, C_{1:n}$
// $q = q_{1:n}$
$q \leftarrow a_1, C_{1:n} \leftarrow 1;$
if $q < 0$ **then**
  $\zeta = 1;$
else
  $\zeta = 0;$
end
for *each* $k \in [1 : n]$ **do**
  if $q == 0$ **then**
    $q \leftarrow \varepsilon$ // ε is a positive small value
  end
  $q \leftarrow a_k - b_{k-1}^2 / q;$
  $C_{1:n} \leftarrow qC_{1:n};$
  if $q < 0$ **then**
    $\zeta \leftarrow \zeta + 1;$
  end
end

Algorithm 2: Computing ST Determinant

Input :a, b^2, n
Output:$C_{1:n-1}, C_{1:n}$
$q \leftarrow a_1, C_{1:n-1} \leftarrow 1;$
for *each* $k \in [1 : n-1]$ **do**
  if $q == 0$ **then**
    $q \leftarrow \varepsilon$ // ε is a positive small value
  end
  $q \leftarrow a_k - b_{k-1}^2 / q;$
  $C_{1:n-1} \leftarrow qC_{1:n-1};$
end
$q \leftarrow a_n - b_{n-1}^2 / q;$
$C_{1:n} \leftarrow qC_{1:n-1}.$

If $u \in (\lambda_\zeta, \lambda_{\zeta+2})$ as discussed in Section 2, we have

$$sign(C_{1:n}) = \begin{cases} (-1)^\zeta, & q_k > b_k^2/p_{n-k}; \\ (-1)^{\zeta+1}, & q_k < b_k^2/p_{n-k}; \\ 0, & q_k = b_k^2/p_{n-k}, \end{cases} \tag{10}$$

according to (2) and Corollary 1. Then, we have

$$\zeta = \begin{cases} \zeta, & q_k \geqslant b_k^2/p_{n-k}; \\ \zeta+1, & q_k < b_k^2/p_{n-k}, \end{cases} \tag{11}$$

and $u = \lambda_{\zeta+1}$ when $q_k = b_k^2/p_{n-k}$. When $q_k p_{n-k} = 0$, which means (10) cannot be calculated, we directly obtain $\zeta = \zeta$ according to Theorem 3. Similarly, we have $u = \lambda_{\zeta+1}$ if q_k and p_{n-k} are both zeros.

In the lower level, $A_{1:k-1}$ is divided into $A_{1:t-1}$ and $A_{t+1:k-1}$. Independently, we calculate

1. $\zeta_{1:t-1}$, $q_t(A_{1:k-1})$, and $C_{1:t-1}$ in $A_{1:t-1}$ by Algorithm 1;
2. $\zeta_{t+1:k-1}$, $p_{k-t-1}(A_{1:k-1})$ and $C_{t+1:k-1}$ in $A_{t+1:k-1}$ by Algorithm 1;
3. $C_{t+2:k-2}$ and $C_{t+1:k-2}$ in $A_{t+1:k-2}$ by Algorithm 2.

And the same in $A_{k+1:n}$.

By substituting these outputs into (2), (10) and (11),

1. $\zeta_{1:k-1}$, $\zeta_{k+1:n}$;
2. $C_{1:k-1}$, q_k;
3. $C_{k+1:n}$, p_{n-k}.

These are determined, and then, we have $\zeta_{1:n}$ finally, completing one Bisection iteration. The new Divisional Bisection iteration method is given by Algorithm 3.

Algorithm 3: Divisional Bisection Iteration

Input $:a, b^2, n, p$
// u is a tentative eigenvalue, p is the number of dividing parts
Output:ζ
distribute a, b^2 into $m + w$ parts evenly such that $m + w = p$;
// so that each pair of a_i and b_i^2 forms a submatrix of A
then get $a_1, \ldots, a_m, a_{m+1}, \ldots, a_{m+w}, b_1^2, \ldots, b_m^2, b_{m+1}^2, \ldots, b_{m+w}^2$;
foreach $i \in [2:m]\&\&i = m+w$ **do**
    reverse a_i, b_i^2;
end
foreach $i \in [1:m+w]$ **do**
    call Algorithm 1 $\Leftarrow a_i$,b_i^2,N_i // N_i is the length of a_i
    then get ζ_i, q_i, C_i;
end
foreach $i \in [2:m] \cap [m+1:m+w-1]$ **do**
    call Algorithm 2 $\Leftarrow a_i(2:end)$,$b_i^2(2:end)$,$N_i - 1$;
    // eliminate 1st component
    then get $C_{2:N_i}$, $C_{2:N_i-1}$;
end
$s \leftarrow 0, C_l \leftarrow C_1, q_l \leftarrow q_1, i \leftarrow 2$;
while $i \leq m$ **do**
    substitute C_l, q_l, C_i, q_i, $C_{2:N_i}$, $C_{2:N_i-1}$ into (2);
    then get C_l, q_l;
    // C_l, q_l is substituted by those of the merged matrix
    $s \leftarrow s$ or $s \leftarrow s+1$ according to (10) and (11), $i \leftarrow i+1$;
end
$C_r \leftarrow C_{m+w}, q_r \leftarrow q_{m+w}, i \leftarrow w+m-1$;
while $i \geq m+1$ **do**
    substitute C_r, q_r, C_i, q_i, $C_{2:N_i}$, $C_{2:N_i-1}$ into (2);
    then get C_r, q_r;
    // C_r, q_r is substituted by those of the merged matrix
    $s \leftarrow s$ or $s \leftarrow s+1$ according to (10) and (11), $i \leftarrow i-1$;
end
substitute C_l, q_l, C_r, q_r into (2);
$s \leftarrow s$ or $s \leftarrow s+1$ according to (10) and (11);
$\zeta \leftarrow s + \sum \zeta_i$.

Algorithm 3 calls Algorithm 2 to compute $p-2$ extra determinants of the submatrices compared to the traditional method. So, the parallel efficiency of Algorithm 3 is $p/(2p-2)$, given that the cost of the merging part is negligible compared to the cost of Algorithms 1 and 2 called during computation. It should be noted that counting non-negative q values instead is more efficient if a high-order eigenvalue is desired. By replacing the iterative process, we give the new Divisional Bisection Algorithm 4 for computing one ST eigenvalue.

Algorithm 4: Computing One ST Eigenvalue

```
Input  : a, b, n, p, r, tol
// compute the rth eigenvalue with the expected precision tol
Output: λ_r
set the original interval [x, y], b ← b^2;
// x, y = ∓||A||_∞, for example
while |y − x| ≥ 2tol do
    u ← (y − x)/2;
    call Algorithm 3 ⇐ a − u, b, n, p
    if any ζ_i ≥ r when executing Algorithm 3 then
        stop Algorithm 3;
        ζ ← r;
    else
        complete Algorithm 3;
        then get ζ
    end
    if ζ ≥ r then
        y ← u;
    else
        x ← u;
    end
end
λ_r ← (y − x)/2.
```

In addition, it can be predicted that a considerable number of Divisional Bisection iterations will end early, especially for the lower or higher order eigenvalues. To find the smallest eigenvalue of a matrix, for example, we can break the iteration in advance if any $\zeta_i \geq 1$, which means the final number will inevitably exceed 1 according to Theorem 3. This strategy can save substantial time in the early computation and more if a larger p is available.

4. Computing All ST Eigenvalues

The Bisection algorithm has many practical advantages but earns the disrepute of being slow when computing all ST eigenvalues. A significant contributor is the excessive number of iterations. The Bisection algorithm permits an eigenvalue to be computed with 53 iterations in IEEE double-precision arithmetic. When an eigenvalue is isolated in an interval, we have some faster root-finders such as Laguerre's method [12,39], the Zeroin scheme [40,41] and the fzero scheme [42] ('fzero' function in Matlab). These competitors can finish the work in less than 10 iterations but seem to stumble when eigenvalues cluster. Another trouble is that so much more has to be completed in the inner loop [39,43] to obtain isolating intervals, costing embarrassingly more time.

Our strategy is to obtain isolating intervals by the eigenvalues of $A_{\ominus k}$. These eigenvalues can be obtained by QR or a Bisection algorithm on each submatrix. The clustering eigenvalues, which can be challenging problems otherwise, accelerate the calculation in our method according to Theorem 3. The submatrix under continuing division (if necessary) has no eigenvalues clustered eventually. Then, we can compute all the eigenvalues by dividing and merging. For convenience, we choose the 'fzero' function in Matlab as the root-finder, which requires an average of 7.5 iterations per root. Our numerical experience supports this conclusion.

It has been found in [31,38] that the deflation properties and techniques of the DC algorithm allow it to converge quickly when the eigenvalues of submatrices cluster or the eigenvectors have zero ends in finite precision arithmetic. These deflation cases are quite common in ST matrices and should be utilized in the Divisional Bisection algorithm. Let *tol* be the expected precision and $s_i(i = 1, \ldots, n-1)$ be the eigenvalues of $A_{\ominus k+1}$, which can be divided into T_1 and T_2. From [38] we have

$$\begin{aligned} A &= QDQ^T \\ &= \begin{bmatrix} 0 & Q_1 & 0 \\ 1 & 0 & 0 \\ 0 & 0 & Q_2 \end{bmatrix} \begin{bmatrix} a_{k+1} & b_k l_k^T & b_{k+1} r_1^T \\ b_k l_k & D_1 & 0 \\ b_{k+1} r_1 & 0 & D_2 \end{bmatrix} \begin{bmatrix} 0 & 1 & 0 \\ Q_1^T & 0 & 0 \\ 0 & 0 & Q_2^T \end{bmatrix} \end{aligned} \tag{12}$$

where

- $T_1 = Q_1 D_1 Q_1^T$ and $T_2 = Q_2 D_2 Q_2^T$ are the eigendecomposition of T_1 and T_2;
- l_k^T is the last row of Q_1;
- r_1^T is the first row of Q_2;
- the diagonals of D_1 and D_2 are arranged in ascending order.

Now, consider how deflation occurs during the calculation and how our algorithm can perceive it. In (12), the close eigenvalues of D_1 and D_2 can be easily detected, since we do the calculation by dividing and merging. However, the connection between zero ends of $b_k l_k$ or $b_{k+1} r_1$ and the intermediate results of Bisection iterations are not easily accessible. Therefore, we give Theorem 4, especially Theorem 4b, to show the deflation properties and to suggest an approach to detecting. First, we introduce the following Lemma 2 as an auxiliary for our proof of Theorem 4.

Lemma 2. *Let A_1 and A_2 be $n \times n$ real symmetric matrices with eigenvalues $\lambda_1^{A_1}, \ldots, \lambda_n^{A_1}$ and $\lambda_1^{A_2}, \ldots, \lambda_n^{A_2}$, respectively. Then*

$$\max_i |\lambda_i^{A_1} - \lambda_i^{A_2}| \leq \|A_1 - A_2\|_2.$$

Proof. See [44]. □

Theorem 4 (Deflation Properties).

a. *If $|\bar{s}_{i+1} - \bar{s}_i| \leq tol$ where $\bar{s}_i$ and $\bar{s}$ are arithmetic approximations of s_i and s_{i+1}, then $\bar{s}_i$ or $\bar{s}_{i+1}$ is an arithmetic approximation of λ_{i+1};*

b. *Let u be an arithmetic approximation to s_i which is one of the $s_j^{T_1}$'s and $s_i = s_h^{T_1} (h \in [1,k])$. If*

   (1) $(C_{1\to k-1}^{T_1}(u)/C_{1\to k}^{T_1}(u))(s_i - u) < 0$;

   (2) $|b_k|\sqrt{\left(1/g - \left|C_{1\to k-1}^{T_1}(u)/C_{1\to k}^{T_1}(u)\right|\right)} < \sqrt{tol}$,

   where $g = \min_{j \neq t} |s_j^{T_1} - u|$, then u is an arithmetic approximate eigenvalue of A, and the similar holds in T_2.

Proof.

a. It can be easily seen from Theorem 3.

b. Without loss of generality, we assume s_i is an isolated eigenvalue of $A_{\ominus k+1}$ because if not, we can turn to Theorem 4a.

From (3) and (4), it shows $1/q_k^{T_1}(u) = (C_{1\to k-1}^{T_1}(u)/C_{1\to k}^{T_1}(u))$ is the last component on the diagonal of $(T_1 - uI)^{-1}$. Then, we have

$$\begin{aligned} & 1/q_k^{T_1}(u) = e_k^T (T_1 - uI)^{-1} e_k, \\ \Rightarrow\ & 1/q_k^{T_1}(u) = e_k^T Q (D_1 - uI)^{-1} Q^T e_k, \\ \Rightarrow\ & 1/q_k^{T_1}(u) = \sum_{j=1}^{k} v_{jk}^2 \frac{1}{s_j^{T_1} - u} \end{aligned} \tag{13}$$

where v_j is the jth eigenvector of T_1.

As $C^{T_1}_{1\to k}(u)$ is the determinant of $T_1 - uI$, $q^{T_1}_k$ should be close to zero when $u \to s_i$. However, in IEEE double precision arithmetic, this is not true if v^2_{ik} is also small when compared to $s_i - u$. (13) can be expressed as

$$1/q^{T_1}_k(u) = \frac{v^2_{ik}}{s_i - u} + \sum_{j=1\neq i}^{k} v^2_{jk}\frac{1}{s_j - u} = v^2_{ik}/(s_i - u) + R_i, \tag{14}$$

where apparently (recall that $g = \min_{j\neq t} |s^{T_1}_j - u|$)

$$|R_i| \in \left[0, \frac{1}{g}\right). \tag{15}$$

Given that u is the previous computation result, we have $|s_i - u| \leq tol$. When $q^{T_1}_k(u)(s_i - u) > 0$, (14) and (15) can be united as

$$\begin{aligned} &\left|v^2_{ik}/(s_i - u)\right| < 1/g + \left|1/q^{T_1}_k\right|, \\ &\Rightarrow |v_{ik}| < \sqrt{(1/q^{T_1}_k + 1/g)tol}. \end{aligned} \tag{16}$$

In addition, we have

$$|v_{ik}| < \sqrt{(1/q^{T_1}_k - 1/g)tol} \tag{17}$$

similarly when $q^{T_1}_k(u)(s_i - u) < 0$.

The condition of Theorem 4b shows $|b_k v_{ik}| < tol$ according to (17). By taking a review of (12) and Lemma 2, the proof is completed. □

Theorem 4 is satisfying because q_i values of T_1 and p_i values of T_2 happen to be accompanying products of Algorithm 2, which can be utilized as the basic iteration of the 'fzero' scheme. The condition of Theorem 4b is sufficient but not necessary, as there are many other possibilities that make $|v_{ik}| < tol$, even when $(C^{T_1}_{1\to k-1}(u)/C^{T_1}_{1\to k}(u))(s_i - u) \geq 0$. A trivial plan is to calculate and check v_{ik} once one s_i is solved and the accompanying $|1/q^{T_1}_i|$ is suspiciously small. Although this idea already saves a large number of unnecessary computations compared to the DC algorithm, we are still concerned that it is too expensive to call the Inverse Iteration algorithm here.

Our scheme is to mark those suspicious small $|1/q^{T_1}_i|$ values by a rough discriminant, for example $|1/q^{T_1}_i| < 1$, then to substitute the corresponding $\bar{s}_i \pm tol$ values into Algorithm 1 to check if deflation is available. We have found in our numerical experiments that it is difficult to cover all the deflation situations by this method, even if we set the discriminant quite loosely. Even filtrating directly by $|v_{ik}|$, as in the DC algorithm, would still leave some out. We applied these methods to 20 randomly generated 2001×2001 matrices for computation, where T_1 and T_2 are both 1000×1000 matrices. The averages were calculated and are shown in Table 1. We collected the hit rate of the DC algorithm by checking how many $\bar{s}_i$ values, which had negligible corresponding v_{ik} values, were really close to λ_i values. In Table 1, the plan 1 refers to "rough discriminant + Inverse Iteration algorithm", the plan 2 refer to "rough discriminant + Algorithm 1", and the hit rates of them were collected similarly. It can be seen that the hit rate and accuracy of our method are acceptable or at least no worse than the DC algorithm. The errors in Table 1 refer to the difference between $\bar{s}_i$ values selected during deflations and $\bar{\lambda}_i$ values obtained by the Bisection method. The data were collected on an Intel Core i5-4590 3.3 GHz CPU and 16 GB RAM machine. All codes were written in Matlab2017b and executed in IEEE double precision. The machine precision is $eps \approx 2.2 \times 10^{-16}$.

Table 1. Comparison of deflation detecting methods (average of 20 2001 × 2001 matrices).

Methods	Time Cost (s)	Hit Rate	Average Error ($\times 10^{-16}$)	Maximum Error ($\times 10^{-16}$)
DC algorithm	/	58.5	1.39	4.44
plan 1	0.30	62.1	1.32	4.44
plan 2	0.19	62.1	0.91	1.00

We give the Divisional Bisection method for all eigenvalues by Algorithm 5 and the following subroutine Algorithm 6.

Algorithm 5: Computing all ST Eigenvalues

Input : a, b, n, p, tol
Output: $\vec{d}$

// all eigenvalues lie in the vector $\vec{d}$ in ascending order
distribute a, b into p parts evenly, $F \leftarrow \max(|a_i| + 2|b_i|)$, **calculate** b^2 in each part;
call PWK version of QR Algorithm in each part;
then get $\vec{d}_1, \ldots, \vec{d}_p$ // eigenvalues of each submatrix lie on $\vec{d}_i$
call Algorithm 2 $\Leftarrow$ each a_i, b_i^2, N_i;
then get q_i's correspondingly;
check deflation, form $\vec{t}_1, \ldots, \vec{t}_{p/2}$ by determined $\vec{d}_i(j)$'s, eliminate corresponding components in each $\vec{d}_i$;
if *there are clustering* $\vec{d}_i(j)$*'s* **then**
  call Algorithm 7 to recheck;
  // Algorithm 7 is provided in Section 5
end
while $p \geq 2$ **do**
  $m \leftarrow p/2, i \leftarrow 1\ s \leftarrow 1$;
  while $i<p$ **do**
    $\vec{v}_s \leftarrow [-F; sort([\vec{d}_i; \vec{d}_{i+1}]); F]$;
    $s \leftarrow s+1, i \leftarrow i+2$;
  end
  call Algorithm 6 $\Leftarrow \vec{v}_1, \ldots, \vec{v}_m$;
  then get $\vec{d}_1, \ldots, \vec{d}_m$ and corresponding q_i's;
  combine each $\vec{d}_j$ and $\vec{t}_j$, $j \in [1:m]$;
  // eigenvalues of each merged matrix lie on $\vec{d}_i$
  check deflation, form $\vec{t}_1, \ldots, \vec{t}_m$ by determined $\vec{d}_i(j)$'s, eliminate corresponding components in each $\vec{d}_i$;
  $p \leftarrow p/2$;
end
combine $\vec{d}_1$ and $\vec{t}_1$, $\vec{d} \leftarrow \vec{d}_1$.

Algorithm 6: Fzero by Determinant

Input : a, b^2, n, V, tol
// searh one root in a isolating interval V
Output: x, q_n
call Algorithm 2 $\Leftarrow a, b^2, n$;
call 'fzero' function in Matlab $\Leftarrow$ Algorithm 2, V, tol;
then get x;
save q_n of the last iteration.

5. Accuracy Analysis and Numerical Results

5.1. Accuracy Analysis

After the eigenvalues of the original submatrices are calculated by the QR Algorithm, as shown by line 3 in Algorithm 5, it is not safe to take $(\bar{s}_i - \bar{s}_{i-1})/2$ as a λ_i if one $\bar{s}_i - \bar{s}_{i-1} \leq tol$, because the QR algorithm is not always as accurate as the Bisection method or fzero scheme. So, in practice, we do an extra check for the selected $\bar{s}_i$ values by Theorem 4a when checking deflation from results of the QR Algorithm. Suppose m sub-eigenvalues (denoted by $s_1, \ldots, s_m$) cluster in the interval $[x, y]$ where $y - x \leq tol$; the process is shown as Algorithm 7.

Algorithm 7: Recheck the Results of QR

```
Input  : clustering sub-eigenvalues s_1, ..., s_m, interval [x, y]
Output: λ_1, ..., λ_m − 1
1  // the subscripts of λ's denote the order in this subroutine, not
      globally
2  Determine how many eigenvalues lie in [x : y] by Algorithm 1 and save the
     number as w; if w = m − 1 then
3      foreach i ∈ [1 : m − 1] do
4          λ_i ← (s_i + s_{i+1})/2;
5      end
6  else
7      foreach i ∈ [1 : w − 1] do
8          λ_i ← x + i * (y − x)/(w − 1);
9      end
10     call Bisection algorithm to search the remain m − 1 − w λ's in
         [x − 10tol, x) ∩ (y, y + 10tol].
11 end
```

In Algorithm 7, $10tol$ is a pessimistic estimation of QR algorithm error, which means it decuples that of the Bisection error. The data in Table 2, which are present in a later paragraph, supports our point. Line 2 in Algorithm 7 costs 2 Bisection iterations for $w - 1$ λ values and line 10 costs 3 to 4 per λ compared to about 7.5 iterations per λ in Algorithm 6 and 53 iterations per λ in the Bisection algorithm.

When arithmetic approximations $\bar{s}_i$ are treated as the boundaries of isolating intervals in the next level, they do not affect the accuracy because if the number of λ's in an interval is not one, Algorithm 6 fails. The troublesome number could be 0 or 2, but it is certainly not bigger than 3. When there are 4 or more λ's in an interval, it means there are clustering $\bar{s}_i$'s of the previous results which can be perceived during the deflation check. For example, if 4 λ's lie in $[\bar{s}_j, \bar{s}_{j+1}]$ as

$$\bar{s}_j < \lambda_{j-1} < s_{j-1} < \lambda_j < s_j < \lambda_{j+1} < s_{j+1} < \lambda_{j+2} < \bar{s}_{j+1}, \tag{18}$$

we have $s_{j-1} - \bar{s}_j < \epsilon$ where ϵ is the previous computation error. (18) shows that $\bar{s}_{j-1}$ and $\bar{s}_j$ both lie in $(s_{j-1} - \epsilon, s_{j-1}]$, which could not happen because we do the deflation check previously.

We regard this as a beneficial situation. It can be seen in (18) that the troublesome number arises only when $\bar{s}_j < \lambda_j$ (or $\bar{s}_j > \lambda_{j+1}$), contrary to Theorem 3. As the accurate $s_j > \lambda_j$ and $s_j - \bar{s}_j \leq \epsilon$, we have $\lambda_j - \bar{s}_j \leq \epsilon$ and then can speed up the calculation. Finally, the accuracy of Theorem 5 is as good as the Bisection algorithm.

We checked the accuracy of Algorithm 5 by computing the eigenvalues of a 2001×2001 Toeplitz ST matrix, which has all 2's on its diagonal and all -1's on its sub-diagonal. The results of each method were then compared with the exact value, i.e., $\lambda_i = 2 - 2\cos(i\pi/2002)$, and are shown in Table 2. In addition, all eigenvalues of 20 randomly generated matrices were calculated for testing the efficiency on serial machines, and we show the average results of 20 in Table 3. We set $p = 2$ in Algorithm 5 for the serial execution.

Table 2. Accuracy Result.

Method	Time Cost (s)	Average Error $\times eps$	Maximum Error $\times eps$
QR	0.10	4.2	32.0
PWK QR	0.09	3.9	32.0
MRRR	0.13	15.1	34.0
Bisection	1.55	1.0	6.0
Our method	0.41	1.0	6.0

Table 3. Time Cost Result.

Method	Time Cost (s) of		
	2500 × 2500 Matrix	5000 × 5000 Matrix	10,000 × 10,000 Matrix
QR	0.16	0.86	2.30
PWK QR	0.13	0.77	1.96
MRRR	0.17	0.92	2.55
Bisection	2.25	12.49	34.10
Our method	0.61	2.30	9.21

Table 2 demonstrates that our method substantially improves the speed of the Bisection method without losing accuracy. In addition, Table 3 confirms that Algorithm 5 is $O(n^2)$ as its iteration based on Algorithm 2. In the following subsections, we illustrate more test results of several different types of matrices. All results in Section 5 were collected on an Intel Core i5-4590 3.3-GHz CPU and 16-GB RAM machine, except for the last figure, which will be introduced in Section 5.4 specifically. All codes were written in Matlab2017b and executed in IEEE double precision. The machine precision is $eps \approx 2.2 \times 1{-}16$.

5.2. Matrices Introduction and Accuracy Test

In the following subsections, we present a numerical comparison among the Divisional Bisection algorithm and four other algorithms for solving the ST eigenvalue problem:

1. Bisection, by calling subroutine 'dstebz' from LAPACK in Matlab;
2. MRRR, by calling subroutine 'dstegr' from LAPACK in Matlab;
3. QR, by calling subroutine 'dsteqr' from LAPACK in Matlab;
4. PWK version of QR (which would be denoted by QR-pwk in the figures), by calling subroutine 'dsterf' from LAPACK in Matlab.

We use the following sets of test $n \times n$ matrices:

1. Matrix A:
$$\text{Matrix A} = \text{tridiagonal}\begin{bmatrix} & 1 & & 1 & & \cdots & 1 & \\ 2 & & 2 & & \cdots & & & 2 \\ & 1 & & 1 & & \cdots & 1 & \end{bmatrix},$$
i.e., the Toeplitz matrix [1,2,1] to test the accuracy and efficiency, which has $\lambda_i = 2 - 2\cos(i\pi/(n+1))$;
2. Matrix T1:
$$\text{Matrix T1} = \text{tridiagonal}\begin{bmatrix} & 1 & & 1 & & \cdots & 1 & \\ 1 & & 0 & & \cdots & & & 0 \\ & 1 & & 1 & & \cdots & 1 & \end{bmatrix},$$
to test the accuracy and efficiency, which has $\lambda_i = -2\cos(2i\pi/(2n+1))$. Matrix T1 is from [45], as well as the following Matrix T2 and T3;

3. Matrix T2 [45]:

$$\text{Matrix T2} = \text{tridiagonal}\begin{bmatrix} & 1 & & 1 & & \cdots & 1 & \\ 1 & & 0 & & \cdots & & & 1 \\ & 1 & & 1 & & \cdots & 1 & \end{bmatrix},$$

to test the accuracy and efficiency, which has $\lambda_i = -2\cos(i\pi/n)$;

4. Matrix T3 [45]:

$$\text{Matrix T3} = \text{tridiagonal}\begin{bmatrix} & 1 & & 1 & & \cdots & 1 & \\ 1 & & 0 & & \cdots & & & -1 \\ & 1 & & 1 & & \cdots & 1 & \end{bmatrix},$$

to test the accuracy and efficiency, which has $\lambda_i = 2\cos((2i-1)\pi/(2n))$;

5. Matrix W [12,46], which has the ith diagonal component equal to $|(n+1)/2 - i|$(n is odd) and all off-diagonal components equal to 1, to test the efficiency only as its exact eigenvalues are not accessible;
6. Random Matrix with both diagonal and off-diagonal elements being uniformly distributed random numbers in [−1,1] to test the efficiency only as its exact eigenvalues are not accessible.

Figures 1–4 present the test results of accuracy, where the Average Errors denote the means of errors of all the calculated eigenvalues and the Maximal Errors denote the maximum. Seven different sizes are used, from 800 × 800 to 3200 × 3200. All errors have been divided by the machine precision *eps* for clarity. It can be seen that the new Divisional Bisection algorithm has the best accuracy as well as the Bisection method, considerably higher than the others.

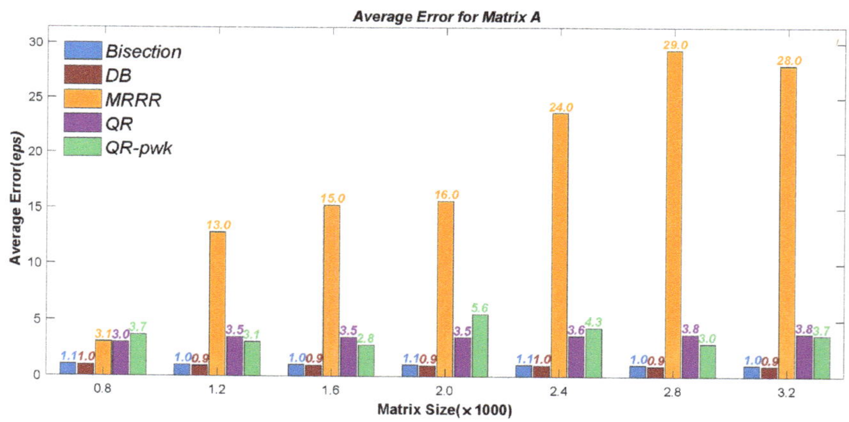

(a)

Figure 1. *Cont.*

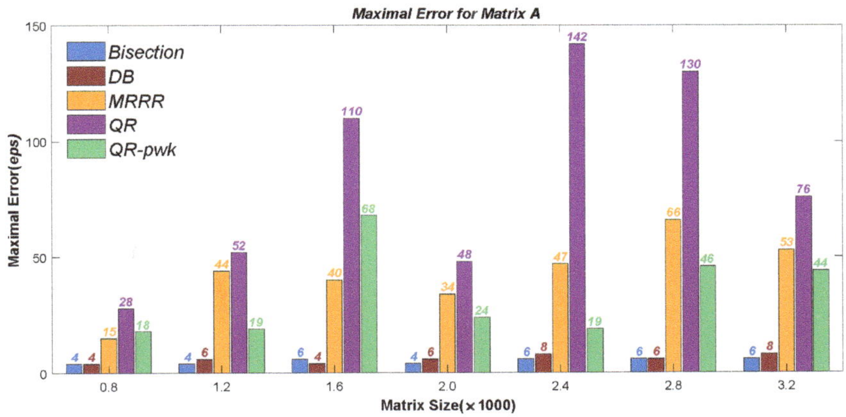

(b)

Figure 1. Results of Matrix A: (**a**) the Average Errors; (**b**) the Maximal Errors.

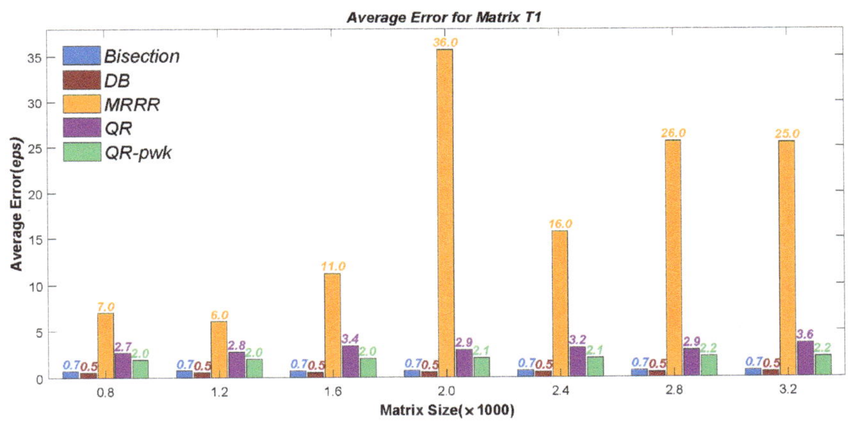

(a)

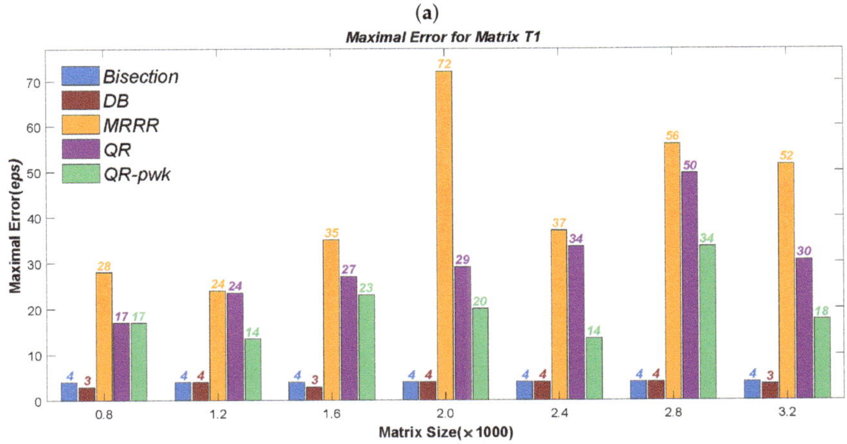

(b)

Figure 2. Results of Matrix T1: (**a**) the Average Errors; (**b**) the Maximal Errors.

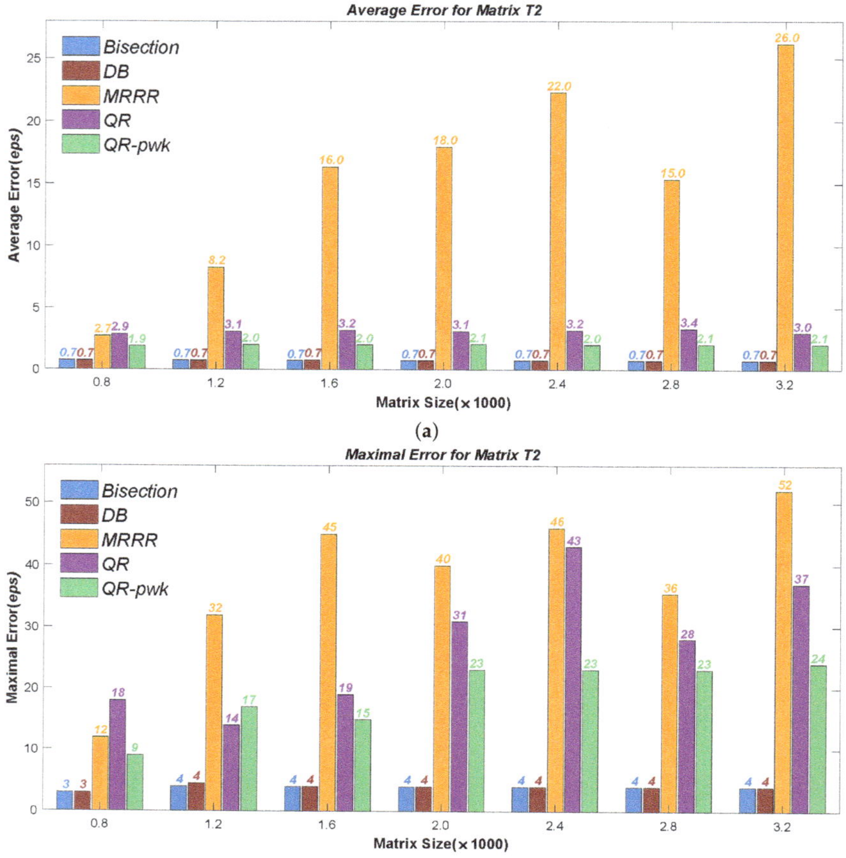

(a)

(b)

Figure 3. Results of Matrix T2: (**a**) the Average Errors; (**b**) the Maximal Errors.

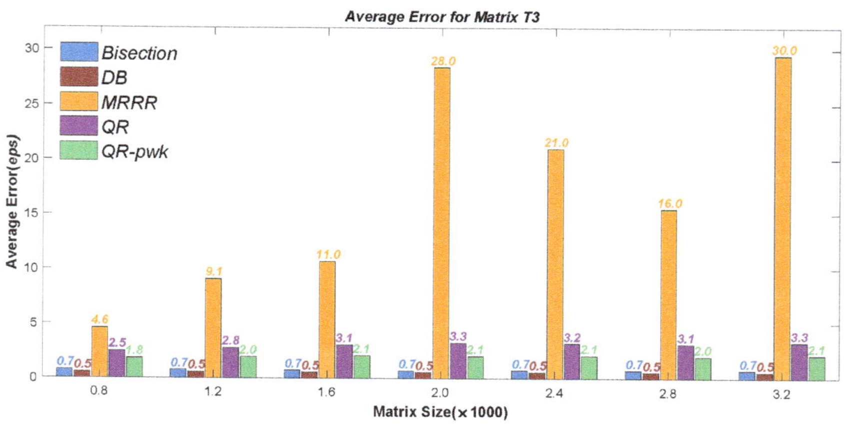

(a)

Figure 4. *Cont.*

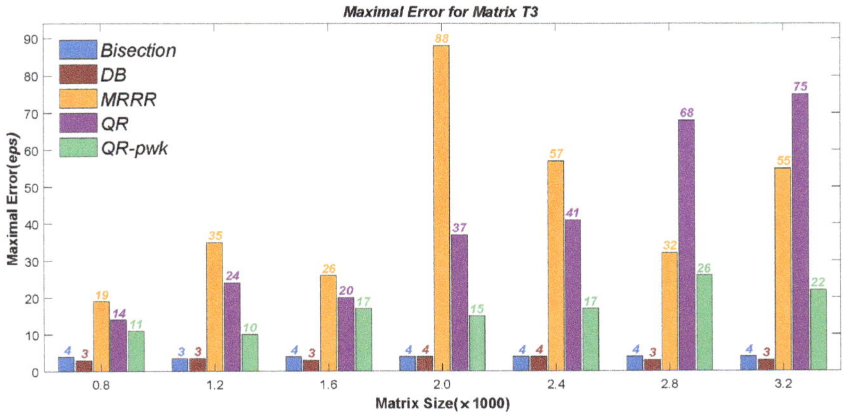

(b)

Figure 4. Results of Matrix T3: (**a**) the Average Errors; (**b**) the Maximal Errors.

5.3. Efficiency Test for Computing all the Eigenvalues

Figure 5 presents the test results of time cost. Seven different sizes are used, from 800×800 to 3200×3200. Note that the results of the Random Matrix of each size are the mean data of 20 tests. Therefore, we use the plural form in the figures.

When the eigenvalues clutter, as in Matrix W, the Divisional Bisection method improves the Bisection method by about 70%. Such a good result can also be in Matrix T1 and Matrix T3. However, the improvement is less than 50% in Matrix A and Matrix T2. The reason is their submatrices have close eigenvalues to the global one but are not equal in finite precision arithmetic. For example, the sub-eigenvalues give an interval for Algorithm 6 and have an upper or lower bound that has a distance between λ_i less than 5×10^{-14}. The 'fzero' scheme uses the linear interpolation to accelerate convergence; such a bound produces poor slopes during the linear interpolation process. As a consequence, more iterations are needed to guarantee convergence, which finally results in the efficiency loss of the Divisional Bisection method. Recall that Algorithm 7 is for checking similar situations. However, a distance of 5×10^{-14} could not be detected, because it does not meet the conditions of Theorem 4.

Nevertheless, we are not pessimistic about the Divisional Bisection method. First, it still improves more than 35% in such cases and performs well for Random Matrices. Secondly, the 'fzero' scheme is not a prerequisite or non-replaceable in our method, which could be modified or substituted by a more powerful competitor in future follow-up studies.

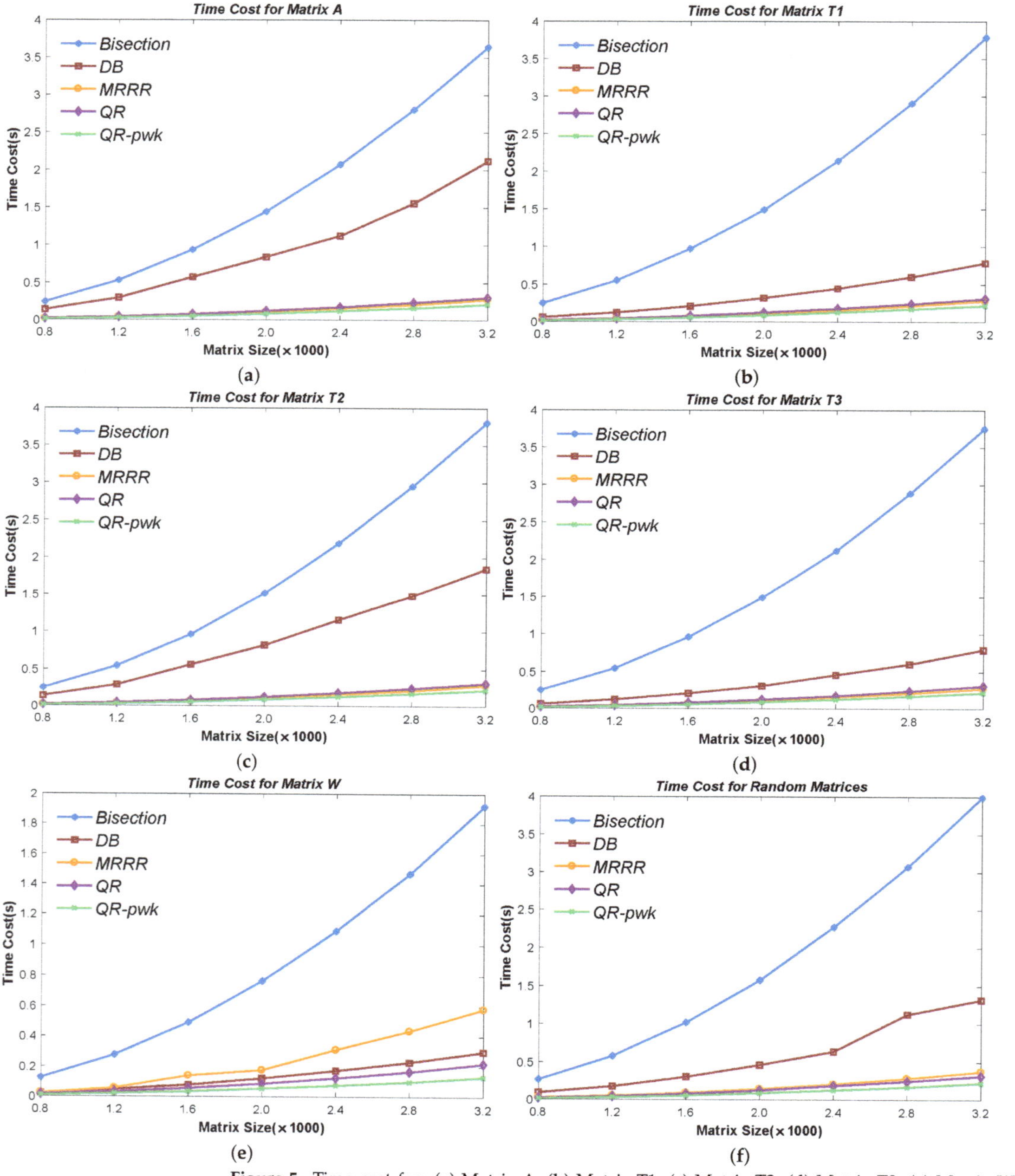

Figure 5. Time cost for: (**a**) Matrix A; (**b**) Matrix T1; (**c**) Matrix T2; (**d**) Matrix T3; (**e**) Matrix W; (**f**) Random Matrices.

5.4. Efficiency Test for Computing a Part of the Eigenvalues

All along, the Bisection method undertakes the task of computing a part of eigenvalues, especially when the size of the matrix is large. When Algorithm 5 obtains all the sub-eigenvalues, as shown in lines 2–11 in Algorithm 5, it is an easy task to calculate any parts of λ_i's. For example, if eigenvalues in a certain interval are wanted, we can drop the sub-eigenvalues which are outside and substitute $\pm F$, in Algorithm 5 line 2 and line 15, with the upper and lower bounds of the given interval. If $r1$th$\sim r2$th eigenvalues are wanted, we need to drop the sub-eigenvalues that are of the order lower than $r1-1$ or higher than $r2$. When s_{r1-1} and s_{r2} are the substitutions of $\pm F$, the problem can be solved.

Figure 6 shows the time cost in Random Matrices of four relatively large size, i.e., 5000×5000, $10{,}000 \times 10{,}000$, $15{,}000 \times 15{,}000$, and $20{,}000 \times 20{,}000$. We calculated 1%, 10%, 30%, and 50% λ_i's of each size. Note the results are mean data of 40 tests, 20 for computing λ_i's in a certain interval and 20 for computing λ_i's in a certain order. Given that there is no evident difference between the test results of calculating λ_i's in an interval or order, we mixed them for averaging.

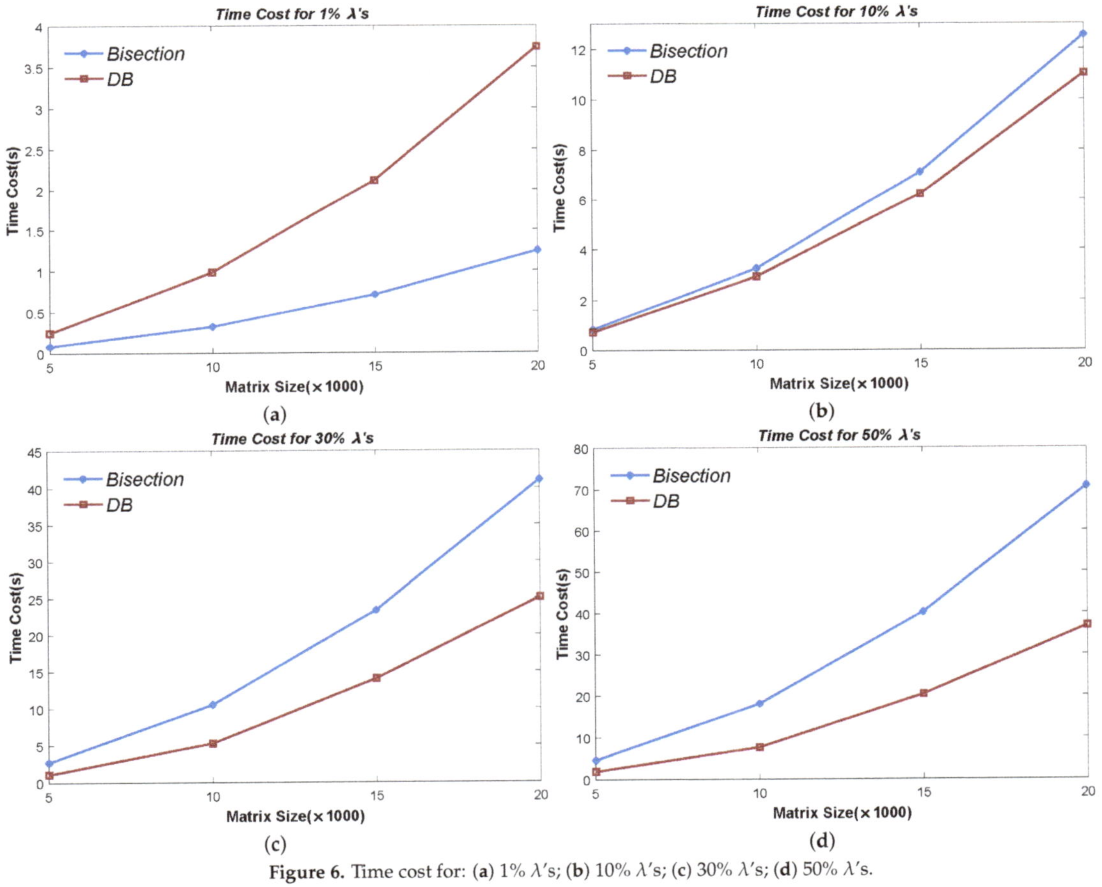

Figure 6. Time cost for: (**a**) 1% λ's; (**b**) 10% λ's; (**c**) 30% λ's; (**d**) 50% λ's.

The results show that the Divisional Bisection method is not suitable for computing a small group of eigenvalues, despite the matrix being relatively large. We consider 10% as an applicable threshold. Although we can replace the QR method with the Bisection method in Algorithm 5 line 3, which could avoid the calculation of all the sub-eigenvalues, the result seems even worse. As the matrix size increases, the efficiency disadvantage of the Bisection method becomes increasingly severe, which could ignore only a quite small number of wanted λ_i, for example, 0.1%. In this case, the 'fzero' loops (line 12 to line 24 in

Algorithm 5) become a heavy burden to the Divisional Bisection method. Therefore, we insist on using the PWK version of the QR method in Algorithm 5.

We now consider the situation of calculating one λ in parallel. The problem also arises when the number of wanted λ is less than the number of CPU cores or not divisible by it. Algorithm 4 solves the problem and makes it available for computing with any number of CPU cores. Of course, the need to compute an eigenvalue in parallel must occur in a very large matrix. Therefore, we use three Random Matrices with sizes of $10^6 \times 10^6$, $10^7 \times 10^7$, and $10^8 \times 10^8$ for the test of parallel efficiency. The results, presented in Figure 7, were collected on an Intel Xeon(R) Core E5-2687 3.1-GHz CPU and 256-GB RAM machine, which has 20 CPU cores. Note that the results are mean data of 20 tests.

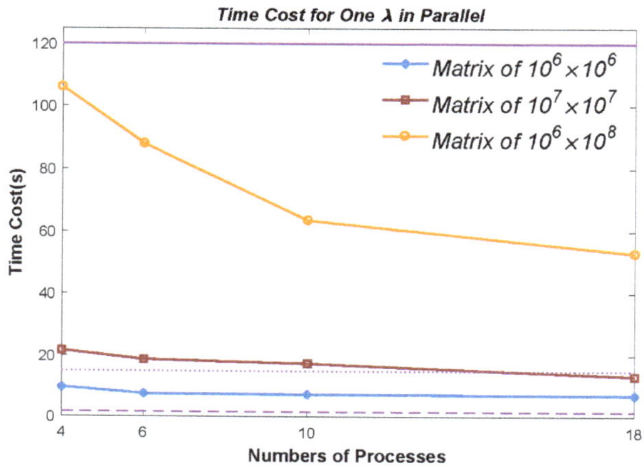

Figure 7. Computing one λ in parallel.

The three purple horizontal lines in Figure 7 denote the time cost of the serial Bisection algorithm. Specifically, the top one denotes the time cost for $10^8 \times 10^8$ Random Matrices, the middle $10^7 \times 10^7$, and the bottom $10^6 \times 10^6$. The parallel efficiency is unsatisfactory, especially for the $10^7 \times 10^7$ and $10^6 \times 10^6$ Random Matrices, which are even worse than the serial Bisection algorithm. The reason is that Matlab is not available for multi-threaded computation. Instead, we run the codes in multi-processes. The task of copying inputs and distributing them to the processes takes up the vast majority of the time. The script time consumption analysis tool in Matlab confirms our point, which shows at least 75% time was consumed during copying and distributing. Therefore, we would focus on the version written in C or Fortran of the Divisional Bisection algorithm in future follow-up studies. Nevertheless, Figure 7 verifies the feasibility of Algorithm 4, which to our knowledge is the only algorithm that works in parallel for computing any one ST eigenvalue. This paper also focuses on the serial version.

6. Conclusions

In this paper, a novel $O(n^2)$ Divisional Bisection method is given for the ST eigenvalue problem by Algorithms 4 and 5. When computing all eigenvalues, the results show that the time cost is reduced by more than 35–70% on serial machines compared to the Bisection algorithm. In addition,

1. The algorithms are easy to implement fully in parallel;
2. By Algorithm 4, even one eigenvalue can be calculated in parallel and distributed on any number of CPU cores;
3. As with the Bisection algorithm, it is flexible to set the expected accuracy and the computing error archives machine precision;
4. By Algorithm 4, it is practicable to calculate a single eigenvalue of any order;

5. Combining Algorithms 4 and 5, it is practicable to calculate eigenvalues in any interval in parallel or any orders.

The Divisional Bisection method offers a novel idea for solving the ST eigenvalue problem and a new choice, especially for readers who care about an algorithm of good parallelization, flexibility, and warranted accuracy.

Author Contributions: Formal analysis, W.C., Y.Z. and H.Y.; investigation, W.C. and Y.Z.; writing—original draft, W.C.; writing—review and editing, H.Y. All authors have read and agreed to the published version of the manuscript.

Funding: This research is funded by the Talent Team Project of Zhangjiang City in 2021 and the R & D and industrialization project of the offshore aquaculture cage nets system of Guangdong Province of China (grant No. 2021E05034). Huazhong University of Science and Technology funds the APC.

Institutional Review Board Statement: Not applicable.

Informed Consent Statement: Not applicable.

Data Availability Statement: Not applicable.

Acknowledgments: The authors would like to thank the editors and reviewers for their constructive comments, which will improve the manuscript.

Conflicts of Interest: The authors declare no conflict of interest.

Abbreviations

The following abbreviations are used in this manuscript:

DC (algorithm)	Divided and Conquer (algorithm)
MRRR (algorithm)	Multiple Relatively Robust Representations (algorithm)
ST (matrix)	Symmetric Tridiagonal (matrix)

References

1. Penke, C.; Marek, A.; Vorwerk, C.; Draxl, C.; Benner, P. High performance solution of skew-symmetric eigenvalue problems with applications in solving the Bethe-Salpeter eigenvalue problem. *Parallel Comput.* **2020**, *96*, 102639. [CrossRef]
2. Xu, W.R.; Bebiano, N.; Chen, G.L. On the construction of real non-self adjoint tridiagonal matrices with prescribed three spectra. *Electron. Trans. Numer. Anal.* **2019**, *51*, 363–386. [CrossRef]
3. Wei, Y.; Zheng, Y.; Jiang, Z.; Shon, S. A Study of Determinants and Inverses for Periodic Tridiagonal Toeplitz Matrices with Perturbed Corners Involving Mersenne Numbers. *Mathematics* **2019**, *7*, 893. [CrossRef]
4. Tanasescu, A.; Carabas, M.; Pop, F.; Popescu, P.G. Scalability of k-Tridiagonal Matrix Singular Value Decomposition. *Mathematics* **2021**, *9*, 3123. [CrossRef]
5. Bala, B.; Manafov, M.D.; Kablan, A. Inverse Spectral Problems for Spectral Data and Two Spectra of N by N Tridiagonal Almost-Symmetric Matrices. *Appl. Appl. Math.* **2019**, *14*, 1132–1144.
6. Bartoll, S.; Jiménez-Munguía, R.R.; Martínez-Avendaño, R.A.; Peris, A. Chaos for the Dynamics of Toeplitz Operators. *Mathematics* **2022**, *10*, 425. [CrossRef]
7. Nesterova, O.P.; Uzdin, A.M.; Fedorova, M.Y. Method for calculating strongly damped systems with non-proportional damping. *Mag. Civ. Eng.* **2018**, *81*, 64–72. [CrossRef]
8. Bahar, M.K. Charge-Current Output in Plasma-Immersed Hydrogen Atom with Noncentral Interaction. *Ann. Der Phys.* **2021**, *533*, 2100111. [CrossRef]
9. Geng, X.; Lei, Y. On the Kirchhoff Index and the Number of Spanning Trees of Linear Phenylenes Chain. *Polycycl. Aromat. Compd.* **2021**. [CrossRef]
10. Neo, V.W.; Naylor, P.A. Second order sequential best rotation algorithm with householder reduction for polynomial matrix eigenvalue decomposition. In Proceedings of the 2019 IEEE International Conference on Acoustics, Speech and Signal Processing (ICASSP), Brighton, UK, 12–17 May 2019, pp. 8043–8047.
11. Vazquez, A. Transition to multitype mixing in d-dimensional spreading dynamics. *Phys. Rev. E* **2021**, *103*, 022309. [CrossRef]
12. Wilkinson. The Algebraic Eigenvalue Problem. In *Handbook for Automatic Computation*; Volume II: Linear Algebra; Oxford University Press: Oxford, UK, 1969.
13. Alqahtani, A.; Gazzola, S.; Reichel, L.; Rodriguez, G. On the block Lanczos and block Golub-Kahan reduction methods applied to discrete ill-posed problems. *Numer. Linear Algebra Appl.* **2021**, *28*, e2376. [CrossRef]
14. Marques, O.; Demmel, J.; Vasconcelos, P.B. Bidiagonal SVD Computation via an Associated Tridiagonal Eigenproblem. *ACM Trans. Math. Softw.* **2020**, *46*, 1–25. [CrossRef]

15. Chen, M.F.; Li, Y.S. Development of powerful algorithm for maximal eigenpair. *Front. Math. China* **2019**, *14*, 493–519. [CrossRef]
16. Coelho, D.F.G.; Dimitrov, V.S.; Rakai, L. Efficient computation of tridiagonal matrices largest eigenvalue. *J. Comput. Appl. Math.* **2018**, *330*, 268–275. [CrossRef]
17. Tang, T.; Yang, J. Computing the Maximal Eigenpairs of Large Size Tridiagonal Matrices with O(1) Number of Iterations. *Numer. Math. Theory Methods Appl.* **2018**, *11*, 877–894. [CrossRef]
18. Francis, J.G. The QR transformation a unitary analogue to the LR transformation—Part 1. *Comput. J.* **1961**, *4*, 265–271. [CrossRef]
19. Francis, J.G. The QR transformation—Part 2. *Comput. J.* **1962**, *4*, 332–345. [CrossRef]
20. Myllykoski, M. Algorithm 1019: A Task-based Multi-shift QR/QZ Algorithm with Aggressive Early Deflation. *ACM Trans. Math. Softw.* **2022**, *48*, 11. [CrossRef]
21. Ortega, J.M.; Kaiser, H.F. The LLT and QR methods for symmetric tridiagonal matrices. *Comput. J.* **1963**, *6*, 99–101. [CrossRef]
22. Parlett, B.N. *The Symmetric Eigenvalue Problem*; SIAM: Philadelphia, PA, USA, 1997.
23. Stewart, G.W. A parallel implementation of the QR-algorithm. *Parallel Comput.* **1987**, *5*, 187–196. [CrossRef]
24. Granat, R.; Kagstrom, B.; Kressner, D. A novel parallel QR algorithm for hybrid distributed memory HPC systems. *SIAM J. Sci. Comput.* **2010**, *32*, 2345–2378. [CrossRef]
25. Matstoms, P. Parallel sparse QR factorization on shared memory architectures. *Parallel Comput.* **1995**, *21*, 473–486. [CrossRef]
26. Kaufman, L. A Parallel QR Algorithm for the Symmetrical Tridiagonal Eigenvalue Problem. *J. Parallel Distrib. Comput.* **1994**, *23*, 429–434. [CrossRef]
27. Ballard, G.; Demmel, J.; Grigori, L.; Jacquelin, M.; Knight, N. A 3d parallel algorithm for qr decomposition. In Proceedings of the 30th on Symposium on Parallelism in Algorithms and Architectures, Vienna, Austria, 16–18 July 2018; pp. 55–65.
28. Dhillon, I.S. A New O (N^2) Algorithm for the Symmetric Tridiagonal Eigenvalue/Eigenvector Problem. Doctoral Thesis, University of California, Berkeley, CA, USA, 1997.
29. Parlett, B.N.; Marques, O.A. An implementation of the dqds algorithm (positive case). *Linear Algebra Its Appl.* **2000**, *309*, 217–259. [CrossRef]
30. Fukuda, A.; Yamamoto, Y.; Iwasaki, M.; Ishiwata, E.; Nakamura, Y. Convergence acceleration of shifted LR transformations for totally nonnegative hessenberg matrices. *Appl. Math.* **2020**, *65*, 677–702. [CrossRef]
31. Cuppen, J.J. A divide and conquer method for the symmetric tridiagonal eigenproblem. *Numer. Math.* **1980**, *36*, 177–195. [CrossRef]
32. Liao, X.; Li, S.; Lu, Y.; Roman, J.E. A Parallel Structured Divide-and-Conquer Algorithm for Symmetric Tridiagonal Eigenvalue Problems. *IEEE Trans. Parallel Distrib. Syst.* **2021**, *32*, 367–378. [CrossRef]
33. Li, S.; Rouet, F.H.; Liu, J.; Huang, C.; Gao, X.; Chi, X. An efficient hybrid tridiagonal divide-and-conquer algorithm on distributed memory architectures. *J. Comput. Appl. Math.* **2018**, *344*, 512–520. [CrossRef]
34. Kahan, W. *Accurate Eigenvalues of a Symmetric Tri-Diagonal Matrix*; Report; Dept. of Computer Science, Stanford University: Stanford, CA, USA, 1966.
35. Ralha, R. Mixed Precision Bisection. *Math. Comput. Sci.* **2018**, *12*, 173–181. [CrossRef]
36. Muir, T.; Metzler, W.H. *A Treatise on the Theory of Determinants*; Dover Publications: Mineola, NY, USA, 1960.
37. Denton, P.; Parke, S.; Tao, T.; Zhang, X. Eigenvectors from eigenvalues: A survey of a basic identity in linear algebra. *Bull. Am. Math. Soc.* **2022**, *59*, 31–58. [CrossRef]
38. Gu, M.; Eisenstat, S.C. A divide-and-conquer algorithm for the symmetric tridiagonal eigenproblem. *SIAM J. Matrix Anal. Appl.* **1995**, *16*, 172–191. [CrossRef]
39. Li, T.Y.; Zeng, Z. The Laguerre iteration in solving the symmetric tridiagonal eigenproblem, revisited. *SIAM J. Sci. Comput.* **1994**, *15*, 1145–1173. [CrossRef]
40. Dekker, T.J. Finding a zero by means of successive linear interpolation. In *Constructive Aspects of the Fundamental Theorem of Algebra*; Wiley: Hoboken, NJ, USA, 1969; pp. 37–51.
41. Wilkinson, J.H. *Two Algorithms Based on Successive Linear Interpolation*; Stanford University: Stanford, CA, USA, 1967.
42. Brent, R.P. *Algorithms for Minimization without Derivatives*; Prentice-Hall: Hoboken, NJ, USA, 1973.
43. Bernstein, H.J. An accelerated bisection method for the calculation of eigenvalues of a symmetric tridiagonal matrix. *Numer. Math.* **1984**, *43*, 153–160. [CrossRef]
44. Bhatia, R. *Perturbation Bounds for Matrix Eigenvalues*; SIAM: Philadelphia, PA, USA, 2007.
45. Da Fonseca, C.M.; Kowalenko, V. Eigenpairs of a family of tridiagonal matrices: Three decades later. *Acta Math. Hung.* **2020**, *160*, 376–389. [CrossRef]
46. Ferreira, C.; Parlett, B. Eigenpairs of Wilkinson Matrices. *SIAM J. Matrix Anal. Appl.* **2020**, *41*, 1388–1415. [CrossRef]

mathematics

Article

An Extrinsic Approach Based on Physics-Informed Neural Networks for PDEs on Surfaces

Zhuochao Tang [1,2], Zhuojia Fu [1,2,3,*] and Sergiy Reutskiy [2]

1 Key Laboratory of Ministry of Education for Coastal Disaster and Protection, Hohai University, Nanjing 210098, China
2 Center for Numerical Simulation Software in Engineering and Sciences, College of Mechanics and Materials, Hohai University, Nanjing 211100, China
3 State Key Laboratory of Mechanics and Control of Mechanical Structures, Nanjing University of Aeronautics and Astronautics, Nanjing 210098, China
* Correspondence: paul212063@hhu.edu.cn

Abstract: In this paper, we propose an extrinsic approach based on physics-informed neural networks (PINNs) for solving the partial differential equations (PDEs) on surfaces embedded in high dimensional space. PINNs are one of the deep learning-based techniques. Based on the training data and physical models, PINNs introduce the standard feedforward neural networks (NNs) to approximate the solutions to the PDE systems. Using automatic differentiation, the PDEs information could be encoded into NNs and a loss function. To deal with the surface differential operators in the loss function, we combine the extrinsic approach with PINNs and then express that loss function in extrinsic form. Subsequently, the loss function could be minimized extrinsically with respect to the NN parameters. Numerical results demonstrate that the extrinsic approach based on PINNs for surface problems has good accuracy and higher efficiency compared with the embedding approach based on PINNs. In addition, the strong nonlinear mapping ability of NNs makes this approach robust in solving time-dependent nonlinear problems on more complex surfaces.

Keywords: machine learning; extrinsic; embedding; intrinsic; surfaces; Laplace–Beltrami operator

MSC: 68T07; 65N99; 65M99

Citation: Tang, Z.; Fu, Z.; Reutskiy, S. An Extrinsic Approach Based on Physics-Informed Neural Networks for PDEs on Surfaces. *Mathematics* **2022**, *10*, 2861. https://doi.org/10.3390/math10162861

Academic Editors: Fajie Wang, Ji Lin and Junseok Kim

Received: 4 July 2022
Accepted: 8 August 2022
Published: 11 August 2022

1. Introduction

Various applications in science and engineering, as a matter of fact, refer to solutions of Partial Differential Equations (PDEs) on curved surfaces or more general manifolds. Such applications include the generation of textures [1] or the visualization of vector fields [2] in image processing, flows and solidification [3] on surfaces in fluid dynamics and evolving surfactants [4] on interfaces in biology, etc.

To solve such surface problems, many numerical methods have been put into operation, including the typical finite difference method (FDM), finite element method (FEM), finite volume method (FVM), phase field (PF) method, radial basis function (RBF) collocation method, meshless generalized finite difference method (GFDM), generalized moving least squares (GMLS) method, etc. Generally, these methods cannot be directly used to handle surface problems because the surface differential operators are defined in tangent space rather than Euclidean space. In order to effectively map surface operators, Ruuth et al. [5] put forward the closest point method based on the closest point representation of the surface and then solved embedded PDEs by standard FDM in Euclidean space; further, Piret [6] presented the orthogonal gradients method, which extends the closest point method to a mesh-free version; Hansbo et al. [7] proposed the cut finite element method to solve PDEs on implicit surfaces via level set methods; Cheung et al. [8] combined the unsymmetric Kansa method and embedding conditions (or constant-along-normal conditions) to construct an overdetermined system for such surface problems; Chen et al. [9,10] used the projection matrix and the idea of pseudospectra to approximate the Laplace–Beltrami operator (also known as surface Laplace operator) only using collocation points on surfaces. These advanced techniques to map surface operators can be roughly divided into three categories: intrinsic approaches [11], embedding approaches [12] and extrinsic approaches [13]. Intrinsic treatment aims to impose global or local parameterization [11] on curved surfaces and then express surface differential operators within new coordinates. The embedding approach aims to make embedding PDE be the analog of the surface PDE and involve only the standard Cartesian operators. The extrinsic approach is to express surface operators in extrinsic form and approximate them extrinsically. In our previous work [14–16], we have combined the meshless GFDM with an extrinsic approach to solve using pattern formation problems, anomalous diffusion problems and the heat and mass transfer problems on surfaces. The extrinsic approach is numerically proved to be a quite effective treatment.

However, traditional numerical methods inevitably need mesh generation or node generation over the whole computational domain. Additionally, the quality of mesh or node distribution more or less has an influence on numerical accuracy [17]. On the contrary, there is no such concept as mesh quality in machine learning methods [18]. In other words, machine learning methods do not require high-quality meshes, but only require relatively uniform data sampling. To overcome the dilemma that conventional neural network methods lack robustness under the small data regime, Tarkhov et al. [19–22] first introduced the PDE information into neural network models with single hidden layers to solve various mathematical problems. Based on this, Raissi et al. [23,24] recently developed a series of deep neural networks based on physical information named physics-informed neural networks (PINNs). PINNs aim to replace the PDE solution with a feedforward neural network and take advantage of information from PDEs and initial/boundary conditions to form an optimized system explicitly. This explicit system originates from the information based on training data and could also be defined as a terminology loss function. By minimizing this system with respect to the parameters (including weights and biases) defined in NNs, PINNs could find one NN which best describes the physical model governed by the PDEs [25–27]. To specify the differential operators acting on the variables, PINNs employ the automatic differentiation technology and classical chain rule. As a matter of fact, Bihlo et al. [28] have applied PINNs to solve shallow-water equations on the sphere. In that paper, they used the latitude–longitude coordinates; i.e., they imposed one smooth parameterization on sphere and then expressed the shallow-water equations in latitude–longitude coordinates. Apparently, the same operation cannot be conducted on more general surfaces. Additionally, Fang et al. [29] first combined the PINNs with the embedding approach to solve time independent PDEs on surface. However, they only considered some of the embedding conditions, and the numerical accuracy can be further improved by applying complete embedding conditions.

In this paper, our main contribution is to propose an extrinsic approach based on the PINNs to solve surface PDEs on curved surfaces or more general manifolds. Compared with surface-type intrinsic approach, although our method is related to the ambient dimension rather than the surface dimension, its capability of handling more complex surfaces makes it more competitive. In addition, we also combined the embedding approach with PINNs to make a direct comparison with the extrinsic approach with regard to computational efficiency. We introduce the complete embedding conditions, which means that more complex optimization function will be formed, resulting in the inefficiency of the approach. This also shows that extrinsic approach performs well in computational efficiency.

The remainder of the paper is organized as follows: Section 2 gives details on PDEs defined on surfaces, introduces the PINNs and describes their implementation. In Section 3, we demonstrate the effectiveness of PINNs under several numerical examples. In this section, we first illustrate the convergence results by using different parameters in PINNs and test the robustness of PINNs by adopting sundry smooth surfaces. In the same section, we also present a comparison of numerical results by using randomly distributed training points and points that are quasi-uniformly distributed in 3D space. Further, we explore the potential of PINNs for time-dependent nonlinear problems on more general surfaces. Finally, the conclusions and discussions are summarized in Section 4.

2. Methodology

In this section, a detailed description of surface differential operators involved in PDEs defined on surfaces, the implementation of physics-informed neural networks and their extrinsic treatment for solving surface PDEs are presented. In addition, a brief procedure of PINNs and its distinguishments from other methods are given.

2.1. Continuous Differential Operators on Surfaces and Its Extrinsic Form

The main difference between surface PDEs defined on surfaces and standard PDEs posed in some bounded domains with flat geometries is that the curvatures of surfaces play vital roles in physical models governed by the PDEs. We first pay attention to the differential operators posed on some sufficiently smooth, connected and compact surface $S \subset \mathbb{R}$ with no boundary and $dim(S) = d - 1$. The dimension $d = 3$ is taken into consideration for notational simplicity, and any other cases with higher d could be extended simply. To specify the relationship between surface differential operators and standard Euclidean differential operators, we denote the unit outward normal vector at any $\mathbf{x} \in S$ as $\mathbf{n} = (n^x, n^y, n^z)$ and the corresponding projection matrix to the tangent space as

$$\mathbf{P}(x) = (\mathbf{I}_3 - \mathbf{n}\mathbf{n}^T) \in \mathbb{R}^{3\times 3}, \tag{1}$$

where $\mathbf{I}$ is the 3-by-3 identity matrix. Then, the surface gradient operator ∇_S could be defined in terms of the standard Euclidean gradient ∇ via projections as

$$\nabla_S := \mathbf{P}\nabla, \tag{2}$$

and similarly, the Laplace–Beltrami operator (also known as surface Laplace operator) Δ_S could be defined as

$$\Delta_S := \nabla_S \cdot \nabla_S. \tag{3}$$

The Laplace–Beltrami operator could be regarded as a divergence-gradient operator. By introducing the extrinsic idea and substituting Equation (2) into Equation (3), the extrinsic (Euclidean) form [8] of the surface gradient operator and Laplace–Beltrami operator acting on any sufficiently smooth function could be derived as

$$\nabla_S u := \nabla u - \mathbf{n}\partial_{\mathbf{n}} u, \tag{4}$$

$$\Delta_S u := \Delta u - H_S \partial_{\mathbf{n}} u - \partial_{\mathbf{n}}^{(2)} u. \tag{5}$$

in which $\partial_{\mathbf{n}} u = \mathbf{n}^T \nabla u, \partial_{\mathbf{n}}^{(2)} u := \mathbf{n}^T J(\nabla u)\mathbf{n}$ and $H_S = \mathrm{trace}\big(J(\mathbf{n})(\mathbf{I} - \mathbf{n}\mathbf{n}^T)\big)$. Here, J means the Jacobian operator in Euclidean space. Obviously, Euclidean space is the one we are most familiar with, and most algorithms are also developed in Euclidean space. Once the extrinsic (Euclidean) form is obtained, the approximations of surface operators are conducted naturally. It should be noted here that the Euclidean way is just one of the extrinsic treatments, and this way makes the approximation be implemented in the ambient dimension rather than the surface dimension.

For better understanding, we give one example to derive the explicit expression of surface differential operators on the unit sphere. Simplifying with the surface $S = x^2 + y^2 + z^2 - 1$, one could naturally obtain the unit normal vector $[x \quad y \quad z]^T$. Putting this into Equations (4) and (5), the extrinsic surface differential operators are represented by

$$\nabla_S = \begin{bmatrix} 1-x^2 & -xy & -xz \\ -xy & 1-y^2 & -yz \\ -xz & -yz & 1-z^2 \end{bmatrix} \begin{bmatrix} \partial_x \\ \partial_y \\ \partial_z \end{bmatrix} = \begin{bmatrix} (1-x^2)\partial_x - xy\partial_y - xz\partial_z \\ -xy\partial_x + (1-y^2)\partial_y - yz\partial_z \\ -xz\partial_x - yz\partial_y + (1-z^2)\partial_z \end{bmatrix}, \tag{6}$$

$$\Delta_S = (1-x^2)\partial_{xx} + (1-y^2)\partial_{yy} + (1-z^2)\partial_{zz} - 2xy\partial_{xy} - 2xz\partial_{xz} - 2yz\partial_{yz} - 2x\partial_x - 2y\partial_y - 2z\partial_z. \tag{7}$$

Once Equations (6) and (7) have been obtained, the approximation for surface operators defined on smooth surfaces could be expressed using some existing methods. For other surfaces, the normal information is different, hence the difference in Equations (6) and (7).

2.2. Physics-Informed Neural Networks (PINNs)

The main aim of PINNs is to approximate the solutions to PDEs. Like other numerical methods, the standard PINNs is derived in standard Euclidean space. In this section, we focus on introducing the basic idea of PINNs and how it solves PDEs on surfaces extrinsically. We use the steady state convective diffusion reaction equation

$$\left(a\Delta_S - \vec{\mathbf{b}}\cdot\nabla_S + c\right)u(x,y,z) = f(x,y,z) \tag{8}$$

with the certain coefficients $a, \vec{\mathbf{b}}, c$ as an illustration.

In the PINNs, there are three different ways to construct the approximate solutions $u(x,y,z)$ to the PDEs [26]. Due to fact that the PDE (8) defined on closed surfaces has no boundary conditions, the direct construction of the approximate solutions is employed in this work as an output of neural networks (NN), namely, $\tilde{u}(x,y,z) = u_{NN}(\mathbf{x};\boldsymbol{\mu})$, $\mathbf{x} \in S(\boldsymbol{\mu} = \{\mathbf{W},\mathbf{B}\})$. The NN, which is parameterized with finitely many weights $\mathbf{W}$ and biases $\mathbf{B}$, acts as a surrogate model of the PDE model to approximate the mapping from the spatial coordinates to the solutions of equation. One NN usually contains multiple hidden layers to obtain more accurate solutions. Here, PINNs seek to optimize the NN's parameters composed of weights and biases by minimizing the so-called loss function. Usually, the loss function is defined as the sum of mean squared error from both governing equations (PDEs) and boundary conditions on the training points. For PDEs defined on surfaces without boundary conditions, the loss function is expressed by the NN parameter $\boldsymbol{\mu}$ as

$$Loss(\boldsymbol{\mu}) = \frac{1}{N}\sum_{k=1}^{N}\left[\left(a\Delta_S - \vec{\mathbf{b}}\cdot\nabla_S + c\right)\tilde{u}(\mathbf{x}_k) - f(\mathbf{x}_k)\right]^2, \tag{9}$$

in which N is the total number of the training points. By substituting Equation (4) and Equation (5) into Equation (9), the loss function in extrinsic form finally could be derived under Cartesian coordinate by the NN parameter as

$$Loss(\boldsymbol{\mu}) = \frac{1}{N}\sum_{k=1}^{N}\left[\left(a(\Delta - H_S\partial_{\mathbf{n}} - \partial_{\mathbf{n}}^{(2)}) - \vec{\mathbf{b}}\cdot(\nabla - \mathbf{n}\partial_{\mathbf{n}}) + c\right)u_{NN}(\mathbf{x}_k;\boldsymbol{\mu}) - f(\mathbf{x}_k)\right]^2. \tag{10}$$

As mentioned in Section 1, the embedding approach based on PINNs is also discussed in this work for comparison with the extrinsic approach. As can be seen in Equations (4) and (5), the surface operators could be completely equal to the standard operator with the constraints $\partial_{\mathbf{n}}u = 0$ and $\partial_{\mathbf{n}}^{(2)}u = 0$. The constraints are embedding conditions. Therefore, the loss function in embedding form could be written as

$$\begin{aligned} Loss(\boldsymbol{\mu}) =& \frac{1}{N}\sum_{k=1}^{N}\left[\left(a\Delta - \vec{\mathbf{b}}\cdot\nabla + c\right)u_{NN}(\mathbf{x}_k;\boldsymbol{\mu}) - f(\mathbf{x}_k)\right]^2 \\ &+ \frac{1}{N}\sum_{k=1}^{N}[\partial_{\mathbf{n}}u_{NN}(\mathbf{x}_k;\boldsymbol{\mu})]^2 + \frac{1}{N}\sum_{k=1}^{N}\left[\partial_{\mathbf{n}}^{(2)}u_{NN}(\mathbf{x}_k;\boldsymbol{\mu})\right]^2. \end{aligned} \tag{11}$$

For PINNs, it is easy to add only two constraints to the optimization function as Equation (11). Although the extrinsic treatment needs many computations, as shown in Equations (4) and (5), they could be pre-computed for a certain surface before the "training", just like Equations (6) and (7) for a unit sphere. Then, the surface operators could be regarded as some specified operators defined in Euclidean space. Once they have been obtained, the loss function could be expressed explicitly only using governing equation without any constraints. Compared with the embedding treatment having extra constraints, the loss function in extrinsic form is simpler in the "training" process.

Then, the original problem (8) becomes an optimization problem, namely,

$$\boldsymbol{\mu}^* = \arg\min_{\boldsymbol{\mu}} Loss(\boldsymbol{\mu}) \tag{12}$$

in which the $\boldsymbol{\mu}^*$ represents the optimal parameters.

Herein the automatic differentiation technique and the chain rule are used in loss function to compute the spatial derivatives of $u_{NN}(\mathbf{x};\boldsymbol{\mu})$. For time-dependent problems, the approximation could be regarded as $u_{NN}(\mathbf{x},t;\boldsymbol{\mu})$, and the temporal derivative could be realized in two ways: similar treatment as a spatial derivative and individual time integration using the method of lines. Then, different optimization algorithms can be used to solve Equation (12). This optimization process is called "training". Additionally, we use multiple sets of initial NN parameters $\boldsymbol{\mu}$ in the following numerical examples to avoid its uncertainty.

2.3. The Procedure of the Extrinsic Approach Based on PINNs

To better understand this extrinsic numerical framework for approximating the surface PDEs and compare it with traditional numerical methods, pseudocode is demonstrated in this section. We first give the steps of some methods, involving linear algebra such as FEM; RBF collocation methods; meshless GFDM; etc. In the implementation of these methods, the process is more or less divided into five steps briefly: firstly, generate the meshes/collocation points on surfaces; secondly, construct the approximate solutions based on respective approximation theory; thirdly, form the stiffness matrix or basis matrix for each mesh/point extrinsically; fourthly, assemble the information on each mesh/point and then obtain a discrete system with respect to the PDE model on surfaces; lastly, solve the algebraic system by using linear solver.

Differently, the pseudocode of the extrinsic approach based on PINNs could be summarized in Algorithm 1.

Algorithm 1 The extrinsic approach based on PINNs.

Require: The training datasets including a group of spatial coordinates and the corresponding solutions; the prescribed number of width and depth in NN; the initialized NN parameters; the convergence tolerance ε and number of iterations N_i;
Ensure: The surrogate NN model with optimized parameters;
Construct the NN with initialized parameters;
Specify the training sets for governing equation;
Specify the loss function in extrinsic form considering the governing equation;
repeat
    $n \leftarrow n+1, n < N_i$;
    Optimization: compute Equation (12);
    Update the loss value;
until Loss value $< \varepsilon$
Determine the optimal parameters;
Substitute test datasets and then acquire the posterior error.

The concept of datasets in PINNs is somewhat similar to the that of collocation points [17]—namely, the PINNs are also meshless. It inherits the advantages of both meshless and neural network methods. In addition, although the numerical accuracy of PINNs in the present study on surface PDEs is usually not as high as those of some collocation methods such as RBF collocation methods, the PINNs is easy implement because neural networks can directly be used to deal with nonlinear problems without introducing iterative algorithms. These two advantages over traditional methods make PINNs quite attractive recently.

3. Numerical Examples

In this section, several different examples are provided. We first explore the convergence and the accuracy of PINNs for Equation (8) on the unit sphere, and then more surfaces and nonlinear PDEs are taken into consideration to verify its robustness. To quantify the accuracy and effectiveness of our approximate solutions, we introduce the L_2 error measures as follows.

$$L_2 = \sqrt{\sum_{k=1}^{N}(u(\mathbf{x}_k) - \tilde{u}(\mathbf{x}_k))^2} \Big/ \sqrt{\sum_{k=1}^{N}(u(\mathbf{x}_k))^2} \tag{13}$$

where $u(\mathbf{x}_k), \tilde{u}(\mathbf{x}_k)$ represent the reference solution and approximate solution at the k-th point. To avoid the uncertainty of different initializations for the network parameters $\boldsymbol{\mu}$ and find an optimal neural network as much as possible, we employed the L-BFGS optimization method and plot the mean for the solution errors from the 10 runs, which we adopted as a new metric of convergence. The Xavier initialization and hyperbolic tangent activation function were taken into consideration, and all the tests were implemented in Python on laptop with CPU i5-8265U @1.60 GHz and RAM 8.00 GB.

Example 1. *Convergence and accuracy test on a unit sphere*

In this example, we used Equation (8), and the coefficients were chosen as $a = 1$, $\vec{\mathbf{b}} = [1\ 1\ 1]^T, c = 5$, and the reference solution was assembled by trigonometric function, which is expressed as

$$u(x, y, z) = \sin x \sin y \sin z. \tag{14}$$

The force term was simply obtained by substituting the reference solution into the equation. A total number of 2500 points were chosen to be distributed on the unit sphere, as shown in Figure 1. Here, we selected N points randomly from these quasi-uniform points and the corresponding solutions from Equation (14) as training data, and all these 2500 points were regarded as test points to test the convergence of PINNs. As derived above in Equations (6) and (7), the loss function on this unit sphere could be obtained easily.

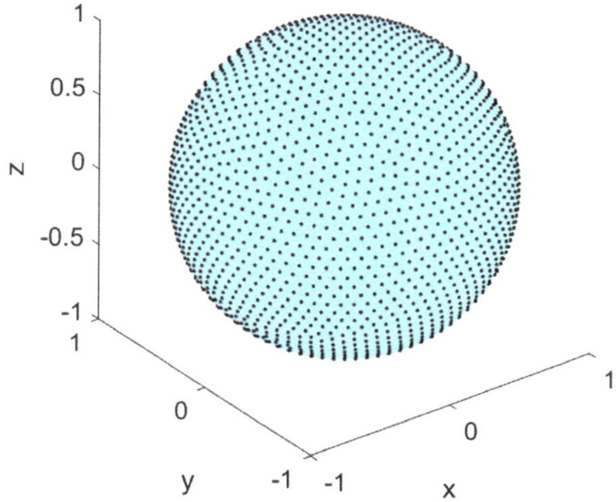

Figure 1. Sketch of the quasi-uniform points distributed on the unit sphere: the point sets could be obtained by using the minimum energy (ME) algorithm [30].

Since we had no idea of how sensitive PINNs approximations are to surface differentiation operators, we attempted to use various NNs with different numbers of hidden layers (also known as the depth of the NN; e.g., four hidden layers' mean depth is five) and neurons (also known as the width of the NN; e.g., 20 neurons' mean width is 20). Figure 2 shows the convergence results, and Figure 3 indicates some snapshots of error distribution by using different parameters. Tables 1 and 2 give some numerical results using smaller width and depth for solving linear problems on surfaces.

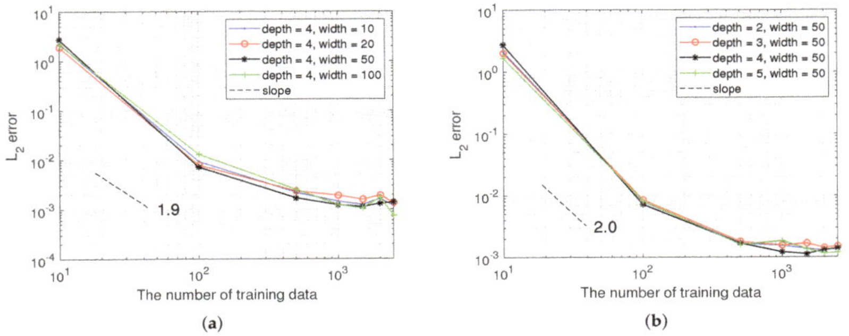

Figure 2. Example 1: Convergence results by using (**a**) different widths and (**b**) different depths.

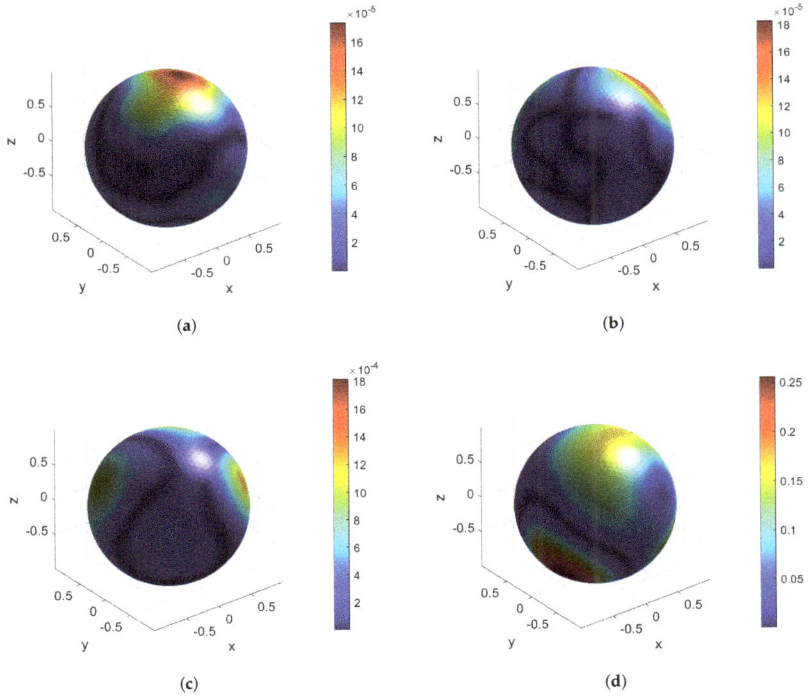

Figure 3. Example 1: Random few snapshots of absolute error distribution under width = 50 and depth = 4 by using (**a**) 2500 training data points; (**b**) 1500 training data points; (**c**) 100 training data points; (**d**) 10 training data points.

Table 1. Example 1: L_2 error and CPU time using different depths under width = 50 and 2000 training data.

Depth	2	3	4	5
L_2 error	1.12×10^{-3}	1.41×10^{-2}	1.34×10^{-3}	1.21×10^{-3}
CPU time	19.96 (s)	29.42 (s)	76.65 (s)	102.26 (s)

Table 2. Example 1: L_2 error and CPU time using different widths under depth = 4, with 2000 training data points.

Width	3	5	10	20	50	100
L_2 error	4.06×10^{-2}	1.02×10^{-2}	1.44×10^{-3}	1.91×10^{-3}	1.34×10^{-3}	1.69×10^{-3}
CPU time	5.47 (s)	8.54 (s)	17.67 (s)	34.63 (s)	76.65 (s)	152.72 (s)

As seen in Figures 2 and 3, we used, respectively, 2, 3, 4 and 5 hidden layers with 10, 20, 50 and 100 neurons to test convergence and accuracy of PINNs in solving Equation (8). The distribution of error could be affected by many factors, such as the width/depth of NNs, the initializations of NNs and the potential noise of training data. Numerical results converged at around $10^{-4} \sim 10^{-3}$ with convergence rates of 1.9 and 2.0. Apparently, we could obtain similar results by using different depths and widths when the number of training data reached 500 or more. In Table 1, we can see that for linear surface PDEs, a network with one hidden layer works fine, and it has the advantages of simplicity and speed of operation. In Table 2, we can see that when using 3 or 5, the numerical accuracy would be reduced to around 10^{-2}. To connect numerical results in Table 2 with those in Table 1, we further considered the case with depth = 2 and width = 3, and its L_2 error is 0.71. We could summarize that the depth, width and number of training data indeed influence the numerical results. Additionally, for surface linear problems, using smaller width and depth is more suitable due to its higher efficiency and for surface nonlinear problems, width and depth should be increased correspondingly. This shows PINN approximation has good adaptability to surface differential operators. Furthermore, we particularly plot the error distribution in Figure 3 to visualize the results, which shows good accuracy of PINNs for explicitly solving surface PDEs.

In addition, we further compare the extrinsic approach with the embedding approach both based on the PINNs. As mentioned in Equation (11), the embedding approach needs other constraints, and in Table 3, one can find that the accuracies of the two techniques show almost no difference, but the computational time varies a lot. This is because the additional constraints of embedding conditions make loss function (11) a more non-convex function. Numerical results prove that PINNs combined with the extrinsic technique is more efficient.

Table 3. Example 1: L_2 error and CPU time by using extrinsic and embedding approaches with different numbers of training data under width = 50 and depth = 4.

N	1000	1500	2000	2500
Extrinsic	1.02×10^{-3} 32.70 (s)	9.88×10^{-4} 65.42 (s)	1.49×10^{-3} 102.26 (s)	9.36×10^{-4} 108.66 (s)
Embedding	3.51×10^{-3} 113.93 (s)	4.80×10^{-3} 237.02 (s)	2.17×10^{-3} 312.26 (s)	1.90×10^{-3} 418.55 (s)

Example 2. *Results on more general surfaces*

In this example, we attempted to test the robustness of PINNs by solving PDEs on more general surfaces, and made a direct comparison by using quasi-uniform distributed training data and randomly distributed training data as shown in Figure 4. The parametric equations or implicit expressions of some surfaces used in this or the following example, including Torus, a constant distance product (CDP) surface, Bretzel2, Orthocircle, Red Blood Cell (RBC) and tooth surface, are provided as

(1) Tours:

$$S = \left(1 - \sqrt{x^2 + y^2}\right)^2 + z^2 - \frac{1}{9}; \tag{15}$$

(2) CDP:

$$\begin{aligned} S = & \sqrt{(x-1)^2 + y^2 + z^2}\sqrt{(x+1)^2 + y^2 + z^2}\sqrt{x^2 + (y-1)^2 + z^2} \\ & \sqrt{x^2 + (y+1)^2 + z^2} - 1.1; \end{aligned} \tag{16}$$

(3) Bretzel2:

$$S = \left(x^2(1-x^2) - y^2\right)^2 + \frac{1}{2}z^2 - \frac{1}{40}; \tag{17}$$

(4) Orthocircle:

$$\begin{aligned} S = & \left((x^2 + y^2 - 1)^2 + z^2\right)\left((y^2 + z^2 - 1)^2 + x^2\right) \\ & \left((z^2 + x^2 - 1)^2 + y^2\right) - 0.075^2\left(1 + 3(x^2 + y^2 + z^2)\right); \end{aligned} \tag{18}$$

(5) RBC:

$$S = \begin{cases} x = 1.15\cos(\lambda)\cos(\theta), \\ y = 1.15\sin(\lambda)\cos(\theta), \\ z = 0.5\sin(\lambda)(0.24 + 2.3\cos(\theta)^2 - 1.3\cos(\theta)^4), \end{cases} \quad -\pi \le \lambda \le \pi, \frac{-\pi}{2} \le \theta \le \frac{\pi}{2}. \tag{19}$$

(6) Tooth:

$$S = x^8 + y^8 + z^8 - (x^2 + y^2 + z^2); \tag{20}$$

In this test, the coefficients in Equation (8) were set as $a = 1, \vec{\mathbf{b}} = [1\ 1\ 1]^T, c = 1$, and the reference solution was changed to $u(x, y, z) = \sin x \cos y \sin z$. We first employed Torus by using 500 quasi-uniform training data and by using 500 randomly distributed training data to make a comparison.

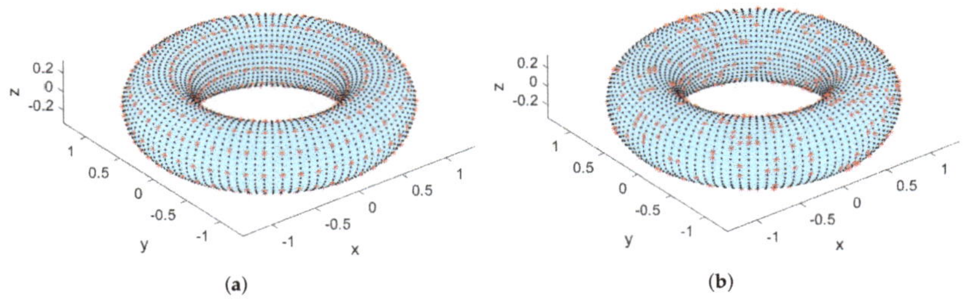

Figure 4. Example 2: Two different selections of training data on Torus: (**a**) quasi-uniform training data; (**b**) random training data generated by combined multiple recursive generator algorithm: red "*" points are selected training data; black points are test points.

It can be found from Figure 5 that the distribution of training data slightly affected the numerical results. Although uniform sampling of the training dataset is always good for results, PINNs are superior to some typical numerical methods to some extent for solving PDEs on high dimensional surfaces because for PINNs combined with the extrinsic approach, only training data are required, rather than generating high quality meshes or regular points. Additionally, the distribution of training data influences the results little.

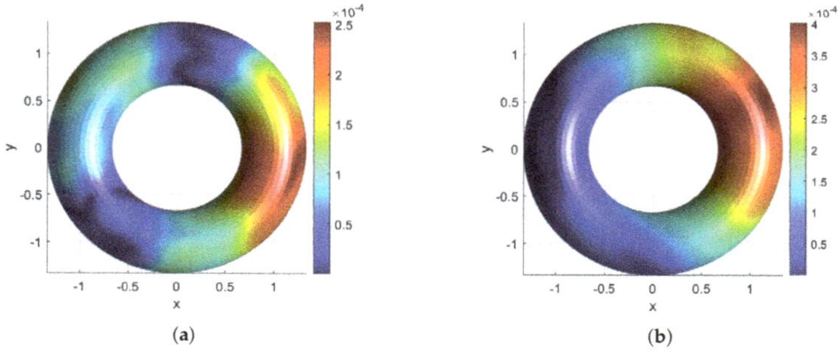

Figure 5. Example 2: Snapshots of absolute error distribution under width = 50 and depth = 4: (**a**) by using quasi-uniform training data and (**b**) by using randomly distributed training data.

In addition, distribution numerical errors and L_2 errors on different surfaces are given, respectively, in Figure 6 and Table 4. The number of training points was chosen as 500, and the total numbers of points corresponding to CDP, Breztel2, Orthocircle and RBC were 3996, 3690, 4286 and 4000. When dealing with PDEs defined on high-dimensional complex surfaces, PINNs combined with the extrinsic approach show good stability and robustness.

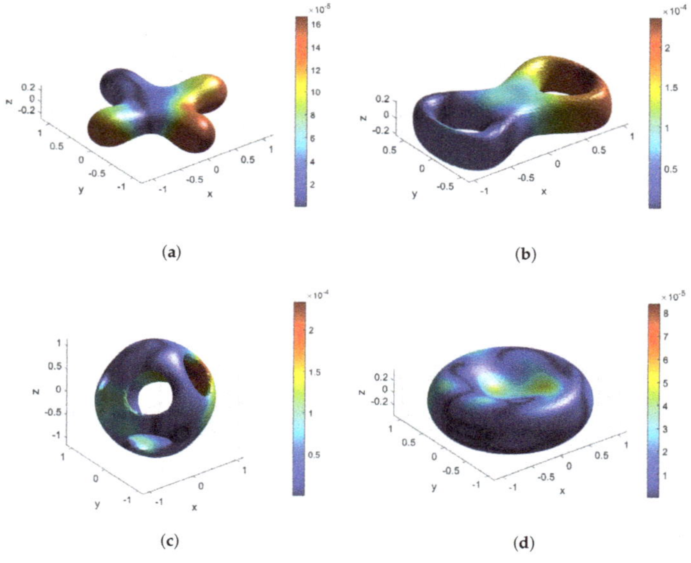

Figure 6. Example 2: Snapshots of absolute error distribution under width = 50 and depth = 4 on various surfaces: (**a**) CDP, (**b**) Bretzel2, (**c**) Orthocircle, (**d**) RBC.

Table 4. Example 2: L_2 error on different surfaces under width = 50 and depth = 4.

Surfaces	CDP	Bretzel2	Orthocircle	RBC
L_2 error	1.18×10^{-3}	1.51×10^{-3}	4.20×10^{-3}	2.37×10^{-3}

Example 3. *Nonlinear PDEs on surfaces*

In order to confront a more complicated model on different surfaces, the nonlinear model is considered in this example. The governing equation is

$$\left(a\Delta_S - \vec{\mathbf{b}} \cdot \nabla_S + c\right)u(x,y,z) + g(u) = f(x,y,z). \tag{21}$$

Herein $g(u) = u^2$ is the nonlinear term, the exact solution was set to $u = e^{x+y}\sin(z)$ and the parameters were $a = 1, \vec{\mathbf{b}} = \mathbf{0}, c = 0$. Similarly, the loss function in extrinsic form could be expressed as Equation (10).

We again performed the convergence analysis for this nonlinear model on a unit sphere, as exhibited in Figure 7. Apparently, compared with the results in Example 1, the numerical results of the nonlinear model are not accurate enough when the depth or width is too small. This means when the number of layers or the number of neurons is too small, the complex nonlinear behavior cannot be perfectly captured in spite of good nonlinear mapping capabilities of neural networks. As the width and depth increase, the numerical results show convergence similarly to the linear problems. We also plot the distribution of absolute error on the unit sphere and tooth surface under depth = 4 and width = 50, as shown in Figure 8, which indicates again that the PINNs combined with extrinsic approach perform well not only for linear problems but also for nonlinear problems on surfaces.

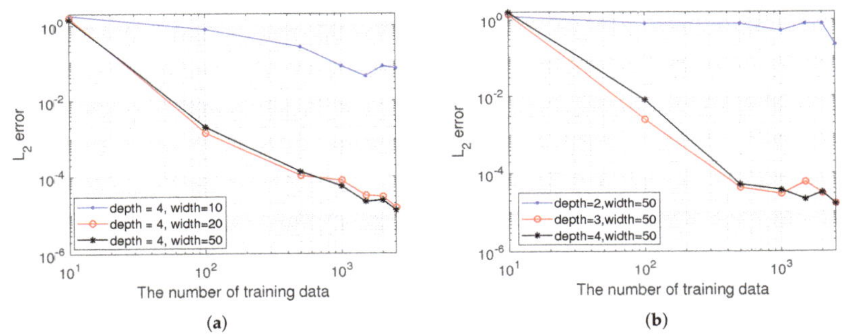

Figure 7. Example 3: Convergence results by using (**a**) different widths and (**b**) different depths.

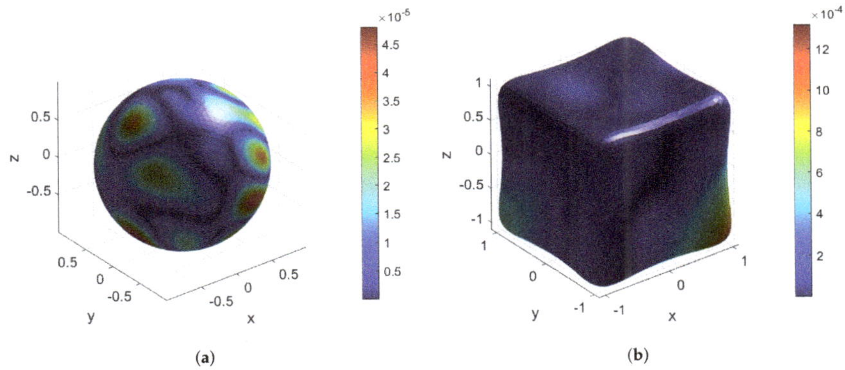

Figure 8. Example 3: Snapshots of absolute error distribution under width = 50 and depth = 4 for nonlinear problems on (**a**) a unit sphere and (**b**) tooth surface.

Example 4. *Time-dependent nonlinear PDEs on surfaces*

In this example, a time-dependent nonlinear convective diffusion reaction equation on a unit sphere is considered as

$$\frac{\partial u}{\partial t} = \left(a\Delta_S - \vec{\mathbf{b}} \cdot \nabla_S + c\right)u(x,y,z,t) + g(u) + f \tag{22}$$

in which $g(u) = u^2$ and $a = 1, \vec{\mathbf{b}} = \mathbf{0}, c = 0$. The exact solution is given as $u = e^{x+y+z}\sin(t)$. Differently from the traditional methods combined with some time integration methods, the variable t in this example is considered as an individual variable, just like the spatial variable in the loss function, i.e.,

$$Loss(\boldsymbol{\mu}) = \frac{1}{N}\sum_{k=1}^{N}\left[\partial_t u_{NN}(\mathbf{x}_k, t_k; \boldsymbol{\mu}) - (a\Delta_S - \vec{\mathbf{b}} \cdot \nabla_S + c)u_{NN}(\mathbf{x}_k, t_k; \boldsymbol{\mu}) - g(\tilde{u}) - f(\mathbf{x}_k)\right]^2 \tag{23}$$

We plot the distribution of absolute error on the unit sphere at $t = 0.1$ as illustrated in Figure 9. The L_2 error is 1.65×10^{-3} using 2500 points with time increment $\Delta t = 0.01$. When considering the continuous time models, the original Equation (22) becomes a 4D problem. We found that PINNs has a good ability to approximate high-dimensional problems, which can be well combined with an extrinsic approach.

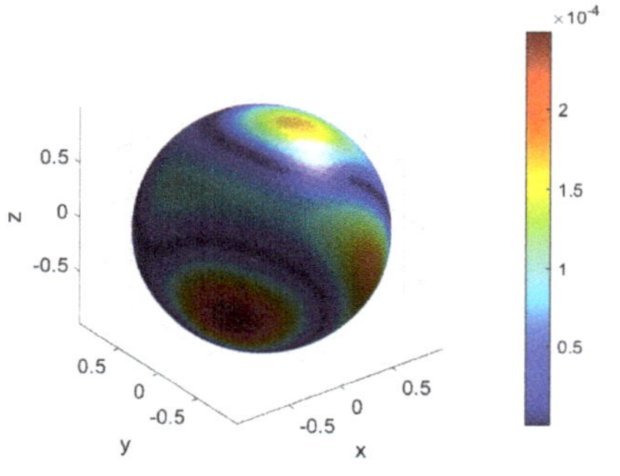

Figure 9. Example 4: Distribution of absolute error under width = 50 and depth = 4 for time-dependent nonlinear problems (22) on the unit sphere.

4. Conclusions and Discussions

In this work, the extrinsic approach based on PINNs is proposed and shows good performance and potential in the solutions of linear or nonlinear partial differential equations (PDEs) on surfaces embedded in high dimensional space. We could conclude from the first example that PINNs converge rapidly at the beginning of the increasing number of training points due to the dominant effect of the discretization error, and the solution will not be obviously improved with the further increase in the number of training points due to the dominant effect of optimization error. The second and third examples show that PINNs, as combinations of machine learning and differential equations, will not lose accuracy as the dimensionality (shape) increases in complexity; and will remain stable regardless of the distribution of training data or the complexity of the problem, as long as the data provided are accurate enough and the depth/width is large enough. This indicates the PINNs have good stability and robustness. In addition, we also compared the embedding approach based on PINNs with the extrinsic approach; the extrinsic approach based on PINNs showed better accuracy and used less computational time.

As a matter of fact, PDEs on curved surfaces or manifolds involve applications in biological pattern formation. In [31] and the references therein, it is proved that the geometry and specifically curvature play vital roles in biological pattern formation on curved surfaces. To deal with those surfaces composed of scatter points in realistic problems, two additional techniques, surface reconstruction [32,33] and the pseudospectral approach [9,16], could be further considered. Additionally, although the continuous time models are fine, they still face a dilemma when dealing with long simulations and large amounts of data, so there is a need to introduce other techniques [34]. We revealed the potential of an extrinsic approach based on PINNs for surface problems in this work and leave the long simulations on complicated surfaces to our future work.

Author Contributions: Conceptualization, Z.F.; methodology, Z.F. and Z.T.; software, Z.T.; validation, Z.F., Z.T. and S.R.; writing—original draft preparation, Z.T.; writing—review and editing, Z.F. and S.R. All authors have read and agreed to the published version of the manuscript.

Funding: The work described in this paper was supported by the National Science Funds of China (grant number 12122205), Fundamental Research Funds for the Central Universities (grant number B220203018) and the Six Talent Peaks Project in Jiangsu Province of China (grant number 2019-KTHY-009).

Data Availability Statement: The data that support the findings of this study are available from the corresponding author (Z.F.) upon reasonable request.

Conflicts of Interest: The authors declare no conflict of interest.

References

1. Witkin, A.; Kass, M. Reaction-Diffusion Textures. *ACM Siggraph Comput. Graph.* **1995**, *25*, 299–308. [CrossRef]
2. Diewald, U.; Preusser, T. Anisotropic diffusion in vector field visualization on Euclidean domains and surfaces. *IEEE Trans. Vis. Comput. Graph* **2000**, *6*, 139–149. [CrossRef]
3. Myers, T.G.; Charpin, J.P.F. A mathematical model for atmospheric ice accretion and water flow on a cold surface. *Int. J. Heat Mass Transf.* **2004**, *47*, 5483–5500. [CrossRef]
4. Xu, J.J.; Zhao, H.K. An Eulerian Formulation for Solving Partial Differential Equations Along a Moving Interface. *J. Sci. Comput.* **2003**, *19*, 573–594. [CrossRef]
5. Ruuth, S.J.; Merriman, B. A simple embedding method for solving partial differential equations on surfaces. *J. Comput. Phys.* **2008**, *227*, 1943–1961. [CrossRef]
6. Piret, C. The orthogonal gradients method: A radial basis functions method for solving partial differential equations on arbitrary surfaces. *J. Comput. Phys.* **2012**, *231*, 4662–4675. [CrossRef]
7. Hansbo, P.; Larson, M.G.; Zahedi, S. A cut finite element method for coupled bulk-surface problems on time-dependent domains. *Comput. Methods Appl. Mech. Eng.* **2016**, *307*, 96–116. [CrossRef]
8. Cheung, K.C.; Ling, L. A Kernel-Based Embedding Method and Convergence Analysis for Surfaces PDEs. *SIAM J. Sci. Comput.* **2018**, *40*, A266–A287. [CrossRef]
9. Chen, M.; Ling, L. Kernel-based collocation methods for heat transport on evolving surfaces. *J. Comput. Phys.* **2019**, *405*, 109166. [CrossRef]
10. Chen, M.; Ling, L. Kernel-Based Meshless Collocation Methods for Solving Coupled Bulk–Surface Partial Differential Equations. *J. Sci. Comput.* **2019**, *81*, 375–391. [CrossRef]
11. Floater, M.S.; Hormann, K. *Surface Parameterization: A Tutorial and Survey*; Springer: Berlin/Heidelberg, Germany, 2005.
12. Macdonald, C.B.; Ruuth, S.J. The implicit closest point method for the numerical solution of partial differential equations on surfaces. *SIAM J. Sci. Comput.* **2010**, *31*, 4330–4350. [CrossRef]
13. Marcelo, B.; Li-Tien, C.; Stanley, O.; Guillermo, S. Variational Problems and Partial Differential Equations on Implicit Surfaces. *J. Comput. Phys.* **2001**, 174, 759–780.
14. Tang, Z.; Fu, Z.; Chen, M.; Ling, L. A localized extrinsic collocation method for Turing pattern formations on surfaces. *Appl. Math. Lett.* **2021**, *122*, 107534. [CrossRef]
15. Tang, Z.; Fu, Z.; Sun, H.; Liu, X. An efficient localized collocation solver for anomalous diffusion on surfaces. *Fract. Calc. Appl. Anal.* **2021**, *24*, 865–894. [CrossRef]
16. Tang, Z.; Fu, Z.; Chen, M.; Huang, J. An efficient collocation method for long-time simulation of heat and mass transport on evolving surfaces. *J. Comput. Phys.* **2022**, *463*, 111310. [CrossRef]
17. Fu, Z.; Tang, Z.; Xi, Q.; Liu, Q.; Gu, Y.; Wang, F. Localized Collocation Schemes and Their Applications. *Acta. Mech. Sin.* **2022**, *38*, 422167.
18. Lecun, Y.; Bengio, Y.; Hinton, G. Deep learning. *Nature* **2015**, *521*, 436. [CrossRef]
19. Tarkhov, D.A.; Vasilyev, A.N. New Neural Network Technique to the Numerical Solution of Mathematical Physics Problems. I: Simple Problems. *Opt. Mem. Neural Netw.* **2005**, *14*, 59–72.
20. Tarkhov, D.A.; Vasilyev, A.N. New Neural Network Technique to the Numerical Solution of Mathematical Physics Problems II: Complicated and Nonstandard Problems. *Opt. Mem. Neural Netw.* **2005**, *14*, 97–122.
21. Tarkhov, D.; Vasilyev, A.N. *Semi-Empirical Neural Network Modeling and Digital Twins Development*; Academic Press: Cambridge, MA, USA, 2019.
22. Antonov, V.; Tarkhov, D.; Vasilyev, A. Unified approach to constructing the neural network models of real objects Part 1. *Math. Methods Appl. Sci.* **2018**, *41*, 9244–9251. [CrossRef]

23. Raissi, M.; Perdikaris, P.; Karniadakis, G.E. Physics-Informed Neural Networks: A Deep Learning Framework for Solving Forward and Inverse Problems Involving Nonlinear Partial Differential Equations. *J. Comput. Phys.* **2018**, *378*, 686–707. [CrossRef]
24. Raissi, M.; Yazdani, A.; Karniadakis, G.E. Hidden fluid mechanics: Learning velocity and pressure fields from flow visualizations. *Science* **2020**, *367*, 1026–1030. [CrossRef]
25. Jagtap, A.D.; Kharazmi, E.; Karniadakis, G.E. Conservative physics-informed neural networks on discrete domains for conservation laws: Applications to forward and inverse problems. *Comput. Methods Appl. Mech. Eng.* **2020**, *365*, 113028. [CrossRef]
26. Pang, G.; Lu, L.; Karniadakis, G.E. fPINNs: Fractional Physics-Informed Neural Networks. *SIAM J. Sci. Comput.* **2019**, *41*, A2603–A2626. [CrossRef]
27. Mao, Z.; Jagtap, A.D.; Karniadakis, G.E. Physics-informed neural networks for high-speed flows. *Comput. Methods Appl. Mech. Eng.* **2020**, *360*, 112789. [CrossRef]
28. Bihlo, A.; Popovych, R.O. Physics-informed neural networks for the shallow-water equations on the sphere. *J. Comput. Phys.* **2022**, *456*, 111024. [CrossRef]
29. Fang, Z.; Zhan, J. A physics-informed neural network framework for PDEs on 3D surfaces: Time independent problems. *IEEE Access* **2019**, *8*, 26328–26335. [CrossRef]
30. Hesse, K.; Sloan, I.H.; Womersley, R.S. Numerical integration on the sphere. In *Handbook of Geomathematics*; Springer: Berlin/Heidelberg, Germany, 2010.
31. Krause, A.L.; Ellis, M.A.; Van Gorder, R.A. Influence of curvature, growth, and anisotropy on the evolution of Turing patterns on growing manifolds. *Bull. Math. Biol.* **2019**, *81*, 759–799. [CrossRef]
32. Zhao, H.K.; Osher, S.; Fedkiw, R. Fast surface reconstruction using the level set method. In Proceedings of the IEEE Workshop on Variational and Level Set Methods in Computer Vision, Vancouver, BC, Canada, 13 July 2001; pp. 194–201.
33. Liu, S.; Wang, C.C. Quasi-interpolation for surface reconstruction from scattered data with radial basis function. *Comput. Aided Geom. Des.* **2012**, *29*, 435–447. [CrossRef]
34. Gorbachenko, V.I.; Lazovskaya, T.V.; Tarkhov, D.A.; Vasilyev, A.N.; Zhukov, M.V. Neural network technique in some inverse problems of mathematical physics. In Proceedings of the International Symposium on Neural Networks, St. Petersburg, Russia, 6–8 July 2016; Springer: Berlin/Heidelberg, Germany, 2016; pp. 310–316.

mathematics

Article

A Modified Radial Point Interpolation Method (M-RPIM) for Free Vibration Analysis of Two-Dimensional Solids

Tingting Sun [1,2], Peng Wang [3], Guanjun Zhang [2] and Yingbin Chai [2,4,*]

1 School of Road Bridge & Harbor Engineering, Nanjing Vocational Institute of Transport Technology, Nanjing 211188, China
2 School of Naval Architecture, Ocean and Energy Power Engineering, Wuhan University of Technology, Wuhan 430063, China
3 Wuhan Second Ship Design and Research Institute, Wuhan 430205, China
4 State Key Laboratory of Ocean Engineering, Shanghai Jiao Tong University, Shanghai 200240, China
* Correspondence: chaiyb@whut.edu.cn

Abstract: The classical radial point interpolation method (RPIM) is a powerful meshfree numerical technique for engineering computation. In the original RPIM, the moving support domain for the quadrature point is usually employed for the field function approximation, but the local supports of the nodal shape functions are always not in alignment with the integration cells constructed for numerical integration. This misalignment can result in additional numerical integration error and lead to a loss in computation accuracy. In this work, a modified RPIM (M-RPIM) is proposed to address this issue. In the present M-RPIM, the misalignment between the constructed integration cells and the nodal shape function supports is successfully overcome by using a fixed support domain that can be easily constructed by the geometrical center of the integration cell. Several numerical examples of free vibration analysis are conducted to evaluate the abilities of the present M-RPIM and it is found that the computation accuracy of the original RPIM can be markedly improved by the present M-RPIM.

Keywords: meshfree numerical technique; free vibration; integration error; numerical integration

MSC: 35A08; 35A09; 35A24; 65L60; 74S05

Citation: Sun, T.; Wang, P.; Zhang, G.; Chai, Y. A Modified Radial Point Interpolation Method (M-RPIM) for Free Vibration Analysis of Two-Dimensional Solids. *Mathematics* **2022**, *10*, 2889. https://doi.org/10.3390/math10162889

Academic Editor: André Nicolet

Received: 21 July 2022
Accepted: 9 August 2022
Published: 12 August 2022

1. Introduction

The classical finite element method (FEM), which is based on the weighted residual technique, is a versatile and well-developed numerical approach in the field of modern computation mechanics [1]. Many mature commercial software packages (such as ANSYS, ABAQUS and NASTRAN) based on the FE approach have been developed and used in various engineering applications. Though the standard FEM has achieved great success in practical engineering computation, the FEM still suffers from several inherent shortcomings compared to other advanced numerical techniques [2–12]. Among them, one important issue is that the FEM is essentially a mesh-based method and the involved problem domain should be firstly discretized into a series of elements that are connected by nodes for FE analysis. Therefore, the additional burdensome tasks for meshing operations cannot always be circumvented. Additionally, the solution accuracy of the FEM is usually sensitive to mesh qualities and the solutions from low-quality meshes are always not sufficiently accurate. To obtain sufficiently fine solutions, more attention should be given to obtain high-quality meshes. These issues will be greater when the standard FEM is employed to manage problems related to dynamic cracks and large deformation of complicated geometric shapes.

To alleviate the dependence of the conventional FE approach on predefined meshes, a series of smoothed FEMs [13–17] and meshfree techniques [18–24] have been proposed, such as the element-free Galerkin method (EFGM) [25,26], the meshless local Petrov–Galerkin method (MLPG) [27], the reproducing kernel particle method (RKPM) [28], the radial point interpolation method (RPIM) [29,30], the general finite difference method GFDM [31–35], and the boundary-based numerical methods [36–40], to name a few. Actually, the meshfree methods can be classified into different types according to different formulation procedures [18]. Among them, several meshless methods are based on the weak form of the governing equation [41–44], while some others are based on the strong weak form [45–51]. In this work, we mainly focus on discussing the meshfree methods based on the well-known Galerkin weighted residual technique (such as the EFEM and RPIM), which are the typical weak-form-based numerical techniques. Compared to the standard FEM, one outstanding advantage of these meshfree methods is that the required nodal shape functions can be built entirely by using a set of scattered nodes, rather than as elements in the conventional FEM. In consequence, the field function approximation also can be constructed by the scattered nodes. This property enables the meshfree methods to have distinct advantages over the conventional FEM in managing the dynamic crack problem and larger deformation problem. In addition, adaptive analysis also can be implemented much more easily in the meshfree framework than in the standard FEM framework. More importantly, the meshfree methods usually possess other excellent features that the standard FEM does not have. A very good comparison and overview on the meshfree methods and the FEM can be found in a published monograph [18].

Although the meshfree methods have achieved considerable success both in theory and practical engineering applications, they still cannot match the classical FEM in terms of universality; further, there still exists several crucial issues that should be addressed very carefully. For example, the radial point interpolation method (RPIM), which is a typical meshfree numerical method, has been employed for solving many engineering problems owing to several excellent features, such as relatively high computation accuracy, good numerical stability and the possession of the Kronecker-delta function property. However, the compatibility of the standard RPIM cannot be automatically ensured, which may lead to numerical integration error. The main reason is that in the standard RPIM the local support domains of nodal interpolation functions are not always in accord with the constructed integration cells for numerical integration. The related issues have been investigated in [52,53] and in the so-called bounding box technique that has been proposed by proposed by Dolbow and Belytschko [52]. The related numerical results show that this scheme is indeed quite effective in addressing the issues mentioned; however, the implementation of this scheme is quite complicated and, hence, it is not very practical in engineering computation.

In this work, a simple and elegant scheme is developed to make the local support domains of the nodal shape functions in RPIM entirely align with the constructed quadrature cells for numerical integration; hence, the possible integration error can be markedly decreased. The main idea of this scheme is to design a new node selection scheme for the field function approximation. In this scheme, a fixed support domain (not a moving support domain in the original RPIM), which is determined by the geometrical center of the quadrature cell, is used for any quadrature point in the integration cell. For the convenience of notation, the proposed scheme in this work is called the modified RPIM (M-RPIM). We have further employed the present M-RPIM to analyze the free vibration of two-dimensional solids. It can be found that the M-RPIM behaves much better than the original RPIM for free vibration analysis, and many more numerical solutions can be provided with the totally identical node distributions.

2. Formulation of the Original RPIM and the Present M-RPIM

Consider a problem domain Ω with boundary Γ, and a field function $u(\mathbf{x})$ is defined on it. A series of scattered field nodes are employed to totally discretize the problem domain and its boundary. For a sampling point in the problem domain, the corresponding field function approximation $u_h(\mathbf{x})$ can be expressed in the following form by using the radial basis function (RBF) and polynomial basis function (PBF) [18]:

$$u_h(\mathbf{x}) = \sum_{i=1}^{n} R_i(\mathbf{x})a_i + \sum_{j=1}^{m} P_j(\mathbf{x})b_j = \mathbf{R}^T(\mathbf{x})\mathbf{a} + \mathbf{P}^T(\mathbf{x})\mathbf{b}, \tag{1}$$

in which $R_i(\mathbf{x})$ stands for the RBF used and $P_j(\mathbf{x})$ represents the PBF used; n denotes the number of RBF used for interpolation, namely, there are n field nodes in the support domain of the sampling point $\mathbf{x}$, m denotes the number of PBF used for interpolation, and the complete linear polynomial ([1 x y]) is used in this work, namely, m = 3; a_i and b_j are the unknown interpolation coefficients.

There are many different types of RBF that can be used to formulate the RPIM, and different RBFs have different features [18]. In this work, the well-known multiquadrics (MQ) function is used to construct the required field function approximation owing to its several excellent characteristics. The expression of the MQ function is as follows [18,21]:

$$R_i(\mathbf{x}) = \left[r_i^2 + (\alpha_c d_c)^2\right]^q, \tag{2}$$

in which r_i denotes the distance from the field node to the sampling point, d_c is the average nodal interval of the field nodes used, and α_c and q denote two undetermined parameters that are closely related to the computation accuracy of the RPIM; q = 1.03 and $\alpha_c = 1$ are used in this work because very good numerical results can always be obtained for solid mechanics with these parameters.

With the aim to determine the coefficients a_i and b_j, Equation (1) should satisfy a series of reasonable constraint conditions. Firstly, it is usually assumed that the constructed field function approximation can exactly pass through the function values of all the nodes located in the support domain of the sampling point $\mathbf{x}$; these constraints can be expressed by:

$$\begin{bmatrix} u_1 & u_2 & \cdots & u_n \end{bmatrix}^T = \mathbf{R}_0\mathbf{a} + \mathbf{P}_0\mathbf{b}, \tag{3}$$

$$\mathbf{R}_0 = \begin{bmatrix} R_1(r_1) & R_2(r_1) & \cdots & R_n(r_1) \\ R_1(r_2) & R_2(r_2) & \cdots & R_n(r_2) \\ \vdots & \vdots & \vdots & \vdots \\ R_1(r_n) & R_2(r_n) & \cdots & R_n(r_n) \end{bmatrix}, \tag{4}$$

$$\mathbf{P}_0^T = \begin{bmatrix} 1 & 1 & \cdots & 1 \\ x_1 & x_2 & \cdots & x_n \\ y_1 & y_2 & \cdots & y_n \\ \vdots & \vdots & \ddots & \vdots \\ q_m(\mathbf{x}_1) & q_m(\mathbf{x}_2) & \cdots & q_m(\mathbf{x}_n) \end{bmatrix}, \tag{5}$$

in which $\mathbf{R}_0$ and $\mathbf{P}_0$ are the so-called moment matrices corresponding to the RBF and PBF, respectively.

To uniquely determine the unknown interpolation coefficients a_i and b_j, the following additional constraints should also be satisfied:

$$\sum_{i=1}^{n} P_j(\mathbf{x}_i)a_i = \mathbf{P}_0^T\mathbf{a} = 0, j = 1, 2, \cdots, m, \tag{6}$$

The combination of all the constraining conditions shown in Equations (2) and (6) can result in the following matrix equation:

$$\begin{bmatrix} \mathbf{u} \\ 0 \end{bmatrix} = \underbrace{\begin{bmatrix} \mathbf{R}_0 & \mathbf{P}_0 \\ \mathbf{P}_0^T & 0 \end{bmatrix}}_{\mathbf{G}} \underbrace{\begin{bmatrix} \mathbf{a} \\ \mathbf{b} \end{bmatrix}}_{\mathbf{a}_0} = \mathbf{G}\mathbf{a}_0, \tag{7}$$

Then, the undetermined interpolation coefficients can be calculated by

$$\begin{bmatrix} \mathbf{a} \\ \mathbf{b} \end{bmatrix} = \mathbf{a}_0 = \mathbf{G}^{-1}\begin{bmatrix} \mathbf{u} \\ 0 \end{bmatrix}, \tag{8}$$

Substituting the interpolation coefficients obtained into Equation (1) and following the standard formulation of the conventional RPIM, the required nodal interpolation shape function can be obtained by

$$\Phi^T(\mathbf{x}) = \begin{bmatrix} \phi_1(\mathbf{x}) & \phi_2(\mathbf{x}) & \cdots & \phi_n(\mathbf{x}) \end{bmatrix} = \begin{Bmatrix} \mathbf{R}^T(\mathbf{x}) & \mathbf{Q}^T(\mathbf{x}) \end{Bmatrix} \mathbf{G}^{-1}|_{1\sim n}, \tag{9}$$

In the standard RPIM, the field nodes participating in building the field function approximation for the sampling point, which are usually quadrature points, are determined by a support domain. The shape of the support domain can be a square or a circle. The sampling point is usually the center of the defined support domain, while the background cells for numerical integration are always constructed independently of the support domain. As a result, the different sampling points (or quadrature points) in one integration cell may have different support domains, namely, the required field nodes to construct the field function approximation are different. In summary, since the moving support domain is used in the traditional RPIM, the support domain of the nodal shape functions always do not align with the background integration cells, which then leads to considerable numerical integration error and degrades the quality of the numerical solutions obtained.

To effectively overcome the abovementioned misalignment between the nodal shape function supports and the background integration cells, in this work a modified RPIM (M-RPIM) is employed to analyze the free vibration of two-dimensional solids. In this M-RPIM, a fixed support domain (as shown in Figure 1) rather than the moving support domain in the standard RPIM is used to select the required field nodes for the construction of the field function approximation. In other words, the identical field nodes are used for interpolation for any quadrature points in one background integration cell. The fixed support domain used can still be a square or a circle (the square support domain is used in this work); however, this fixed support domain is always centered by the geometrical center of the integration cell, not centered by the sampling points (which are usually the quadrature points) as in the conventional RPIM. The difference between the original RPIM and the present M-RPIM in constructing the field function approximation can be shown as follows:

$$\begin{cases} u_h(\mathbf{x})_{\mathrm{RPIM}} = \sum \phi_i u_i, x_i \in \Omega^Q \\ u_h(\mathbf{x})_{\mathrm{M-RPIM}} = \sum \phi_i u_i, x_i \in \Omega^* \end{cases}, \tag{10}$$

in which Ω^Q stands for the moving support domains, which are centered by the quadrature points in one background cell, Ω^* represents the fixed support domains that are directly centered by the centroids of the background integration cells.

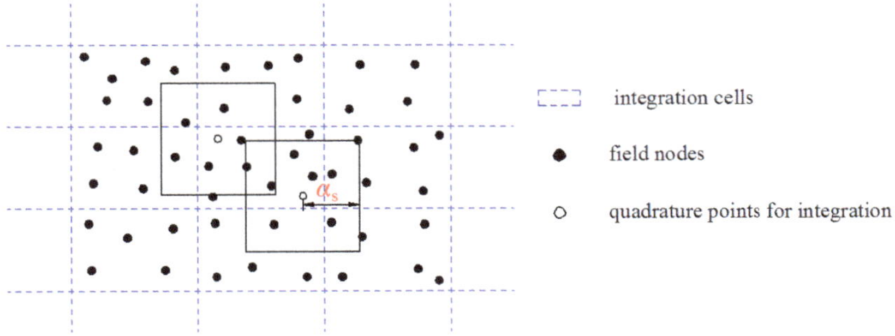

(**a**)

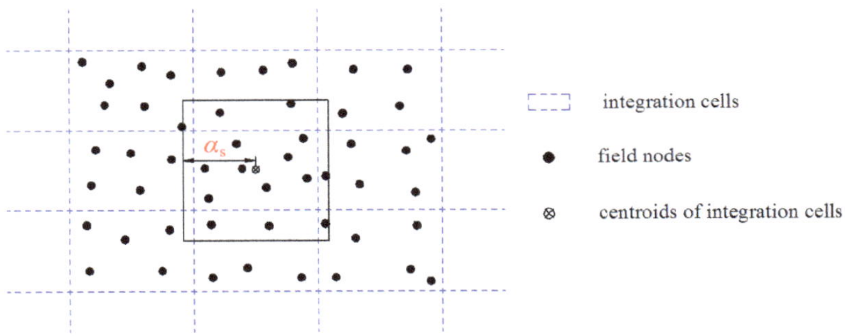

(**b**)

Figure 1. Comparison of the original RPIM and the present M-RPIM for node selection in the numerical approximation. (**a**) The node selection scheme in the original RPIM. (**b**) The node selection scheme in the present M-RPIM.

3. Formulation of the Elastodynamics of Two-Dimensional Solids

Based on the small displacement assumption, the partial differential equation (PDE) of the boundary-value problem for the elastodynamics of solids can be written by

$$\nabla\sigma + \mathbf{b} = \rho\ddot{\mathbf{u}} \text{ in } \Omega, \tag{11}$$

in which Ω denotes the problem domain considered, $\mathbf{b}$ stands for the body force, σ represents the stress tensor, ρ is the mass density, $\mathbf{u}$ is the displacement vector and $\ddot{\mathbf{u}}$ signifies second derivatives of $\mathbf{u}$.

As usual, the following two kinds of boundary conditions are always considered for the two-dimensional elastodynamics of solids:

$$\begin{cases} \mathbf{u} = \overline{\mathbf{u}}, & \text{on } \Gamma_E \\ \sigma \cdot \mathbf{n} = \overline{\mathbf{t}}, & \text{on } \Gamma_N \end{cases}, \tag{12}$$

in which Γ_E and Γ_N denote the essential boundary condition and the natural boundary condition, respectively; $\overline{\mathbf{u}}$ and $\overline{\mathbf{t}}$ are the imposed displacement vector and traction vector on the corresponding boundary conditions.

Using the boundary conditions shown in Equation (12) and following the virtual displacement principle, the weak form of Equation (11) for the elastodynamics of two-dimensional solids can be obtained by

$$\int_{\Omega} \rho \delta \mathbf{u} \ddot{\mathbf{u}} \mathrm{d}\Omega + \int_{\Omega} \delta \boldsymbol{\varepsilon} \boldsymbol{\sigma} \mathrm{d} = \int_{\Gamma_N} \delta \mathbf{u}\, \bar{\mathbf{t}} \mathrm{d}\Gamma + \int_{\Omega} \delta \mathbf{u} \mathbf{b} \mathrm{d}\Omega, \tag{13}$$

in which $\delta \mathbf{u}$ and $\delta \boldsymbol{\varepsilon}$ stand for the virtual displacement and strain, respectively.

Using the Galerkin weighted residual techniques and the field function approximation shown in Equation (1), the matrix equation for the weak form shown in Equation (13) can be obtained [1,18] by the following relationship:

$$\mathbf{M}\ddot{\mathbf{u}} + \mathbf{C}\dot{\mathbf{u}} + \mathbf{K}\mathbf{u} = \mathbf{F}, \tag{14}$$

in which $\mathbf{M}$ is the usual mass matrix, $\mathbf{K}$ is the usual stiffness matrix, $\mathbf{F}$ is the applied force vector and $\mathbf{C}$ is the matrix containing the damping effects.

Without considering the damping effects and the external force, Equation (14) reduces to

$$\mathbf{M}\ddot{\mathbf{u}} + \mathbf{K}\mathbf{u} = 0, \tag{15}$$

Equation (15) is the governing matrix equation obtained for the free vibration analysis of two-dimensional solids.

Assuming that the displacement solution to Equation (15) is time harmonic, namely,

$$\mathbf{u} = \mathbf{U}\exp(j\omega t), \tag{16}$$

in which $j = \sqrt{-1}$, ω denotes the angular frequency, and $\mathbf{U}$ is the amplitude of the displacement distribution.

Substituting Equation (16) into Equation (15), then Equation (15) can be rewritten as

$$\left[\mathbf{K} - \omega^2 \mathbf{M}\right]\mathbf{U} = 0, \tag{17}$$

From Equation (17), we can observe that the typical eigenvalue problem should be solved to perform the analysis of free vibration problems.

4. Numerical Example

In this section, several typical numerical examples are considered to assess the capability of the proposed M-RPIM in free vibration analysis of the two-dimensional solids. For the convenience of discussion, the natural frequency values from the present M-RPIM are compared to those from the original RPIM and the standard finite element approach with bilinear quadrilateral elements (FEM-Q4). In all the numerical examples considered, identical node arrangements are employed for these three different numerical methods (M-RPIM, RPIM and FEM-Q4). For simplification, the quadrilateral meshes used are directly employed as the background cells to perform the numerical integration for the RPIM and M-RPIM, unless otherwise noted. To effectively examine and compare the accuracy and convergence of numerical solutions from the different numerical methods, the following relative error indicator is employed in this work:

$$\mathrm{Re} = \left| \frac{f_{num} - f_{ref}}{f_{ref}} \right| \times 100\%, \tag{18}$$

in which f_{num} denotes the natural frequency results from the numerical methods (M-RPIM, RPIM and FEM-Q4) and f_{ref} represents the reference natural frequency results, which are usually obtained from the commercial finite element software packages with a very refined mesh.

4.1. Free Vibration Analysis of the Cantilever Beam

Firstly, the free vibration of a cantilever beam is considered here. As shown in Figure 2, the geometric configuration of the cantilever beam has length L = 100 mm and height D = 10 mm. A unit thickness (t = 1 mm) is considered for this beam and, hence, this numerical example can be simplified as a plane stress problem. The material constants of this beam are taken as Young's modulus $E = 2.1 \times 10^{11}$ Pa, Poisson's ratio $v = 0.3$ and mass density $\rho = 8 \times 10^3$ kg/m^3. The regular node arrangements are used to discretize the problem domain of this cantilever beam for the three different numerical methods. For a detailed analysis and discussion, a series of different node arrangement patterns with different nodal intervals are used here (see Figure 3).

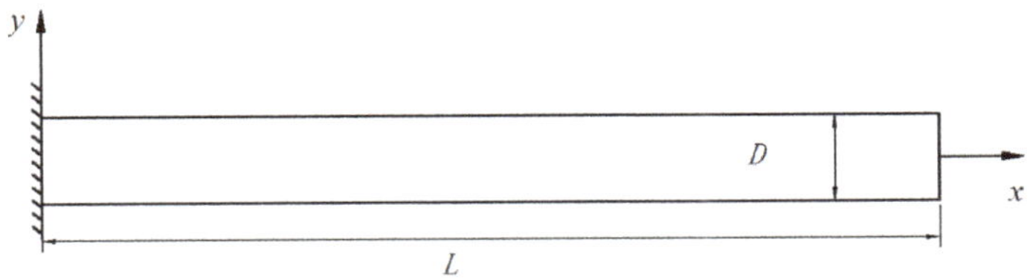

Figure 2. The geometric configuration of the cantilever beam in plane stress condition.

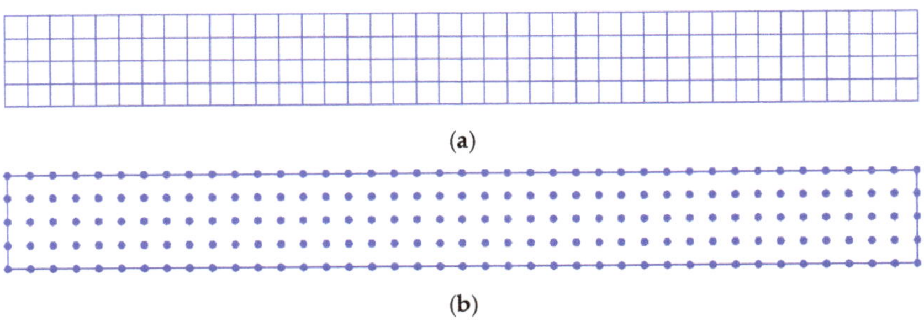

Figure 3. The different node arrangement patterns that are employed to discretize the cantilever beam for different numerical methods: (**a**) uniform mesh pattern, which is used to discretize the cantilever beam for the standard FEM-Q4; (**b**) node arrangement pattern used to discretize the cantilever beam for the RPIM and M-RPIM.

4.1.1. Computation Accuracy Study

Utilizing a series of different node arrangement patterns, the first twelve natural frequency solutions from the three numerical methods are listed in Tables 1–4. Among them, the corresponding RPIM and M-RPIM solutions are obtained when the size of the nodal support domain is taken as $\alpha_s = 2.5h$ (h denotes average nodal interval of the meshes used). The reference solutions from eight-node quadrilateral element (FEM-Q8) with a very refined mesh pattern (average nodal interval h = 0.1 mm) are also provided in the tables for comparison.

Table 1. The first twelve natural frequency solutions from the three numerical methods using the node arrangement pattern with average nodal space h = 2 mm.

Mode	FEM-Q4	Error (%)	RPIM	Error (%)	M-RPIM	Error (%)	Ref.
1	830.567	1.003	815.423	0.839	825.213	0.351	822.322
2	4989.034	1.132	4909.931	0.471	4952.383	0.389	4933.177
3	12,826.933	0.022	12,826.322	0.017	12,825.428	0.010	12,824.145
4	13,167.852	1.336	13,035.277	0.316	13,025.003	0.237	12,994.215
5	23,992.489	1.604	23,772.722	0.673	23,725.015	0.471	23,613.775
6	36,701.000	1.910	36,492.012	1.329	36,197.042	0.510	36,013.226
7	38,467.305	0.059	38,461.345	0.044	38,450.819	0.016	38,444.488
8	50,697.394	2.248	50,570.105	1.991	49,854.144	0.547	49,582.799
9	64,062.116	0.225	64,045.638	0.199	63,984.254	0.103	63,918.563
10	65,590.504	2.524	65,609.724	2.554	64,290.994	0.493	63,975.503
11	81,118.869	3.012	81,334.286	3.286	79,233.413	0.618	78,746.943
12	89,562.090	0.252	89,514.438	0.199	89,345.277	0.010	89,336.686

Table 2. The first twelve natural frequency solutions from the three numerical methods using the node arrangement pattern with average nodal space h = 1 mm.

Mode	FEM-Q4	Error (%)	RPIM	Error (%)	M-RPIM	Error (%)	Ref.
1	824.304	0.241	819.913	0.293	822.800	0.058	822.322
2	4946.701	0.274	4924.719	0.171	4936.588	0.069	4933.177
3	12,824.618	0.004	12,824.955	0.006	12,824.496	0.003	12,824.145
4	13,036.557	0.326	13,008.259	0.108	13,004.647	0.080	12,994.215
5	23,706.655	0.393	23,657.845	0.187	23,635.380	0.091	23,613.775
6	36,182.573	0.470	36,152.539	0.387	36,049.829	0.102	36,013.226
7	38,449.523	0.013	38,447.183	0.007	38,445.401	0.002	38,444.488
8	49,857.999	0.555	49,874.211	0.588	49,637.697	0.111	49,582.799
9	63,996.004	0.121	63,990.287	0.112	63,976.475	0.091	63,918.563
10	64,332.241	0.558	64,422.173	0.698	63,994.651	0.030	63,975.503
11	79,334.621	0.746	79,524.455	0.987	78,846.611	0.127	78,746.943
12	89,391.481	0.061	89,377.038	0.045	89,336.977	0.000	89,336.686

Table 3. The first twelve natural frequency solutions from the three numerical methods using the node arrangement pattern with average nodal space h = 0.67 mm.

Mode	FEM-Q4	Error (%)	RPIM	Error (%)	M-RPIM	Error (%)	Ref.
1	823.104	0.095	821.051	0.155	822.413	0.011	822.322
2	4938.559	0.109	4928.453	0.096	4933.920	0.015	4933.177
3	12,824.010	0.001	12,823.612	0.004	12,823.953	0.001	12,824.145
4	13,011.299	0.131	12,992.024	0.017	12,996.698	0.019	12,994.215
5	23,651.752	0.161	23,631.689	0.076	23,619.234	0.023	23,613.775
6	36,083.214	0.194	36,074.813	0.171	36,022.821	0.027	36,013.226
7	38,445.687	0.003	38,444.328	0.000	38,443.843	0.002	38,444.488
8	49,697.499	0.231	49,714.721	0.266	49,597.527	0.030	49,582.799
9	63,982.840	0.101	63,979.749	0.096	63,939.314	0.032	63,918.563
10	64,092.160	0.182	64,149.033	0.271	63,974.133	0.002	63,975.503
11	78,994.780	0.315	79,104.908	0.455	78,774.275	0.035	78,746.943
12	89,358.561	0.024	89,351.356	0.016	89,334.272	0.003	89,336.686

Table 4. The first twelve natural frequency solutions from the three numerical methods using the node arrangement pattern with average nodal space $h = 0.5$ mm.

Mode	FEM-Q4	Error (%)	RPIM	Error (%)	M-RPIM	Error (%)	Ref.
1	822.674	0.043	821.486	0.102	822.279	0.005	822.322
2	4935.637	0.050	4929.842	0.068	4932.985	0.004	4933.177
3	12,823.747	0.003	12,823.464	0.005	12,823.711	0.003	12,824.145
4	13,002.246	0.062	12,991.382	0.022	12,993.901	0.002	12,994.215
5	23,632.124	0.078	23,621.334	0.032	23,613.557	0.001	23,613.775
6	36,047.788	0.096	36,044.602	0.087	36,013.347	0.000	36,013.226
7	38,444.192	0.001	38,443.250	0.003	38,443.144	0.003	38,444.488
8	49,640.417	0.116	49,653.240	0.142	49,583.475	0.001	49,582.799
9	63,977.974	0.093	63,975.937	0.090	63,920.007	0.002	63,918.563
10	64,006.958	0.049	64,044.242	0.107	63,973.057	0.004	63,975.503
11	78,874.387	0.162	78,944.368	0.251	78,749.088	0.003	78,746.943
12	89,346.670	0.011	89,342.201	0.006	89,332.973	0.004	89,336.686

From the results listed in the tables, we can observe that the original RPIM cannot always provide more accurate solutions than the standard FEM-Q4 in calculating the natural frequency values of this cantilever beam, although the higher order interpolation (not the bilinear interpolation in the FEM-Q4) is employed in the RPIM when the nodal support domain $\alpha_s = 2.5h$. This is mainly caused by the misalignment between the constructed integration cells and the local support domains of the nodal interpolation functions. Owing to this misalignment, the integrands obtained in the original RPIM are not always continuously differentiable, then considerable numerical integration error is generated and leads to an additional loss in computation accuracy. However, from the tables we can observe that very good agreement between the M-RPIM solutions and the reference solutions can be achieved, and the M-RPIM solutions are much more accurate than the RPIM solutions. The main reason for this is that in the M-RPIM a fixed nodal support domain (not a moving support domain), which is built by the centroids of the integration cells, is directly used to perform the required numerical integration; then, the abovementioned misalignment between the integration cells and the local nodal support domains can be easily removed. As a result, the integrands obtained are completely continuously differentiable in the integration cells, so the numerical integration error can be markedly reduced and the computation accuracy can be significantly improved by the present M-RPIM for free vibration analysis. In addition, the vibration modes of the cantilever beam corresponding to the first twelve natural frequency values from the present M-RPIM are plotted in Figure 4; we can observe that the vibration modes obtained are quite stable and the physical mode shapes can be accurately achieved.

4.1.2. Convergence Study

In this subsection, the convergence performance of the numerical solutions from different numerical approaches is investigated in great detail. As shown in Figure 5, the comparison of the relative error (Re) results of the computed natural frequency values from different numerical methods versus the nodal interval ($1/h$) are given; the sign R in the legend of Figure 5 denotes the convergence rate of different numerical techniques. For simplicity, only the first two natural frequency values (Mode 1 and Mode 2) are considered here. From Figure 5, it can be observed that the convergence rate of the original RPIM is unexpectedly lower than the standard FEM-Q4 when the size of the nodal interpolation function support domain is taken as $\alpha_s = 2.5h$. This observation indicates that the misalignment between the integration cells and the local support domain of the nodal shape function in the original RPIM indeed can result in considerable numerical integration error; thus, the convergence rate can be markedly reduced.

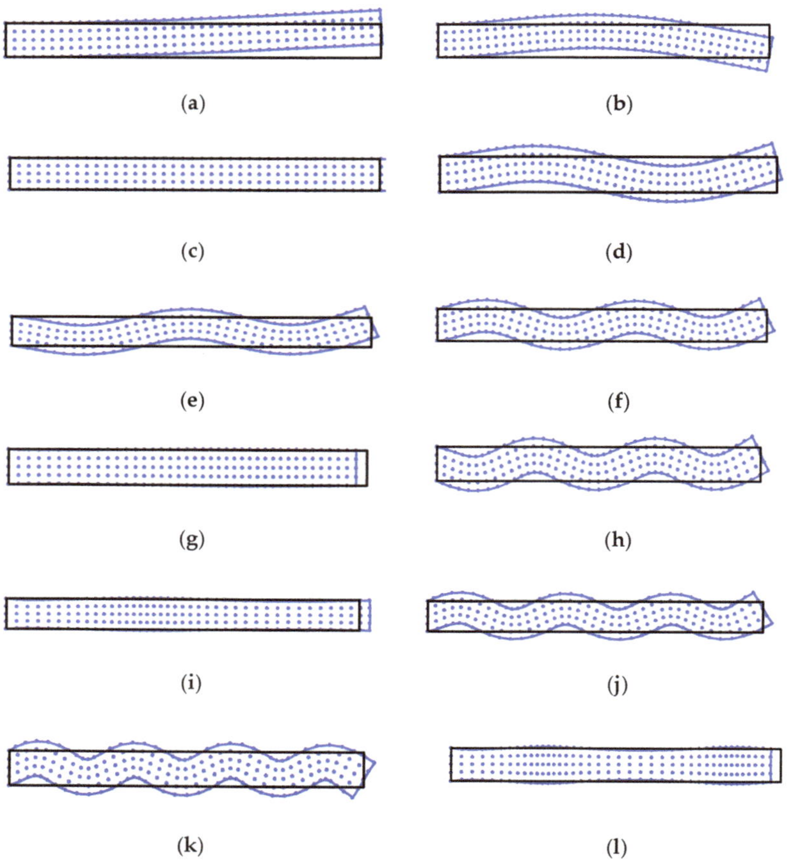

Figure 4. The free vibration modes of cantilever beam corresponding to the first twelve natural frequency values from the present M-RPIM: (**a**) Mode 1; (**b**) Mode 2; (**c**) Mode 3; (**d**) Mode 4; (**e**) Mode 5; (**f**) Mode 6; (**g**) Mode 7; (**h**) Mode 8; (**i**) Mode 9; (**j**) Mode 10; (**k**) Mode 11; (**l**) Mode 12.

However, from Figure 5 we also can see that the present M-RPIM is able to achieve a higher convergence rate than the original RPIM and standard FEM-Q4. These findings again demonstrate that the proposed program in this paper overcomes the misalignment between the constructed integration cells, and that the nodal shape function indeed effectively supports suppression of possible numerical integration error. For free vibration analysis of solids, therefore, the present M-RPIM has a higher convergence rate than the original RPIM and standard FEM-Q4.

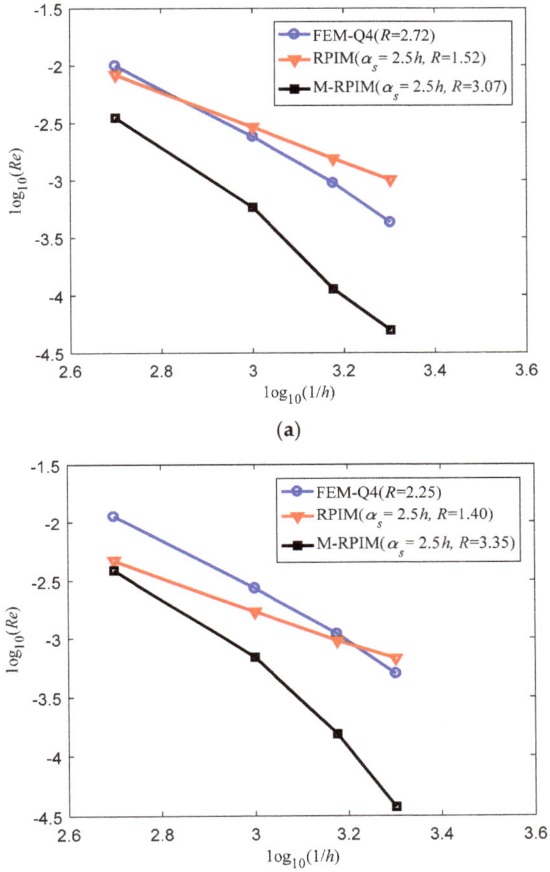

Figure 5. Comparison of the relative error (Re) results of the computed natural frequency values from different numerical methods versus the nodal interval ($1/h$): (**a**) Mode 1; (**b**) Mode 2.

4.1.3. Computation Efficiency Study

From the analysis and discussion above, it can be observed that the present M-RPIM behaves better than the original RPIM and standard FEM-Q4 in terms of computation accuracy and convergence properties. However, the computation efficiency of the proposed M-RPIM is not yet studied. Note that computation efficiency is also a crucial index to assess the capabilities of numerical methods in engineering computation; comparison of the computation efficiency for the three different numerical methods is performed here. To analyze the computation efficiency, a series of different node arrangement schemes shown in Figure 3 are again employed.

Figure 6 gives the comparison of the relative error results (Re) of the natural frequency values versus the computation cost for the three numerical methods. For simplicity, we still only consider the first two modes. From Figure 6, we can observe that the required computational cost for the standard FEM-Q4 is much less than for the original RPIM and the present M-RPIM when the identical node arrangement scheme is employed. This is because many more quadrature points are used to perform the numerical integration in RPIM and M-RPIM compared to standard FEM-Q4. Nevertheless, the computation accuracy of the standard FEM-Q4 cannot surpass the M-RPIM because a higher local approximation is used in this meshless numerical technique.

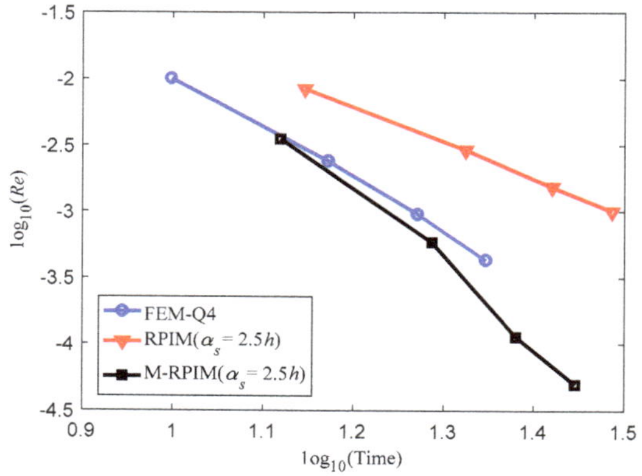

(a)

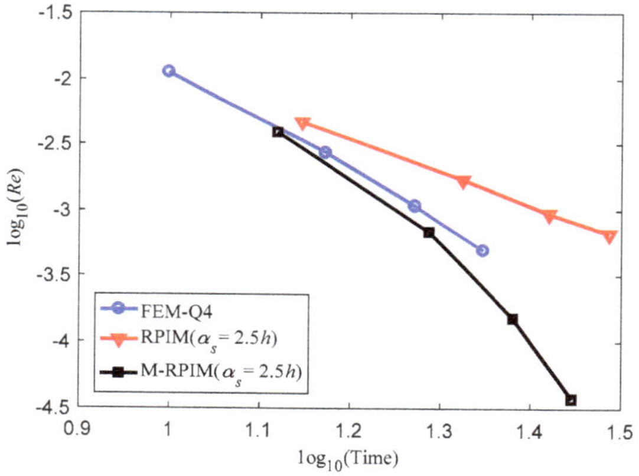

(b)

Figure 6. Comparison of the relative error results (Re) of the natural frequency values versus the computation cost for the three different numerical methods: (**a**) Mode 1; (**b**) Mode 2.

From Figure 6, we also can observe that the original RPIM is actually numerically more expensive than the M-RPIM for the identical node arrangement scheme. This is because a moving support domain is used for different quadrature points in the original RPIM. In other words, for each quadrature point, the related operation in determining the support domain (namely the node selection for interpolation) should be performed once, while in the present M-RPIM, a fixed support domain is employed for any quadrature points within one integration cell; hence, the required operation in determining the support domain only should be performed once for each integration cell. Thus, in the M-RPIM, less computational cost is required in the node selection compared to the RPIM. Note that the present M-RPIM also has higher computation accuracy than the original RPIM; hence, the present M-RPIM also possesses higher computation efficiency than the original RPIM in engineering computation. This point can be clearly seen in Figure 6.

4.2. Free Vibration Analysis of the Cantilever Beam with Variable Cross-Section

The second numerical example considered here is a cantilever beam with variable cross-section. The geometric configuration of the variable cross-section beam is shown in Figure 7 and the related material constants are taken as Young's modulus $E = 3 \times 10^7$ Pa, Poisson's ratio $v = 0.3$ and mass density $\rho = 1$ kg/m^3. The regular node arrangement scheme is used to discretize this variable cross-section beam and the corresponding node distributions for the standard FEM-Q4 and the two meshless methods (RPIM and M-RPIM) are given in Figure 8. The first twelve natural frequency values computed using different numerical methods are listed in Table 5. Similar to the first numerical example, the corresponding natural frequency results from the eight-node quadrilateral element (FEM-Q8) with a very refined mesh pattern (5151 nodes and 5000 elements) are also provided as the reference solutions. It is clearly seen that the accuracy of FEM-Q4 results is worse than the original RPIM and the present M-RPIM results. However, the RPIM results are not more accurate than the M-RPIM ones, and the most accurate natural frequency solutions of this variable cross-section cantilever beam can be provided by the present M-RPIM. In addition, the first twelve mode shapes of this variable cross-section cantilever beam obtained from the proposed M-RPIM are depicted in Figure 9. It is easy to find that the eigenmode of this variable cross-section cantilever beam can be accurately predicted by the present M-RPIM. This numerical example demonstrates that the abilities of the original RPIM in engineering computation can be markedly improved by the present M-RPIM.

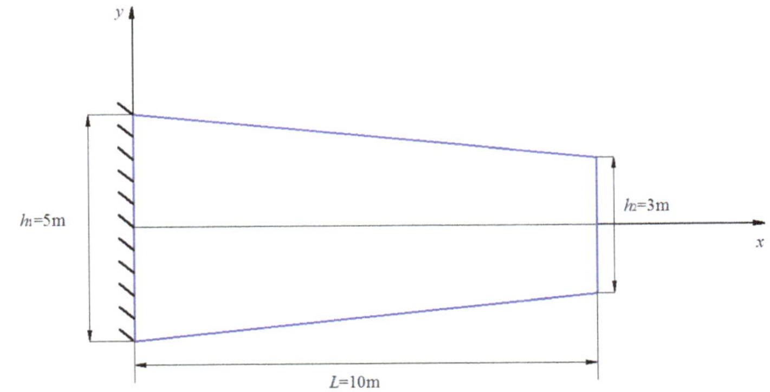

Figure 7. The geometric configuration of the variable cross-section beam in plane stress condition.

Table 5. The first twelve natural frequency values for the variable cross-section cantilever beam computed using different numerical methods.

Mode	FEM-Q4	Error (%)	RPIM	Error (%)	M-RPIM	Error (%)	Ref.
1	41.771	0.333	41.536	0.233	41.678	0.109	41.633
2	147.202	0.781	146.826	0.523	146.335	0.187	146.062
3	151.597	0.058	151.511	0.002	151.532	0.015	151.508
4	298.805	1.349	298.048	1.092	295.483	0.222	294.829
5	412.666	0.326	412.032	0.172	411.396	0.017	411.327
6	442.931	1.685	441.428	1.340	436.366	0.178	435.592
7	528.614	1.053	526.132	0.578	523.667	0.107	523.108
8	601.857	2.143	598.737	1.614	590.187	0.163	589.229
9	619.528	1.005	613.227	0.023	613.441	0.012	613.365
10	671.507	1.529	662.514	0.170	662.167	0.117	661.392
11	710.007	2.389	705.817	1.785	695.000	0.225	693.441
12	713.997	0.802	710.025	0.241	708.647	0.046	708.320

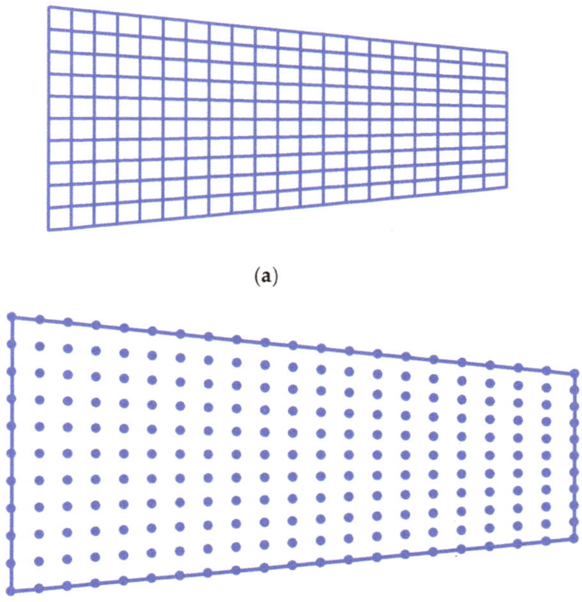

(**a**)

(**b**)

Figure 8. The different node arrangement patterns that are employed to discretize the variable cross-section cantilever beam for different numerical methods: (**a**) mesh pattern used to discretize the variable cross-section cantilever beam for the standard FEM-Q4; (**b**) node arrangement patterns used to discretize the variable cross-section cantilever beam for the RPIM and M-RPIM.

4.3. Free Vibration Analysis of the Cantilever Beam with Holes

The last numerical example is also a cantilever beam in plane stress condition. Unlike the previous numerical examples, the cantilever beam considered here has three identical holes (see Figure 10). The geometric parameters of this beam are given in Figure 10 and the material constants are taken as Young's modulus $E = 2.1 \times 10^{11}$ Pa, Poisson's ratio $v = 0.3$ and mass density $\rho = 8 \times 10^3$ kg/m^3. The node arrangement scheme for the different numerical methods are plotted in Figure 11, and the average nodal interval $h = 0.002$ m. Similar to the previous two numerical examples, the first twelve natural frequency values from the different numerical methods are listed in Table 6, and the corresponding mode shapes from the present M-RPIM are given in Figure 12. In Table 6, the reference solutions are also computed from the eight-node quadrilateral element (FEM-Q8) with a very refined mesh pattern (average node interval $h = 0.0001$ m). Similarly, Table 6 and Figure 12 show that we obtain results similar to those in the previous two numerical examples, namely, the present M-RPIM can generate much more accurate numerical solutions than the original RPIM and FEM-Q4 for free vibration analysis; the present method has great potential for more complicated engineering computation.

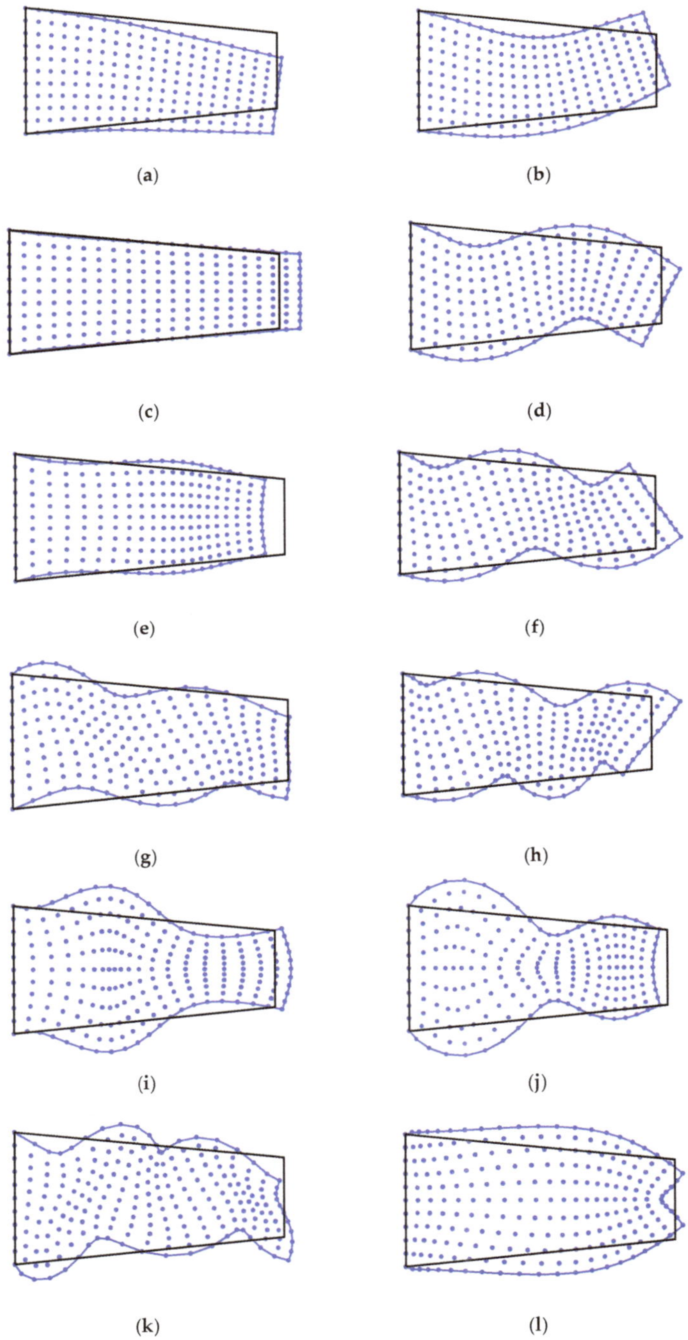

Figure 9. The free vibration modes of the variable cross-section cantilever beam corresponding to the first twelve natural frequency values from the present M-RPIM: (**a**) Mode 1; (**b**) Mode 2; (**c**) Mode 3; (**d**) Mode 4; (**e**) Mode 5; (**f**) Mode 6; (**g**) Mode 7; (**h**) Mode 8; (**i**) Mode 9; (**j**) Mode 10; (**k**) Mode 11; (**l**) Mode 12.

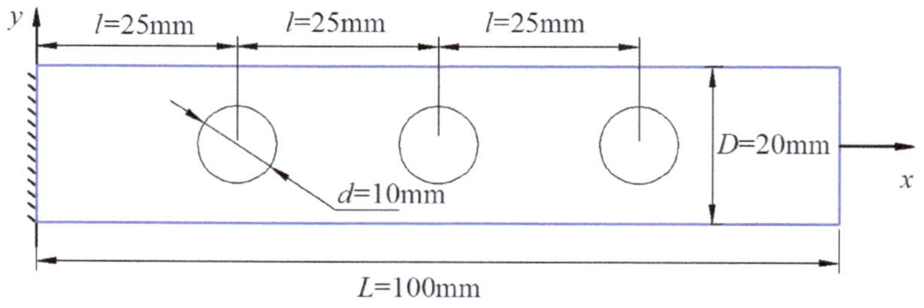

Figure 10. The cantilever beam with three identical holes and in plane stress condition.

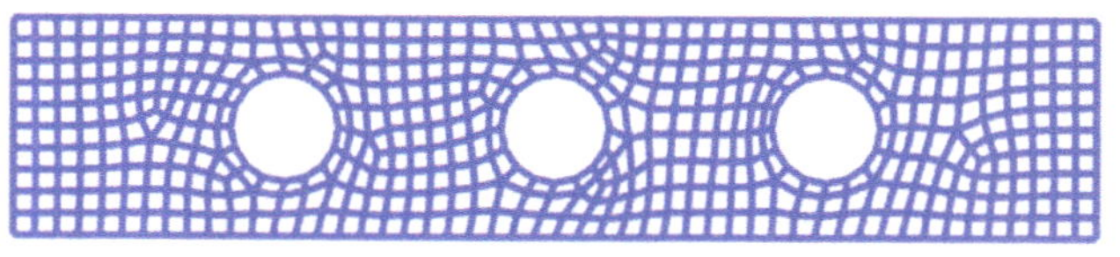

(**a**)

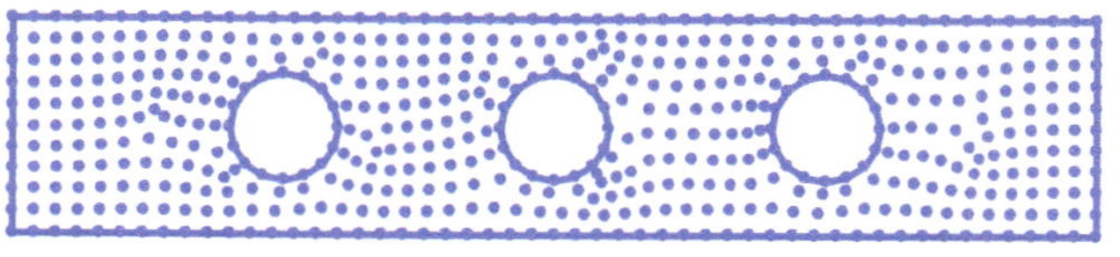

(**b**)

Figure 11. The node arrangement patterns employed to discretize the cantilever beam with three identical holes for the different numerical methods: (**a**) mesh pattern used to discretize the cantilever beam with three identical holes for the standard FEM-Q4; (**b**) node arrangement pattern used to discretize the cantilever beam with three identical holes for the RPIM and M-RPIM.

Table 6. The first twelve natural frequency values computed using different numerical methods for the cantilever beam with three identical holes.

Mode	FEM-Q4	Error (%)	RPIM	Error (%)	M-RPIM	Error (%)	Ref.
1	1626.190	0.617	1612.353	0.239	1618.711	0.154	1616.218
2	8272.300	0.174	8246.759	0.135	8268.312	0.126	8257.923
3	11,373.419	0.791	11,239.656	0.395	11,302.342	0.161	11,284.188
4	19,395.928	1.595	19,004.812	0.454	19,101.194	0.051	19,091.435
5	33,523.877	1.273	33,233.174	0.395	33,231.319	0.390	33,102.326
6	33,972.380	1.786	33,568.275	0.575	33,472.489	0.288	33,376.214
7	37,191.685	2.943	36,443.890	0.873	36,333.778	0.568	36,128.559
8	52,155.832	2.894	51,179.337	0.968	51,042.893	0.699	50,688.744
9	52,582.353	3.420	51,249.812	0.799	51,117.100	0.538	50,843.699
10	55,474.223	2.473	54,470.879	0.620	54,276.585	0.261	54,135.295
11	67,782.825	2.359	66,555.530	0.505	66,471.730	0.379	66,220.863
12	75,775.407	1.343	75,309.818	0.721	74,789.424	0.025	74,771.060

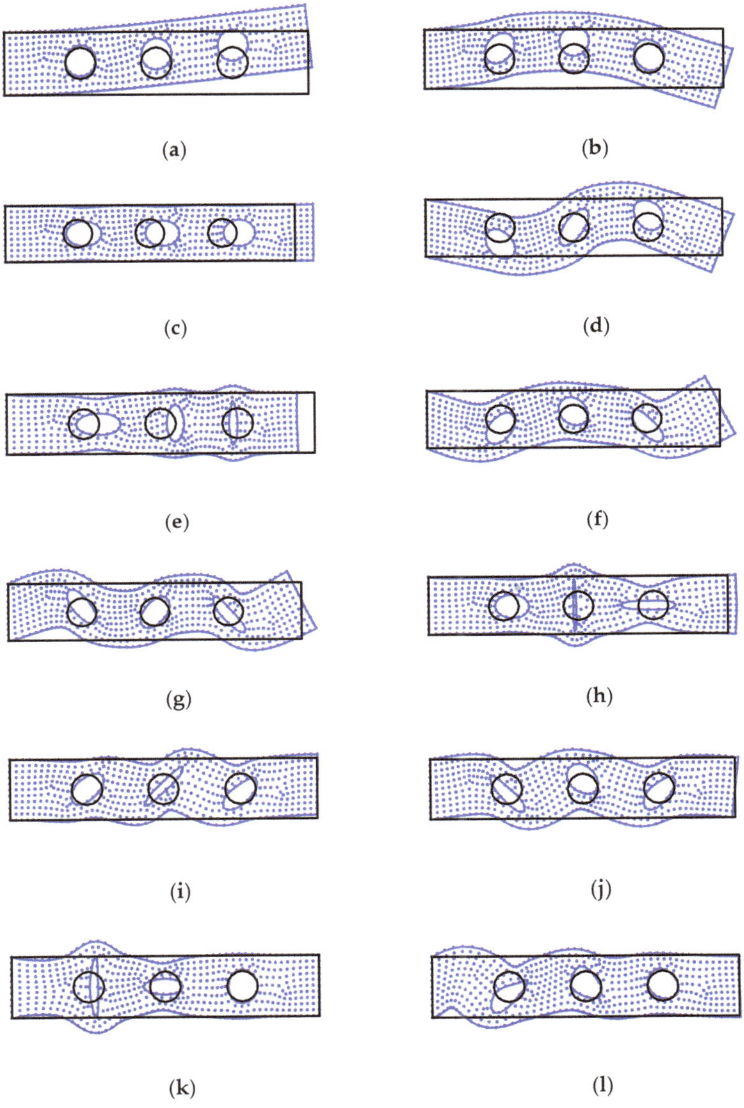

Figure 12. The free vibration modes of the cantilever beam with three identical holes corresponding to the first twelve natural frequency values from the present M-RPIM: (**a**) Mode 1; (**b**) Mode 2; (**c**) Mode 3; (**d**) Mode 4; (**e**) Mode 5; (**f**) Mode 6; (**g**) Mode 7; (**h**) Mode 8; (**i**) Mode 9; (**j**) Mode 10; (**k**) Mode 11; (**l**) Mode 12.

5. Conclusions

In this work, a modified radial point interpolation method (M-RPIM) is proposed to enhance the capacities of the original RPIM for the free vibration analysis of two-dimensional solids. In the present M-RPIM, the numerical approximation established in integration cells is continuously differentiable while the corresponding numerical approximation in the original RPIM is always not continuously differentiable. Therefore, the possible numerical integration error in the original RPIM can be markedly reduced by the present M-RPIM.

Several supporting numerical examples are employed to investigate fully and in detail the performance of the proposed M-RPIM in solving free vibration problems. It is demonstrated that the proposed M-RPIM not only is able to surpass the original RPIM and the standard FEM-Q4 in terms of computation accuracy and convergence properties when the identical node arrangement scheme is employed, but the proposed method also has higher computation efficiency. This is because the fixed support domain is employed for any quadrature points in the integration cells; hence, the additional operations to determine the support domain for each quadrature point are not required. Owing to these excellent features, the present M-RPIM has great potential for solving more complex problems in practical engineering application.

Author Contributions: Conceptualization, T.S. and Y.C.; methodology, Y.C.; software, P.W.; validation, T.S. and Y.C.; formal analysis, T.S.; investigation, T.S.; resources, Y.C.; data curation, T.S.; writing—original draft preparation, T.S.; writing—review and editing, T.S.; visualization, T.S.; supervision, Y.C.; funding acquisition, G.Z. All authors have read and agreed to the published version of the manuscript.

Funding: This research was funded by the State Key Laboratory of Ocean Engineering (Shanghai Jiao Tong University) (Grant No. GKZD010081); the National Natural Science Foundation of China (Grant No. 51909201); the Open Fund of Key Laboratory of High Performance Ship Technology (Wuhan University of Technology), Ministry of Education (Grant No. gxnc21112701 and No. gxnc18041401); and the National Key Laboratory on Ship Vibration and Noise (Grant No. 6142204210208).

Institutional Review Board Statement: Not applicable.

Informed Consent Statement: Not applicable.

Data Availability Statement: The data used to support the findings of this study are available from the corresponding author upon request.

Acknowledgments: We thank Qiang Gui for the helpful suggestions to revise the present paper.

Conflicts of Interest: The authors declare no conflict of interest.

References

1. Bathe, K.J. *Finite Element Procedures*, 2nd ed.; Prentice Hall: Watertown, MA, USA, 2014.
2. Li, J.P.; Fu, Z.J.; Gu, Y.; Qin, Q.H. Recent advances and emerging applications of the singular boundary method for large-scale and high-frequency computational acoustics. *Adv. Appl. Math. Mech.* **2022**, *14*, 315–343. [CrossRef]
3. Wu, F.; Zhou, G.; Gu, Q.Y.; Chai, Y.B. An enriched finite element method with interpolation cover functions for acoustic analysis in high frequencies. *Eng. Anal. Bound. Elem.* **2021**, *129*, 67–81. [CrossRef]
4. Gu, Y.; Fan, C.M.; Fu, Z.J. Localized method of fundamental solutions for three-dimensional elasticity problems: Theory. *Adv. Appl. Math. Mech.* **2021**, *13*, 1520–1534.
5. Liu, C.S.; Qiu, L.; Lin, J. Simulating thin plate bending problems by a family of two-parameter homogenization functions. *Appl. Math. Model.* **2020**, *79*, 284–299. [CrossRef]
6. Li, J.P.; Zhang, L.; Qin, Q.H. A regularized method of moments for three-dimensional time-harmonic electromagnetic scattering. *Appl. Math. Lett.* **2021**, *112*, 106746. [CrossRef]
7. Qiu, L.; Lin, J.; Wang, F.J.; Qin, Q.H.; Liu, C.S. A homogenization function method for inverse heat source problems in 3D functionally graded materials. *Appl. Math. Model.* **2021**, *91*, 923–933. [CrossRef]
8. Gu, Y.; Lei, J. Fracture mechanics analysis of two-dimensional cracked thin structures (from micro- to nano-scales) by an efficient boundary element analysis. *Results Math.* **2021**, *11*, 100172. [CrossRef]
9. Li, J.P.; Gu, Y.; Qin, Q.H.; Zhang, L. The rapid assessment for three-dimensional potential model of large-scale particle system by a modified multilevel fast multipole algorithm. *Comput. Math. Appl.* **2021**, *89*, 127–138. [CrossRef]
10. Chai, Y.B.; Bathe, K.J. Transient wave propagation in inhomogeneous media with enriched overlapping triangular elements. *Comput. Struct.* **2020**, *237*, 106273. [CrossRef]
11. Chai, Y.B.; Li, W.; Liu, Z.Y. Analysis of transient wave propagation dynamics using the enriched finite element method with interpolation cover functions. *Appl. Math. Comput.* **2022**, *412*, 126564. [CrossRef]
12. Li, Y.C.; Dang, S.N.; Li, W.; Chai, Y.B. Free and Forced Vibration Analysis of Two-Dimensional Linear Elastic Solids Using the Finite Element Methods Enriched by Interpolation Cover Functions. *Mathematics* **2022**, *10*, 456. [CrossRef]
13. Liu, M.Y.; Gao, G.J.; Zhu, H.F.; Jiang, C. A cell-based smoothed finite element method stabilized by implicit SUPG/SPGP/Fractional step method for incompressible flow. *Eng. Anal. Bound. Elem.* **2021**, *124*, 194–210. [CrossRef]

14. Chai, Y.B.; Gong, Z.X.; Li, W.; Li, T.Y.; Zhang, Q.F.; Zou, Z.H.; Sun, Y.B. Application of smoothed finite element method to two dimensional exterior problems of acoustic radiation. *Int. J. Comput. Methods* **2018**, *15*, 1850029. [CrossRef]
15. Liu, M.Y.; Gao, G.J.; Zhu, H.F.; Jiang, C.; Liu, G.R. A cell-based smoothed finite element method (CS-FEM) for three-dimensional incompressible laminar flows using mixed wedge-hexahedral element. *Eng. Anal. Bound. Elem.* **2021**, *133*, 269–285. [CrossRef]
16. Wang, T.T.; Zhou, G.; Jiang, C.; Shi, F.C.; Tian, X.D.; Gao, G.J. A coupled cell-based smoothed finite element method and discrete phase model for incompressible laminar flow with dilute solid particles. *Eng. Anal. Bound. Elem.* **2022**, *143*, 190–206. [CrossRef]
17. Li, W.; Gong, Z.X.; Chai, Y.B.; Cheng, C.; Li, T.Y.; Zhang, Q.F.; Wang, M.S. Hybrid gradient smoothing technique with discrete shear gap method for shell structures. *Comput. Math. Appl.* **2017**, *74*, 1826–1855. [CrossRef]
18. Liu, G.R. *Mesh Free Methods: Moving Beyond the Finite Element Method*; CRC Press: Boca Raton, FL, USA, 2009.
19. Cheng, S.F.; Wang, F.J.; Wu, G.Z.; Zhang, C.X. semi-analytical and boundary-type meshless method with adjoint variable formulation for acoustic design sensitivity analysis. *Appl. Math. Lett.* **2022**, *131*, 108068. [CrossRef]
20. Lin, J. Simulation of 2D and 3D inverse source problems of nonlinear time-fractional wave equation by the meshless homogenization function method. *Eng. Comput.* **2021**. [CrossRef]
21. Lin, J.; Bai, J.; Reutskiy, S.; Lu, J. A novel RBF-based meshless method for solving time-fractional transport equations in 2D and 3D arbitrary domains. *Eng. Comput.* **2022**. [CrossRef]
22. Lin, J.; Zhang, Y.H.; Reutskiy, S.; Feng, W. A novel meshless space-time backward substitution method and its application to nonhomogeneous advection-diffusion problems. *Appl. Math. Comput.* **2021**, *398*, 125964. [CrossRef]
23. Wang, C.; Wang, F.J.; Gong, Y.P. Analysis of 2D heat conduction in nonlinear functionally graded materials using a local semi-analytical meshless method. *AIMS Math.* **2021**, *6*, 12599–12618. [CrossRef]
24. Gu, Y.; Sun, H.G. A meshless method for solving three-dimensional time fractional diffusion equation with variable-order derivatives. *Appl. Math. Model.* **2020**, *78*, 539–549. [CrossRef]
25. Li, X.; Li, S. A fast element-free Galerkin method for the fractional diffusion-wave equation. *App. Math. Lett.* **2021**, *122*, 107529. [CrossRef]
26. Li, X.; Li, S. A linearized element-free Galerkin method for the complex Ginzburg–Landau equation. *Comput. Math. Appl.* **2021**, *90*, 135–147. [CrossRef]
27. Atluri, S.N.; Kim, H.G.; Cho, J.Y. Critical assessment of the truly meshless local PetrovGalerkin (MLPG), and local boundary integral equation (LBIE) methods. *Comput. Mech.* **1999**, *24*, 348–372. [CrossRef]
28. Liu, W.K.; Jun, S.; Zhang, Y.F. Reproducing kernel particle methods. *Int. J. Numer. Methods Fluids* **1995**, *20*, 1081–1106. [CrossRef]
29. Qu, J.; Dang, S.N.; Li, Y.C.; Chai, Y.B. Analysis of the interior acoustic wave propagation problems using the modified radial point interpolation method (M-RPIM). *Eng. Anal. Bound. Elem.* **2022**, *138*, 339–368. [CrossRef]
30. Gui, Q.; Zhang, Y.; Chai, Y.B.; You, X.Y.; Li, W. Dispersion error reduction for interior acoustic problems using the radial point interpolation meshless method with plane wave enrichment functions. *Eng. Anal. Bound. Elem.* **2022**, *143*, 428–441. [CrossRef]
31. Qu, W.Z.; He, H. A GFDM with supplementary nodes for thin elastic plate bending analysis under dynamic loading. *Appl. Math. Lett.* **2022**, *124*, 107664. [CrossRef]
32. Qu, W.Z.; Gao, H.W.; Gu, Y. Integrating Krylov deferred correction and generalized finite difference methods for dynamic simulations of wave propagation phenomena in long-time intervals. *Adv. Appl. Math. Mech.* **2021**, *13*, 1398–1417.
33. Xi, Q.; Fu, Z.J.; Li, Y.; Huang, H. A hybrid GFDM–SBM solver for acoustic radiation and propagation of thin plate structure under shallow sea environment. *J. Theor. Comput. Acous.* **2020**, *28*, 2050008. [CrossRef]
34. Fu, Z.J.; Xie, Z.Y.; Ji, S.Y.; Tsai, C.C.; Li, A.L. Meshless generalized finite difference method for water wave interactions with multiple-bottom-seated-cylinder-array structures. *Ocean Eng.* **2020**, *195*, 106736. [CrossRef]
35. Zheng, Z.Y.; Li, X.L. Theoretical analysis of the generalized finite difference method. *Comput. Math. Appl.* **2022**, *120*, 1–14. [CrossRef]
36. Wang, F.; Fan, C.M.; Zhang, C.; Lin, J. A localized space-time method of fundamental solutions for diffusion and convection-diffusion problems. *Adv. Appl. Math. Mech.* **2020**, *12*, 940–958. [CrossRef]
37. Fu, Z.J.; Xi, Q.; Li, Y.; Huang, H.; Rabczuk, T. Hybrid FEM–SBM solver for structural vibration induced underwater acoustic radiation in shallow marine environment. *Comput. Methods Appl. Mech. Eng.* **2020**, *369*, 113236. [CrossRef]
38. Fu, Z.J.; Chen, W.; Wen, P.H.; Zhang, C.Z. Singular boundary method for wave propagation analysis in periodic structures. *J. Sound Vib.* **2018**, *425*, 170–188. [CrossRef]
39. Li, J.P.; Zhang, L. High-precision calculation of electromagnetic scattering by the Burton-Miller type regularized method of moments. *Eng. Anal. Bound. Elem.* **2021**, *133*, 177–184. [CrossRef]
40. Li, J.P.; Zhang, L.; Qin, Q.H. A regularized fast multipole method of moments for rapid calculation of three-dimensional time-harmonic electromagnetic scattering from complex targets. *Eng. Anal. Bound. Elem.* **2022**, *142*, 28–38. [CrossRef]
41. Zhang, Y.O.; Dang, S.N.; Li, W.; Chai, Y.B. Performance of the radial point interpolation method (RPIM) with implicit time integration scheme for transient wave propagation dynamics. *Comput. Math. Appl.* **2022**, *114*, 95–111. [CrossRef]
42. You, X.Y.; Li, W.; Chai, Y.B. A truly meshfree method for solving acoustic problems using local weak form and radial basis functions. *Appl. Math. Comput.* **2020**, *365*, 124694. [CrossRef]
43. Chai, Y.B.; You, X.Y.; Li, W. Dispersion Reduction for the Wave Propagation Problems Using a Coupled "FE-Meshfree" Triangular Element. *Int. J. Comput. Methods* **2020**, *17*, 1950071. [CrossRef]

44. Li, W.; Zhang, Q.; Gui, Q.; Chai, Y.B. A coupled FE-Meshfree triangular element for acoustic radiation problems. *Int. J. Comput. Methods* **2021**, *18*, 2041002. [CrossRef]
45. Wang, F.; Zhao, Q.; Chen, Z.; Fan, C.M. Localized Chebyshev collocation method for solving elliptic partial differential equations in arbitrary 2D domains. *Appl. Math. Comput.* **2021**, *397*, 125903. [CrossRef]
46. Xi, Q.; Fu, Z.J.; Zhang, C.Z.; Yin, D.S. An efficient localized Trefftz-based collocation scheme for heat conduction analysis in two kinds of heterogeneous materials under temperature loading. *Comput. Struct.* **2021**, *255*, 106619. [CrossRef]
47. Xi, Q.; Fu, Z.J.; Wu, W.J.; Wang, H.; Wang, Y. A novel localized collocation solver based on Trefftz basis for Potential-based Inverse Electromyography. *Appl. Math. Comput.* **2021**, *390*, 125604. [CrossRef]
48. Li, X.; Li, S. A finite point method for the fractional cable equation using meshless smoothed gradients. *Eng. Anal. Bound. Elem.* **2022**, *134*, 453–465. [CrossRef]
49. Fu, Z.J.; Yang, L.W.; Xi, Q.; Liu, C.S. A boundary collocation method for anomalous heat conduction analysis in functionally graded materials. *Comput. Math. Appl.* **2021**, *88*, 91–109. [CrossRef]
50. Tang, Z.; Fu, Z.J.; Sun, H.; Liu, X. An efficient localized collocation solver for anomalous diffusion on surfaces. *Fract. Calc. Appl. Anal.* **2021**, *24*, 865–894. [CrossRef]
51. Xi, Q.; Fu, Z.J.; Rabczuk, T.; Yin, D. A localized collocation scheme with fundamental solutions for long-time anomalous heat conduction analysis in functionally graded materials. *Int. J. Heat Mass Tran.* **2021**, *180*, 121778. [CrossRef]
52. Dolbow, J.; Belytschko, T. Numerical integration of the Galerkin weak form in meshfree methods. *Comput. Mech.* **1999**, *23*, 219–230. [CrossRef]
53. Liu, G.R.; Gu, Y.T. Assessment and applications of point interpolation methods for computational mechanics. *Int. J. Numer. Meth. Engng.* **2004**, *59*, 1373–1397. [CrossRef]

mathematics

MDPI

Article

A Modified Inverse Iteration Method for Computing the Symmetric Tridiagonal Eigenvectors

Wei Chu [1], Yao Zhao [1,2] and Hua Yuan [1,2,*]

[1] School of Naval Architecture and Ocean Engineering, Huazhong University of Sciences and Technology, Wuhan 430074, China
[2] Hubei Key Laboratory of Naval Architecture and Ocean Engineering Hydrodynamics (HUST), Wuhan 430074, China
* Correspondence: yuanhua@hust.edu.cn; Tel.: +86-027-8754-3258

Abstract: This paper presents a novel method for computing the symmetric tridiagonal eigenvectors, which is the modification of the widely used Inverse Iteration method. We construct the corresponding algorithm by a new one-step iteration method, a new reorthogonalization method with the general Q iteration and a significant modification when calculating severely clustered eigenvectors. The numerical results show that this method is competitive with other existing methods, especially when computing part eigenvectors or severely clustered ones.

Keywords: symmetric tridiagonal matrix; eigenvector solver; clustered eigenpairs; orthogonalization; general Q iteration

MSC: 65F15

Citation: Chu, W.; Zhao, Y.; Yuan, H. A Modified Inverse Iteration Method for Computing the Symmetric Tridiagonal Eigenvectors. *Mathematics* **2022**, *10*, 3636. https://doi.org/10.3390/math10193636

Academic Editor: Michael Voskoglou

Received: 26 August 2022
Accepted: 29 September 2022
Published: 5 October 2022

1. Introduction

Computing the symmetric tridiagonal (ST) eigenvector is an important task in many research fields, such as the computational quantum physics [1], mathematics [2,3], dynamics [4], computational quantum chemistry [5], etc. The ST eigenvector problem also arises while solving any symmetric eigenproblem because it is a common practice to reduce the generalized symmetric eigenproblems to an ST one.

The Divide and Conquer (DC) algorithm [6] has a considerable advantage when calculating all the eigenpairs of an ST matrix. It is quite remarkable that the DC method, which is efficient for parallel computation, can also be faster than other implementations on a serial computer. However, this method does not support computing part eigenpairs or computing eigenvectors only. In practice, it is rare to compute the full eigenvectors of a large ST matrix. The famous QR method [7] has the same shortage while costing more time and is hard to be parallelized. This paper focuses on modifying the solution of computing part eigenvectors and gives a new method for eigenvectors of good accuracy and orthogonality.

Once an accurate eigenvalue approximation is known, the Inverse Iteration method [8] always computes an accurate eigenvector with an acceptable time cost. However, it does not guarantee the orthogonality when eigenvalues are close. A commonly used remedy is to reorthogonalize each approximate eigenvector, by the modified Gram–Schmidt method, against previously computed eigenvectors in the cluster. This remedy increases up to $2n^3$ operations if all the eigenvalues cluster, while the time cost for the eigenvectors themselves is only $O(n^2)$.

Dhillion proposed the Multiple Relatively Robust Representations (MRRR) algorithm [9] to avoid reorthogonalization. This is an ambitious attempt as the MRRR algorithm computes all the accurate and numerically orthogonal eigenvectors with a time cost of

$O(n^2)$. Nevertheless, the MRRR algorithm can fail in calculating severely clustered eigenvalues of a large group, such as the glued Wilkinson matrices [10]. Dhillion fixed the problem and modified the MRRR method subtly and cleverly [11], without increasing its time complexity. However, this modified MRRR method, which applies the perturbation to the root representation of the ST matrix, costs even more time than the Inverse Iteration method with the modified Gram–Schmidt process. Even when computing random matrices, the MRRR algorithm has no advantage compared with the Inverse Iteration method. In addition, when computing part eigenvectors, the MRRR algorithm needs considerably accurate eigenvalues to guarantee natural orthogonality and thus calls the time-consuming Bisection method to obtain them. As a consequence, except for those cases with many eigenvalues clusters, the Inverse Iteration method is more efficient. More related details are presented in Section 6.

Mastronardi and Van Dooreen [12] proposed an ingenious method to determine the accurate eigenvector of a symmetric tridiagonal matrix once an approximation of the eigenvalue is known. In addition, they applied this method to calculate the weights of the Gaussian quadrature rules [3].

Our strategy is to improve the Inverse Iteration method with the three main modifications:

- We replace the iteration process with a new one that only costs one step to guarantee convergence, similar to the MRRR method;
- The envelope vector theory [13] is utilized to compute accurate and naturally orthogonal eigenvectors when the eigenvalues severely cluster. By combining the new iteration process, the time cost is even less than the cost of calculating isolated eigenvectors. In other words, the severely clustered eigenvalues accelerate the convergence;
- We give a new orthogonalization method for the generally clustered groups of severely clustered eigenvalues. For k clustered eigenvalues in such a case, the new orthogonalization method decreases the time cost from $O(nk^2)$ to $O(nk)$.

The numerical results confirm our promise of accuracy and orthogonality. In addition, our new method supports computing part eigenvectors and embarrassingly parallelization, significantly improving the computational efficiency.

This paper focuses on the symmetric tridiagonal eigenvector problem. According to Weyl's theorem, the real symmetric eigenvalue problem $Ax = x\lambda$ is well posed, in an absolute sense because an eigenvalue can change by no more than the spectral norm of the change in the matrix A [14]. However, for an unsymmetric matrix $\hat{A}$, some of its eigenvalues may be extremely sensitive to uncertainty in the matrix entries. Consequently, the assessment of error becomes a major concern. Some specific conclusions were introduced in [14]. Readers can also see more unsymmetric examples in [15,16].

The organization of the rest of this paper is as follows: Section 2 gives the modified iteration of the new method and an algorithm to compute an isolated eigenvector. Section 3 studies the computation of clustered eigenvectors. Section 4 introduces the general Q iteration and the new orthogonalization method. Section 5 concerns the overflow and underflow. Several corresponding pseudocodes are provided in the above sections. Section 6 shows some examples and numerical results. Finally, we discuss and assess the Modified Inverse Iteration method in Section 7.

2. Compute Isolated Eigenvectors

2.1. Theoretical Background

Consider a $n \times n$ real unreduced ST matrix A (all the ST matrices discussed in this paper are real and unreduced), which has eigenvalues $\lambda_1 \sim \lambda_n$ in the increasing order and the corresponding eigenvectors $v_1 \sim v_n$. Once an accurate eigenvalue approximation $u \to \lambda_j$ is known, we have

$$(A - uI_{n\times n})\tilde{v}_j = T\tilde{v}_j = 0, \tag{1}$$

where $\tilde{v}_j$ is the eigenvector approximation and $I_{n\times n}$ denotes the $n \times n$ identity matrix.

When u is the exact eigenvalue, T has a rank of $n-1$ and (1) can be solved by ignoring any one of its n rows. However, since $u \neq \lambda_j$, T is not singular and thus (1) has no nonzero solution. If one still solves (1) by ignoring one of its n rows, say, the kth row, the actually solved equation is

$$Tz^k = e_k, \tag{2}$$

where e_k is the kth column of $I_{n\times n}$, and z^k denotes the solution when ignoring the k row. It is obvious that z^k is the kth column of T^{-1}. From [10], we have

$$z^k = r_j v_j/(\lambda_j - u) + \sum_{i\neq j} r_i v_i/(\lambda_i - u), \tag{3}$$

where $r_i (i \in [1,n])$ is the kth component of v_i, which can also be denoted by $v_i(k)$.

The main idea of the Inverse Iteration is to solve (2), substitute the result into the right side, and go on. As $u \to \lambda_j$, z^k will finally approach v_j. If λ_j is an isolated eigenvalue, (3) shows that the degree of approximation of z^k and v_j depends on the absolute value of $v_j(k)$. For example, if $|v_j(k)|$ approximates to zero, z^k has nearly no ingredient of v_j. As a consequence, the iterations hardly converge. Therefore, the traditional Inverse Iteration method uses a vector with all components equal to 1 to be the original right side of (1). Within about two or three steps, the traditional Inverse Iteration method calculates an accurate eigenvector approximation $\tilde{v}_j$.

2.2. One-Step Iteration

To accelerate the iteration process, our task is to find the biggest $|v_j(k)| (k \in [1,n])$ and to guarantee convergence in one step. From [9], we have

$$\frac{1}{\gamma_k} = e_k^T (A - uI)^{-1} e_k = \frac{|v_j(k)|^2}{\lambda_j - u} + \sum_{i\neq j} \frac{|v_i(k)|^2}{\lambda_i - u} \tag{4}$$

where $1/\gamma_k$ is the kth component on the diagonal of $(A-uI)^{-1}$, i.e., the kth component of z^k, and its absolute value reflects $|v_j(k)|$ (recall $u \to \lambda_j$). The MRRR method finds the smallest $|\gamma_k|$ by the twisted triangular factorization, while we give a new method in this section.

We denote the ith sequential principal minor of a ST matrix A by $A_{1:i}$. The submatrix of A in rows i through j is denoted by $A_{i:j}$ and its determinant by $det(A)$. We denote the characteristic polynomial $det(A-uI)$ by $C_{1:n}$, $C_{1:n}(u)$, or $C^A_{1:n}(u)$ if necessary. a_i and b_i denote the ith component on the diagonal and sub-diagonal of A, respectively. According to [17], we have

$$z^k = \begin{bmatrix} C_{k+1:n}(\prod_{t=1}^{k-1} -b_t) \\ C_1 C_{k+1:n}(\prod_{t=2}^{k-1} -b_t) \\ \cdots \\ C_{1:k-2} C_{k+1:n}(-b_{k-1}) \\ C_{1:k-1} C_{k+1:n} \\ C_{1:k-1} C_{k+2:n}(-b_k) \\ \cdots \\ C_{1:k-1} C_n(\prod_{t=k}^{n-2} -b_t) \\ C_{1:k-1}(\prod_{t=k}^{n-1} -b_t) \end{bmatrix} / C_{1:n} \tag{5}$$

and

$$
\begin{aligned}
C_{1:n} &= det(A - uI) \\
&= -b_{k-1}^2 C_{1:k-2} C_{k+1:n} + (a_k - u) C_{1:k-1} C_{k+1:n} - b_k^2 C_{1:k-1} C_{k+2:n} \\
&= C_{1:k-1} C_{k+1:n} (C_{1:k} / C_{1:k-1} - b_k^2 C_{k+2:n} / C_{k+1:n}).
\end{aligned} \tag{6}
$$

Remark 1. *(5) is also introduced in [9], but in an incorrect form as missing the negative sign before each b_i. Dhillion worried about the overflow and underflow issues when calculating z^k by (5) and thus did not discuss it further. This paper will give a more practical form of (5), reduce its computational cost and solve the overflow or underflow problem (in Section 5).*

By (5) and (6), we have

$$\gamma_k = q_k - b_k^2 / p_{n-k} \tag{7}$$

where $q_i = C_i / C_{i-1}$ and $p_i = C_{n-i+1} / C_{n-i+2}$. As the sequential principal minors of an ST matrix form a Sturm sequence, we have [18]

$$
\begin{aligned}
q_0 = 1, q_1 = a_1 - u, q_i = a_i - u - b_{i-1}^2 / q_{i-1}; \\
p_0 = 1, p_1 = a_n - u, p_i = a_{n+1-i} - u - b_{n+1-i}^2 / p_{i-1}.
\end{aligned} \tag{8}
$$

(5) and (8) can be expressed as

$$
z^k = x_1 \alpha + x_2 \beta = \begin{bmatrix} 1 \\ q_1/(-b_1) \\ q_1 q_2 / ((-b_1)(-b_2)) \\ \cdots \\ \prod_{i=1}^{k-1} q_i/(-b_i) \\ 0 \\ \cdots \\ 0 \\ 0 \end{bmatrix} \alpha + \begin{bmatrix} 0 \\ 0 \\ \cdots \\ 0 \\ \prod_{i=1}^{n-k-1} p_i/(-b_{n-i}) \\ \cdots \\ p_1 p_2 / ((-b_{n-1})(-b_{n-2})) \\ p_1/(-b_{n-1}) \\ 1 \end{bmatrix} \beta, \tag{9}
$$

where x_1 and x_2 are both $n \times 1$ vectors, the $(k+1) \sim n$th components of x_1 are zeros while the $1 \sim k$th components of x_2 are zeros. α and β are two coefficients to be determined.

It can be seen that (9) satisfies (2), except for the kth and $(k+1)$th rows. As we only care about the direction of z^k, only the $(k+1)$th row needs to be considered when determining α and β. Then, we have

$$\alpha b_k \prod_{i=1}^{k-1} q_i/(-b_i) + \beta \left((a_{k+1} - u) (\prod_{i=1}^{n-k-1} p_i/(-b_{n-i})) + b_{k+1} (\prod_{i=1}^{n-k-2} p_i/(-b_{n-i})) \right) = 0.$$

Therefore, our scheme is to calculate q_i's and p_i's by (8) first, then find the smallest $|\gamma_k|$ by (7). Note that (7) would not cost extra division operations if we save the b_i^2/p_{n-i}'s when calculating p_i's by (8). Finally, we choose the corresponding k of the smallest $|\gamma_k|$ and obtain z^k by (9). Our modified iteration method to calculate one isolated eigenvector is shown by Algorithm 1.

If b_i^2 and $1/b_i$ are calculated and stored in advance, Algorithm 1 costs $8n \sim 8.5n$ operations (note the cost of calculating $a - u$ is shared in step 3 of Algorithm 1) per eigenvector while the version in [9] costs $11n$.

Note that (8) computes p and q with no time cost savings per se. The two main contributors are: first, (7) reduces the cost of searching min $|\gamma_k|$; second, (9) divides the eigenvector computation into two parts, and even under the most adverse condition of $k = n/2$, (9) can still reduce the multiplication operations by half compared to (5).

Algorithm 1: Compute one isolated eigenvector.

Input : a, b, n, u
// a is the diagonal of A, b is the sub-diagonal, n is the size and u is the approximation to λ_i
Output: z
// z is the approximation to v_i
calculate q and p by (8);
calculate $|\gamma_i|(i \in [1, n])$ by (7);
find the smallest $|\gamma_i|$ and save the corresponding i;
$k \leftarrow i$, construct a $k \times 1$ vector x_1 and a $(n-k) \times 1$ vector x_2;
$x_1(1) \leftarrow 1, x_2(1) \leftarrow 1$;
for *each* $i \in [2, k]$ **do**
  $x_1(i) \leftarrow x_1(i-1)q_{i-1} / -b_{i-1}$;
end
for *each* $i \in [2, n-k]$ **do**
  $x_2(i) \leftarrow x_2(i-1)p_{i-1} / -b_{n+1-i}$;
end
flip x_2;
if $x_1(k) = 0$ **then**
  $P \leftarrow 1$;
else
  if $k == n$ **then**
    $P \leftarrow -a_{k+1}x_2(1) / (b_k x_1(k))$
    // to satisfy the $k+1$th row of (2)
  else
    $P \leftarrow -(a_{k+1}x_2(1) + b_{k+1}x_2(2)) / (b_k x_1(k))$
    // to satisfy the $k+1$th row of (2)
  end
end
$z \leftarrow [Px_1; x_2]$;
$z \leftarrow z/\|z\|$ // if normalization is needed

2.3. Accuracy Analysis of Algorithm 1

Let R denote the residual norm, i.e., $R_k = \left\|Tz^k\right\| / \left\|z^k\right\|$, then we have

$$
\begin{aligned}
R_k &= \frac{\left\|Tz^k\right\|}{\left\|z^k\right\|} = \frac{|\gamma_k|}{\left\|z^k\right\|} \\
&= \sqrt{\frac{\gamma_k^2}{\gamma_k^2 e_k^T (A-uI)^{-1}(A-uI)^{-1} e_k}} \\
&= \left(\sum \frac{v_i^2(k)}{(\lambda_i - u)^2}\right)^{-1/2} = \frac{|\lambda_j - u|}{|v_j(k)|}\left(1 + \sum \frac{(\lambda_j - u)^2}{(\lambda_i - u)^2}\frac{v_i^2(k)}{v_j^2(k)}\right)^{-1/2} \\
&\leq \frac{|\lambda_j - u|}{|v_j(k)|}.
\end{aligned}
\tag{10}
$$

As Algorithm 1 ensures that $|v_j(k)|$ is the biggest one among all the $|v_j(i)|(i \in [1, n])$, it is guaranteed that $|v_j(k)| \geq \sqrt{1/n}$. Then, according to (10), we have $R_k \leq \sqrt{n}\epsilon$ where ϵ is the machine precision.

3. Computing Severely Clustered Eigenvectors

Now consider the case when eigenvalues clusters severely, for example, p eigenvalues that are equal in finite precision arithmetic. We will define "severely clustering" later in this section.

First, we introduce the two following lemmas from [13] to state our theorems.

Lemma 1 (The Envelope Vector). *Define $\mathcal{S} = span\{v_1, v_2, \ldots, v_p\}$, and the envelope vector of $\mathcal{S}$ is $\mathcal{E}$ given by*

$$\mathcal{E}_i = \max\{\mathcal{V}_i : \mathcal{V} \in \mathcal{S}, \|\mathcal{V}\| = 1\}.$$

For p clustered eigenvalues, the envelope vector will undulate with p high hills separated by $p-1$ low valleys.

Lemma 2. *For an ST matrix A that has p clustered eigenvalues $\lambda_1 \sim \lambda_p$, divide A into p submatrices: $A_{1:\eta_1}$, $A_{\eta_2^l:\eta_2^r}$, $\ldots$, $A_{\eta_{p-1}^l:\eta_{p-1}^r}$ and $A_{\eta_p:n}$. Note that these submatrices can have overlaps. Then, for each submatrix, there exists at least one A_{sub}, among all the possibilities of divisions that satisfies:*

1. *A_{sub} has an isolated sub-eigenvalue $\kappa \in [\lambda_1, \lambda_p]$;*
2. *For the 2nd to $(p-1)$th submatrices, the corresponding sub-eigenvector $s_i (i \in [2, p-1])$ (with respect to κ) has small components at both its ends. For $A_{1:\eta_1}$, $s_1(\eta_1) \to 0$ and for $A_{\eta_p:n}$, $s_p(1) \to 0$.*

Supplement zero components to obtain $\tilde{v}_s = [s; 0]$, $[0; s; 0]$, or $[0; s]$, which has the size of $n \times 1$. Then, the p $\tilde{v}_s$'s are approximations to $v_t (t \in [1, p])$. These eigenvector approximations are numerical orthogonal and satisfy $\|Tv_s\| < \sqrt{n/p}(\lambda_p - \lambda_1)/p$.

See the proofs and more details in [13].

Let us take a typical example of clustered eigenvalues to illustrate. Let α_0 be a 200×1 vector and $\alpha_0(i) = i (i \in [1, 200])$ and then construct $\alpha \leftarrow [flip(\alpha_0); 0; \alpha_0]$. Then, repeat $\alpha \leftarrow [\alpha; \alpha_0]$ by eight times totally. Finally, we obtain a 2001×1 vector α. Consider an ST matrix Φ, which has the diagonal equal to α and all the components on its sub-diagonal equal to 1. Φ is similar to the glued Wilkinson matrices in [11] and its biggest eight eigenvalues ($\lambda_1 \sim \lambda_8$) cluster severely. Let $u_1 \sim u_8$ denote the approximations of the biggest eight eigenvalues of Φ; it shows $u_8 - u_1 = 0$ in Matlab, i.e., $\lambda_1 \sim \lambda_8$ severely clusters.

Let $u = u_1$ and calculate $|\gamma_k| (k \in [1, 2001])$ of Φ. The results are shown in Figure 1. According to Lemma 1, the low valley entries of the envelope vector correspond to small components of $v_i (i \in [1, p])$. Note that this means all the p eigenvectors have small components at this entry, thus the corresponding $|\gamma_k|$ must be a big value according to (4). The case of high hills is similar. In other words, the $|\gamma_k|$ curve undulates with p low valleys separated by $p-1$ high hills. Note these extreme points may not be exactly the same as the envelope vector. We show $|\gamma_k| (k \in [1, 2001])$ of Φ in Figure 1. A logarithmic scale on the y-axis has been used to emphasize the small entries. The results confirm our point.

We give a method to find the applicable submatrices of Lemma 2 by Theorem 1.

Theorem 1. *If a submatrix satisfies Lemma 2, then the corresponding entries contain and only contain one low valley of the $|\gamma_k|$ curve.*

Proof. Take the first submatrix $A_{1:\eta_1}$ (which is assumed to satisfy Lemma 2) as an example because the proofs of the others are similar.

Let X denote the eigenvector approximation from Lemma 2, and we have $X = \sum_{t=1}^{p} x_t v_t = [s; 0]$. Thus, the corresponding entries of $A_{1:\eta_1}$ must contain at least one low valley, if not all the x_t's will be small values and violate the equation $\sum_{t=1}^{p} x_t^2 = 1$.

If the corresponding entries of $A_{1:\eta_1}$ contain more than one low valley, say, two, it will also contain one high hill of the $|\gamma_k|$ curve. This means X has a small component at the corresponding entry of the hill. In addition, X contains at least two major ingredients of v_i

that has big components at the two valleys, respectively, or X contains one major ingredient of v_i that has big components at both entries. According to [10], if an eigenvector has one part that has both small ends, the corresponding eigenvalue must have a close neighbor. Therefore, if the corresponding entries of $A_{1:\eta_1}$ contain more than one low valley, $A_{1:\eta_1}$ has clustered sub-eigenvalues that $\in [\lambda_1, \lambda_p]$.

With the above conclusions, the proof is completed. □

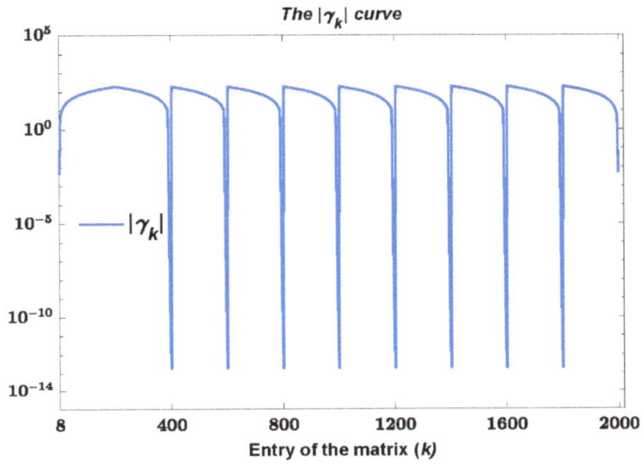

Figure 1. The $|\gamma_k|$ curve of Φ.

To illustrate Theorem 1 more intuitively, and as a complementary argument to the above proof, we performed the following numerical test. We calculated the distances between λ_{2001} of Φ and the last two sub-eigenvalues of $\Phi_{1:\eta}(\eta \in [2, 2000])$. Because by the Interlacing Property from [17], the close sub-eigenvalues to λ_{2001} must be the last ones. The result is shown in Figure 2. A logarithmic scale on the y-axis has been used to emphasize the small entries. In Figure 2, $\Phi_{1:\eta}$ starts to have one close eigenvalue when $\eta > 400$, which is the first low valley of the $|\gamma_k|$ curve, and two close eigenvalues when $\eta > 600$, which is the second valley. We also present the results of the last eight sub-eigenvalues of $\Phi_{1:\eta}(\eta \in [8, 2000])$ in Figure 3. It can be seen that, whenever $\Phi_{1:\eta}$ "crosses" a low valley of $|\gamma_k|$, the clustered sub-eigenvalues are one more. Figures 2 and 3 confirm Theorem 1 well. See more and detailed numerical examples and results for accuracy in Section 6.

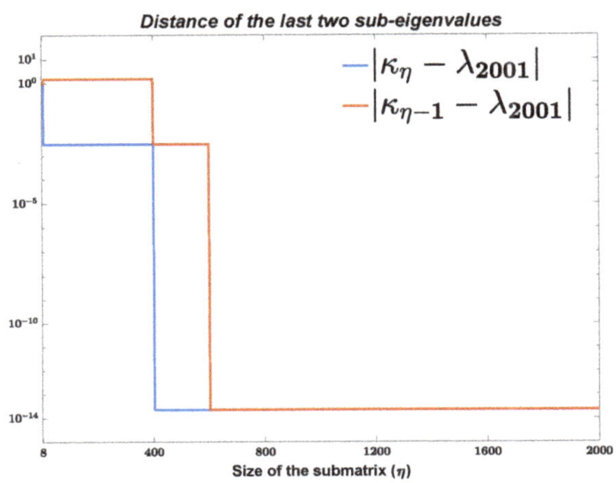

Figure 2. The distances of the last two sub-eigenvalues.

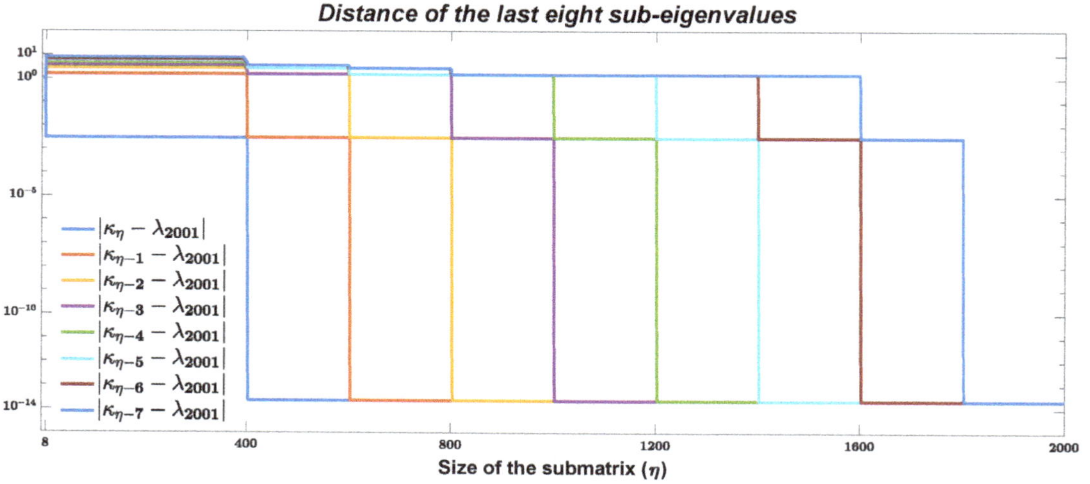

Figure 3. The distances of the last eight sub-eigenvalues.

According to [13], we have that (recall $\mathcal{E}$ is the envelope vector from Lemma 1)

$$b_j |s_1(j)| \mathcal{E}(j+1) \approx V,$$

where V is independent of j. This means that a big $\mathcal{E}(j+1)$ corresponds to a small $|s_1(j)|$.

Therefore, our computation strategy of clustered eigenvalues is shown as follows:

1. Every submatrix has one low valley of the $|\gamma_k|$ curve.
2. The ends of the submatrix are the closest entries to the adjacent valleys.
3. According to Lemma 2, $(\lambda_p - \lambda_1) < p\sqrt{p}\|A\|\epsilon$ ensures $\|T\tilde{v}_s\| < \sqrt{n}\epsilon$, thus it can be used as the "clustering" threshold.

We show the method for computing severely clustered eigenvalues by the following pseudocode Algorithm 2.

Algorithm 2: Compute severely clustered eigenvalues.

Input : a, b, n, d

`// ` d ` is a ` $p \times 1$ ` vector where ` p ` severely clustered eigenvalues are its components`

Output: z

`// ` z ` is the approximation to ` $v_{(:,1:p)}$ ` where the subscripts denote the ` $1 \sim p$ ` columns of ` v

$u \leftarrow mean(d)$;

calculate $|\gamma_i| (i \in [1, n])$ by (7) and (8);

find the p low valleys of $|\gamma_i|$ and save the corresponding entries in K;

`// ` K ` is a ` $p \times 1$ ` vector`

$K \leftarrow [K; n+1], l \leftarrow 1$;

for *each* $i \in [1, p]$ **do**

    $r \leftarrow K(i+1) - 1$;

    call Algorithm 1 $\Leftarrow a(l:r), b(l:r), r-l+1, u$;

    then get $z_{(:,i)}$;

    $z_{(:,i)} \leftarrow z_{(:,i)} / \left\| z_{(:,i)} \right\|$ `// if normalization is needed`

    $l \leftarrow K(i) + 1$;

end

Assume that the p valleys are arranged uniformly. The cost calculation of p severely clustered λ's by Algorithm 2 is twice as large as the cost of one isolated λ by Algorithm 1, while the Inverse Iteration method needs p times cost and a reorthogonalization. This means that Algorithm 2 saves time compared to the Inverse Iteration method even when disregarding its expensive orthogonal cost.

For the matrix Φ, we calculated R's (recall $R = \|Tz\| / \|z\|$, the residual norm) and the dot products of its last eight eigenvector approximations obtained by Algorithm 2. We show the mean and maximal results in Table 1 and compare them to the results of the Inverse Iteration method and the MRRR method. The results were collected on an Intel Core i5-4590 3.3-GHz CPU and a 16-GB RAM machine. All codes were written in Matlab2017a and executed in IEEE double precision. The machine precision is $\epsilon \approx 2.2 \times 10^{-16}$. It can be seen that all the eight eigenvector approximations are accurate and numerically orthogonal. See more examples and numerical results in Section 6.

Table 1. Accuracy and orthogonality.

Method	Mean $R(\times\varepsilon\|\Phi\|)$	Max $R(\times\varepsilon\|\Phi\|)$	Mean Dot Product $(\times\epsilon^{-1})$	Max Dot Product $(\times\epsilon^{-1})$	Time Cost $(\times 10^{-2}$ s)
Algorithm 2	1.5	1.5	0	0	0.1
Inverse Iteration	1.2	1.2	0	0.05	2.9
MRRR	1.2	1.2	0	0	4.2

4. Reorthogonalization

4.1. General Q Iteration

For severely clustered eigenvalues, Algorithm 2 saves considerable time and avoids reorthogonalization. However, if the group of clustering p eigenvalues has a close eigenvalue neighbor or another group of clustering eigenvalues with the distance $\in (\, p\sqrt{p}\epsilon, 10^{-3})\|A\|$ (note $p\sqrt{p}\|A\|\epsilon$ is the threshold of severely clustering), Algorithm 2 can not ensure the orthogonality between them. Therefore, a reorthogonalization is needed. This is quite frustrating, not only because of the high cost of orthogonalization but also because using the modified Gram–Schmidt method for orthogonalization destroys the orthogonality of the eigenvectors obtained by Algorithm 2. In other words, the method we proposed in the previous section is meaningless. For example, two groups of severely eigenvalues have approximations u_1 and u_2, respectively, while $u_1 - u_2 < 10^{-3}\|A\|$. Each group's eigenvectors are orthogonal, but Algorithm 2 can not ensure the orthogonality of two from different groups. If one uses the modified Gram–Schmidt method to reorthogonalize them, it makes no difference whether the original vectors are orthogonal in groups. Therefore, we give a new reorthogonalization method in this section.

In [9], Dhillon introduced the twisted Q factorization. For an $n \times n$ ST matrix $T = A - \lambda_1(\lambda_1$ is one eigenvalue of $A)$ and a certain number $k (k \in [1, n])$, implement the Givens rotation to its columns to eliminated $1 \sim (k-1)$th components on its super-diagonal and $k \sim (n-1)$th components on the sub-diagonal. Finally, a singleton in the kth column is left. The process is shown in Figure 4 (from [9]), where $n = 5$ and $k = 3$.

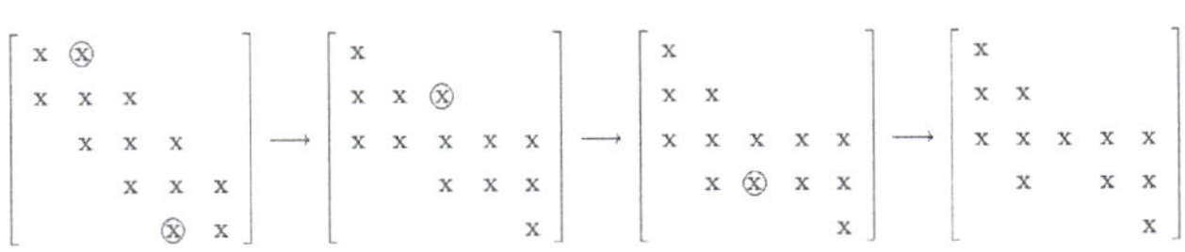

Figure 4. The twisted Q factorization.

Let W denote the final form of the twisted Q factorization, and we have

$$\begin{aligned} TQ &= W; \\ T &= WQ^T; \\ Q &= G_1 G_2 \ldots G_{n-1}, \end{aligned}$$

where $G_1 \sim G_{n-1}$ are Givens rotation matrices. Obviously, $W_{k,k} = R_k$. Therefore, at least one k satisfies $\zeta = W_{k,k} \leq \sqrt{n}\epsilon$ according to Section 2.3.

Now, we introduce our so-called general Q iteration. For such a k that satisfies $\zeta \leq \sqrt{n}\epsilon$, we implement the corresponding Givens rotations to the rows of W. Using the example from Figure 4, the process is shown by

$$\begin{aligned}
G_1^T TQ = \begin{bmatrix} \times & \times & & & \\ \times & \times & & & \\ \times & \times & \zeta & \times & \times \\ & \times & & \times & \times \\ & & & & \times \end{bmatrix} &\Rightarrow G_2^T \ldots TQ = \begin{bmatrix} \times & \times & & & \\ \times & \times & s_2\zeta & \times & \times \\ & \times & c_2\zeta & \times & \times \\ & \times & & \times & \times \\ & & & & \times \end{bmatrix} \\
\Rightarrow G_3^T \ldots TQ &= \begin{bmatrix} \times & \times & & & \\ \times & \times & s_2\zeta & \times & \times \\ & s_2\zeta & c_3c_2\zeta & \times & \times \\ & \times & -s_3c_2\zeta & \times & \times \\ & \times & & & \times \end{bmatrix} \\
\Rightarrow G_4^T \ldots TQ &= \begin{bmatrix} \times & \times & & & \\ \times & \times & s_2\zeta & \times & \times \\ & s_2\zeta & c_3c_2\zeta & -c_4s_3c_2\zeta & s_4s_3c_2\zeta \\ & \times & -c_4s_3c_2\zeta & \times & \times \\ & \times & s_4s_3c_2\zeta & \times & \times \end{bmatrix} = Q^T TQ
\end{aligned} \tag{11}$$

where c_i and s_i constitutes G_i, i.e.,

$$G_i := \begin{bmatrix} c_i & -s_i \\ s_i & c_i \end{bmatrix}.$$

Note that, in the last rotation of (11), the components on $(3,4)$ and $(3,5)$ have not changed. We obtain their values according to symmetry.

Finally, we have

$$A_1 = Q^T TQ + \lambda_1$$

and complete one step of the general Q iteration. Obviously, A_1 has the same eigenpairs to A. As all $|c_i|$'s and $|c_i|$'s are less than 1, all the rest components of the kth rows and columns of A_1 are less than ζ. Therefore, deflation can arise as

$$A_1 = \begin{bmatrix} \times & \times & & & \\ \times & \times & & \times & \times \\ & & \lambda_1 & & \\ & \times & & \times & \times \\ & \times & & \times & \times \end{bmatrix} \Rightarrow \begin{bmatrix} \times & \times & & \\ \times & \times & \times & \times \\ & \times & \times & \times \\ & \times & \times & \times \end{bmatrix} = B.$$

Thus, B has the numerical equal eigenvalues to $\lambda_2 \sim \lambda_5$ and the corresponding eigenvectors can be calculated similarly to the QR method. For example, if $s_2 = [x_1, x_2, x_3, x_4]^T$ is the eigenvector of B with respect to λ_2, then $v_2 = Qs_2$. These v_i's are certainly orthogonal. Note that B can be transferred to an ST matrix by chasing and eliminating its bulge (for example, the $(2,4)$ and $(4,2)$ components of B) with Givens rotations. Therefore, it costs at most 1.5 times operations compared to the QR (or QL) iteration, which is the exceptional case when $k = n$ or 1.

Therefore, the general Q iteration is to fulfill a deflation of a certain λ by QR-like transformation. For a normal ST matrix and one accurate approximation to λ, $k = 1$ or n is enough. Thus, the cost of chasing the bulge can be saved. However, in some special cases, $|\gamma_1|$ or $|\gamma_n|$ can both be small, which means it costs numerous QR-like iterations to converge. This is similar to the solution of (2) by inverse iterations, considering the strong relationship between the Inverse Iteration method and the QR (or QL) method [7]. Recall that we give the one-step inverse iteration in Section 2, and the general Q iteration can be regarded as a one-step QR-like iteration. In our numerical experience, the case that several QR iterations (which use an accurate eigenvalue approximation as the shift) can not obtain convergence is not rare. For example, for a random 2000×2000 ST matrix, its most λ_i's can ensure one-step converges by QR iteration, but some λ_i's may cost more than 50 steps. In addition, this case almost arises in every random matrix.

Mastronardi and Van Dooreen discovered this instability when obtaining an ST eigenvector and solved the problem by a modified implicit QR decomposition method [12]. Their method can ensure an accurate calculation. However, this paper uses a modified inverse iteration method to calculate the eigenvector. The implicit QR decomposition in our paper is used for deflation and guarantee of orthogonality in the case that the eigenvalues cluster generally.

The corresponding pseudocode for computing generally clustered eigenvectors is given in Algorithm 3. The generally clustering denotes that the span of the p clustered eigenvalues is not big enough to guarantee orthogonality of its corresponding eigenvectors (calculated by the Inverse Iteration method or Algorithms 1 and 2), i.e., $\lambda_p - \lambda_1 \leq 10^{-3}\|A\|$.

Algorithm 3: Computing generally clustered eigenvectors.

```
   Input  :a, b, n, d
 1 // d is a p×1 vector where p generally clustered eigenvalues are
      its components
   Output:z
 2 for each i ∈ [1, p] do
 3     if i = p then
 4         v ← e_1 // e_1 is the first column of the n×n identity matrix
 5     else
 6         call Algorithm 1 ⇐ a, b, n, d(i);
 7         then get v;
 8         implement the deflation by the general Q iteration with the shift of d(i);
 9         then get ā, b̄ // the length of ā is n−i and b̄ is n−1−i
10         save all the Givens rotation matrices in G^(i);
11         a ← ā, b ← b̄, n ← n − 1;
12     end
13     if i > 1 then
14         for each j ∈ [1, i−1] do
15             implement every Givens rotation in G^(j) to v
16         end
17     end
18     z_{:,i} = v;
19 end
```

4.2. Cost of Reorthogonalization

This subsection concerns the cost of reorthogonalization in Algorithm 3. For k clustered eigenvalues, the last obtained v (line 7 in Algorithm 3) is a $(n+1-k) \times 1$ vector. v has to be premultiplied $n-k$ Givens rotation matrices to transfer to $(n+2-k) \times 1$. Repeat this process until the length reaches n. For every Givens rotation, the cost is six operations. Therefore, the total cost is

$$\begin{aligned} &6 \times ((n-k) \times 1 + (n+1-k) \times 2 + (n+2-k) \times 3 + \ldots + (n-2) \times (k-1)) \\ &= 6 \times n \times (1+2+\ldots+k-1) - 6 \times (k \times 1 + (k-1) \times 2 + \ldots + 2 \times (k-1)) \\ &= 3nk^2 - \left(k^3 + 3k^2 - 4k + 3n\right). \end{aligned} \tag{12}$$

At first sight, (12) is hardly satisfactory, as the modified Gram–Schmidt method costs only $4n \times (1+2+3+\ldots+k) = 2nk^2$ operations. Only when k is close to n, our method matches the efficiency of the modified Gram–Schmidt method. Moreover, those cases where we need to use the general Q iteration (the QR-like iterations cannot converge at one step) have not been considered. However, the cost will slump for cases with many severely clustered eigenvalues within groups.

For example, if m eigenvalues are severely clustered among the k eigenvalues, the cost is

$$3n(k-m)^2 - \left((k-m)^3 + 3(k-m)^2 - 4(k-m) + 3n\right) + 6(n-m)m, \tag{13}$$

which decreases from $O(nk^2)$ to $O(nk)$ if m is close to k. In addition, the cost for the modified Gram–Schmidt method, in this case, is $4n(m+m+1+\ldots+k) = 2n(m+k)(k-m)$.

If the k eigenvalues can be divided into two severely clustering groups, the cost is

$$6(n-m)m, \tag{14}$$

which decreases from $O(nk^2)$ to $O(nm)$. In addition, the cost for the modified Gram–Schmidt method, in this case, is $2n(m+k)(k-m)$.

Therefore, Algorithm 3 calls the deflation method with the general Q iteration or the modified Gram–Schmidt method according to an advanced prediction by (12)–(14). However, both methods are time-consuming in cases where k is very close to n, and the eigenvalues have few severely clustering groups. In this case, the best method is the MRRR method. See more examples and numerical details in Section 6.

4.3. Modification of QR-Like Iteration

The general Q iteration can be seen as starting a QL iteration from the left of the matrix, stopping it at column k, and then doing a QR iteration from the right of the matrix till there is a singleton in the kth column. We give a subtle modification to the QR or QL iteration with the implicit shift to save some operations. Take the QR iteration as an example, and the traditional process is shown in Algorithm 4.

One step of QR iteration implemented into a 4×4 ST matrix is shown as follows:

$$\begin{aligned} &\begin{bmatrix} c_1 & s_1 \\ -s_1 & c_1 \end{bmatrix} \begin{bmatrix} a_1 & b_1 & & \\ b_1 & a_2 & b_2 & \\ & b_2 & a_3 & b_3 \\ & & b_3 & a_4 \end{bmatrix} \begin{bmatrix} c_1 & -s_1 \\ s_1 & c_1 \end{bmatrix} \\ \Rightarrow &\begin{bmatrix} \times & \times & s_1 b_2 & \\ -s_1\delta & \pi_2 + c_1\delta & c_1 b_2 & \\ & b_2 & a_3 & b_3 \\ & & b_3 & a_4 \end{bmatrix} \begin{bmatrix} c_1 & -s_1 \\ s_1 & c_1 \end{bmatrix} \\ \Rightarrow &\begin{bmatrix} \bar{a}_1 & s_1\pi_2 & s_1 b_2 & \\ s_1\pi_2 & c_1\pi_2 + \delta & c_1 b_2 & \\ s_1 b_2 & c_1 b_2 & a_3 & b_3 \\ & & b_3 & a_4 \end{bmatrix} \end{aligned} \tag{15}$$

Algorithm 4: QR iteration with the implicit shift.

Input :a, b, n, δ

1 // δ is the shift

Output:$\bar{a}, \bar{b}$

2 // $\bar{a}$ is the diagonal after transformation and $\bar{b}$ is the diagonal

3 $\omega \leftarrow a_1 - \delta, N \leftarrow \sqrt{\omega^2 + b_1^2}, c \leftarrow \omega/N, s \leftarrow b_1/N;$

4 $\pi \leftarrow c(a_2 - \delta) - sb_1, \bar{\pi} \leftarrow c\pi;$

5 $a_1 \leftarrow \omega + a_2 - \bar{\pi};$

6 $\omega \leftarrow \bar{\pi};$

7 **for** *each* $i \in [2, n-1]$ **do**

8 $\quad N \leftarrow \sqrt{\pi + b_i^2}, b_{i-1} \leftarrow Ns, s \leftarrow b_i/N;$

9 $\quad b_i \leftarrow cb_i, c \leftarrow \pi/N;$

10 $\quad \pi \leftarrow c(a_{i+1} - \delta) - sb_i, \bar{\pi} \leftarrow c\pi;$

11 $\quad a_i \leftarrow \omega + a_{i+1} - \bar{\pi};$

12 $\quad \omega \leftarrow \bar{\pi};$

13 **end**

14 $b_{n-1} \leftarrow s\pi, a_n \leftarrow c\pi + \delta;$

15 $\bar{a} \leftarrow a, \bar{b} \leftarrow b;$

In (15), π_{i+1} is updated by $\pi_{i+1} = c_i(a_{i+1} - \delta) - s_i b_i$, which corresponds to line 10 in Algorithm 4. This equation can be rewritten as

$$\begin{aligned}\pi_{i+1}/c_i &= (a_{i+1} - \delta) - s_i b_i / c_i \\ &= (a_{i+1} - \delta) - b_i c_{i-1} b_i / \pi_i \\ &= (a_{i+1} - \delta) - b_i^2 / (\pi_i / c_{i-1})\end{aligned}$$

Without loss of generality, assume that $c_0 = 1$, then $\pi_1/c_0 = a_1 - \delta = q_1$ (recall q_i is the Sturm sequence from (8)). Finally, we have

$$\pi_{i+1}/c_i = q_{i+1}(i \in [0, n-1]). \tag{16}$$

Note all the q_i's have been calculated in advance when searching the smallest $|\gamma_k|$ in our methods; thus, we can use (16) to update π's instead. We show the modified QR iteration algorithm in Algorithm 5.

Algorithm 5 costs $6n$ multiplications, $2n$ divisions, and $(n-1)$ square roots while Algorithm 4 costs $9n$ multiplications, $2n$ divisions, and $(n-1)$ square roots. Thus, our modification saves $3n$ multiplications.

Algorithm 5: Modified QR iteration with the implicit shift.

Input : a, b, n, δ, q

// q is the Sturm sequence from (8)

Output: $\bar{a}, \bar{b}$

// $\bar{a}$ is the diagonal after transformation and $\bar{b}$ is the diagonal

$\omega \leftarrow q_1, N \leftarrow \sqrt{\omega^2 + b_1^2}, c \leftarrow \omega/N, s \leftarrow b_1/N;$

$\pi \leftarrow cq_2, \bar{\pi} \leftarrow c\pi;$

$a_1 \leftarrow \omega + a_2 - \bar{\pi};$

$\omega \leftarrow \bar{\pi};$

for *each* $i \in [2, n-1]$ **do**

  $N \leftarrow \sqrt{\pi + b_i^2}, b_{i-1} \leftarrow Ns, s \leftarrow b_i/N;$

  $b_i \leftarrow cb_i, c \leftarrow \pi/N;$

  $\pi \leftarrow cq_{i+1}, \bar{\pi} \leftarrow c\pi;$

  $a_i \leftarrow \omega + a_{i+1} - \bar{\pi};$

  $\omega \leftarrow \bar{\pi};$

end

$b_{n-1} \leftarrow s\pi, a_n \leftarrow c\pi + \delta;$

$\bar{a} \leftarrow a, \bar{b} \leftarrow b;$

5. Avoiding Overflow and Underflow

Our new method obtains an eigenvector essentially by the cumulative products of q's, as shown in lines 9 and 12 of Algorithm 1. As is well known, the products can grow or decay rapidly; hence, the recurrences to compute them are susceptible to severe overflow and underflow problems. This section gives a relatively cheap algorithm to avoid overflow and underflow.

Let f denotes the overflow threshold, for example, $f = 2^{1023}$ in IEEE double precision arithmetic. Whenever one intermediate product during the recurrences exceeds f, multiply it by f^{-1} to normalize and continue the iteration. Similarly, whenever one $\leq f^{-1}$, multiply it by f. At the same time, we save the corresponding entry and mark 1 for overflow and -1 for underflow.

Assume y positions, which divide the eigenvector approximation $\tilde{v}$ into $y+1$ parts, are marked when the iteration is completed. Then, we have a $y \times 1$ vector Y, with components of 1's and -1's. For any certain position, the mark 1 means the components of $\tilde{v}$ from it to the end are shrunk by a factor of f compared to v. In addition, the mark -1 means amplification by f. The mark before the first component of $\tilde{v}$ is zero. Thus, we have $Y \leftarrow [0; Y]$.

Calculate the cumulative sums of Y from the first component to everyone and save the results at each entry. In this way, each component of Y corresponds to each part of $\tilde{v}$, and its value represents the specific degree to which the corresponding part has been enlarged or reduced. A positive value of m means that this part has been reduced by f^m times, while a negative value means enlarged. The corresponding part is not enlarged or reduced when the value is zero.

Revisiting $\tilde{v}$, all the components have not overflowed but are just to be restored to their true values. In addition, the biggest part after restoration corresponds to the biggest component of Y (recall each component of Y corresponds to each part of $\tilde{v}$) because it is reduced by the most significant times. Since $\tilde{v}$ is ultimately normalized, we take the biggest part as the benchmark. Thus, the second biggest component of Y corresponds to the second biggest part of $\tilde{v}$ after restoration, which should be divided by f. The rest parts, if they exist, need to be divided by f^2 or more, thus directly taking zeros as its components.

We give the corresponding pseudocode in Algorithm 6, which corresponds to the details of lines 9 and 12 of Algorithm 1.

Algorithm 6: Compute $\prod q$ without overflow and underflow.

```
Input  : n, q
// q is a n × 1 vector
Output: x
// x_i = ∏_{t=1}^{i} q_t
x ← zeros(n, 1), y ← zeros(n, 1);
// zeros(n, 1) is a vector constituted by n zeros
f_1 ← 2^2013, f_2 ← 2^-2013;
// We set two f's to avoid divisions when scaling
x_1 ← 1, y ← 0;
for each i ∈ [2, n] do
    T ← q_{i-1}xi − 1, T_2 ← |T|;
    if T_2 > f_1 then
        s ← s + 1, x_i ← T f_2;
        y_s = i;
    else if T_2 < f_1 then
        s ← s + 1, x_i ← T f_1;
        y_s = −i;
    else
        x_i ← T;
    end
end
if s = 1 then
    i ← y_s;
    if y_s > 0 then
        x_{1:(i-1)} ← f_2 × x_{1:(i-1)};
    else
        x_{i:n} ← f_2 × x_{i:n};
    end
else if s > 1 then
    χ ← [1; |y_{1:s}|; (n + 1)];
    y ← the cumulative sum of sign(y_{1:s});
    y ← ([0; y] − max_{i=1}^{s} y_i);
    for each part of x corresponded by y_i < −1(i ∈ [1, (s + 1)]) do
        x_{(y<−1)} ← zeros(length(x_{(y<−1)}), 1) ;
    end
    for each part corresponded by y_i = −1(i ∈ [1, (s + 1)]) do
        x_{(y=−1)} ← f_2 × x_{(y=−1)} ;
    end
end
x ← x/||x||// if normalization is needed
```

Finally, we give the complete modified Inverse Iteration method by Algorithm 7.

Algorithm 7: Modified Inverse Iteration method.

Input : a, b, n, d
// d is a vector contains the eigenvalues
Output: v
// v is the eigenvectors with respect to d
$F \leftarrow \max_{i=1}^{n}(|a_i| + 2|b_i|)$ // $F = \|A\|_\infty$, the substitution of $\|A\|$
$r \leftarrow length(d)$;
compare every $d_{i+1} - d_i (i \in [1, n-1])$ to $10^{-3}F$, **then**
distribute d into isolated and clustered parts;
for every clustered parts of d, mark the severely clustered groups by $(\lambda_{p+j} - \lambda_{j+1}) < p\sqrt{p}F\epsilon$;
if $r \geq 0.9n$ && *the number of generally clustered eigenvalues is close to* r **then**
    call the MRRR method to compute all the eigenpairs;
    save the corresponding eigenvectors (with respect to d) in v;
    return;
end
for *every isolated part of* d **do**
    call Algorithm 1 to calculate the corresponding eigenvectors;
    call Algorithm 6 to avoid overflow and underflow;
    save the results in v;
end
for *every clustered part of* d **do**
    call Algorithm 2 and 3 to calculate the corresponding eigenvectors;
    call Algorithm 6 to avoid overflow and underflow;
    save the results in v;
end

6. Numerical Results

In this section, we present a numerical comparison among the modified Inverse Iteration method and four other widely used algorithms for computing eigenvectors:

1. the Inverse Iteration method, by calling subroutine "dstein" from LAPACK in Matlab;
2. the MRRR method, by calling subroutine "dstegr" from LAPACK in Matlab;
3. the QR method, by calling subroutine "dsteqr" from LAPACK in Matlab;
4. the DC method, by calling subroutine "dstedc" from LAPACK in Matlab.

Since the MRRR, QR, and DC methods compute the eigenpairs instead of only eigenvectors, we compared the total cost for eigenpairs in this section. To obtain eigenvalues for Algorithm 7 and the Inverse Iteration method, we use the PWK version of the QR method (by calling subroutine 'dsterf' from LAPACK in Matlab) when calculating more than 5% eigenpairs, otherwise use the Bisection method (by calling subroutine 'dstebz' from LAPACK in Matlab). Note the QR and DC methods are only available when computing all the eigenpairs and thus will not be compared in the cases when computing parts of the eigenpairs.

We use the following five types of $n \times n$ matrices for tests:

1. Matrix Φ_1, which is constructed similarly to Φ in Section 3 with $\alpha_0 = (1{:}200)$. We change the repeat times of $\alpha \leftarrow [\alpha; \alpha_0]$ to adjust the size of Matrix Φ_1. Note this matrix has many groups of clustered eigenvalues (severely and generally clusterings both exist) and has overflow issues if calculated directly.
2. Matrix Φ_2, which is constructed similarly to Φ_1 with $\alpha_0 = (1{:}80)$. This matrix also has many groups of clustered eigenvalues (severely and generally clusterings both exist) but has no overflow issue if calculated directly.

3. Matrix W_1, the famous Wilkinson matrix, which has the ith diagonal component equal to $|(n+1)/2 - i|(n$ is odd) and all off-diagonal components equal to 1. All its eigenvalues severely cluster in pairs.
4. Matrix W_2, another form of the Wilkinson matrix, which has the ith ($i \in [1,(n+1)/2]$) diagonal component equal to $|(n+1)/2 - i|(n$ is odd), the ith ($i \in [(n+1)/2+1, n]$) diagonal component equal to $-|(n+1)/2 - i|$ and all off-diagonal components equal to 1. Its eigenvalues do not cluster if the size is less than 2000.
5. Random Matrix with both diagonal and off-diagonal elements being uniformly distributed random numbers in $[-1, 1]$. Note that all the Random Matrix results in this section are mean data of 20 times tests.

The results were collected on an Intel Core i5-4590 3.3-GHz CPU and 16-GB RAM machine. All codes were written in Matlab2017a and executed in IEEE double precision. The machine precision is $\epsilon \approx 2.2 \times 10^{-16}$.

6.1. Accuracy Test

Figures 5–9 present the results of the residual norms, i.e., $R = T\tilde{v}/\|v\|$, where the Average Errors denote the means of R's of all the calculated eigenvectors and the Maximal Errors denote the maximum. The results of dot products of the calculated eigenvectors are also presented to show orthogonality. Different sizes are used in our test, from 400×400 to 2000×2000. We denote the corresponding 2-norm of the tested matrix, for example, $F = \|\Phi_1\|$ in Figure 5. The results confirm that Algorithm 7 computes accurate and numerical orthogonal eigenvectors.

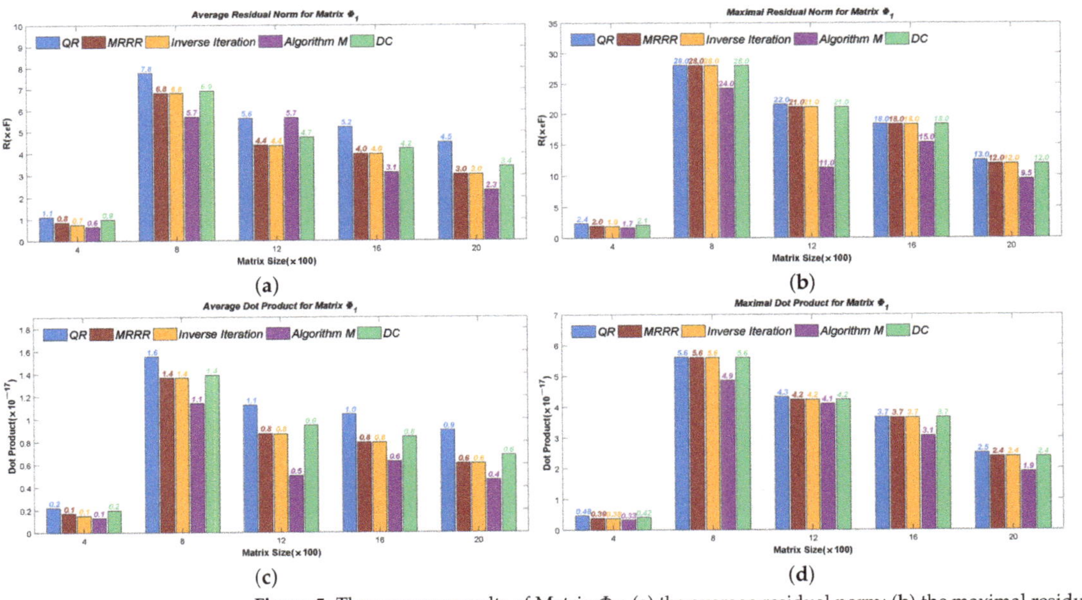

Figure 5. The accuracy results of Matrix Φ_1: (**a**) the average residual norm; (**b**) the maximal residual norm; (**c**) the average dot product; (**d**) the maximal dot product.

6.2. Efficiency Test of Part Eigenpairs

Figures 10–14 show the time cost for computing 10%, 30%, 50%, and 70% eigenpairs of the above five types of matrices in each size. Note the cost of the Inverse Iteration method surges in Figure 12 because the eigenvalues start to cluster and need an expensive reorthogonalization by the modified Gram–Schmidt method as the size of Matrix W_1 rises. The MRRR method costs the most in every matrix because it needs more accurate eigenvalues and calls the Bisection method, while the Inverse Iteration and Algorithm 7 call the PWK version of the QR method to obtain all eigenvalues. Finally, the results show that the modified Inverse Iteration method always costs the least time and has a surpassing efficiency when eigenvalues severely cluster, which confirms our points in Section 3.

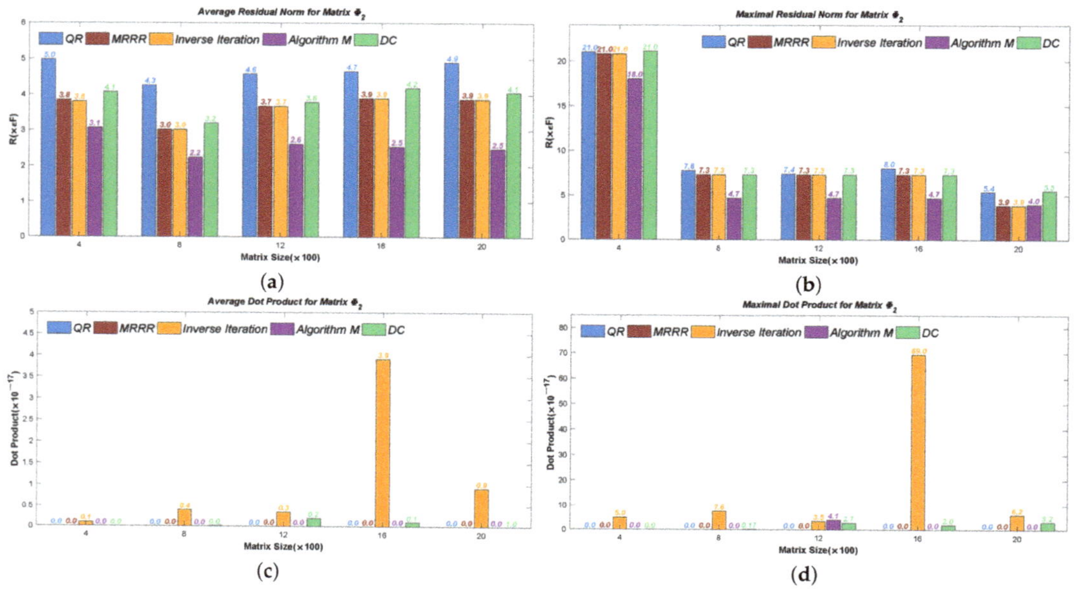

Figure 6. The accuracy results of Matrix Φ_2: (**a**) the average residual norm; (**b**) the maximal residual norm; (**c**) the average dot product; (**d**) the maximal dot product.

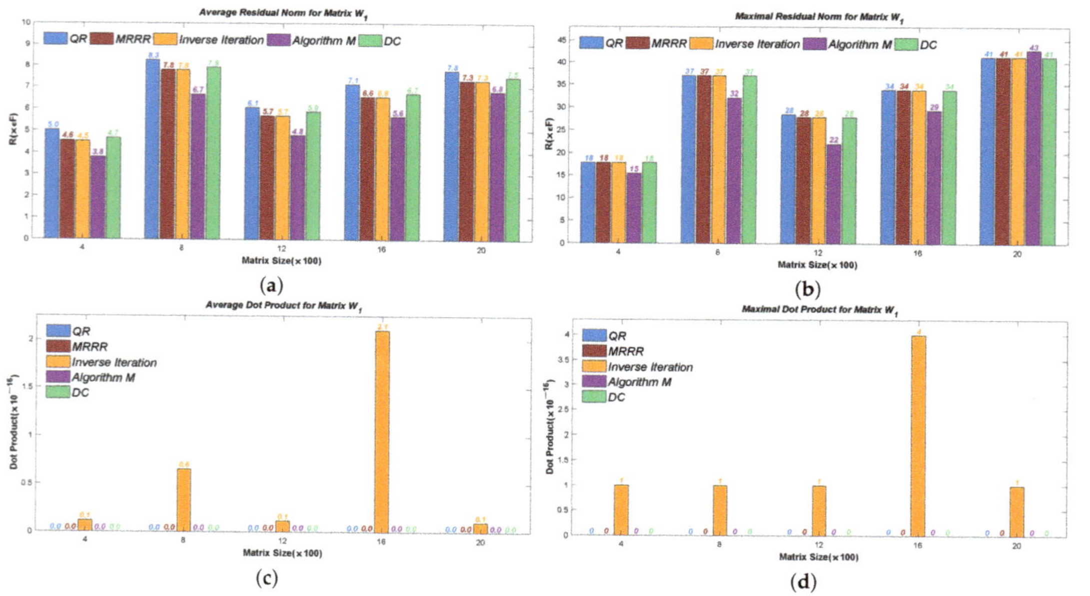

Figure 7. The accuracy results of Matrix W_1: (**a**) the average residual norm; (**b**) the maximal residual norm; (**c**) the average dot product; (**d**) the maximal dot product.

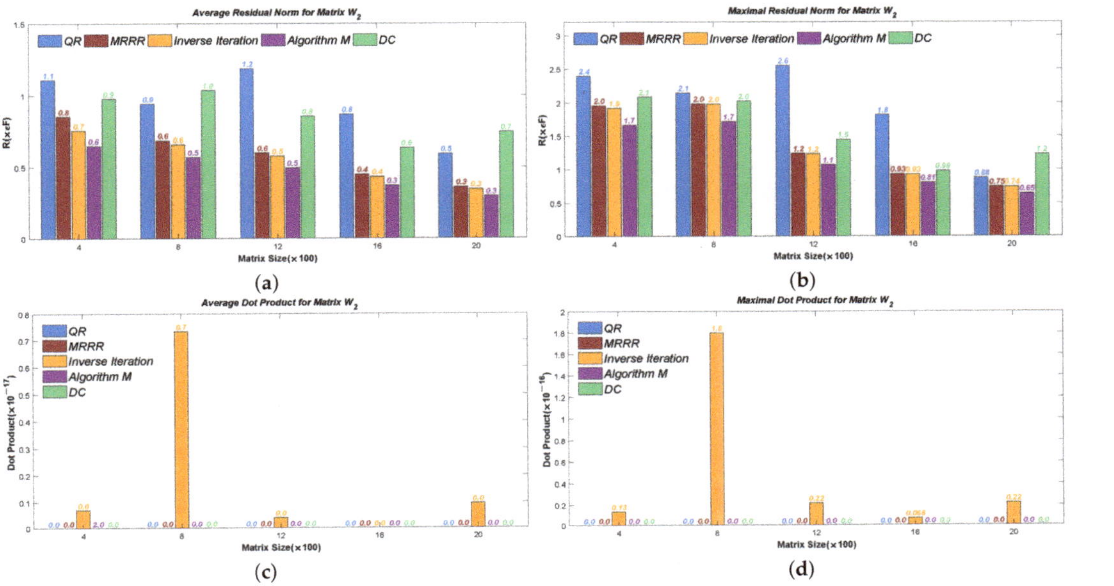

Figure 8. The accuracy results of Matrix W_2: (**a**) the average residual norm; (**b**) the maximal residual norm; (**c**) the average dot product; (**d**) the maximal dot product.

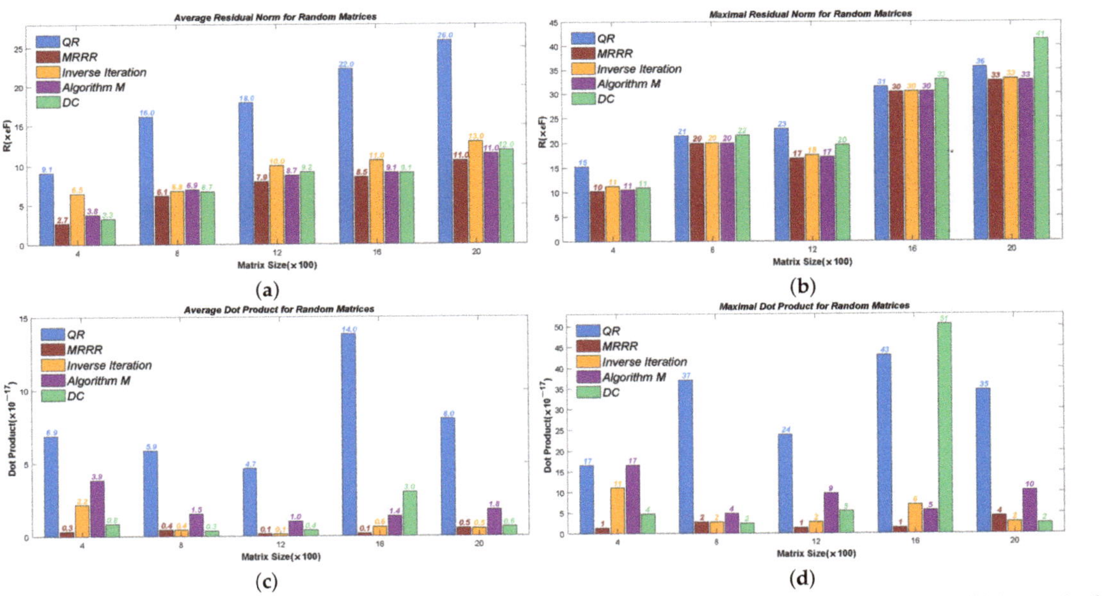

Figure 9. The accuracy results of Random Matrices: (**a**) the average residual norm; (**b**) the maximal residual norm; (**c**) the average dot product; (**d**) the maximal dot product.

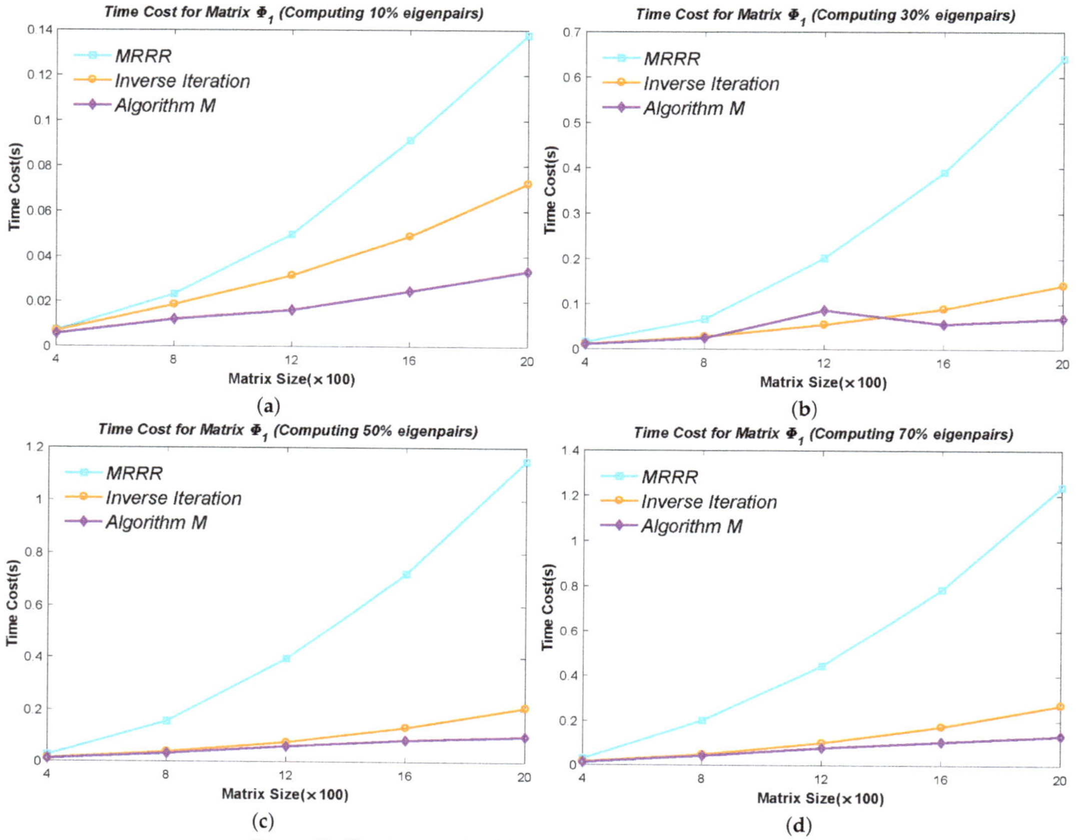

Figure 10. The time cost for Matrix Φ_1 when calculating part eigenpairs: (**a**) 10%; (**b**) 30%; (**c**) 50%; (**d**) 70%.

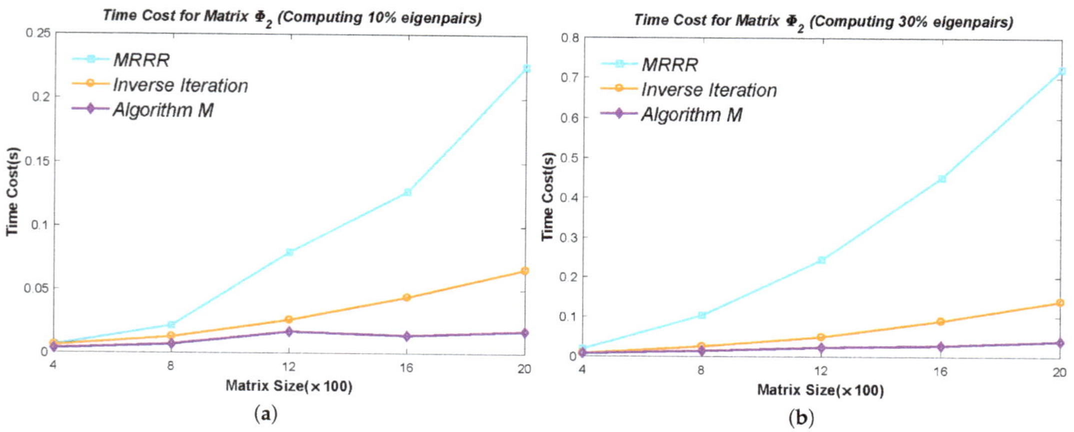

Figure 11. *Cont.*

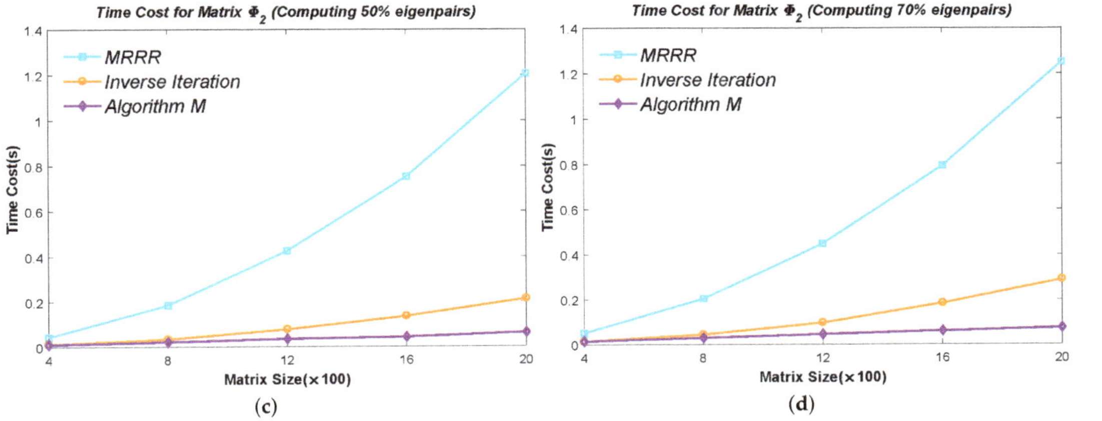

Figure 11. The time cost for Matrix Φ_2 when calculating part eigenpairs: (**a**) 10%; (**b**) 30%; (**c**) 50%; (**d**) 70%.

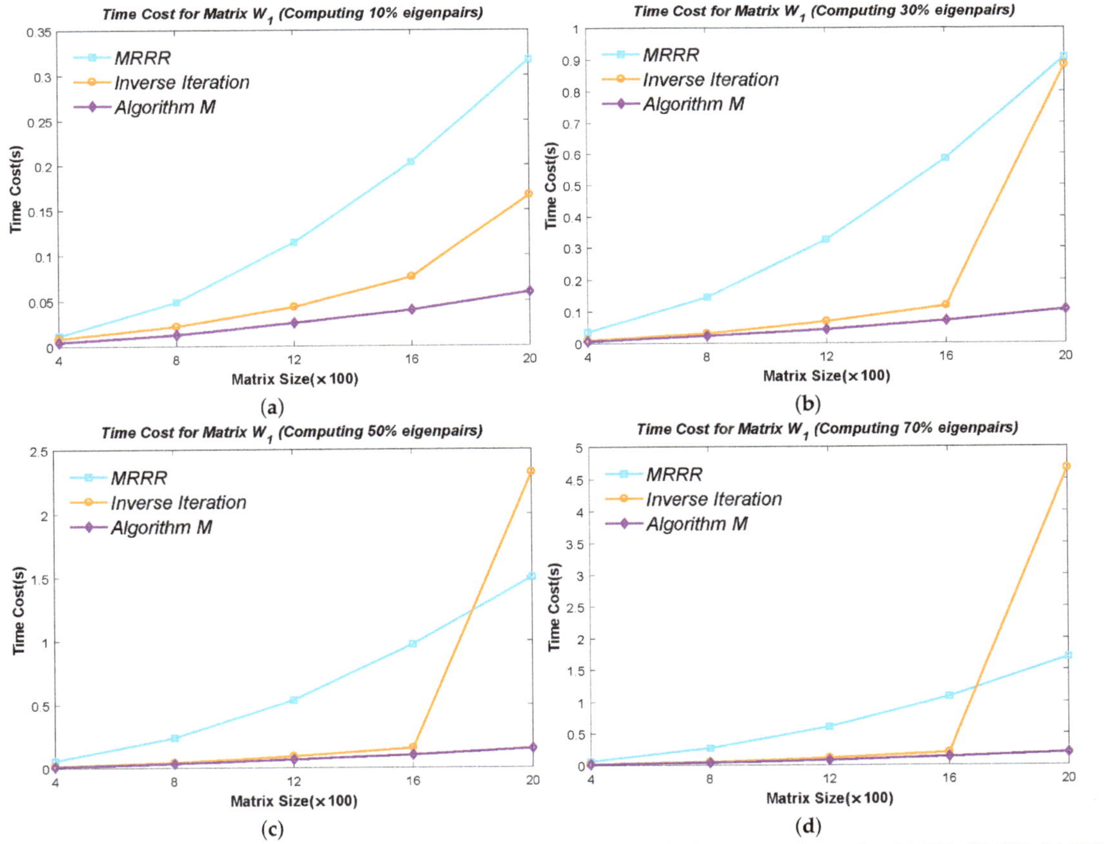

Figure 12. The time cost for Matrix W_1 when calculating part eigenpairs: (**a**) 10%; (**b**) 30%; (**c**) 50%; (**d**) 70%.

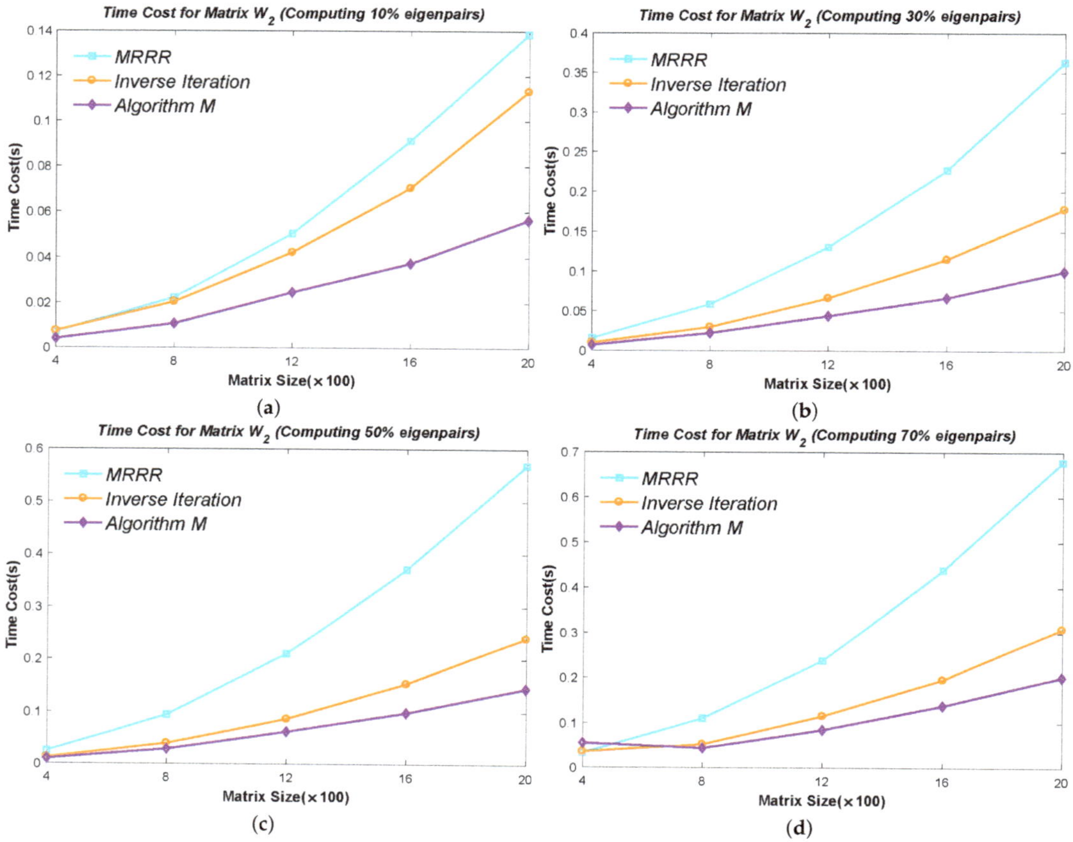

Figure 13. The time cost for Matrix W_2 when calculating part eigenpairs: (**a**) 10%; (**b**) 30%; (**c**) 50%; (**d**) 70%.

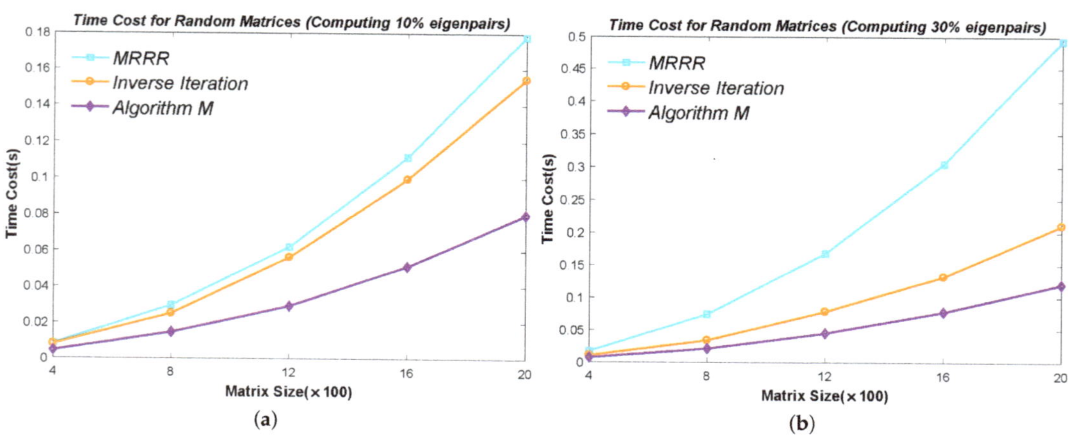

Figure 14. *Cont.*

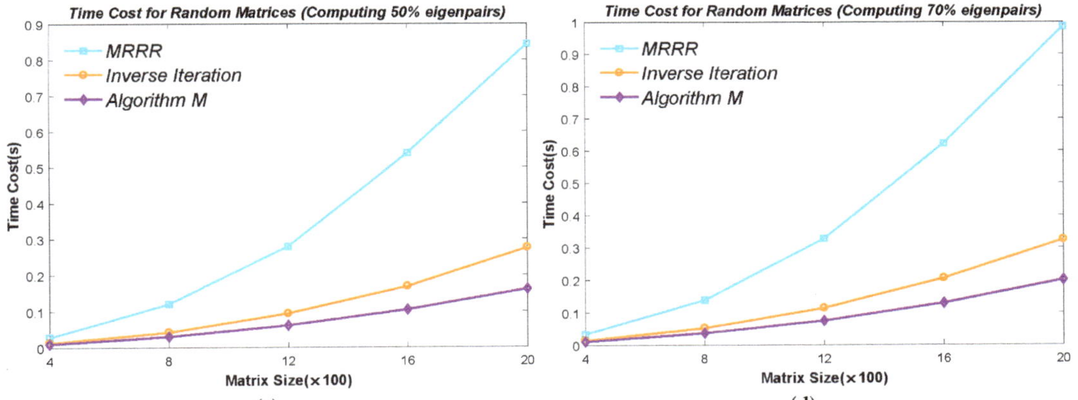

(c) (d)

Figure 14. The time cost for Random Matrix when calculating part eigenpairs: (**a**) 10%; (**b**) 30%; (**c**) 50%; (**d**) 70%.

6.3. Efficiency Test of Minor Eigenpairs

When it comes to a minor set of eigenpairs, it is inadvisable to calculate all the eigenvalues by the PWK version of the QR method for the Inverse Iteration and Algorithm 7. We use the Bisection method instead, similar to the MRRR algorithm. Thus, the result is more convictive in this case because all the methods obtain the eigenvalues at an identical cost.

We calculated 0.2%, 0.4%, 0.6%, 0.8%, and 1% eigenpairs of the above five types of matrices and used two sizes: 2001×2001 and 10001×10001. The results are presented in Figure 15 and 16. It can be seen that the cost of the MRRR method is close to the Inverse Iteration method when computing clustered eigenpairs but higher in other cases. Once again, the modified Inverse Iteration prevails in all cases.

6.4. Efficiency Test of All Eigenpairs

As discussed in previous sections, Algorithm 7 is not suitable for computing all the eigenvectors because the DC method has a significant advantage in this case. Nevertheless, we also performed the corresponding test and show the results in Figure 17. It can be seen in Figure 17b,c that the modified Inverse Iteration method has a close time cost to the DC method. The efficiency increase comes from the computation process for severely clustered eigenvectors, which is recurrent in Matrix Φ_2 and W_1. The acceleration is not that distinct in Figure 17a (where many eigenvectors also cluster severely) because it takes extra operations to avoid overflows and underflows in Matrix ε_1, which will not arise in Matrix ε_2. However, the DC method is still recommended when computing all the eigenpairs.

6.5. Comparing with Mastronardi's Method

Mastronardi [3,12] developed a procedure for computing an eigenvector of a symmetric tridiagonal matrix once its associate eigenvalue is known and gave the corresponding Matlab codes in [12].

We tested the Matlab routine, collected the residual norm errors (denoted by R), dot product errors, and time cost on the test matrices, and compared them with our new method. The results are shown in Table 2. Note that Mastronardi's method is for one ST eigenvector; thus, we calculated the maximal eigenpairs of the test matrices. All the matrices in Table 2 have a size of 2001. The residual norm data have been scaled by the product of the machine precision and the 2-norm of the tested matrix.

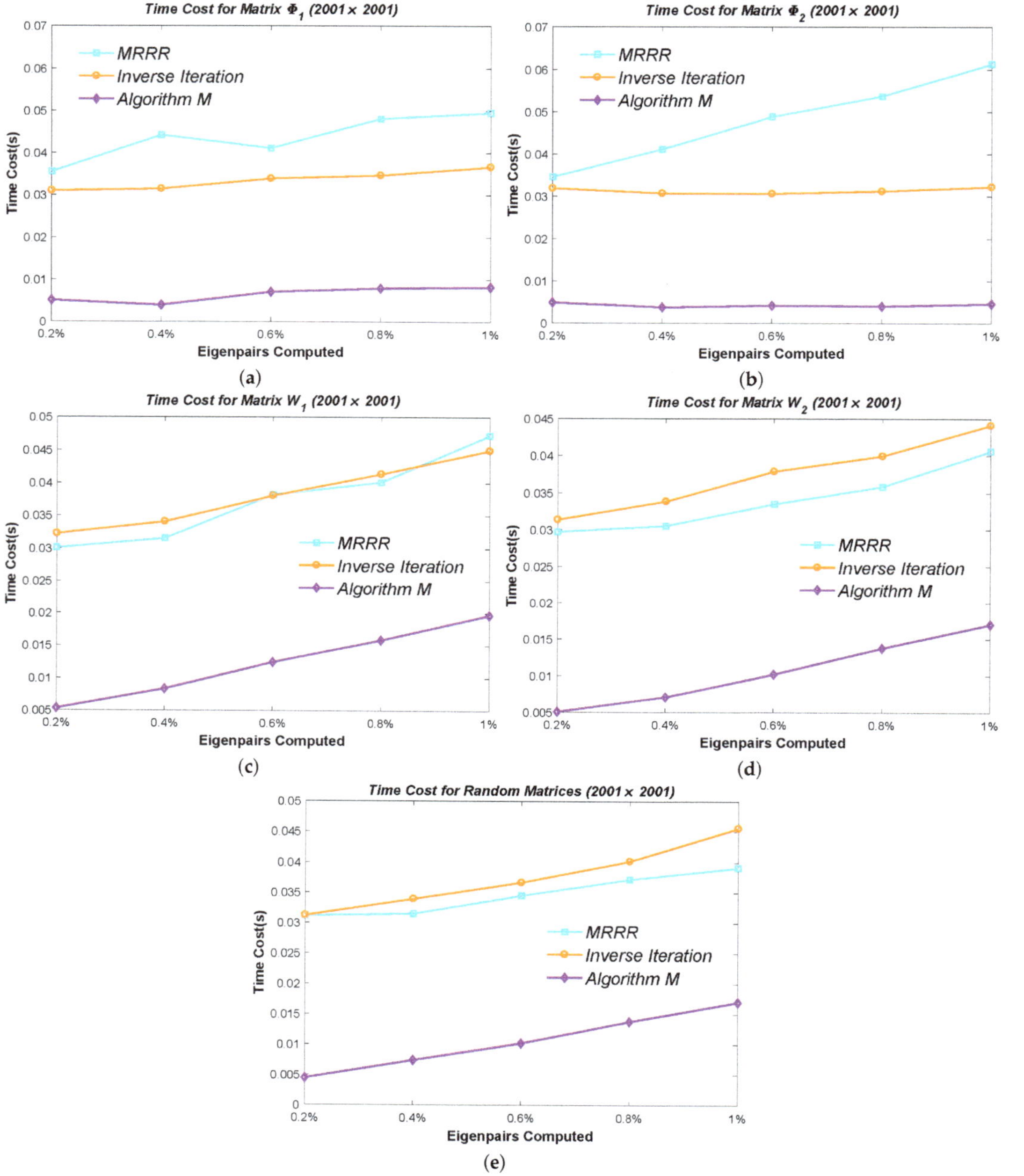

Figure 15. The time cost for minor eigenpairs in 2001 × 2001: (**a**) Matrix Φ_1; (**b**) Matrix Φ_2; (**c**) Matrix W_1; (**d**) Matrix W_2; (**e**) Random Matrix.

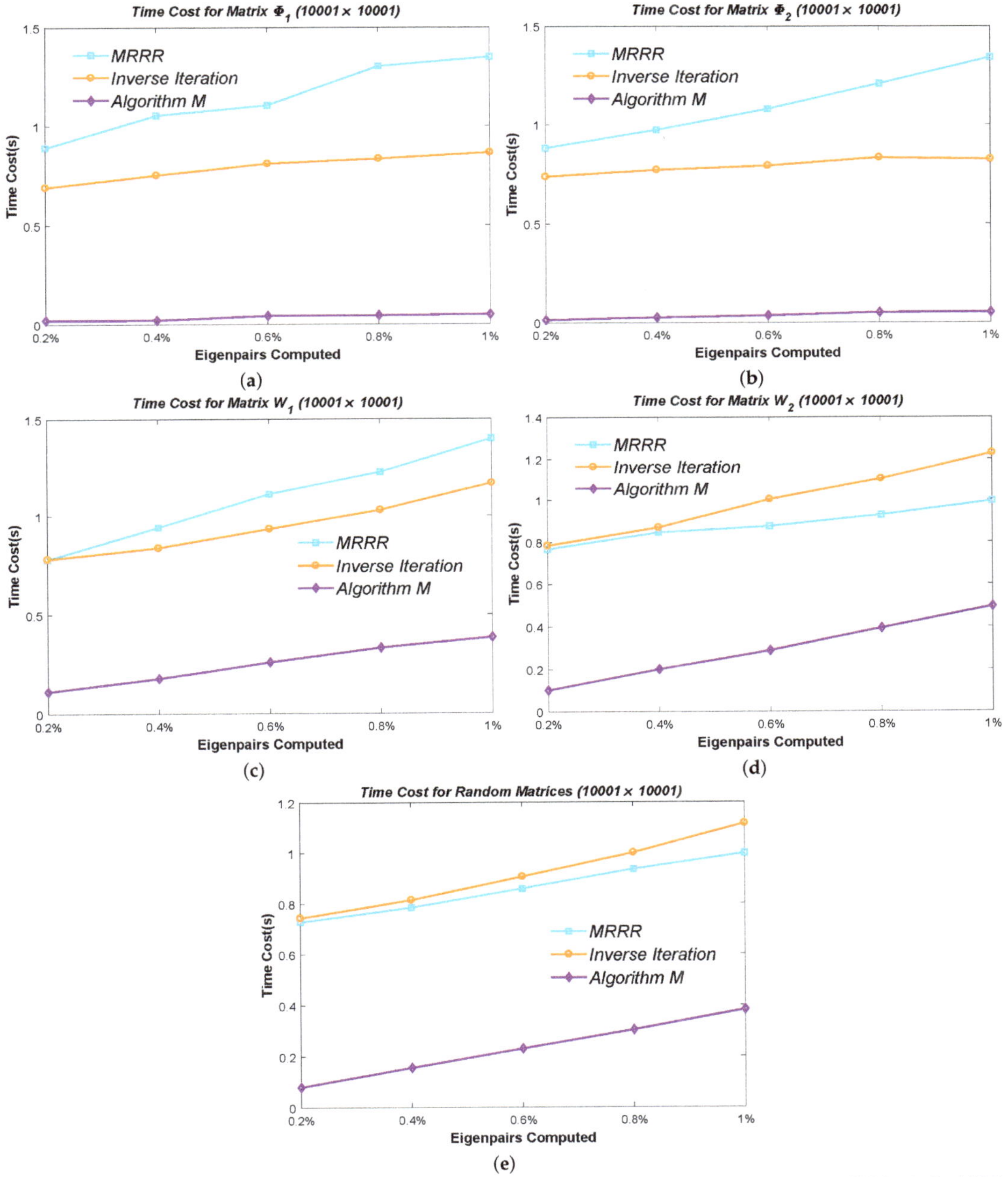

Figure 16. The time cost for minor eigenpairs in 10001 × 10001: (**a**) Matrix Φ_1; (**b**) Matrix Φ_2; (**c**) Matrix W_1; (**d**) Matrix W_2; (**e**) Random Matrix.

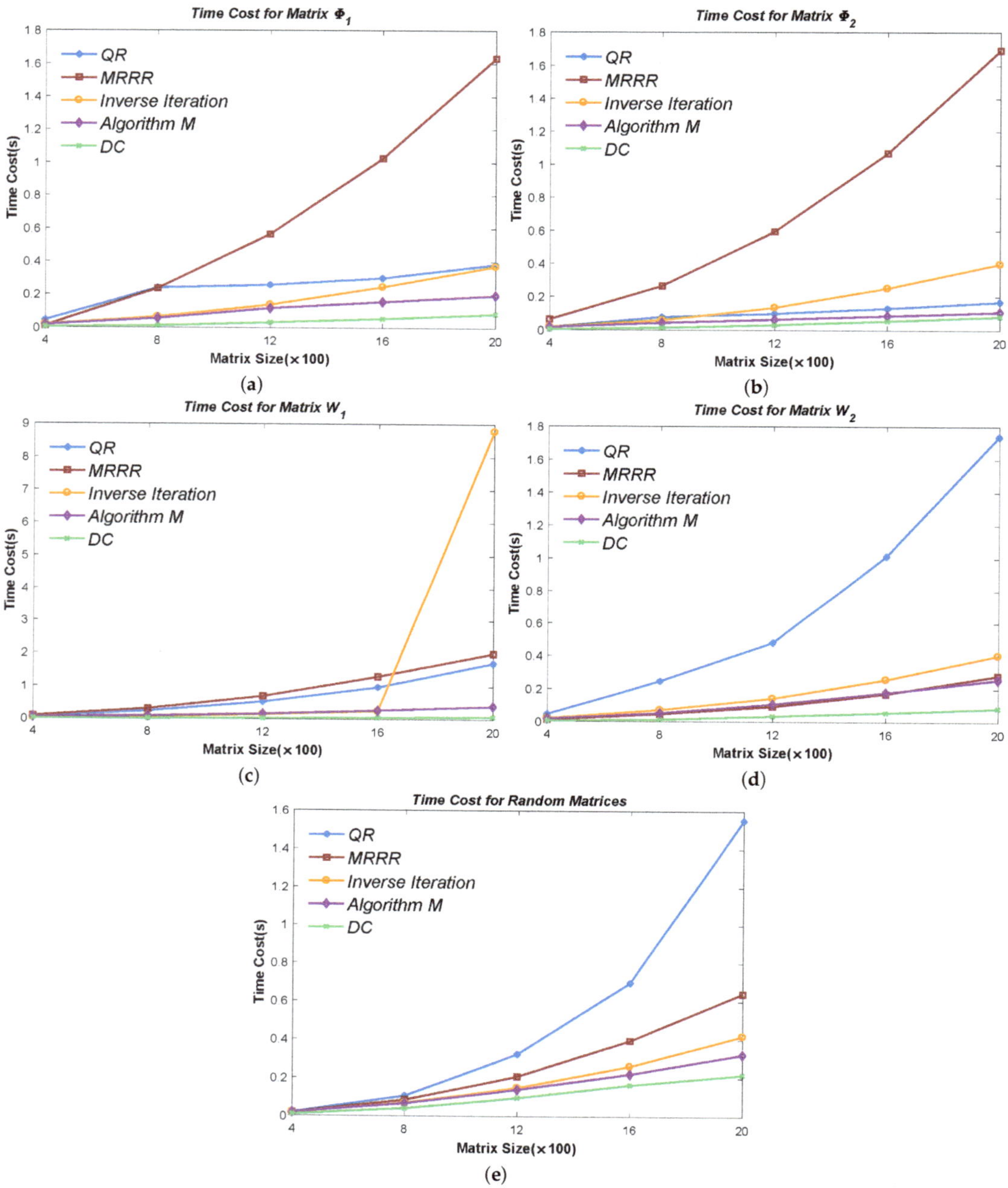

Figure 17. The time cost for all eigenpairs in: (**a**) Matrix Φ_1; (**b**) Matrix Φ_2; (**c**) Matrix W_1; (**d**) Matrix W_2; (**e**) Random Matrix.

Table 2. Comparing with Mastronardi's method when calculating one eigenvector.

Matrix	Method	$R(\times\varepsilon\|A\|)$	Max Dot Product ($\times\epsilon^{-1}$)	Time Cost (s)
Φ_1	Mastronardi's	-	-	-
	Algorithm M	3.42	1.2	5.5×10^{-4}
Φ_2	Mastronardi's	2.86	1.5	0.24
	Algorithm M	3.01	0.7	4.0×10^{-4}
W_1	Mastronardi's	-	-	-
	Algorithm M	0.27	1.4	4.6×10^{-3}
W_2	Mastronardi's	18.7	0	0.29
	Algorithm M	0.27	1.2	4.8×10^{-4}
Random	Mastronardi's	24.6	2.1	0.30
	Algorithm M	12.2	0	5.5×10^{-4}

Table 2 shows that Mastronardi's method can provide a better result in Matrix W_2 when considering orthogonality. However, Algorithm 7 has a significant advantage in time cost. In addition, Mastronardi seems unstable when computing the eigenvector (corresponding to the maximal eigenvalue) of Matrix Φ_1 and W_1: the Matlab routine provided in [12] failed to converge. The instability also arises in computing some eigenvectors of the random matrices. As a consequence, we did not present the corresponding results of Matrix Φ_1 and W_1 in Table 2.

The test for calculating all eigenvectors stuck because of the instability too. However, the time cost of Mastronardi's method is easy to conclude to be much more expensive than Algorithm 7, as the costs for one eigenvector have such a significant difference as shown in Table 2. In addition, Mastronardi's method is unsuitable for computing all the eigenvectors, as the deflation process costs $O(2n^3)$ operations [12] while it could not benefit from the sub-diagonal "zero"s like the traditional QR method.

7. Discussion

Algorithm 7 is a modified version of the MRRR, certainly of the Inverse Iteration method essentially, as the MRRR method implements inverse iterations in bidiagonal forms. The key improvements are:

1. the one-step iteration method with Algorithm 6 to avoid overflow and underflow. Although the MRRR method uses another version of one-step iteration, the accompanying operations of square and square root slow down the routine.
2. computing severely eigenvectors by the envelope vector theory. The severely clustering eigenvalues, which make the cost of the MRRR and Inverse Iteration method surge, bring a significant acceleration, on the contrary, for our new method. The scheme of the MRRR method for clustered eigenvalues is ingenious with time complexity of $O(n^2)$, but costs too many operations when searching the so-called "Relatively Robust Representation". In terms of results, it is even the slowest when severely clustering eigenvalues arise.
3. the novel reorthogonalization method. Dhillion also tried the envelope vectors when the MRRR method was stuck by the glued Wilkinson Matrices [11] but gave up because of the general clustering of severely clustered groups. This paper solves the problem by the general Q iteration. Note we also accelerate the QR-like iteration itself by Algorithm 5.

The results in Section 6 show that the modified Inverse Iteration method is suitable for computing part eigenpairs, especially the severely clustered ones. When computing a minor set, our new method is significantly faster. As the computations for every eigenpair are independent, our new method is flexible in calculating in any given order. However, when eigenvalues generally cluster without severely clustering groups, one should use the MRRR method. In addition, the DC method is absolutely the champion for computing all the eigenpairs in almost every type of matrix. Nevertheless, considering it is rare to calculate all the eigenpairs of a large matrix in practice, this paper provides a novel, practical, flexible, and fast method.

Algorithm 7 can be divided into roughly three steps: finding the smallest $|\gamma_k|$; computing the isolated or clustered eigenvectors; reorthogonalizing by premultiplying Givens' rotation matrices. The consumption of the other calculation parts is not comparable to these three steps. Note that all these main steps can be implemented in parallel. Therefore, Algorithm 7 is suitable for parallel computation. We will focus on the parallel version of the modified Inverse Iteration method in our future research work.

Author Contributions: Formal analysis, W.C., Y.Z., and H.Y.; investigation, W.C. and Y.Z.; writing—original draft, W.C.; writing—review and editing, H.Y. All authors have read and agreed to the published version of the manuscript.

Funding: This research is funded by the Talent Team Project of Zhangjiang City in 2021 and the R & D and industrialization project of the offshore aquaculture cage nets system of Guangdong Province of China (Grant No. 2021E05034). Huazhong University of Science and Technology funds the APC.

Data Availability Statement: Not applicable.

Acknowledgments: The authors would like to thank the editors and reviewers for their constructive comments, which will improve the manuscript.

Conflicts of Interest: The authors declare no conflict of interest.

Abbreviations

The following abbreviations are used in this manuscript:

ST (matrix)	Symmetric Tridiagonal (matrix)
DC (algorithm)	Divided and Conquer (algorithm)
MRRR (algorithm)	Multiple Relatively Robust Representations (algorithm)

References

1. Xu, W.R.; Bebiano, N.; Chen, G.L. On the construction of real non-self adjoint tridiagonal matrices with prescribed three spectra. *Electron. Trans. Numer. Anal.* **2019**, *51*, 363–386. [CrossRef]
2. Van Dooren, P.; Laudadio, T.; Mastronardi, N. Computing the Eigenvectors of Nonsymmetric Tridiagonal Matrices. *Comput. Math. Math. Phys.* **2021**, *61*, 733–749. [CrossRef]
3. Laudadio, T.; Mastronardi, N.; Van Dooren, P. Computing Gaussian quadrature rules with high relative accuracy. *Numer. Algorithms* **2022**. [CrossRef]
4. Nesterova, O.P.; Uzdin, A.M.; Fedorova, M.Y. Method for calculating strongly damped systems with non-proportional damping. *Mag. Civ. Eng.* **2018**, *81*, 64–72. [CrossRef]
5. Bahar, M.K. Charge-Current Output in Plasma-Immersed Hydrogen Atom with Noncentral Interaction. *Ann. Phys.* **2021**, *533*. [CrossRef]
6. Gu, M.; Eisenstat, S.C. A divide-and-conquer algorithm for the symmetric tridiagonal eigenproblem. *SIAM J. Matrix Anal. Appl.* **1995**, *16*, 172–191. [CrossRef]
7. Parlett, B.N. *The Symmetric Eigenvalue Problem*; SIAM: Philadelphia, PA, USA, 1997.
8. Peters, G.; Wilkinson, J.H., The calculation of specified eigenvectors by inverse iteration. In *Handbook for Automatic Computation*; Springer: Berlin/Heidelberg, Germany, 1971; pp. 418–439.
9. Dhillon, I.S. A New O(n^2) Algorithm for the Symmetric Tridiagonal Eigenvalue/Eigenvector Problem. Ph.D. Thesis, University of California, Berkeley, CA, USA, 1997.
10. Wilkinson. The Algebraic Eigenvalue Problem. In *Handbook for Automatic Computation, Volume II, Linear Algebra*; Oxford University Press: Oxford, UK, 1969.
11. Dhillon, I.S.; Parlett, B.N.; Vömel, C. Glued matrices and the MRRR algorithm. *SIAM J. Sci. Comput.* **2005**, *27*, 496–510. [CrossRef]
12. Mastronardi, N.; Taeter, H.; Dooren, P. On computing eigenvectors of symmetric tridiagonal matrices. *Springer INdAM Ser.* **2019**, *30*, 181–195. [CrossRef]
13. Parlett, B.N. Invariant subspaces for tightly clustered eigenvalues of tridiagonals. *BIT Numer. Math.* **1996**, *36*, 542–562. [CrossRef]
14. Parlett, B.; Dopico, F.M.; Ferreira, C. The inverse eigenvector problem for real tridiagonal matrices. *SIAM J. Matrix Anal. Appl.* **2016**, *37*, 577–597. [CrossRef]
15. Kovačec, A. Schrödinger's tridiagonal matrix. *Spec. Matrices* **2021**, *9*, 149–165. [CrossRef]

16. da Fonseca, C.M.; Kılıç, E. A new type of Sylvester–Kac matrix and its spectrum. *Linear Multilinear Algebra* **2021**, *69*, 1072–1082. [CrossRef]
17. Chu, W.; Zhao, Y.; Yuan, H. A Novel Divisional Bisection Method for the Symmetric Tridiagonal Eigenvalue Problem. *Mathematics* **2022**, *10*, 2782. [CrossRef]
18. Barth, W.; Martin, R.; Wilkinson, J. Calculation of the eigenvalues of a symmetric tridiagonal matrix by the method of bisection. *Numer. Math.* **1967**, *9*, 386–393. [CrossRef]

mathematics

MDPI

Article

The Shortest-Edge Duplication of Triangles

Miguel Ángel Padrón †, Francisco Perdomo †, Ángel Plaza † and José Pablo Suárez *,†

IUMA Information and Communications System, University of Las Palmas de Gran Canaria, 35017 Canary Islands, Spain

* Correspondence: josepablo.suarez@ulpgc.es

† These authors contributed equally to this work.

Abstract: We introduce a new triangle transformation, the shortest-edge (SE) duplication, as a natural way of mesh derefinement suitable to those meshes obtained by iterative application of longest-edge bisection refinement. Metric properties of the SE duplication of a triangle in the region of normalised triangles endowed with the Poincare hyperbolic metric are studied. The self-improvement of this transformation is easily proven, as well as the minimum angle condition. We give a lower bound for the maximum of the smallest angles of the triangles produced by the iterative SE duplication $\alpha = \frac{\pi}{6}$. This bound does not depend on the shape of the initial triangle.

Keywords: triangulations; shortest edge; finite element method; triangle shape

MSC: 65L50; 68R99

Citation: Padrón, M.Á.; Perdomo, F.; Plaza, Á.; Suárez, J.P. The Shortest-Edge Duplication of Triangles. *Mathematics* **2022**, *10*, 3643. https://doi.org/10.3390/math10193643

Academic Editors: Fajie Wang and Ji Lin

Received: 26 August 2022
Accepted: 29 September 2022
Published: 5 October 2022

1. Introduction

Adaptive meshing is a fundamental component of adaptive finite element methods. This includes refining and coarsening meshes locally [1,2]. As the mesh is enriched through the refinement process, the solution on a given mesh provides an accurate starting iterate for the next mesh. Frequently, it is needed not only to enrich the mesh but also to coarsen it by some derefinement or coarsening strategy [3,4] in such a way that the nodes are located in the places where it is necessary for a more accurate solution while the number of unknowns remains bound. Mesh coarsening and mesh refinement are usually combined to provide a flexible approach for the adaptation of time-dependent problems [5].

In the context of adaptive finite element methods, both in two and three dimensions, longest-edge bisection-based algorithms have been largely studied in the last years [6–8]. These algorithms guarantee the construction of high-quality triangulations [9,10], assuring the maximum angle condition [11] and the non-degeneracy of the obtained meshes [10]. Non-degeneracy of the meshes means that the minimum angle generated is bounded away from zero, and it is closely related to the finite number of similarly different triangles or tetrahedra generated. Further, some longest-edge bisection-based partitions show a mesh quality improvement property, meaning that the generated meshes not only do not degenerate but also present better quality than the previously obtained mesh as the refinement is applied.

For coarsening a refined mesh, we may consider different approaches, such as removing nodes, swapping edges, or amplifying elements [2]. Here we study the shortest-edge duplication of a triangle as a simple procedure to be applied to those triangles for coarsening a triangular mesh that has been obtained by the iterative application of local refinements based on longest-edge bisection. This method shows to be effective at coarsening meshes while improving the smallest angle. On the other hand, if it is desired to maintain the resolution of the mesh while improving the smallest angles, the method can be combined with a local refinement strategy to improve high-order mesh quality while maintaining sufficient resolution, for example, by the self-similar refinement scheme [2,12], albeit this issue will not be tackled in this paper. It should be underlined, however, that there have been recent approaches, such as the *hr*-adaptivity, which are able to address this problem [13].

Our goal in the paper is to study the metric properties of the shortest-edge duplication, in the sequel SE duplication, of a triangle. To this end, we will employ the results of hyperbolic geometry and particularly the Poincare half-plane model, which has demonstrated its utility in similar triangle partitions [14,15].

Given an initial triangle, a new triangle is obtained by doubling the shortest edge, maintaining the longest edge as unaltered. The SE duplication will be explicitly set up in the next definition.

Definition 1. *Let $t_0(A, B, C)$ denote triangle t_0 with vertices A, B and C. Let us assume that the shortest edge of t_0 is edge AB, while the longest one is edge BC. Then, the SE SE duplication of t_0 is $t_1(A_1, B, C)$, where $A_1 = B + 2\overrightarrow{BA}$.*

Notice that the SE duplication is a transformation of triangles that may be applied recursively. For example, and continuing with the triangle in Definition 1, if the shortest-edge of triangle t_1 is A_1B, and the longest one is BC, the SE duplication of t_1 is triangle $t_2(A_2, B, C)$, where $A_2 = B + 2\overrightarrow{BA_1}$. See Figure 1.

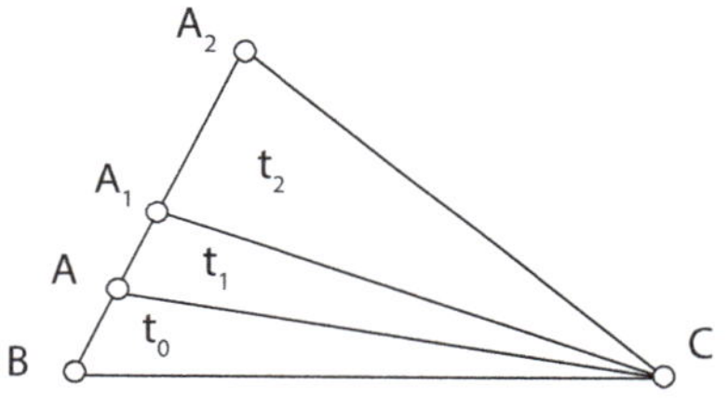

Figure 1. First SE duplications of triangle t_0.

It is clear that by the SE duplication of a triangle, the two shortest edges of the triangle increase, while the longest edge remains unaltered.

Let τ be a locally refined triangular mesh obtained by a longest-edge bisection-based refinement. One could apply the SE duplication of some triangles in order to coarsen the mesh. This procedure consists of locally changing a triangle by SE duplication. As a matter of example, Figure 2 shows the application of SE duplication to a refined mesh obtained by the longest-edge bisection so that a derefined mesh appears.

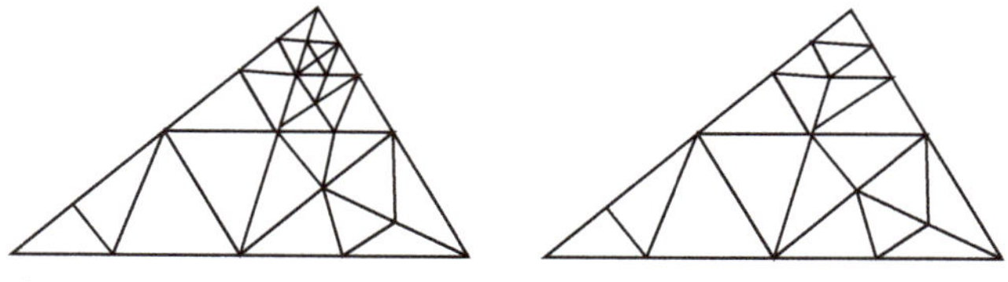

Figure 2. SE duplication procedure as a derefinement process.

2. Normalised Region for Triangles and Piecewise Function for the SE Duplication

For any arbitrary triangle, a similar triangle can be found by performing suitable symmetries, scaling, translations and rotations such that the normalised triangle has the longest edge with vertices $(0,0)$ and $(1,0)$, and the opposite vertex, z, in the upper plane at the left of the vertical line $x = \frac{1}{2}$; that is, with the shortest edge to the left with vertices $(0,0)$ and z [12]. Using this procedure, all similar triangles are represented by a unique complex number $z \in \Sigma$, where Σ is the set of the complex plane $\Sigma = \{z/ \operatorname{Im} z > 0,\ \operatorname{Re} z \leq \frac{1}{2},\ |z-1| \leq 1\}$. Σ is called the space of triangular shapes. See Figure 3, where Σ is in grey.

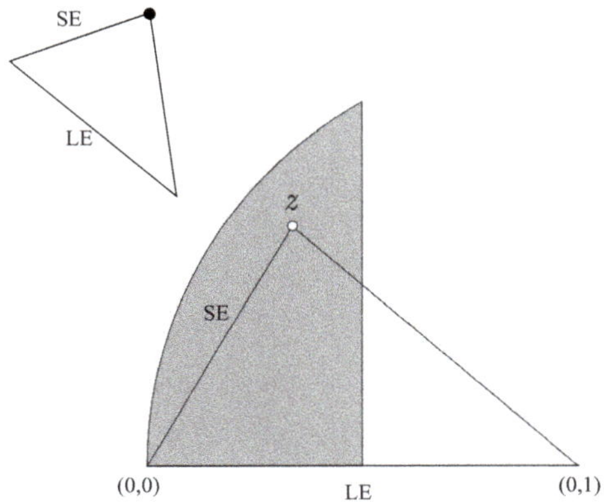

Figure 3. Normalised triangle and normalised region $\Sigma = \{z/\ \mathrm{Im}\, z > 0,\ \mathrm{Re}\, z \le \frac{1}{2},\ |z-1| \le 1\}$.

For any point $z \in \Sigma$, let $w(z)$ be its image in Σ by the shortest-edge duplication transformation. $w(z)$ is a piecewise function that depends on the location of z in Σ. Explicitly, function $w(z)$ is defined as follows, depending on which subregion point z is in according to the subregions in Figure 4.

$$w(z) = \begin{cases} w_V(z) = 2z & \text{if } z \in V, \\ w_{VI}(z) = 1 - 2\bar{z} & \text{if } z \in VI, \\ w_{III}(z) = \dfrac{2\bar{z}}{2\bar{z}-1} & \text{if } z \in III, \\ w_{IV}(z) = \dfrac{2z-1}{2z} & \text{if } z \in IV, \\ w_{II}(z) = \dfrac{1}{1-2z} & \text{if } z \in II, \\ w_I(z) = \dfrac{1}{2\bar{z}} & \text{if } z \in I. \end{cases}$$

Figure 4 shows the subdomains in Σ needed to define function $w(z)$.

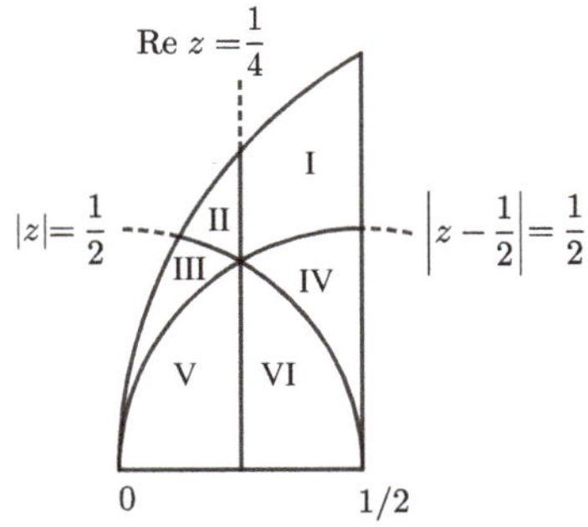

Figure 4. Circles and straight lines defining the subregions for the piecewise function w.

The values of function w, depending on the position of point z in each sub-region, may be easily deduced. As a matter of example, Figure 5 shows the definition of function $w(z)$ for z in the first two lower subregions of the space of triangular shapes. Similar figures may be found for the other subregions. In Figure 5 right, $w(z) = 2z$, while in Figure 5 left,

$w(z) = 1 - 2\bar{z}$ in order to normalise the triangle to have its shortest edge on the left side, so that $w(z)$ belongs to Σ.

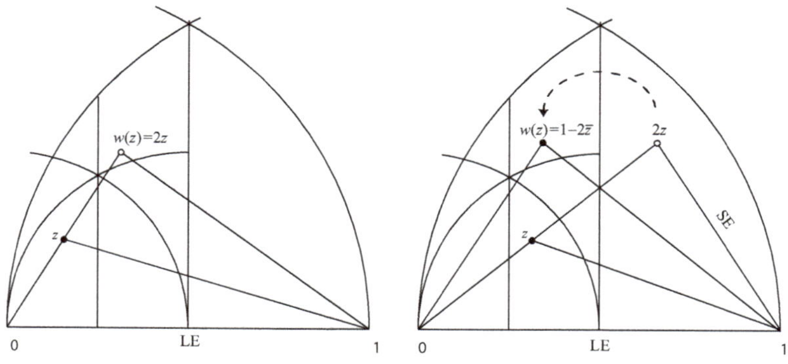

Figure 5. Definition of w for $z \in V$ on the **left**, and for $z \in VI$ on the **right**.

Using hyperbolic geometry, such as the Poincare half-plane model, see [14–17], the circumferences and straight lines in the definition of the piecewise function w are orthogonal to $\operatorname{Im} z = 0$ and, therefore, are geodesics in the Poincare half-plane. The expressions for function w are isometries in the half-plane hyperbolic model because they have the form $\frac{az+b}{cz+d}$ or $\frac{a(\bar{z})+b}{c(\bar{z})+d}$ with real coefficients $ad - bc > 0$. Function w is invariant with respect to the inversion of the circumferences $|z| = 1/2$ and $|z - 1/2| = 1/2$, and under symmetry with respect to the straight line $\operatorname{Re} z = 1/2$. We recall here the expression of these transformations in [18]. Let K be an arbitrary circle with centre q and radius R. Then the inversion in K, written $z \mapsto \tilde{z} = \mathcal{I}_K(z)$, is equal to

$$\mathcal{I}_K(z) = \frac{R^2}{\bar{z} - \bar{q}} + q = \frac{q\bar{z} + (R^2 - |q|^2)}{\bar{z} - \bar{q}}.$$

In particular, for K_1, circle $|z| = 1/2$, we have $\mathcal{I}_{K_1}(z) = \frac{1}{4\bar{z}}$, while for K_2, circle $|z - 1/2| = 1/2$, we have $\mathcal{I}_{K_2}(z) = \frac{\bar{z}}{2\bar{z} - 1}$.

On the other hand, ff $\bar{\alpha}z + \alpha\bar{z} = r$ is a line in the complex plane such that z_1 is the reflection of z_2 in the given line, then $r = \bar{z_1}\alpha + z_2\bar{\alpha}$. In particular, for the straight line L with equation $\operatorname{Re} z = 1/2$, the expression of the reflection in line L, say $\mathcal{R}_L(z)$, is $\mathcal{R}_L(z) = \frac{1}{2} - \bar{z}$.

Theorem 1. *Function w is invariant with respect to the inversion of the two circumferences, $|z - 1/2| = 1/2$ and $|z| = 1/2$, and under symmetry with respect to the straight line $\operatorname{Re} z = 1/2$ that appears in its definition.*

Proof. The proof follows easily by checking that

$$\begin{cases} w_I(\mathcal{R}_L(z)) = w_{II}(z) \;\; \forall z \in II, & w_{II}(\mathcal{R}_L(z)) = w_I(z) \;\; \forall z \in I, \\ w_{III}(\mathcal{R}_L(z)) = w_{IV}(z) \;\; \forall z \in IV, & w_{IV}(\mathcal{R}_L(z)) = w_{III}(z) \;\; \forall z \in III, \\ w_V(\mathcal{R}_L(z)) = w_{VI}(z) \;\; \forall z \in VI, & w_{VI}(\mathcal{R}_L(z)) = w_V(z) \;\; \forall z \in V. \end{cases}$$

Similarly, for inversions $\mathcal{I}_{K_i}(z)$, with $i = 1, 2$, it holds, in closed form, that

$$w_J(\mathcal{I}_{K_i}(z)) = w_{\mathcal{I}_{K_i}(J)}(z) \;\; \forall z \in \mathcal{I}_{K_i}(z)$$

where J represents any subregion in the definition of function w. □

If z_1 and z_2 are such that Im $z_i > 0$, then the hyperbolic distance d between z_1 and z_2, $d(z_1, z_2)$, is

$$d(z_1, z_2) = \cosh^{-1}\left(1 + \frac{|z_1 - z_2|}{2\text{Im } z_1 \text{ Im } z_2}\right).$$

On the other hand, if Re z_1 = Re z_2, then

$$d(z_1, z_2) = \left|\ln\left(\frac{\text{Im } z_1}{\text{Im } z_2}\right)\right|.$$

Let z_1 and z_2 be points in a geodesic circumference, and z_2 be the upper point located over the centre of the circumference, the hyperbolic length of the segment in the geodesic from z_1 to z_2, say l, verifies

$$\theta = 2\arctan(e^{-l})$$

where θ is the difference between $\pi/2$ and the central angle is determined by the segment from z_1 to z_2 over the geodesic. See Figure 6.

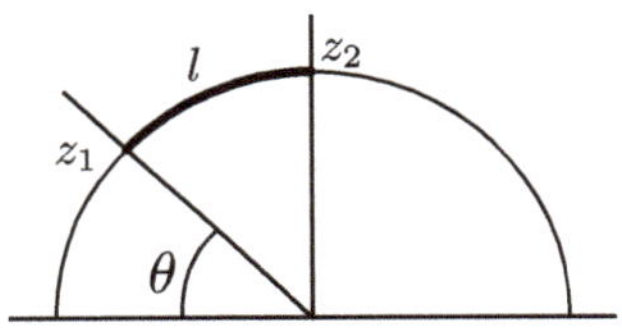

Figure 6. Hyperbolic length l from z_1 to z_2 verifies $\theta = 2\arctan(e^{-l})$.

Definition 2. *A region $\Omega \subset \Sigma$ is called a closed region for SE duplication if $w(z) \in \Omega \;\; \forall z \in \Omega$.*

Lemma 1 (non-increasing property). *If $z_1, z_2 \in \Sigma$, then $d(w(z_1),\, w(z_2)) \leq d(z_1,\, z_2)$.*

Proof. Let us first assume that z_1 and z_2 are in a region with the same definition of w, then $d(z_1, z_2) = d(w(z_1), w(z_2))$. This may be checked easily and also follows because w is an isometry in Σ.

Suppose now that z_1 and z_2 are not in a region with the same definition of w. z_1 and z_2 may be in two regions sharing a common boundary. In this case, there is z_1' in the region of z_2 with $w(z_1) = w(z_1')$ because of the symmetry of w with respect to the boundary. Let γ be the geodesic line that joins z_1 and z_2. γ intersects the boundary at a point, say z^*. Then, since points z_1, z^* and z_2 are in the same geodesic, $d(z_1, z_2) = d(z_1, z^*) + d(z^*, z_2)$. Further, $d(z_1, z^*) = d(z_1', z^*)$ because z_1 and z_1' are symmetrical points with respect to the boundary containing z^*. See Figure 7.

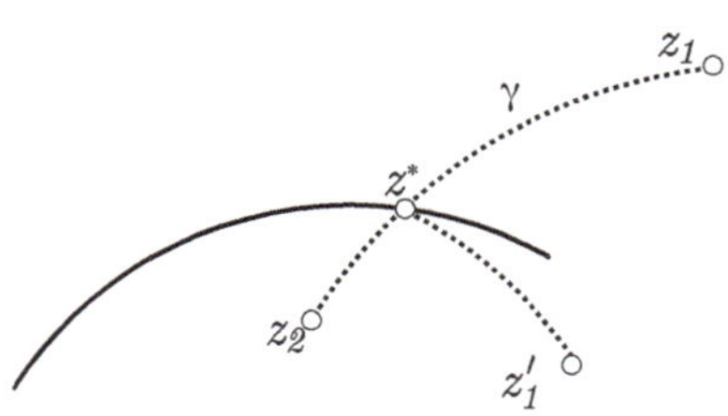

Figure 7. The geodesic line joining z_1 and z^* is an image by reflection of the segment joining z_1' with z^*, and so $d(z_1, z^*) = d(z_1', z^*)$.

Therefore, by the triangular inequality,

$$d(z_1, z_2) = d(z_1, z^*) + d(z^*, z_2) = d(z_1', z^*) + d(z^*, z_2) > d(z_1', z_2).$$

Thus, $d(w(z_1), w(z_2)) = d(w(z_1'), w(z_2)) = d(z_1', z_2) < d(z_1, z_2)$.

If, z_1 and z_2 are in different regions not sharing a common boundary, we may apply the previous process to bring both z_1 and z_2 into the same region and the proof is finished. □

Definition 3. *Let z be in Σ. The orbit of z by the SE duplication, $\Gamma(z)$, is the set as $\Gamma(z) = \cup_{n\geq 0} w^{(n)}(z)$, where $w^{(0)}(z) = z$, and $w^{(n)}(z) = w\left(w^{(n-1)}(z)\right)$.*

For $\zeta = \frac{1}{2} + \frac{1}{2}i$, $\Gamma(\zeta) = \{\zeta\}$, since $w(\zeta) = \zeta$. Other fixed points for w are $x_1 = \frac{1}{4} + \frac{\sqrt{7}}{4}i$ and $q_1 = \frac{3}{8} + \frac{\sqrt{23}}{8}i$. In sub-region I, as denoted in Figure 8, $w(z) = \frac{1}{2\bar{z}}$, which is an inversion with respect to the circumference of equation $|z| = \frac{\sqrt{2}}{2}$, or $x^2 + y^2 = \frac{1}{2}$. Therefore, for z in the arc of that circumference which is in region I, $|\Gamma(z)| = 1$. It may be easily verified that these are the only fixed points for $w \in \Sigma$. Notice that although $(0,0)$ is another fixed point, that triangle is invalid and does not belong to the space of triangular shapes Σ where it is required Im $z > 0$. Further, it follows that for $z \in I$, $|\Gamma(z)| \leq 2$. For example, for $v_0 = \frac{1}{2} + \frac{\sqrt{3}i}{2}$, which corresponds to the equilateral triangle, then $\Gamma(v_0) = \{v_0, v_1\}$, where $v_1 = \frac{1}{4} + \frac{\sqrt{3}}{4}i$.

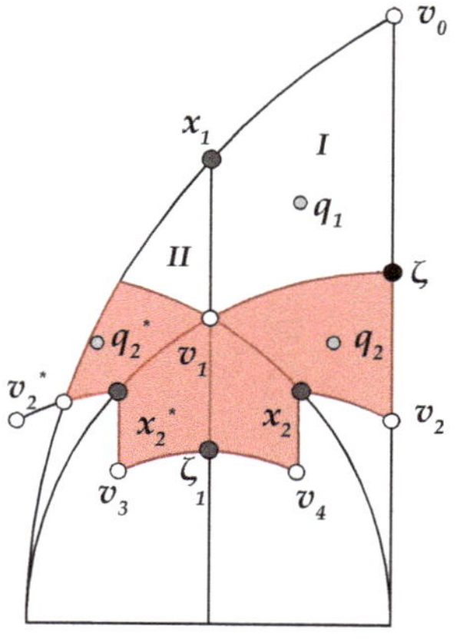

Figure 8. Regions for Lemma 2.

In order to prove that the orbit for any point z is finite, we will use the division of the normalised region is shown in Figure 8. We consider the sets $w_J^{-1}(I)$, with $J = III, V, VI, IV$, where $w_J^{-1}(I) = \left\{w_J^{-1}(z) \text{ for } z \in I\right\}$. It is clear that $w_J^{-1}(I) \subset J$. These sets are the coloured subsets in Figure 8. The points labelled in the figure are $x_1 = \frac{1}{4} + \frac{\sqrt{7}}{4}i$, $x_2 = \frac{3}{8} + \frac{\sqrt{7}}{8}i$ and $x_2^* = \frac{1}{8} + \frac{\sqrt{7}}{8}i$ are pre-images of x_1. Similarly, $v_1 = w^{-1}(v_0)$, $v_2 = w_{IV}^{-1}(v_1)$, $v_2^* = w_{III}^{-1}(v_1)$, $v_3 = w_V^{-1}(v_1)$, and $v_4 = w_{VI}^{-1}(v_1)$. Further, q_2 is the pre-image of q_1 in region IV; that is, $q_2 = \frac{5}{12} + \frac{\sqrt{23}}{12}i$, while $q_2^* = \frac{1}{12} + \frac{\sqrt{23}}{12}i = w_{III}^{-1}(q_1)$.

Lemma 2. *$S = I \cup II \cup w_{III}^{-1}(I) \cup w_V^{-1}(I) \cup w_{VI}^{-1}(I) \cup w_{IV}^{-1}(I)$ is a closed region. Further, if $z \in S$, then $|\Gamma(z)| \leq 3$.*

Proof. Let $z \in S$. If $z \in I$, $w(z) = w_I(z) = \frac{1}{2\bar{z}}$ is an inversion with respect to the circumference of equation $|z| = \frac{\sqrt{2}}{2}$, then $w(z \in I) = z' \in I$. Therefore, for $z \in I$, $|\Gamma(z)| \leq 2$. Further, by construction, $w\left(w_J^{-1}(I)\right) \subset I$, with $J = III, V, VI, IV$, so $|\Gamma(z)| \leq 3$ for $z \in w_{III}^{-1}(I) \cup w_V^{-1}(I) \cup w_{VI}^{-1}(I) \cup w_{IV}^{-1}(I)$. Finally, by the symmetry of function w about line Re $z = \frac{1}{4}$, then for $z \in II$, $w(z) = \frac{-1}{2\bar{z}-1} \in I$, and, therefore, $|\Gamma(z)| \leq 3$ for $z \in II$. □

The argument of the last lemma may be applied recursively, considering each of the pre-images of the last sets by w_J, with $J = III, V, VI, IV$. In that way, since the pre-images of the lowest vertices considered tend to the horizontal line $\text{Im}(z) = 0$, it follows that $|\Gamma(z)| < \infty$, $\forall z \in \Sigma$. This fact will also be shown experimentally by a Monte Carlo experiment later.

Lemma 3. *There is $\varepsilon' > 0$ such that for every $z \in \Sigma$ such that the hyperbolic distance to any of the points v_0, v_1, v_2 or v_2^* is less than or equal to ε' then $|\Gamma(z)| < \infty$.*

Proof. Notice that ε' may be chosen such that every hyperbolic circle with centre v_0, v_1, v_2 or v_2^* and radius ε' intersects only the geodesic lines defining w that pass through their centres, as Figure 9 shows.

Let us first suppose that $z \in \Sigma$ with $d(z, v_0) \leq \varepsilon'$. In that case, $z \in I$ so $|\Gamma(z)| \leq 2$.

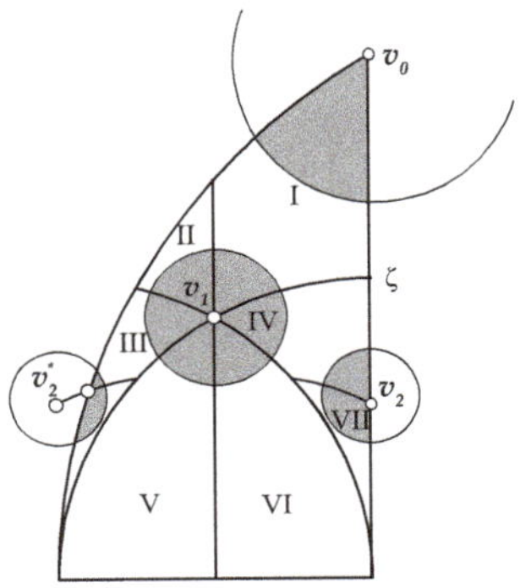

Figure 9. ε' is such that every hyperbolic circle with a centre at v_0, v_1 and v_2 intersects only with the geodesic lines in the definition of $w(z)$ passing through its centres.

On the other hand, if $d(z, v_1) \leq \varepsilon'$, $w(z) \in I$, so $|\Gamma(z)| \leq 3$. Finally, if $d(z, v_2) \leq \varepsilon'$ or $d(z, v_2^*) \leq \varepsilon'$, then $d(w(z), v_1) \leq \varepsilon'$, so it is reduced to the previous case. □

Lemma 4. *Let $q_1 = \frac{3}{8} + \frac{\sqrt{23}}{8}i$ and $r = d(q_1, v_1)$. Then there exists $\varepsilon > 0$ such that for every $z \in \Sigma$ with $d(q_1, z) \leq r + \varepsilon$, then $|\Gamma(z)| < \infty$.*

Proof. Let us consider that $\varepsilon > 0$ is small enough so that the hyperbolic circle with a centre at q_1 and radius $r + \varepsilon$ does not intersect with region VII. This is possible because $d(q_1, v_1) < d(q_1, x_2)$, as it is shown in Figure 10. With such a ε, we may assure that the region of z such that $d(q_1, z) \leq r + \varepsilon$ is contained in $I \cup IV$ along with a small hyperbolic circle with its centre at v_1, so it is inside region S from Lemma 2. It follows that $|\Gamma(z)| < \infty$. □

Lemma 5. *Let $\varepsilon > 0$ as in the previous lemma, and $r = d(q_1, v_1)$. Let K be a compact set contained in the normalised region Σ such that for every $z \in K$ it holds that $d(z, q_1) > r + \varepsilon$. Then, there exists a value A, where $0 < A < 1$ such that for every $z \in K$, $d(w(z), q_1) < A \cdot d(z, q_1)$.*

Proof. Function
$$\phi(z) = \frac{d(w(z), q_1)}{d(z, q_1)}$$
is continuous in K. Since K is compact, there exists A, the maximum value of $\phi(z)$ in K. By not increasing the distance and since $w(q_1) = q_1$, then $d(w(z), q_1) \leq d(z, q_1)$. In addition, if $z \in K$, z is not in region I, and the inequality between the distances is strict. In particular, this happens for the value of $z \in K$ in where the maximum is attained, where $A < 1$. □

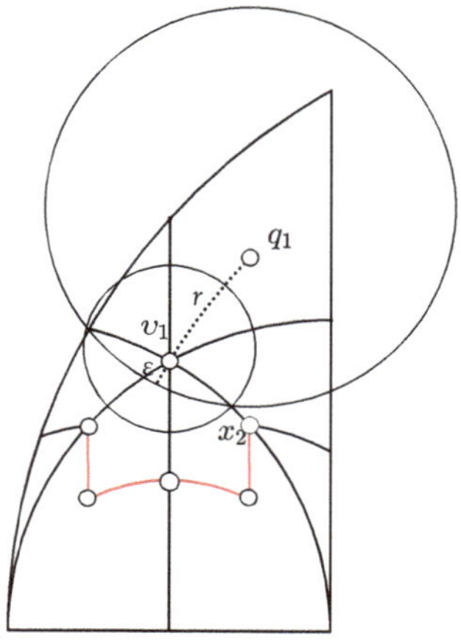

Figure 10. For a suitable ε, a circle with its centre at q_1 and radius $d(q_1, v_1) + \varepsilon$ is in region S from Lemma 2.

Theorem 2. *If $z \in \Sigma$, then $|\Gamma(z)| < \infty$.*

Proof. Let r and ε be as in the previous lemmas. If $d(z, q_1) \leq r + \varepsilon$, then $|\Gamma(z)| < \infty$, by Lemma 5. Let us suppose, therefore, that $d(z, q_1) > r + \varepsilon$. Let K be the compact set given by the points $u \in \Sigma$ such that $d(u, q_1) \leq d(z, q_1)$ with $d(u, q_1) \geq r + \varepsilon$, and also $d(u, q_2) \leq d(z, q_2)$ with $d(u, q_2) \geq r + \varepsilon$. In Figure 11, K is grey. By Lemma 5, there exists A such that for every $u \in K$, $d(w(u), q_1) \leq A \cdot d(u, q_1)$. Therefore, $d(w(z), q_1) \leq A \cdot d(z, q_1)$ with $A < 1$. By the non-increasing property, $d(w(z), q_2) \leq A \cdot d(z, q_2)$. Therefore, either $w(z) \in K$ or the orbit $|\Gamma(w(z))| < \infty$. By iterating this process, the orbit $|\Gamma(z)|$ is described as a finite set and a finite number of finite orbits of points with a distance to q_1 of less than or equal to $r + \varepsilon$. Therefore, by Lemma 4 these orbits are also finite. □

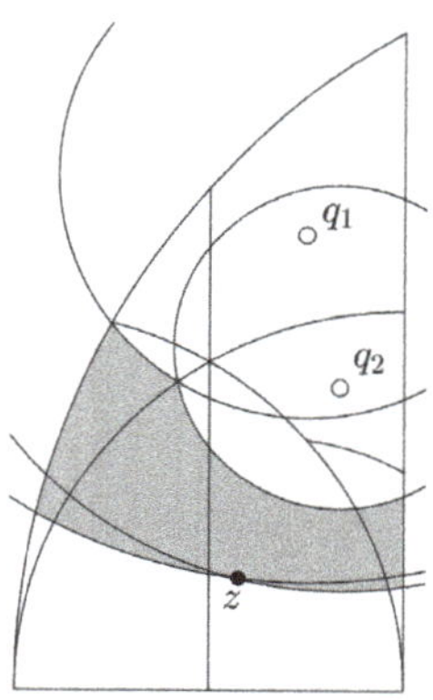

Figure 11. In grey are the points $u \in \Sigma$ with $d(u, q_i) \leq d(z, q_i)$ and $d(u, q_i) \geq r + \varepsilon$, for $i = 1, 2$.

3. Classes of Triangles

Here, we focus on the number of dissimilar triangles that are produced in the SE duplication scheme. Our goal in this section is to study the number of dissimilar triangles so that we can get a classification of the triangles. Let class C_n be the set of triangles for which the SE duplication produces exactly n dissimilar triangles.

We develop a Monte Carlo experiment that can be used to visually represent the classes of triangles according to the number of dissimilar triangles generated.

The process can be described in three phases: (1) Pick a point within the mapping domain defined by the horizontal base and by the two bounding exterior circular arcs. This point $z = (x, y)$ is the apex of a target triangle. (2) Apply SE duplication to the triangle defined by z and its successors and stop when no new shapes appear. (3) The number of steps until termination defines the number of dissimilar triangles for z. This process is recursively applied to a large sample of triangles uniformly over the domain. The output of the experiment is a graph where all of the dissimilar triangles are represented using a colour map to obtain the result in Figure 12.

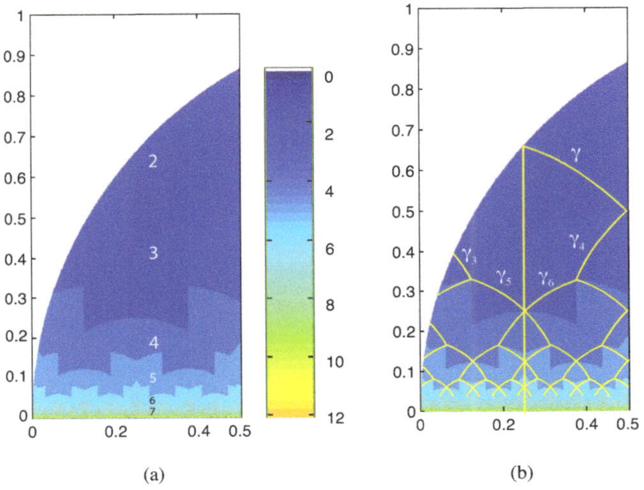

Figure 12. (a) Dissimilar triangle classes generated by a Monte Carlo computational experiment for the SE duplication. (b) Lines inside each nth triangle class with $\Gamma(z) = n - 1$.

Note that the number of dissimilar triangles has been drawn within several coloured regions. For instance, label 2 stands for the two dissimilar triangles and is associated with the targeted triangles within the region above the pair of arcs that intersect on the vertical line of symmetry near the point $y = 0.3$. Label 3 is in the region below for the 3 dissimilar triangles. A graph is then constructed in this manner that fills a completely coloured diagram. It should be noted that triangles with needle-like shapes located close to the baseline will require a higher number of SE duplications until new dissimilar triangles no longer appear.

Note that the region where all the trajectories end in the diagram is located at the dark blue region. Therefore, we can determine a lower bound of the maximum of the smallest angles for the last generated triangles of $\alpha = 30°$, which are related to the apex with $\text{Re}\, z = 1/4$. It can be seen that the smallest angle in each of the regions generated by duplicating its shortest edge is bounded from below with total independence of the initial point of the respective trajectories. This is a salient property in comparison with the evolution of the angles in other longest-edge schemes, for example, in the 4T-LE partition. In the case of 4T-LE partition, these lower bounds depend on the geometry of the initial triangle. See [9,10] for details on the evolution properties of the angles when the 4T-LE partition is recursively applied. In Table 1, the minimum angles generated in the process are listed.

Table 1. Sequences of dissimilar triangles obtained by SE duplication.

	Triangle 1 # of Dissimilar Triangles 7			Triangle 2 # of Dissimilar Triangles 8		
It. n	γ_n	β_n	α_n	γ_n	β_n	α_n
0	145.455	32.595	1.950	173.972	5.423	0.605
1	143.291	32.595	4.114	173.216	5.423	1.361
2	138.199	32.595	9.206	170.950	5.423	3.627
3	123.933	32.595	23.472	153.690	20.887	5.423
4	77.683	69.722	32.595	144.929	20.887	14.184
5	69.722	59.153	51.126	102.859	56.254	20.887
6	84.036	59.153	36.811	78.056	56.254	45.690
7	69.722	59.153	51.126	81.241	56.254	42.504
8				78.056	56.254	45.690

	Triangle 3 # of Dissimilar Triangles 7			Triangle 4 # of Dissimilar Triangles 4		
It. n	γ_n	β_n	α_n	γ_n	β_n	α_n
0	169.900	8.572	1.528	114.624	54.900	10.475
1	167.719	8.572	3.708	102.074	54.900	23.025
2	158.613	12.814	8.572	74.625	54.900	50.475
3	125.395	41.790	12.814	86.502	54.900	38.598
4	106.818	41.790	31.390	74.625	54.900	50.475
5	75.424	62.784	41.790			
6	73.181	62.784	44.033			
7	75.424	62.784	41.790			

In addition, we may find curves inside each coloured region that appear from the trajectories of the triangles in the diagram. Figure 12b shows some of these curves of interest as follows.

It has already been proven that for $z \in I, \Gamma(z) \leq 2$. In this sub-region, $w(z) = \frac{1}{2\bar{z}}$ is an inversion with respect to the circumference of $|z| = \frac{\sqrt{2}}{2}$, or $x^2 + y^2 = \frac{1}{2}$. Therefore, for z in the arc of circumference $w(z) = z$ so $|\Gamma(z)| = 1$.

Similarly to the points in region I, where $|\Gamma(z)| = 1$, there exist points in lower regions such that $|\Gamma(z)| = 2$. These points will be those where $w(z)$ is precisely in the arc of circumference, say γ, of equation $|z| = \frac{\sqrt{2}}{2}$. That is, by studying the pre-images of w for $z \in \gamma$, the corresponding arcs in lower regions of σ may be found as follows

- If $z \in II$, $w(z) = \frac{-1}{2z-1}$. If $w(z) \in \gamma$, then $\left|z - \frac{1}{2}\right| = \frac{\sqrt{2}}{2}$, which is the arc of a circumference with centre $(\frac{1}{2}, 0)$ and radius $\frac{\sqrt{2}}{2}$. Notice that this circumference is out of Σ, and, therefore, there is no point in region II where $|\Gamma(z)| = 2$.
- If $z \in III$, $w(z) = \frac{2\bar{z}}{2\bar{z}-1}$. If $w(z) \in \gamma$, then $\left|\frac{2\bar{z}}{2\bar{z}-1}\right| = \frac{1}{\sqrt{2}}$. If $z = (x, y)$, we have $(x + \frac{1}{2})^2 + y^2 = \frac{1}{2}$, which is the arc of a circumference with centre $(-\frac{1}{2}, 0)$ and radius $\frac{\sqrt{2}}{2}$, arc γ_3 in the figure.
- If $z \in IV$, $w(z) = \frac{2z-1}{2z}$. If $w(z) \in \gamma$, then $\left|\frac{2z-1}{2z}\right| = \frac{1}{\sqrt{2}}$. If $z = (x, y)$, $(x-1)^2 + y^2 = \frac{1}{2}$, which is the arc of a circumference with centre $(1, 0)$ and radius $\frac{\sqrt{2}}{2}$, arc γ_4 in the figure.
- If $z \in V$, $w(z) = 2z$. If $w(z) \in \gamma$, then $|z| = \frac{\sqrt{2}}{4}$, which is a circumference with centre $(0, 0)$ and radius $\frac{\sqrt{2}}{4}$, arc γ_5 in the figure.
- If $z \in VI$, $w(z) = 1 - 2\bar{z}$. If $w(z) \in \gamma$, then $|1 - 2\bar{z}| = \frac{1}{\sqrt{2}}$, so $\left|z - \frac{1}{2}\right| = \frac{\sqrt{2}}{4}$, arc of a circumference with centre $(\frac{1}{2}, 0)$ and radius $\frac{\sqrt{2}}{4}$, arc γ_6 in the figure.

The analysis of subsequent lines where $|\Gamma(z)| = n$, for $n \geq 3$ is analogous to those already carried out by considering the pre-images of the circular arcs already studied. The first of these arcs is depicted in Figure 12b.

It is worth noting here that the fractal appearance of these arcs, in the diagram of triangular shapes is similar to that of the fractal appearance of the boundary of the regions depending on the number of dissimilar triangles generated by SE duplication.

4. Improvement Properties

The non-degeneracy property has been very relevant in the approximation properties of finite element spaces and the convergence issues of multigrid and multilevel algorithms [19]. The non-degeneracy is held when the interior angles of all elements are bounded uniformly away from zero. This property should be assured in refinement and remeshing strategies. It is well-known that the longest-edge bisection algorithms guarantee the construction of high-quality triangulations [10,15].

However, the most interesting property of SE duplication is the self-improvement property, as the following theorem establishes.

Theorem 3 (self-improvement property). *Let t_0 be an initial obtuse triangle in which SE duplication is iteratively applied. Then a (finite) sequence of dissimilar triangles, one per iteration, is obtained: $\{t_0, t_1, \ldots t_{N-1}, t_N, \ldots t_{N+M}\}$, where triangles $t_0, t_1, t_2, \ldots, t_{N-1}$ are obtuse, triangle t_N is nonobtuse, and the SE duplication of t_N produces a finite number of new, not obtuse triangles t_{N+1} and t_{N+M}.*

The iterative SE duplication transformation applied to an initial obtuse triangle produces a finite sequence of 'better' triangles in the sense that the new triangle is 'less obtuse' than the previous one, and its minimum angle is greater than the minimum angle of the previous triangle, until triangle t_N becomes nonobtuse.

This process results in one of the situations illustrated in the next diagram:

(1)	t_{N-1} obtuse	$\rightarrow$	t_N ↺ nonobtuse					
(2)	t_{N-1} obtuse	$\rightarrow$	t_N nonobtuse	$\rightleftharpoons$	t_{N+1} nonobtuse			
(3)	t_{N-1} obtuse	$\rightarrow$	t_N nonobtuse	$\rightarrow \cdots$	t_{N+M-1} nonobtuse	$\rightleftharpoons$	t_{N+M} nonobtuse	

THE THREE ENDINGS TO AN ORBIT BY THE SE DUPLICATION.

The first situation corresponds to the orbit ending in a fixed point for the SE duplication. In the other two possibilities, the orbit also ends in region I but not at a fixed point of w. Since function $w(z)$ is an inversion in I $w^2(z) = z$. The only difference between the two last scenarios is that in (2), the first nonobutse triangle is in I, while in (3), it is not in I. See Figures 8 and 12. We will show some examples in the next section.

5. Numerical Examples

In this section, we present the evolution of the iterative application of the SE duplication to some initial test triangles. The first four initial triangles were also chosen and studied by Rivara and Iribarren in [9] and Plaza et al. in [10] in the context of the 4-triangle longest-edge partition. Table 1 shows the different-shaped triangles obtained by SE duplication of these triangles. The evolution of the generated triangles is visible at a glance in Figure 13.

Table 2 shows the evolution by the SE duplication applied to four more triangles sharing the same minimum angle, 5°. It should be noted that, as before, the generated triangles are better shaped than the previous ones until the respective orbit ends in subregion I%. We observe that triangle 8 is an acute isosceles, and all triangles of its orbit are acute.

The evolution of the generated triangles is visible at a glance in Figure 14. Notice that once a nonobtuse triangle appears in the sequence all its sucessors in orbit are also nonobtuse.

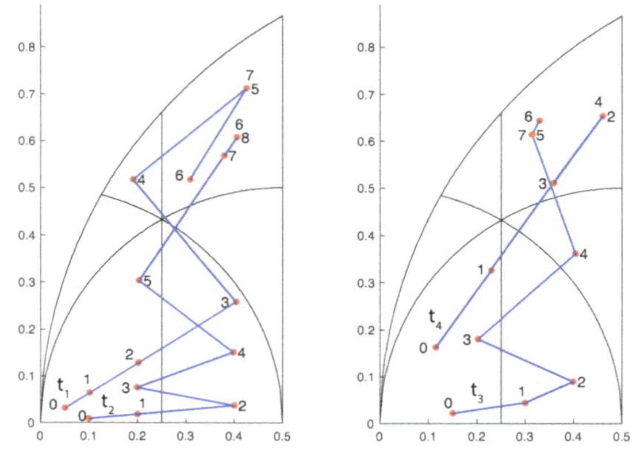

Figure 13. Evolution of SE duplication for the four different triangles in Table 1.

Table 2. Sequences of triangles obtained by SE duplication from initial triangles with the same minimum angle α_0.

	Triangle 5 # of Dissimilar Triangles 6			Triangle 6 # of Dissimilar Triangles 5		
It. n	γ_n	β_n	α_n	γ_n	β_n	α_n
0	146.875	28.125	5.000	123.75	51.250	5.000
1	140.057	28.125	11.817	118.092	51.250	10.658
2	117.363	34.512	28.125	104.840	51.250	23.910
3	78.236	67.252	34.512	74.750	54.002	51.25
4	67.252	62.637	50.111	87.821	54.002	38.177
5	80.958	62.637	36.405	74.750	54.002	51.25
6	67.252	62.784	50.111			
	Triangle 7 # of Dissimilar Triangles 4			**Triangle 8 # of Dissimilar Triangles 4**		
It. n	γ_n	β_n	α_n	γ_n	β_n	α_n
0	100.625	74.375	5.000	87.500	87.500	5.000
1	95.456	74.375	10.169	87.500	82.538	9.962
2	84.935	74.375	20.690	82.538	77.685	19.777
3	74.375	65.442	40.183	77.685	64.346	37.968
4	70.022	65.442	44.537	68.170	64.346	47.483
5	74.375	65.442	40.183	77.685	64.346	37.968

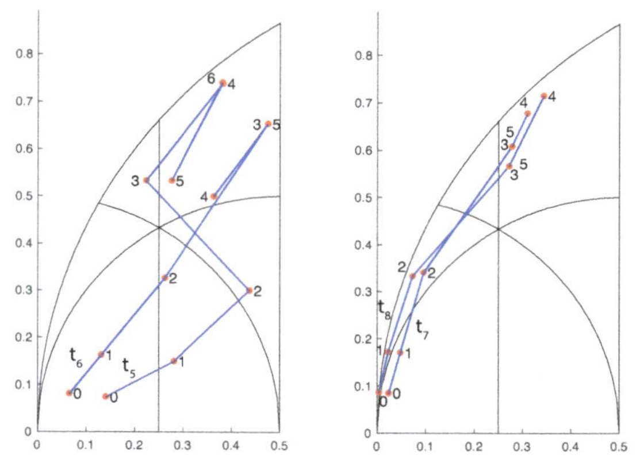

Figure 14. Evolution of SE duplication for the four different triangles in Table 2.

6. Conclusions

In this paper, a new triangle transformation, the shortest-edge duplication of triangles, has been defined. This transformation may be seen as the natural counterpart of the longest-edge partition of a triangle. Metric properties of the SE duplication of a triangle in the region of normalised triangles endowed with the Poincare hyperbolic metric have been studied. The self-improvement of this transformation has been easily proven, as well as the minimum angle condition. A lower bound for the maximum of the smallest angles of the triangles obtained by iterative SE duplication has been obtained with the value $\alpha = \frac{\pi}{6}$. This value does not depend on the shape of the initial triangle. Finally, some numerical examples have been shown to be in total agreement with the mathematical analysis.

Author Contributions: All authors contributed equally to this work. All authors have read and agreed to the published version of the manuscript.

Funding: This research was funded by 'Fundación Parque Científico y Tecnológico de la ULPGC' grant number 'F2021/05 FEI Innovación y Transferencia empresarial en material científico tecnológica en la rama Geoinformática y datos'.

Institutional Review Board Statement: Not applicable.

Informed Consent Statement: Not applicable.

Data Availability Statement: Not applicable.

Conflicts of Interest: The authors declare no conflict of interest.

References

1. Bank, R.E.; Xu, J. An algorithm for coarsening unstructured meshes. *Numer. Math.* **1996**, *73*, 1–36. [CrossRef]
2. Carey, G. *Computational Grids: Generation, Refinement and Solution Strategies*; CRC Press: Boca Raton, FL, USA, 1997.
3. De, J.; Gago, S.; Kelly, D.; Zienkiewicz, O.; Babuşka, I. A posteriori error analysis and adaptive processes in the finite element method: Part II—Adaptive mesh refinements. *Int. J. Numer. Methods Eng.* **1983**, *19*, 1621–1656. [CrossRef]
4. Funken, S.A.; Schmidt, A. A coarsening algorithm on adaptive red-green-blue refined meshes. *Numer. Algorithms* **2021**, *87*, 1147–1176. [CrossRef]
5. Baker, T.J. Mesh deformation and modification for time dependent problems. *Int. J. Numer. Methods Eng. Fluids* **2003**, *43*, 747–768. [CrossRef]
6. Rivara, M. Mesh refinement based on the generalized bisection of simplices. *SIAM J. Numer. Anal.* **1984**, *21*, 604–613. [CrossRef]
7. Rivara, M.C.; Levin, C. A 3-D refinement algorithm suitable for adaptive and multi-grid techniques. *Commun. Appl. Numer. Methods* **1992**, *8*, 281–290. [CrossRef]
8. Plaza, A.; Carey, G. Local refinement of simplicial grids based on the skeleton. *Appl. Numer. Math.* **2000**, *32*, 195–218. [CrossRef]
9. Rivara, M.; Iribarren, G. The 4-triangles longest-side partition of triangles and linear refinement algorithms. *Math. Comput.* **1996**, *65*, 1485–1502. [CrossRef]
10. Plaza, A.; Suárez, J.P.; Falcón, S.; Amieiro, D. Mesh quality improvement and other properties in the four-triangles longest-edge partition. *Comput. Aided Geom. Des.* **2004**, *22*, 353–369. [CrossRef]
11. Korotov, S.; Fredrik, L.; Vatne, J.E. Improved Maximum Angle Estimate for Longest-Edge Bisection. *Int. J. Comput. Geom. Appl.* **2015**, *31*, 183–192. [CrossRef]
12. Plaza, A.; Suárez, J.P.; Carey, G.F. A geometric diagram and hybrid scheme for triangle subdivision. *Comput. Aided Geom. Des.* **2007**, *24*, 19–27. [CrossRef]
13. Askes, H.; Rodriguez-Ferran, A. A combined *rh*-adaptive scheme based on domain subdivision. Formulation and linear examples. *Int. J. Numer. Methods Eng.* **1996**, *51*, 253–273. [CrossRef]
14. Perdomo, F. Dynamics of the Longest-Edge Partitions in a Triangle Space Endowed with an Hyperbolic Metric. Ph.D. Thesis, Universidad de Las Palmas de Gran Canaria, Las Palmas, Spain, 2013. Available online: http://hdl.handle.net/10553/11286 (accessed on 25 August 2022). (In Spanish)
15. Perdomo, F.; Plaza, A. Properties of triangulations obtained by the longest-edge bisection. *Cent. Eur. J. Math.* **2014**, *12*, 1796–1810. [CrossRef]
16. Iversen, B. *Hyperbolic Geometry*; Cambridge University Press: Cambridge, UK, 1992.
17. Stahl, S. *The Poincar Half-Plane: A Gateway to Modern Geometry*; Jones & Bartlett Learning: Burlington, MA, USA, 1993.
18. Needham, T. *Visual Complex Analysis*; Clarendon Press: Oxford, UK, 1997.
19. Rosenberg, I.; Stenger, F. A lower bound on the angles of triangles constructed by bisecting the longest side. *Math. Comput.* **1975**, *29*, 390–395. [CrossRef]

mathematics

MDPI

Article

The Finite Element Method with High-Order Enrichment Functions for Elastodynamic Analysis

Xunbai Du [1,2], Sina Dang [3], Yuzheng Yang [4] and Yingbin Chai [5,6,*]

1 School of Ship and Ocean Engineering, Jiangsu Maritime Institute, Nanjing 211170, China
2 Mechanical and Electrical College, Nanjing University of Aeronautics and Astronautics, Nanjing 211106, China
3 Air and Missile Defense School, Air Force Engineering University, Xi'an 710051, China
4 School of Naval Architecture and Ocean Engineering, Huazhong University of Science and Technology, Wuhan 430074, China
5 School of Naval Architecture, Ocean and Energy Power Engineering, Wuhan University of Technology, Wuhan 430063, China
6 State Key Laboratory of Ocean Engineering, Shanghai Jiao Tong University, Shanghai 200240, China
* Correspondence: chaiyb@whut.edu.cn

Abstract: Elastodynamic problems are investigated in this work by employing the enriched finite element method (EFEM) with various enrichment functions. By performing the dispersion analysis, it is confirmed that for elastodynamic analysis, the amount of numerical dispersion, which is closely related to the numerical error from the space domain discretization, can be suppressed to a very low level when quadric polynomial bases are employed to construct the local enrichment functions, while the amount of numerical dispersion from the EFEM with other types of enrichment functions (linear polynomial bases or first order of trigonometric functions) is relatively large. Consequently, the present EFEM with a quadric polynomial enrichment function shows more powerful capacities in elastodynamic analysis than the other considered numerical techniques. More importantly, the attractive monotonic convergence property can be broadly realized by the present approach with the typical two-step Bathe temporal discretization technique. Three representative numerical experiments are conducted in this work to verify the abilities of the present approach in elastodynamic analysis.

Keywords: high-order enrichment functions; numerical methods; numerical dispersion; transient analysis; wave propagation

MSC: 35A08; 35A09; 35A24; 65L60; 74S05

Citation: Du, X.; Dang, S.; Yang, Y.; Chai, Y. The Finite Element Method with High-Order Enrichment Functions for Elastodynamic Analysis. *Mathematics* **2022**, *10*, 4595. https://doi.org/10.3390/math10234595

Academic Editor: Fernando Simoes

Received: 28 October 2022
Accepted: 2 December 2022
Published: 4 December 2022

1. Introduction

The transient responses of engineering structures under time-varying excitation force are very common problems in engineering practice [1,2]. Meanwhile, the solutions of these elastodynamics are also of great importance in practical applications. Due to the limitations of analytical methods, sufficiently reliable and accurate solutions to complex elastodynamic problems are always very difficult to obtain. In these cases, we usually resort to numerical techniques.

Over the past few decades, many numerical techniques have been developed for determining solutions to elastodynamic problems, such as the finite element method (FEM) [1,2] and smoothed FEM [3–11], the finite difference method (FDM) [12–17], the spectral method [18,19], the boundary element or boundary-based methods [20–33] and various meshless numerical techniques [34–51]. Nevertheless, these numerical approaches usually exhibit some shortcomings in one way or another when practical and complex elastodynamic problems are considered. For example, the FDM is always numerically effective in elastodynamic analysis, but there always exist difficulties when complex and irregular problem domains are involved [52]. In addition, the imposition of a Neumann boundary condition is usually quite complicated. Compared to the FDM, better generality can be achieved using the classical FEM, and very complex elastodynamic problems can be directly and effectively handled by the FEM. Unfortunately, the corresponding numerical solutions from the FEM usually suffers from considerable numerical errors [53–55]. Meanwhile, the numerical anisotropy issue is also a main block we have to confront when the FEM is utilized for elastodynamic analysis [53]. The spectral method, indeed, behaves very well in improving the solution accuracy in elastodynamic analysis; however, it also shows obvious restrictions in tackling very complex problems. Meshless numerical techniques are usually able to yield relatively high-quality numerical solutions, but the related formulations in a mesh-free framework are always very complicated, and the required computational efforts are also very numerically expensive.

The enriched FEM (EFEM), which was proposed and developed by Babuška and co-workers, can be regarded as an advanced and generalized version of the conventional FEM [56], and it has been employed in a wide range of practical engineering computation fields. Since extra enrichment functions are introduced to the constructed numerical approximation, high-order approximation can be achieved by the EFEM without adding additional nodes, even if simple linear elements are employed. This numerical feature clearly distinguishes the EFEM from the conventional FEM [57]. Moreover, it is also very flexible to construct the employed enrichment functions. We can construct specific enrichment functions according to the practical problems solved. In consequence, enrichment functions can be designed to contain the solution knowledge of the considered problems, then the solution accuracy can be markedly increased.

In general, polynomial bases are always utilized as enrichment functions in formulating the EFEM. However, the intractable linear dependence (LD) issue is always encountered when this type of enrichment function is employed [58–60]. As a result, the resultant system matrices are always singular; hence, it is always quite difficult to obtain sufficiently stable and reliable numerical solutions. To address this issue, Duarte et al. developed a specific solver to tackle singular system matrices [61]. Though very accurate and stable numerical solutions can be yielded by a specifically designed solver, extra numerical treatments are also required; this, of course, will increase the required computational cost. Recently, Chai and Gui investigated the LD issue of the EFEM in depth, and the root of the LD was analyzed using mathematical analysis [57,62]. More importantly, they also developed a simple and direct method to completely eliminate the LD issue in the EFEM, and the corresponding proofs were also provided in their work.

In addition to discretization in the space domain, discretization in the time domain also plays a very important role in elastodynamic analysis. Direct time integration schemes are commonly employed approaches for temporal discretization in practice. The frequently employed direct time integration techniques include the central difference method, the Houbolt method [63], the Wilson-θ method [64], the Newmark method [65] and the Bathe method [66–68]. Among them, the Bathe method usually shows more excellent numerical features and is increasingly employed in practical engineering computation, because the proper numerical damping effects can be introduced to the numerical model, and the inaccurate high-order modes from the spatial discretization can be effectively suppressed. As a result, quite accurate and reliable numerical solutions can then be yielded. At present, the Bathe temporal discretization scheme has been widely employed in tackling linear and nonlinear structural dynamic problems; in addition, the Bathe method is a typical two-stage composite time integration scheme and is always unconditionally stable; the satisfaction of the critical time step criterion is not required in the Bathe method. Owing to the abovementioned good numerical features, the Bathe method was employed to perform discretization in the time domain for the elastodynamic analysis in this work.

This work was organized with the aim of investigating the numerical performance of the EFEM with a Bathe time integration scheme when different orders of polynomial bases were utilized to construct the enrichment functions. The possible LD issue and the treatment of the boundary conditions are handled by using the procedure proposed by Chai and Gui [57,62]. The obtained numerical results demonstrate that the present EFEM is able to yield sufficiently small spatial discretization errors when the second order of polynomial bases are exploited as the enrichment function. According to the conclusions obtained in Ref. [57], it can be concluded that in these cases the EFEM with the Bathe time integration scheme will basically possesses the valuable monotonic convergence property in elastodynamic analysis. Then the solution accuracy can be increased continuously by directly utilizing the decreasing temporal discretization steps, this numerical feature can effectively overcome the shortcomings of the FEM in elastodynamic analysis. A number of representative numerical experiments are considered to demonstrate the performance of the present approach in elastodynamic analysis. It should be noted that the nonreflecting boundary conditions are not employed in all numerical examples due to the fact that all the involved waves do not reach the boundary of the problem domain for the considered simulation time. Additionally, in all numerical examples the fixed temporal discretization step sizes are employed to perform the required time integration. Note that several researcher have shown that the variable step sizes (VSS) can produce better numerical solutions [69–71], the performance of the present numerical approaches with the variable time integration step sizes will be investigated in future work.

2. Formulation of the EFEM

Note that the formulation of the present EFEM is closely related to the classical FEM; hence, the numerical approximation in the EFEM is provided here in great detail by comparing the corresponding numerical approximation in the standard FEM. For a general problem domain Ω in two-dimensional space, assuming that the standard three-node triangular elements are utilized to perform the required spatial discretization, then the involved problem domain Ω is represented by n_E elements with n_I nodes. Let $u(\mathbf{x})$ be a scalar field function defined in the two-dimensional problem domain; in the standard FEM, the employed field function approximation is usually constructed by [56]:

$$u_h(\mathbf{x}) = \sum_{i \in n_I} N_i(\mathbf{x}) u_i = \mathbf{N}(\mathbf{x})\mathbf{u}, \tag{1}$$

in which $N_i(\mathbf{x})$ stands for the usual interpolation function for node i, and u_i denotes the corresponding nodal unknown coefficient. In this work, we only considered the linear interpolation function for the triangular mesh, namely:

$$\begin{cases} N_1(\mathbf{x}) = \frac{1}{2A}[(x_2y_3 - x_3y_2) + (y_2 - y_3)x + (x_3 - x_2)y] \\ N_2(\mathbf{x}) = \frac{1}{2A}[(x_3y_1 - x_1y_3) + (y_3 - y_1)x + (x_1 - x_3)y] \\ N_3(\mathbf{x}) = \frac{1}{2A}[(x_1y_2 - x_2y_1) + (y_1 - y_2)x + (x_2 - x_1)y] \end{cases}, \tag{2}$$

in which x_i and y_i (i = 1, 2, 3) represent the coordinate values of three vertexes for one triangular element; A denotes the area of this element.

In the EFEM framework, the structure of the employed field function approximation can be expressed by [56]:

$$u_h(\mathbf{x}) = \sum_{i \in n_I} N_i(\mathbf{x}) u_i + \sum_{i \in n_I} N_i^*(\mathbf{x}) \psi_i(\mathbf{x}) a_i, \tag{3}$$

in which $N_i^*(\mathbf{x})$ denotes the enrichment term for node i; $\psi_i(\mathbf{x})$ and a_i are the corresponding enrichment function and the extra nodal unknown coefficient.

It should be noted that the nodal enrichment term should satisfy the partition of the unity property, namely:

$$\sum_{i \in n_I} N_i^*(\mathbf{x}) = 1, \tag{4}$$

The nodal enrichment term $N_i^*(\mathbf{x})$ can be designed differently from the standard nodal interpolation function $N_i(\mathbf{x})$ in the FEM; however, in this work, we directly choose the standard nodal interpolation function $N_i(\mathbf{x})$ as the nodal enrichment term for brevity, namely, $N_i^*(\mathbf{x}) = N_i(\mathbf{x})$.

In Equation (3), the first term corresponds to the standard numerical approximation in the FEM, and the second term is the additional enriched numerical approximation. The computational accuracy of the EFEM is closely related to the enrichment function $\psi_i(\mathbf{x})$. To enhance the numerical performance of the EFEM, different enrichment functions can be designed for solving different problems [56].

From Equation (3), one important observation we can obtain is that the employed numerical approximation in the EFEM actually contains two parts; the first part is the standard FE numerical approximation, which is linear, and the second part is the additional high-order numerical approximation. Owing to the additional high-order numerical approximation, the original linear approximation space in the FEM can be effectively enriched, then the computation accuracy can be markedly increased. In addition, it should be noted that the above-mentioned enriched numerical approximation space is constructed without requiring the additional nodes, this numerical feature clearly distinguishes the EFEM from the standard high-order finite elements in which the additional mid-edge-points are always required to construct the numerical approximation.

In general, the constructed numerical approximation in Equation (3) does not satisfy the Kronecker-delta function property, namely, $u_h(\mathbf{x}_i) \neq u(\mathbf{x}_i)$. In consequence, the treatment of the essential boundary condition in the present EFEM is usually quite difficult. In addition, the condition number of the system matrices from Equation (3) is always very large; then, the obtained numerical solutions are not sufficiently stable. To make the numerical approximation in Equation (3) have the Kronecker-delta function property and improve its numerical stability, the original numerical approximation in Equation (3) is usually modified by the following form [56]:

$$u_h(\mathbf{x}) = \sum_{i \in n_I} N_i(\mathbf{x}) u_i + \sum_{i \in n_I} N_i^*(\mathbf{x}) [\psi_i(\mathbf{x}) - \psi_i(\mathbf{x}_i)] a_i, \tag{5}$$

From Equation (5), we can see that the additional enriched numerical approximation (namely, the second term) will vanish at all nodes, and the important Kronecker-delta function property can be successfully recovered. Additionally, it is demonstrated that the condition number of the resultant system matrices can be significantly reduced by the modified numerical approximation shown in Equation (5) [56].

In practice, the enrichment function in Equations (3) and (5) can be designed according to the specific problems solved. In this work, the frequently used polynomial bases are exploited to construct the enrichment functions; hence, the used numerical approximation in EFEM for a two-dimensional problem can be given by:

$$u_h(\mathbf{x}) = \sum_{i \in n_I} N_i(\mathbf{x}) u_i + \sum_{i \in n_I} N_i^*(\mathbf{x}) \mathbf{H}_i(\overline{\mathbf{x}}) \mathbf{a}_i, \tag{6}$$

in which $\mathbf{H}_i(\overline{\mathbf{x}})$ is the enrichment function matrix constructed by the polynomial bases and has the following form in two-dimensional space:

$$\mathbf{H}_i(\overline{\mathbf{x}}) = \begin{bmatrix} \overline{x} & \overline{y} & \overline{x}^2 & \overline{xy} & \overline{y}^2 & \cdots & \overline{x}^n & \overline{x}^{n-1}\overline{y} & \cdots & \overline{xy}^{n-1} & \overline{y}^n \end{bmatrix}, \tag{7}$$

in which $\overline{x} = (x - x_i)/h$ and $\overline{y} = (y - y_i)/h$ (h is the characteristic length of the used triangular mesh) represent the nondimensional coordinate values, which are designed to make the constructed numerical approximations have the Kronecker-delta function property.

For the wave propagation elastodynamic problems considered in this work, the enrichment functions can also be designed by [72]:

$$\mathbf{H}_i\left(\overline{\mathbf{x}}\right) = \begin{bmatrix} \cos\left(\frac{2\pi\overline{x}_i}{\lambda_x}\right), & \sin\left(\frac{2\pi\overline{x}_i}{\lambda_x}\right), & \cos\left(\frac{2\pi\overline{y}_i}{\lambda_y}\right), & \sin\left(\frac{2\pi\overline{y}_i}{\lambda_y}\right), \\ \cos\left(\frac{2\pi\overline{x}_i}{\lambda_x}+\frac{2\pi\overline{y}_i}{\lambda_y}\right), & \sin\left(\frac{2\pi\overline{x}_i}{\lambda_x}+\frac{2\pi\overline{y}_i}{\lambda_y}\right), & \cos\left(\frac{2\pi\overline{x}_i}{\lambda_x}-\frac{2\pi\overline{y}_i}{\lambda_y}\right), & \sin\left(\frac{2\pi\overline{x}_i}{\lambda_x}-\frac{2\pi\overline{y}_i}{\lambda_y}\right), \\ \cdots & & & \\ \cos\left(\frac{2\pi q\overline{x}_i}{\lambda_x}\right), & \sin\left(\frac{2\pi q\overline{x}_i}{\lambda_x}\right), & \cos\left(\frac{2\pi q\overline{y}_i}{\lambda_y}\right), & \sin\left(\frac{2\pi q\overline{y}_i}{\lambda_y}\right), \\ \cos\left(\frac{2\pi q\overline{x}_i}{\lambda_x}+\frac{2\pi q\overline{y}_i}{\lambda_y}\right), & \sin\left(\frac{2\pi q\overline{x}_i}{\lambda_x}+\frac{2\pi q\overline{y}_i}{\lambda_y}\right), & \cos\left(\frac{2\pi q\overline{x}_i}{\lambda_x}-\frac{2\pi q\overline{y}_i}{\lambda_y}\right), & \sin\left(\frac{2\pi q\overline{x}_i}{\lambda_x}-\frac{2\pi q\overline{y}_i}{\lambda_y}\right) \end{bmatrix}, \tag{8}$$

in which λ_x and λ_y are the fundamental wave lengths; q is the order of the used trigonometric functions.

From Equations (5)–(8), it is obvious that more additional nodal unknowns will be introduced into the numerical approximation when the high-order polynomial or trigonometric functions are employed to create the local enrichment functions, leading to more computational efforts. Note that there exist three or six nodal unknowns when the linear or quadric polynomial bases are employed as the enrichment functions; hence, we used EFEM-N3 and EFEM-N6 to represent these two different numerical approaches. Similarly, EFEM-N9 was employed to denote the EFEM with the first order of the trigonometric enrichment functions. Additionally, it should be noted that the implementation of the present enriched FEM is quite similar as for the standard finite element analysis (FEA). The only difference is that there are more unknowns for each node. The process of performing the required numerical integration, the assembling of the system stiffness and the mass matrices are identical to the related operations in the standard finite element implementation.

3. Governing Equation of the Transient Wave Propagations

Assuming that the considered wave propagation medium is isotropic with wave speed c, the governing partial differential equation (PDE) can be directly obtained by:

$$\nabla^2 u - \frac{1}{c^2}\frac{\partial^2 u}{\partial t^2} = 0, \tag{9}$$

in which u denotes the used field function variable (such as the pressure, displacement or velocity potential) to describe the considered transient wave propagation dynamic problems.

According to the principle of virtual work, from Equation (9), the following equation in integration form can be arrived at:

$$\int_\Omega \overline{u}\left(\nabla^2 u - \frac{1}{c^2}\frac{\partial^2 u}{\partial t^2}\right)\mathrm{d}\Omega = 0, \tag{10}$$

in which Ω stands for the involved problem domain; $\overline{u}$ represents the virtual field function variable.

Using the divergence theorem and performing the integration in Equation (10) in part, we have:

$$\int_{\Omega_i} \nabla\overline{u}\cdot\nabla u\mathrm{d}\Omega + \frac{1}{c^2}\int_\Omega \overline{u}\frac{\partial^2 u}{\partial t^2}\mathrm{d}\Omega - \int_\Gamma \overline{u}(\nabla u\cdot\mathbf{n})\mathrm{d}\Gamma = 0, \tag{11}$$

in which Γ denotes the problem domain boundary; $\mathbf{n}$ is the outward unit normal vector.

Following the formulations in the standard Galerkin-weighted residual method and using the constructed numerical approximation in Equation (5), the governing equation in the following matrix form can be arrived at for the transient wave propagation dynamic problems:

$$\mathbf{M}\ddot{\mathbf{u}} + c^2\mathbf{K}\mathbf{u} = \mathbf{F}, \tag{12}$$

in which the overdots stand for the time derivatives; $\mathbf{M} = \int_\Omega \mathbf{N}^T\mathbf{N}\mathrm{d}\Omega$ is the system mass matrix; $\mathbf{K} = \int_\Omega (\nabla\mathbf{N})^T\nabla\mathbf{N}\mathrm{d}\Omega$ is the system stiffness matrix; $\mathbf{F} = \int_{\Gamma_N} \mathbf{N}^T v_n\mathrm{d}\Gamma$ is the external excitation force vector; Γ_N is the involved Neumann boundary condition; and v_n is the corresponding prescribed data on the boundary.

4. Dispersion Analysis

The process of solving elastodynamic problems usually contains two parts, namely, the discretization in the space and time domains. Both of these two parts are able to give rise to considerable numerical errors and affect the solution accuracy of the obtained numerical solutions. In this work, the EFEM was employed for the discretization in the space domain, and the standard implicit Bathe time integration technique was used for the discretization in the time domain. The numerical performance of the different methods in addressing the numerical dispersion error is investigated in this section, and the dispersion errors corresponding to the spatial discretization are firstly studied here.

Assuming that the considered transient wave propagation dynamic problem in this work is time-harmonic, namely, the time-dependent field function variable u can be expressed by:

$$u = U(\mathbf{x})e^{j\omega t}, \tag{13}$$

in which $j = \sqrt{-1}$, $U(\mathbf{x})$ is the amplitude distribution of the field function variable u; ω stands for the angular frequency.

Using the above expression, the governing equation in Equation (9) for transient wave propagations can be rewritten as:

$$\nabla^2 u + k^2 u = 0, \tag{14}$$

in which $k = \omega / c$ is the wave number.

Equation (14) is the well-known Helmholtz equation, which is the steady-state form of the governing equation for wave analysis.

Using the constructed field function approximation shown in Equation (5) to discretize Equation (14), we can arrive at the following matrix equation when the additional boundary conditions are not applied:

$$\left(\mathbf{K} - k^2\mathbf{M}\right)\mathbf{U} = 0, \tag{15}$$

In two-dimensional space, the general plane wave solution to Equation (15) is $u = Ae^{jkh(x\cos\theta + y\sin\theta)}$, and the corresponding numerical solution can be expressed by:

$$u = \mathbf{A}e^{jk_h h(x\cos\theta + y\sin\theta)}, \tag{16}$$

in which θ stands for the angle of wave travel; k_h and k denote the numerical and exact wave number, respectively.

In Equation (16), $\mathbf{A}$ is a vector listing the unknown solution coefficients, which are related to the field function amplitudes for each node. For the present EFEM, the structure of vector $\mathbf{A}$ is of the following form [72]:

$$\mathbf{A} = \begin{bmatrix} A_1 & A_2 & \cdots & A_{n_p}, & A_1 & A_2 & \cdots & A_{n_p}, & \cdots \end{bmatrix}, \tag{17}$$

in which n_p is the number of DOFs at one node.

Here, we employed the regular triangular mesh (see Figure 1) to perform the dispersion analysis. By substituting the above expression of the numerical solution into Equation (15), we can obtain:

$$\left[\mathbf{D}_{\text{stiff}} - k^2\mathbf{D}_{\text{mass}}\right]\mathbf{A}_i = 0, \tag{18}$$

in which $\mathbf{A}_i = \begin{bmatrix} A_1 & A_2 & \cdots & A_{n_p} \end{bmatrix}^T$ lists the unknown solution coefficients for node i; $\mathbf{D}_{\text{stiff}}$ and $\mathbf{D}_{\text{mass}}$ are the resultant matrices which can be calculated by:

$$\begin{array}{rl} \mathbf{D}_{\text{stiff}} = & \mathbf{K}_{n,n} + \mathbf{K}_{n,n-1}e^{-jk_h h\cos\theta} + \mathbf{K}_{n,n+1}e^{jk_h h\cos\theta} + \\ & \mathbf{K}_{n,n-2}e^{jk_h h(\cos\theta - \sin\theta)} + \mathbf{K}_{n,n+2}e^{jk_h h(-\cos\theta + \sin\theta)} + \\ & \mathbf{K}_{n,n-3}e^{-jk_h h\sin\theta} + \mathbf{K}_{n,n+3}e^{jk_h h\sin\theta} + \\ & \mathbf{K}_{n,n-4}e^{jk_h h(-\cos\theta - \sin\theta)} + \mathbf{K}_{n,n+4}e^{jk_h h(\cos\theta + \sin\theta)} \end{array}, \tag{19}$$

$$\begin{aligned}\mathbf{D}_{\text{mass}} = &\mathbf{M}_{n,n} + \mathbf{M}_{n,n-1}e^{-jk_h h\cos\theta} + \mathbf{M}_{n,n+1}e^{jk_h h\cos\theta} + \\ &\mathbf{M}_{n,n-2}e^{jk_h h(\cos\theta-\sin\theta)} + \mathbf{M}_{n,n+2}e^{jk_h h(-\cos\theta+\sin\theta)} + \\ &\mathbf{M}_{n,n-3}e^{-jk_h h\sin\theta} + \mathbf{M}_{n,n+3}e^{jk_h h\sin\theta} + \\ &\mathbf{M}_{n,n-4}e^{jk_h h(-\cos\theta-\sin\theta)} + \mathbf{M}_{n,n+4}e^{jk_h h(\cos\theta+\sin\theta)}\end{aligned}, \tag{20}$$

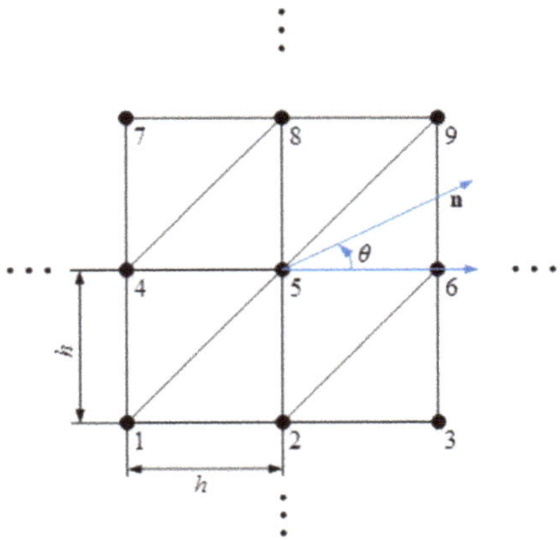

Figure 1. The uniform triangular mesh in the analysis of the numerical dispersion.

If nontrivial solutions to Equation (18) exist, the following relationship is required:

$$\det\left[\mathbf{D}_{\text{stiff}} - k^2\mathbf{D}_{\text{mass}}\right] = 0, \tag{21}$$

From Equations (19) and (20), it is obvious that the numerical wave number k_h is the unique unknown variable in $\mathbf{D}_{\text{stiff}}$ and $\mathbf{D}_{\text{mass}}$; hence, Equation (21) actually offers the relationship between k_h and k. Using Equation (21) for any k_h, the corresponding k can be computed by:

$$k = \text{eig}\sqrt{\frac{\mathbf{D}_{\text{mass}}}{\mathbf{D}_{\text{stiff}}}}, \tag{22}$$

In general, the computed k does not match k_h very well owing to the discretization error in the space domain; in this work, we employed the following indicator to assess the calculated numerical dispersion error from the spatial discretization:

$$\varepsilon = \frac{k}{k_h}, \tag{23}$$

For several varying wave travel angles, the numerical dispersion error solutions versus the nondimensional wave number kh from the various numerical techniques are displayed in Figure 2. It should be noted that all of these numerical dispersion errors were computed using a totally identical mesh pattern. It is easy to observe that the computed numerical dispersion errors from the standard FEM were quite large. More importantly, the numerical dispersion errors will become even larger with the increase in the considered nondimensional wave numbers. A similar trend can also be observed in the EFEM-N3 results; however, the numerical dispersion errors from the EFEM-N3 were clearly smaller than those from the FEM. Although the EFEM-N9 is able to offer much smaller numerical dispersion errors than the FEM, its numerical performance in suppressing the numerical dispersion error is still not sufficiently fine, because considerable dispersion errors can still be found with the nondimensional wave number $kh < \pi$. Among all of the considered numerical techniques, the performance of the EFEM-N6 in suppressing the numerical dispersion from the spatial discretization is the best, because almost no dispersion errors from the discretization in the space domain can be seen for the considered nondimensional wave number. More importantly, the numerical dispersion errors from the EFEM-N6 were very close to zero in all considered wave travel angles, namely, the numerical anisotropy issue also can be largely alleviated by the present EFEM-N6, while this intractable phenomenon can clearly be seen in the results from the other mentioned numerical techniques (i.e., FEM, EFEM-N3 and EFEM-N9). These findings indicate that the present EFEM with the quadric polynomial enrichment functions is basically sufficient to generate adequately small numerical dispersion errors for the wave analysis. Though more accurate solutions, indeed, can be yielded when the higher order of the polynomial bases are employed to create the enrichment functions, more computational expenses are also required. To reduce the computational efforts as much as possible, in this work we only considered the enrichment functions that are created by linear and quadric polynomial bases.

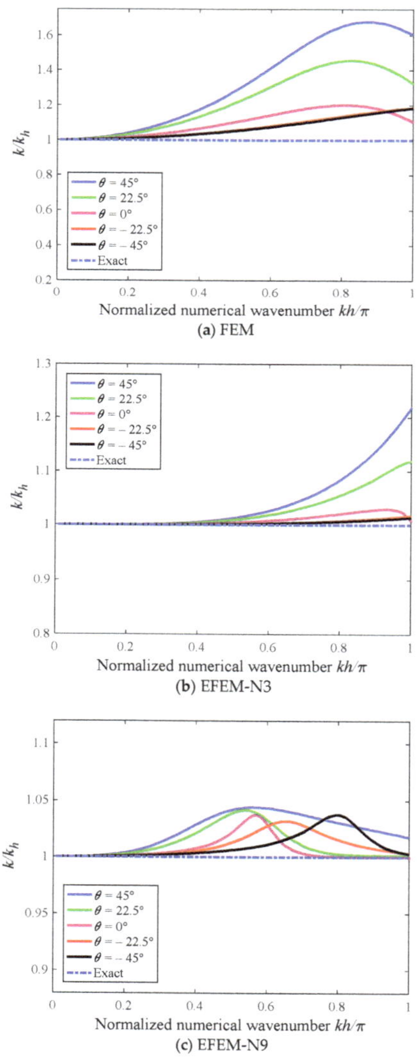

Figure 2. *Cont.*

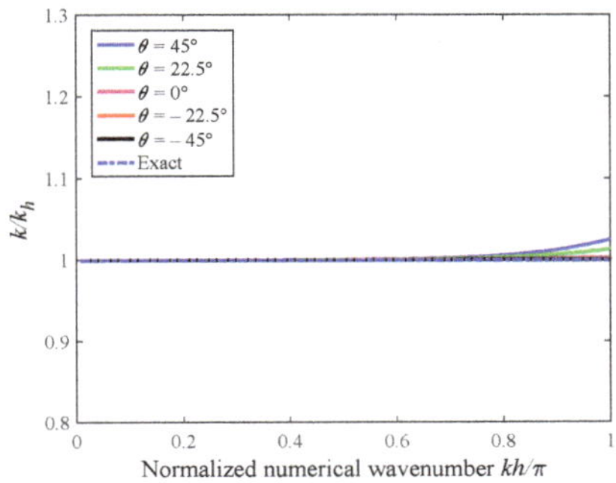

(**d**) EFEM-N6

Figure 2. The numerical dispersion error solutions versus the nondimensional wave number kh from the various numerical techniques.

Apart from the discretization in the space domain, the discretization in the time domain is also a major source that produces numerical errors in solving elastodynamic problems. Here, the numerical error affected by the time integration scheme was also taken into consideration in the dispersion analysis.

Owing to the fact that the recently developed Bathe implicit temporal discretization technique always shows very excellent numerical features in handling linear and nonlinear structural dynamic problems, in this work the standard Bathe was employed for the discretization in the time domain. In the standard Bathe method, the following assumptions are employed:

$$\begin{cases} {}^{t+\Delta t/2}\dot{\mathbf{u}} = {}^{t}\dot{\mathbf{u}} + \frac{\Delta t}{4}\left({}^{t}\ddot{\mathbf{u}} + {}^{t+\Delta t/2}\ddot{\mathbf{u}}\right) \\ {}^{t+\Delta t/2}\mathbf{u} = {}^{t}\mathbf{u} + \frac{\Delta t}{4}\left({}^{t}\dot{\mathbf{u}} + {}^{t+\Delta t/2}\dot{\mathbf{u}}\right) \\ {}^{t+\Delta t}\dot{\mathbf{u}} = \frac{1}{\Delta t}{}^{t}\mathbf{u} - \frac{4}{\Delta t}{}^{t+\Delta t/2}\mathbf{u} + \frac{3}{\Delta t}{}^{t+\Delta t}\mathbf{u} \\ {}^{t+\Delta t}\ddot{\mathbf{u}} = \frac{1}{\Delta t}{}^{t}\dot{\mathbf{u}} - \frac{4}{\Delta t}{}^{t+\Delta t/2}\dot{\mathbf{u}} + \frac{3}{\Delta t}{}^{t+\Delta t}\dot{\mathbf{u}} \end{cases}, \tag{24}$$

Using the assumptions in the above equation to the discretize matrix equation shown in Equation (12) and following the similar steps in References [72–75], the total dispersion error in the elastodynamic analysis can be expressed by:

$$\frac{c_h}{c} = \frac{\omega_h/k_h}{c} = \frac{\omega_h \Delta t}{k_h c \Delta t} = \frac{\omega_h \Delta t}{k_h h\mathrm{CFL}} = \frac{f(\omega \Delta t)}{k_h h\mathrm{CFL}} = \frac{f(kh\mathrm{CFL})}{k_h h\mathrm{CFL}}, \tag{25}$$

in which c stands for the wave speed; the subscript h means that the corresponding variables are from the numerical solutions; Δt denotes the interval of temporal discretization; CFL represents the Courant–Friedrichs–Lewy number, which is defined by CFL = $c\Delta t/h$; $f()$ is a defined function with respect to the parameter $k_h h$CFL.

Using the Taylor series expansion, Equation (25) can be rewritten by:

$$\begin{aligned} \frac{c_h}{c} &= \frac{\omega_h/k_h}{c} = \frac{\omega_h \Delta t}{k_h c \Delta t} = \frac{\omega_h \Delta t}{k_h h\mathrm{CFL}} = \frac{f(kh\mathrm{CFL})}{k_h h\mathrm{CFL}} \\ &= \frac{1}{k_h h\mathrm{CFL}}\left[f(0) + f'(0)(kh\mathrm{CFL}) + \frac{f''(0)}{2!}(kh\mathrm{CFL})^2 + \cdots\right], \\ &= \frac{k}{k_h}\left(1 - \frac{1}{24}(kh\mathrm{CFL})^2 + \frac{61}{17280}(kh\mathrm{CFL})^4 + \cdots\right) \end{aligned} \tag{26}$$

From Equation (25), we also can obtain

$$\frac{c_h}{c} = \frac{\omega_h/k_h}{c} = \frac{\omega_h/k_h}{\omega/k} = \frac{k}{k_h}\frac{\omega_h}{\omega} = \frac{k}{k_h}\frac{T}{T_h}, \tag{27}$$

in which T stands for the period of one considered wave mode.

By comparing Equations (26) and (27), the total numerical error in the elastodynamic analysis can be expressed in the following form:

$$\frac{c_h}{c} = \frac{k}{k_h}\frac{T}{T_h} = \frac{k}{k_h}\underbrace{\left(1 - \frac{1}{24}(kh\text{CFL})^2 + \frac{61}{17280}(kh\text{CFL})^4 + \cdots\right)}_{\text{Temporal dispersion error } T/T_h}, \tag{28}$$

From Equations (25)–(28), it is very interesting to observe that both the discretizations in the space and time domains are able to result in numerical errors in the final numerical solutions for the elastodynamic analysis. The first term in Equation (27) is the defined indicator to assess the spatial discretization error. From the above formulation and analysis, it is seen that the error k/k_h, indeed, mainly comes from the discretization in the space domain, and it is determined by the used field function approximation in the space domain. The second term T/T_h in Equation (27) represents the additional effects from the temporal discretization, and it is closely associated with the employed the time integration scheme. In this work, the standard Bathe method was exploited for the temporal discretization, and it has been proved that T/T_h is actually a monotonic function with respect to the nondimensional temporal discretization interval CFL. Therefore, the total numerical error can be continuously decreased by reducing the used CFL numbers as long as the spatial discretization error k/k_h is adequately small; then, the so-called monotonic convergence property can be reached. From the previous analysis, it is seen that the EFEM-N6 can basically meet this requirement, while the other mentioned numerical techniques (i.e., FEM, EFEM-N3 and EFEM-N9) cannot generate adequately small spatial discretization errors. In the next section, several supporting numerical experiments are conducted to verify that the present EFEM-N6 with the Bathe method, indeed, possesses the important monotonic convergence property with respect to the nondimensional temporal discretization step CFL, while the other numerical approaches do not have this very valuable numerical feature.

5. The Implementation of the EFEM for the Transient Wave Analysis

From the above formulation, we can find that the implementation of the present EFEM is quite similar to the standard FEM in solving transient wave propagations, and the general procedure mainly consists of the following steps:

(1) Perform the required spatial discretization using the standard mesh as in the FEM. In general, the triangular elements and tetrahedron elements are employed for two-dimensional and three-dimensional problems, respectively.

(2) Create the required field function approximation for the considered problem. In creating the numerical approximation, compared to the standard FEM, more unknown coefficients for each node are involved in the local interpolation, and various basis functions can be employed for the local numerical approximation.

(3) Assemble the system mass and stiffness matrices. In this step, the required numerical integration is still performed using the Gauss integration rule. However, the scale of the obtained system matrices will be clearly larger than those from the standard FEM, because more unknowns are involved for each node.

(4) Remove the possible linear dependence of the obtained matrix equation. Note that linear dependent nodal shape functions are possibly employed to construct the required field function approximation; then, the linear dependent matrix equation will be generated. For stable and reliable numerical solutions, extra numerical treatments are required to remove the possible linear dependence of the obtained matrix equation.

(5) Impose the involved boundary conditions and perform the required temporal discretization. Usually, direct time integration techniques are employed to perform the required time integration. This step is almost the same as in the standard FEM.

(6) Solve the finally obtained matrix equation and assess the obtained numerical results; this process is also quite similar as in the standard FEM.

6. Numerical Example

6.1. The Scalar Wave Propagation in a Clamped-Free Elastic Bar

We firstly consider the transient scalar wave propagation in an elastic bar with a length $L = 1$ m and width $b = 0.1$ m. The left end of this elastic bar is free, and the other end is clamped (see Figure 3a). The considered wave travel speed in this bar is $c = 1$ m/s. To solve this problem, the required discretization in the space domain is accomplished by using the uniform triangular mesh with the node interval $h = 0.0125$ m (see Figure 3b). This transient wave propagation problem is excited by using the following initial conditions:

$$u(\mathbf{x}, t = 0) = 0\ \mathrm{m}, \dot{u}(\mathbf{x}, t = 0) = 0\ \mathrm{m/s}, \dot{u}(\mathbf{x}, t > 0) = 1\ \mathrm{m/s},, \tag{29}$$

in which u denotes the considered displacement variable, and the overdot stands for the time derivative.

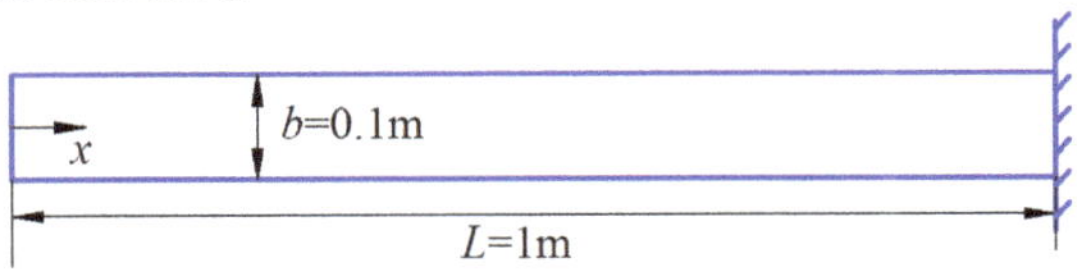

(a)

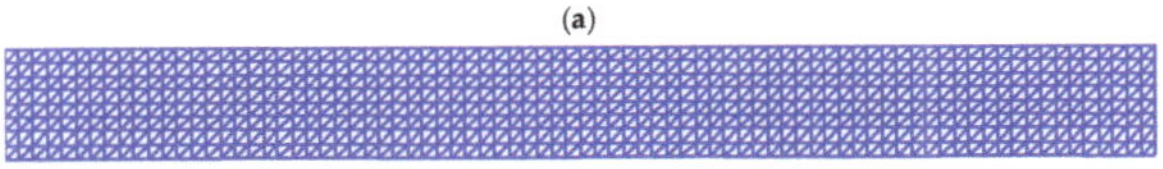

(b)

Figure 3. The description of the scalar wave propagation in a clamped-free elastic bar: (**a**) geometric shape of the elastic bar; (**b**) employed uniform triangular mesh.

The computed velocity distributions of this elastic bar were employed to investigate this simple transient wave propagation problem. For the nondimensional temporal discretization step CFL = 0.1 and the considered time point $t = 0.6$ s, the calculated velocity distributions of this elastic bar from various numerical approaches together with the exact solutions are displayed in Figure 4. It is seen from the figure that the numerical solution from the standard FEM was not sufficiently accurate, and many unwanted peaks can be found in the solutions. In contrast to the standard FEM, the EFEM-N3 and EFEM-N9 are able to generate more accurate solutions despite several relatively small spurious peaks that can still be seen in the solutions. Among all of the considered numerical approaches, the numerical performance of the proposed EFEM-N6 is the best, since the resultant numerical solutions of the velocity distributions agreed very well with the exact solutions, and almost no spurious peaks can be seen in the solutions.

Furthermore, this numerical experiment was studied by exploiting the varying nondimensional time integration steps (CFL = 1, CFL = 0.5, CFL = 0.25 and CFL = 0.1), and the relevant computed velocity distributions are plotted in Figure 5. Here, the abovementioned four different numerical approaches were again employed, and the considered time point was still $t = 0.6$ s. By carefully comparing the computed velocity distributions shown in Figure 5, we can observe that the present EFEM-N6 has the ability to continuously increase the solution accuracy by employing the decreasing nondimensional time integration steps, because the EFEM-N6 solutions will converge to the exact solutions when the employed CFL numbers become smaller. On the contrary, the EFEM-N3, EFEM-N6 and the standard FEM do not have this ability, because the corresponding velocity distributions can become unexpectedly worse when decreasing CFL numbers are utilized for time integration. These observations can be broadly explained by two factors; one factor is that the EFEM-N6 can produce close-to-zero spatial discretization errors, while the corresponding spatial discretization errors from the other three numerical approaches are relatively large (See Figure 2); the other factor is that the additional numerical error from the time integration is actually a monotonic decreasing function of the nondimensional time integration steps. These two factors can ensure that the EFEM-N6 has the monotonic convergence property in the transient wave analysis. From the above analysis, it is demonstrated that the numerical performance of the EFEM-N6 clearly outperforms the other three numerical approaches in solving transient wave propagations.

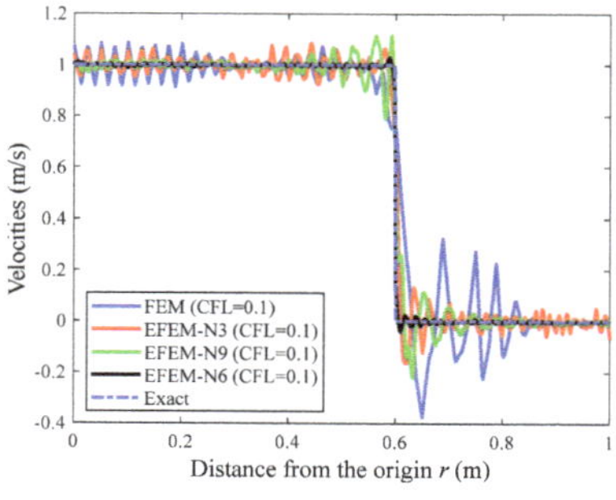

Figure 4. The calculated velocity distributions of this elastic bar from various numerical approaches when the time point t = 0.6 s.

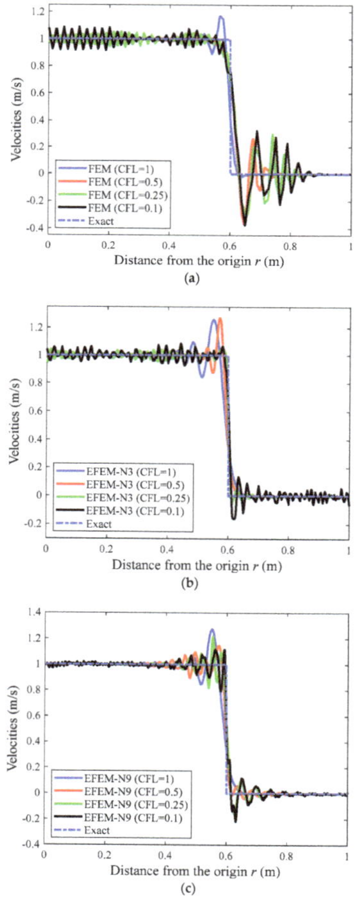

Figure 5. *Cont.*

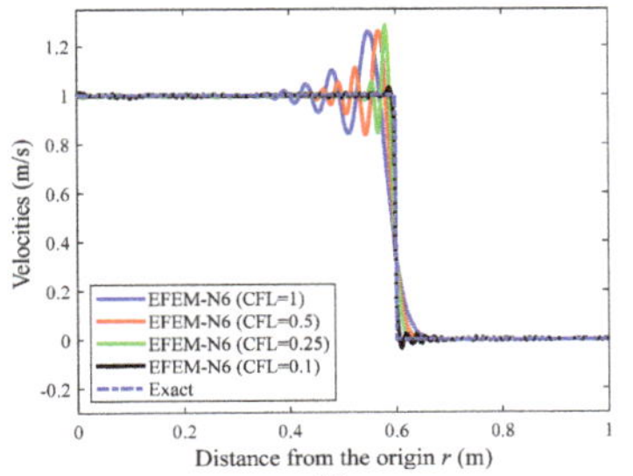

(d)

Figure 5. The velocity distributions of this elastic bar from various numerical approaches using the varying nondimensional time integration steps: (**a**)FEM; (**b**) EFEM-N3; (**c**) EFEM-N9; (**d**) EFEM-N6.

6.2. The Scalar Wave Propagation in a Square Pre-Stressed Membrane

The numerical experiment on scalar wave propagation in a two-dimensional square pre-stressed membrane is investigated in this section. The geometric configuration of the problem domain is sketched in Figure 6, and the wave speed for this numerical experiment was $c = 1$ m/s. We employed a regular mesh pattern with a nodal interval $h = 0.025$ m to discretize the membrane. The point load was at the middle of the square domain, and the excitation load was of the following Ricker wavelet form [72,73]:

$$F_c = 0.5\left[1 - 2\pi^2 f_s^2 (t - t_s)^2\right] \exp\left[-\pi^2 f_s^2 (t - t_s)^2\right], \tag{30}$$

in which $t_s = 0.25$ s and $f_s = 5$ Hz stand for the time and frequency parameters.

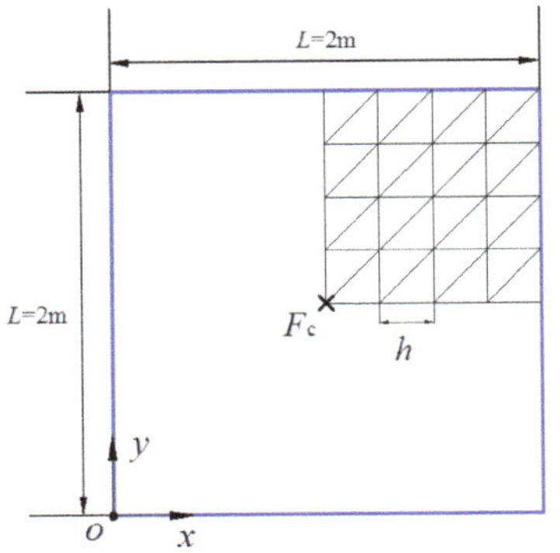

Figure 6. The geometric configuration and spatial discretization pattern of the square pre-stressed membrane.

Considering the symmetry feature of this numerical experiment, in practical computation processes, only the partial problem domain is needed to model (see Figure 6). Here, the transient displacement responses from the different numerical techniques were examined. When the nondimensional time step CFL = 0.1 and the time point $t = 0.9$ s were chosen, the displacement responses along two disparate angles ($\theta = 0°$ and $\theta = 45°$) are depicted in Figure 7. Note that the exact solution to this problem is available; hence, it is also plotted in the figures. It can be observed that the amount of numerical error in the FEM solutions is quite large. Though the EFEM-N3 and EFEM-N9, indeed, can suppress the numerical error to some degree, the EFEM-N6 solutions are the most accurate. These findings indicate that the use of quadric polynomials as an enrichment function is more effective than the linear polynomial and first order of the trigonometric function to control the amount of numerical error for the wave analysis.

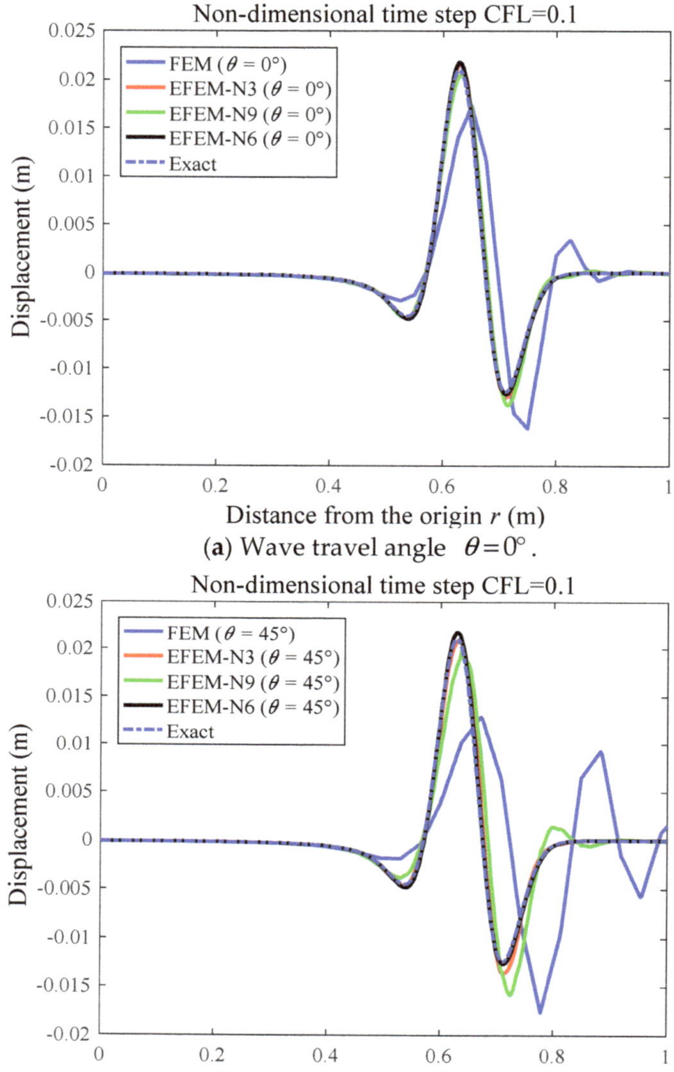

Figure 7. The displacement responses of the square membrane along two disparate angles of wave travel.

Furthermore, the numerical analysis of the problem was performed by considering the varying angles, and the related displacement responses at the time point t = 0.9 s from various methods are displayed in Figure 8. It is clear that the varying angles can visibly affect the accuracy of the solutions from FEM, EFEM-N3 and EFEM-N9, namely, the so-called numerical anisotropy issue can be obviously seen, while the EFEM-N6 solutions are almost insensitive to the angles, and very reliable solutions can still be yielded for all considered angles.

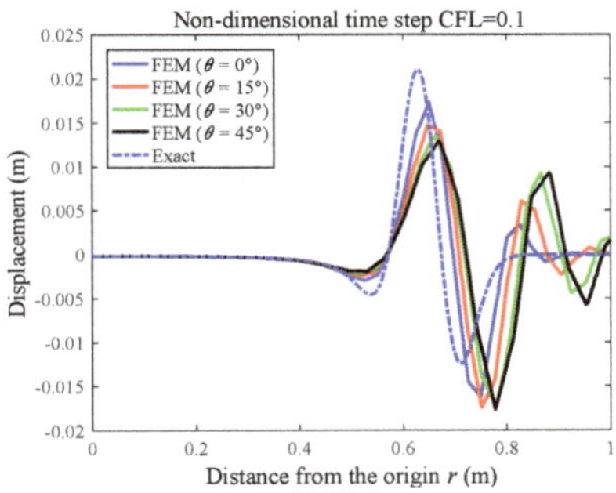

(**a**) FEM.

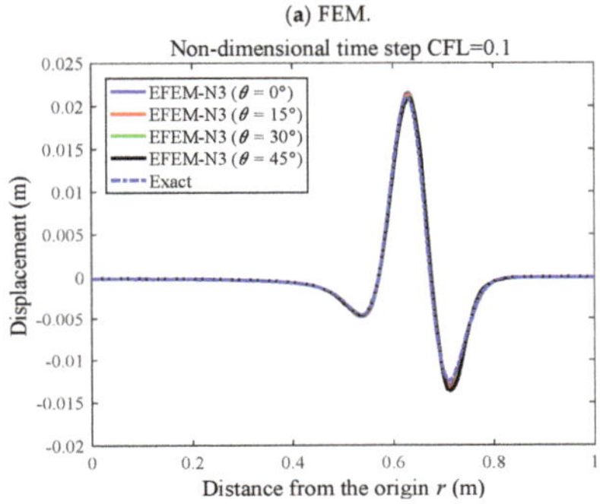

(**b**) EFEM-N3.

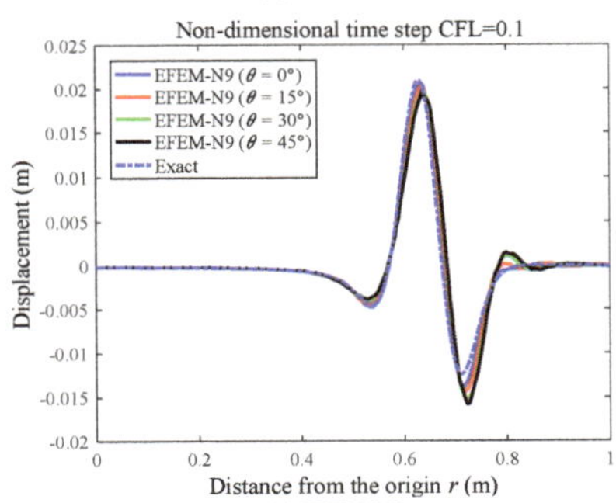

(**c**) EFEM-N9.

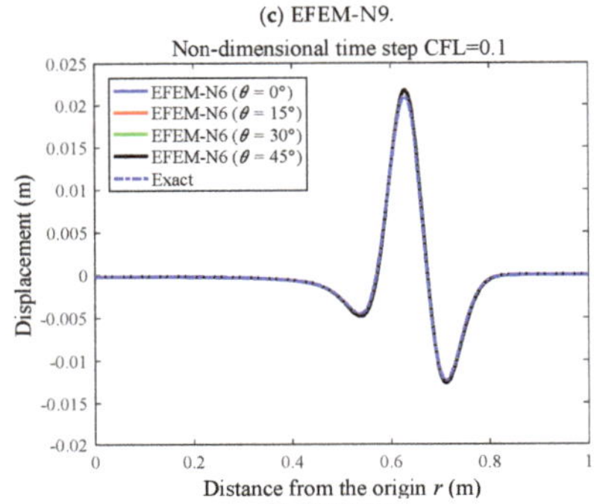

(**d**) EFEM-N6.

Figure 8. The displacement responses of the square membrane from various numerical techniques by varying the considered angles of wave travel.

In more detail, several varying nondimensional time step CFL numbers were considered here to perform an overall analysis of this numerical experiment. Similar to the previous discussion, for two disparate angles ($\theta = 0^\circ$ and $\theta = 45^\circ$), the displacement responses at the time point $t = 0.9$ s from the various methods are given in Figures 9–12. These figures show that the FEM, EFEM-N3 and EFEM-N9 always failed to continuously increase the solution quality by decreasing the employed CFL numbers, namely, the monotonic convergence property for the transient wave analysis cannot be achieved. On the contrary, it is very interesting to find that the EFEM-N6 basically has the monotonic convergence property, and the corresponding numerical solutions will become more accurate when the employed CFL number becomes smaller. A possible cause for these observations is that the EFEM-N6 can produce adequately small spatial dispersion errors, while the errors from other methods are relatively large, which have been seen in the dispersion analysis. With this good numerical feature, the present EFEM-N6 obviously has stronger abilities than the other numerical techniques in handling very complicated wave propagations in practice.

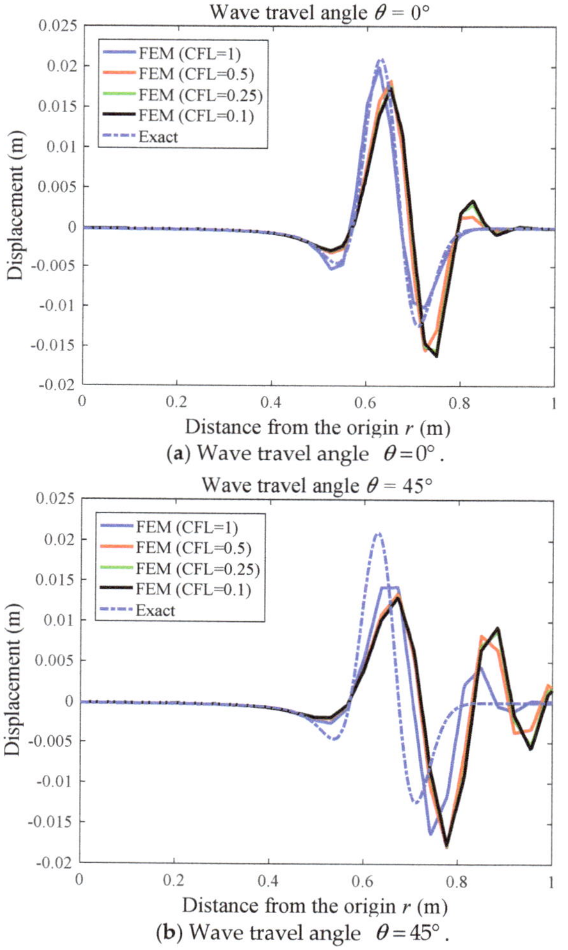

(**a**) Wave travel angle $\theta = 0^\circ$.

(**b**) Wave travel angle $\theta = 45^\circ$.

Figure 9. The displacement responses of the square membrane from the FEM by varying the employed nondimensional temporal discretization interval.

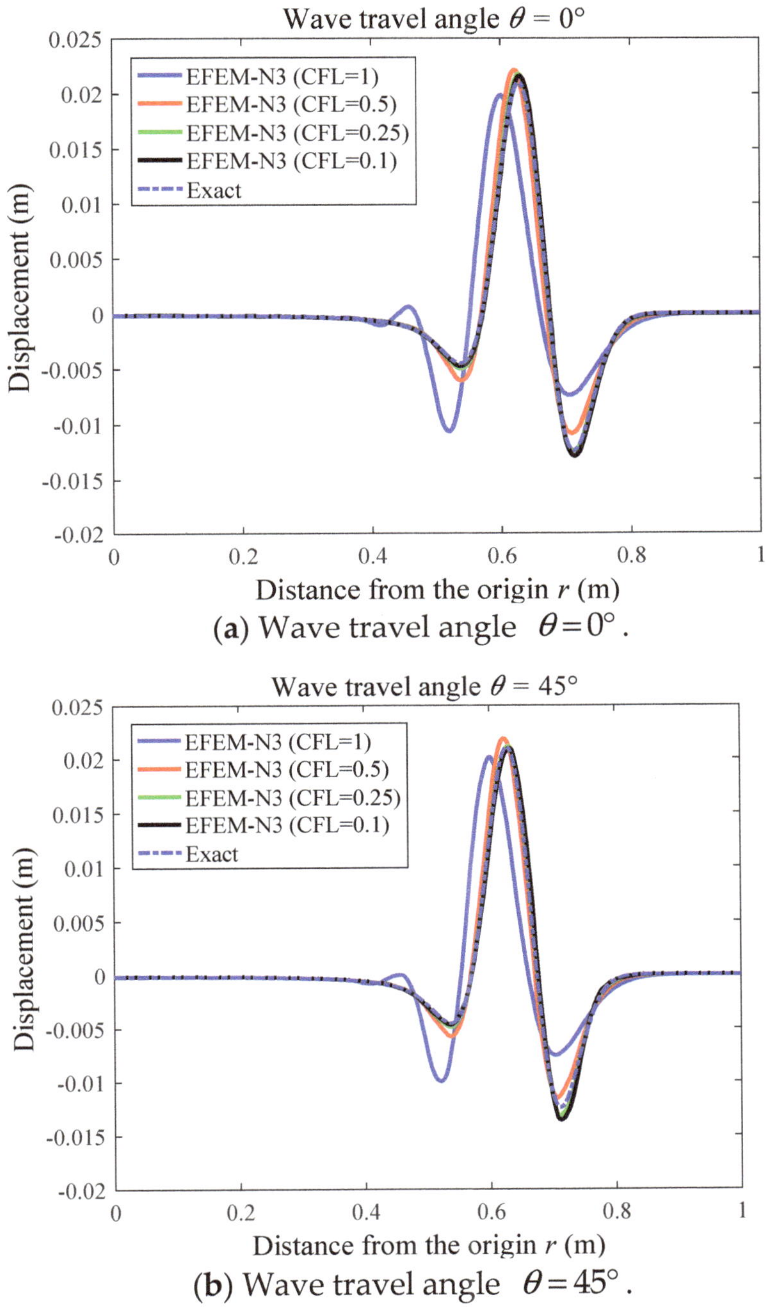

Figure 10. The displacement responses of the square membrane from the EFEM-N3 by varying the employed nondimensional temporal discretization interval.

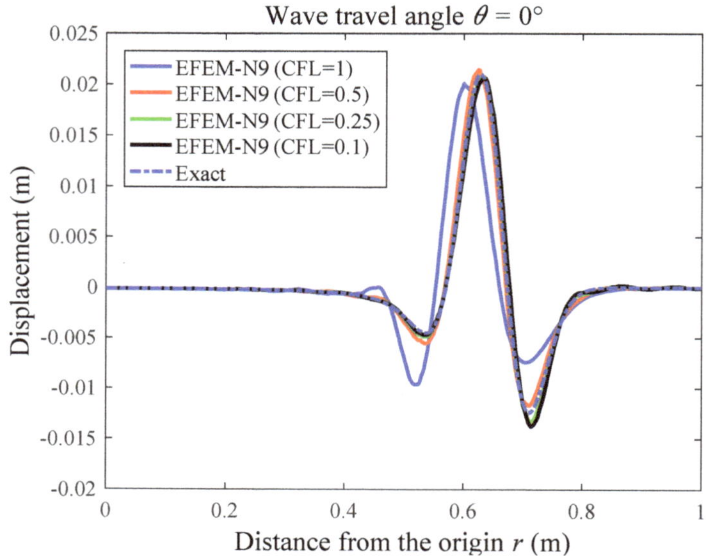

(**a**) Wave travel angle $\theta = 0^\circ$.

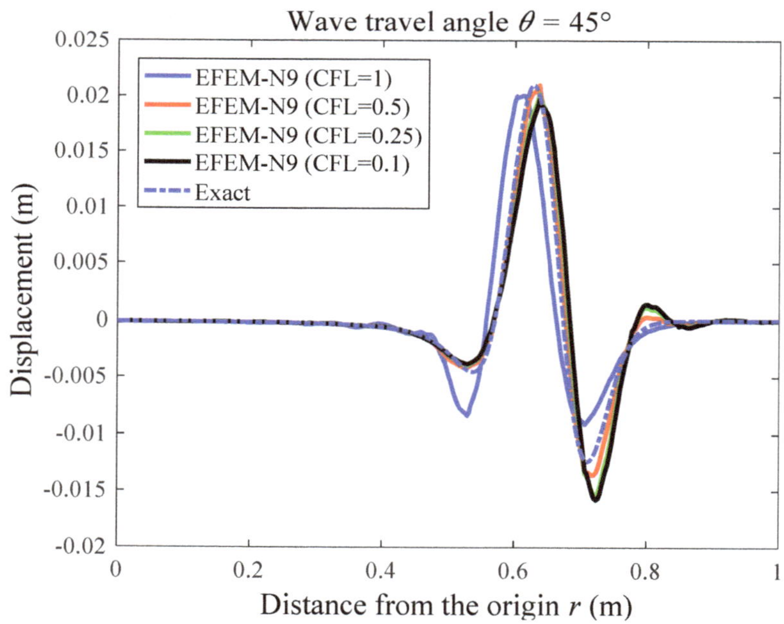

(**b**) Wave travel angle $\theta = 45^\circ$.

Figure 11. The displacement responses of the square membrane from the EFEM-N9 by varying the employed nondimensional temporal discretization interval.

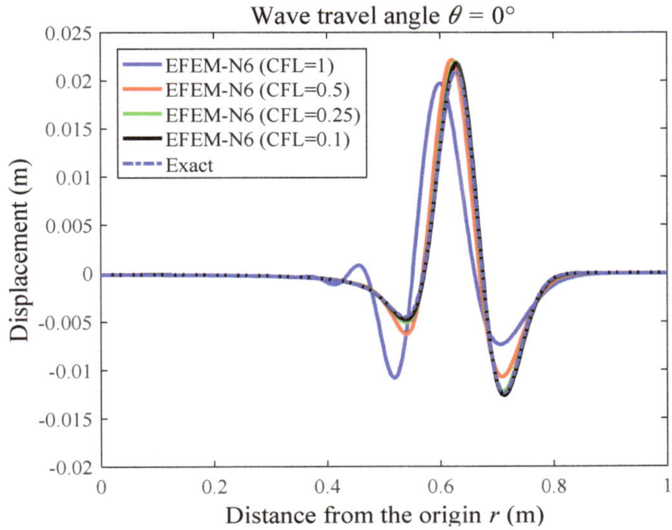

(**a**) Wave travel angle $\theta = 0°$.

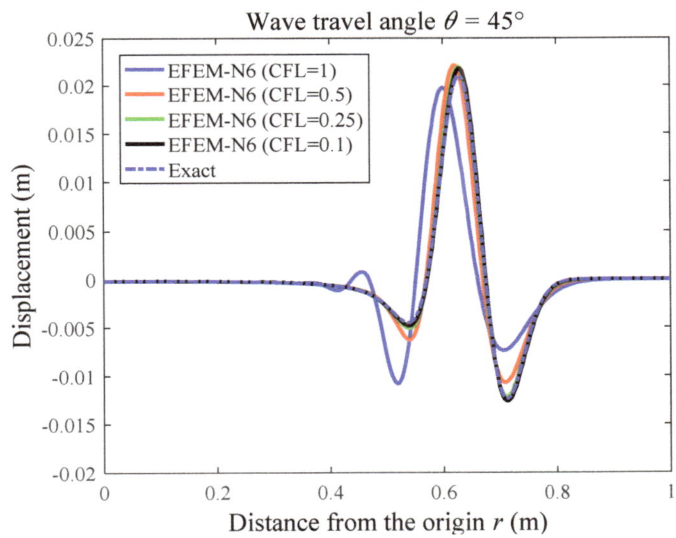

(**b**) Wave travel angle $\theta = 45°$.

Figure 12. The displacement responses of the square membrane from the EFEM-N6 by varying the employed nondimensional temporal discretization interval.

6.3. The Scalar Wave Propagation in a Membrane with Holes

In the last numerical experiment, we still consider the scalar wave propagation with a wave speed $c = 1$ m/s in a square pre-stressed membrane, while in this case the membrane had several evenly placed holes (see Figure 13). Similar to the previous numerical experiment, only the partial problem domain was needed to model this problem, owing to the symmetry feature. The triangular mesh pattern with an average nodal interval $h = 0.02$ m was employed here. The point load at the middle of this membrane was still a Ricker wavelet with an amplitude A = 0.4 N, time parameter t_s = 0.1 s and frequency parameter f_s = 10 Hz.

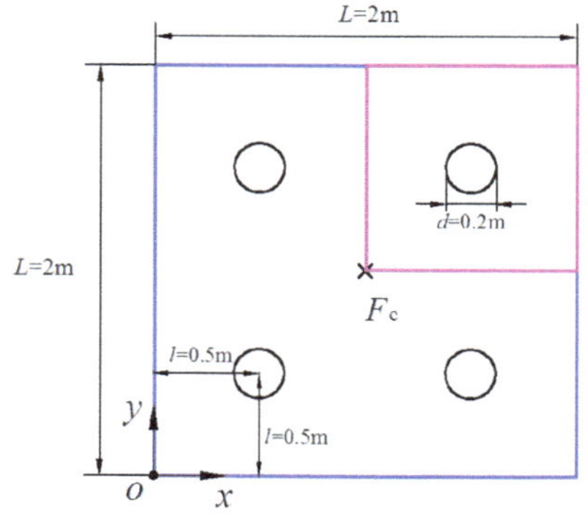

Figure 13. The square membrane with a number of evenly placed holes.

With a wave travel angle $\theta = 30°$, nondimensional temporal discretization interval CFL = 0.1 and time point t = 1 s, Figure 14 displays the displacement distribution responses using various numerical techniques. With the aim to examine the accuracy of the obtained solutions, the reference solution from the commercial software package ABAQUS with very refined mesh is also presented here to investigate this numerical experiment. Figure 14 shows very good agreements of the EFEM-N6 solutions with the reference ones, while the other three methods clearly failed to yield very accurate solutions.

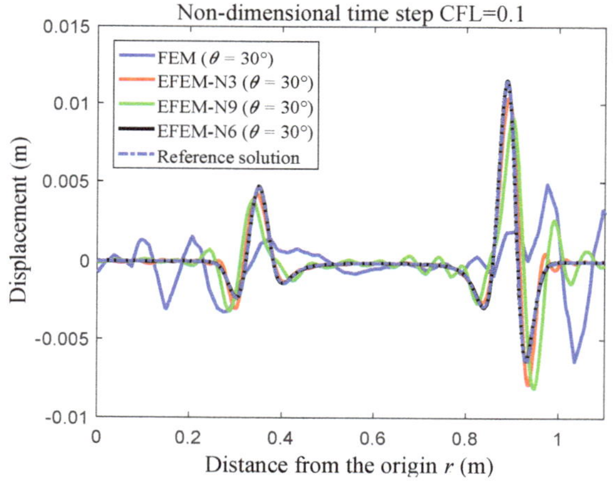

Figure 14. The displacement distribution responses of the membrane with holes from various numerical techniques when the considered time point t = 1 s.

Additionally, we also perform the numerical analysis of this wave problem by employing the varying nondimensional temporal discretization intervals and the related displacement distribution responses are shown in Figure 15. Here the wave travel angle $\theta = 30°$. It is again confirmed from these figures that the proposed EFEM-N6 can yield monotonic convergence solutions when the CFL number trends to zero, while the other three methods obviously did not exhibit this good numerical feature. As discussed and analyzed in the previous sections, this good numerical feature can be obtained because the EFEM-N6 can yield sufficiently small numerical dispersion errors in the space domain discretization, while the related errors from the other methods were relatively large.

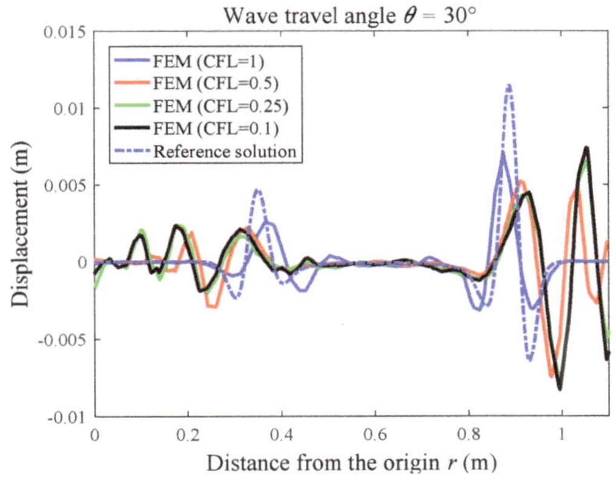

(**a**) FEM.

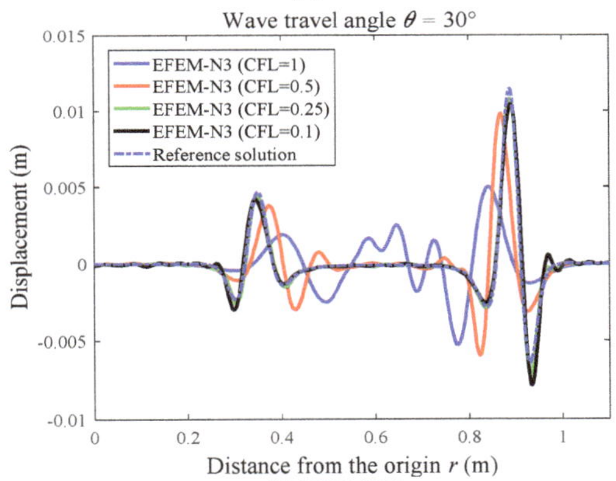

(**b**) EFEM-N3.

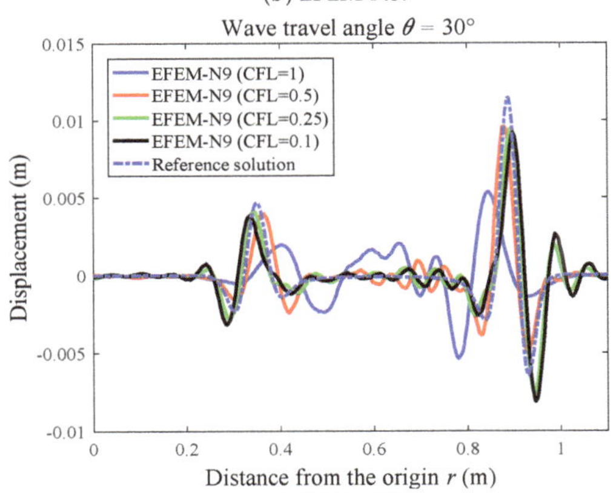

(**c**) EFEM-N9.

Figure 15. *Cont.*

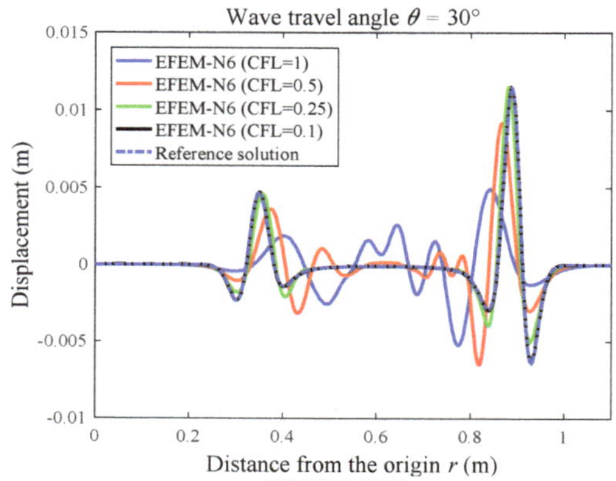

(**d**) EFEM-N6.

Figure 15. The displacement responses of the square membrane with holes from various methods by varying the employed nondimensional temporal discretization interval.

6.4. Study on the Computational Cost

From the previous three numerical experiments, we can clearly obtain that the proposed EFEM-N6 showed much more excellent numerical performance than the other three mentioned numerical approaches (i.e., FEM, EFEM-N3 and EFEM-N9) for the analysis of transient wave propagationsm and the close-to-exact numerical solutions can be generated by utilizing the decreasing time integration steps. However, the detailed computational cost of the different numerical approaches in solving the transient wave propagations has still not been taken into consideration so far. In this section, the computational cost and the computational efficiency of all of the considered numerical approaches is investigated in great detail. To comprehensively and fairly compare the obtained results, the identical meshes and the following relative error norm was used to measure the accuracy of the obtained numerical solutions.

$$e_r = \sqrt{\frac{\int_V (u_e - u_h)^2 \mathrm{d}V}{\int_V {u_e}^2 \mathrm{d}V}}, \tag{31}$$

in which V denotes the involved total problem domain; u_e and u_h represent the exact and numerical solutions, respectively.

For a series of varying nondimensional time integration steps (CFL = 1, CFL = 0.5, CFL = 0.25 and CFL = 0.1), the detailed computational cost, which is represented by the CPU time (s) and the relative error results from the different numerical approaches in solving the previous two numerical experiments with exact solutions are given in Tables 1 and 2. In this work, all the numerical computations were performed using a laptop with a single core Intel 2.2 GHz CPU and 2 GB RAM. From the tables, the following valuable points can be observed:

(1) When the identical mesh patterns were employed, the number of required degree of freedoms (DOFs) and nonzero entities in the system matrices from the standard FEM were much larger than that of the proposed EFEM. This was because more nodal unknowns for each node were employed to construct the required field function approximation in the EFEM.

(2) Compared to the standard FEM, in the transient wave analysis the required computational cost for the EFEM was much more expensive. As a result, the computational efficiency of the EFEM was clearly lower than the standard FEM.

(3) For the three considered EFEMs (i.e., EFEM-N3, EFEM-N6 and EFEM-N9), more additional nodal unknowns were involved for each node, and the obtained EFEM will be

more numerically expensive, leading to the lower computation efficiency in the transient wave analysis.

(4) In solving transient wave propagations using numerical approaches, the total required computational cost mainly consisted of two different parts, namely, the CPU time for the spatial and temporal discretizations, respectively. Additionally, it was also clear that the required computational cost for the temporal discretization was much more expensive than that for the spatial discretization.

(5) When the standard FEM was employed for the transient wave analysis, the relative numerical error did not become lower for the smaller used nondimensional time integration steps. As discussed in the previous text, this was because the standard FEM cannot provide sufficiently low spatial discretization errors. Likewise, very similar observations can also be found when the EFEM-N3 and EFEM-N9 were employed.

(6) Among all of the considered four different numerical approaches, the numerical performance of the EFEM-N6 was quite ideal, because the obtained numerical solution accuracy can be broadly improved by using decreasing nondimensional time integration steps. This also makes the EFEM-N6 specifically suitable for the analysis of complex transient wave propagation problems.

Table 1. Comparisons of the computational cost and computational efficiency of the different numerical approaches in solving the scalar wave propagation in a clamped-free elastic bar.

Methods	Number of DOFs	Nonzero Entities in the System Matrices	CPU Time for Spatial Discretization (s)	Nondimensional Time Steps	CPU Time for Temporal Discretization (s)	Total CPU Time (s)	Total Numerical Error (%)
FEM-T3	729	3465	0.66	CFL = 1	2.63	3.29	7.16
				CFL = 0.5	5.36	6.02	11.51
				CFL = 0.25	9.52	10.18	12.69
				CFL = 0.1	13.32	13.98	13.14
EFEM-N3	2187	41411	2.64	CFL = 1	9.75	12.39	11.14
				CFL = 0.5	16.57	19.21	8.28
				CFL = 0.25	29.03	31.67	5.09
				CFL = 0.1	54.35	56.99	7.12
EFEM-N9	6561	382975	7.65	CFL = 1	19.21	26.86	11.01
				CFL = 0.5	34.21	41.86	6.53
				CFL = 0.25	54.38	62.03	6.68
				CFL = 0.1	95.48	103.13	7.32
EFEM-N6	4374	169496	4.16	CFL = 1	13.26	17.42	11.16
				CFL = 0.5	22.01	26.17	8.45
				CFL = 0.25	36.13	40.29	5.43
				CFL = 0.1	65.93	70.09	2.01

Table 2. Comparisons of the computational cost and computational efficiency of different numerical approaches in solving the scalar wave propagation in a square pre-stressed membrane.

Methods	Number of DOFs	Nonzero Entities in the System Matrices	CPU Time for Spatial Discretization (s)	Nondimensional Time Steps	CPU Time for Temporal Discretization (s)	Total CPU Time (s)	Total Numerical Error (%)
FEM-T3	1681	8241	1.49	CFL = 1	7.03	8.52	52.33
				CFL = 0.5	10.55	12.04	87.73
				CFL = 0.25	20.19	21.68	95.38
				CFL = 0.1	37.84	39.33	97.31
EFEM-N3	5043	99751	11.68	CFL = 1	13.77	25.45	59.39
				CFL = 0.5	24.23	35.91	39.89
				CFL = 0.25	43.62	55.3	11.95
				CFL = 0.1	82.19	93.87	19.69
EFEM-N9	15129	923,343	37.89	CFL = 1	41.28	79.17	51.29
				CFL = 0.5	81.62	119.51	13.82
				CFL = 0.25	147.82	185.71	19.54
				CFL = 0.1	347.38	385.27	22.76

Table 2. *Cont.*

Methods	Number of DOFs	Nonzero Entities in the System Matrices	CPU Time for Spatial Discretization (s)	Nondimensional Time Steps	CPU Time for Temporal Discretization (s)	Total CPU Time (s)	Total Numerical Error (%)
EFEM-N6	10086	408614	29.62	CFL = 1	27.16	56.78	60.85
				CFL = 0.5	47.71	77.33	22.57
				CFL = 0.25	89.93	119.55	9.41
				CFL = 0.1	208.58	238.2	3.26

7. Conclusions

The enriched FEM (EFEM) with disparate types of enrichment functions was presented to investigate elastodynamic problems. Since the original linear approximation space in the traditional FEM can be effectively enriched by local enrichment functions, more accurate and reliable numerical solutions can be yielded. From the analysis of the numerical dispersion and several representative numerical experiments, we can see that the EFEM enriched by quadric polynomial enrichment functions (EFEM-N6) can ensure that the amount of numerical dispersion errors from the discretization in the space domain can be suppressed to a sufficiently small level, while the corresponding errors are relatively large when other types of enrichment functions are employed. Moreover, the proposed EFEM-N6 can effectively overcome the numerical anisotropy issue in the wave analysis, because the solutions generated by the EFEM-N6 were almost totally identical, even though varying angles of wave travel were considered.

From the viewpoint of a practical engineering application, the numerical experiments in this work also show that the monotonic convergence property with respect to the nondimensional time integration step CFL can be basically realized by the proposed EFEM-N6; hence, the obtained numerical solution accuracy can be continuously increased by decreasing the employed nondimensional time integration steps, while the other mentioned numerical techniques do not have this good numerical feature. It is exactly this important numerical property that makes the proposed EFEM-N6 specifically suitable to handle a wide range of complicated elastodynamic problems.

Author Contributions: Conceptualization, X.D. and Y.C.; methodology, Y.C.; software, S.D.; validation, X.D. and Y.Y.; formal analysis, X.D.; investigation, X.D.; resources, Y.Y.; data curation, X.D.; writing—original draft preparation, X.D.; writing—review and editing, X.D.; visualization, X.D.; supervision, Y.C.; funding acquisition, Y.C. All authors have read and agreed to the published version of the manuscript.

Funding: This research was funded by the State Key Laboratory of Ocean Engineering (Shanghai Jiao Tong University) (Grant No. GKZD010081) and the Open Fund of Key Laboratory of High Performance Ship Technology (Wuhan University of Technology), Ministry of Education (Grant No. gxnc21112701).

Data Availability Statement: Thee data used to support the findings of this study are available from the corresponding author upon request.

Acknowledgments: We thank Gui for the helpful suggestions for revising the present paper.

Conflicts of Interest: The authors declare no conflict of interest.

References

1. Bathe, K.J. *Finite Element Procedures*, 2nd ed.; Prentice Hall: Watertown, MA, USA, 2014.
2. Zienkiewicz, O.C.; Taylor, R.L. *The Finite Element Method for Solid and Structural Mechanics*; Elsevier: Amsterdam, The Netherlands, 2005.
3. Liu, M.Y.; Gao, G.J.; Zhu, H.F.; Jiang, C. A cell-based smoothed finite element method stabilized by implicit SUPG/SPGP/Fractional step method for incompressible flow. *Eng. Anal. Bound. Elem.* **2021**, *124*, 194–210. [CrossRef]
4. Chai, Y.B.; Gong, Z.X.; Li, W.; Li, T.Y.; Zhang, Q.F.; Zou, Z.H.; Sun, Y.B. Application of smoothed finite element method to two dimensional exterior problems of acoustic radiation. *Int. J. Comput. Methods* **2018**, *15*, 1850029. [CrossRef]
5. Liu, M.Y.; Gao, G.J.; Zhu, H.F.; Jiang, C.; Liu, G.R. A cell-based smoothed finite element method (CS-FEM) for three-dimensional incompressible laminar flows using mixed wedge-hexahedral element. *Eng. Anal. Bound. Elem.* **2021**, *133*, 269–285. [CrossRef]

6. Wang, T.T.; Zhou, G.; Jiang, C.; Shi, F.C.; Tian, X.D.; Gao, G.J. A coupled cell-based smoothed finite element method and discrete phase model for incompressible laminar flow with dilute solid particles. *Eng. Anal. Bound. Elem.* **2022**, *143*, 190–206. [CrossRef]
7. Li, W.; Gong, Z.X.; Chai, Y.B.; Cheng, C.; Li, T.Y.; Zhang, Q.F.; Wang, M.S. Hybrid gradient smoothing technique with discrete shear gap method for shell structures. *Comput. Math. Appl.* **2017**, *74*, 1826–1855. [CrossRef]
8. Chai, Y.B.; Li, W.; Gong, Z.X.; Li, T.Y. Hybrid smoothed finite element method for two-dimensional underwater acoustic scattering problems. *Ocean Eng.* **2016**, *116*, 129–141. [CrossRef]
9. Chai, Y.B.; Li, W.; Gong, Z.X.; Li, T.Y. Hybrid smoothed finite element method for two dimensional acoustic radiation problems. *Appl. Acoust.* **2016**, *103*, 90–101. [CrossRef]
10. Chai, Y.B.; You, X.Y.; Li, W.; Huang, Y.; Yue, Z.J.; Wang, M.S. Application of the edge-based gradient smoothing technique toacoustic radiation and acoustic scattering from rigid and elastic structures in two dimensions. *Comput. Struct.* **2018**, *203*, 43–58. [CrossRef]
11. Li, W.; Chai, Y.B.; Lei, M.; Li, T.Y. Numerical investigation of the edge-based gradient smoothing technique for exterior Helmholtz equation in two dimensions. *Comput. Struct.* **2017**, *182*, 149–164. [CrossRef]
12. Zheng, Z.Y.; Li, X.L. Theoretical analysis of the generalized finite difference method. *Comput. Math. Appl.* **2022**, *120*, 1–14. [CrossRef]
13. Xi, Q.; Fu, Z.J.; Li, Y.; Huang, H. A hybrid GFDM–SBM solver for acoustic radiation and propagation of thin plate structure under shallow sea environment. *J. Theor. Comput. Acous.* **2020**, *28*, 2050008. [CrossRef]
14. Ju, B.R.; Qu, W.Z. Three-dimensional application of the meshless generalized finite difference method for solving the extended Fisher–Kolmogorov equation. *Appl. Math. Lett.* **2023**, *136*, 108458. [CrossRef]
15. Qu, W.Z.; He, H. A GFDM with supplementary nodes for thin elastic plate bending analysis under dynamic loading. *Appl. Math. Lett.* **2022**, *124*, 107664. [CrossRef]
16. Qu, W.Z.; Gao, H.W.; Gu, Y. Integrating Krylov deferred correction and generalized finite difference methods for dynamic simulations of wave propagation phenomena in long-time intervals. *Adv. Appl. Math. Mech.* **2021**, *13*, 1398–1417.
17. Fu, Z.J.; Xie, Z.Y.; Ji, S.Y.; Tsai, C.C.; Li, A.L. Meshless generalized finite difference method for water wave interactions with multiple-bottom-seated-cylinder-array structures. *Ocean Eng.* **2020**, *195*, 106736. [CrossRef]
18. Komatitsch, D.; Barnes, C.; Tromp, J. Simulation of anisotropic wave propagation based upon a spectral element method. *Geophysics* **2000**, *65*, 1251–1260. [CrossRef]
19. Seriani, G.; Oliveira, S.P. Dispersion analysis of spectral element methods for elastic wave propagation. *Wave Motion* **2008**, *45*, 729–744. [CrossRef]
20. Li, J.P.; Fu, Z.J.; Gu, Y.; Qin, Q.H. Recent advances and emerging applications of the singular boundary method for large-scale and high-frequency computational acoustics. *Adv. Appl. Math. Mech.* **2022**, *14*, 315–343. [CrossRef]
21. Gu, Y.; Lei, J. Fracture mechanics analysis of two-dimensional cracked thin structures (from micro- to nano-scales) by an efficient boundary element analysis. *Results Math.* **2021**, *11*, 100172. [CrossRef]
22. Li, J.P.; Gu, Y.; Qin, Q.H.; Zhang, L. The rapid assessment for three-dimensional potential model of large-scale particle system by a modified multilevel fast multipole algorithm. *Comput. Math. Appl.* **2021**, *89*, 127–138. [CrossRef]
23. Chen, Z.; Wang, F. Localized Method of Fundamental Solutions for Acoustic Analysis Inside a Car Cavity with Sound-Absorbing Material. *Adv. Appl. Math. Mech.* **2022**, *15*, 182–201. [CrossRef]
24. Li, J.P.; Zhang, L.; Qin, Q.H. A regularized fast multipole method of moments for rapid calculation of three-dimensional time-harmonic electromagnetic scattering from complex targets. *Eng. Anal. Bound. Elem.* **2022**, *142*, 28–38. [CrossRef]
25. Gu, Y.; Fan, C.M.; Fu, Z.J. Localized method of fundamental solutions for three-dimensional elasticity problems: Theory. *Adv. Appl. Math. Mech.* **2021**, *13*, 1520–1534.
26. Liu, C.S.; Qiu, L.; Lin, J. Simulating thin plate bending problems by a family of two-parameter homogenization functions. *Appl. Math. Model.* **2020**, *79*, 284–299. [CrossRef]
27. Wei, X.; Luo, W. 2.5D singular boundary method for acoustic wave propagation. *App. Math. Lett.* **2021**, *112*, 106760. [CrossRef]
28. Wei, X.; Rao, C.; Chen, S.; Luo, W. Numerical simulation of anti-plane wave propagation in heterogeneous media. *App. Math. Lett.* **2023**, *135*, 108436. [CrossRef]
29. Fu, Z.J.; Xi, Q.; Li, Y.; Huang, H.; Rabczuk, T. Hybrid FEM–SBM solver for structural vibration induced underwater acoustic radiation in shallow marine environment. *Comput. Methods Appl. Mech. Eng.* **2020**, *369*, 113236. [CrossRef]
30. Cheng, S.F.; Wang, F.J.; Wu, G.Z.; Zhang, C.X. Semi-analytical and boundary-type meshless method with adjoint variable formulation for acoustic design sensitivity analysis. *Appl. Math. Lett.* **2022**, *131*, 108068. [CrossRef]
31. Li, J.P.; Zhang, L. High-precision calculation of electromagnetic scattering by the Burton-Miller type regularized method of moments. *Eng. Anal. Bound. Elem.* **2021**, *133*, 177–184. [CrossRef]
32. Cheng, S.; Wang, F.J.; Li, P.W.; Qu, W. Singular boundary method for 2D and 3D acoustic design sensitivity analysis. *Comput. Math. Appl.* **2022**, *119*, 371–386. [CrossRef]
33. Chen, Z.; Sun, L. A boundary meshless method for dynamic coupled thermoelasticity problems. *App. Math. Lett.* **2022**, *134*, 108305. [CrossRef]
34. Liu, G.R. *Mesh Free Methods: Moving beyond the Finite Element Method*; CRC Press: Boca Raton, FL, USA, 2009.
35. Li, X.; Li, S. A finite point method for the fractional cable equation using meshless smoothed gradients. *Eng. Anal. Bound. Elem.* **2022**, *134*, 453–465. [CrossRef]

36. Lin, J. Simulation of 2D and 3D inverse source problems of nonlinear time-fractional wave equation by the meshless homogenization function method. *Eng. Comput.* **2022**, *38*, 3599–3608. [CrossRef]
37. Lin, J.; Bai, J.; Reutskiy, S.; Lu, J. A novel RBF-based meshless method for solving time-fractional transport equations in 2D and 3D arbitrary domains. *Eng. Comput.* **2022**. [CrossRef]
38. Lin, J.; Zhang, Y.H.; Reutskiy, S.; Feng, W. A novel meshless space-time backward substitution method and its application to nonhomogeneous advection-diffusion problems. *Appl. Math. Comput.* **2021**, *398*, 125964. [CrossRef]
39. Wang, C.; Wang, F.J.; Gong, Y.P. Analysis of 2D heat conduction in nonlinear functionally graded materials using a local semi-analytical meshless method. *AIMS Math.* **2021**, *6*, 12599–12618. [CrossRef]
40. Gu, Y.; Sun, H.G. A meshless method for solving three-dimensional time fractional diffusion equation with variable-order derivatives. *Appl. Math. Model.* **2020**, *78*, 539–549. [CrossRef]
41. Li, X.; Li, S. A fast element-free Galerkin method for the fractional diffusion-wave equation. *App. Math. Lett.* **2021**, *122*, 107529. [CrossRef]
42. Li, X.; Li, S. A linearized element-free Galerkin method for the complex Ginzburg–Landau equation. *Comput. Math. Appl.* **2021**, *90*, 135–147. [CrossRef]
43. Atluri, S.N.; Kim, H.G.; Cho, J.Y. Critical assessment of the truly meshless local PetrovGalerkin (MLPG), and local boundary integral equation (LBIE) methods. *Comput. Mech.* **1999**, *24*, 348–372. [CrossRef]
44. Liu, W.K.; Jun, S.; Zhang, Y.F. Reproducing kernel particle methods. *Int. J. Numer. Methods Fluids* **1995**, *20*, 1081–1106. [CrossRef]
45. Qu, J.; Dang, S.N.; Li, Y.C.; Chai, Y.B. Analysis of the interior acoustic wave propagation problems using the modified radial point interpolation method (M-RPIM). *Eng. Anal. Bound. Elem.* **2022**, *138*, 339–368. [CrossRef]
46. Gui, Q.; Zhang, Y.; Chai, Y.B.; You, X.Y.; Li, W. Dispersion error reduction for interior acoustic problems using the radial point interpolation meshless method with plane wave enrichment functions. *Eng. Anal. Bound. Elem.* **2022**, *143*, 428–441. [CrossRef]
47. Fu, Z.J.; Tang, Z.C.; Xi, Q.; Liu, Q.G.; Gu, Y.; Wang, F.J. Localized collocation schemes and their applications. *Acta. Mech. Sin.* **2022**, *38*, 422167. [CrossRef]
48. Fu, Z.J.; Yang, L.W.; Xi, Q.; Liu, C.S. A boundary collocation method for anomalous heat conduction analysis in functionally graded materials. *Comput. Math. Appl.* **2021**, *88*, 91–109. [CrossRef]
49. Tang, Z.; Fu, Z.J.; Sun, H.; Liu, X. An efficient localized collocation solver for anomalous diffusion on surfaces. *Fract. Calc. Appl. Anal.* **2021**, *24*, 865–894. [CrossRef]
50. You, X.Y.; Li, W.; Chai, Y.B. A truly meshfree method for solving acoustic problems using local weak form and radial basis functions. *Appl. Math. Comput.* **2020**, *365*, 124694. [CrossRef]
51. Xi, Q.; Fu, Z.J.; Rabczuk, T.; Yin, D. A localized collocation scheme with fundamental solutions for long-time anomalous heat conduction analysis in functionally graded materials. *Int. J. Heat Mass Tran.* **2021**, *180*, 121778. [CrossRef]
52. Liu, G.R.; Gu, Y.T. A meshfree method: Meshfree weak–strong (MWS) form method for 2-D solids. *Comput. Mech.* **2003**, *33*, 2–14. [CrossRef]
53. Noh, G.; Ham, S.; Bathe, K.J. Performance of an implicit time integration scheme in the analysis of wave propagations. *Comput. Struct.* **2013**, *123*, 93–105. [CrossRef]
54. Chai, Y.B.; You, X.Y.; Li, W. Dispersion Reduction for the Wave Propagation Problems Using a Coupled "FE-Meshfree" Triangular Element. *Int. J. Comput. Methods* **2020**, *17*, 1950071. [CrossRef]
55. Li, W.; Zhang, Q.; Gui, Q.; Chai, Y.B. A coupled FE-Meshfree triangular element for acoustic radiation problems. *Int. J. Comput. Methods* **2021**, *18*, 2041002. [CrossRef]
56. Fries, T.P.; Belytschko, T. The extended/generalized finite element method: An overview of the method and its applications. *Int. J. Numer. Methods Eng.* **2010**, *84*, 253–304. [CrossRef]
57. Chai, Y.B.; Li, W.; Liu, Z.Y. Analysis of transient wave propagation dynamics using the enriched finite element method with interpolation cover functions. *Appl. Math. Comput.* **2022**, *412*, 126564. [CrossRef]
58. Tian, R.; Yagawa, G.; Terasaka, H. Linear dependence problems of partition of unity-based generalized FEMs. *Comput. Methods Appl. Mech. Eng.* **2006**, *195*, 4768–4782. [CrossRef]
59. Wu, F.; Zhou, G.; Gu, Q.Y.; Chai, Y.B. An enriched finite element method with interpolation cover functions for acoustic analysis in high frequencies. *Eng. Anal. Bound. Elem.* **2021**, *129*, 67–81. [CrossRef]
60. Li, Y.C.; Dang, S.N.; Li, W.; Chai, Y.B. Free and Forced Vibration Analysis of Two-Dimensional Linear Elastic Solids Using the Finite Element Methods Enriched by Interpolation Cover Functions. *Mathematics* **2022**, *10*, 456. [CrossRef]
61. Duarte, C.A.; Babuška, I.; Oden, J.T. Generalized finite element methods for three-dimensional structural mechanics problems. *Comput. Struct.* **2000**, *77*, 215–232. [CrossRef]
62. Gui, Q.; Zhang, G.Y.; Chai, Y.B.; Li, W. A finite element method with cover functions for underwater acoustic propagation problems. *Ocean Eng.* **2022**, *243*, 110174. [CrossRef]
63. Soroushian, A.; Farjoodi, J. A unified starting procedure for the Houbolt method. *Commun. Numer. Meth. Eng.* **2008**, *24*, 1–13. [CrossRef]
64. Noh, G.; Bathe, K.J. Further insights into an implicit time integration scheme for structural dynamics. *Comput. Struct.* **2018**, *202*, 15–24. [CrossRef]
65. Roy, D.; Dash, M.K. A stochastic newmark method for engineering dynamical systems. *J. Sound Vib.* **2002**, *249*, 83–100. [CrossRef]

66. Bathe, K.J. Conserving energy and momentum in nonlinear dynamics: A simple implicit time integration scheme. *Comput. Struct.* **2007**, *85*, 437–445. [CrossRef]
67. Malakiyeh, M.M.; Shojaee, S.; Bathe, K.J. The Bathe time integration method revisited for prescribing desired numerical dissipation. *Comput. Struct.* **2019**, *212*, 289–298. [CrossRef]
68. Li, J.; Yu, K.; Tang, H. Further Assessment of Three Bathe Algorithms and Implementations for Wave Propagation Problems. *Int. J. Struct. Stab. Dyn.* **2021**, *21*, 2150073. [CrossRef]
69. Rufai, M.A.; Ramos, H. A variable step-size fourth-derivative hybrid block strategy for integrating third-order IVPs, with applications. *Int. J. Comput. Math.* **2022**, *99*, 292–308. [CrossRef]
70. Ramos, H.; Rufai, M.A. An adaptive one-point second-derivative Lobatto-type hybrid method for solving efficiently differential systems. *Int. J. Comput. Math.* **2022**, *99*, 1687–1705. [CrossRef]
71. Ramos, H.; Rufai, M.A. An adaptive pair of one-step hybrid block Nyström methods for singular initial-value problems of Lane–Emden–Fowler type. *Math. Comput. Simulat.* **2022**, *193*, 497–508. [CrossRef]
72. Chai, Y.B.; Bathe, K.J. Transient wave propagation in inhomogeneous media with enriched overlapping triangular elements. *Comput. Struct.* **2020**, *237*, 106273. [CrossRef]
73. Zhang, Y.O.; Dang, S.N.; Li, W.; Chai, Y.B. Performance of the radial point interpolation method (RPIM) with implicit time integration scheme for transient wave propagation dynamics. *Comput. Math. Appl.* **2022**, *114*, 95–111. [CrossRef]
74. Sun, T.T.; Wang, P.; Zhang, G.J.; Chai, Y.B. Transient analyses of wave propagations in nonhomogeneous media employing the novel finite element method with the appropriate enrichment function. *Comput. Math. Appl.* **2023**, *129*, 90–112. [CrossRef]
75. Li, Y.; Liu, C.; Li, W.; Chai, Y.B. Numerical investigation of the element-free Galerkin method (EFGM) with appropriate temporal discretization techniques for transient wave propagation problems. *Appl. Math. Comput.* **2023**. [CrossRef]

mathematics

MDPI

Article

C^1-Cubic Quasi-Interpolation Splines over a CT Refinement of a Type-1 Triangulation

Haithem Benharzallah [1], Abdelaziz Mennouni [1] and Domingo Barrera [2,*]

[1] Department of Mathematics, LTM, University of Batna 2, Mostefa Ben Boulaïd, Fesdis, Batna 05078, Algeria
[2] Department of Applied Mathematics, University of Granada, 18071 Granada, Spain
* Correspondence: dbarrera@ugr.es

Abstract: C^1 continuous quasi-interpolating splines are constructed over Clough–Tocher refinement of a type-1 triangulation. Their Bernstein–Bézier coefficients are directly defined from the known values of the function to be approximated, so that a set of appropriate basis functions is not required. The resulting quasi-interpolation operators reproduce cubic polynomials. Some numerical tests are given in order to show the performance of the approximation scheme.

Keywords: Bernstein–Bézier coefficients; quasi-interpolation; type-1 triangulation; Clough–Tocher split

MSC: 41A15; 65D07

Citation: Benharzallah, H.; Mennouni, A.; Barrera, D. C^1-Cubic Quasi-Interpolating Splines in the Bernstein Basis over a Clough–Tocher Refinement of a Type-1 Triangulation. *Mathematics* **2023**, *11*, 59. https://doi.org/10.3390/math11010059

Academic Editors: Fajie Wang and Ji Lin

Received: 5 October 2022
Revised: 13 December 2022
Accepted: 19 December 2022
Published: 23 December 2022

1. Introduction

A novel, non-standard technique for constructing bivariate quasi-interpolating splines over uniform partitions was proposed by T. Sorokina and F. Zeilfelder in [1,2] (see also [3,4]). The essential idea of this methodology is to define the quasi-interpolant by directly providing the coefficients of the Bernstein–Bézier (BB-) form of its restriction to each of the subsets forming the partition.

In [2], the construction of C^1 quartic quasi-interpolants over a type-1 triangulation is addressed, so that the largest polynomial space is reproduced, namely the space $\mathbb{P}_3$ of polynomials of total degree less than or equal to three (see Figure 1). The coefficients of the quasi-interpolant on each triangle are linear combinations of function values at vertices and midpoints in a neighborhood of the triangle. The quasi-interpolant is constructed from them.

In [1], the same strategy is applied to construct C^1 quadratic quasi-interpolants on a triangulation which the authors called of type-2. Starting from a decomposition of the plane into squares, each of them is divided into eight micro-triangles by means of its diagonals and the straight lines parallel to the coordinate axes passing through the center of the square (see Figure 1).

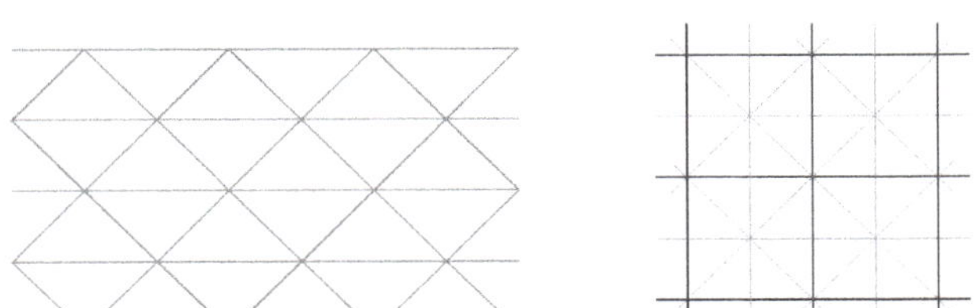

Figure 1. From left to right, type-1 and type-2 triangulations on which C^1-continuous quasi-interpolants are constructed in [1,2]: quartic and exact on $\mathbb{P}_3$, and quadratic and exact on $\mathbb{P}_2$, respectively.

The problem addressed in [2] is studied in detail in [5], proving that the approximation scheme proposed in [2] is a particular choice in a 19-parametric family of schemes. Moreover, different strategies for assigning values to the parameters are provided. In both [2] and [5], the quasi-interpolating splines interpolate the values at the vertices and the masks associated with the domain points that are key to the construction are applied taking into account the symmetries of the triangulation involved. Since the triangulation is uniform, these masks are independent of the specific triangle on which the quasi-interpolant is calculated (see also [6]).

Later, the cubic case was dealt with in [7], on the same triangulation used to construct quartic quasi-interpolants. The aim was to construct a C^1 cubic one, exact on $\mathbb{P}_2$, from the values at vertices and midpoints. Since it is not possible to define a quasi-interpolant that interpolates values at vertices, the authors opted to find specific masks for key domain points, including vertices, without imposing any symmetry. It was proved that there are unique masks that satisfy the required properties. Not being possible to achieve exactness on $\mathbb{P}_3$, this paper presents a construction on a refinement of the initial type-1 triangulation in order to achieve the optimal approximation order. Specifically, we work on a Clough–Tocher (CT-) refinement [8], which produces a subdivision into six micro-triangles of each square formed by two macro-triangles sharing an edge.

The rest of the paper is structured as follows. In Section 2, a type-1 triangulation endowed with a Clough–Tocher refinement is introduced, as well as the space of C^1 cubic splines defined over it. Further, a partition of the domain points associated with the micro-triangles is provided. In Section 3, the construction of quasi-interpolating splines is given and the general solution of the resulting problem. In Section 4, a method for selecting parameters based on the minimization of an upper bound of the quasi-interpolation error associated with the quartic monomials is proposed. In Section 5, the results of some numerical tests are given to illustrate the performance of the quasi-interpolation operator relative to the selected parameters. Finally, some details are included in Appendix A.

2. Bernstein–Bézier Form of Cubic Splines on a Type-1 Triangulation

Let us suppose that the triangulation is spanned by the vectors $e_1 := (h,h)$ and $e_2 := (h,-h)$, with $h > 0$. Its vertices are $v_{i,j} := ie_1 + je_2$, which define the lattice $\mathcal{V} := \{v_{i,j}, i,j \in \mathbb{Z}\}$. These vertices define squares which can be decomposed into the triangles $\mathbb{T}_{i,j}\langle v_{i,j}, v_{i+1,j+1}, v_{i+1,j}\rangle$ and $\mathbb{B}_{i,j}\langle v_{i,j}, v_{i+1,j+1}, v_{i,j+1}\rangle$ (see Figure 2). Therefore, a type-1 triangulation results:

$$\Delta := \bigcup_{i,j\in\mathbb{Z}} (\mathbb{T}_{i,j} \cup \mathbb{B}_{i,j}).$$

When there is no need to distinguish between the types of triangles in Δ, we denote by $\mathbb{T}$ any one of them.

To define the refinement of Δ to be used, let

$$t_{i,j} := \frac{1}{3}(v_{i,j} + v_{i+1,j+1} + v_{i+1,j}) \quad \text{and} \quad b_{i,j} := \frac{1}{3}(v_{i,j} + v_{i+1,j+1} + v_{i,j+1})$$

be the barycenters of $\mathbb{T}_{i,j}$ and $\mathbb{B}_{i,j}$, respectively. Then, the CT-refinement of each triangle is obtained by joining its vertices with its barycenter [8]. Each macro-triangle $\mathbb{T}_{i,j}$ and $\mathbb{B}_{i,j}$ is, respectively, divided into the following micro-triangles:

$$\begin{array}{lll} t_1^+ = \langle v_{i,j}, v_{i+1,j+1}, t_{i,j}\rangle, & t_2^+ = \langle v_{i+1,j+1}, v_{i+1,j}, t_{i,j}\rangle, & t_3^+ = \langle v_{i+1,j}, v_{i,j}, t_{i,j}\rangle, \\ t_1^- = \langle v_{i,j}, v_{i,j+1}, b_{i,j}\rangle, & t_2^- = \langle v_{i,j+1}, v_{i+1,j+1}, b_{i,j}\rangle, & t_3^- = \langle v_{i+1,j+1}, v_{i,j}, b_{i,j}\rangle. \end{array} \tag{1}$$

They are shown in Figure 2, bottom, where any reference to the subscripts of the micro-triangles has been avoided. As in the case of macro-triangles, the lower case letter t will be used to represent any of the micro-triangles of Δ_{CT}.

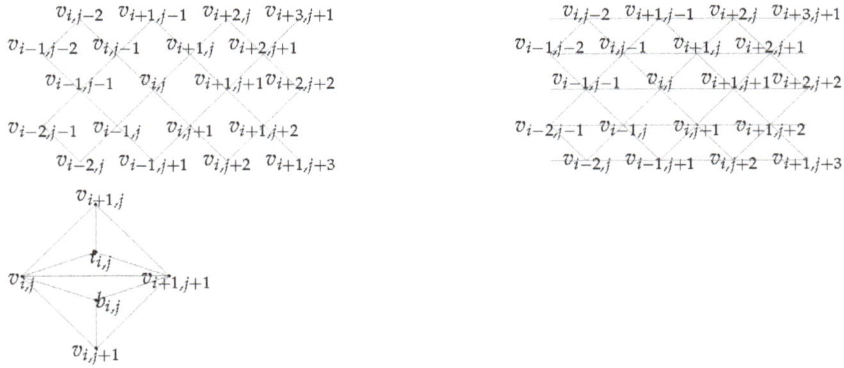

Figure 2. Top, from left to right, decomposition into squares induced by the vertices of Δ, type-1 triangulation. Bottom, CT-refinements of macro-triangles $T_{i,j}$ and $B_{i,j}$.

In this paper, we consider the space of C^1 cubic splines on Δ_{CT} defined by

$$S_3^1(\Delta_{\mathrm{CT}}) := \left\{ s \in C^1\left(\mathbb{R}^2\right) : s_{|t} \in \mathbb{P}_3 \quad \text{for all } t \in \Delta_{\mathrm{CT}} \right\}.$$

where the restriction is $s_{|t}$ of $s \in S_3^1(\Delta_{\mathrm{CT}})$ to a micro-triangle $t = \langle V_1, V_2, V_3 \rangle \in \Delta_{\mathrm{CT}}$ a cubic polynomial, it can be represented using the cubic Bernstein polynomials

$$B_{\beta,t}(p) := \frac{3!}{\beta!}\tau^\beta = \frac{6}{\beta_1!\beta_2!\beta_3!}\tau_1^{\beta_1}\tau_2^{\beta_2}\tau_3^{\beta_3},$$

where the multi-index notations $\beta := (\beta_1, \beta_2, \beta_3) \in \mathbb{N}_0^3$, $|\beta| := \beta_1 + \beta_2 + \beta_3$ and $\beta! := \beta_1!\beta_2!\beta_3!$ have been used, and $\tau := (\tau_1, \tau_2, \tau_3)$ provides the barycentric coordinates of point $p \in \mathbb{R}^2$ with respect to t, i.e., $p = \sum_{i=1}^3 \tau_i V_i$ and $\sum_{i=1}^3 \tau_i = 1$. The coordinates τ_1, τ_2 and τ_3 are non-negative whenever p belongs to t.

Every polynomial $q \in \mathbb{P}_3$ can be expressed on t in terms of the cubic Bernstein basis polynomials $B_{\beta,t}$, $|\beta| = 3$, i.e., there exist values b_β such that

$$q(x,y) = q(\tau) = \sum_{|\beta|=3} b_{\beta,t}\, B_{\beta,t}(\tau).$$

Coefficients in $D_t := \left\{ b_{\beta,t}, |\beta| = 3 \right\}$ are said to be the Bernstein–Bézier (BB-) coefficients of q. They are linked to the domain points $\xi_{\beta,t}$ determined by the barycentric coordinates $\left(\frac{\beta_{1,t}}{3}, \frac{\beta_{2,t}}{3}, \frac{\beta_{3,t}}{3}\right)$ with respect to t. They determine the lattice $L_3(t)$. The graph of q on t is included in the convex hull of $\left\{ \left(\left(\xi_{\beta,t}, b_{\beta,t}\right), |\beta| = 3 \right\}$.

On each micro-triangle, an element $s \in S_3^1(\Delta_{\mathrm{CT}})$ is uniquely determined by ten BB-coefficients, associated with the corresponding domain points. When all macro-triangles are taken into account, a subset of domain points is obtained, which we note $\mathcal{D}_3(\Delta_{\mathrm{CT}})$, i.e., $\mathcal{D}_3(\Delta_{\mathrm{CT}}) = \bigcup_{t\in\Delta_{\mathrm{CT}}} L_3(t)$, where the union is formed without taking repetitions into account. To determine s, it is necessary to give the BB-coefficients associated with all the points of $\mathcal{D}_3(\Delta_{\mathrm{CT}})$. As the triangulation is uniform, following the approach in [2,4–6], it is sufficient to establish a partition $\left\{ D_{i,j}, i,j \in \mathbb{Z} \right\}$ of $\mathcal{D}_3(\Delta_{\mathrm{CT}})$ and define the BB-coefficients linked to the domain points in $D_{i,j}$.

Figure 3 shows the twenty-seven domain points forming $D_{i,j}$, which are linked to vertex $v_{i,j}$. Each of them has the subscripts of $v_{i,j}$. The vertices and barycenter have already been defined. They remaining domain points in $D_{i,j}$ are given next:

$$
\begin{array}{rlrl}
u_{i,j}^{1,1} := & \frac{1}{3}(2v_{i,j} + v_{i+1,j+1}), & u_{i,j}^{1,0} := & \frac{1}{3}(2v_{i,j} + v_{i+1,j}), \\
u_{i,j}^{2,1} := & \frac{1}{3}(2v_{i,j} + t_{i,j}), & u_{i,j}^{-1,-1} := & \frac{1}{3}(2v_{i,j} + v_{i-1,j-1}), \\
u_{i,j}^{1,-1} := & \frac{1}{3}(2v_{i,j} + b_{i,j-1}), & u_{i,j}^{0,-1} := & \frac{1}{3}(2v_{i,j} + v_{i,j-1}), \\
u_{i,j}^{-1,-2} := & \frac{1}{3}(2v_{i,j} + t_{i-1,j-1}), & u_{i,j}^{-2,-1} := & \frac{1}{3}(2v_{i,j} + b_{i-1,j-1}), \\
u_{i,j}^{-1,0} := & \frac{1}{3}(2v_{i,j} + v_{i-1,j}), & u_{i,j}^{-1,1} := & \frac{1}{3}(2v_{i,j} + t_{i-1,j}), \\
u_{i,j}^{0,1} := & \frac{1}{3}(2v_{i,j} + v_{i,j+1}), & u_{i,j}^{1,2} := & \frac{1}{3}(2v_{i,j} + b_{i,j}), \\
x_{i,j}^{1,1} := & \frac{1}{3}(v_{i,j} + v_{i+1,j+1} + b_{i,j}), & x_{i,j}^{1,0} := & \frac{1}{3}(v_{i,j} + v_{i+1,j} + b_{i,j-1}), \\
x_{i,j}^{0,1} := & \frac{1}{3}(v_{i,j} + v_{i,j+1} + b_{i,j}), & y_{i,j}^{2,1} := & \frac{1}{3}(v_{i,j} + 2t_{i,j}), \\
y_{i,j}^{1,-1} := & \frac{1}{3}(v_{i,j} + 2b_{i,j-1}), & y_{i,j}^{-1,-2} := & \frac{1}{3}(v_{i,j} + 2t_{i-1,j-1}), \\
y_{i,j}^{-2,-1} := & \frac{1}{3}(v_{i,j} + 2b_{i-1,j-1}), & y_{i,j}^{-1,1} := & \frac{1}{3}(v_{i,j} + 2t_{i-1,j}) \\
y_{i,j}^{1,2} := & \frac{1}{3}(v_{i,j} + 2b_{i,j}), & z_{i,j}^{1,1} := & \frac{1}{3}(v_{i,j} + v_{i+1,j+1} + t_{i,j}), \\
z_{i,j}^{1,0} := & \frac{1}{3}(v_{i,j} + v_{i+1,j} + t_{i,j}), & z_{i,j}^{0,1} := & \frac{1}{3}(v_{i,j} + v_{i,j+1} + t_{i-1,j}).
\end{array}
$$

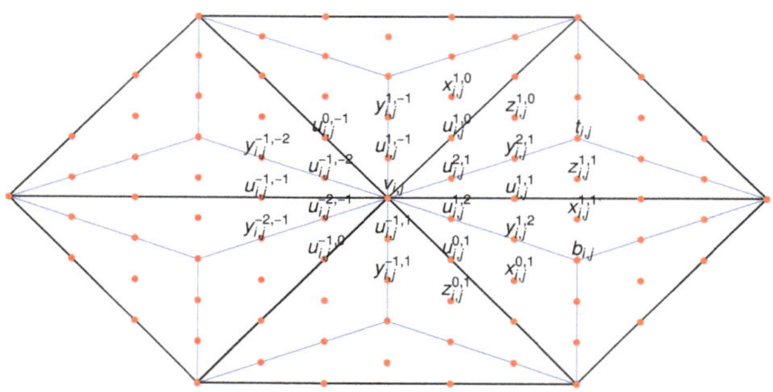

Figure 3. Domain points forming the subset $D_{i,j}$ corresponding to $v_{i,j}$.

Figure 4 shows the domain points in D lying in the hexagon formed by the six triangles sharing the vertex $v_{i,j}$.

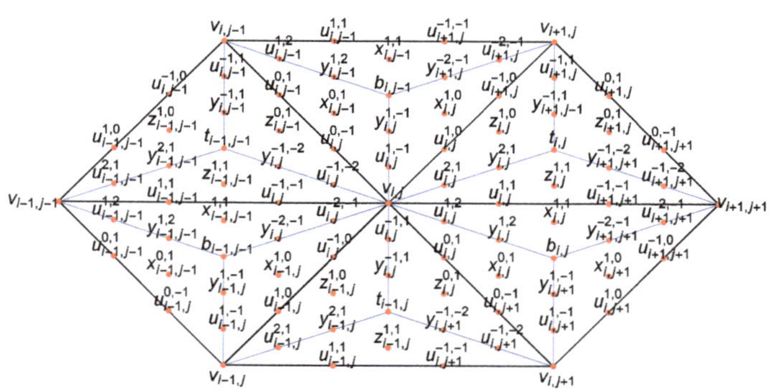

Figure 4. Domain points lying in the hexagon formed by the triangles sharing vertex $v_{i,j}$. Each shows the subscripts of the vertex to which it is linked.

3. C^1 Quasi-Interpolating Splines on a Clough–Tocher Refinement

The main objective of this work is to construct a quasi-interpolation operator for $S_3^1(\Delta_{CT})$ that is exact on $\mathbb{P}_3$ in order to improve the result obtained in [7]. Let us denote it as $\mathcal{Q}$. It is assumed that the values of a function f are known at the domain points in $\mathcal{D}_3(\Delta_{CT})$.

The quasi-interpolant $\mathcal{Q}f \in S_3^1(\Delta_{CT})$ of f should be constructed in such a way that the BB-coefficients of the restriction $\mathcal{Q}f_{|t}$ to each micro-triangle $t \in \Delta_{CT}$ are defined as combinations of those values of f. In other words, $\mathcal{Q}f_{|t}$ is written in the basis of Bernstein polynomials $B_{\beta,t}$, $|\beta| = 3$, as

$$\mathcal{Q}f_{|t} = \sum_{\gamma \in \Delta_3} P_\gamma B_{\gamma,t},$$

where P_γ denotes the BB-coefficient associated with the domain point $p_\gamma \in t$, Δ_3 is the set of indices with length equal to 3 written in the lexicographical order, i.e.,

$$\Delta_3 = \{(3,0,0),(2,1,0),(2,0,1),(1,2,0),(1,1,1),\\(1,0,2),(0,3,0),(0,2,1),(0,1,2),(0,0,3)\}$$

and the vertices of each micro-triangle follow in the order they appear in (1).

For instance, with regard to the micro-triangle t_1^+ of $\mathbb{T}_{i,j}$ (see Figure 5) we write

$$\mathcal{Q}f_{|t_1^+} = V_{i,j}B_{(3,0,0),t_1^+} + U_{i,j}^{1,1}B_{(2,1,0),t_1^+} + U_{i,j}^{2,1}B_{(2,0,1),t_1^+} + U_{i+1,j+1}^{-1,-1}B_{(1,2,0),t_1^+}\\ + Z_{i,j}^{1,1}B_{(1,1,1),t_1^+} + Y_{i,j}^{2,1}B_{(1,0,2),t_1^+} + V_{i+1,j+1}B_{(0,3,0),t_1^+}\\ + U_{i+1,j+1}^{-1,-2}B_{(0,2,1),t_1^+} + Y_{i+1,j+1}^{-1,-2}B_{(0,1,2),t_1^+} + T_{i,j}B_{(0,0,3),t_1^+}.$$

Similar expressions are obtained for the restrictions of $\mathcal{Q}f$ to the other two micro-triangles of $\mathbb{T}_{i,j}$ and those three into which $\mathbb{B}_{i,j}$ is divided.

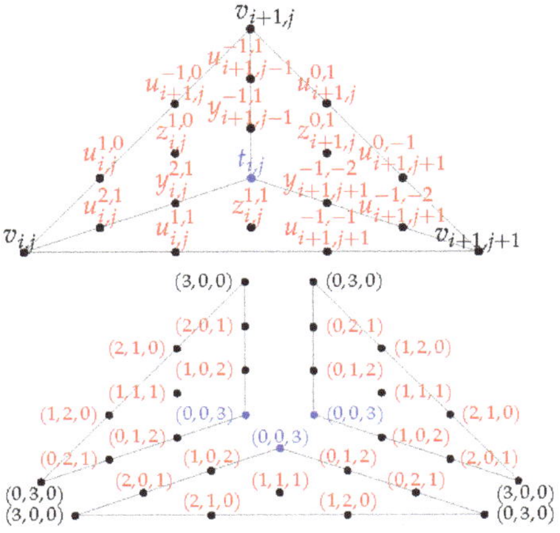

Figure 5. Top, the domain points associated with the three micro-triangles of the macro-triangle $\mathbb{T}_{i,j}$. They are denoted as shown in Figure 4 bottom; the indices corresponding to each micro-triangle, whose orientation is determined by the vertex ordering given by (1).

The BB-coefficients involved in the definition of $\mathcal{Q}f$ on each micro-triangle of $\mathbb{T}_{i,j}$ and $\mathbb{B}_{i,j}$ will be linear combinations of f at the specific domain points for cubic polynomials lying in the hexagon defined by the triangles sharing vertex $v_{i,j}$. Specifically, the union without repetitions $\mathcal{D}_3(\Delta) := \bigcup_{\mathbb{T}\in\Delta} L_3(\mathbb{T})$ is formed and decomposed as

$$\mathcal{D}_3(\Delta) = \bigcup_{i,j\in\mathbb{Z}} S_{i,j},$$

where the ordered subset $S_{i,j}$ consists of the thirty-seven domain points given below:

$$\begin{aligned} S_{i,j} := \Big\{ & v_{i,j}, u_{i,j}^{1,1}, u_{i,j}^{1,0}, u_{i,j}^{0,-1}, u_{i,j}^{-1,-1}, u_{i,j}^{-1,0}, u_{i,j}^{0,1}, u_{i+1,j+1}^{-1,-1}, t_{i,j}, u_{i+1,j}^{-1,0}, b_{i,j-1}, \\ & u_{i,j-1}^{0,-1}, t_{i-1,j-1}, u_{i-,j-1}^{-1,-1}, b_{i-1,j-1}, u_{i-1,j}^{1,0}, t_{i-1,j}, u_{i,j+1}^{0,-1}, b_{i,j}, v_{i+1,j+1}, u_{i+1,j+1}^{0,-1}, \\ & u_{i+1,j}^{0,1}, v_{i+1,j}, u_{i+1,j}^{-1,-1}, u_{i,j-1}^{1,1}, v_{i,j-1}, u_{i,j-1}^{-1,0}, u_{i-1,j-1}^{1,0}, v_{i-1,j-1}, u_{i-1,j-1}^{0,1}, u_{i-1,j}^{0,-1}, \\ & v_{i-1,j}, u_{i-1,j}^{1,1}, u_{i,j+1}^{-1,-1}, v_{i,j+1}, u_{i,j+1}^{1,0}, u_{i+1,j+1}^{-1,0} \Big\}. \end{aligned}$$

The BB-coefficient P of a domain point p is a linear combination of values of f at points in $S_{i,j}$, its coefficients give rise to a vector $M(p)$, ordered as $S_{i,j}$, which is said to be the mask of p. If $f(S_{i,j}) := \{f(p), p \in S_{i,j}\}$ is also ordered as $S_{i,j}$, then

$$P = M(p) \cdot f(S_{i,j}) := \sum_{\ell=1}^{37} M(p)_\ell f(S_{i,j})_\ell,$$

where $M(p)_\ell$ and $f(S_{i,j})_\ell$ stand for the ℓ-th entries of $M(p)$ and $f(S_{i,j})$, respectively.

In the following, we state the problem that is the object of this work.

Problem 1. *Find masks for the domain points in $D_{i,j}$ such that the associated quasi-interpolation operator $\mathcal{Q}$ is exact on $\mathbb{P}_3$ and produces C^1 quasi-interpolating splines.*

The following result holds.

Proposition 2. *Problem 1 has a 17-parametric family of solutions.*

Proof. Given an arbitrary function f, C^1 continuity of $\mathcal{Q}f$ across segment $[v_{i,j}, v_{i+1,j}]$ is equivalent to the following conditions [9] (Thm. 2.28) (see Figure 6 and the notations used for the domain points in Figures 3 and 4):

$$\begin{aligned} V_{i,j} + U_{i,j}^{1,0} - U_{i,j}^{1,-1} - U_{i,j}^{2,1} &= 0, \\ U_{i,j}^{1,0} + U_{i+1,j}^{-1,0} - X_{i,j}^{1,0} - Z_{i,j}^{1,0} &= 0, \\ U_{i+1,j}^{-1,0} + V_{i+1,j} - U_{i+1,j}^{2,1} - U_{i+1,j}^{-1,1} &= 0. \end{aligned}$$

For $[v_{i,j}, v_{i+1,j+1}]$,

$$\begin{aligned} V_{i,j} + U_{i,j}^{1,1} - U_{i,j}^{2,1} - U_{i,j}^{1,2} &= 0, \\ U_{i,j}^{1,1} + U_{i+1,j+1}^{-1,-1} - X_{i,j}^{1,1} - Z_{i,j}^{1,1} &= 0, \\ U_{i+1,j+1}^{-1,-1} + V_{i+1,j+1} - U_{i+1,j+1}^{-1,-2} - U_{i+1,j+1}^{2,1} &= 0. \end{aligned}$$

And for $[v_{i,j}, v_{i,j+1}]$,

$$\begin{aligned} V_{i,j} + U_{i,j}^{0,1} - U_{i,j}^{-1,1} - U_{i,j}^{1,2} &= 0, \\ U_{i,j}^{0,1} + U_{i,j+1}^{0,-1} - Z_{i,j}^{0,1} - X_{i,j}^{0,1} &= 0, \\ U_{i,j+1}^{0,-1} + V_{i,j+1} - U_{i,j+1}^{-1,-2} - U_{i,j+1}^{1,-1} &= 0. \end{aligned}$$

Regarding micro-edges, C^1 continuity across $[v_{i,j}, t_{i,j}]$ is equivalent to conditions

$$U_{i,j}^{2,1} - \frac{1}{3}\left(V_{i,j} + U_{i,j}^{1,0} + U_{i,j}^{1,1}\right) = 0,\ Y_{i,j}^{2,1} - \frac{1}{3}\left(U_{i,j}^{2,1} + Z_{i,j}^{1,0} + Z_{i,j}^{1,1}\right) = 0.$$

Similarly, it is satisfied across $[v_{i+1,j}, t_{i,j}]$ and $[v_{i+1,j+1}, t_{i,j}]$, respectively, if and only if

$$U_{i+1,j}^{-1,1} - \frac{1}{3}\left(V_{i+1,j} + U_{i+1,j}^{-1,0} + U_{i+1,j}^{0,1}\right) = 0,$$
$$Y_{i+1,j+1}^{-1,-1} - \frac{1}{3}\left(U_{i+1,j}^{-1,1} + Z_{i,j}^{1,0} + Z_{i+1,j}^{0,1}\right) = 0,$$

and

$$U_{i+1,j+1}^{-1,-2} - \frac{1}{3}\left(V_{i+1,j+1} + U_{i+1,j+1}^{-1,-1} + U_{i+1,j+1}^{0,-1}\right) = 0,$$
$$Y_{i+1,j+1}^{-1,-2} - \frac{1}{3}\left(U_{i+1,j+1}^{-1,-2} + Z_{i,j}^{1,1} + Z_{i+1,j}^{0,1}\right) = 0.$$

For the micro-sides of macro-triangle $\mathbb{B}_{i,j}$, six new conditions are involved. For $[v_{i,j}, b_{i,j}]$, $[v_{i,j+1}, b_{i,j}]$ and $[v_{i+1,j+1}, b_{i,j}]$, C^1 regularity is equivalent to

$$U_{i,j}^{1,2} - \frac{1}{3}\left(V_{i,j} + U_{i,j}^{0,1} + U_{i,j}^{1,1}\right) = 0,\ Y_{i,j}^{1,2} - \frac{1}{3}\left(U_{i,j}^{1,2} + X_{i,j}^{1,1} + X_{i,j}^{0,1}\right) = 0,$$

$$U_{i,j+1}^{1,-1} - \frac{1}{3}\left(V_{i,j+1} + U_{i,j+1}^{0,-1} + U_{i,j+1}^{1,0}\right) = 0,$$
$$Y_{i,j+1}^{1,-1} - \frac{1}{3}\left(U_{i,j+1}^{1,-1} + X_{i,j}^{0,1} + X_{i,j+1}^{1,0}\right) = 0,$$

and

$$U_{i+1,j+1}^{2,-1} - \frac{1}{3}\left(V_{i+1,j+1} + U_{i+1,j+1}^{-1,-1} + U_{i+1,j+1}^{-1,0}\right) = 0,$$
$$Y_{i+1,j+1}^{-2,-1} - \frac{1}{3}\left(U_{i+1,j+1}^{2,1} + X_{i,j}^{1,1} + X_{i,j+1}^{1,0}\right) = 0,$$

respectively. Finally, C^1 continuity at the barycenters of $\mathbb{T}_{i,j}$ and $\mathbb{B}_{i,j}$ is obtained if and only if

$$T_{i,j} - \frac{1}{3}\left(Y_{i,j}^{2,1} + Y_{i+1,j+1}^{-1,-2} + Y_{i+1,j-1}^{-1,1}\right) = 0,$$
$$B_{i,j} - \frac{1}{3}\left(Y_{i,j}^{1,2} + Y_{i+1,j+1}^{-2,-1} + Y_{i,j+1}^{-1,-1}\right) = 0.$$

These are all equalities involving the values $f(p)$, $p \in S_{i,j}$, so $\mathcal{Q}f$ is C^1 continuous if and only if all the coefficients of the f-values in these equalities are zero. Therefore, the requirements on the C^1 continuity are equivalent to a system of equations having a 122-parametric family of solutions. To these equations must be added those related to the exactness of the operator on $\mathbb{P}_3$. They are obtained by imposing that the BB-coefficients on each microtriangle of the monomials of degree less than or equal to three and those of their quasi-interpolants are equal. The resulting system can be solved with a Computer Algebra System, namely, Mathematica, obtaining the existence of a 17-parametric family of solutions. The free parameters are entries with indices 1, 2, 3, 4, 5, 6, 7, 8, 9, 10, 11, 12, 18, 19, 20, 21, and 22 of the mask $M(b_{i,j})$. □

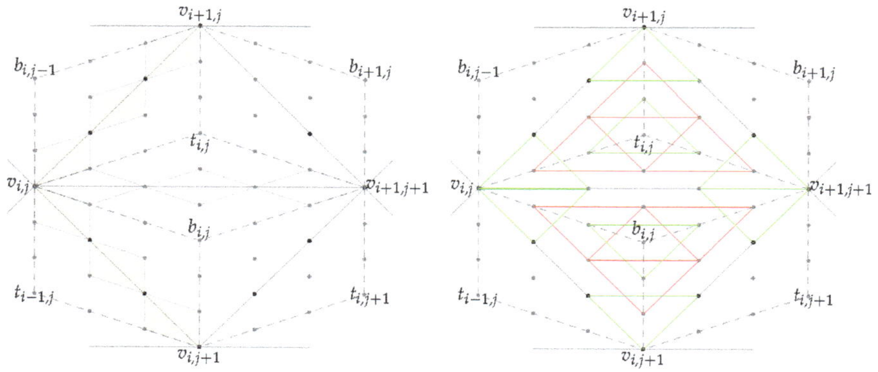

Figure 6. Schematic representation of the conditions to be imposed to achieve C^1 continuity on the macro-interval edges (top) and on the micro-edges and at barycenters (bottom). In each of the shaded parallelograms in the figure on the left, it must be fulfilled that the sum of the BB-coefficients of two opposite domain points must be equal to that of the other two. The C^1 continuity across the micro-edges of the triangle $\mathbb{T}_{i,j}$ is obtained if, in each of the two green and red $\triangle$-triangles closest to each vertex, it is satisfied that the BB-coefficient corresponding to the interior domain point is equal to one-third of the sum of those of the three vertices of the triangle. The same condition must be fulfilled for the ∇-triangles of $\mathbb{B}_{i,j}$.

Figure 7 shows the mask relative to vertex $v_{i,j}$. The entries of the masks for $u_{i,j}^{0,-1}$, $u_{i,j}^{-1,-2}$, $u_{i,j}^{-2,-1}$ and $u_{i,j}^{-1,0}$ are almost all zero, and the following expressions for their BB-coefficients are found:

$$
\begin{aligned}
U_{i,j}^{-1,0} &= -\frac{5}{6}f(v_{i,j}) + 3f\left(u_{i,j}^{-1,0}\right) - \frac{3}{2}f\left(u_{i,j-1}^{0,-1}\right) + \frac{1}{3}f(v_{i,j-1}),\\
U_{i,j}^{0,-1} &= -\frac{5}{6}f(v_{i,j}) - \frac{3}{2}f\left(u_{i,j}^{-1,0}\right) + 3f\left(u_{i,j-1}^{0,-1}\right) + \frac{1}{3}f(v_{i+1,j+1}),\\
U_{i,j}^{-1,-2} &= -\frac{5}{6}f(v_{i,j}) + f\left(u_{i,j}^{-1,0}\right) + 2f\left(u_{i,j}^{0,-1}\right) - \frac{1}{2}f\left(u_{i,j-1}^{0,-1}\right)\\
&\quad - f\left(u_{i+1,j}^{-1,0}\right) + \frac{2}{9}f(v_{i+1,j+1}) + \frac{1}{9}f(v_{i,j-1}),\\
U_{i,j}^{-2,-1} &= -\frac{5}{6}f(v_{i,j}) + 2f\left(u_{i,j}^{-1,0}\right) + f\left(u_{i,j}^{0,-1}\right) - f\left(u_{i,j-1}^{0,-1}\right)\\
&\quad - \frac{1}{2}f\left(u_{i+1,j}^{-1,0}\right) + \frac{1}{9}f(v_{i+1,j+1}) + \frac{2}{9}f(v_{i,j-1}).
\end{aligned}
$$

Fourteen of the masks relative to the remaining twenty-two domain points in $D_{i,j}$ do not depend on any parameters and appear in Appendix A. Those of $t_{i,j}$, $b_{i,j}$, $y_{i,j}^{1,2}$, $y_{i,j}^{2,1}$, $y_{i,j}^{-1,-2}$, $y_{i,j}^{-2,-1}$, $x_{i,j}^{1,1}$, and $z_{i,j}^{1,1}$ have very long entries and will not be given.

$$\frac{4484399224513}{6514447513140} \quad -\frac{2552223421511}{1085741252190} \quad \frac{5169718992073}{1085741252190} \quad -\frac{8031525079}{232658839755}$$

$$-\frac{64504080325}{868593001752} \quad -\frac{3505392583699}{4342965008760} \quad -\frac{27952071335903}{2895310005840} \quad -\frac{3505392583699}{4342965008760} \quad \frac{5169718992073}{1085741252190}$$

$$\frac{36832622942}{542870626095} \quad \frac{120096488429}{482551667640} \quad \frac{519419554543}{310211786340} \quad -\frac{533680265081}{1447655002920} \quad \frac{120096488429}{482551667640} \quad -\frac{2552223421511}{1085741252190}$$

$$-\frac{6955013524199}{13028895026280} \quad -\frac{144225313868}{1628611878285} \quad \frac{382180214323}{100531597425} \quad -\frac{176728557928}{232658839755} \quad -\frac{285439445629}{1085741252190} \quad \frac{6856655665381}{8685930017520} \quad \frac{4484399224513}{6514447513140}$$

$$\frac{2095907565527}{2171482504380} \quad -\frac{2725154777111}{4342965008760} \quad \frac{519419554543}{310211786340} \quad -\frac{533680265081}{1447655002920} \quad -\frac{64504080325}{868593001752} \quad \frac{343799911081}{1085741252190}$$

$$-\frac{2725154777111}{4342965008760} \quad \frac{2095907565527}{2171482504380} \quad -\frac{6955013524199}{13028895026280} \quad \frac{36832622942}{542870626095} \quad \frac{343799911081}{1085741252190}$$

$$-\frac{31932271589}{120637916910} \quad -\frac{31932271589}{120637916910} \quad \frac{73887390529}{5211558010512} \quad -\frac{25733502500393}{130288950262800}$$

Figure 7. Mask $M(v_{i,j})$.

Remark 1. *It can be proved that it is not possible to obtain quasi-interpolants with the required characteristics if the BB-coefficients are linear combinations of function values at the vertices lying in the hexagon $H_{i,j}$ determined by the six triangles sharing vertex $v_{i,j}$, and the midpoints of the edges of $H_{i,j}$. Neither is it possible to construct C^1 cubic quasi-interpolants exact on $\mathbb{P}_3$ in this way if function values at $v_{i,j}$ and at the eighteen vertices closest to it are used.*

Moreover, quasi-interpolation error estimates are found using a standard procedure [2].

Proposition 3. *There exists an absolute constant K such that for every $f \in C^{m+1}(\mathbb{R}^2)$, $0 \le m \le 2$,*

$$\|D^\gamma(f - \mathcal{Q}f)\|_{\infty,\mathbb{T}} \le K h^{m+1-|\gamma|} \left\|D^{m+1} f\right\|_{\infty,\Omega_{\mathbb{T}}}, \tag{2}$$

for all $0 \le |\gamma| \le 1$, $\gamma = (\gamma_1, \gamma_2)$, with $\Omega_{\mathbb{T}}$ denoting the union of the triangles in Δ having a non-empty intersection with T.

4. Selecting Parameters

An obvious choice is to make all parameters equal to zero. However, a reasonable strategy is to minimize an upper bound of the quasi-interpolation error for monomials of smaller degree non reproduced by the quasi-interpolation operator, namely $m_{k,4-k}(x,y) := x^k y^{4-k}$, $k = 0,1,2,3,4$. Let us suppose that the BB-coefficients of $m_{k,4-k}$ relative to each micro-triangle t_ℓ^+, $\ell = 1,2,3$, of $\mathbb{T}_{i,j}$ are μ_{k,β,t_ℓ^+}, $|\beta| = 4$, and that those of the cubic quasi-interpolant $\mathcal{Q}m_{k,4-k}$ are b_{k,γ,t_ℓ^+}, $|\gamma| = 4$. By degree elevation, $\mathcal{Q}m_{k,4-k|t_\ell^+}$ can be represented as a quartic polynomial having BB-coefficients b_{k,β,t_ℓ^+}, $|\beta| = 4$, which depend on parameters $z_r := M(b_{i,j})_r$, $1 \le r \le 12$, and $z_r := M(b_{i,j})_{r+5}$, $13 \le r \le 17$. Therefore, the BB-coefficients of the restriction of $m_{k,4-k} - \mathcal{Q}m_{k,4-k}$ to t_ℓ^+ have the form

$$\sigma_{k,t_\ell^+}(z) = c_{k,t_\ell^+} + \sum_{r=1}^{17} c_{k,t_\ell^+}^{(r)} z_r$$

for real values c_{k,t_ℓ^+} and $c_{k,t_\ell^+}^{(r)}$, where $z := (z_1, \dots, z_{17})$. Since the Bernstein polynomials relative to t_ℓ^+ form a partition of unity, then the infinity norm of $m_{k,4-k} - \mathcal{Q}m_{k,4-k}$ is bounded by

$$\max\left\{\left|\sigma_{k,t_\ell^+}(z)\right|,\ \ell = 1,2,3\right\}.$$

Consequently, an upper bound for the quasi-interpolation errors for quartic monomials in the macro-triangle $\mathbb{T}_{i,j}$ is

$$U_+(z) := \max\left\{\left|\sigma_{k,t_\ell^+}(z)\right|,\ \ell = 1,2,3;\ k = 0,1,2,3,4\right\}.$$

Analogously, an upper bound of such errors in the macro-triangle $\mathbb{B}_{i,j}$ is written as

$$U_-(z) := \max\left\{\left|\sigma_{k,t_\ell^-}(z)\right|,\ \ell = 1,2,3;\ k = 0,1,2,3,4\right\},$$

where

$$\sigma_{k,t_\ell^-}(z) = c_{k,t_\ell^-} + \sum_{r=1}^{17} c_{k,t_\ell}^{(r)} z_r,$$

for real values c_{k,t_ℓ^-} and $c_{k,t_\ell}^{(r)}$. In short, the function

$$U(z) := \max\{U_+(z), U_-(z)\}$$

is an upper bound for the quasi-interpolation errors for quartic monomials in the square $\mathbb{T}_{i,j} \bigcup \mathbb{B}_{i,j}$.

Function U can be rewritten as

$$U(z) = \max_{1 \leq \alpha \leq 30} \frac{1}{c_\alpha} \left(d_\alpha + \sum_{\beta=1}^{17} e_{\alpha,\beta} |f_{\alpha,\beta} \cdot z| \right),$$

where $c_\alpha, d_\alpha, e_{\alpha,\beta} \in \mathbb{N}$, $f_{\alpha,\beta} \in \mathbb{Z}^{17}$ and $A \cdot B := \sum_{s=1}^{17} A_s B_s$. The number of terms involved in each sum depends on α, because some of them will be zero. Therefore, the minimization of U is equivalent to the following linear programming problem:

$$\text{Minimize} \quad \mu$$
$$\text{such that} \quad \begin{cases} d_\alpha + \sum_{\beta=1}^{17} e_{\alpha,\beta}(u_{\alpha,\beta} + v_{\alpha,\beta}) - c_\alpha \mu \leq 0, & 1 \leq \alpha \leq 30, \\ f_{\alpha,\beta} \cdot (Z^+ - Z^-) - u_{\alpha,\beta} + v_{\alpha,\beta} = 0, & 1 \leq \alpha \leq 30,\ 1 \leq \beta \leq 17, \\ u_{p,n}, v_{p,n}, X_1, X_2, Y_1, Y_2, Z_1, Z_2, \mu \geq 0, & \end{cases}$$

where it has been used that each variable z_r can be written as $z_r = z_r^+ - z_r^-$, $z_r^+, z_r^- \geq 0$, therefore $Z = Z^+ - Z^-$, with $Z^+ := \left(z_1^+, \ldots, z_{17}^+\right)$ and $Z^- := \left(z_1^-, \ldots, z_{17}^-\right)$. The solution of this problem has been exactly determined by using Mathematica, and the minimum value $\mu = \frac{35971348390906381}{87945041427390}$ is reached at

$$\begin{aligned} Z_3^+ &= \tfrac{33654106472661220639}{24647711830550794440}, & Z_6^- &= \tfrac{289311192782870590597 81}{79874153306877553434720}, \\ Z_7^- &= \tfrac{1477134152647983512 89}{4929542366110158888 0}, & Z_9^- &= \tfrac{716874104646429666 11}{4929542366110158888 0}, \\ Z_{10}^- &= \tfrac{372356219454533971909 5199}{111823814629628574808 6080}, & Z_{12}^- &= \tfrac{345992170811097165259 3}{122883312779811620668 80}, \\ Z_{13}^- &= \tfrac{143791532332224502212 1277}{186373024382714291347 6800}, & Z_{15}^+ &= \tfrac{933461094140338011503 5381}{100641433166665717327 74720}, \end{aligned}$$

being equal to zero all the remaining values. Therefore, the minimum is attained at point $z^*$with components $z_r^* = 0$ for $r \in \{1, 2, 4, 5, 8, 11, 14, 16, 17\}$, and

$$\begin{aligned} z_3^* &= \tfrac{33654106472661220639}{24647711830550794440}, & z_6^* &= -\tfrac{28931119278287059059781}{79874153306877553434720}, \\ z_7^* &= -\tfrac{147713415264798351289}{49295423661101588880}, & z_9^* &= -\tfrac{71687410464642966611}{49295423661101588880}, \\ z_{10}^* &= -\tfrac{3723562194545339719095199}{1118238146296285748086080}, & z_{12}^* &= -\tfrac{34599217081109716525 93}{12288331277981162066880}, \\ z_{13}^* &= -\tfrac{1437915323322245022121277}{1863730243827142913476800}, & z_{15}^* &= \tfrac{9334610941403380115035381}{10064143316666571732774720}. \end{aligned}$$

5. Numerical Tests

In this section, the performance of the quasi-interpolation operator Q^* defined by the masks provided by the solution above is tested. To perform this, we consider Franke's function

$$f_1(x_1, x_2) = \frac{3}{4} \exp\left(-\frac{(9x_1 - 2)^2}{4} - \frac{(9x_2 - 2)^2}{4} \right) + \frac{3}{4} \exp\left(-\frac{(9x_1 + 1)^2}{49} - \frac{9x_2 + 1}{10} \right)$$
$$+ \frac{1}{2} \exp\left(-\frac{(9x_1 - 7)^2}{4} - \frac{(9x_2 - 3)^2}{4} \right) - \frac{1}{5} \exp\left(-(9x_1 - 4)^2 - (9x_2 - 7)^2 \right)$$

and Nielson's function

$$f_2(x_1, x_2) = \frac{x_2}{2} \cos^4\left(4(x_1^2 + x_2 - 1) \right)$$

to produce quasi-interpolants on the unit square [10,11]. The plots of f_1 and f_2 are shown in Figure 8, together with those of their quasi-interpolants obtained by diving the unit interval into 256 equal parts.

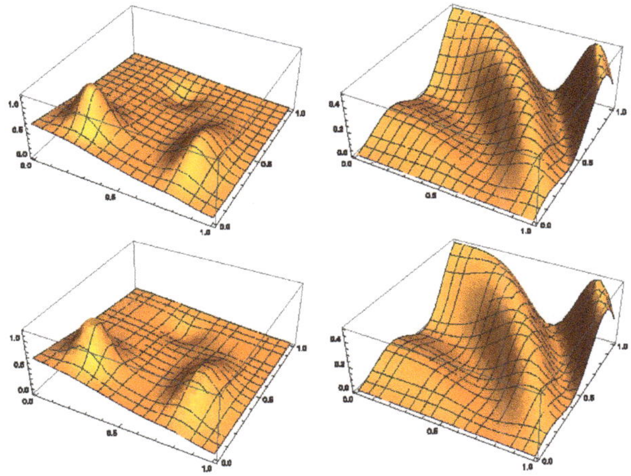

Figure 8. Top, from left to right, plots of the test functions. Bottom, the ones of their respective quasi-interpolants $Q^* f_1$ and $Q^* f_2$ with $h = 1/256$.

The quasi-interpolation error is estimated as

$$\max_{k,\ell=1,\ldots,400} |\mathbb{Q}^* f(x_k, y_\ell) - f(x_k, y_\ell)|,$$

x_k and y_ℓ being equally spaced points in $[0,1]$. The numerical convergence order (NCO) is given by the rate

$$\mathrm{NCO} := \log\left(\frac{\mathtt{E}(h_2)}{\mathtt{E}(h_1)}\right) / \log\left(\frac{h_2}{h_1}\right),$$

where $\mathtt{E}(h)$ stands for the estimated error associated with the step length h.

The quasi-interpolation errors are estimated for different values of the step length h and the NCO are calculated. The results are shown in Table 1. They confirm the theoretical ones.

Table 1. Errors and NCOs for functions f_1 and f_2 with $h = 1/n$, $n = 20, 40, 80, 160$.

	f_1		f_2	
n	**Estimated Error**	**NCO**	**Estimated Error**	**NCO**
16	7.07377×10^{-1}	–	1.47146×10^{-1}	–
32	4.49051×10^{-2}	3.97753	1.44799×10^{-2}	3.34512
64	3.14830×10^{-3}	3.83423	8.62813×10^{-4}	4.06886
128	1.76965×10^{-4}	4.15304	5.36388×10^{-5}	4.00770
256	1.07615×10^{-5}	4.03951	3.48823×10^{-6}	3.94271

6. Conclusions

In this work, C^1 cubic quasi-interpolants have been defined on a Clough–Tocher refinement of a type-1 triangulation, providing directly their BB-coefficients on each of the micro-triangles of the sub-triangulation, which are linear combinations of the values taken by the approximated function at specific points in a neighborhood of each macro-triangle. Cubic polynomials are reproduced. The general problem has a 17-parametric family of solutions and a specific solution has been chosen, which minimizes an upper bound of the quasi-interpolation errors associated with the quartic monomials.

The results improve on those available for cubic quasi-interpolation over a type-1 triangulation since the quasi-interpolation operator is now exact on $\mathbb{P}_3$ instead of $\mathbb{P}_2$.

Author Contributions: Conceptualization, D.B.; Investigation, H.B., A.M. and D. Barrera; Writing—original draft, D.B.; Writing—review & editing, H.B. and A.M. All authors have read and agreed to the published version of the manuscript

Funding: Not applicable

Institutional Review Board Statement: Not applicable

Informed Consent Statement: Not applicable

Data Availability Statement: Not applicable

Acknowledgments: The authors wish to thank the anonymous referees for their very pertinent and useful comments which helped them to improve the original manuscript.

Conflicts of Interest: The authors declare no conflicts of interest.

Appendix A. Masks

This appendix includes the masks provided by Proposition 2 and which do not depend on the parameters indicated. Further, the remaining ones corresponding to the parameters values z_r^* were performed. They have been obtained by minimizing the considered upper bound of the quasi-interpolation errors of the quartic monomials. They are very lengthy expressions, but are included to provide the reader with as much information as possible.

Appendix A.1. Masks That Do Not Depend on Parameters

Mask of $u_{i,j}^{1,1}$:

$$\left(-\frac{47473646953}{77552946585}, -\frac{2854394445629}{361913750730}, -\frac{533680265081}{482551667640}, \frac{209207768203}{103403928780}, \frac{382180214323}{33510532475},\right.$$
$$\frac{209207768203}{103403928780}, -\frac{533680265081}{482551667640}, \frac{6856655665381}{2895310005840}, \frac{120096488429}{160850555880}, -\frac{1333910079319}{1447655002920},$$
$$-\frac{27952071335903}{9651033335280}, -\frac{1333910079319}{1447655002920}, \frac{120096488429}{160850555880}, -\frac{144225313868}{542870626095}, -\frac{2725154777111}{1447655002920},$$
$$\frac{2095907565527}{723827501460}, -\frac{6955013524199}{4342965008760}, \frac{36832622942}{180956875365}, -\frac{64504080325}{289531000584}, \frac{3760571723053}{2171482504380},$$
$$-\frac{2552223421511}{361913750730}, \frac{5169718992073}{361913750730}, -\frac{8031525079}{77552946585}, \frac{5169718992073}{361913750730}, -\frac{2552223421511}{361913750730},$$
$$\frac{3760571723053}{2171482504380}, -\frac{64504080325}{289531000584}, \frac{36832622942}{180956875365}, -\frac{6955013524199}{4342965008760}, \frac{2095907565527}{723827501460},$$
$$-\frac{2725154777111}{1447655002920}, -\frac{31932271589}{40212638970}, -\frac{31932271589}{40212638970}, \frac{73887390529}{1737186003504}, -\frac{25733502500393}{43429650087600},$$
$$\left.\frac{343799911081}{361913750730}, \frac{343799911081}{361913750730}\right)$$

Mask of $u_{i,j}^{-1,-1}$:

$$\left(-\frac{211036174997}{232658839755}, \frac{2854394445629}{1085741252190}, \frac{533680265081}{1447655002920}, \frac{411215804477}{310211786340}, -\frac{382180214323}{100531597425},\right.$$
$$\frac{411215804477}{310211786340}, \frac{533680265081}{1447655002920}, -\frac{6856655665381}{8685930017520}, -\frac{120096488429}{482551667640}, -\frac{3009054929441}{4342965008760},$$
$$\frac{27952071335903}{2895310005840}, -\frac{3009054929441}{4342965008760}, -\frac{120096488429}{482551667640}, \frac{144225313868}{1628611878285}, \frac{2725154777111}{4342965008760},$$
$$-\frac{2095907565527}{2171482504380}, \frac{6955013524199}{13028895026280}, -\frac{36832622942}{542870626095}, \frac{64504080325}{868593001752}, -\frac{2312916720133}{6514447513140},$$
$$\frac{2552223421511}{1085741252190}, -\frac{5169718992073}{1085741252190}, \frac{8031525079}{232658839755}, -\frac{5169718992073}{1085741252190}, \frac{2552223421511}{1085741252190},$$
$$-\frac{2312916720133}{6514447513140}, \frac{64504080325}{868593001752}, -\frac{36832622942}{542870626095}, \frac{6955013524199}{13028895026280}, -\frac{2095907565527}{2171482504380},$$
$$\frac{2725154777111}{4342965008760}, \frac{31932271589}{120637916910}, \frac{31932271589}{120637916910}, -\frac{73887390529}{5211558010512}, \frac{25733502500393}{130288950262800},$$
$$\left.-\frac{343799911081}{1085741252190}, -\frac{343799911081}{1085741252190}\right)$$

Mask of $u_{i,j}^{2,1}$:

$$\left(-\frac{319149498787}{465317679510}, -\frac{285439445629}{542870626095}, -\frac{533680265081}{723827501460}, \frac{364313661373}{155105893170}, \frac{764360428646}{100531597425},\right.$$
$$\frac{209207768203}{155105893170}, -\frac{533680265081}{723827501460}, \frac{6856655665381}{4342965008760}, \frac{120096488429}{241275833820}, -\frac{2419651331509}{2171482504380},$$
$$-\frac{27952071335903}{1447655002920}, -\frac{1333910079319}{2171482504380}, \frac{120096488429}{241275833820}, -\frac{288450627736}{1628611878285}, -\frac{2725154777111}{2171482504380},$$
$$\frac{2095907565527}{1085741252190}, -\frac{6955013524199}{6514447513140}, \frac{73665245884}{542870626095}, -\frac{64504080325}{434296500876}, \frac{4122485473783}{3257223756570},$$
$$-\frac{2552223421511}{542870626095}, \frac{5169718992073}{542870626095}, -\frac{16063050158}{232658839755}, \frac{5169718992073}{542870626095}, -\frac{2552223421511}{542870626095},$$
$$\frac{3760571723053}{3257223756570}, -\frac{64504080325}{434296500876}, \frac{73665245884}{542870626095}, -\frac{6955013524199}{6514447513140}, \frac{2095907565527}{1085741252190},$$
$$-\frac{2725154777111}{2171482504380}, -\frac{31932271589}{60318958455}, -\frac{31932271589}{60318958455}, \frac{73887390529}{2605779005256}, -\frac{25733502500393}{65144475131400},$$
$$\left.\frac{343799911081}{542870626095}, \frac{343799911081}{542870626095}\right)$$

Mask of $u_{i,j}^{1,0}$:

$$\left(-\frac{319149498787}{465317679510}, -\frac{285439445629}{542870626095}, -\frac{533680265081}{723827501460}, \frac{519419554543}{155105893170}, \frac{764360428646}{100531597425},\right.$$
$$\frac{54101875033}{155105893170}, -\frac{533680265081}{723827501460}, \frac{6856655665381}{4342965008760}, \frac{120096488429}{241275833820}, -\frac{3505392583699}{2171482504380},$$
$$-\frac{27952071335903}{1447655002920}, -\frac{248168827129}{2171482504380}, \frac{120096488429}{241275833820}, -\frac{288450627736}{1628611878285}, -\frac{2725154777111}{2171482504380},$$
$$\frac{2095907565527}{1085741252190}, -\frac{6955013524199}{6514447513140}, \frac{73665245884}{542870626095}, -\frac{64504080325}{434296500876}, \frac{4484399224513}{3257223756570},$$
$$-\frac{2552223421511}{542870626095}, \frac{5169718992073}{542870626095}, -\frac{16063050158}{232658839755}, \frac{5169718992073}{542870626095}, -\frac{2552223421511}{542870626095},$$
$$\frac{3398657972323}{3257223756570}, -\frac{64504080325}{434296500876}, \frac{73665245884}{542870626095}, -\frac{6955013524199}{6514447513140}, \frac{2095907565527}{1085741252190},$$
$$-\frac{2725154777111}{2171482504380}, -\frac{31932271589}{60318958455}, -\frac{31932271589}{60318958455}, \frac{73887390529}{2605779005256}, -\frac{25733502500393}{65144475131400},$$
$$\left.\frac{343799911081}{542870626095}, \frac{343799911081}{542870626095}\right)$$

Mask of $u_{i,j}^{1,-1}$:

$$\left(-\frac{176728557928}{232658839755}, -\frac{285439445629}{1085741252190}, -\frac{533680265081}{1447655002920}, \frac{829631340883}{310211786340}, \frac{382180214323}{100531597425},\right.$$
$$\frac{209207768203}{310211786340}, -\frac{533680265081}{1447655002920}, \frac{6856655665381}{8685930017520}, \frac{120096488429}{482551667640}, -\frac{5676875088079}{4342965008760},$$
$$-\frac{27952071335903}{2895310005840}, -\frac{1333910079319}{4342965008760}, \frac{120096488429}{482551667640}, -\frac{144225313868}{1628611878285}, -\frac{2725154777111}{4342965008760},$$
$$\frac{2095907565527}{2171482504380}, -\frac{6955013524199}{13028895026280}, \frac{36832622942}{542870626095}, -\frac{64504080325}{868593001752}, \frac{5208226725973}{6514447513140},$$
$$-\frac{2552223421511}{1085741252190}, \frac{5169718992073}{1085741252190}, -\frac{8031525079}{232658839755}, \frac{5169718992073}{1085741252190}, -\frac{2552223421511}{1085741252190},$$
$$\frac{3760571723053}{6514447513140}, -\frac{64504080325}{868593001752}, \frac{36832622942}{542870626095}, -\frac{6955013524199}{13028895026280}, \frac{2095907565527}{2171482504380},$$
$$-\frac{2725154777111}{4342965008760}, -\frac{31932271589}{120637916910}, -\frac{31932271589}{120637916910}, \frac{73887390529}{5211558010512}, -\frac{25733502500393}{130288950262800},$$
$$\left.\frac{343799911081}{1085741252190}, \frac{343799911081}{1085741252190}\right)$$

Mask of $u_{i,j}^{-1,1}$:

$$\left(-\frac{176728557928}{232658839755}, -\frac{285439445629}{1085741252190}, -\frac{533680265081}{1447655002920}, \frac{209207768203}{310211786340}, \frac{382180214323}{100531597425},\right.$$
$$\frac{829631340883}{310211786340}, -\frac{533680265081}{1447655002920}, \frac{6856655665381}{8685930017520}, \frac{120096488429}{482551667640}, -\frac{1333910079319}{4342965008760},$$
$$-\frac{27952071335903}{2895310005840}, -\frac{5676875088079}{4342965008760}, \frac{120096488429}{482551667640}, -\frac{144225313868}{1628611878285}, -\frac{2725154777111}{4342965008760},$$
$$\frac{2095907565527}{2171482504380}, -\frac{6955013524199}{13028895026280}, \frac{36832622942}{542870626095}, -\frac{64504080325}{868593001752}, \frac{3760571723053}{6514447513140},$$
$$-\frac{2552223421511}{1085741252190}, \frac{5169718992073}{1085741252190}, -\frac{8031525079}{232658839755}, \frac{5169718992073}{1085741252190}, -\frac{2552223421511}{1085741252190},$$
$$\frac{5208226725973}{6514447513140}, -\frac{64504080325}{868593001752}, \frac{36832622942}{542870626095}, -\frac{6955013524199}{13028895026280}, \frac{2095907565527}{2171482504380},$$
$$-\frac{2725154777111}{4342965008760}, -\frac{31932271589}{120637916910}, -\frac{31932271589}{120637916910}, \frac{73887390529}{5211558010512}, -\frac{25733502500393}{130288950262800},$$
$$\left.\frac{343799911081}{1085741252190}, \frac{343799911081}{1085741252190}\right)$$

Mask of $u_{i,j}^{0,1}$:

$$\left(-\frac{319149498787}{465317679510}, -\frac{285439445629}{542870626095}, -\frac{533680265081}{723827501460}, \frac{54101875033}{155105893170}, \frac{764360428646}{100531597425},\right.$$
$$\frac{519419554543}{155105893170}, -\frac{533680265081}{723827501460}, \frac{6856655665381}{4342965008760}, \frac{120096488429}{241275833820}, -\frac{248168827129}{2171482504380},$$
$$-\frac{27952071335903}{1447655002920}, -\frac{3505392583699}{2171482504380}, \frac{120096488429}{241275833820}, -\frac{288450627736}{1628611878285}, -\frac{2725154777111}{2171482504380},$$
$$\frac{2095907565527}{1085741252190}, -\frac{6955013524199}{6514447513140}, \frac{73665245884}{542870626095}, -\frac{64504080325}{434296500876}, \frac{3398657972323}{3257223756570},$$
$$-\frac{2552223421511}{542870626095}, \frac{5169718992073}{542870626095}, -\frac{16063050158}{232658839755}, \frac{5169718992073}{542870626095}, -\frac{2552223421511}{542870626095},$$
$$\frac{4484399224513}{3257223756570}, -\frac{64504080325}{434296500876}, \frac{73665245884}{542870626095}, -\frac{6955013524199}{6514447513140}, \frac{2095907565527}{1085741252190},$$
$$-\frac{2725154777111}{2171482504380}, -\frac{31932271589}{60318958455}, -\frac{31932271589}{60318958455}, \frac{73887390529}{2605779005256}, -\frac{25733502500393}{65144475131400},$$
$$\left.\frac{343799911081}{542870626095}, \frac{343799911081}{542870626095}\right)$$

Mask $u_{i,j}^{1,2}$:

$$\left(-\frac{319149498787}{465317679510}, -\frac{285439445629}{542870626095}, -\frac{533680265081}{723827501460}, \frac{209207768203}{155105893170}, \frac{764360428646}{100531597425},\right.$$
$$\frac{364313661373}{155105893170}, -\frac{533680265081}{723827501460}, \frac{6856655665381}{4342965008760}, \frac{120096488429}{241275833820}, -\frac{1333910079319}{2171482504380},$$
$$-\frac{27952071335903}{1447655002920}, -\frac{2419651331509}{2171482504380}, \frac{120096488429}{241275833820}, -\frac{288450627736}{1628611878285}, -\frac{2725154777111}{2171482504380},$$
$$\frac{2095907565527}{1085741252190}, -\frac{6955013524199}{6514447513140}, \frac{73665245884}{542870626095}, -\frac{64504080325}{434296500876}, \frac{3760571723053}{3257223756570},$$
$$-\frac{2552223421511}{542870626095}, \frac{5169718992073}{542870626095}, -\frac{16063050158}{232658839755}, \frac{5169718992073}{542870626095}, -\frac{2552223421511}{542870626095},$$
$$\frac{4122485473783}{3257223756570}, -\frac{64504080325}{434296500876}, \frac{73665245884}{542870626095}, -\frac{6955013524199}{6514447513140}, \frac{2095907565527}{1085741252190},$$
$$-\frac{2725154777111}{2171482504380}, -\frac{31932271589}{60318958455}, -\frac{31932271589}{60318958455}, \frac{73887390529}{2605779005256}, -\frac{25733502500393}{65144475131400},$$
$$\left.\frac{343799911081}{542870626095}, \frac{343799911081}{542870626095}\right).$$

Mask of $y_{i,j}^{1,-1}$:

$$\Big(-\frac{176522697979}{827231430240}, -\frac{285439445629}{6514447513140}, \frac{17550007242871}{13028895026280}, \frac{43682365976659}{52115580105120}, -\frac{3914887523587}{26057790052560}, 0,$$
$$0, \frac{6856655665381}{52115580105120}, \frac{23609319453817}{52115580105120}, -\frac{4979513337263}{52115580105120}, \frac{8038657526531}{26057790052560}, 0, 0,$$
$$-\frac{72112656934}{4885835634855}, -\frac{2725154777111}{26057790052560}, \frac{2095907565527}{13028895026280}, -\frac{41401785965929}{78173370157680}, \frac{48774214262167}{52115580105120},$$
$$-\frac{231734735789}{325722375657}, \frac{12969882253997}{156346740315360}, \frac{7618392504781}{26057790052560}, -\frac{8209241769433}{52115580105120}, -\frac{2520438176729}{19543342539420},$$
$$0, 0, 0, 0, 0, 0, 0, 0, -\frac{31932271589}{723827501460}, 0, 0, 0, -\frac{26064240688}{180956875365}, 0\Big)$$

Mask of $y_{i,j}^{-1,1}$:

$$\Big(-\frac{176522697979}{827231430240}, -\frac{285439445629}{6514447513140}, 0, 0, -\frac{3914887523587}{26057790052560}, \frac{43682365976659}{52115580105120}, \frac{17550007242871}{13028895026280},$$
$$\frac{6856655665381}{52115580105120}, 0, 0, \frac{8038657526531}{26057790052560}, -\frac{4979513337263}{52115580105120}, \frac{23609319453817}{52115580105120}, -\frac{72112656934}{4885835634855},$$
$$0, 0, 0, 0, 0, 0, 0, 0, -\frac{2520438176729}{19543342539420}, -\frac{8209241769433}{52115580105120}, \frac{7618392504781}{26057790052560}, \frac{12969882253997}{156346740315360},$$
$$-\frac{231734735789}{325722375657}, \frac{48774214262167}{52115580105120}, -\frac{41401785965929}{78173370157680}, \frac{2095907565527}{13028895026280},$$
$$-\frac{2725154777111}{26057790052560}, 0, -\frac{31932271589}{723827501460}, 0, 0, 0, -\frac{26064240688}{180956875365}\Big).$$

Mask of $z_{i,j}^{1,0}$:

$$\Big(-\frac{16044311288503}{10423116021024}, -\frac{285439445629}{434296500876}, -\frac{19207698623}{32170111176}, \frac{7517711285213}{1737186003504}, \frac{13541457918013}{1206379169100},$$
$$\frac{105803839423}{103403928780}, -\frac{533680265081}{482551667640}, \frac{6856655665381}{3474372007008}, \frac{948342242035}{1158124002336}, -\frac{1604093855459}{496338858144},$$
$$-\frac{2302892888971}{80425277940}, -\frac{610082577859}{1447655002920}, \frac{120096488429}{160850555880}, -\frac{72112656934}{325722375657}, -\frac{2725154777111}{1737186003504},$$
$$\frac{2095907565527}{868593001752}, -\frac{5562426555557}{5211558010512}, -\frac{1095500413283}{1737186003504}, \frac{1089486754079}{868593001752}, \frac{505619067587}{1302889502628},$$
$$-\frac{521386636583}{144765500292}, \frac{2085546546332}{180956875365}, \frac{364490450669}{542870626095}, \frac{5169718992073}{361913750730}, -\frac{2552223421511}{361913750730},$$
$$\frac{3519295889233}{2171482504380}, -\frac{64504080325}{289531000584}, \frac{36832622942}{180956875365}, -\frac{6955013524199}{4342965008760}, \frac{2095907565527}{723827501460},$$
$$-\frac{2725154777111}{1447655002920}, -\frac{31932271589}{48255166764}, -\frac{31932271589}{40212638970}, \frac{73887390529}{1737186003504}, -\frac{25733502500393}{43429650087600},$$
$$\frac{521386636583}{723827501460}, \frac{343799911081}{361913750730}\Big)$$

Mask of $z_{i,j}^{0,1}$:

$$\Big(\frac{61848672613411}{52115580105120}, \frac{285439445629}{2171482504380}, \frac{533680265081}{1447655002920}, -\frac{209207768203}{310211786340}, -\frac{4369132774261}{1206379169100},$$
$$- - \frac{8501061371657}{8685930017520}, \frac{339213799501}{206807857560}, -\frac{6856655665381}{17371860035040}, -\frac{120096488429}{482551667640}, \frac{1333910079319}{4342965008760},$$
$$\frac{2700000133115}{289531000584}, \frac{28100144271473}{17371860035040}, \frac{15512464547161}{5790620011680}, \frac{72112656934}{1628611878285}, \frac{2725154777111}{4342965008760},$$
$$-\frac{2095907565527}{2171482504380}, \frac{6955013524199}{13028895026280}, -\frac{36832622942}{542870626095}, \frac{64504080325}{868593001752}, -\frac{3760571723053}{6514447513140},$$
$$\frac{2552223421511}{1085741252190}, -\frac{5169718992073}{1085741252190}, -\frac{1205912703113}{1628611878285}, -\frac{1086920646923}{542870626095}, -\frac{2388094137299}{2171482504380},$$
$$\frac{6440703111091}{6514447513140}, -\frac{1218494914729}{868593001752}, \frac{6656146000559}{8685930017520}, -\frac{21722746362811}{26057790052560}, -\frac{2095907565527}{4342965008760},$$
$$\frac{2725154777111}{8685930017520}, \frac{31932271589}{120637916910}, \frac{31932271589}{241275833820}, -\frac{73887390529}{5211558010512}, \frac{25733502500393}{130288950262800},$$
$$-\frac{343799911081}{1085741252190}, -\frac{37792053085}{434296500876}\Big)$$

Mask of $x_{i,j}^{1,0}$:

$$\left(\frac{61848672613411}{52115580105120}, \frac{285439445629}{2171482504380}, -\frac{339213799501}{206807857560}, -\frac{8501061371657}{8685930017520}, -\frac{4369132774261}{1206379169100},\right.$$
$$-\frac{209207768203}{310211786340}, \frac{533680265081}{1447655002920}, -\frac{6856655665381}{17371860035040}, \frac{15512464547161}{5790620011680}, \frac{28100144271473}{17371860035040},$$
$$\frac{2700000133115}{289531000584}, \frac{1333910079319}{4342965008760}, -\frac{120096488429}{482551667640}, \frac{72112656934}{1628611878285}, \frac{2725154777111}{8685930017520},$$
$$-\frac{2095907565527}{4342965008760}, -\frac{21722746362811}{26057790052560}, \frac{6656146000559}{8685930017520}, -\frac{1218494914729}{868593001752}, \frac{6440703111091}{6514447513140},$$
$$-\frac{2388094137299}{2171482504380}, -\frac{1086920646923}{542870626095}, -\frac{1205912703113}{1628611878285}, -\frac{5169718992073}{1085741252190}, \frac{2552223421511}{1085741252190},$$
$$-\frac{3760571723053}{6514447513140}, \frac{64504080325}{868593001752}, -\frac{36832622942}{542870626095}, \frac{6955013524199}{13028895026280}, -\frac{2095907565527}{2171482504380},$$
$$\frac{2725154777111}{4342965008760}, \frac{31932271589}{241275833820}, \frac{31932271589}{120637916910}, -\frac{73887390529}{5211558010512}, \frac{25733502500393}{130288950262800},$$
$$\left.-\frac{37792053085}{434296500876}, -\frac{343799911081}{1085741252190}\right)$$

Mask of $x_{i,j}^{0,1}$:

$$\left(-\frac{16044311288503}{10423116021024}, -\frac{285439445629}{434296500876}, -\frac{533680265081}{482551667640}, \frac{105803839423}{103403928780}, \frac{13541457918013}{1206379169100},\right.$$
$$\frac{7517711285213}{1737186003504}, -\frac{19207698623}{32170111176}, \frac{6856655665381}{3474372007008}, \frac{120096488429}{160850555880}, -\frac{610082577859}{1447655002920},$$
$$-\frac{2302892888971}{80425277940}, -\frac{1604093855459}{4963388858144}, \frac{948342242035}{1158124002336}, -\frac{72112656934}{325722375657}, -\frac{2725154777111}{1447655002920},$$
$$\frac{2095907565527}{723827501460}, -\frac{6955013524199}{4342965008760}, \frac{36832622942}{180956875365}, -\frac{64504080325}{289531000584}, \frac{3519295889233}{2171482504380},$$
$$-\frac{2552223421511}{361913750730}, \frac{5169718992073}{361913750730}, \frac{364490450669}{542870626095}, \frac{2085546546332}{180956875365}, -\frac{521386636583}{144765500292},$$
$$\frac{505619067587}{1302889502628}, \frac{1089486754079}{868593001752}, -\frac{1095500413283}{1737186003504}, -\frac{5562426555557}{5211558010512}, \frac{2095907565527}{868593001752},$$
$$-\frac{2725154777111}{1737186003504}, -\frac{31932271589}{40212638970}, -\frac{31932271589}{48255166764}, \frac{73887390529}{1737186003504}, -\frac{25733502500393}{43429650087600},$$
$$\left.\frac{343799911081}{361913750730}, \frac{521386636583}{723827501460}\right).$$

Masks associated with the parameter values z_r^*

Mask of $t_{i,j}$:

$$\left(-\frac{4531890127703}{13028895026280}, \frac{36006119259559}{39086685078840}, -\frac{20242568383524532937}{70422033801573698400}, \frac{17297520671281}{13028895026280},\right.$$
$$\frac{29593026919579}{5428706260950}, \frac{26994849992255621402765}{15974830661375510686944}, \frac{9165456190681132751}{6161927957637698610}, \frac{30904875065308}{24429178174275},$$
$$\frac{6402823528855197916 9}{24647711830550794440}, \frac{5763346201075045008969 35}{22364762925925714961721 6}, -\frac{361472787357233}{26057790052560},$$
$$-\frac{5791606797469437299171}{12288331277981162066880}, -\frac{9645124685875037347 9}{49295423661101588880}, \frac{9488658832619183459}{7783487946489724560},$$
$$\frac{3994283936045967 67}{37919556662385837 60}, -\frac{21206215098462805471}{49295423661101588880}, -\frac{888284192303734585}{1556697589297944912},$$
$$\frac{1354491661355237551055957}{1863730243827142913476800}, \frac{1387013003869}{8685930017520}, -\frac{2878083358530960513494389}{10064143316666571732774720},$$
$$-\frac{1681864799399}{558381215412}, \frac{4586462085623}{697976519265}, \frac{179554805254886612513}{221829406474957149960 0},$$
$$\frac{5674250490552090470842 19}{1490984195061714330781 44}, \frac{72692170759927858695516 7}{79874153306877553434720 0}, -\frac{108722974607171930519712 7}{629008957291660733298420},$$
$$\frac{7013088865869552773812 9}{31949661322751021373888}, -\frac{5574602285095942873064 3}{27955953657407143702152 0}, -\frac{292198896309538327}{972935993311215570},$$
$$\frac{14888455883830641356 9}{49295423661101588880}, -\frac{7135795471566067417}{1895977833119291880}, -\frac{1112520265706788528800107}{3354714438888885724425824 0},$$
$$\frac{1767938963792804738010533}{6709428877777714488516480}, -\frac{232977362971875229}{341276009961472538 40}, -\frac{48551848730147429474011}{276487453754576146504800},$$
$$\left.-\frac{2318866060366412313392359}{8386786097222143110645 60}, -\frac{7657959982383155961476047}{33547144388888857244258240}\right)$$

Mask of $b_{i,j}$:

$$\Big(0,0,\frac{33654106472661220639}{246477118305507944440},0,0,-\frac{289311192782870590597781}{7987415330687755343472O},-\frac{14771341526479835128 9}{492954236611015888880},$$

$$0,-\frac{71687410464642966611}{492954236611015888880},-\frac{372356219454533397190951 99}{11182381462962857480860 80},0,-\frac{345992170811097165259 3}{122883312779811620668 80},$$

$$\frac{10915736212229383229}{3521101690078684920},-\frac{17837846075447753051}{7783487946489724560},-\frac{2964129356331035}{27085397615989884},$$

$$\frac{80572693526252875501}{492954236611015888880},-\frac{584083821479971933}{1945871986622431140},-\frac{1437915323322245022121277}{18637302438271429134768 00},0,$$

$$\frac{933461094140338011503538 1}{100641433166665717327747 20},0,0,\frac{65479845261671636 65}{887317625899828599 84},\frac{20615656792515848815700 09}{74549209753085716539072 0},$$

$$-\frac{3132760642018231502419567}{798741533068775534347200},\frac{1490762720001245530293439}{629008957291660733298420},-\frac{3251450300041228327569 77}{15974830661375510686944 0},$$

$$\frac{8646494711181661614169}{559119073148142874043 04},-\frac{4440165076962254041}{7783487946489724560},-\frac{895180804105163435 39}{492954236611015888880},$$

$$\frac{14256041226850386701}{3791955666238583760},-\frac{2818467836914786993979 89}{33547144388888857244258240},-\frac{91133461251786783888134 5}{134188577555554289770329 6},$$

$$\frac{352952140065170249}{6825520199229450768},-\frac{606565515626167530063 1}{552974907509152293009 60},\frac{268106510964236440057425 1}{838678609722214311064560},$$

$$\frac{1821351235897392862040723}{670942887777771448851648}\Big)$$

Mask of $y_{i,j}^{2,1}$:

$$\Big(-\frac{12271780430239}{11167624308240},\frac{23115036621721}{13028895026280},-\frac{697752284589655474}{146712570419945205},\frac{19233346304581}{5211558010512},$$

$$\frac{29593026919579}{1809568753650},\frac{269948499922556214027 65}{5324943553791836895648},\frac{31613815182159137939}{164318078870338629 60},\frac{123384121964447}{65144475131400},$$

$$\frac{7928485881111597527}{20539759858792328 70},\frac{2940388026606543576781849}{372746048765428582695360},-\frac{361472787357233}{8685930017520},$$

$$-\frac{5791606797469437299171}{409611042599372068896 0},-\frac{89635388032606534969}{328636157740677259 20},\frac{23919500601269859 55}{10377983928652966 08},$$

$$-\frac{833558368032964139}{6319926110397639 60},\frac{2966315162024509075}{6572723154813545184},\frac{4586462085623}{232658839755},-\frac{869086434956909083}{6486239955408103 80},$$

$$\frac{1447826441014520643970577}{621243414609047637825600},\frac{444445950829}{2605779005256},-\frac{2445437288558816620140901}{33547144388888857244258240},$$

$$-\frac{1681864799399}{186127071804},\frac{3280256906864456103 53}{14788627098330476664 00},\frac{5674250490552090470842 19}{496994731687238110260 48},$$

$$\frac{72692170759927858695516 7}{266247177689591844782400},-\frac{108722974607171930519712 7}{209669652430553577766140},\frac{70130888658695527738129}{106498871075836737912 96},$$

$$-\frac{557460228509594287306 43}{931865121913571456738 40},-\frac{2370991526403268243}{25944959821632415 20},\frac{17805640243921011986 9}{328636157740677259 20},$$

$$-\frac{40037025445563025 61}{631992611039763960},-\frac{95145411039889983536881 1}{111823814629628574808608 0},\frac{176793896379280473801053 3}{223647629259257149617216 0},$$

$$\frac{8956702739347499}{5687933499357875640},-\frac{4855184873014742947401 1}{921624845848587155016 00},-\frac{231886606036641231339235 9}{279559536574071437021520},$$

$$-\frac{7657959982383155961476047}{11182381462962857480860 80}\Big),$$

Mask of $y_{i,j}^{-1,-2}$:

$$\Big(\frac{279021003241424923}{148256913266470944},0,-\frac{2095907565527}{13028895026280},\frac{2987873000594748871}{252797044415905584 0},\frac{251548442921233}{260577900525600},$$

$$-\frac{391511615876220607}{78999076379970495},0,0,\frac{2725154777111}{26057790052560},-\frac{61670773096205223361}{328636157740677259 20},\frac{11080236034699}{6514447513140},$$

$$\frac{119712715237402707269}{32863615774067725920},0,-\frac{358415383500814 61}{16251238569593930 40},0,0,\frac{72112656934}{4885835634855},-\frac{6856655665381}{52115580105120},$$

$$\frac{285439445629}{6514447513140},-\frac{822872808792542327}{5188991964326483040},\frac{20342292042566996155}{6572723154813545184},-\frac{123959409326402622509}{32863615774067725920},$$

$$-\frac{1437666942653}{52115580105120},\frac{41709834343289924069}{16431807887033862960},-\frac{103267105684894211989}{32863615774067725920},\frac{33400355926961627}{2594495982163241520},$$

$$0,0,0,0,0,0,0,0,\frac{31083919823327614673}{1478862709833047666400},\frac{31932271589}{723827501460},0\Big)$$

Mask of $y_{i,j}^{-2,-1}$:

$$\left(-\frac{3512153958923412841}{1037798392865296608}, 0, 0, \frac{132824112520673051}{252797044415905584}, -\frac{5398434624971}{5790620011680}, \frac{3368897166768107761}{5055940888318111168},\right.$$
$$-\frac{2095907565527}{13028895026280}, 0, 0, \frac{5140084992534916920 1}{32863615774067725920}, \frac{2771608293079}{8685930017520}, -\frac{12998263840825876142 9}{32863615774067725920},$$
$$\frac{2725154777111}{26057790052560}, \frac{74797826319829301}{1137586699871575128}, 0, 0, 0, 0, 0, \frac{34028298205171069}{2594495982163241520},$$
$$-\frac{7850326929078680512 1}{32863615774067725920}, \frac{4837764506653326713}{2053975985879232870}, \frac{5150734764713}{10423116021024}, -\frac{12997484590652924323 9}{32863615774067725920},$$
$$\frac{1806789951527748394 9}{4694802253438246560}, -\frac{821616924236123443}{5188991964326483040}, \frac{285439445629}{6514447513140}, -\frac{6856655665381}{52115580105120},$$
$$\left.\frac{72112656934}{4885835634855}, 0, 0, 0, 0, 0, \frac{3045745544524018757}{29577254196660953328 0}, 0, \frac{31932271589}{723827501460}\right)$$

Mask of $y_{i,j}^{1,2}$:

$$\left(-\frac{22557725931173}{39086685078840}, \frac{10223953983883}{26057790052560}, \frac{14303048446047913787}{8215903943516931480}, 0, 0, -\frac{7343052350198304428891}{5324943553791836895648},\right.$$
$$-\frac{811559741641047234 53}{16431807887033862960}, -\frac{47075659357}{13028895026280}, -\frac{6487155163849912810 1}{32863615774067725920},$$
$$-\frac{372356219454533971909519 9}{372746048765428582695360}, 0, -\frac{2814702740319531297679}{4096110425993720688960}, \frac{758098052459464836 5}{1643180788703386296},$$
$$-\frac{3073350921486401347}{1037798392865296608}, -\frac{215819734497942031}{252797044415905584}, \frac{10974453712715658180 1}{32863615774067725920},$$
$$-\frac{2370363584125058801}{2594495982163241520}, -\frac{1437915323322245022121277}{621243414609047637825600}, 0, \frac{933461094140338011503538 1}{335471443888885724425824 0},$$
$$0, 0, \frac{8919157102449659699}{4225322028094421904 0}, \frac{2061565679251584881570009}{2484973658436190551302 40}, -\frac{3132760642018231502419567}{2662471776895918447824 00},$$
$$\frac{3794507748436261309070 08}{5241741310763839444153 5}, -\frac{6831442640606235780506 5}{1064988710758367379129 6}, \frac{2861634525240038600401 9}{4659325609567857283692 0},$$
$$-\frac{347571779754942689}{259449598216324152}, -\frac{5348028950193099269 3}{32863615774067725920}, \frac{526118968055696668 9}{1263985222079527920},$$
$$-\frac{2818467836914786993979 89}{1118238146296285748086 080}, -\frac{4234540751973561807544133}{2236476292592571496172160}, \frac{203356487425511647}{227517339974315025 6},$$
$$\left.-\frac{6065655515626167530063 1}{1843249691697174310032 0}, \frac{2681065109642364400574251}{2795595365740714370215 20}, \frac{1821351235897392862040723}{223647629259257149617216}\right)$$

Mask of $z_{i,j}^{1,1}$:

$$\left(-\frac{55838625716687}{52115580105120}, \frac{28252946643043}{4342965008760}, -\frac{3541977685067376326 3}{27386346478389771 60}, \frac{340862589821}{77552946585},\right.$$
$$\frac{36472270777393}{12063791691 00}, \frac{2278456774419731489904 5}{1774981184597278965216}, \frac{41709834343289924069}{5477269295677954320}, \frac{184986982915643}{86859300175200},$$
$$\frac{16061835113666299907}{15649340844794155 20}, \frac{6960779820048589013942 27}{2484973658436190551302 4}, -\frac{222664500682471}{2895310005840},$$
$$-\frac{4377474382328624429291}{1365370141997906896320}, -\frac{1032671056848942119 89}{1095453859135590864 0}, \frac{126490342282778972 63}{17296639881088276 80},$$
$$-\frac{954829982212037 57}{84265681471968528}, -\frac{3274820030539396707 7}{1095453859135590864 0}, -\frac{162996908964716752 3}{86483199405441384 0},$$
$$\frac{1550315458679682817567037}{2070811382030158792752 00}, -\frac{64504080325}{108574125219}, -\frac{4294689070651846383297973}{1118238146296285748086080},$$
$$-\frac{10208893686044}{542870626095}, \frac{20678875968292}{542870626095}, \frac{31083919823327614673}{4929542366110158888 00}, \frac{1730212107893740329498 83}{1656649105624127034201 6},$$
$$\frac{1770022110879746120192767}{887490592298639482608 00}, -\frac{3202974039104927951977 03}{1747247103587946481384 5}, \frac{7144903799533175173912 9}{3549962369194557930432},$$
$$-\frac{6628353554071922205368 3}{3106217073045238189128 0}, -\frac{6269208785686213 3}{86483199405441384 0}, \frac{1251899845330806615 89}{1095453859135590864 0},$$
$$-\frac{417844641336210772}{26333025459990165}, -\frac{5074657885263635628527 63}{3727460487654285826953 60}, \frac{2754579679065107565823973}{745492097530857165390720},$$
$$-\frac{35841538350081461}{54170795231979768 0}, -\frac{1821333930266442717510 1}{3072082819495290516720 0}, -\frac{2445005075701749729458923}{931865121913571456738 40},$$
$$\left.-\frac{8248110067234692639264367}{372746048765428582695360}\right)$$

Mask of $x_{i,j}^{1,1}$:

$$\Big(\frac{25735396581967}{52115580105120}, \frac{20499774026527}{86859300175520}, \frac{48377645066653326713}{684658661959744290}, -\frac{147165410935}{62042357268}, -\frac{4542756612353}{241275833820},$$
$$-\frac{95967048423019818088417}{88749059229863948260800}, -\frac{10549610284487262413}{78246704223970776O}, -\frac{61898203625857}{17371860035040},$$
$$-\frac{785032692907868O5121}{10954538591355908640}, -\frac{35948761447675257479361 19}{124248682921809527565120}, \frac{69404143337381}{1447655002920},$$
$$\frac{3119383890644764638467}{1365370141997906896320}, \frac{1371966821897715O6217}{10954538591355908640}, -\frac{1467747067978903 9247}{1729663988108827680},$$
$$\frac{485584310487O4523}{842656814719685 28}, \frac{5687811922102712352 1}{10954538591355908640}, -\frac{62064145578652691}{864831994054413840},$$
$$-\frac{1508165407920643644274877}{2070811382030158792752 00}, \frac{322520401625}{868593001752}, \frac{6231253028279350105536421}{1118238146296285748086080}, \frac{2552223421511}{217148250438},$$
$$-\frac{5169718992073}{217148250438}, \frac{30457455445240187 57}{985908473222031777 60}, \frac{3181054608506348776535 93}{828324552812063517100 80},$$
$$-\frac{2395882352848026640135327}{8874905922986394826080 0}, \frac{280444972598738032686143}{139779768287035718510 76},$$
$$-\frac{7223992759731348613972 9}{354996236919455793043 2}, \frac{7260604315457509804750 7}{3106217073045238189128 0}, -\frac{1629341147368958081}{864831994054413840},$$
$$-\frac{20212013123489501029}{2190907718271181728}, \frac{3225445712758438091}{2106642036799213 20}, \frac{2114735739446727145087 31}{3727460487654285826953 60},$$
$$-\frac{3346564108228489262512037}{745492097530857165390720}, \frac{74797826319829301}{379195566623858376}, \frac{20467292349251591 51}{614416563899058103344 0},$$
$$\frac{2533527588429480231127171}{931865121913571456738 40}, \frac{860220011814561464593735 9}{372746048765428582695360}\Big)$$

References

1. Sorokina, T.; Zeilfelder, F. Optimal quasi-interpolation by quadratic C^1 splines on four-directional meshes. In *Approximation Theory*; Chui, C.K., Neamtu, M., Schumaker, L.L., , Eds.; Nashboro Press: Brentwood, TN, USA, 2005; Volume XI, pp. 423–438.
2. Sorokina, T.; Zeilfelder, F. An explicit quasi-interpolation scheme based on C^1 quartic splines on type-1 triangulations. *Comput. Aided Geom. Des.* **2008**, *25*, 1–13. [CrossRef]
3. Nürnberger, G.; Rössl, C.; Seidel, H.-P.; Zeilfelder, F. Quasi-Interpolation by quadratic piecewise polynomials in three variables. *Comput. Aided Geom. Des.* **2005**, *22*, 221–249. [CrossRef]
4. Sorokina, T.; Zeilfelder, F. Local Quasi-Interpolation by cubic C^1 splines on type-6 tetrahedral partitions. *IMA J. Numer. Anal.* **2007**, *27*, 74–101. [CrossRef]
5. Barrera, D.; Dagnino, C.; Ibáñez, M.J.; Remogna, S. Quasi-interpolation by C^1 quartic splines on type-1 triangulations. *J. Comput. Appl. Math.* **2019**, *349*, 225–238. [CrossRef]
6. Barrera, D.; Conti, C.; Dagnino, C.; Ibáñez, M.J.; Remogna, S. C^1-Quartic Butterfly-spline interpolation on type-1 triangulations. In *Approximation Theory XVI, Proceedings of the Conference on Mathematics & Statistics, Nashville, TN, USA, 19–22 May 2019*; Fasshauer, G.E., Neamtu, M., Schumaker, L.L., Eds.; Springer Nature Switzerland AG : Cham, Switzerland, 2021; Volume 336, Chapter 2, pp. 11–26.
7. Barrera, D.; Dagnino, C; Ibáñez, M.J.; Remogna, S. Point and differential C^1 quasi-interpolation on three direction meshes. *J. Comput. Appl. Maths.* **2019**, *354*, 373–389. [CrossRef]
8. Clough, R.W.; Tocher, J.L. Finite element stiffness matrices for analysis of plates in bending. In Proceedings of the Conference on Matrix Methods in Structural Mechanics, Wright Patterson Air Force Base, OH, USA, 26–28 October 1965; Przemieniecki, J.S., Ed.; Wright-Patterson Air Force Base: Dayton, OH, USA, 1967; pp. 515–545.
9. Lai, M.-J.; Schumaker, L.L. *Spline Functions on Triangulations. Encyclopedia of Mathematics and Its Applications, 110*; Cambridge University Press: Cambridge, UK, 2007.
10. Franke, R. Scattered data interpolation: Tests of some methods. *Math. Comput.* **1982**, *38*, 181–200.
11. Nielson, G.M. A first order blending method for triangles based upon cubic interpolation. *Int. J. Numer. Meth. Eng.* **1978**, *15*, 308–318. [CrossRef]

mathematics

MDPI

Article

The Novel Analytical–Numerical Method for Multi-Dimensional Multi-Term Time-Fractional Equations with General Boundary Conditions

Ji Lin [1,†], Sergiy Reutskiy [2,†], Yuhui Zhang [1,†], Yu Sun [3,†] and Jun Lu [3,*,†]

1 College of Mechanics and Materials, Hohai University, Nanjing 210098, China
2 A. Pidhornyi Institute of Mechanical Engineering Problems of NAS of Ukraine, 2/10 Pozharsky Street, 61046 Kharkiv, Ukraine
3 Nanjing Hydraulic Research Institute, Nanjing 210029, China
* Correspondence: lujun@nhri.cn
† These authors contributed equally to this work.

Abstract: This article presents a simple but effective two-step analytical–numerical algorithm for solving multi-dimensional multi-term time-fractional equations. The first step is to derive an analytic representation that satisfies boundary requirements for 1D, 2D, and 3D problems, respectively. The second step is the meshless approximation where the Müntz polynomials are used to form the approximate solution and the unknown parameters are obtained by imposing the approximation for the governing equations. We illustrate first the detailed derivation of the analytic approximation and then the numerical implementation of the solution procedure. Several numerical examples are provided to verify the accuracy, efficiency, and adaptability to problems with general boundary conditions. The numerical results are compared with exact solutions and numerical methods reported in the literature, showing that the algorithm has great potential for multi-dimensional multi-term time-fractional equations with various boundary conditions.

Keywords: multi-dimensional fractional equations; multi-term fractional equations; meshless method; collocation method; analytic representation

MSC: 65D05; 34K37

Citation: Lin, J.; Reutskiy, S.; Zhang, Y.; Sun, Y.; Lu, J. The Novel Analytical–Numerical Method for Multi-Dimensional Multi-Term Time-Fractional Equations with General Boundary Conditions. *Mathematics* **2023**, *11*, 929. https://doi.org/10.3390/math11040929

Academic Editor: Andrey Amosov

Received: 5 January 2023
Revised: 7 February 2023
Accepted: 10 February 2023
Published: 12 February 2023

1. Introduction

In recent years, many mathematical models with time-fractional multi-term derivatives have been studied in physics, hydrology, chemistry, etc. Hilfer [1] provided a collection of fractional calculus applications in physics. Molz [2] reviewed some fundamental properties of fractional motion and applications in hydrology. Singh [3] analyzed a chemical kinetics system pertaining to a fractional derivative. Furthermore, the applications of fractional equations can also be found in [4]. The well-known cable equations with fractional-order temporal operators belong to this class. They were introduced to model electronic properties of spiny neuronal dendrites [5,6]. The time-fractional partial differential equations (TFPDEs) can also include the Sobolev equations, which have been used to model many phenomena, such as the migration of moisture in soil, thermodynamics, and the motion of fluid in various media [7,8]. The equations of different models of heat transfer, whether the classical or dual-phase-lagging ones, undoubtedly also fall into this group [9]. Fractional differential equations have broad applications for the fact that fractional operators can describe physical phenomena more precisely than classical integral operators for some practical problems. The collection of real world applications of fractional differential equations can be seen in [10] and references therein.

Solutions to fractional partial differential equations are crucial for representing physical phenomena. Some analytical methods have been proposed that can be useful for parametric study. Liu carried out an analytical study for magnetohydrodynamic flow using fractional derivatives [11]. Ming derived the analytical solution for the problems containing multi-term time-fractional diffusion [12]. Ding proposed an analytical solution to the multi-term TFPDEs considering the non-local damping term [13] and also the fractional delay PDEs with mixed boundary conditions [14]. Jong used the analytic expression of the multi-term fractional integral operators to obtain the analytical expressions for the fractional equations [15]. Jiang investigated the multi-term fractional diffusion equations and obtained the analytical solutions by the method of separation variables [16]. In [17], the Laplace transform method was used to derive the solution to the time-fractional distributed-order heat conduction law. The Adomian decomposition method was also being used in [18]. Despite the fact that so many analytical techniques have been developed, the explicit forms of analytical or semi-analytical solutions are rare only for some problems under certain idealized conditions. For the further prospects of engineering applications, the numerical methods are still necessary and useful tools in this field. Numerical methods have already been used to observe some important mathematical models. Liu investigated the fluid mechanics for semiconductor circuit breakers based on finite element analysis [19]. Yang, Liu, and Xu applied functional differential equations to analyze the problems in financial accounting [20–22]. A computational heuristic was designed to solve the nonlinear Lienard differential model [23]. The nonuniform difference scheme was applied to study the distributed-order fractional parabolic equations with fractional Laplacian in [24]. A fast Fourier spectral exponential time-differencing method was used to solve time-fractional mobile–immobile equations [25]. A fast difference scheme was proposed to solve the fractional equations considering non-smooth data [26]. Some other works can be found in [27–29] and references therein. Among them, the most popular methods are mesh-based methods. Some of the references and studies are listed below. Dehghan [30] proposed a high-order numerical algorithm based on the finite difference scheme for multi-term time-fractional diffusion wave problems. The Galerkin finite element method [31] was proposed for the approximation of the multi-term time-fractional diffusion equations. The finite difference and the finite element method were used to solve the multi-term time-fractional equations that are mixed by the sub-diffusion and diffusion-wave equation [32]. The fast algorithm combined with the finite difference method was used to solve multi-term time-fractional reaction–diffusion wave equations with stability analysis and error analysis [33]. The second-order numerical method was proposed for the problems with non-smooth solutions [34]. As implied by the name, mesh-based methods require the mesh of the whole domain and also information about the nodal topology that may introduce some unreasonable constraints on the problems. The automatic and efficient approach to constructing mesh for 3D complicated domains has long been the challenge for computational mechanics. Spectral methods [35,36] and spectral-based methods, especially those based on the collocation method, have been published recently [37,38]. The spectral-based method has also been used to solve the distributed order time-fractional diffusion equations in [39]. A pseudo-spectral method based on the reproducing kernel has been proposed to study the time-fractional diffusion-wave equation [40].

In this paper, considering the advantages of analytical and numerical methods, a novel analytical–numerical method is proposed for solving multi-term TFPDEs with boundary conditions of general kinds. First, we apply the Fourier method, which can also be regarded as an expansion method over the eigenfunctions, in order to remove the partial derivatives with respect to the space variables and transform the original TFPDE into fractional ordinary differential equations (FODEs) without truncation error. In the general case of the time-dependent non-homogeneous boundary conditions, the solutions with the features of separation of spatial variables are not available naturally. The time-dependent non-homogeneous term in the equation also poses a problem for the application of the Fourier method. To deal with the time dependence boundary conditions and the source term, the Green function method and the operational methods such as the Laplace transform method are used [41]. A similar technique has been proposed for the time-fractional

PDEs [42,43]. Then, we apply the recently proposed meshless collocation method, the backward substitution method (BSM) [44–46], to solve each FODE individually. In [44], the BSM was also applied to solve systems of FODEs. The BSM technique can also deal with the non-homogeneous time-dependent source term. The BSM is a newly developed meshless method. By introducing special analytical functions or numerical approximations that satisfy the boundary conditions, the original problem is degenerated into a homogeneous one. Then, the BSM attempts to form an orthogonal basis system that satisfies the homogeneous boundary conditions in a general way. The approximated solution is formed using the proposed basis system where the weighted parameters are determined by backward substituting the approximation into the governing equations. This improvement has significantly increased the accuracy and stability of the usual collocation methods. Recently, some variants of the BSM have been proposed, such as the space-time BSM [47], the localized BSM [48], and the Fourier-based BSM [49]. In order to apply the BSM for the fractional differential equations, some special bases should be used. Firstly, the solution of the fractional equations can contain the fractional-power terms where the common bases cannot be used for such purpose. Secondly, in terms of the BSM, the collocation method is applied. In order to apply the collocation method, it is critical that derivatives of the trial functions should be approximated by the same trial bases where the common polynomial bases cannot be used. In order to match the two requirements, the Müntz polynomials can be considered as alternative bases. The reasons behind this is to apply the critical feature that a fractional derivative of a Müntz polynomial is again a Müntz polynomial. Therefore, we can hope to obtain a good approximation for the fractional derivatives by the Müntz polynomial approximation. Due to these outstanding features, Müntz polynomials have been widely used for the solution of fractional equations in literature. Esmaeili [50] provided the solution for fractional differential equations with the Müntz polynomial collocation method. Mokhtary [51] solved the fractional problems with the Müntz polynomial Tau method. Bahmanpour discussed the Müntz polynomial wavelets collocation method for fractional equations [52]. Recently, Maleknejad discussed the Müntz–Legendre wavelet approach [53]. The Müntz polynomial has also been absorbed in the BSM to solve fractional equations [46].

The remainder of this paper is organized as follows. Section 2 contains a brief definition of the problems to be solved and also a brief description of the solution process. Section 3 contains the derivation of the analytical approximations satisfying the general boundary conditions. This technique for the orthogonal basis is described in detail in Section 4. Following the main algorithm in Section 5, numerical examples that illustrate the presented procedure are placed in Section 6. Finally, a brief conclusion is drawn in Section 7.

2. Preliminaries

In the present work, our goal is to find an effective solution to the following multi-dimensional multi-term time-fractional partial differential equations (TFPDEs):

$$\mathcal{L}_t[u] = \mathcal{M}_t\left[\nabla^2 u\right] + f(\mathbf{x},t),\ t \in [0,T],\ \mathbf{x} \in \Omega^d = [0,1]^d, d = 1,2,3, \tag{1}$$

where

$$\mathcal{L}_t = D_t^{(\mu)} + \sum_{k=1}^{I} a_k(t) D_t^{(\mu_k)},\ \mathcal{M}_t = \sum_{k=I+1}^{K} a_k(t) D_t^{(\mu_k)}, \tag{2}$$

in which $\mu \in (l-1,l]$, $0 \leq \mu_k < \mu$, $D_t^{(0)}[\varphi] \equiv \varphi$ is the identical operator, and $a_k(t)$, $k = 1,\ldots,K$. Some initial conditions (ICs) should be prescribed in advance for the time-dependent problems

$$u(\mathbf{x},0) = u_0(\mathbf{x}),\ \frac{\partial u(\mathbf{x},0)}{\partial t} = u_1(\mathbf{x}),\ldots,\ \frac{\partial^{l-1} u(\mathbf{x},0)}{\partial t^{l-1}} = u_{l-1}(\mathbf{x}), \tag{3}$$

where l is the highest integer derivative of the considered problem.

The operator $D_t^{(\nu)}$, which has the following form,

$$D_t^{(\nu)}[\xi(x,t)] = \begin{cases} \frac{1}{\Gamma(n-\nu)} \int_0^x \frac{\partial_t^{(n)} \xi(x,\tau) d\tau}{(t-\tau)^{\nu-n+1}}, & n-1 < \nu < n, \\ \partial_t^{(n)} \xi(x,t), & \nu = n, \end{cases} \tag{4}$$

is the Caputo fractional derivative of the order ν. In particular, if $\xi(x,t)$ is the power function t^z, we have

$$D_t^{(\nu)}[t^z] = 0, \tag{5}$$

if $z \in \mathcal{N}_0$ and $z < n$, and

$$D_t^{(\nu)}[t^z] = \frac{\Gamma(z+1)}{\Gamma(z+1-\nu)} t^{z-\nu}, \tag{6}$$

if $z \in \mathcal{N}_0$ and $z \geq n$ or $z \notin \mathcal{N}_0$ and $z > n-1$. Further, $\mathcal{N}_0$ denotes the set of all non-negative integers.

In order to solve Equation (1), suitable boundary conditions have to be prescribed to ensure the solvability of the problems. In the present work, we address general forms of boundary conditions:

$$B_i[u] = \alpha_i \frac{\partial u(\mathbf{x},t)}{\partial n_i} + \beta_i u(\mathbf{x},t) = g_i(\mathbf{x},t),\ \mathbf{x} \in \partial\Omega^d,\ \Omega^d = [0,1]^d,\ \alpha_i^2 + \beta_i^2 \neq 0, \tag{7}$$

where $\partial u(\mathbf{x},t)/\partial n_i$ denotes differentiation along the outward unit normal direction of the surface boundary, and $i = 1,2$, for $d = 1$, $i = 1,\ldots,4$ for $d = 2$, and $i = 1,\ldots,6$ for $d = 3$.

It is known to all that in mathematics and engineering applications, the Fourier expansion in eigenfunctions of the differential operator is an efficient numerical method in the case of homogeneous BCs when the solution can be represented as a linear combination of eigenfunctions $\psi_{n_1}^{(1)}(x_1)$, $\psi_{n_2}^{(2)}(x_2)$, $\psi_{n_3}^{(3)}(x_3)$,

$$u(\mathbf{x},t) = \sum_{n_1,n_2,n_3=1}^{\infty} U_{n_1,n_2,n_3}(t) \psi_{n_1}^{(1)}(x_1) \psi_{n_2}^{(2)}(x_2) \psi_{n_3}^{(3)}(x_3), \tag{8}$$

and the unknowns can be determined by substituting the expression into the initial conditions using the orthogonality property of eigenfunctions with different eigenvalues. It should be emphasized that, for the application of the Fourier method, we have to transform the original problem into a homogeneous problem. In this case, our main goal is to calculate the analytic function $v_g(\mathbf{x},t)$ that exactly satisfies the boundary conditions of Equation (7) for any given α_i, β_i, $g_i(\mathbf{x},t)$ at each t in Equation (7). This function can be used to solve the problem of the non-homogeneous boundary conditions cardinally. Suppose that the solution can be approximated by the following approximation:

$$u(\mathbf{x},t) = v_g(\mathbf{x},t) + w(\mathbf{x},t). \tag{9}$$

Substituting the above equation into Equations (1), (3), and (7), we have:

$$\mathcal{L}_t[w] = \mathcal{M}_t\left[\nabla^2 w\right] + f_1(\mathbf{x},t),\ t \in [0,T],\ \mathbf{x} \in \Omega^d, \tag{10}$$

$$\frac{\partial^i w(\mathbf{x},0)}{\partial t^i} = w_i(\mathbf{x}),\ i = 0,\ldots,l-1, \tag{11}$$

$$B_i[w] = \alpha_i \frac{\partial w(\mathbf{x},t)}{\partial n_i} + \beta_i w(\mathbf{x},t) = 0,\ \mathbf{x} \in \partial\Omega^d. \tag{12}$$

It is evident that the boundary conditions have been transformed into the homogeneous one, which makes it possible to use the Fourier-series expansion as follows:

$$w(\mathbf{x},t) = \sum_{n=1}^{\infty} w_{\mathbf{n}}(t)\psi_{\mathbf{n}}(\mathbf{x}), \tag{13}$$

where the orthonormal basis $\psi_{\mathbf{n}}(\mathbf{x})$ is corresponding to the BC Equation (12), which satisfies

$$\nabla^2\psi_{\mathbf{n}}(\mathbf{x}) = -\lambda_{\mathbf{n}}^2\psi_{\mathbf{n}}(\mathbf{x}),\ \mathbf{x} \in \Omega^d,\ B_i[\psi_{\mathbf{n}}(\mathbf{x})] = 0,\ \mathbf{x} \in \partial\Omega^d. \tag{14}$$

This orthonormal basis will be described in Section 4. By substituting Equation (13) into Equation (10) and projecting $\langle \ldots, \psi_{\mathbf{n}} \rangle$, we have

$$\mathcal{L}_t[w_{\mathbf{n}}(t)] = -\lambda_{\mathbf{n}}^2\mathcal{M}_t[w_{\mathbf{n}}(t)] + \theta_{\mathbf{n}}(t),\ t \in [0,T] \tag{15}$$

for the approximation of each $w_{\mathbf{n}}$, which will be described in detail in the following several sections.

3. The Algorithm for Computing $v_g(\mathbf{x},t)$

Construction of the analytic function $v_g(\mathbf{x},t)$, which exactly satisfies the BCs of the original problem, is the main subject of the proposed method. In this section, we will propose an approach to derive $v_g(\mathbf{x},t)$ for the $(1+1)$-dimensional problems, $(2+1)$-dimensional problems, and $(3+1)$-dimensional problems, respectively.

3.1. $(1+1)$-*Dimensional Problems*

In this case, the problem of finding the function $v_g(x,t)$, which conforms the BC

$$L_W\left[v_g(x,t)\right](x=0) = \alpha_W\frac{\partial v_g}{\partial x}(0,t) + \beta_W v_g(0,t) = g_W(t), \tag{16}$$

$$L_E\left[v_g(x,t)\right](x=1) = \alpha_E\frac{\partial v_g}{\partial x}(1,t) + \beta_E v_g(1,t) = g_E(t), \tag{17}$$

at the endpoints of the interval $\Omega^1 = [0,1]$ is a trivial one. Indeed, one can prove easily that the following functions

$$\theta_E(x) = \frac{\alpha_W - \beta_W x}{\alpha_W\beta_E - \beta_W(\alpha_E + \beta_E)}, \tag{18}$$

$$\theta_W(x) = \frac{\beta_E x - (\alpha_E + \beta_E)}{\alpha_W\beta_E - \beta_W(\alpha_E + \beta_E)}, \tag{19}$$

satisfy the conditions

$$L_W(x)[\theta_W(x)](0) = 1,\ L_E(x)[\theta_W(x)](1) = 0, \tag{20}$$

$$L_W(x)[\theta_E(x)](0) = 0,\ L_E(x)[\theta_E(x)](1) = 1. \tag{21}$$

Then, the function

$$v_g(x,t) = \theta_E(x)g_E(t) + \theta_W(x)g_W(t) \tag{22}$$

satisfies the BCs of Equations (16) and (17).

3.2. $(2+1)$-Dimensional Problems

For the $(2+1)$-dimensional problem, we intend to obtain the v_g satisfying the BCs in a square domain; for example:

$$L_W(x)[v_g] \equiv \alpha_W \frac{\partial v_g}{\partial x} + \beta_W v_g = g_W(y,t),\, x = 0, 0 \le y \le 1, \tag{23}$$

$$L_E(x)[v_g] \equiv \alpha_E \frac{\partial v_g}{\partial x} + \beta_E v_g = g_E(y,t),\, x = 1, 0 \le y \le 1, \tag{24}$$

$$L_S(y)[v_g] \equiv \alpha_S \frac{\partial v_g}{\partial y} + \beta_S v_g = g_S(x,t),\, 0 \le x \le 1, y = 0, \tag{25}$$

$$L_N(y)[v_g] \equiv \alpha_N \frac{\partial v_g}{\partial y} + \beta_N v_g = g_N(x,t),\, 0 \le x \le 1, y = 1. \tag{26}$$

We assume that the desired function $v_g(x,y,t)$ is smooth enough and so the functions $g_W(y,t)$, $g_E(y,t)$, $g_S(x,t)$, and $g_N(x,t)$ guarantee continuity condition at the apexes $(0,0)$, $(0,1)$, $(1,0)$, and $(1,1)$ of the unit square $[0,1]^2$:

$$L_S(y)[g_W(y,t)] = L_W(x)[g_S(x,t)] \text{ at } (0,0), \tag{27}$$

$$L_N(y)[g_W(y,t)] = L_W(x)[g_N(x,t)] \text{ at } (0,1), \tag{28}$$

$$L_S(y)[g_E(y,t)] = L_E(x)[g_S(x,t)] \text{ at } (1,0), \tag{29}$$

$$L_N(y)[g_E(y,t)] = L_E(x)[g_N(x,t)] \text{ at } (1,1). \tag{30}$$

Let us define the functions

$$\theta_N(y) = \frac{\alpha_S - \beta_S y}{\alpha_S \beta_N - \beta_S(\alpha_N + \beta_N)}, \tag{31}$$

$$\theta_S(y) = \frac{\beta_N y - (\alpha_N + \beta_N)}{\alpha_S \beta_N - \beta_S(\alpha_N + \beta_N)}, \tag{32}$$

which are similar to the functions $\theta_E(x)$, $\theta_W(x)$. They satisfy the boundary conditions

$$L_S(y)[\theta_S(y)](0) = 1, L_N(y)[\theta_S(y)](1) = 0, \tag{33}$$

$$L_S(y)[\theta_N(y)](0) = 0, L_N(y)[\theta_N(y)](1) = 1. \tag{34}$$

Let us define the function

$$v_1 = \theta_E(x) g_E + \theta_W(x) g_W. \tag{35}$$

One can easily prove that v_1 satisfies Equations (23) and (24):

$$L_W(x)[v_1(x,y,t)]_{x=0} = g_W(y,t), 0 \le y \le 1, \tag{36}$$

$$L_E(x)[v_1(x,y,t)]_{x=1} = g_E(y,t), 0 \le y \le 1. \tag{37}$$

This follows directly from Definitions (20) and (21). Additionally, we define $g_{N1}(x,t)$ and $g_{S1}(x,t)$ as follows:

$$g_{N1}(x,t) = g_N(x,t) - L_N(y)[v_1(x,y,t)]_{y=1}, \tag{38}$$

$$g_{S1}(x,t) = g_S(x,t) - L_S(y)[v_1(x,y,t)]_{y=0}. \tag{39}$$

Finally, we can prove that the following combination,

$$v_g(x,y,t) = v_1(x,y,t) + \theta_N(y) g_{N1}(x,t) + \theta_S(y) g_{S1}(x,t), \tag{40}$$

satisfies Equations (23)–(26).

3.3. (3 + 1)-Dimensional Problems

For (3 + 1)-dimensional problems, we try to seek a smooth analytical function v_g that satisfies

$$L_W(x)[v_g] \equiv \alpha_W \frac{\partial v_g}{\partial x} + \beta_W v_g = g_W(y,z,t),\ x = 0, \tag{41}$$

$$L_E(x)[v_g] \equiv \alpha_E \frac{\partial v_g}{\partial x} + \beta_E v_g = g_E(y,z,t),\ x = 1, \tag{42}$$

$$L_S(y)[v_g] \equiv \alpha_S \frac{\partial v_g}{\partial y} + \beta_S v_g = g_S(x,z,t),\ y = 0, \tag{43}$$

$$L_N(y)[v_g] \equiv \alpha_N \frac{\partial v_g}{\partial y} + \beta_N v_g = g_N(x,z,t),\ y = 1, \tag{44}$$

$$L_T(z)[v_g] \equiv \alpha_T \frac{\partial v_g}{\partial z} + \beta_T v_g = g_T(x,y,t),\ z = 1, \tag{45}$$

$$L_B(z)[v_g] \equiv \alpha_B \frac{\partial v_g}{\partial z} + \beta_B v_g = g_B(x,y,t),\ z = 0, \tag{46}$$

where $0 \le x,\ y,\ z \le 1$ if the variables $x,\ y,\ z$ are not defined in the above equations. Without loss of generality, the operators $L_E(x)$ and $L_N(y)$ hold the general property $L_E(x)[L_N(y)[u]] = L_N(y)[L_E(x)[u]]$ in the presence of any given smooth function u for $x = 1, y = 1, 0 \le z \le 1$. It follows that

$$\begin{aligned} L_E(x)[L_N(y)[u]]_{x=1,y=1} &= L_N(y)[L_E(x)[u]]_{x=1,y=1} \Rightarrow L_E(x)\left[L_N(y)[u]_{y=1}\right]_{x=1} \\ &= L_N(y)[L_E(x)[u]_{x=1}]_{y=1} \Rightarrow L_E(x)[g_N(x,z,t)]_{x=1} = L_N(y)[g_E(y,z,t)]_{y=1}. \end{aligned} \tag{47}$$

The above condition is obviously fulfilled for the remaining 11 edges. Let us define the functions $\theta_T(z), \theta_B(z)$ as

$$\theta_T(z) = \frac{\alpha_B - \beta_B z}{\beta_T \alpha_B - \beta_B(\alpha_T + \beta_T)}, \tag{48}$$

$$\theta_B(z) = \frac{\beta_T z - (\alpha_T + \beta_T)}{\beta_T \alpha_B - \beta_B(\alpha_T + \beta_T)}, \tag{49}$$

similar to Equations (18), (19), (31), and (32), which satisfy the boundary conditions

$$L_T(z)[\theta_T(z)](1) = 1, L_B(z)[\theta_T(z)](0) = 0, \tag{50}$$

$$L_T(z)[\theta_B(z)](1) = 0, L_B(z)[\theta_B(z)](0) = 1. \tag{51}$$

Let us now try to construct the set of auxiliary functions along with their linear combinations

$$v_1 = \theta_T(z) g_T(x,y,t) + \theta_B(z) g_B(x,y,t), \tag{52}$$

$$g_{N1} = g_N(x,z,t) - L_N(y)[v_1(x,y,z,t)]_{y=1}, \tag{53}$$

$$g_{S1} = g_S(x,z,t) - L_S(y)[v_1(x,y,z,t)]_{y=0}, \tag{54}$$

$$v_2 = v_1 + \theta_N(y) g_{N1} + \theta_S(y) g_{S1}, \tag{55}$$

where $\theta_N(y)$ and $\theta_S(y)$ can be defined according to Equations (31) and (32). Then, let us define

$$g_{E1}(y,z,t) = g_E(y,z,t) - L_E(x)[v_2(x,y,z,t)]_{x=1}, \tag{56}$$
$$g_{W1}(y,z,t) = g_W(y,z,t) - L_W(x)[v_2(x,y,z,t)]_{x=0}, \tag{57}$$

and, finally,

$$v_g(x,y,z,t) = v_2(x,y,z,t) + \theta_E(x)g_{E1}(y,z,t) + \theta_W(x)g_{W1}(y,z,t), \tag{58}$$

which determines the objective function that satisfies the BC Equations (41)–(46). Note also that there are not any problems in the derivation of v_g for various boundary conditions, including the boundary conditions of the third kind. Furthermore, it is noteworthy that the v_g obtained in this section is not unique. In the present work, we show a simple form of the formulas for easy application. Other methods such as numerical methods can also be used for such purposes that are not reported in the present work.

4. Orthogonal Basis for the Fourier Expansion

This section deals with the application of the Fourier method to the solution of corresponding homogeneous problems. As mentioned earlier, once we obtain the function $v_g(\mathbf{x},t)$, the original equation can be transformed into the following homogeneous system by substituting the $v_g(\mathbf{x},t)$ into the governing equations and boundary conditions

$$\mathcal{L}_t[w] = \mathcal{M}_t\left[\nabla^2 w\right] + f_1(\mathbf{x},t),\ f_1(\mathbf{x},t) = f(\mathbf{x},t) + \mathcal{M}_t\left[\nabla^2 v_g(\mathbf{x},t)\right] - \mathcal{L}_t[v_g(\mathbf{x},t)], \tag{59}$$

which satisfies homogeneous BC

$$B_i[w] = \alpha_i \frac{\partial w(\mathbf{x},t)}{\partial n_i} + \beta_i w(\mathbf{x},t) = 0,\ \mathbf{x} \in \partial\Omega^d, \tag{60}$$

where the solution can now be approximated with the following functional form,

$$w(\mathbf{x},t) = \sum_{n=1}^{\infty} w_{\mathbf{n}}(t)\psi_{\mathbf{n}}(\mathbf{x}), \tag{61}$$

over the orthonormal basis $\psi_{\mathbf{n}}(\mathbf{x})$, corresponding to BC Equation (60),

$$\nabla^2\psi_{\mathbf{n}}(\mathbf{x}) = -\lambda_{\mathbf{n}}^2\psi_{\mathbf{n}}(\mathbf{x}),\ B_i[\psi_{\mathbf{n}}(\mathbf{x})] = 0,\ \ \mathbf{x} \in \partial\Omega^d. \tag{62}$$

In this section, we describe the orthonormal basis $\psi_{\mathbf{n}}(\mathbf{x})$ and begin with the $(1+1)$-dimensional problem as an example.

4.1. (1 + 1)-Dimensional Problems

Let us consider the following Sturm–Liouville problem:

$$\frac{d^2\psi}{dx^2} = -\mu\psi, \tag{63}$$
$$L_W(x)[\psi]_{x=0} = \left(\alpha_W \frac{d\psi}{dx} + \beta_W\psi\right)_{x=0} = 0,\ L_E(x)[\psi]_{x=1} = \left(\alpha_E \frac{d\psi}{dx} + \beta_E\psi\right)_{x=1} = 0, \tag{64}$$

where we describe some possible forms of the eigenfunctions corresponding to Equations (63) and (64).

1. First, let us consider the general case $\alpha_W \neq 0$, $\alpha_E \neq 0$. We write the boundary conditions in the traditional form for transport problems:

$$\frac{d\psi}{dx} - b_1\psi|_{x=0} = 0,\ \frac{d\psi}{dx} + b_2\psi|_{x=1} = 0,\ b_1, b_2 \geq 0. \tag{65}$$

The change of the sign is connected to the different direction of the outward normal at the endpoints $x = 0$ and $x = 1$ [41].

From Equation (63), it follows:

$$\begin{aligned} \mu \int_0^1 \psi^2 dx = & -\int_0^1 \frac{d^2\psi}{dx^2}\psi dx = \int_0^1 \left[\left(\frac{d\psi}{dx}\right)^2 dx - d\left(\psi\frac{d\psi}{dx}\right)\right] \\ = & -\left(\psi\frac{d\psi}{dx}\right)|_0^1 + \int_0^1 \left(\frac{d\psi}{dx}\right)^2 dx \\ = & \psi(0)\frac{d\psi(0)}{dx} - \psi(1)\frac{d\psi(1)}{dx} + \int_0^1 \left(\frac{d\psi}{dx}\right)^2 dx. \end{aligned} \tag{66}$$

Using Equation (65), one gets:

$$\mu \int_0^1 \psi^2 dx = b_1\psi^2(0) + b_2\psi^2(1) + \int_0^1 \left(\frac{d\psi}{dx}\right)^2 dx. \tag{67}$$

Thus, under the condition $b_1, b_2 \geq 0$, the values of μ are positive, and we denote $\mu = \lambda^2$. The function

$$\psi_{1,n}(x) = \frac{1}{\mathcal{R}_n}\left[\cos(\lambda_n x) + \frac{b_1}{\lambda_n}\sin(\lambda_n x)\right], \tag{68}$$

where

$$\mathcal{R}_n = \sqrt{\frac{1}{2}\left(1 + \frac{b_1^2}{\lambda_n^2}\right) + \frac{b_1}{2\lambda_n^2} + \frac{b_2}{2\lambda_n^2}\frac{\lambda_n^2 + b_1^2}{\lambda_n^2 + b_2^2}} \tag{69}$$

and where λ_n is the nth solution that can be obtained by solving the following system of transcendental equation

$$\left(\lambda^2 - b_1 b_2\right)\tan(\lambda) = (b_1 + b_2)\lambda, \tag{70}$$

where $\psi_{1,n}(x)$ constructs an orthonormal basis in the Hilbert space $L([0,1])$, and the following identity holds for different bases

$$\langle \psi_{1,n}, \psi_{1,m} \rangle = \int_0^1 \psi_{1,n}(x)\psi_{1,m}(x)dx = \delta_{n,m}. \tag{71}$$

2. Let us consider the case $\alpha_W = 0$, $\alpha_E \neq 0$. We get the Dirichlet condition at the left endpoint $x = 0$:

$$\psi|_{x=0} = 0, \ \frac{d\psi}{dx} + b_2\psi|_{x=1} = 0, \ b_2 \geq 0. \tag{72}$$

The function

$$\psi_{2,n}(x) = \frac{1}{\mathcal{R}_n}\sin(\lambda_n x), \tag{73}$$

is an eigenfunction of Sturm–Liouville Problems (63) and (72). Here

$$\mathcal{R}_n = \sqrt{\frac{1}{2}\left(1 - \frac{\sin(2\lambda_n)}{2\lambda_n}\right)}, \tag{74}$$

and λ_n is the nth solution of the transcendental equation

$$\lambda\cos(\lambda) + b_2\sin(\lambda) = 0. \tag{75}$$

Function $\psi_{2,n}(x)$ satisfies $\langle \psi_{2,n}, \psi_{2,m} \rangle = \delta_{n,m}$.

3. Let us consider the case $\alpha_W \neq 0$, $\alpha_E = 0$. We get the Dirichlet condition at the right endpoint $x = 1$:

$$\frac{d\psi}{dx} - b_1\psi|_{x=0} = 0,\ \psi|_{x=1} = 0,\ b_1 \geq 0. \tag{76}$$

The function

$$\psi_{3,n}(x) = \frac{1}{\mathcal{R}_n}\left[\sin(\lambda_n x) + \frac{\lambda_n}{b_1}\cos(\lambda_n x)\right] \tag{77}$$

is an eigenfunction of Sturm–Liouville Problems (63) and (76). Here

$$\mathcal{R}_n = \sqrt{\frac{1}{2}\left(1 - \frac{\sin(2\lambda_n)}{2\lambda_n}\right) + \frac{1}{2b_1}(1 - \cos(2\lambda_n)) + \frac{\lambda_n^2}{2b_1^2}\left(1 + \frac{\sin(2\lambda_n)}{2\lambda_n}\right)}, \tag{78}$$

and λ_n is the nth solution of the transcendental equation

$$\lambda\cos(\lambda) + b_1\sin(\lambda) = 0. \tag{79}$$

Function $\psi_{3,n}(x)$ satisfies $\langle\psi_{3,n}, \psi_{3,m}\rangle = \delta_{n,m}$.

4. The case $\alpha_W = 0$, $\alpha_E = 0$ corresponds to the Dirichlet conditions at both endpoints of the interval $[0, 1]$. The function

$$\psi_{4,n}(x) = \sqrt{2}\sin n\pi x,\ n = 1, 2, \ldots, \tag{80}$$

also satisfies the property $\langle\psi_{4,n}, \psi_{4,m}\rangle = \delta_{n,m}$.

5. Finally, let us consider the following case $\alpha_W, \alpha_E, \beta_E \neq 0$, $\beta_W = 0$. Using Equation (65), the boundary conditions can be expressed as

$$\frac{d\psi}{dx} = 0,\ \frac{d\psi}{dx} + b_2\psi|_{x=1} = 0,\ b_1, b_2 \geq 0. \tag{81}$$

Thus, we get the Neumann condition at the left-hand side endpoint. The function

$$\psi_{5,n}(x) = \frac{1}{\mathcal{R}_n}\cos(\lambda_n x), \tag{82}$$

satisfies $\langle\psi_{5,n}, \psi_{5,m}\rangle = \delta_{n,m}$. Here

$$\mathcal{R}_n = \sqrt{\frac{1}{2}\left(1 + \frac{b_2}{\lambda_n^2 + b_2^2}\right)}, \tag{83}$$

and λ_n is the nth solution of the transcendental equation

$$\lambda\sin(\lambda) = b_2\cos(\lambda). \tag{84}$$

4.2. $(2+1)$ *and* $(3+1)$*-Dimensional Problems*

We use the products $\psi_{i_1,n_1}(x)\psi_{i_2,n_2}(y)$ and $\psi_{i_1,n_1}(x)\psi_{i_2,n_2}(y)\psi_{i_3,n_3}(z)$ as the basis function for solving $(2+1)$ and $(3+1)$-dimensional problems. Here, the first index $i_1, i_2, i_3 = 1, 2, 3, 4, 5$ indicates the type of the basis function as described in the last subsection; the second index n_1, n_2, n_3 indicates the harmonic number. These functions satisfy the equations:

$$\nabla^2_{x,y}\psi_{i_1,n_1}(x)\psi_{i_2,n_2}(y) = -\left(\lambda^2_{i_1,n_1} + \lambda^2_{i_2,n_2}\right)\psi_{i_1,n_1}(x)\psi_{i_2,n_2}(y), \tag{85}$$

$$\nabla^2_{x,y,z}\psi_{i_1,n_1}(x)\psi_{i_2,n_2}(y)\psi_{i_3,n_3}(z) = -\left(\lambda^2_{i_1,n_1} + \lambda^2_{i_2,n_2} + \lambda^2_{i_3,n_3}\right)\psi_{i_1,n_1}(x)\psi_{i_2,n_2}(y)\psi_{i_3,n_3}(z). \tag{86}$$

Below they are used in the Fourier transformation of governing Equation (59).

5. The Solution Procedure

In this section, we demonstrate the solution procedure for the proposed method for the multi-dimensional fractional equations by utilizing the analytic function v_g and the orthogonal basis derived in the last section. At first, we discuss the solution for the one-dimensional problem with a single harmonic.

5.1. $(1+1)$ *Problem with a Single Spatial Harmonic*

Now, for the $(1+1)$-dimensional TFPDE with a specific source term,

$$L_t[w] = M_t\left[\frac{\partial^2 w}{\partial x^2}\right] + \theta_n(t)\psi_n(x), \tag{87}$$

$\psi_n(x)$ denotes the eigenfunctions given by Equations (68), (73), (77), (80), or (82). Suppose that the equation is subjected to the BCs and ICs, which conform the chosen eigenfunction $\psi_n(x)$:

$$L_W(x)[w]_{x=0} = 0,\ L_E(x)[w]_{x=1} = 0, \tag{88}$$

$$w(x,0) = w_0\psi_n(x),\ \frac{\partial w(x,0)}{\partial t} = w_1\psi_n(x), \ldots, \frac{\partial^{l-1} w(x,0)}{\partial t^{l-1}} = w_{l-1}\psi_n(x). \tag{89}$$

We see the solution as

$$w(x,t) = w_n(t)\psi_n(x). \tag{90}$$

Then, we get the multi-term FODE

$$L_t[w_n] = -\lambda_n^2 M_t[w_n] + \theta_n(t). \tag{91}$$

Using Equation (2), we rewrite the equation in the expanded form

$$D_t^{(\mu)}[w_n] = -\sum_{k=1}^{K} b_k(t) D_t^{(\mu_k)}[w_n] + \theta_n(t), \tag{92}$$

where $b_k(t) = a_k(t)$, $k = 1,\ldots,I$, $b_k(t) = \lambda_n^2 a_k(t)$, $k = I+1,\ldots,K$, and $\mu \in (l-1,l]$, $0 \le \mu_k < \mu$. The considered initial conditions from Equation (89) are as follows:

$$w_n(0) = w_0,\ \frac{dw_n(0)}{dt} = w_1, \ldots, \frac{d^{l-1}w_n(0)}{dt^{l-1}} = w_{l-1}. \tag{93}$$

Supposing that the right-hand side of Equation (92) can be approximated by the linear combination of φ, as shown below,

$$-\sum_{k=1}^{K} b_k(t) D_t^{(\mu_k)}[w_n] + \theta_n(t) = \sum_{m=1}^{\infty} q_m \varphi_m(t), \tag{94}$$

where the φ is the chosen basis and q_m are unknown coefficients to be determined. In this way, Equation (92) is transformed into

$$D_t^{(\mu)}[w_n(t)] = \sum_{m=1}^{\infty} q_m \varphi_m(t), \tag{95}$$

where $\varphi_m(t)$ and $\phi_m(t)$ holds

$$D_t^{(\mu)}[\phi_m(t)] = \varphi_m(t). \tag{96}$$

It is easy to verify that the Müntz polynomial basis (MPB) proposed in [46,50–53] meets the requirement given in Equation (96). The explicit expression of such functions is as follows:

$$\varphi_m(t) = t^{\delta_m},\ \delta_m = \sigma(m-1), \tag{97}$$

where σ is an auxiliary variable within $(0,\ 1]$, and m is a positive integer. From the preceding numerical examples in [44], we set $\sigma = 0.25$ for this paper.

It follows that the function

$$\phi_m(t) = \frac{\Gamma(\delta_m+1)}{\Gamma(\delta_m+\mu+1)} t^{\delta_m+\mu} \tag{98}$$

satisfies the following equality:

$$D^{(\mu)}[\phi_m(t)] = \varphi_m(t). \tag{99}$$

As far as $l-1 < \mu \le l$, the function $\phi_m(t)$ satisfies zero ICs:

$$\phi_m^{(i)}(0) = 0,\ i = 0, 1, \ldots, l-1. \tag{100}$$

From Equations (97), (99), and (100) it can be seen that the series

$$w_{h,n}(t, \mathbf{q}) = \sum_{m=1}^{\infty} q_m \phi_m(t) \tag{101}$$

satisfies Equation (95) with any $\{q_m\}_{m=1}^{\infty} \equiv \mathbf{q}$.

Let us define the following approximation:

$$w_{p,n}(t) = w_0 + w_1 t + \cdots + w_{l-1}\frac{t^{l-1}}{(l-1)!} = \sum_{i=0}^{l-1} \frac{w_i}{i!} t^i. \tag{102}$$

The function $w_{p,n}(t)$ satisfies IC Equation (93). In this way, the following approximation

$$w_n(t, \mathbf{q}) = w_{p,n}(t) + w_{h,n}(t, \mathbf{q}) = w_{p,n}(t) + \sum_{m=1}^{\infty} q_m \phi_m(t) \tag{103}$$

satisfies Equations (95) and (93) with any $\{q_m\}_{m=1}^{\infty}$. Additionally, the unknown weighted parameter q_m is determined by backward substituting the $w_n(t, \mathbf{q})$ into Equation (94):

$$\sum_{m=1}^{\infty} q_m \left[\varphi_m(t) + \sum_{k=1}^{K} b_k(t) D_t^{(\mu_k)}[\phi_m(t)] \right] = \theta_n(t) - \sum_{k=1}^{K} b_k(t) D_t^{(\mu_k)}\left[w_p(t)\right] \equiv F_n(t), \tag{104}$$

where we denote

$$\begin{aligned} D_t^{(\mu_k)}[\phi_m(t)] &= \frac{\Gamma(\delta_m+1) D_t^{(\mu_k)}\left[t^{\delta_m+\mu}\right]}{\Gamma(\delta_m+\mu+1)} \\ &= \frac{\Gamma(\delta_m+1)\Gamma(\delta_m+\mu+1) t^{\delta_m+\mu-\mu_k}}{\Gamma(\delta_m+\mu+1)\Gamma(\delta_m+\mu+1-\mu_k)} = \frac{\Gamma(\delta_m+1) t^{\delta_m+\mu-\mu_k}}{\Gamma(\delta_m+\mu+1-\mu_k)}, \end{aligned} \tag{105}$$

$$D_t^{(\mu_k)}\left[w_p(t)\right] = \sum_{i=1}^{l-1} \frac{w_i}{i!} D_t^{(\mu_k)}\left[t^i\right] = \sum_{i=1}^{l-1} \frac{w_i \Gamma(i+1) t^{i-\mu_k}}{i!\Gamma(i+1-\mu_k)} = \sum_{i \ge \mu_k}^{l-1} \frac{w_i t^{i-\mu_k}}{\Gamma(i+1-\mu_k)}. \tag{106}$$

We consider the truncated series of Equation (103),

$$w_n(t, M, \mathbf{q}) = w_{p,n}(t) + \sum_{m=1}^{M} q_m \phi_m(t), \tag{107}$$

which also satisfies the modified Equation (95):

$$D^{(\mu)}[w_n(t, M, \mathbf{q})] = \sum_{m=1}^{M} q_m \varphi_m(t). \tag{108}$$

The unknown parameters $q_1, \ldots, q_M$ should satisfy the truncated version of Equation (104),

$$\sum_{m=1}^{M} q_m \left[\varphi_m(t) + \sum_{k=1}^{K} b_k(t) D_t^{(\mu_k)}[\phi_m(t)] \right] = F_n(t), \tag{109}$$

by the collocation method as follows:

$$\sum_{m=1}^{M} q_m \left[\varphi_m(t_j) + \sum_{k=1}^{K} b_k(t_j) D_t^{(\mu_k)}[\phi_m(t_j)] \right] = F_n(t_j), \tag{110}$$

where

$$t_j = 0.5T[1 + \cos(\pi(2j-1)/2N_c)] \in [0, T], j = 1, 2, \ldots N_c \geq M, \tag{111}$$

are the Gauss–Chebyshev (GC) collocation points on the time interval $[0, T]$. It is important to note that in the framework of the presented method, the $F_n(t)$ are required at several time steps t_j given in Equation (111) only. As it follows from Equation (104), the same is true for time function $\theta_n(t)$. As a result, the Fourier expansion of the $f_1(\mathbf{x}, t)$ of Equation (10) also should be performed at the same time moments t_j only.

5.2. $(1+1)$-*Dimensional Problems of the General Case*

Consider the following equation:

$$L_t[u] = M_t\left[\frac{\partial^2 u}{\partial x^2}\right] + f(x,t),\ x \in [0,1], t \in [0,T]. \tag{112}$$

The substitution

$$u = v_g + w, \tag{113}$$

with $v_g(x,t)$, gives us

$$L_t[w] = M_t\left[\frac{\partial^2 w}{\partial x^2}\right] + f_1(x,t), \tag{114}$$

$$L_W(x)[w]_{x=0} = 0,\ L_E(x)[w]_{x=1} = 0, \tag{115}$$

and IC

$$\frac{\partial^i w(x,0)}{\partial t^i} = u_i(x) - \frac{\partial^i v_g(x,0)}{\partial^i t} = w_i(x), i = 0, \ldots, l-1. \tag{116}$$

Here,

$$f_1(x,t) = f(x,t) - L_t[v_g(x,t)] + M_t\left[\frac{\partial^2 v_g(x,t)}{\partial x^2}\right]. \tag{117}$$

We seek the solution of the problem in Equations (114)–(116) using the following linear combination,

$$w_N(x,t) = \sum_{n=1}^{N} w_n(t)\psi_n(x), \tag{118}$$

where $\psi_n(x)$ denotes one of the eigenfunctions given by Equations (68), (73), (77), (80), and (82). Substituting Equation (118) into Equation (114), we have

$$L_t[w_n] = -\lambda_n^2 M_t[w_n] + \theta_n(t), n = 1, \ldots, N, \tag{119}$$

where

$$\theta_n(t) = \int_0^1 f_1(x,t)\psi_n(x)dx. \tag{120}$$

Further, w_n holds

$$\frac{d^i w_n(0)}{dt^i} = \int_0^1 w_i(x)\psi_n(x)dx = w_{i,n}, \, i = 0,\ldots,l-1, \tag{121}$$

which follows from Equation (116). The solution of w_n can be given by

$$w_n(t, M, \mathbf{q}_n) = w_{p,n}(t) + \sum_{m=1}^{M} q_{n,m}\phi_m(t), \; \mathbf{q}_n = \{q_{n,m}\}_{m=1}^{M}. \tag{122}$$

Therefore, the solution $u_{appro}(x,t)$ to the origin problem is given by

$$u_{appro} = v_g(x,t) + \sum_{n=1}^{N} w_{p,n}(t)\psi_n(x) + \sum_{m=1}^{M} Q_m(x)\phi_m(t), \tag{123}$$

where the $Q_m(x)$ is given by

$$Q_m(x) = \sum_{n=1}^{N} q_{n,m}\psi_n(x). \tag{124}$$

5.3. $(2+1)$-*Dimensional Problems*

Consider the following $(2+1)$-dimensional problem:

$$L_t[u] = M_t\left[\nabla^2 u\right] + f(x,y,t), (x,y) \in [0,1]^2, t \in [0,T]. \tag{125}$$

The substitution

$$u = v_g + w, \tag{126}$$

with $v_g(x,y,t)$ given by Equation (40) gives us

$$L_t[w] = M_t\left[\nabla^2 w\right] + f_1(x,y,t), \tag{127}$$

and the homogeneous BCs

$$L_W(x)[w]_{x=0} = 0, \; L_E(x)[w]_{x=1} = 0, \; L_S(y)[u]_{y=0} = 0, \; L_N(y)[u]_{y=1} = 0, \tag{128}$$

and ICs

$$\frac{\partial^i w(x,y,0)}{\partial t^i} = u_i(x,y) - \frac{\partial^i v_g(x,y,0)}{\partial t^i} = w_i(x,y), \; i = 0,\ldots,l-1. \tag{129}$$

The approximate solution to Problems (127)–(129) is approximated as follows:

$$w_N(\mathbf{x},t) = \sum_{n_1,n_2=1}^{N} w_{n_1,n_2}(t)\psi_{n_1,n_2}(x_1,x_2) = \sum_{\mathbf{n}=1}^{N} w_{\mathbf{n}}(t)\psi_{\mathbf{n}}(\mathbf{x}). \tag{130}$$

Here, $\psi_{n_1,n_2}(x_1,x_2) = \psi_{\mathbf{n}}(\mathbf{x}) = \psi_{n_1}(x_1)\psi_{n_2}(x_2)$ is the product of the eigenfunctions given by Equations (68), (73), (77), (80), or (82), and we use the following short notations: $\mathbf{n} = (n_1,n_2)$, $\mathbf{x} = (x_1,x_2) = (x,y)$.

Substituting $w_N(\mathbf{x},t)$ in (127), we have

$$\mathcal{L}_t[w_{\mathbf{n}}(t)] = -\left(\lambda_{n_1}^2 + \lambda_{n_2}^2\right)\mathcal{M}_t[w_{\mathbf{n}}(t)] + \theta_{\mathbf{n}}(t), \; t \in [0,T], \tag{131}$$

where

$$\theta_{\mathbf{n}}(t) = \int_0^1 \int_0^1 f_1(x_1, x_2, t)\psi_{n_1,n_2}(x_1, x_2)dx_1dx_2. \tag{132}$$

The harmonic $w_{\mathbf{n}}(t) = w_{n_1,n_2}(t)$ satisfies

$$\frac{\partial^i w_{0,\mathbf{n}}(0)}{\partial t^i} = w_{i,\mathbf{n}} = \int_0^1 \int_0^1 w_i(x_1, x_2)\psi_{n_1,n_2}(x_1, x_2)dx_1dx_2, i = 0, 1, \ldots, l-1, \tag{133}$$

which follows from Equation (129). The approximate solution

$$w_{\mathbf{n}}(t, M, \mathbf{q_n}) = w_{p,\mathbf{n}}(t) + \sum_{m=1}^{M} q_{\mathbf{n},m}\phi_m(t), \ \mathbf{q_n} = \{\mathbf{q}_{\mathbf{n},m}\}_{m=1}^M = \{q_{n_1,n_2,m}\}_{m=1}^M, \tag{134}$$

can be obtained obviously for each harmonic. Then, the $u_{N,M}(\mathbf{x}, t)$ can be approximated as follows:

$$\begin{aligned} u_{N,M}(\mathbf{x}, t) &= v_g(\mathbf{x}, t) + \sum_{n_1,n_2=1}^{N} w_{M,n_1,n_2}(t)\psi_{n_1,n_2}(x_1, x_2) \\ &= v_g(\mathbf{x}, t) + \sum_{n_1,n_2=1}^{N} w_{p,n_1,n_2}(t)\psi_{n_1,n_2}(x_1, x_2) + \sum_{m=1}^{M} Q_m(\mathbf{x})\phi_m(t), \end{aligned} \tag{135}$$

where

$$Q_m(\mathbf{x}) = \sum_{n_1,n_2=1}^{N} q_{n_1,n_2,m}\psi_{n_1,n_2}(x_1, x_2). \tag{136}$$

5.4. $(3+1)$-*Dimensional Problems*

Now let us move to the $(3+1)$-dimensional problems

$$L_t[u] = M_t\left[\nabla^2 u\right] + f, \ (x, y, z) \in [0, 1]^3, t \in [0, T]. \tag{137}$$

Using the substitution

$$u = v_g + w, \tag{138}$$

with v_g given by Equation (58), we have

$$L_t[w] = M_t\left[\nabla^2 w\right] + f_1(x, y, z, t), \tag{139}$$

subjected to

$$\begin{aligned} L_W(x)[w]_{x=0} = 0, \ L_E(x)[w]_{x=1} = 0, \ L_S(y)[u]_{y=0} = 0, \ L_N(y)[u]_{y=1} = 0, \\ L_B(z)[u]_{z=0} = 0, \ L_T(z)[u]_{z=1} = 0, \end{aligned} \tag{140}$$

and IC

$$\frac{\partial^i w(x, y, z, 0)}{\partial t^i} = u_i(x, y, z) - \frac{\partial^i v_g(x, y, z, 0)}{\partial t^i} = w_i(x, y, z), \ i = 0, \ldots, l-1, \tag{141}$$

in which

$$f_1 = f - L_t[v_g] + M_t\left[\nabla^2 v_g\right]. \tag{142}$$

With the same technology, the approximated solution of $w_N(\mathbf{x}, t)$ can be expressed in the following functional form,

$$w_N(\mathbf{x}, t) = \sum_{\mathbf{n}=1}^{N} w_{\mathbf{n}}(t)\psi_{\mathbf{n}}(\mathbf{x}), \tag{143}$$

where $\mathbf{n} = (n_1, n_2, n_3)$, $\mathbf{x} = (x, y, z) = (x_1, x_2, x_3)$, $\psi_{\mathbf{n}}(\mathbf{x}) = \psi_{n_1,n_2,n_3}(x_1, x_2, x_3)$ is the product of the eigenfunctions $\psi_{n_1}(x)\psi_{n_2}(y)\psi_{n3}(z)$ given by Equations (68), (73), (77), (80), or (82).

Substituting $w_N(\mathbf{x}, t)$ in Equation (127), we have

$$\mathcal{L}_t[w_{\mathbf{n}}(t)] = -\left(\lambda_{n_1}^2 + \lambda_{n_2}^2 + \lambda_{n_3}^2\right)\mathcal{M}_t[w_{\mathbf{n}}(t)] + \theta_{\mathbf{n}}(t),\ t \in [0, T], \tag{144}$$

where

$$\theta_{\mathbf{n}}(t) = \int_0^1 \int_0^1 \int_0^1 f_1(\mathbf{x}, t)\psi_{n_1,n_2,n_3}(\mathbf{x})d\mathbf{x}. \tag{145}$$

It is important to note that in the context of the present method, the Fourier expansion of the source term $f_1(\mathbf{x}, t)$ over the eigenfunction basis should be performed at several fixed time moments t_j only. This follows from the algorithm of the backward substitution technique (see Equations (104) and (121)).

The harmonic $w_{\mathbf{n}}(t) = w_{n_1,n_2,n_3}(t)$ satisfies

$$\frac{\partial^i w_{0,\mathbf{n}}(0)}{\partial t^i} = w_{i,\mathbf{n}} = \int_0^1 \int_0^1 \int_0^1 w_i(\mathbf{x})\psi_{\mathbf{n}}(\mathbf{x})d\mathbf{x},\ i = 0, \ldots, l-1. \tag{146}$$

Then, the solution is approximated as

$$\begin{aligned} u_{N,M}(\mathbf{x}, t) &= v_g + \sum_{\mathbf{n}=(1,1,1)}^{N} w_{M,\mathbf{n}}(t)\psi_{\mathbf{n}}(\mathbf{x}) \\ &= v_g + \sum_{\mathbf{n}=(1,1,1)}^{N} w_{p,\mathbf{n}}(t)\psi_{\mathbf{n}}(\mathbf{x}) + \sum_{m=1}^{M} Q_m(\mathbf{x})\phi_m(t), \end{aligned} \tag{147}$$

where

$$Q_m(\mathbf{x}) = \sum_{n\mathbf{n}=(1,1,1)}^{N} q_{\mathbf{n},m}\psi_{\mathbf{n}}(\mathbf{x}). \tag{148}$$

6. Numerical Examples

In this section, the feasibility of the proposed method is experimentally verified. The maximum absolute error (MAE) and the $E_{H^1}(t)$ error containing the derivatives were used as numerical criteria, as shown below:

$$E_{\max}(t) = \max_{1 \le i \le N_t} |u_{N,M}(\mathbf{x}_i, t) - u_{ex}(\mathbf{x}_i, t)|, \tag{149}$$

$$E_{H^1}(t) = \sqrt{\frac{1}{N_t}\sum_{i=1}^{N}\left[(u_{N,M}(\mathbf{x}_i, t) - u_{ex}(\mathbf{x}_i, t))^2 + \left(\frac{\partial u_{N,M}}{\partial t}(\mathbf{x}_i, t) - \frac{\partial u_{ex}}{\partial t}(\mathbf{x}_i, t)\right)^2\right]}, \tag{150}$$

where $u_{N,M}(\mathbf{x}_i, t)$ indicates the approximate solutions obtained by the presented analytical–numerical method for the compared solution $u_{ex}(\mathbf{x}_i, t)$, and N_t is the total number of test nodes.

For the 1D problems, we used the number of test nodes $N_t = 4N$, where N is the number of spatial harmonics; i.e., we use 4 testing nodes per harmonic. For the 2D examples, the errors were carried using the $N_t = 4000$ test nodes distributed in the solution domain.

For the 3D problem, we have transformed it into the FODE analytically so that we only have to check the solution accuracy in the time domain.

As for the total number of collocation nodes, we have to illustrate that, in this paper, the derivation of v_g can be done analytically. Therefore, we do not have to place nodes on the boundary. Using the approximate solution in the form of the Fourier series over the eigenfunction, we transform the TFPDE into the set of the FODEs for each of the Fourier harmonics. Therefore, we do not have to place collocation nodes inside the domain. The collocation nodes are placed in the time domain only.

The collocation points t_j, $j = 1, 2, \ldots, N_c$, in the time interval $[0, T]$ are used to form the collocation system for solving each FODE. In all the examples, we use the number of collocation nodes $N_c = 2M$ in the time domain, where M is the number of the Müntz polynomials that are used in the approximate solution of the FODEs. The parameter M defines the accuracy of the approximation in time.

6.1. $(1+1)$-Dimensional Problem

6.1.1. Example 1

For the first example, the following time fractional cable equation is studied under the Dirichlet boundary condition

$$\frac{\partial u(x,t)}{\partial t} = D_t^{(1-\gamma_1)}\left[\frac{\partial^2 u}{\partial x^2}(x,t)\right] - D_t^{(1-\gamma_2)}[u(x,t)] + f(x,t), x \in (0,1), t \in (0,1), \quad (151)$$

$$u(x,0) = 0,\ u(0,t) = 0,\ u(1,t) = 0, \quad (152)$$

where the source term $f(x,t)$ can be computed by substituting the analytic solution $u(x,t)$

$$u(x,t) = t^2 \sin \pi x, \quad (153)$$

into the governing equation, which yields

$$f(x,t) = 2\left(t + \frac{\pi^2 t^{1+\gamma_1}}{\Gamma(2+\gamma_1)} + \frac{t^{1+\gamma_2}}{\Gamma(2+\gamma_2)}\right) \sin \pi x = F(t) \sin \pi x. \quad (154)$$

Thus, the problem considered is a special 1D case with a single spatial harmonic, which was considered in Section 4.1. As it is shown there, the problem can be reduced to a single FODE,

$$\frac{dw(t)}{dt} = -\pi^2 D_t^{(1-\gamma_1)}[w(t)] - D_t^{(1-\gamma_2)}[w(t)] + F(t), \quad (155)$$

for the sole harmonic.

To illustrate the effects of the error in M, Table 1 shows the behavior of the maximum absolute error with respect to M for the approximation of the source terms in Equations (97), (98), and (107). The approximate solution is sought as a truncated series Equation (107) over the function $\phi_m(t)$: $D^{(\mu)}[\phi_m(t)] = \varphi_m(t)$ and so belongs to the linear span $S(\mu, \sigma, M) = Span\left(1, t^{\mu+\sigma(m-1)}\right)_{m=1}^{M}$. In the case considered, $\mu = 1$ and $S(1, \sigma, M) = Span\left(1, t^{1+\sigma(m-1)}\right)_{m=1}^{M}$. For $\sigma = 0.25$, $S(1, 0.25, M) = Span\left(1, t, t^{1.25}, \ldots, t^{1+0.25(M-1)}\right)$. Therefore, as it comes from Equation (153), the exact solution $w(t) = t^2$ belongs to $S(1, 0.25, M)$ for $M \geq 5$. The data in Table 1 demonstrate that, for this particular case, the results of the proposed analytical–numerical method converge to the exact solution for the parameter $M \geq 5$ and reach the computer rounding errors. Let us consider the case $\sigma = 0.5$. Here, $w(t) = t^2$ belongs to $S(1, 0.5, M)$ for $M \geq 3$. The data in Table 1 illustrate this situation.

Table 1. The MAE versus the M at $t = 1$ for different σ.

M	1	2	3	4	5	6	10
$\sigma = 0.25$	1.19×10^{-2}	1.93×10^{-3}	1.97×10^{-4}	3.73×10^{-5}	1.22×10^{-16}	1.22×10^{-16}	-
$\sigma = 0.50$	1.19×10^{-2}	1.47×10^{-3}	1.22×10^{-16}	1.22×10^{-16}	-	-	-
$\sigma = 0.33$	1.19×10^{-2}	1.83×10^{-3}	1.21×10^{-4}	9.35×10^{-7}	5.44×10^{-8}	6.38×10^{-9}	3.12×10^{-1}

It is easy to verify that for $\sigma = 0.33$ (the bottom row of the table), there is no such M that the exact solution $w(t)$ belongs to $S(1, 0.33, M)$. As a result, for $\sigma = 0.33$, the error decreases gradually with the growth of M, while for $\sigma = 0.25$ and $\sigma = 0.50$, it decreases sharply when the exact solution belongs to the corresponding range $S(\alpha, \sigma, M)$. The calculations have been performed for $(\gamma_1 = 0.5, \gamma_2 = 0.5)$, $(\gamma_1 = 0.3, \gamma_2 = 0.9)$, and $(\gamma_1 = 0.7, \gamma_2 = 0.6)$ which have produced the same results. Thus, if the parameters σ of the Müntz polynomial basis are chosen in such a way that exact solution belongs to $S(\mu, \sigma, M)$, then the present method provides the exact solution up to the rounding errors of the computer. This problem has been considered by Yang, Jiang, and Zhang in [54] using the spectral Legendre–Tau method. The most accurate result that has been achieved there has the error $E_{max} = 9.3019 \times 10^{-6}$ when 13 Legendre's polynomials were used for the spatial and temporal approximations.

6.1.2. Example 2

Let us consider the following problem that has been studied using the time-space spectral tau method in [54]:

$$\frac{\partial u(x,t)}{\partial t} = D_t^{(1-\gamma_1)}\left[\frac{\partial^2 u}{\partial x^2}(x,t)\right] - D_t^{(1-\gamma_2)}[u(x,t)] + f(x,t), \tag{156}$$

subjected to the following conditions:

$$u(0,t) - \frac{\partial u(0,t)}{\partial x} = -\pi t^{2+\gamma_1}, \tag{157}$$

$$u(1,t) + \frac{\partial u(1,t)}{\partial x} = -\pi t^{2+\gamma_1} + 2et^{1+\gamma_2}. \tag{158}$$

The BCs, the source term, and the IC can be computed from the corresponding exact solution:

$$u(x,t) = t^{2+\gamma_1}\sin \pi x + t^{1+\gamma_2}e^x. \tag{159}$$

In order to show the effects of N and M on the accuracy, Table 2 displays the MAE, elapsed computational time, and the order of convergence with respect to parameter N:

$$CO_N = \frac{\log(E_{max}(N)/E_{max}(2N))}{\log 2}, \tag{160}$$

for $M = 7$ and $M = 15$ with $\sigma = 0.25$, $\gamma_1 = 0.6$, and $\gamma_2 = 0.9$. From this table, it is clearly seen that, for the case $M = 7$, the error decreases shapely with the increase of parameter N up to the value $N = 128$. For larger $N > 128$, the results of the proposed method do not change, and the solution accuracy remains at 10^{-7}. In the case of $M = 15$, the error decreases monotonically over the whole range of N, and the final accuracy comes to 10^{-11}. The order of convergence is three. Table 2 tabulates the solutions given in [54] by the usage of the spectral Legendre–Tau method for comparison. The data correspond to the case where 13 Legendre's polynomials are used for the spatial and temporal approximations. From the comparison, it can be seen obviously that the proposed analytical–numerical method leads to a better solution even for small values of M and N from the point of view of standard accuracy.

Table 2. The MAE, CO_N, and the elapsed time versus the N using M = 7 (left) and $M = 15$ (right).

	$M = 7$			$M = 15$		
N	$E_{\max}$	CO_N	*CPU, s*	$E_{\max}$	CO_N	*CPU, s*
2	9.37×10^{-2}	-	0.02	9.37×10^{-2}	-	0.11
4	7.31×10^{-3}	3.68	0.07	7.31×10^{-3}	3.68	0.17
8	6.81×10^{-4}	3.42	0.16	6.81×10^{-4}	3.42	0.33
16	7.30×10^{-5}	3.22	0.36	7.22×10^{-5}	3.24	0.66
32	9.09×10^{-6}	3.01	0.61	8.30×10^{-6}	3.12	1.0
64	1.78×10^{-6}	2.35	0.98	9.94×10^{-7}	3.06	1.9
128	9.97×10^{-7}	0.84	1.84	1.22×10^{-7}	3.03	4.1
256	9.94×10^{-7}	0.04	3.18	1.51×10^{-8}	3.01	9.0
512	9.94×10^{-7}	«1	6.5	1.89×10^{-9}	2.99	19
1024	9.94×10^{-7}	«1	13	2.57×10^{-10}	2.88	44
2048	9.94×10^{-7}	«1	24	5.36×10^{-11}	2.26	74
	[54], Table 2 , $E_{\max} = 3.2279 \times 10^{-5}$					

Table 3 displays the MAE and convergence order with respect to the parameter M for the fixed values N = 32, 128, 512. Here the convergence order is defined as:

$$CO_M = \frac{\log(E_{\max}(M_1)/E_{\max}(M_2))}{\log(M_2/M_1)}. \quad (161)$$

When M is small enough, it defines the accuracy of the approximate solution for all values of N. For $N = 32$, the accuracy remains the same for the growth of $M > 8$. On the other hand, when $N = 512$, the calculated error decreases with the increase of M in the whole range $2 \leq M \leq 12$. This means that 512 Fourier's harmonics provide an accurate approximation and the main error here is caused by the solving of FODEs. From the last row of this table, it can be seen evidently that the proposed method has high rates of convergence for the MAE, which provides reasonably accurate approximations for the unknown variables. It should be noted here that, with the increasing of M and N, the CO becomes flat, which means that the errors do not change for very large M or N. The proposed algorithm converges to the stable results.

Table 3. The MAE and CO_M versus the M with the fixed number of harmonics N.

	$N = 32$		$N = 128$		$N = 512$	
M	$E_{\max}$	CO_M	$E_{\max}$	CO_M	$E_{\max}$	CO_M
2	1.87×10^{-1}	-	1.87×10^{-1}	-	1.87×10^{-1}	-
3	4.02×10^{-2}	3.79	4.02×10^{-2}	3.79	4.02×10^{-2}	3.79
4	6.69×10^{-3}	6.23	6.69×10^{-3}	6.23	6.69×10^{-3}	6.23
5	6.66×10^{-4}	10.3	6.66×10^{-4}	10.3	6.66×10^{-4}	10.3
6	1.82×10^{-5}	19.7	1.24×10^{-5}	21.8	1.24×10^{-5}	21.8
7	9.09×10^{-6}	4.5	9.97×10^{-7}	16.4	9.97×10^{-7}	16.4
8	8.33×10^{-6}	0.66	1.51×10^{-7}	14.1	3.72×10^{-8}	24.6
9	8.30×10^{-6}	«1	1.27×10^{-7}	1.47	7.42×10^{-9}	13.7
10	8.30×10^{-6}	«1	1.23×10^{-7}	0.08	3.22×10^{-9}	7.92
11	8.30×10^{-6}	«1	1.22×10^{-7}	«1	2.33×10^{-9}	3.39
12	8.30×10^{-6}	«1	1.22×10^{-7}	«1	1.96×10^{-9}	0.63

In Figure 1, the observed behavior of the error is shown in more detail. Let us consider the left-hand side of Figure 1. The graphics $log(Emax(N))$ have the same origin for all fixed M. With the growth of N, the curves $log(Emax(N))$ change shape depending on the fixed value of M.

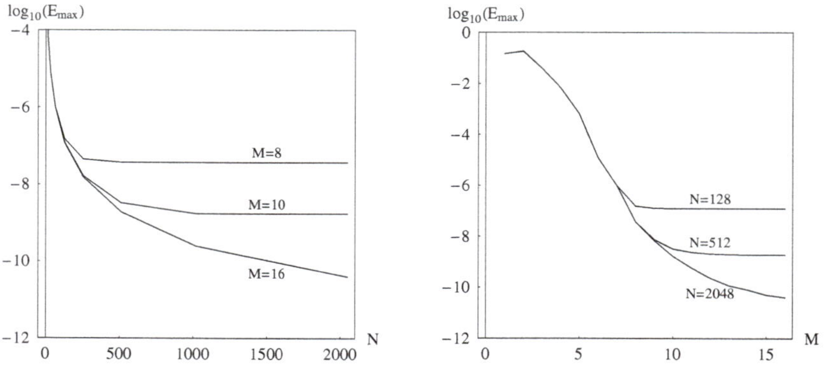

Figure 1. The MAE with respect to the parameters M and N.

6.1.3. Example 3

The third example solved here is the high order TFPDE

$$D_t^{(\alpha)}[u(x,t)] + \frac{\sin(t)}{1+t} D_t^{(\alpha_1)}[u(x,t)] + \frac{\cos(t)}{1+t} D_t^{(\alpha_2)}[u(x,t)] + \log(1+t)u(x,t)$$
$$= \frac{\sinh(t)}{1+t} D_t^{(\alpha_3)}\left[\frac{\partial^2 u}{\partial x^2}(x,t)\right] + \frac{\cosh(t)}{1+t} D_t^{(\alpha_4)}\left[\frac{\partial^2 u}{\partial x^2}(x,t)\right] + \left(1+t^2\right)\frac{\partial^2 u}{\partial x^2}(x,t) + f(x,t), \quad (162)$$

where $\alpha = \sqrt{21}$, $\alpha_1 = \pi$, $\alpha_2 = \sqrt{5}$, $\alpha_3 = \sqrt{3}$, $\alpha_4=\sqrt{2}$. As far as $4 < \alpha = \sqrt{21} < 5$, the TFPDE needs the following five ICs:

$$\frac{\partial^i u}{\partial t^i}(x, t=0) = u_i(x), i = 0,1,2,3,4. \quad (163)$$

The equation is subjected to the BC

$$\frac{\partial u}{\partial x}(x=0,t) - \pi^2 u(x=0,t) = g_W(t), \; \frac{\partial u}{\partial x}(x=1,t) + e^2 u(x=1,t) = g_E(t), \quad (164)$$

where the functions $f(x,t), u_i(x), g_W(t), g_E(t)$ can be easily computed from the following exact solution

$$u(x,t) = \cos(t)[\cos(x) + \cosh(x)]. \quad (165)$$

Table 4 presents the maximum absolute errors of the solution and its first derivative in time with the increase in N for $M = 16$ and $M = 24$. In the case when $M = 24$, the errors decrease sharply for $100 \leq N \leq 2000$. For $M = 16$, the errors are the same for $N > 500$. In Figure 2, this behavior of the error is shown in more detail.

Table 4. The MAE of the u and $\partial u/\partial t$ versus N using M = 16 (left) and 24 (right).

	$M=16$			$M=24$		
N	$E_{\max}(u)$	$E_{\max}(\partial u/\partial t)$	E_{H^1}	$E_{\max}(u)$	$E_{\max}(\partial u/\partial t)$	E_{H^1}
100	3.53×10^{-8}	5.51×10^{-8}	8.43×10^{-9}	3.53×10^{-8}	5.51×10^{-8}	8.42×10^{-9}
200	4.36×10^{-9}	6.92×10^{-9}	8.16×10^{-10}	4.39×10^{-9}	6.84×10^{-9}	7.33×10^{-10}
300	1.27×10^{-9}	2.10×10^{-9}	3.93×10^{-10}	1.30×10^{-9}	2.02×10^{-9}	1.76×10^{-10}
400	5.21×10^{-10}	9.31×10^{-10}	3.56×10^{-10}	5.47×10^{-10}	8.51×10^{-10}	6.42×10^{-11}
500	2.54×10^{-10}	5.15×10^{-10}	3.51×10^{-10}	2.80×10^{-10}	4.36×10^{-10}	2.94×10^{-11}
1000	5.80×10^{-11}	1.94×10^{-10}	3.50×10^{-10}	3.49×10^{-11}	5.44×10^{-11}	2.59×10^{-12}
2000	5.80×10^{-11}	1.94×10^{-10}	3.50×10^{-10}	4.35×10^{-12}	6.81×10^{-12}	2.65×10^{-13}

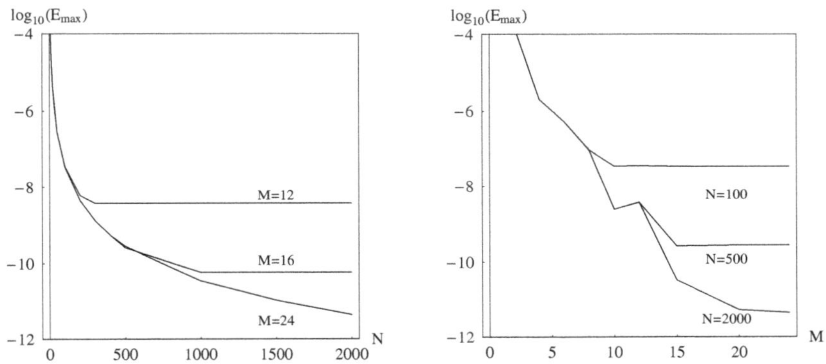

Figure 2. The MAE with respect to the parameters M and N.

6.2. $(2+1)$-Dimensional Problems

6.2.1. Example 4

Let us consider the following two-dimensional multi-term time-fractional mixed sub-diffusion and diffusion-wave equation defined in the unit square

$$D_t^{(\alpha)}[u(x,y,t)] + \frac{\partial u}{\partial t}(x,y,t) + D_t^{(\alpha_1)}[u(x,y,t)] + u(x,y,t)$$
$$= \nabla^2 u(x,y,t) + D_t^{(\alpha_2)}\left[\nabla^2 u(x,y,t)\right] + f(x,y,t),\ (x,y)\in[0,1]^2, \tag{166}$$

with the exact solution

$$u(x,y,t) = \left(1+t^3\right)\sin(\pi x)\sin(\pi y) \equiv w(t)\psi_{1,1}(x,y), \tag{167}$$

for the case $\alpha = 1.6$, $\alpha_1 = 0.7$, and $\alpha_2 = 0.3$.

The initial and Dirichlet boundary conditions of function $f(x,y,t)$ conform the exact solution. Thus, we get the TFPDE with a single spatial harmonic corresponding to the eigenfunction $\psi_{1,1}(x,y) = 2\sin(\pi x)\sin(\pi y)$. As it is shown above, the problem can be reduced to the single FODE

$$D_t^{(\alpha)}[w(t)] + \frac{dw(t)}{dt} + D_t^{(\alpha_1)}[w(t)] + w(t)$$
$$= -2\pi^2 w(t) - 2\pi^2 D_t^{(\alpha_2)}[w(t)] + F(t), \tag{168}$$

with initial conditions $w(0) = w_0$, $dw(0)/dt = w_1$.

Table 5 shows the behavior of the MAE versus the M in $\varphi_m(t) = t^{\delta_m}$, $\delta_m = \sigma(m-1)$. As shown in the previous section (see Equations (97), (98) and (107)), the approximate solution $w(t,M)$ belongs to the linear span $S(\alpha,\sigma,M) = Span\left(1, t, t^{\alpha+\sigma(m-1)}\right)_{m=1}^{M}$. It is easy to check that for $\alpha = 1.6, \sigma = 0.25$, there is no such M that the exact $w(t)$ (see Equation (167)) belongs to $S(\alpha,\sigma,M)$. On the other hand, $w(t) \in S(1.6, 0.35, M \geq 5)$ and $w(t) \in S(1.6, 0.7, M \geq 3)$. The data placed in Table 5 illustrate this situation. For $\sigma = 0.25$, the error decreases step-by-step with the growth of M, while it decreases sharply for $\sigma = 0.35$ and $\sigma = 0.7$ when the exact solution belongs to the corresponding manifold $S(\alpha,\sigma,M)$. Feng, Liu, and Turner have considered this problem [32] and constructed two finite element schemes for its numerical solution. Ezz-Eldien et al. [55] have studied this problem by the use of the combination of the shifted Legendre polynomials with the time-space spectral collocation method. The comparison of the two methods presented in Table 4 of [55] shows that most accurate result that has been achieved there has the error $E_{\max} = 1.407 \times 10^{-3}$ for the first technique and $E_{\max} = 1.807 \times 10^{-6}$ for the second one.

Table 5. The MAE and the computational time versus the M at $t = 1$.

M	1	2	3	4	5	6	10	15
$\sigma = 0.25$	4.3×10^{-1}	4.8×10^{-2}	1.1×10^{-2}	1.7×10^{-3}	8.5×10^{-5}	2.2×10^{-6}	8.1×10^{-11}	5.4×10^{-13}
$\sigma = 0.35$	4.3×10^{-1}	3.6×10^{-2}	5.2×10^{-3}	4.9×10^{-4}	1.8×10^{-15}	1.1×10^{-15}	-	-
$\sigma = 0.70$	4.3×10^{-1}	1.8×10^{-2}	1.1×10^{-15}	2.0×10^{-15}	-	-	-	-

6.2.2. Example 5

In this example, the problem solved here is to show the applicability of the proposed algorithm for the multi-term time-fractional diffusion-wave equation in the unit square $[0,1]^2$ [56]

$$D_t^{(\alpha)}[u] + \frac{\partial u}{\partial t} + D_t^{(\alpha_1)}[u] + u = \nabla^2 u + f(x,y,t). \tag{169}$$

The initial conditions, the Dirichlet BC, and the source term f correspond to the exact solution

$$u(x,y,t) = t^2 \sin(1-x)(e^x - 1)\sin(1-y)(e^y - 1). \tag{170}$$

The data shown in Table 6 are obtained using $\alpha = 1.3$, $\alpha_1 = 0.3$, $\sigma = 0.25$, and the numbers of the Müntz polynomials are $M = 5$ and $M = 10$. The same problem was considered by Shen, Liu, and Anh in [56] using an implicit difference method. From this table, it is clearly stated that our new approach is generally more accurate than others, even with a small number of N and M.

Table 6. The MAE and the elapsed time versus the N at $t = 1$ using $M = 5$ (left) and 10 (right).

	$M = 5$			$M = 10$		
N	$E_{\max}(u)$	$E_{\max}(\partial u/\partial t)$	CPU, s	$E_{\max}(u)$	$E_{\max}(\partial u/\partial t)$	CPU, s
100	1.443×10^{-6}	3.105×10^{-6}	9	1.452×10^{-6}	2.903×10^{-6}	14
200	2.018×10^{-7}	1.553×10^{-6}	23	2.100×10^{-7}	4.200×10^{-7}	35
300	1.203×10^{-7}	1.522×10^{-6}	56	6.445×10^{-8}	1.289×10^{-7}	97
400	1.231×10^{-7}	1.514×10^{-6}	89	2.756×10^{-8}	5.510×10^{-8}	154
500	1.241×10^{-7}	1.511×10^{-6}	153	1.420×10^{-8}	2.839×10^{-8}	260
600	1.245×10^{-7}	1.510×10^{-6}	204	8.247×10^{-9}	1.649×10^{-8}	352
[56], Table 1, $E_{\max}(u) = 6.145893072032060 \times 10^{-6}$						

6.3. $(3+1)$-*Dimensional Problems*
Example 6

Let us consider the following time-fractional telegraph equation in three dimensions

$$D_t^{(\alpha+1)}[u] + D_t^{(\alpha)}[u] + u = \nabla^2 u + f(x,y,z,t), 0 \le t \le 1, \tag{171}$$

in the domain $(x,y,z) \in [0,\pi]^3$ with zero Dirichlet boundary conditions and the source term corresponding to the exact solution

$$u(x,y,z,t) = \frac{t^{\alpha+2}}{\Gamma(\alpha+3)} \sin 2x \sin 2y \sin 2z. \tag{172}$$

Using the transform $(x,y,z) \to (\pi x, \pi y, \pi z)$, the equation is transformed into

$$D_t^{(\alpha+1)}[u] + D_t^{(\alpha)}[u] + u = \frac{1}{\pi^2}\nabla^2 u + f(x,y,z,t), \tag{173}$$

with the solution

$$u(x,y,z,t) = \frac{t^{\alpha+2}}{\Gamma(\alpha+3)} \sin 2\pi x \sin 2\pi y \sin 2\pi z. \tag{174}$$

Thus, we get a single spatial harmonic TFPDE. Substituting

$$u(x,y,z,t) = w(t) \sin 2\pi x \sin 2\pi y \sin 2\pi z, \tag{175}$$

we get the FODE

$$D_t^{(\alpha+1)}[w] + D_t^{(\alpha)}[w] + 13w = F(t), 0 \le t \le 1, \tag{176}$$

with the source term and ICs corresponding to the exact solution

$$w(t) = \frac{t^{\alpha+2}}{\Gamma(\alpha+3)}. \tag{177}$$

Table 7 shows the behavior of the absolute errors with the growth of M for two cases: $\sigma = 0.23$ and $\sigma = 0.25$. The results tabulated in the table are obtained by using $\alpha = 0.9$. As shown above (see Equations (97), (98) and (107)), the approximate solution $w(t,M)$ belongs to the linear span $S(\alpha,\sigma,M) = Span\left(1, t, t^{\alpha+\sigma(m-1)}\right)_{m=1}^{M}$. It is easy to check that for $\sigma = 0.23$ there is no such M that the exact solution $w(t)$ belongs to $S(\alpha,\sigma,M)$. On the other hand, $w(t) \in S(\alpha, 0.25, M \ge 5)$. Indeed, $\alpha + 0.25 \times (5-1) = \alpha + 2$. The data placed in the table illustrate this situation. For $\sigma = 0.23$, the error decreases step-by-step with the growth of M, while it decreases sharply for $\sigma = 0.25$ when the exact solution belongs to the corresponding manifold $S(\alpha,\sigma,M)$. Yang et al. have considered this problem in [57] using an ADI finite difference scheme. The most accurate result shown in Table 2 of the reference has the error 1.1243×10^{-3}.

Table 7. The MAE versus M at $t = 1$ for different σ.

M	1	2	3	4	5	6	10	15
σ = 0.23	4.6×10^{-2}	2.4×10^{-2}	3.4×10^{-3}	1.2×10^{-4}	1.6×10^{-6}	1.2×10^{-7}	2.4×10^{-10}	3.9×10^{-12}
σ = 0.25	4.6×10^{-2}	2.3×10^{-2}	3.0×10^{-3}	8.2×10^{-5}	1.1×10^{-17}	2.8×10^{-17}	-	-

7. Conclusions

In the present work, an accurate method that can reach the computer rounding errors has been proposed for solving multi-term time-fractional equations. Let us note that the proposed analytical–numerical method collides with two key issues. The first one is the method to handle non-homogeneous time-dependent boundary conditions, which is critical to the derivation of v_g. The second problem is the method to handle the non-homogeneous time-dependent source term of the equation. The derived function v_g solves the first problem cardinally. This article presents the analytical function v_g exactly satisfying the boundary conditions. Let us note that this function is not unique because one can locally change it inside the cube. The algorithm can give the function in the explicit analytical form with the help of math software packages like Maple or Mathematica if needed. The method of the Laplace transform and the Green function method are traditionally used for solving the second one. The BSM technique can also handle the non-homogeneous time-dependent source term. As mentioned above, in the solution procedure of the present method, one gets the system of the equation for each Fourier harmonic. The FODEs were solved independently with the help of Müntz polynomial bases. Additionally, the Fourier expansion of the source term over the eigenfunction basis should be performed at several fixed time moments t_j only. The number of these points is proportional to M. The value of M is not too large. As the numerical experiment shows, even $M = 10$ for Müntz's basis functions are enough for a rather precise approximate solution of the $(3+1)$ multi-term FPDE of the high order. And the convergence order with respect to the M and N is larger than 3. Generally speaking, $M > 10$ and $N > 100$ are sufficient to provide accurate results for the tested problems.

In this paper, the method is demonstrated by solving an important class of fractional problems described in the Introduction. This technique can also be extended onto iterative quasi-linear PDEs and onto the problems in other orthogonal coordinate systems. The main drawback of this work is that the derivation of v_g is only applicable for regular domains. Actually, numerical methods can be used for this purpose. This is the subject of further study.

Author Contributions: Conceptualization, J.L. (Ji Lin), S.R. and J.L. (Jun Lu); methodology, Y.Z.; writing—original draft preparation, S.R.; writing—review and editing, J.L. (Ji Lin) and Y.S.; visualization, J.L. (Ji Lin); funding acquisition, J.L. (Jun Lu). All authors have read and agreed to the published version of the manuscript.

Funding: This research was funded by the National Key Research and Development Program of China (No. 2021YFB2600704), the National Natural Science Foundation of China (Nos. 12072103, 52171272), and the Significant Science and Technology Project of the Ministry of Water Resources of China (No. SKS-2022112).

Data Availability Statement: No data were analyzed or generated during the study.

Conflicts of Interest: The authors declare no conflict of interest.

References

1. Hilfer, R. *Applications of Fractional Calculus in Physics*; World Scientific: Singapore, 2000.
2. Molz, F.-J.; Liu, H.-H.; Szulga, J. Fractional Brownian motion and fractional Gaussian noise in subsurface hydrology: A review, presentation of fundamental properties, and extensions. *Water Resour. Res.* **1997**, *33*, 2273–2286. [CrossRef]
3. Singh, J.; Kumar, D.; Baleanu, D. On the analysis of chemical kinetics system pertaining to a fractional derivative with Mittag-Leffler type kernel. *Chaos Interdiscip. J. Nonlinear Sci.* **2017**, *27*, 103113. [CrossRef]
4. Podlubny, I. *Fractional Differential Equations*; Academic Press: Cambridge, MA, USA, 1999.
5. Langlands, T.-A.-M.; Henry, B.I.; Wearne, S.L. Fractional cable equation models for anomalous electrodiffusion in nerve cells: Finite domain solutions. *Siam J. Appl. Math.* **2011**, *71*, 1168–1203. [CrossRef]
6. Chen, Y.; Chen, C.-M. Novel numerical method of the fractional cable equation. *J. Appl. Math. Comput.* **2020**, *62*, 663–683. [CrossRef]
7. Dehghan, M.; Shafieeabyaneh, N.; Abbaszadeh, M. Application of spectral element method for solving Sobolev equations with error estimation. *Appl. Numer. Math.* **2020**, *158*, 439–462. [CrossRef]
8. Zhao, J.; Fang, Z.; Li, H.; Liu, Y. A Crank–Nicolson Finite Volume Element Method for Time Fractional Sobolev Equations on Triangular Grids. *Mathematics* **2020**, *8*, 1591. [CrossRef]
9. Lin, J.; Zhang, Y.-H.; Reutskiy, S. A semi-analytical method for 1D, 2D and 3D time fractional second order dual-phase-lag model of the heat transfer. *Alex. Eng. J.* **2021**, *60*, 5879–5896. [CrossRef]
10. Sun, H.-G.; Zhang, Y.; Baleanu, D.; Chen, W.; Chen, Y.-Q. A new collection of real world applications of fractional calculus in science and engineering. *Commun. Nonlinear Sci. Numer. Simul.* **2018**, *64*, 213–231. [CrossRef]

11. Liu, Y.; Zheng, L.; Zhang, X. Unsteady MHD Couette flow of a generalized Oldroyd-B fluid with fractional derivative. *Comput. Math. Appl.* **2011**, *61*, 443–450. [CrossRef]
12. Ming, C.; Liu, F.-W.; Zheng, L.; Turner, I.; Anh, V. Analytical solutions of multi-term time fractional differential equations and application to unsteady flows of generalized viscoelastic fluid. *Comput. Math. Appl.* **2016**, *72*, 2084–2097. [CrossRef]
13. Ding, X.-L.; Nieto, J.-J. Analytical solutions for multi-term time-space fractional partial differential equations with nonlocal damping terms. *Fract. Calc. Appl. Anal.* **2018**, *21*, 312–335.
14. Ding, X.-L.; Jiang, Y.-J. Analytical solutions for multi-term time-space coupling fractional delay partial differential equations with mixed boundary conditions. *Commun. Nonlinear Sci. Numer. Simul.* **2018**, *65*, 231–247. [CrossRef]
15. Jong, S.-G.; Choe, H.-C.; Ri, Y.-D. A new approach for an analytical solution for a system of multi-term linear fractional differential equations. *Iran. J. Sci. Technol. Trans. Sci.* **2021**, *45*, 955–964. [CrossRef]
16. Jiang, H.; Liu, F.; Turner, I.; Burrage, K. Analytical solutions for the multi-term time-fractional diffusion-wave/diffusion equations in a finite domain. *Comput. Math. Appl.* **2012**, *64*, 3377–3388. [CrossRef]
17. Zeli, V.; Zorica, D. Analytical and numerical treatment of the heat conduction equation obtained via time-fractional distributed-order heat conduction law. *Phys. Stat. Appl.* **2018**, *492*, 2316–2335. [CrossRef]
18. Ama, E.-S.; El-Kalla, I.-L.; Ziada, E. Analytical and numerical solutions of multi-term nonlinear fractional orders differential equations. *J. Appl. Math. Comput.* **2010**, *60*, 788–797.
19. Liu, D.; He, W. Numerical simulation analysis mathematics of fluid mechanics for semiconductor circuit breaker. *Appl. Math. Nonlinear Sci.* **2021**, *7*, 331–342. [CrossRef]
20. Yang, Y. Application of numerical method of functional differential equations in fair value of financial accounting. *Appl. Math. Nonlinear Sci.* **2022**, *7*, 533–540. [CrossRef]
21. Liu, Q.; Dai, B.; Katib, I.; Alhamami, M.-A. Financial accounting measurement model based on numerical analysis of rigid normal differential equation and rigid generalised functional equation. *Appl. Math. Nonlinear Sci.* **2022**, *7*, 541–548. [CrossRef]
22. Xu, L.; Aouad, M. Application of Lane-Emden differential equation numerical method in fair value analysis of financial accounting. *Appl. Math. Nonlinear Sci.* **2021**, *7*, 669–676. [CrossRef]
23. Yan, L.; Sabir, Z.; Ilhan, E.; Gao, W. Design of a computational heuristic to solve the nonlinear Liénard differential model: Nonlinear Liénard differential model. *CMES-Comput. Model. Eng. Sci.* **2023**, *136*, 201–221.
24. Fardi, M.; Zaky, M.-A.; Hendy, A.-S. Nonuniform difference schemes for multi-term and distributed-order fractional parabolic equations with fractional Laplacian. *Math. Comput. Simul.* **2023**, *206*, 614–635. [CrossRef]
25. Mohammadi, S.; Ghasemi, M.; Fardi, M. A fast Fourier spectral exponential time-differencing method for solving the time-fractional mobile–immobile advection–dispersion equation. *Comput. Appl. Math.* **2022**, *41*, 264. [CrossRef]
26. Fardi, M.; Khan, Y. A fast difference scheme on a graded mesh for time-fractional and space distributed-order diffusion equation with nonsmooth data. *Int. J. Mod. Phys. B* **2022**, *36*, 2250076. [CrossRef]
27. Fardi, M.; Alidousti, J. A Legendre spectral-finite difference method for Caputo–Fabrizio time-fractional distributed-order diffusion equation. *Math. Sci.* **2022**, *16*, 417–430. [CrossRef]
28. Fardi, M.; Ghasemi, M. A numerical solution strategy based on error analysis for time-fractional mobile/immobile transport model. *Soft Comput.* **2021**, *25*, 11307–11331. [CrossRef]
29. Fardi, M.; Khan, Y. A novel finite difference-spectral method for fractal mobile/immobiletransport model based on Caputo–Fabrizio derivative. *Chaos Solitons Fractals* **2021**, *143*, 110573. [CrossRef]
30. Dehghan, M.; Safarpoor, M.; Abbaszadeh, M. Two high-order numerical algorithms for solving the multi-term time fractional diffusion-wave equations. *J. Comput. Appl. Math.* **2015**, *290*, 174–195. [CrossRef]
31. Jin, B.; Lazarov, R.; Liu, Y.; Zhou, Z. The Galerkin finite element method for a multi-term time-fractional diffusion equations. *J. Comput. Phys.* **2015**, *281*, 825–843. [CrossRef]
32. Feng, L.-B.; Liu, F.-W.; Turner, I. Finite difference/finite element method for a novel 2D multi-term time-fractional mixed sub-diffusion and diffusion-wave equation on convex domains. *Commun. Nonlinear Sci. Numer. Simul.* **2019**, *70*, 354–371. [CrossRef]
33. Yin, B.-L.; Liu, Y.; Li, H.; Zeng, F.-H. A class of efficient time-stepping methods for multi-term time-fractional reaction-diffusion-wave equations. *Appl. Numer. Math.* **2021**, *165*, 56–82. [CrossRef]
34. Zeng, F.; Zhang, Z.; Karniadakis, G.E. Second-order numerical methods for multi-term fractional differential equations: Smooth and non-smooth solutions. *Comput. Methods Appl. Mech. Eng.* **2017**, *327*, 478–502. [CrossRef]
35. Zheng, M.; Liu, F.; Anh, V.; Turner, I. A high-order spectral method for the multi-term time-fractional diffusion equations. *Appl. Math. Model.* **2016**, *40*, 4970–4985. [CrossRef]
36. Rashidinia, J.; Mohmedi, E. Approximate solution of the multi-term time fractional diffusion and diffusion-wave equations. *Comput. Math. Appl.* **2020**, *39*, 216. [CrossRef]
37. Soltani, J.-A.; Derakhshan, M.-H.; Marasi, H.-R. An efficient hybrid numerical method for multi-term time fractional partial differential equations in fluid mechanics with convergence and error analysis. *Commun. Nonlinear Sci. Numer.* **2022**, *114*, 106620.
38. Alsuyuti, M.-M.; Doha, E.-H.; Ezz-Eldien, S.-S. Galerkin operational approach for multi-dimensions fractional differential equations. *Commun. Nonlinear Sci. Numer.* **2022**, *114*, 106608. [CrossRef]
39. Fardi, M. A kernel-based pseudo-spectral method for multi-term and distributed order time-fractional diffusion equations. *Numer. Methods Partial. Differ. Equations* **2022**. [CrossRef]

40. Fardi, M.; Al-Omari, S.-K.-Q.; Araci, S. A pseudo-spectral method based on reproducing kernel for solving the time-fractional diffusion-wave equation. *Adv. Contin. Discret. Model.* **2022**, *2022*, 54. [CrossRef]
41. Carslaw, H.-S.; Jaeger, J.-C. *Conduction of Heat in Solids*; Clarendon Press: Oxford, UK, 1959.
42. Alquran, M.; Ali, M.; Alsukhour, M.; Jaradat, I. Promoted residual power series technique with Laplace transform to solve some time-fractional problems arising in physics. *Results Phys.* **2020**, *19*, 103667. [CrossRef]
43. Kamran, K.; Shah, Z.; Kumam, P.; Alreshidi, N.-A. A Meshless Method Based on the Laplace Transform for the 2D Multi-Term Time Fractional Partial Integro-Differential Equation. *Mathematics* **2020**, *8*, 1972. [CrossRef]
44. Reutskiy, S.-Y.; Fu, Z.-J. A semi-analytic method for fractional-order ordinary differential equations: Testing results. *Fract. Calc. Appl. Anal.* **2018**, *21*, 1598–1618. [CrossRef]
45. Hong, Y.-X.; Lin, J.; Chen, W. A typical backward substitution method for the simulation of Helmholtz problems in arbitrary 2D domains. *Eng. Anal. Bound. Elem.* **2018**, *93*, 167–176. [CrossRef]
46. Safari, F.; Azarsa, P. Backward substitution method based on Müntz polynomials for solving the nonlinear space fractional partial differential equations. *Math. Methods Appl. Sci.* **2020**, *43*, 847–864. [CrossRef]
47. Zhang, Y.; Rabczuk, T.; Lu, J.; Lin, S.; Lin, J. Space-time backward substitution method for nonlinear transient heat conduction problems in functionally graded materials. *Comput. Math. Appl.* **2022**, *124*, 98–110. [CrossRef]
48. Lin, J.; Xu, Y.; Zhang, Y. Simulation of linear and nonlinear advection–diffusion–reaction problems by a novel localized scheme. *Appl. Math. Lett.* **2020**, *99*, 106005. [CrossRef]
49. Lin, J.; Xu, Y.; Reutskiy, S.; Lu, J. A novel Fourier-based meshless method for (3 + 1)-dimensional fractional partial differential equation with general time-dependent boundary conditions. *Appl. Math. Lett.* **2023**, *135*, 108441. [CrossRef]
50. Esmaeili, S.; Shamsi, M.; Luchko, Y. Numerical solution of fractional differential equations with a collocation method based on Mü ntz polynomials. *Comput. Math. Appl.* **2011**, *62*, 918–929. [CrossRef]
51. Mokhtary, P.; Ghoreishi, F.; Srivastava, H.M. The Mü ntz-Legendre Tau method for fractional differential equations. *Appl. Math. Model.* **2016**, *40*, 671–684. [CrossRef]
52. Bahmanpour, M.; Tavassoli-Kajani, M.; Maleki, M. A Müntz wavelets collocation method for solving fractional differential equations. *Comput. Math. Appl.* **2018**, *37*, 5514–5526. [CrossRef]
53. Maleknejad, K.; Rashidinia, J.; Eftekhari, T. Numerical solutions of distributed order fractional differential equations in the time domain using the Müntz–Legendre wavelets approach. *Numer. Methods Partial. Differ. Equations* **2021**, *37*, 707–731. [CrossRef]
54. Yang, X.; Jiang, X.Y.; Zhang, H. A time–space spectral tau method for the time fractional cable equation and its inverse problem. *Appl. Numer. Math.* **2018**, *130*, 95–111. [CrossRef]
55. Ezz-Eldien, S.-S.; Doha, E.-H.; Wang, Y.; Cai, W. A numerical treatment of the two-dimensional multi-term time-fractional mixed sub-diffusion and diffusion-wave equation. *Commun. Nonlinear Sci. Numer. Simul.* **2020**, *91*, 105445. [CrossRef]
56. Shen, S.; Liu, F.-W.; Anh, V.-V. The analytical solution and numerical solutions for a two-dimensional multi-term time fractional diffusion and diffusion-wave equation. *J. Comput. Appl. Math.* **2019**, *345*, 515–534. [CrossRef]
57. Yang, X.-H.; Qiu, W.-L.; Zhang, H.-X.; Tang, L. An efficient alternating direction implicit finite difference scheme for the three-dimensional time-fractional telegraph equation. *Comput. Math. Appl.* **2021**, *102*, 233–247. [CrossRef]

mathematics

Article

Numerical Analysis and Structure Optimization of Concentric GST Ring Resonator Mounted over SiO_2 Substrate and Cr Ground Layer

Khaled Aliqab [1,*], Bo Bo Han [2], Ammar Armghan [1,*], Meshari Alsharari [1], Jaymit Surve [3] and Shobhit K. Patel [4]

1 Department of Electrical Engineering, College of Engineering, Jouf University, Sakaka 72388, Saudi Arabia
2 Department of Information and Communication Technology, Marwadi University, Rajkot 360003, India
3 Department of Electrical Engineering, Marwadi University, Rajkot 360003, India
4 Department of Computer Engineering, Marwadi University, Rajkot 360003, India
* Correspondence: kmaliqab@ju.edu.sa (K.A.); aarmghan@ju.edu.sa (A.A.)

Abstract: Since the introduction of Metal-Insulator-Metal (MIM) absorbers, most of the structures demonstrated a narrowband absorption response which is not suitable for potential applications in photovoltaic systems, as it requires higher energy to enhance its performance. Very little research is being conducted in this direction; to address this issue, we exhibit a broadband solar absorber designed using a concentric GST ring resonator placed upon a silicon dioxide substrate layer with chromium used as a ground plane. It was analyzed using the finite element method. The design is also optimized by using a nonlinear parametric optimization algorithm. Comparatively less work has been focused on solar absorbers designed with the help of GST material, and here we have compared the effect of two different phases of GST, i.e., amorphous (aGST) and crystalline (cGST); the results indicate the higher performance of aGST phase. Parametric optimization has been adapted to identify the optimal design to attain high performance at minimal resources. The absorption response is angle insensitive for 0 to 60 degrees, and at the same time for both TE and TM modes, the design provides identical results, indicating the polarization-insensitive properties. The electric field intensity changes at the six peak wavelengths are also demonstrated for the authentication of the high performance. Thus, the proposed concentric GST ring resonator solar absorber can present a higher solar energy absorption rate than other solar structure designs. This design can be applied for improving the performance of photovoltaic systems.

Keywords: numerical analysis; structure optimization; parametric optimization; GST; chromium; SiO_2; Photovoltaic applications

MSC: 65K10; 78-10; 00A06

Citation: Aliqab, K.; Han, B.B.; Armghan, A.; Alsharari, M.; Surve, J.; Patel, S.K. Numerical Analysis and Structure Optimization of Concentric GST Ring Resonator Mounted over SiO_2 Substrate and Cr Ground Layer. *Mathematics* **2023**, *11*, 1257. https://doi.org/10.3390/math11051257

Academic Editors: Fajie Wang and Ji Lin

Received: 13 February 2023
Revised: 28 February 2023
Accepted: 2 March 2023
Published: 5 March 2023

1. Introduction

Nowadays, many appliances are used to ease our daily lives, but the power supplies for these appliances need to be considered, as they contribute significantly towards the major issues of climate change and global warming. To solve this problem, solar energy plays an important role [1]. Photonics defines the technology of light, and the main function of photonic technology is to encompass generating, manipulating, amplifying, guiding, and detecting light [2]. Moreover, it can be used in our phones, such as lasers, cameras, optical fibers, and screens. Optical tweezers and lighting are also used in cars, homes, TVs, and computers [3]. Photonic devices are used in the medical field and for a large generation of power in the industrial field [4]. Photonic devices play an important role in our daily lives; therefore, by studying photonic technology, we can improve many other science fields, such as optical, microwave, wireless communication, solar energy systems, and so on [5]. One of the main reasons to develop the solar energy system is to reduce the damage to our natural environment and stop the toxic gases produced by large industries [6]. The solar energy system intends to reduce the greenhouse effect we have been facing for the last decade [7]. Several numerical algorithms have also been employed for photovoltaic cell analysis [8,9].

Engineers have developed many techniques to improve the absorption rate of photovoltaic cells, including a multi-layer structure with several types of layers using various types of suitable materials [10]. Using a multi-layer structure provides better results than other structures and can produce better energy absorption output [11]. Before designing a good solar absorber, engineers need to consider the properties of the metamaterials that will be used in the developed solar absorbers [12–16]. The greater the number of solar absorber layers, the greater the absorption rate [17,18]. The number of solar absorber layers is directly proportional to the absorption rate. Nevertheless, the three-layer solar absorber type is the most popular because of its efficiency and cost [19]. According to Wang and co-authors, at a frequency between 20.59 GHz and 43.73 GHz, the metamaterial absorber can provide an absorption rate of over 83% and an absorption rate of 79.5% in full width. Moreover, a metamaterial absorber is ultra-thin at the center frequency and has only 10% of the wavelength [20]. John and co-authors found that under the visible region between 450 THz and 750 THz, a novel circular ring resonator solar energy absorber has a more suitable operating range in the polarization insensitive property for solar cells [21]. Zhao's theory optimized that a three-layer coating solar absorber has an absorptance value of 0.97 at 2.5 μm [22]. Wu and co-author proposed an ultra-broadband solar absorber with an absorption above 90% ranging between 685 and 4071 nm by a split-ring resonator design [23]. The average absorption rate is above 94.3 between the wavelength range 600 and 4200 nm [24]. Yu observed that the absorption rate is over 90% by using surface plasmon resonance at 1759 nm [25]. Wanger and co-authors found that metallic chromium (Cr) and chromium oxide (Cr_2O_3) absorptance values are more than 90.0% by XRD, resulting in diffraction peaks [26]. To date, many materials have been employed for solar absorber designs for solar thermophotovoltaic (STPV) applications. Naveed et al. reported a MIM structure with a SiO_2 insulator and nickel ground and resonator layer. The resonator was a combination of multiple hexagonal structures, and the authors achieved an overall absorption of 80% in the entire solar spectrum [27]. The authors also varied the metallic layers in the range of Al, Au, Cr, Ag, W, and Ni, and the highest performing material was Ni. Shafique and co-authors proposed a vanadium-nitride-inspired MIM absorber for STPV application and achieved >98% absorptance in UV and visible regions [28]. Kondaiah and investigators reported an Al_2O_3/TaC/Ti-based structure for a solar thermal absorber which is stable for 2 h at 500 °C [29]. A tungsten-nanowire-assisted MIM structure is presented for subwavelength domain with near perfect absorption in UV, and 85% in visible range is observed [30].

The available structures of solar absorbers either depict the single band or multiband response, which is not feasible for several solar energy harvesting related applications, and for this specific need, we require a broadband solar absorber that can absorb the solar energy under the whole solar spectrum. Hence, the objective of this study is to design a solar absorber which can absorb the solar energy over the whole solar spectrum from UV to MIR with large angular and polarization-independent characteristics. Furthermore, the objective is to obtain an optimal structure by applying parametric optimization and comparing the absorption response for various phases of GST. This work is among the few works which have utilized GST materials for a solar absorber structure and achieved the broadband absorption response, and here resides the novelty of this work. We examined the GST material for this study, which makes this work interesting, as previously, most of the GST-based works are reported in the IR band.

The proposed structure is designed with three layers, including a ground layer, the substrate layer, and the resonator to overcome the narrowband absorption response and achieve the broadband absorption response. We used the structure with a concentric ring designed to obtain a high absorption rate and good quality [31]. At the ground layer, we used Cr, and at the substrate layer, we used SiO_2 and GST resonators, respectively. The proposed GST ring structure can provide a high absorption rate compared to other designs because of its concentric ring resonators [32]. In this paper, we are going to demonstrate the changes in absorption rates in the ultraviolet (UV) regions, visible (V) regions, and infrared (IR) regions. The electromagnetic spectrum in the ultraviolet region starts from 10 nm to 400 nm and is shorter than the visible region [33]. The visible region is the region that the electromagnetic spectrum in the range the human eye can see, and the wavelength range is between 380 and 700 nm [34]. The IR wavelength is longer than visible light, generally from around 1 mm [35]. The developed design will show the average absorption rates for the TE and TM modes. The TE mode is the propagation of the direction of the electric field traveled concerning the normal direction of a magnetic field [36]. The TM mode is the propagation of the direction of the magnetic field traveled concerning the normal direction of a magnetic field [37]. The section below discusses the design and parameters of construction, the results and discussion of the proposed design absorption rate, and the comparison of average absorption rates between the developed design and the formerly published works.

2. Methodology

This section discusses the design and modeling of the proposed structure. The materials used for designing the proposed structure, parameters, and the structure optimization process are discussed in detail. The optical properties of the utilized materials are discussed to demonstrate their advantage in the proposed structure. The structure is first designed by introducing every layer. The importance of those layers is demonstrated for obtaining the ultrawideband absorption. The structure optimization is then carried out to identify the best parameters to achieve the highest possible broadband absorption response with the help of the proposed structure. The ideal characteristics, including angular and polarization insensitivity, are investigated to demonstrate the absorber's response similar to an ideal absorber. At last, the proposed absorber structure is compared with available designs to depict its high performance compared to those structures.

2.1. Design and Modeling

The design and modeling process of the proposed broadband solar absorber is described through a flowchart in Figure 1. Figure 2a shows the top view for the GST ring resonator. Figure 2b represents the 3D shape of the concentric GST ring resonator-based solar absorber. Figure 2c represents the front view for the GST ring resonator with the respective parameters such as the structure length L = 500 nm; the ground layer thickness, P_B is 500 nm; the substrate layer thickness, P_S is 600 nm; and the GST ring resonator thickness, P_R is also 500 nm. Figure 2d shows the radius of the rings, respectively. The radius of the central circle R_1 is 25 nm. The first ring radius R_2 is 50 nm, the second ring radius R_3 is 125 nm, and the third ring radius R_4 is 200 nm. To investigate the concentric ring resonator design, we used COMSOL Multiphysics software [38]. The refractive index of Cr is 3.212 and the silicon dioxide SiO_2 refractive index is 1.5175 [39]. The proposed design is developed with a SiO_2 substrate layer over the Cr ground layer and a GST ring resonator is placed over the SiO_2 layer. Figure 2e,f represent the refractive index output for aGST and cGST with real and imaginary parts, respectively. A SiO_2 material as a substrate is chosen due to its dielectric properties [40,41]. Due to its remarkable optical properties and high melting point, chromium metal is selected as the ground layer [39].

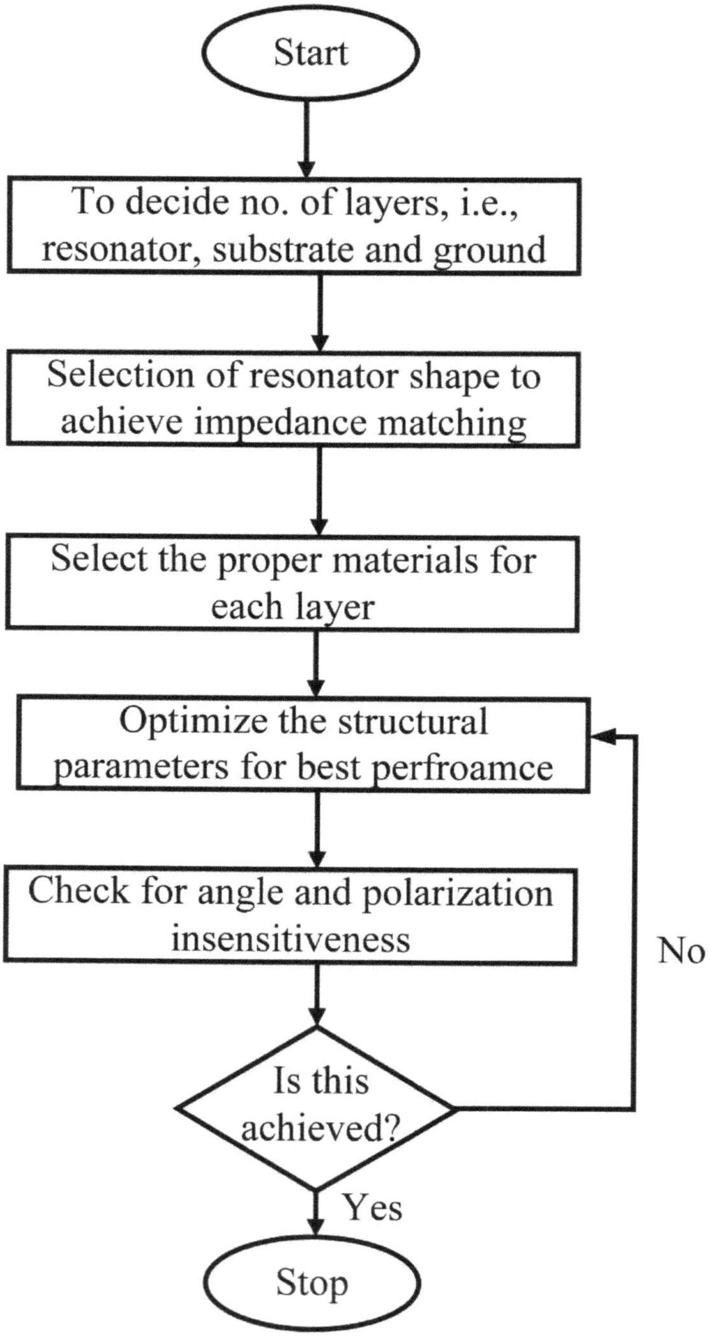

Figure 1. Flowchart describing the design process of the proposed broadband solar absorber.

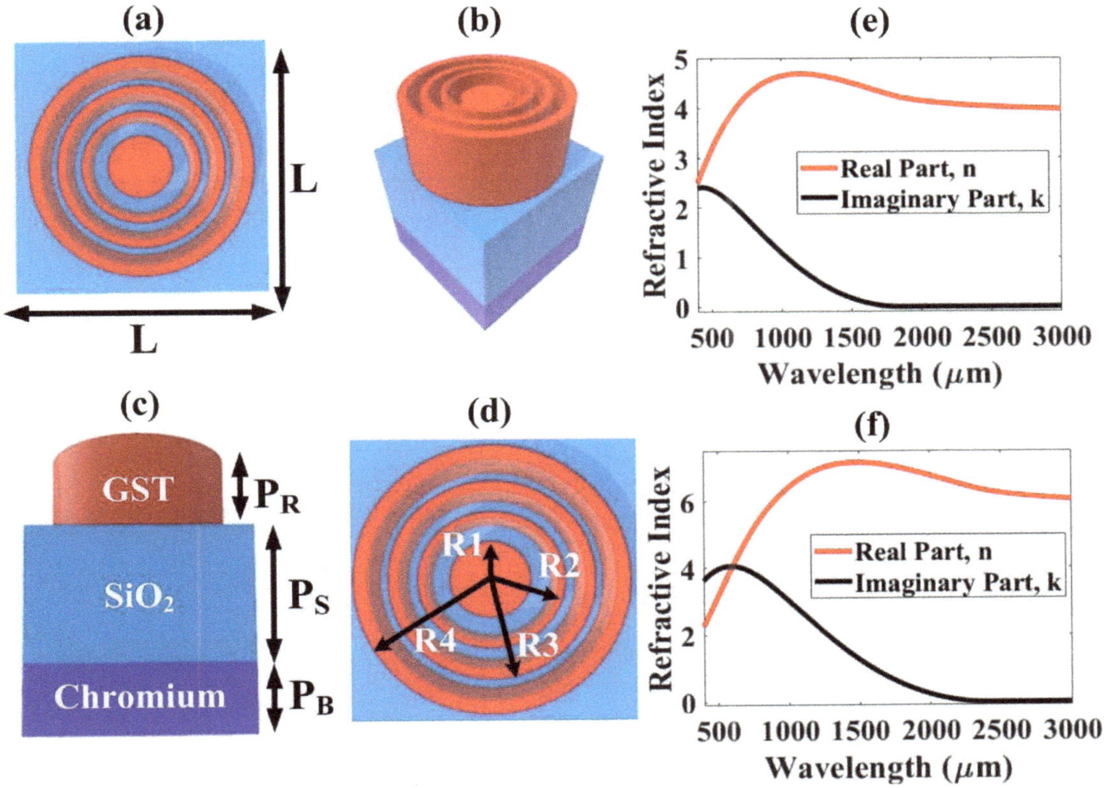

Figure 2. Structure of the concentric GST ring resonator-based solar absorber. (**a**) the top view for the ring resonator, (**b**) the 3D view for the solar absorber, (**c**) the front view for the solar absorber with the respective parameters, (**d**) top view with ring parameters, (**e**) real (n) and imaginary (k) parts of refractive index for aGST, (**f**) real (n) and imaginary (k) parts of refractive index for cGST.

2.2. Structure Optimization

The main importance and novelty of the proposed concentric ring resonator is its symmetrical shape, which in return gives the polarization insensitive response which is a necessity for a solar absorber. Furthermore, the material used to fabricate ring resonators is less compared to circular resonators, and it is also easy to fabricate with the help of photolithography. Figure 3a presents the process of optimizing a developed structure by simulating and checking the importance of each layer and how they contribute towards improving the absorption response step by step. First, we built a Cr ground layer. On the Cr ground layer, we placed a SiO_2 layer, and we constructed the ring resonator over the SiO_2 layer. Then, the second ring resonator, third ring resonator, and finally the one cylinder were constructed concentrically. Figure 3b–h represents the situations of absorptance, reflectance, and transmittance of the developed designs of Figure 3a. The average absorption rates of the various structures were calculated by the FEM method [42].

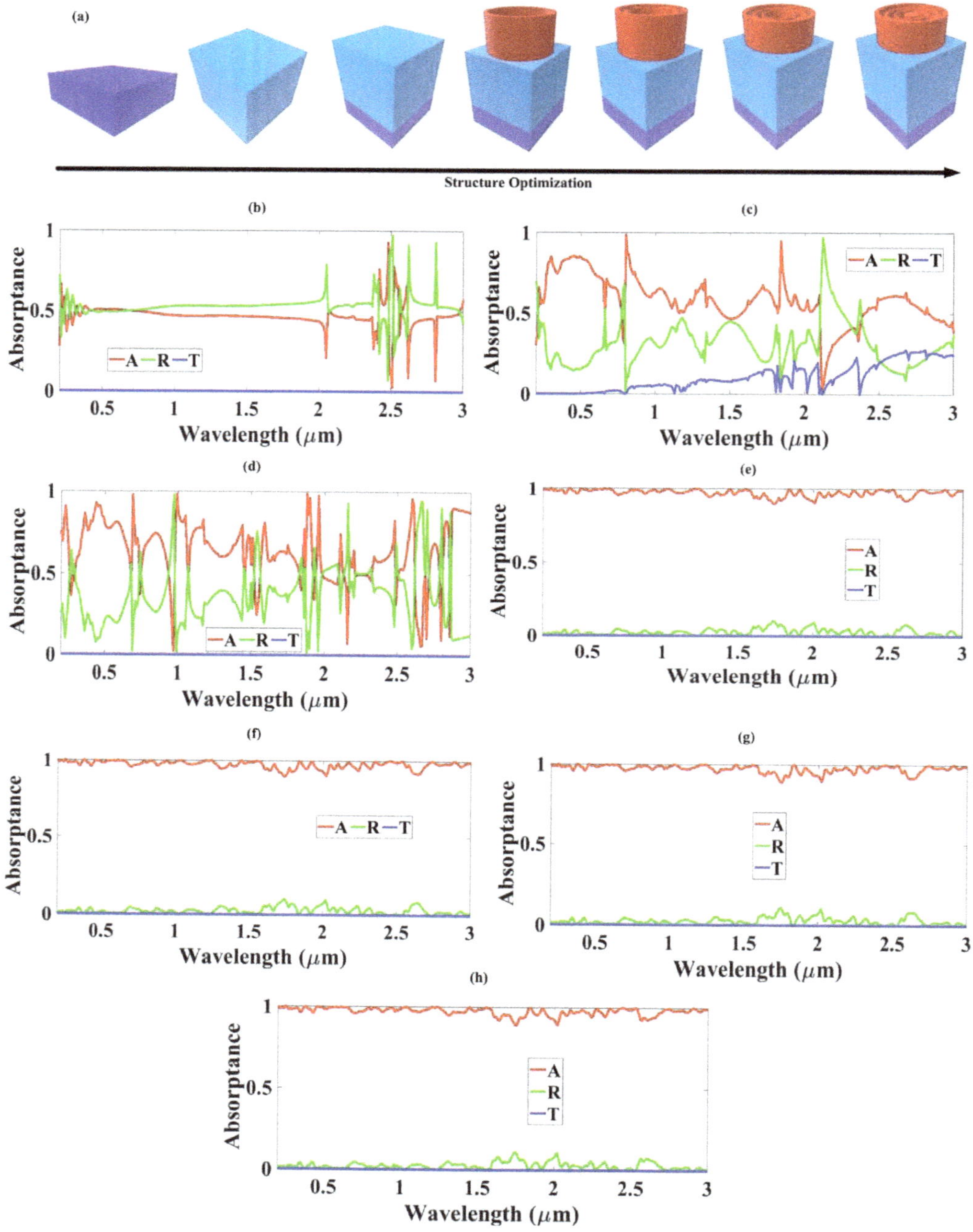

Figure 3. (**a**) Construction for the GST ring resonator configuration process step by step, (**b**) absorptance (A), reflectance (R), and transmittance (T) lines for the Cr ground layer, (**c**) A, R, and T lines for the SiO_2 layer, (**d**) A, R, and T lines of the construction of both the Cr ground layer and SiO_2 layer, (**e**–**h**) A, R, and T lines by inserting the first GST ring resonator, second GST ring resonator, third GST ring resonator, and the cylinder constructed on the Cr ground layer, and SiO_2 layer respectively.

In Figure 3b, the average absorption rate of the Cr ground layer in UV, V, NIR, and MIR regions is presented. The absorption rates are 48.28%, 50.45%, 46.41%, and 45.76% in the mentioned ranges, respectively, with an overall absorption rate of 46.96%. Figure 3c examines the average absorption rate of the SiO_2 substrate layer in UV, V, NIR, and MIR regions, and the absorption rates are 70.77%, 77.53%, 54.79%, and 53.83%, respectively, with the overall absorption rate of 58.16%. The absorption rate of the design comprised both the Cr ground layer and SiO_2 substrate layer and is shown in Figure 3d. In this figure, the absorption rates are 68.24%, 78.66%, 60.77%, and 62.27% in UV, V, NIR, and MIR regions, respectively, and the overall average absorption rate is 63.48%. Then, we continued to develop the GST ring resonator with the first ring, and the absorption rate is shown in Figure 3e. In this figure, the average absorption rate is significantly higher than the previous structures with 98.52%, 98.47%, 96.92%, and 97.44% in UV, V, NIR, and NIR, respectively. The overall average absorption rate is also increased to 97.3%. The second ring resonator is then included, and the absorption rates are 98.49%, 98.43%, 96.18%, and 97.38% in UV, V, NIR, and MIR, respectively, and the overall absorption rate mentioned is 97.32%, as shown in Figure 3f. The absorption results of the third ring structure are presented in Figure 3g including 98.47%, 98.44%, 97.97%, and 97.58% in UV, V, NIR, and MIR regions, respectively, and the average overall rate is 97.35%. In Figure 3h, the overall design is developed, and the absorption results are 98.52%, 98.45%, 97.15%, and 97.45% in UV, V, NIR, and MIR regions, respectively. The overall average absorption rate is 97.36%, so the average absorption rate gets higher when we develop the new layers in the proposed design. One interesting trend that we observed is when we removed the ground plane, the transmittance started to increase, as we can observe in Figure 3c; this is since the ground layer transmits back the electromagnetic (EM) waves and in absence of this, the EM waves are reflected. The flowchart presented in Figure 4 describes the process of optimizing the structural parameters used for the proposed study.

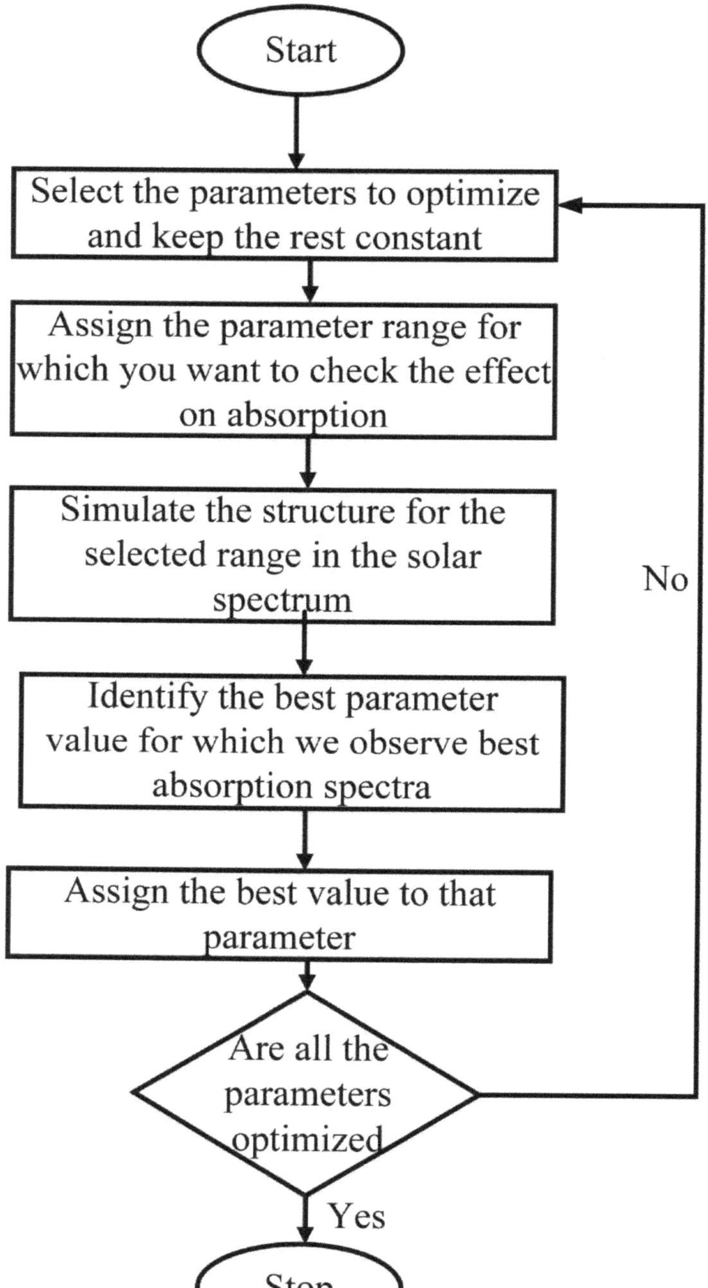

Figure 4. Flowchart describing the process of structural parameter optimization.

3. Results and Discussion

In this part, the effect of various structural parameters and the phases of GST are investigated, with the corresponding results discussed in detail. Figure 5a shows the absorptance (A), reflectance (R), and transmittance (T) of the aGST concentric ring resonator solar absorber. For the wavelength range between 0.2 and 1.59 µm, the absorption rate is above 97% with a bandwidth of 1390 nm; the average absorption is 98.18% for this particular bandwidth. The absorption rate is also above 97% in the wavelength between 1.84 and 3 µm with a bandwidth of 1160 nm and a mean absorption of 97.14%. The overall wavelength ranges between 0.2 and 3 µm from UV to MIR and shows an absorption rate above 95% with a bandwidth of 2800 nm. We can assign six peak wavelengths (in micrometers) to show the unity absorption rate of the aGST ring resonator solar absorbers such as $\lambda_1 = 0.25$, $\lambda_2 = 0.61$, $\lambda_3 = 1.24$, $\lambda_4 = 1.84$, $\lambda_5 = 2.53$, and $\lambda_6 = 2.91$. Figure 5b presents the average absorptance, reflectance, and transmittance for the cGST concentric ring resonator solar absorber with the same parameters as aGST. We can see the decreased absorption rate and increased reflectance rate in the cGST compared to the aGST results. Therefore, the absorption rate in the ring resonator solar absorber using aGST is better than cGST.

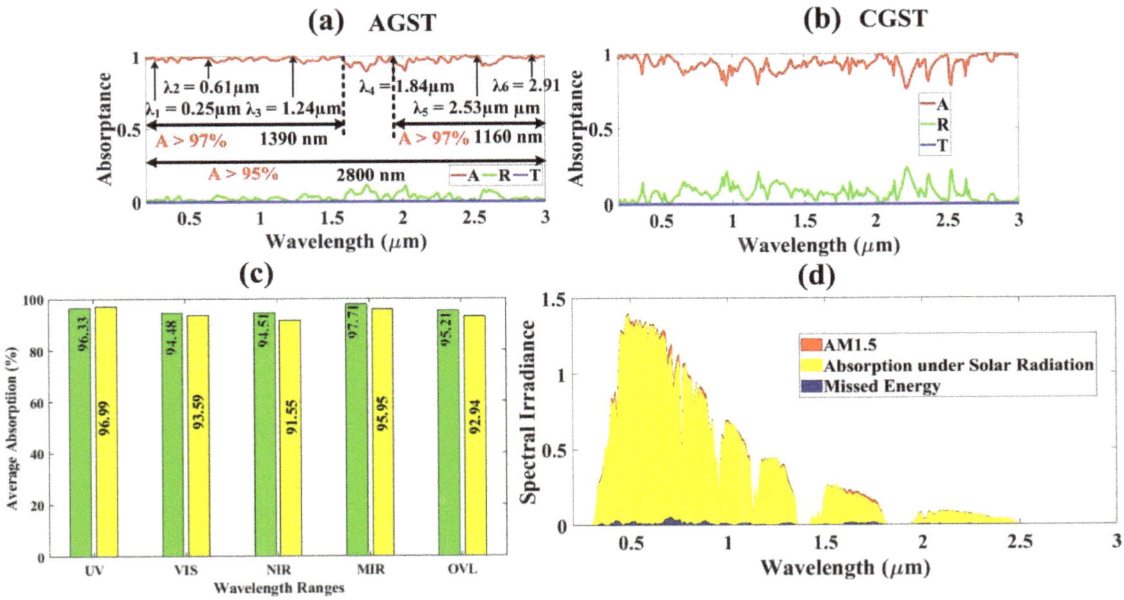

Figure 5. (**a**) The absorption rate of aGST concentric ring resonator solar absorber between 0.2 and 3 µm, (**b**) The absorptance, transmittance, and reflectance of cGST, (**c**) The comparison data plot of absorption rate between aGST in green color and cGST in yellow color for UV, V, NIR, MIR, and overall ranges, (**d**) aGST absorption under solar radiation missed solar energy concerning AM1.5.

Figure 5c shows the comparison data flow chart of the average absorption rate of aGST and cGST in UV, V, NIR, MIR, and overall ranges. In the data plot, the absorption rate of aGST is represented by the color green and cGST is represented by the color yellow. The average absorption rate in aGST is decreased compared to the cGST in the UV region; however, the average absorption rate in aGST is increased compared to the cGST consisting of V, NIR, MIR, and overall regions. In the UV region, the absorption rate of aGST is 96.33% and cGST is 96.99%, which is a very slight difference. In V, NIR, and MIR regions, the absorption rate of aGST is 94.48%, 94.51%, and 97.71%, respectively; on the other hand, the decreased absorption rate of cGST is 93.59%, 91.55%, and 95.95%, respectively. Therefore, we can observe that the overall average absorption rate in cGST is slightly decreased compared to the aGST in the data plot.

The proposed aGST concentric ring resonator solar absorber can be examined by the AM1.5 radiation systems mentioned in Figure 5d. In this figure, the AM1.5 section is in red, the absorption section under the solar radiation region is in yellow, and the regions of missed solar energy are in blue. By using Equation (1), we can obtain the numerical values of the absorption section and missed solar energy [43]. To develop the good efficiency and higher absorption rate of the proposed aGST concentric ring resonator solar absorber, we need to improve the absorbed solar energy under the solar radiation region and reduce the missed solar energy nearly to zero for all the ranges from ultraviolet to MIR regions [44]. To calculate the amount of solar energy radiated from the sun, we need to use the following AM1.5 equation [45].

$$\eta_A = \frac{\int_{\lambda_{min}}^{\lambda_{max}} (1 - R(\omega)).I_{AM1.5}(\omega).d\omega}{\int_{\lambda_{min}}^{\lambda_{max}} I_{AM1.5}(\omega).d\omega} \quad (1)$$

From the above equation, the ultra-broadband absorption rate under normal solar radiation conditions is assigned by A, IAM for an air mass 1.5 irradiances, and the reflectance of solar energy is denoted by R [46].

The difference between the conventional and proposed optimization technique is as follows:

There are two main methods for optimization used by researchers based on their behavior [47].

1. Linear Parametric Optimization
2. Nonlinear Parametric Optimization

As our response has behaved nonlinearly with wavelength, we have used the nonlinear parametric optimization technique for optimizing our structural parameters, such as GST concentric ring resonator thickness, substrate thickness, and Cr ground layer thickness.

We can analyze the absorption rate of the developed ultra-broadband GST ring resonator design by changing the numerous parameters of the GST resonator thickness, SiO_2 substrate layer, and Cr ground layer as shown in Figure 6. The output of the absorption rate changes by increasing the GST resonator thickness from 500 nm to 1000 nm, shown in Figure 6a,b with the help of line plots as well as the fermi plot. At the first peak wavelength λ_1, the average absorption rate increases from 96.48% to 97.79% by changing the aGST resonator thickness from 500 nm to 1000 nm. For the next three peak wavelengths λ_2, λ_3, and λ_4, the absorption rate also increases from 91.01%, 88.88%, and 93.61% to 96.93%, 97.62%, and 97.47% when the aGST resonator thickness changes to between 500 nm and 1000 nm, respectively. The absorption rate of the last two peak wavelengths λ_5 and λ_6 decreases from 99.58% and 99.92% to 98.54% and 98.85%, respectively. So, the overall ranges of aGST resonator thickness from 500 nm to 1000 nm decreases from 95.47% to 94.05%, and also slightly decreases in the ultraviolet, violet, NIR, and MIR regions. The fermi plot of the absorption rate changes by the GST resonator thickness from 500 to 1000 nm is shown in Figure 6b.

The output of the absorption rates by the substrate thickness changes between 500 nm and 1000 nm at the six peak wavelength ranges between 0.2 and 3 μm is shown in Figure 6c,d, shown by the fermi plot. The increased average absorption rate of the substrate thickness from 500 nm to 1000 nm at the first four wavelengths λ_1, λ_2, λ_3, and λ_4 is 96.67%, 92.78%, 91.28%, and 98.32% from 96.48%, 91.01%, 88.88%, and 93.61%, respectively. The absorption rate of the substrate thickness decreased from 99.58% and 99.92% to 96.43% and 99.63% at the λ_5 and λ_6, respectively. When we increased the substrate thickness from 500 nm to 1000 nm, the overall absorption rate showed just a little change from 95.47% to 95.92%; this was also the same situation in the UV, V, NIR, and MIR regions.

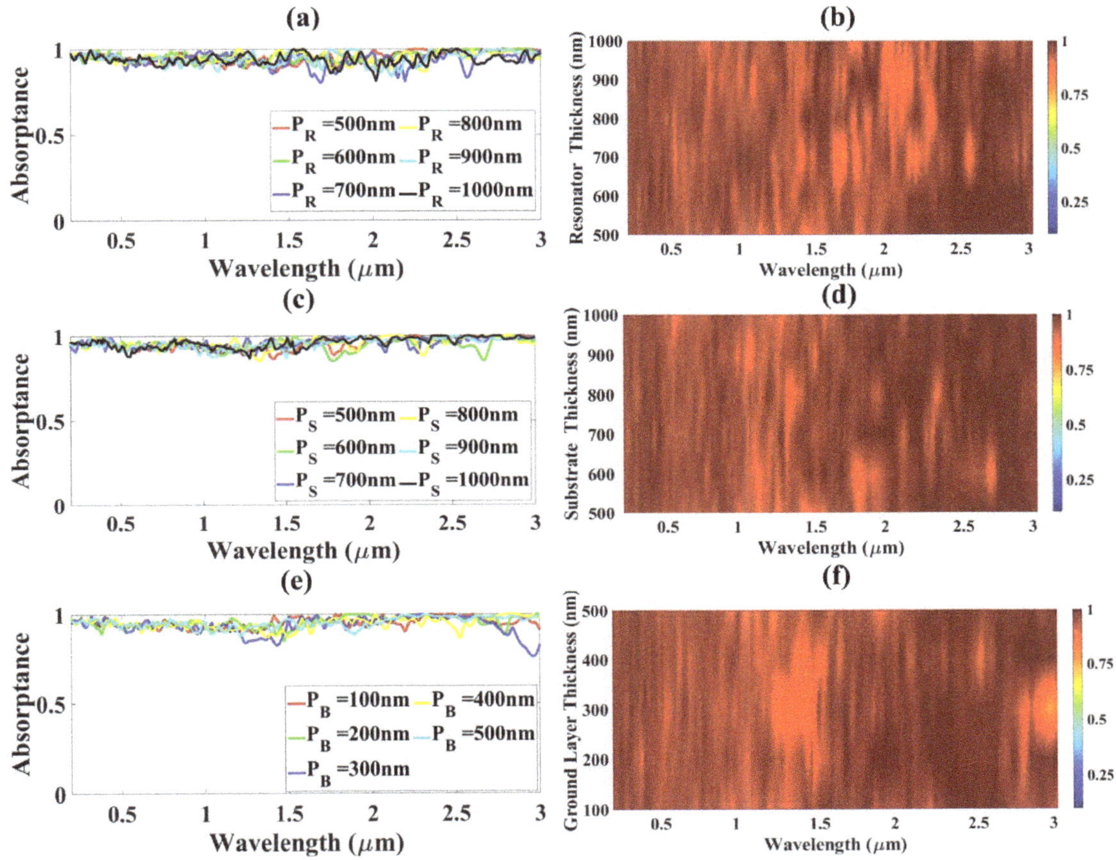

Figure 6. The proposed concentric GST ring resonator solar absorber's absorption rate (**a**) absorption rate of concentric GST ring resonator solar absorber by increasing the GST ring structural height, P_R, (**b**) absorption rate of concentric GST ring resonator solar absorber by increasing the GST ring structural height, P_R demonstrated by fermi plot, (**c**) absorption rate of concentric GST ring resonator solar absorber by increasing the SiO_2 substrate layer thickness, P_S, (**d**) absorption rate of concentric GST ring resonator solar absorber by increasing the SiO_2 substrate layer thickness, P_S demonstrated by fermi plot, (**e**) absorption rate of concentric GST ring resonator solar absorber by increasing the Cr ground layer thickness, P_B, (**f**) absorption rate of concentric GST ring resonator solar absorber by increasing the Cr ground layer thickness, P_B, demonstrated by the color plot.

When we increased the ground layer thickness between 500 nm and 900 nm at the six peak wavelength ranges between 0.2 and 3 μm, the output of the absorption rate changes is shown in Figure 6e, and the fermi plot is shown in Figure 6f. At the first peak wavelength λ_1, the absorption rate is increased from 95.96% to 96.74% when the ground layer thickness changes between 100 nm and 500 nm. On the other hand, the absorption rates decreased from 94.88%, 91.04%, 93.27%, 98.46, and 97.14% to the absorption rates 92.55%, 90.36%, 91.68%, 96.35%, and 96.37%, respectively, when we changed the ground layer thickness from 100 nm to 500 nm at another five peak wavelengths λ_2, λ_3, λ_4, λ_5, and λ_6. The overall absorption rate is equal to the absorption rate of 95.2%, and the absorption rates at the UV, V, NIR, and MIR regions are also equal at the increased ground layer thickness between 100 nm and 500 nm with the six peak wavelengths ranging between 0.2 and 3 μm. The fermi plot of the absorption rate changes when we increased the ground layer thickness from 100 nm to 500 nm is presented in Figure 6f.

To develop the ultra-broadband GST ring solar absorber with a good average absorption rate, we need to analyze some sections such as GST resonator, SiO_2 substrate layer thickness, Cr ground layer thickness, and incidence angles in (TE) and (TM) modes by changing the structural parameters numerically [48]. The absorption rate of the concentric GST ring solar absorber in the TE mode with the angle of incidence changes from 0 to 60 degrees at the wavelength range from 0.2 to 3 μm is presented in Figure 7a and by the fermi plot in Figure 7b. The five peak wavelengths λ_1, λ_2, λ_4, λ_5, and λ_6 (all except λ_3) show decreased absorption rates from 95.96%, 93.24%, 89.97%, 96.99%, and 97.62% to 67.49%, 73.52%, 91.79%, 87.41%, and 84.71%, respectively.

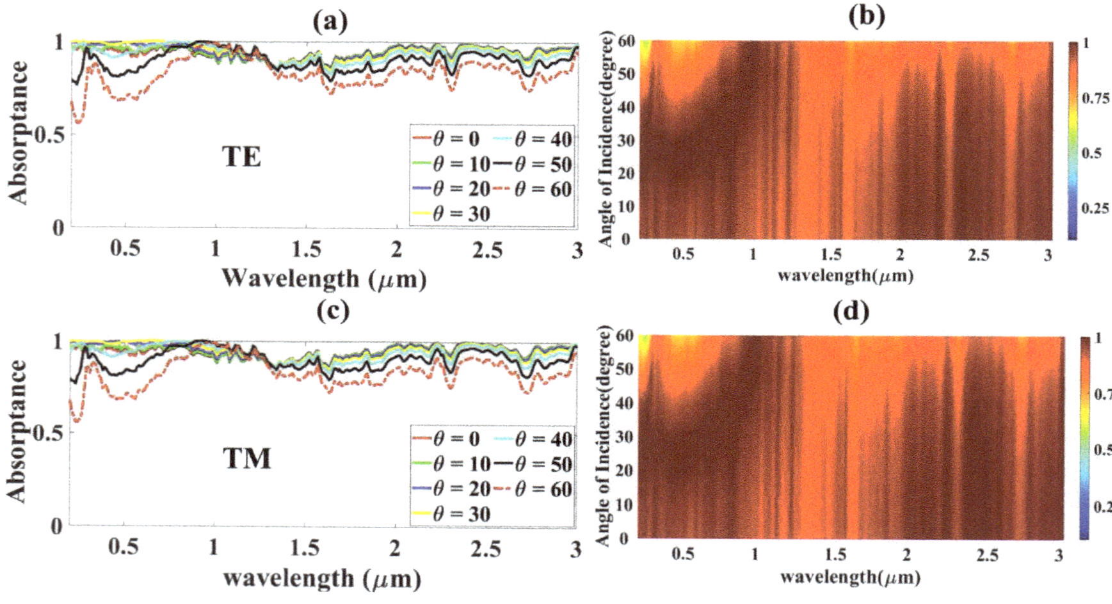

Figure 7. Concentric GST ring solar absorber's absorption rates (**a**) the absorption rate changes of concentric GST ring solar absorber between 0 and 60 degrees in TE mode, (**b**) the absorption rate changes of concentric GST ring solar absorber between 0 and 60 degrees in TE mode demonstrated by the fermi plot, (**c**) the absorption rate changes of concentric GST ring solar absorber between 0 and 60 degrees in TM mode, (**d**) the absorption rate changes of concentric GST ring solar absorber between 0 and 60 degrees in TM mode demonstrated by the fermi plot.

Only one wavelength λ_3 shows an increased absorption rate from 89.97% to 91.79%. The absorption rate of the concentric GST ring solar absorber in TE mode by the fermi plot is presented in Figure 7b. The average absorption rate of the concentric GST ring solar absorber in TM mode with the angle of incidence changes from 0 to 60 degrees at the wavelength range from 0.2 to 3 μm is shown in Figure 7c and by the fermi plot in Figure 7d. The results of the absorption rates in the TE mode also changed, as in the TM mode. In the TM mode, the output of five peak wavelengths λ_1, λ_2, λ_4, λ_5, and λ_6 (all except λ_3) show decreased absorption rates from 95.96%, 93.24%, 96.15%, 98.32%, and 98.53% to 67.49%, 73.52%, 82.77%, 89.43%, and 83.42%, respectively. Only one wavelength, also λ_3, shows an increased absorption rate from 90.01% to 91.83%. The absorption rate of the concentric GST ring solar absorber in TM mode by the fermi plot is exhibited in Figure 7d. From the comparison of the TE and TM modes, we can see the overall absorption rates do not have many changes in percentages. For the TE mode, the overall absorption rate significantly decreased from 94.45% to 83.19%. For the TM mode, the overall absorption rate significantly also decreased from 94.78% to 83.31%. In the ultraviolet region for both TE and TM modes, the absorption rate decreased from 96.04% to 73.27%. In the TE mode, the absorption rate of V, NIR, and MIR decreased from 94.9%, 93.71%, and 96.28% to 85.8%, 83.89%, and 83.9%, respectively. Comparing the TE mode to the TM mode, the absorption rates in V, NIR, and MIR also decreased from 94.9%, 94.03%, and 96.99% to 86.08%, 83.59%, and 83.6%, respectively. Therefore, in both the TE mode and TM mode, the absorption rate is above 95% in the UV and MIR regions and above 90% in the V and NIR regions by changing the angle of incidences (degrees) from 0 to 60 with the wavelength range of 0.2–3 μm. In Table 1, we can express the absorption rate in percentages with the respective bandwidth by changing the angle insensitive in the UV, V, NIR, and MIR regions with a wavelength range of 0.2 to 3 μm. The proposed structure demonstrates an almost identical response for 0 to 60 degrees, after which the response gets affected and the absorption decreases after 60 degrees. This limitation can be avoided by creating a platform to place a solar absorber structure to avoid solar energy coming from more than 60 degrees of the incidence angle.

Table 1. Proposed Absorber's Performance comparison with the available literature.

MIM Absorber Design	Overall Absorption Rate	Bandwidth (Absorption > 95%)	Bandwidth (Absorption > 97%)	Angle Insensitive	Polarization Insensitive
$Ni/SiO_2/Ni$ inspired structure [27]	More than 80%	-	1700 nm	0° to 60°	Yes
Refractory metal VN based structure [28]	-	-	>98% (500 nm)	-	Yes
$W/SiO_2/W$ structure [30]	85% (visible)	-	Near perfect in UV region	0° to 60°	Yes
TiN & TiO_2 disk arrays on SiO_2 layer [49]	More than 90%	1110 (>90%)	-	0° to 40°	Yes
Ti/Silica/Ti double lattice structure [50]	91.4%	1007 (>90%)	-	0° to 45°	-
Multilayer structure of $SiO_2/Ti/SiO_2/Ti$ (elliptical nanodisc of Ti) [51]	93.26%	1650 (>90%)	-	0° to 70°	Yes
All ceramic structure [52]	More than 90%	1310 (>90%)	-	0° to 60°	Yes
Phase change material based structure [53]	More than 90%	1000 (>90%)	-	-	Yes
TiO_2/TiN resonator with SiO_2 and TiN as a substrate and ground plane [54]	More than 90%	1264 (>90%)	-	0° to 45°	-
Proposed concentric GST ring inspired structure	**95.21%**	**2800 nm**	**2550 nm**	**0° to 60°**	**Yes**

The situations of electric field intensity changes in the concentric ring aGST resonator for the six peak wavelengths in micrometers (μm) such as $\lambda_1 = 0.25$, $\lambda_2 = 0.61$, $\lambda_3 = 1.24$, $\lambda_4 = 1.84$, $\lambda_5 = 2.53$, and $\lambda_6 = 2.91$ are exhibited in Figure 8a–f, respectively. The amount of the electric field intensity is also important for developing the absorption rate of the GST ring resonators in UV, V, NIR, and MIR. The electric field intensity changes in the x-y and x-z planes are mentioned in Figure 8a,b. At the first peak wavelength $\lambda_1 = 0.25$ μm, the amount of the electric field intensity is better at the inner part of the ring resonator and at the top of the absorber layer, as shown in Figure 8a in both the x-y and x-z planes, and the absorption rate is 96.74%. At the second peak wavelength $\lambda_2 = 0.61$ μm, the amount of electric field intensity is better at the resonator rings compared to the other parts of the proposed broadband design, and the top absorber layer is presented in Figure 8b in both the x-y and x-z planes, and the absorption rate is 92.55%. At the wavelengths of $\lambda_3 = 1.24$ μm and $\lambda_4 = 1.84$ μm, the decreased amount of the electric field intensity to the other wavelengths of the proposed design is presented in Figure 8c,d in both the x-y and x-z planes, and the absorption rate is 90.36% and 91.68%, respectively. In Figure 8e,f, the amount of electric field intensity is significantly increased at the ring resonators and gives the higher absorption rate of 96.35% and 96.37% at the wavelengths of $\lambda_5 = 2.53$ μm and $\lambda_6 = 2.91$ μm in the UV, V, NIR, and MIR ranges, respectively. In Table 1, we have compared the proposed design's absorption rate to the other published papers, and it can be found that the developed GST ring resonator design can provide better results than the other published paper's results. Therefore, the proposed concentric GST ring resonator design can be used to develop many photonic devices with a higher absorption rate. The absorption characteristics depend on the electromagnetic field, as discussed in Figure 5 above. To better understand the best factors affecting absorption, we analyzed the significance of the angles of incidence (IAS) for both the TE and TM modes.

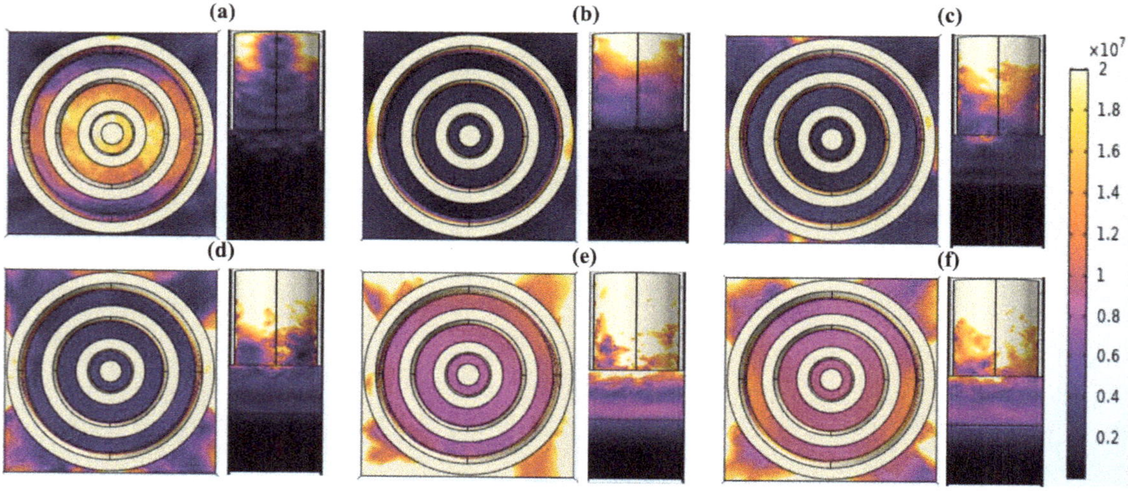

Figure 8. The amount of electric field strength in x-y and x-z planes of GST ring resonators at six peak wavelengths in micrometers (μm). (**a**) $\lambda_1 = 0.25$, (**b**) $\lambda_2 = 0.61$, (**c**) $\lambda_3 = 1.24$, (**d**) $\lambda_4 = 1.84$, (**e**) $\lambda_5 = 2.53$, and (**f**) $\lambda_6 = 2.91$.

4. Conclusions

A MIM solar energy absorber has been simulated, designed, and theoretically proven and is achieving an optimal average absorption response of 96.52% in the visible region and a maximum absorptivity of 99.98%. Chromium metal is utilized as the ground layer because of its transmittance blocking properties; the substrate layer of SiO_2 dielectric insulator is used since it provides lossless resonance characteristics, and the concentric ring resonator is made of GST, as it has good impedance matching characteristics. The proposed aGST ring resonator solar absorber represents a good absorption rate over the wavelength range from 0.2 to 3 μm. For the bandwidth range of 2550 nm, the solar absorption rate is located above 97% between the wavelength range 0.2 and 1.59 μm and 1.84 to 3 μm, and the average absorption rate is 98.18%, and 97.14%, respectively. The overall wavelength between 0.2 and 3 μm from UV to MIR regions shows an absorption rate above 95% with a bandwidth of 2800 nm. A broadband absorption response is achieved, which is the combination of multiple near-perfect absorption peaks that can be validated by the electric field distribution plots. We have developed a good quality structural design with a higher absorption rate with wide angle and polarization insensitiveness, a lower reflectance rate, and zero transmittance. This design can be applied for improving the performance of thermoelectric photovoltaic systems.

Author Contributions: Conceptualization, S.K.P. and K.A.; methodology, B.B.H. and J.S.; software, B.B.H., J.S. and K.A.; validation, B.B.H., M.A. and A.A.; formal analysis, K.A., M.A., A.A. and J.S.; investigation, K.A., S.K.P., J.S. and A.A.; resources, A.A. and B.B.H.; writing—original draft preparation, All Authors; writing—review and editing, K.A., S.K.P. and J.S.; visualization, B.B.H. and J.S.; supervision, S.K.P. and K.A. All authors have read and agreed to the published version of the manuscript.

Funding: This research received no external funding.

Institutional Review Board Statement: Not applicable.

Informed Consent Statement: Not applicable.

Data Availability Statement: The data will be made available at a reasonable request to corresponding author.

Conflicts of Interest: The authors declare no conflict of interest.

References

1. Lønborg, C.; Carreira, C.; Jickells, T.; Álvarez-Salgado, X.A. Impacts of Global Change on Ocean Dissolved Organic Carbon (DOC) Cycling. *Front. Mar. Sci.* **2020**, *7*, 466. [CrossRef]
2. Gamon, J.A.; Huemmrich, K.F.; Wong, C.Y.S.; Ensminger, I.; Garrity, S.; Hollinger, D.Y.; Noormets, A.; Peñuelask, J. A remotely sensed pigment index reveals photosynthetic phenology in evergreen conifers. *Proc. Natl. Acad. Sci. USA* **2016**, *113*, 13087–13092. [CrossRef] [PubMed]
3. Park, Y.; Kim, J.; Roh, Y.G.; Park, Q.H. Optical slot antennas and their applications to photonic devices. *Nanophotonics* **2018**, *7*, 1617–1636. [CrossRef]
4. Fang, T.; Gao, X.; Wang, X.; Liu, J. Design of gate-tunable graphene electro-optical reflectors based on an optical slot-antenna coupled cavity. *J. Phys. Photonics* **2021**, *3*, 045003. [CrossRef]
5. Zhou, J.; Leaño, J.L.; Liu, Z.; Jin, D.; Wong, K.L.; Liu, R.S.; Bünzli, J.C.G. Impact of Lanthanide Nanomaterials on Photonic Devices and Smart Applications. *Small* **2018**, *14*, 1801882. [CrossRef]
6. Liu, Z.; Zhang, H.; Fu, G.; Liu, G.; Liu, X.; Yuan, W.; Xie, Z.; Tang, C. Colloid templated semiconductor meta-surface for ultra-broadband solar energy absorber. *Sol. Energy* **2020**, *198*, 194–201. [CrossRef]
7. Krumme, J.-P.; Hack, R.A.A.; Raaijmakers, I.J.M.M.; Cazzaniga, A.; Crovetto, A.; Ettlinger, R.B.; Canulescu, S.; Hansen, O.; Pryds, N.; Schou, J.J.; et al. Photovoltaic Energy Conversion, 2003. Proceedings of 3rd World Conference on. *Thin Solid Films* **2011**, *3*, 1–4.
8. Jalal, R.; Shihab, S.; Alhadi, M.A.; Rasheed, M. Spectral Numerical Algorithm for Solving Optimal Control Using Boubaker-Turki Operational Matrices. *J. Phys. Conf. Ser.* **2020**, *1660*, 012090. [CrossRef]
9. Rasheed, M.; Mohammed, O.Y.; Shihab, S.; Al-Adili, A. A comparative Analysis of PV Cell Mathematical Model. *J. Phys. Conf. Ser.* **2021**, *1795*, 012042. [CrossRef]
10. Ding, F.; Cui, Y.; Ge, X.; Jin, Y.; He, S. Ultra-broadband microwave metamaterial absorber. *Appl. Phys. Lett.* **2012**, *100*, 103506. [CrossRef]
11. Nuru, Z.Y.; Arendse, C.J.; Muller, T.F.; Khamlich, S.; Maaza, M. Thermal stability of electron beam evaporated AlxO y/Pt/AlxOy multilayer solar absorber coatings. *Sol. Energy Mater. Sol. Cells* **2014**, *120*, 473–480. [CrossRef]
12. Zaversky, F.; Aldaz, L.; Sánchez, M.; Ávila-Marín, A.L.; Roldán, M.I.; Fernández-Reche, J.; Füssel, A.; Beckert, W.; Adler, J. Numerical and experimental evaluation and optimization of ceramic foam as solar absorber—Single-layer vs multi-layer configurations. *Appl. Energy* **2018**, *210*, 351–375. [CrossRef]
13. Patel, S.K.; Udayakumar, A.K.; Mahendran, G.; Vasudevan, B.; Surve, J.; Parmar, J. Highly efficient, perfect, large angular and ultrawideband solar energy absorber for UV to MIR range. *Sci. Rep.* **2022**, *12*, 18044. [CrossRef] [PubMed]
14. Patel, S.K.; Surve, J.; Katkar, V.; Parmar, J. Optimization of Metamaterial-Based Solar Energy Absorber for Enhancing Solar Thermal Energy Conversion Using Artificial Intelligence. *Adv. Theory Simul.* **2022**, *5*, 2200139. [CrossRef]
15. Patel, S.K.; Surve, J.; Prajapati, P.; Taya, S.A. Design of an ultra-wideband solar energy absorber with wide-angle and polarization independent characteristics. *Opt. Mater.* **2022**, *131*, 112683. [CrossRef]
16. Patel, S.K.; Surve, J.; Parmar, J.; Katkar, V.; Jadeja, R.; Taya, S.A.; Ahmed, K. Graphene-based metasurface solar absorber design for the visible and near-infrared region with behavior prediction using Polynomial Regression. *Optik* **2022**, *262*, 169298. [CrossRef]
17. Thomas, N.H.; Chen, Z.; Fan, S.; Minnich, A.J. Semiconductor-based Multilayer Selective Solar Absorber for Unconcentrated Solar Thermal Energy Conversion. *Sci. Rep.* **2017**, *7*, 5362. [CrossRef]
18. Patel, S.K.; Surve, J.; Jadeja, R.; Katkar, V.; Parmar, J.; Ahmed, K. Ultra-Wideband, Polarization-Independent, Wide-Angle Multilayer Swastika-Shaped Metamaterial Solar Energy Absorber with Absorption Prediction using Machine Learning. *Adv. Theory Simul.* **2022**, *5*, 2100604. [CrossRef]
19. AL-Rjoub, A.; Rebouta, L.; Costa, P.; Vieira, L.G. Multi-layer solar selective absorber coatings based on W/WSiAlNx /WSiAlOyNx/SiAlOx for high temperature applications. *Sol. Energy Mater. Sol. Cells* **2018**, *186*, 300–308. [CrossRef]

20. Xin, W.; Binzhen, Z.; Wanjun, W.; Junlin, W.; Junping, D. Design and characterization of an ultrabroadband metamaterial microwave absorber. *IEEE Photonics J.* **2017**, *9*, 1–13. [CrossRef]
21. Du John, H.V.; Jose, T.; Jone, A.A.A.; Sagayam, K.M.; Pandey, B.K.; Pandey, D. Polarization Insensitive Circular Ring Resonator Based Perfect Metamaterial Absorber Design and Simulation on a Silicon Substrate. *Silicon* **2022**, *14*, 9009–9020. [CrossRef]
22. Niranjan, K.; Kondaiah, P.; Biswas, A.; Kumar, V.P.; Srinivas, G.; Barshilia, H.C. Spectrally selective solar absorber coating of w/walsin/sion/sio2 with enhanced absorption through gradation of optical constants: Validation by simulation. *Coatings* **2021**, *11*, 334. [CrossRef]
23. Wu, B.; Liu, Z.; Du, G.; Shi, L.; Liu, X.; Liu, M.; Zhan, X. Ultra-broadband electromagnetic wave absorber based on split-ring resonators. *J. Opt. Soc. Am. B* **2019**, *36*, 3573. [CrossRef]
24. IEEE MTT-S International Microwave and RF Conference 2014, IMaRC 2014—Collocated with Intemational Symposium on Microwaves, ISM 2014. 2015, p. 406. Available online: https://www.scimagojr.com/journalsearch.php?q=21100379733&tip=sid&clean=0 (accessed on 12 February 2023).
25. Yu, P.; Yang, H.; Chen, X.; Yi, Z.; Yao, W.; Chen, J.; Yi, Y.; Wu, P. Ultra-wideband solar absorber based on refractory titanium metal. *Renew. Energy* **2020**, *158*, 227–235. [CrossRef]
26. Wu, P.; Wei, K.; Xu, D.; Chen, M.; Zeng, Y.; Jian, R. Ultra-wideband and wide-angle perfect solar energy absorber based on titanium and silicon dioxide colloidal nanoarray structure. *Nanomaterials* **2021**, *11*, 2040. [CrossRef]
27. Naveed, M.A.; Bilal, R.M.H.; Baqir, M.A.; Bashir, M.M.; Ali, M.M.; Rahim, A.A. Ultrawideband fractal metamaterial absorber made of nickel operating in the UV to IR spectrum. *Opt. Express* **2021**, *29*, 42911–42923. [CrossRef]
28. Shafique, A.; Naveed, M.A.; Ijaz, S.; Zubair, M.; Mehmood, M.Q.; Massoud, Y. Highly efficient Vanadium Nitride based metasurface absorber/emitter for solar-thermophotovoltaic system. *Mater. Today Commun.* **2023**, *34*, 105416. [CrossRef]
29. Kondaiah, P.; Niranjan, K.; John, S.; Barshilia, H.C. Tantalum carbide based spectrally selective coatings for solar thermal absorber applications. *Sol. Energy Mater. Sol. Cells* **2019**, *198*, 26–34. [CrossRef]
30. Bilal, R.M.H.; Baqir, M.A.; Choudhury, P.K.; Naveed, M.A.; Ali, M.M.; Rahim, A.A. Ultrathin broadband metasurface-based absorber comprised of tungsten nanowires. *Results Phys.* **2020**, *19*, 103471. [CrossRef]
31. Zhang, Z.; Yang, J.; He, X.; Zhang, J.; Huang, J.; Chen, D.; Han, Y. Plasmonic refractive index sensor with high figure of merit based on concentric-rings resonator. *Sensors* **2018**, *18*, 116. [CrossRef]
32. Liu, P.; Yan, S.; Ren, Y.; Zhang, X.; Li, T.; Wu, X.; Shen, L.; Hua, E. A mim waveguide structure of a high-performance refractive index and temperature sensor based on fano resonance. *Appl. Sci.* **2021**, *11*, 10629. [CrossRef]
33. Rio, Y.; Rodríguez-Morgade, M.S.; Torres, T. Modulating the electronic properties of porphyrinoids: A voyage from the violet to the infrared regions of the electromagnetic spectrum. *Org. Biomol. Chem.* **2008**, *6*, 1877–1894. [CrossRef] [PubMed]
34. Stauber, T.; Peres, N.M.R.; Geim, A.K. Optical conductivity of graphene in the visible region of the spectrum. *Phys. Rev. B Condens. Matter Mater. Phys.* **2008**, *78*, 085432. [CrossRef]
35. Rio, Y.; Rodriguez-Morgade, M.S.; Torres, T. ChemInform Abstract: Modulating the Electronic Properties of Porphyrinoids: A Voyage from the Violet to the Infrared Regions of the Electromagnetic Spectrum. *Org. Biomol. Chem.* **2008**, *39*. [CrossRef]
36. Amiri, M.; Tofigh, F.; Shariati, N.; Lipman, J.; Abolhasan, M. Wide-angle metamaterial absorber with highly insensitive absorption for TE and TM modes. *Sci. Rep.* **2020**, *10*, 13638. [CrossRef] [PubMed]
37. Volke-Sepulveda, K.; Ley-Koo, E. General construction and connections of vector propagation invariant optical fields: TE and TM modes and polarization states. *J. Opt. A Pure Appl. Opt.* **2006**, *8*, 867–877. [CrossRef]
38. *COMSOL Multiphysics®*, Version 6.0; COMSOL, Inc.: Stockholm, Sweden, 2021.
39. Rakić, A.D.; Djurišić, A.B.; Elazar, J.M.; Majewski, M.L. Optical properties of metallic films for vertical-cavity optoelectronic devices. *Appl. Opt.* **1998**, *37*, 5271. [CrossRef] [PubMed]
40. Ramesh, S.; Kim, H.S.; Lee, Y.J.; Hong, G.W.; Jung, D.; Kim, J.H. Synthesis of cellulose-L-tyrosine-SiO2/ZrO2 hybrid nanocomposites by sol-gel process and its potential. *Int. J. Precis. Eng. Manuf.* **2017**, *18*, 1297–1306. [CrossRef]
41. Azad, M.M.; Ejaz, M.; Shah, A.u.R.; Afaq, S.K.; Song, J. A bio-based approach to simultaneously improve flame retardancy, thermal stability and mechanical properties of nano-silica filled jute/thermoplastic starch composite. *Mater. Chem. Phys.* **2022**, *289*, 126485. [CrossRef]
42. Zhou, Y.; Li, H.; Li, L.; Cai, Y.; Zeyde, K.; Han, X. Efficient HIE-FDTD method for designing a dual-band anisotropic terahertz absorption structure. *Opt. Express* **2021**, *29*, 18611. [CrossRef]
43. Khare, P.; Wadhvani, R.; Shukla, S. Missing Data Imputation for Solar Radiation Using Generative Adversarial Networks. In *Proceedings of International Conference on Computational Intelligence: ICCI 2020*; Springer: Singapore, 2022; pp. 1–14.
44. Li, Y.; Zhang, L.; Torres-Pardo, A.; González-Calbet, J.M.; Ma, Y.; Oleynikov, P.; Terasaki, O.; Asahina, S.; Shima, M.; Cha, D.; et al. Cobalt phosphate-modified barium-doped tantalum nitride nanorod photoanode with 1.5% solar energy conversion efficiency. *Nat. Commun.* **2013**, *4*, 2566. [CrossRef]
45. Zhao, B.; Hu, M.; Ao, X.; Pei, G. Performance analysis of enhanced radiative cooling of solar cells based on a commercial silicon photovoltaic module. *Sol. Energy* **2018**, *176*, 248–255. [CrossRef]
46. Rana, A.S.; Zubair, M.; Danner, A.; Mehmood, M.Q. Revisiting tantalum based nanostructures for efficient harvesting of solar radiation in STPV systems. *Nano Energy* **2021**, *80*, 105520. [CrossRef]
47. Kler, A.M.; Zharkov, P.V.; Epishkin, N.O. Parametric optimization of supercritical power plants using gradient methods. *Energy* **2019**, *189*, 116230. [CrossRef]

48. Radhakrishnan, S.; Kumar, D.S.; Raja, G.T. Design and Simulation Analysis on TM–Pass GST-Assisted Asymmetric Directional Coupler-Based Polarizer. *Silicon* **2022**, *14*, 6351–6362. [CrossRef]
49. Liu, Z.; Liu, G.; Huang, Z.; Liu, X.; Fu, G. Ultra-broadband perfect solar absorber by an ultra-thin refractory titanium nitride meta-surface. *Sol. Energy Mater. Sol. Cells* **2018**, *179*, 346–352. [CrossRef]
50. Liu, Z.; Liu, G.; Liu, X.; Wang, Y.; Fu, G. Titanium resonators based ultra-broadband perfect light absorber. *Opt. Mater.* **2018**, *83*, 118–123. [CrossRef]
51. Gao, H.; Peng, W.; Chu, S.; Cui, W.; Liu, Z.; Yu, L.; Jing, Z. Refractory ultra-broadband perfect absorber from visible to near-infrared. *Nanomaterials* **2018**, *8*, 1038. [CrossRef] [PubMed]
52. Soydan, M.C.; Ghobadi, A.; Yildirim, D.U.; Erturk, V.B.; Ozbay, E. All Ceramic-Based Metal-Free Ultra-broadband Perfect Absorber. *Plasmonics* **2019**, *14*, 1801–1815. [CrossRef]
53. Tian, X.; Li, Z.-Y. Visible-near infrared ultra-broadband polarization-independent metamaterial perfect absorber involving phase-change materials. *Photonics Res.* **2016**, *4*, 146. [CrossRef]
54. Yu, P.; Chen, X.; Yi, Z.; Tang, Y.; Yang, H.; Zhou, Z.; Duan, T.; Cheng, S.; Zhang, J.; Yi, Y. A numerical research of wideband solar absorber based on refractory metal from visible to near infrared. *Opt. Mater.* **2019**, *97*, 109400. [CrossRef]

Σ mathematics

MDPI

Article

Defect Analysis of a Non-Iterative Co-Simulation

Slaven Glumac [1,*] and Zdenko Kovačić [2]

[1] Spyrosoft Solutions d.o.o., Ulica Grada Vukovara 284, 10000 Zagreb, Croatia
[2] Faculty of Electrical Engineering and Computing, University of Zagreb, Unska Ulica 3, 10000 Zagreb, Croatia
* Correspondence: sgl@spyro-soft.com; Tel.: +385-915968929

Abstract: This article presents an analysis of co-simulation defects for a system of coupled ordinary differential equations. The research builds on the theorem that the co-simulation error is bounded if the co-simulation defect is bounded. The co-simulation defect can be divided into integration, output, and connection defects, all of which can be controlled. This article proves that the output and connection defect can be controlled by the co-simulation master by varying the communication step size. A non-iterative co-simulation method with variable communication step size is presented to demonstrate the applicability of the presented research. The orders of the interpolation polynomials used in the co-simulation method are varied in the experimental analysis. The experimental analysis shows how each component of a co-simulation defect affects the co-simulation error. The analysis presented is used to verify the applicability of the proposed approach and to provide guidelines for the configuration of the co-simulation.

Keywords: co-simulation; defect analysis; error bounds; variable step-size

MSC: 65L80

Citation: Glumac, S.; Kovačić, Z. Defect Analysis of a Non-Iterative Co-Simulation. *Mathematics* **2023**, *11*, 1342. https://doi.org/10.3390/math11061342

Academic Editors: Fajie Wang and Ji Lin

Received: 20 January 2023
Revised: 25 February 2023
Accepted: 6 March 2023
Published: 9 March 2023

1. Introduction

In practice, a network of co-simulation slaves is often used to model complex systems by coupling subsystems on the behavioral description level [1]. The usefulness of this approach comes from the fact that a co-simulation slave can be exported from a simulation tool. Multi-disciplinary teams can use co-simulation to combine information from already developed models from multiple domains. A recent overview of existing co-simulation research can be found in [2]. A Functional Mock-up Interface (FMI) [3,4] has been introduced to standardize the co-simulation interface. This effort allows the coupling of a growing number of commercial simulators [5].

A co-simulation master is an algorithm responsible for the simulation of a co-simulation network. The master calculates the approximation of input signals and controls the execution of slaves. Each slave has a solver of the internal model to calculate its own state and output updates. The responsibility for the quality of co-simulation results is shared between the master and the solvers. The main objective of this article is to develop a practical co-simulation quality assessment and to illustrate its use in a variable-step co-simulation.

An implicit co-simulation master repeats the simulation steps of the slaves until the coupled inputs and outputs match. An explicit co-simulation master executes a single step and continues the execution regardless of the connection error. A comparison of implicit and explicit masters using the example of a two-mass oscillator can be found in [6]. The comparison shows that implicit approaches have larger regions of stability than explicit approaches. Furthermore, Ref. [1] states implicit co-simulation is zero-stable if zero-stable [7] solvers are used. However, an implicit co-simulation requires the option to roll back a step of a co-simulation slave. That option is defined in the FMI standard but is rarely supported in practice. For this reason, only the explicit co-simulation is analyzed in this article.

Another very important reason to focus on explicit co-simulation is that hardware-in-the-loop simulation [8,9] is explicit co-simulation. Hardware co-simulation slaves included in the simulation loop cannot repeat a simulation step. Furthermore, there are very few techniques that can be applied to assess the quality of such a co-simulation. An energy-based quality assessment of an engine-in-the-loop simulation is presented in [10]. In comparison, this article tries to provide an analysis of the whole co-simulation including integration and output equations, and not just the connections. The quality assessment in [10] shows how the quality of power bonds [11] can be analyzed. This article provides a quality assessment applicable to a wider range of co-simulation systems. Connections do not have to be pairs of effort and flow signals. One example of systems that can have connections that are not power bonds is kinematic models in robotics [12].

Error estimation techniques used in ordinary differential equations provide suggestions for evaluating the simulation quality. Most algorithms for solving ordinary differential equations attempt to control either the local error or the defect of a numerical solution [13]. Local error estimation techniques based on Richardson extrapolation for the co-simulation have been presented in [14]. Assuming perfect subsystem integration, that article shows that the global error is bounded in terms of extrapolation error. That technique, however, requires the option to roll back a step of a co-simulation slave.

This article presents a co-simulation quality assessment based on the defect calculation [15–17]. The research presented is the continuation of the work presented in [15]. There, the numerical defect of the co-simulation is analyzed. That analysis showed that for co-simulation, when numerical defects are limited, numerical errors are limited. The main parts of this analysis are referenced in the next section.

The analysis in this article and [15] is based on coupled ordinary differential equations. Coupled ordinary differential equations are a special case of differential and algebraic equations. An example of such a system is shown in Figure 1. Ordinary differential equations are used to represent the state equations of systems modeled by co-simulation slaves. Algebraic equations are divided into output and connection equations. This is performed to reflect co-simulation practice, where co-simulation slaves are typically black boxes. State and output equations are not available to the co-simulation master and are therefore colored gray in Figure 1.

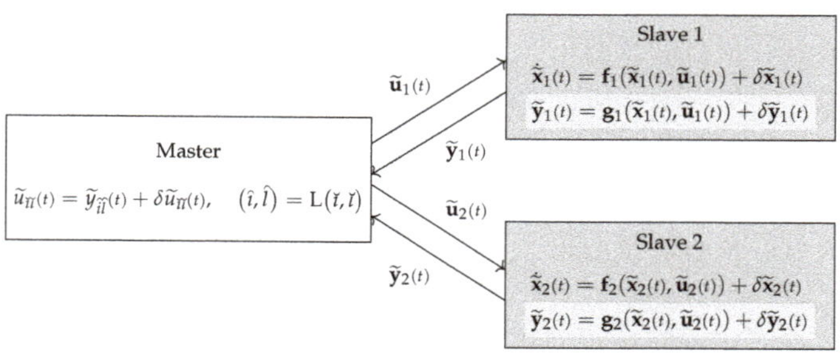

Figure 1. The underlying model for the analysis in this article is coupled ordinary differential equations [15]. Co-simulation slave equations are colored gray because they are not available to the master. Output equations are lighter colored because this article suggests that the master should estimate the output defect.

This article proposes an explicit variable step co-simulation method based on numerical defect control. A co-simulation slave is responsible for generating its output signals, while the co-simulation master is responsible to solve the connection equation (Figure 1). The state and output equations are grayed out to indicate that they are usually not available to the co-simulation master. However, the output defect depends on the co-simulation step size controlled by the co-simulation master. This is why this article assumes that the output defect should be estimated by the co-simulation master and why the output equations in Figure 1 are lighter colored.

Ref. [15] provides the basis for the defect analysis of the co-simulation. This article continues that work and proposes how to adapt a step size controller [18] to co-simulation defect control. Non-iterative co-simulation in [15] is a fixed-step, multi-rate co-simulation that uses zero-order hold. This article presents a non-iterative single-rate variable-step co-simulation using higher-order interpolation.

The next section shows the basis for the analysis in this work, carried over from [15]. The defect control section introduces an explicit co-simulation variable-step method. That section shows how to calculate the connection defect and estimate the output defect. The proposed method controls the error by varying the communication step size using the PI controller. A simple application of the method is presented in the example section. This application serves to highlight some of the effects of using different orders of interpolation polynomials in co-simulation. The final section of the article contains conclusions and ideas for future work.

2. Error Bounds

This article extends the work performed in [15] with variable step co-simulation presented in the next section and experimental analysis in the following section. There, coupled ordinary differential Equation (1) and their numerical solution (2) are used to analyze numerical errors of the co-simulation. An important result of [15] is Theorem 1. It states that the global error of the co-simulation is limited when the co-simulation defect is limited. It is worth noting that a similar statement is proved in [19] for a system of differential and algebraic equations. The main difference is that algebraic equations in this article are divided into output and connection equations (Figure 1). This section repeats the expressions for coupled ordinary differential equations and the error bounds theorem from [15] (Theorem 1). Coupled ordinary differential equations are the basis for the step size analysis and Theorem 1 justifies the error control presented in the next section.

A co-simulation models a system partitioned into N subsystems connected by the connection function L

$$\dot{\mathbf{x}}_i(t) = \mathbf{f}_i(\mathbf{x}_i(t), \mathbf{u}_i(t)) \tag{1a}$$

$$\mathbf{y}_i(t) = \mathbf{g}_i(\mathbf{x}_i(t), \mathbf{u}_i(t)) \tag{1b}$$

$$\mathbf{x}_i(0) = \mathbf{x}_{0i} \tag{1c}$$

$$u_{\breve{\imath}\breve{l}}(t) = y_{\widehat{\imath l}}(t), \quad (\hat{\imath}, \hat{l}) = \mathrm{L}(\breve{\imath}, \breve{l}) \tag{1d}$$

where i is the subsystem index, $\mathbf{x}_i$ is the state signal, $\mathbf{y}_i$ is the output signal, $\mathbf{u}_i$ is the input signal, and $\mathbf{x}_{0i}$ is the initial state of the subsystem. The numerical solution of the system satisfies the following equations

$$\dot{\widetilde{\mathbf{x}}}_i(t) = \mathbf{f}_i(\mathbf{x}_i(t), \mathbf{u}_i(t)) + \delta\widetilde{\mathbf{x}}_i(t) \tag{2a}$$

$$\widetilde{\mathbf{y}}_i(t) = \mathbf{g}_i(\mathbf{x}_i(t), \mathbf{u}_i(t)) + \delta\widetilde{\mathbf{y}}_i(t) \tag{2b}$$

$$\widetilde{\mathbf{x}}_i(0) = \mathbf{x}_{0i} \tag{2c}$$

$$\widetilde{u}_{\breve{\imath}\breve{l}}(t) = \widetilde{y}_{\widehat{\imath l}}(t) + \delta\widetilde{u}_{\breve{\imath}\breve{l}}(t), \quad (\hat{\imath}, \hat{l}) = \mathrm{L}(\breve{\imath}, \breve{l}) \tag{2d}$$

where the numerical solution of the state, output, and input signals is denoted as $\widetilde{\mathbf{x}}_i$, $\widetilde{\mathbf{y}}_i$, and $\widetilde{u}_{\breve{\imath}\breve{l}}$, respectively. The signals found by the numerical solution are assumed to be piecewise continuous. The defect introduced to the numerical solution is partitioned into integration $\delta\widetilde{\mathbf{x}}_i$, output $\delta\widetilde{\mathbf{y}}_i$, and connection defect $\delta\widetilde{u}_{\breve{\imath}\breve{l}}$. The system (1) represents the equations solved by the co-simulation and the system (2) represents the behavior of the solution obtained by the co-simulation.

The numerical solution (1) can be rewritten to

$$\dot{\widetilde{\mathbf{x}}}(t) = \mathbf{f}(\widetilde{\mathbf{x}}(t), \widetilde{\mathbf{u}}(t)) + \delta\widetilde{\mathbf{x}}(t) \tag{3a}$$

$$\widetilde{\mathbf{y}}(t) = \mathbf{g}(\widetilde{\mathbf{x}}(t), \widetilde{\mathbf{u}}(t)) + \delta\widetilde{\mathbf{y}}(t) \tag{3b}$$

$$\widetilde{\mathbf{u}}(t) = \mathbf{L}\widetilde{\mathbf{y}}(t) + \delta\widetilde{\mathbf{u}}(t) \tag{3c}$$

where signals of all subsystems in (2) are grouped into large column vector signals

$$\begin{aligned} \mathbf{x}^T(t) &= \begin{bmatrix} \mathbf{x}_1^T(t) & \mathbf{x}_2^T(t) & \cdots & \mathbf{x}_N^T(t) \end{bmatrix} \\ \mathbf{y}^T(t) &= \begin{bmatrix} \mathbf{y}_1^T(t) & \mathbf{y}_2^T(t) & \cdots & \mathbf{y}_N^T(t) \end{bmatrix} \\ \mathbf{u}^T(t) &= \begin{bmatrix} \mathbf{u}_1^T(t) & \mathbf{u}_2^T(t) & \cdots & \mathbf{u}_N^T(t) \end{bmatrix} \end{aligned} \tag{4}$$

The error of the numerical solution (3) is defined as the difference between the numerical and the analytic solution of the system (1)

$$\Delta\widetilde{\mathbf{x}}(t) = \widetilde{\mathbf{x}}(t) - \mathbf{x}(t), \quad \Delta\widetilde{\mathbf{y}}(t) = \widetilde{\mathbf{y}}(t) - \mathbf{y}(t), \quad \Delta\widetilde{\mathbf{u}}(t) = \widetilde{\mathbf{u}}(t) - \mathbf{u}(t) \tag{5}$$

where $\Delta\widetilde{\mathbf{x}}$ is the integration error, $\Delta\widetilde{\mathbf{y}}$ the output error and $\Delta\widetilde{\mathbf{u}}$ the input error of the numerical solution.

Definition 1 (Lipschitz Continuity). *A function* $\mathbf{f}$ *is said to be Lipschitz continuous if there exist constant* $K_{\mathbf{f}} > 0$ *such that for all* $\mathbf{x}_1, \mathbf{x}_2 \in \mathbb{R}^{|\mathbf{x}|}$*:*

$$\|\mathbf{f}(\mathbf{x}_2) - \mathbf{f}(\mathbf{x}_1)\| \leqslant K_{\mathbf{f}}\|\mathbf{x}_2 - \mathbf{x}_1\| \tag{6}$$

The constant $K_{\mathbf{f}}$ *is called the Lipschitz constant of the function* $\mathbf{f}$.

Definition 1 introduces Lipschitz continuity, which is used to describe the conditions for the uniqueness of the solution for (1) [15]. It is used to formulate Assumption 1 and Theorem 1.

Assumption 1. *Assume that there exists a Lipschitz continuous function* $\mathbf{G}$ *that explicitly calculates the input signals*

$$\widetilde{\mathbf{u}}(t) = \mathbf{G}(\widetilde{\mathbf{x}}(t), \delta\widetilde{\mathbf{y}}(t), \delta\widetilde{\mathbf{u}}(t)) \tag{7}$$

Assume that the aggregated state transition function $\mathbf{f}$ *(3a) is Lipschitz continuous. Assume that the aggregated output function* $\mathbf{g}$ *(3b) is Lipschitz continuous. Assume that the numerical solution (2) is continuous in every subinterval* $(t_{\kappa-1}, t_\kappa]$.

Theorem 1 (Error Bounds = Theorem 2.12 in [15]). *Suppose Assumption (1) holds. Then, the integration error is limited*

$$\|\Delta\widetilde{\mathbf{x}}(t)\| \leqslant e^{K_{\mathbf{f}}(t-t_0)}\|\Delta\widetilde{\mathbf{x}}(t_0)\| + \frac{1}{K_{\mathbf{f}}}(e^{K_{\mathbf{f}}(t-t_0)} - 1)\delta^{(t_0,t]} \tag{8}$$

the input error satisfies is limited

$$\begin{aligned} \|\Delta\widetilde{\mathbf{u}}(t)\| \leqslant & K_{\mathbf{G}}e^{K_{\mathbf{f}}(t-t_0)}\|\Delta\widetilde{\mathbf{x}}(t_0)\| + \frac{K_{\mathbf{G}}}{K_{\mathbf{f}}}\left(e^{K_{\mathbf{f}}(t-t_0)} - 1\right)\delta^{(t_0,t]} \\ & + K_{\mathbf{G}}\|\delta\widetilde{\mathbf{y}}(t)\| + K_{\mathbf{G}}\|\delta\widetilde{\mathbf{u}}(t)\| \end{aligned} \tag{9}$$

and the output error satisfies is limited

$$\begin{aligned}\|\Delta\widetilde{\mathbf{y}}(t)\| \leqslant & K_{\mathbf{g}}(1+K_{\mathbf{G}})e^{K_{\mathbf{f}}(t-t_0)}\|\Delta\widetilde{\mathbf{x}}(t_0)\| \\ & + \frac{K_{\mathbf{g}}}{K_{\mathbf{f}}}(1+K_{\mathbf{G}})\left(e^{K_{\mathbf{f}}(t-t_0)}-1\right)\delta^{(t_0,t]} \\ & + (1+K_{\mathbf{g}}K_{\mathbf{G}})\|\delta\widetilde{\mathbf{y}}(t)\| + K_{\mathbf{g}}K_{\mathbf{G}}\|\delta\widetilde{\mathbf{u}}(t)\|\end{aligned} \tag{10}$$

In [15], it is shown that Theorem 1 requires the same conditions as the uniqueness of the solution for (1). In addition, the numerical solution obtained by co-simulation (2) must be piecewise continuous. This theorem provides the justification for the defect control presented next.

3. Defect Control

Theorem 1 suggests that the step size control of the co-simulation defect can be used to limit the global error of the co-simulation. According to [3], a communication step size is the "distance between two subsequent communication points (also known as sampling rate or macro step size)", where communication points are "time grid for data exchange between master and slaves in a co-simulation environment (also known as sampling points or synchronization points)". This section describes how to control the communication step size of a slave using a non-iterative variant of the Jacobi co-simulation method (Algorithm 1). The proposed co-simulation method is shown in Figure 2. The variable-step variant of the method generates a sequence of communication step sizes $H : \mathbb{N} \to \mathbb{R}_{\geqslant 0}$ with the explicit version of the PI control procedure introduced in [18]. The defect controlled by the proposed method is based on the connection defect (2d) and/or the output defect (2b).

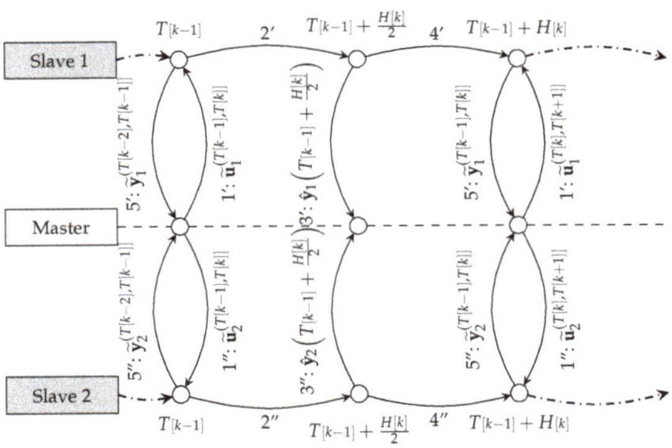

Figure 2. This article uses a non-iterative variant of the Jacobi co-simulation method with variable steps to demonstrate co-simulation defect control.

The numerical defect must be limited to ensure that the co-simulation error is limited. Theorems 2 and 3 show that the defect can be limited by reducing the communication step size. This section shows how to calculate the connection defect and estimate the output defect. Theorem 4 shows that the output defect estimate used is asymptotically correct.

The sequence of communication points $T : \mathbb{N}_0 \to \mathbb{R}_{\geqslant 0}$ is determined by the communication step sizes

$$T[k] = T[k-1] + H[k] \tag{11}$$

The sequence of points t_κ at which a numeric solution discontinuity can occur is marked differently than the sequence of communication points $T[k]$. The reason is that discontinuities in the numeric solution may occur during slave integration. Each slave can perform the integration with different individual integration steps (sometimes referred to as a micro step size). It is assumed that the internal solver of the slave takes over the responsibility for the control of the integration step size. Control of the integration step size may be used to reduce the integration error [16,17]. Theorem 1 suggests that integration defect reduction is an important factor for the quality of co-simulation. This article focuses on controlling the size of the communication step with respect to output and connection defects. This choice respects the black box character of co-simulation slaves (Figure 1) and leaves the integration defects in the responsibility of internal slave solvers.

Co-simulation is the simulation of a continuous time model with a computer, a discrete system. The co-simulation generates samples of the signal and its derivatives at communication points. This description is consistent with [3]. The reconstruction of output signals from such samples can be obtained using the Taylor polynomial

$$\widetilde{\mathbf{y}}_i^{(T[k-1],T[k])}(t) = \sum_{n=0}^{n_i} \frac{\mathrm{d}^n \widetilde{\mathbf{y}}_i^{(T[k-1],T[k])}}{\mathrm{d}t^n}(T[k]) \frac{(t - T[k])^n}{n!} \tag{12}$$

where the samples of the output signal and its derivatives are determined by the co-simulation slave. The output signal of the ith co-simulation slave is a piecewise polynomial signal

$$\widetilde{\mathbf{y}}_i(t) = \widetilde{\mathbf{y}}_i^{(T[k-1],T[k])}(t), \quad T[k-1] < t \leqslant T[k] \tag{13}$$

The inputs of the ith co-simulation slave are extrapolated with the following polynomial

$$\widetilde{\mathbf{u}}_i^{(T[k-1],T[k])}(t) = \sum_{m=0}^{m_i} \frac{\mathrm{d}^m \widetilde{\mathbf{u}}_i^{(T[k-1],T[k])}}{\mathrm{d}t^m}(T[k-1]) \frac{(t - T[k-1])^m}{m!} \tag{14}$$

where the samples of the input signal and its derivatives are determined by the co-simulation master. A non-iterative Jacobi co-simulation master (Figure 2) determines the input signals in the kth step with the connected output signals from the $(k-1)^{st}$ step

$$\begin{aligned} \frac{\mathrm{d}^m \widetilde{u}_{\check{\imath}\check{l}}^{(T[k],T[k+1])}}{\mathrm{d}t^m}(T[k-1]) &= \frac{\mathrm{d}^m \widetilde{y}_{\hat{\imath}\hat{l}}^{(T[k-2],T[k-1])}}{\mathrm{d}t^m}(T[k-1]), \\ &(\hat{\imath},\hat{l}) = \mathrm{L}(\check{\imath},\check{l}), \quad m \leqslant m_{\check{\imath}}, \quad m \leqslant n_{\hat{\imath}} \end{aligned} \tag{15}$$

The input signal of the ith co-simulation slave is a piecewise polynomial signal

$$\widetilde{\mathbf{u}}_i(t) = \widetilde{\mathbf{u}}_i^{(T[k-1],T[k])}(t), \quad T[k-1] < t \leqslant T[k] \tag{16}$$

The connection defect (2d) can be calculated by comparing the extrapolation polynomials for the output (12) and input (14) signals, i.e.,

$$\delta \widetilde{u}_{\check{\imath}\check{l}}^{(T[k-1],T[k])}(t) = \widetilde{u}_{\check{\imath}\check{l}}^{(T[k-1],T[k])}(t) - \widetilde{y}_{\hat{\imath}\hat{l}}^{(T[k-1],T[k])}(t), \quad (\hat{\imath},\hat{l}) = \mathrm{L}(\check{\imath},\check{l}) \tag{17}$$

where individual scalar signals are selected according to the connection function.

This article assumes that the output signal and all its derivatives are perfectly sampled, i.e., the output defect can only deviate from zero between the communication points

$$\frac{\mathrm{d}^n \widetilde{\mathbf{y}}_i^{(T[k-1],T[k])}}{\mathrm{d}t^n}(T[k]) = \left. \frac{\mathrm{d}^n \mathbf{g}_i(\widetilde{\mathbf{x}}_i(t), \widetilde{\mathbf{u}}_i(t))}{\mathrm{d}t^n} \right|_{t=T[k]}, \quad n = 0, \ldots, n_i \tag{18}$$

Lemma 1. *Assume that the numerical solution for the input signals is bounded $\|\widetilde{\mathbf{u}}_{\hat{\imath}}(t)\| \leqslant B_{\widetilde{\mathbf{u}}_{\hat{\imath}}}$, the numerical solution for the state signal is bounded $\|\widetilde{\mathbf{x}}_{\hat{\imath}}(t)\| \leqslant B_{\widetilde{\mathbf{x}}_{\hat{\imath}}}$, the integration defects are $\delta\widetilde{\mathbf{x}}_{\hat{\imath}}(t) = \mathcal{O}(H^{N_i[k]})$, and the state transition function $\mathbf{f}_{\hat{\imath}}$ is Lipschitz continuous (Definition 1). Then*

$$\lim_{H[k]\to 0} \left\|\widetilde{\mathbf{x}}_{\hat{\imath}}(T[k]) - \widetilde{\mathbf{x}}_{\hat{\imath}}(T[k-1])\right\| = 0 \tag{19}$$

Proof. Since $\delta\widetilde{\mathbf{x}}_{\hat{\imath}}(t) = \mathcal{O}(H^{N_i}[k])$ there exists $C, H_0 \in \mathbb{R}_{>0}$ such that for all $H[k] \leqslant H_0$

$$\|\delta\widetilde{\mathbf{x}}_{\hat{\imath}}(t)\| \leqslant CH_0^{N_i} \tag{20}$$

By the integration of (2a)

$$\widetilde{\mathbf{x}}_{\hat{\imath}}(T[k]) - \widetilde{\mathbf{x}}_{\hat{\imath}}(T[k-1]) = \int_{T[k-1]}^{T[k]} \mathbf{f}(\widetilde{\mathbf{x}}_{\hat{\imath}}(\tau), \widetilde{\mathbf{u}}_{\hat{\imath}}(\tau)) + \delta\widetilde{\mathbf{x}}_{\hat{\imath}}(\tau)\, \mathrm{d}\tau \tag{21}$$

the following inequality is obtained

$$\|\widetilde{\mathbf{x}}_{\hat{\imath}}(T[k]) - \widetilde{\mathbf{x}}_{\hat{\imath}}(T[k-1])\| \leqslant \int_{T[k-1]}^{T[k-1]+H[k]} K_{\mathbf{f}}\, B_{\widetilde{\mathbf{x}}_{\hat{\imath}}} + K_{\mathbf{f}} B_{\widetilde{\mathbf{u}}_{\hat{\imath}}} + CH_0^{N_i}\, \mathrm{d}\tau \tag{22}$$

The statement of the lemma (19) follows from the previous inequality

$$\|\widetilde{\mathbf{x}}_{\hat{\imath}}(T[k]) - \widetilde{\mathbf{x}}_{\hat{\imath}}(T[k-1])\| \leqslant \left(K_{\mathbf{f}}\, B_{\widetilde{\mathbf{x}}_{\hat{\imath}}} + K_{\mathbf{f}} B_{\widetilde{\mathbf{u}}_{\hat{\imath}}} + CH_0^{N_i}\right) H[k] \tag{23}$$

□

Theorem 2 (Connection defect). *Assume that the numerical solution for the input signals is bounded $\|\widetilde{\mathbf{u}}_{\hat{\imath}}(t)\| \leqslant B_{\widetilde{\mathbf{u}}_{\hat{\imath}}}$, the numerical solution for the state signal is bounded $\|\widetilde{\mathbf{x}}_{\hat{\imath}}(t)\| \leqslant B_{\widetilde{\mathbf{x}}_{\hat{\imath}}}$, the integration defects are $\delta\widetilde{\mathbf{x}}_{\hat{\imath}}(t) = \mathcal{O}(H^{N_{\hat{\imath}}}[k])$, the state transition function $\mathbf{f}_{\hat{\imath}}$ is Lipschitz continuous (Definition 1), the output function of the $\hat{\imath}^{th}$ subsystem is*

$$\mathbf{g}_{\hat{\imath}}(\widetilde{\mathbf{x}}_{\hat{\imath}}(t), \widetilde{\mathbf{u}}_{\hat{\imath}}(t)) = \mathbf{g}_{\hat{\imath}}(\widetilde{\mathbf{x}}_{\hat{\imath}}(t)) \tag{24}$$

and the step sizes of connected simulators $\hat{\imath}, \check{\imath} \in IF$. The connection defect (2d) of a numerical solution converges in terms of the communication step size

$$\lim_{H[k]\to 0} \left(\delta\widetilde{u}_{\check{\imath}\check{l}}^{(T[k-1],T[k]]}(t)\right) = 0 \tag{25}$$

Proof. From (14)–(18) and (24) it follows that

$$\begin{aligned}
\delta\widetilde{u}_{\check{\imath}\check{l}}^{(T[k-1],T[k]]}(t) = & \sum_{m=0}^{\min(m_{\check{\imath}},n_{\hat{\imath}})} \left.\frac{\mathrm{d}^m g_{\hat{\imath}\hat{l}}(\widetilde{\mathbf{x}}_{\hat{\imath}}(t))}{\mathrm{d}t^m}\right|_{t=T[k-1]} \frac{(t-T[k-1])^m}{m!} \\
& - \sum_{n=0}^{n_{\hat{\imath}}} \left.\frac{\mathrm{d}^n g_{\hat{\imath}\hat{l}}(\widetilde{\mathbf{x}}_{\hat{\imath}}(t))}{\mathrm{d}t^n}\right|_{t=T[k]} \frac{(t-T[k])^n}{n!} \\
= & g_{\hat{\imath}\hat{l}}(\widetilde{\mathbf{x}}_{\hat{\imath}}(T[k-1])) - g_{\hat{\imath}\hat{l}}(\widetilde{\mathbf{x}}_{\hat{\imath}}(T[k])) + \mathcal{O}(H[k])
\end{aligned} \tag{26}$$

where $(\hat{\imath}, \hat{l}) = \mathrm{L}(\check{\imath}, \check{l})$. Since $\mathbf{g}_{\hat{\imath}}$ is Lipschitz continuous it follows that

$$\left\|g_{\hat{\imath}\hat{l}}(\widetilde{\mathbf{x}}_{\hat{\imath}}(T[k-1])) - g_{\hat{\imath}\hat{l}}(\widetilde{\mathbf{x}}_{\hat{\imath}}(T[k]))\right\| \leqslant K_{\mathbf{g}_{\hat{\imath}}} \|\widetilde{\mathbf{x}}_{\hat{\imath}}(T[k-1]) - \widetilde{\mathbf{x}}_{\hat{\imath}}(T[k])\| \tag{27}$$

The statement of the theorem follows from Lemma 1, (26) and (27). □

Theorem 2 specifies the conditions under which the connection defect converges with respect to the communication step size. A number of simplifications are adopted to prove Theorem 2. In (26), the higher order terms are ignored to simplify the proof. The goal was to prove that the connection defect was converging in terms of communication step size, rather than finding the smallest limit. The next section shows the order of convergence of the connection defect in a simple example. Bounded inputs and state signals are reasonable assumptions for a stable system and a stable co-simulation. The assumptions (24), however, restrict the models used to those that have no direct output dependency on input signals. If this simplification is not applied, it is possible to construct a system with an algebraic loop that makes the co-simulation unstable. The subject of future work will be to analyze how some or all of these simplifications can be discarded or at least relaxed.

Theorem 3 (Output defect). *Suppose the function $\mathbf{g}_i$ is continuously differentiable and the calculated state signal $\widetilde{\mathbf{x}}_i$ is continuously differentiable. Then, the output defect (2b) is*

$$\delta\widetilde{\mathbf{y}}_i(t) = \mathcal{O}\left(H^{n_i+1}[k]\right) \tag{28}$$

Proof. From (14) and the fact that $\mathbf{g}_i$ and $\widetilde{\mathbf{x}}_i$ are continuously differentiable, it follows that

$$\mathbf{g}\left(\widetilde{\mathbf{x}}_i(t), \widetilde{\mathbf{u}}_i(t)\right) = \sum_{n=0}^{n_i} \frac{\mathrm{d}^{n_i}\mathbf{g}\left(\widetilde{\mathbf{x}}_i(\tau), \widetilde{\mathbf{u}}_i(\tau)\right)}{\mathrm{d}\tau^{n_i}}\Bigg|_{\tau=T[k]} \frac{\left(t - T[k]\right)^n}{n!} + \mathcal{O}\left(H^{n_i+1}[k]\right) \tag{29}$$

for $T(k-1) < t \leqslant T[k]$ The expression (28) follows from (2b), (12) and (18). □

Theorem 3 shows that the output defect can be controlled by reducing the communication step size. Theorem 2 and Theorem 3 justify the communication step size control. Numerical solvers are expected to minimize the remaining component of the numerical defect, the integration defect (2a). The rest of the section analyzes how to estimate the output defect.

For the purpose of estimating the output defect between the communication points, a Hermite interpolation polynomial [20] is łintroduced

$$\hat{\mathbf{y}}_i^{(T[k-1],T[k])}(t) = \widetilde{\mathbf{y}}_i(t) + \frac{(T[k]-t)^{n_i+1}}{(0.5H[k])^{n_i+1}}\left[\mathbf{g}_i\left(\widetilde{\mathbf{x}}_i\left(T[k]-\tfrac{H[k]}{2}\right), \widetilde{\mathbf{u}}_i\left(T[k]-\tfrac{H[k]}{2}\right)\right) - \widetilde{\mathbf{y}}_i\left(T[k]-\tfrac{H[k]}{2}\right)\right] \tag{30}$$

A Hermite interpolation polynomial is consistent with multiple samples of the signals and their derivatives. The polynomial used in this paper is consistent with signal values at two communication points and signal derivatives at the later point

$$\begin{aligned}
\hat{\mathbf{y}}_i^{(T[k-1],T[k])}\left(T[k]-\tfrac{H[k]}{2}\right) &= \mathbf{g}_i\left(\widetilde{\mathbf{x}}_i\left(T[k]-\tfrac{H[k]}{2}\right), \widetilde{\mathbf{u}}_i\left(T[k]-\tfrac{H[k]}{2}\right)\right) \\
\frac{\mathrm{d}^n\hat{\mathbf{y}}_i^{(T[k-1],T[k])}}{\mathrm{d}t^n}(T[k]) &= \frac{\mathrm{d}^n\mathbf{g}_i(\widetilde{\mathbf{x}}_i(t), \widetilde{\mathbf{u}}_i(t))}{\mathrm{d}t^n}\Bigg|_{t=T[k]}, \quad n = 0, \ldots, n_i
\end{aligned} \tag{31}$$

The Hermite interpolation polynomial is used to obtain an asymptotically correct estimate of the output defect.

Theorem 4 (Estimate of the Output Defect). *The estimation of the output defect is defined as the difference between interpolation polynomials (30) and (12)*

$$\hat{\delta\widetilde{\mathbf{y}}}_i^{(T[k-1],T[k])}(t) = \widetilde{\mathbf{y}}_i^{(T[k-1],T[k])}(t) - \hat{\mathbf{y}}_i^{(T[k-1],T[k])}(t) \tag{32}$$

Suppose the function $\mathbf{g}_i$ is n_i+1 times continuously differentiable on the interval $t \in (T[k-1], T[k]]$ and

$$\widetilde{\mathbf{x}}_i^{(T[k-1],T[k])}(t) = \sum_{n=0}^{n_i+1} \frac{\mathrm{d}^n\widetilde{\mathbf{x}}_i}{\mathrm{d}t^n}(T[k])\frac{(t - T[k])^n}{n!} + \mathcal{O}\left(H^{n_i+2}[k]\right) \tag{33}$$

Then, the estimate of the output defect (32) is asymptotically correct, i.e., for each $\alpha \in (0,1]$

$$\lim_{H[k]\to 0} \frac{\hat{\delta\widetilde{\mathbf{y}}}_i^{(T[k-1],T[k])}(t)}{\delta\widetilde{\mathbf{y}}_i^{(T[k-1],T[k])}(t)} = 1, \quad t = T[k-1] + \alpha H[k] \tag{34}$$

Proof. Since $\mathbf{g}_i$ is continuously differentiable, it is also Lipschitz continuous. Lipschitz continuity and (33) imply

$$\mathbf{g}_i\left(\widetilde{\mathbf{x}}_i^{(T[k-1],T[k]]}(t),\widetilde{\mathbf{u}}_i^{(T[k-1],T[k]]}(t)\right)=\sum_{n=0}^{n_i+1}\left[\frac{\mathrm{d}^n\mathbf{g}_i(\widetilde{\mathbf{x}}_i(t),\widetilde{\mathbf{u}}_i(t))}{\mathrm{d}t^n}\bigg|_{t=T[k]}\frac{(t-T[k])^n}{n!}\right]+\mathcal{O}(H^{n_i+2}[k]) \tag{35}$$

The output defect (3b) is the difference between the numerical output signal (12) and the output signal without defect (35). The output defect on the interval $(T[k-1],T[k]]$ is equal to

$$\delta\widetilde{\mathbf{y}}_i(t)=\widetilde{\mathbf{y}}_i(t)-\mathbf{g}_i(\widetilde{\mathbf{x}}_i(t),\widetilde{\mathbf{u}}_i(t))=\frac{\mathrm{d}^{n_i+1}\mathbf{g}_i(\widetilde{\mathbf{x}}_i(t),\widetilde{\mathbf{u}}_i(t))}{\mathrm{d}t^{n_i+1}}\bigg|_{t=T[k]}\frac{(t-T[k])^{n_i+1}}{(n_i+1)!}+\mathcal{O}(H^{n_i+2}[k]) \tag{36}$$

The estimate of the output defect on the interval $(T[k-1],T[k]]$ is equal to

$$\begin{aligned}\hat{\delta\widetilde{\mathbf{y}}}_i^{(T[k-1],T[k]]}(t)&=\frac{(T[k]-t)^{n_i+1}}{(0.5H[k])^{n_i+1}}\left[\mathbf{g}_i\left(\widetilde{\mathbf{x}}_i\left(T[k]-\tfrac{H[k]}{2}\right),\widetilde{\mathbf{u}}_i\left(T[k]-\tfrac{H[k]}{2}\right)\right)-\widetilde{\mathbf{y}}_i\left(T[k]-\tfrac{H[k]}{2}\right)\right]\\&=\frac{(T[k]-t)^{n_i+1}}{(0.5H[k])^{n_i+1}}\left[\frac{\mathrm{d}^{n_i+1}\mathbf{g}_i(\widetilde{\mathbf{x}}_i(t),\widetilde{\mathbf{u}}_i(t))}{\mathrm{d}t^{n_i+1}}\bigg|_{t=T[k]}\frac{(-0.5H[k])^{n_i+1}}{(n_i+1)!}+\mathcal{O}\left(H[k]^{n_i+2}\right)\right]\\&=\frac{\mathrm{d}^{n_i+1}\mathbf{g}_i(\widetilde{\mathbf{x}}_i(t),\widetilde{\mathbf{u}}_i(t))}{\mathrm{d}t^{n_i+1}}\bigg|_{t=T[k]}\frac{(t-T[k])^{n_i+1}}{(n_i+1)!}+\mathcal{O}\left(H^{n_i+2}[k]\right)\end{aligned} \tag{37}$$

The Equation (34) follows directly from (36) and (37). □

The output defect estimate (32) is obtained by adding communication points during co-simulation. The additional points are added in the middle of the interval $(T[k-1],T[k]]$ shown in Figure 2. These points are used to obtain a higher order interpolation polynomial (30) for use in the output defect estimate. Theorem 4 gives the conditions (33) under which the output defect estimate (32) is asymptotically correct. The integration should have a higher order of local error than the order of the output interpolation polynomial (12).

The connection defect calculation (17) and the output defect estimate (32) are used to define the controlled co-simulation defect

$$\epsilon[k]=\max\left(\max_{i,j}\left(\underset{T[k-1]<t\leqslant T[k]}{RMS}(\delta\widetilde{u}_{ij})\right),\max_{i,j}\left(\underset{T[k-1]<t\leqslant T[k]}{RMS}(\hat{\delta\widetilde{y}}_{ij})\right)\right) \tag{38}$$

The calculation of the co-simulation defect is used in a step size control approach similar to the one introduced in [18]. The approach uses a PI controller for the logarithm of an error measurement

$$\begin{aligned}e[k]&=\log(tol)-\log(\epsilon[k])\\I'[k]&=I[k-1]+K_Ie[k]\\H'[k]&=\exp\left(I'[k]+K_Pe[k]\right)\\H[k]&=\begin{cases}\theta_{max}H[k-1], & H'[k]>\theta_{max}H[k-1]\\H'[k], & otherwise\end{cases}\\I[k]&=I'[k]+\log(H[k])-\log(H'[k])\\H[1]&=H_1,\quad I[1]=\log(H_1)\end{aligned} \tag{39}$$

where $\epsilon:\mathbb{N}\rightarrow\mathbb{R}$ is the controlled error approximation. Such a method has already been used for co-simulation [21]. The difference to the method presented in this article is the controlled error estimate. In [21], the authors have used an explicit step size control procedure to control the local co-simulation error of the output signal. In this article, the method controls the maximum of the connection defect and the output defect estimate (38).

The co-simulation method used for demonstrating the communication step size control is defined in Algorithm 1. It is also shown in Figure 2 to simplify the introduction. Like any other co-simulation master, the method solves the connection Equation (1d) and controls the execution of the co-simulation slaves. The connection equation is solved by the assignment of input signal derivatives (15). The presented co-simulation method allows a parallel execution with a distribution of the calculation performed in for-loops. The communication step sizes are controlled using the PI controller (39) to keep the co-simulation defect (38) constant.

4. Numerical Example

This section presents an example of using the proposed variable-step co-simulation method (Algorithm 1). The example system is a two mass oscillator that is commonly used to benchmark co-simulation master algorithms [6,21–25]. The slaves are implemented in the C programming language using Functional Mock-up Interface (FMI) [3,4]. The proposed connection defect calculation (17) and the output defect estimation (32) are illustrated in this example.

Algorithm 1 The pseudocode describes a non-iterative Jacobi co-simulation method. In the variable-step variant, the step size $H[k]$ is computed with the PI controller (17), (32), (38) and (39). In the fixed-step variant, the step size is constant $H[k] = H[k-1] = H_1$.

Require: a partitioned system (1) without algebraic loops, an initial step size H_1, defect tolerance *tol*

$k := 0$, $T[k] := 0$, $H[1] = H_1$
calculate the initial output signals by solving the Equations (1b) and (1d)
repeat
  $k := k + 1$
  for $i \leftarrow 1$ to N **do**
    assign the input signals (15)
  for $i \leftarrow 1$ to N **do**
    integrate the Equation (1a) on the interval $\left(T[k-1], T[k-1] + \frac{H[k]}{2}\right]$
  for $i \leftarrow 1$ to N **do**
    obtain the output signal samples at $T[k-1] + \frac{H[k]}{2}$
  for $i \leftarrow 1$ to N **do**
    integrate the Equation (1a) on the interval $\left(T[k-1] + \frac{H[k]}{2}, T[k]\right]$
  for $i \leftarrow 1$ to N **do**
    obtain the output signal samples at $T[k]$
  compute $H[k]$
  $T[k] := T[k-1] + H[k]$
until $T[k] \leqslant t_{end}$

The algorithms presented in this article and the code used to generate the results in this section are published at [26]. The models are implemented in C, the algorithms are implemented in C++, and the figures are created in Python. In the repository [26] an interested reader can find

- a C++ implementation of Algorithm 1 in the template function `fmi::jacobi_co_simulation` (*src/fmi.h*),
- an implementation of the step size controller (39) in the method `VariableStepSize::next` (*src/fmi.cpp*),
- an implementation of the Hermite polynomial calculation (30) in the method `FMU::get_hermite` (*src/fmi.cpp*),
- an implementation of the output defect calculation in the function `fmi::calculate_output_defects` (*src/fmi.cpp*),
- an implementation of connection defect calculation in the function `fmi::calculate_connection_defects` (*src/fmi.cpp*),
- an implementation of co-simulation slaves according to the FMI 2.0 standard [3] in the directories *src/OscillatorOmega2Tau* and *src/OscillatorTau2Omega*,

- an implementation of the reference solution in the directory *src/TwoMassRotationalOscillator*,
- and the code to create the images presented in this section in the Python script *scripts/results_analysis.py*.

The implementation of the co-simulation slaves (Figure 3b) follows the FMI standard [3]. Since slaves are compiled together with the master, the shared library and the interface description are not packaged together for ease of implementation. Models solved by the slaves are described in the following equations.

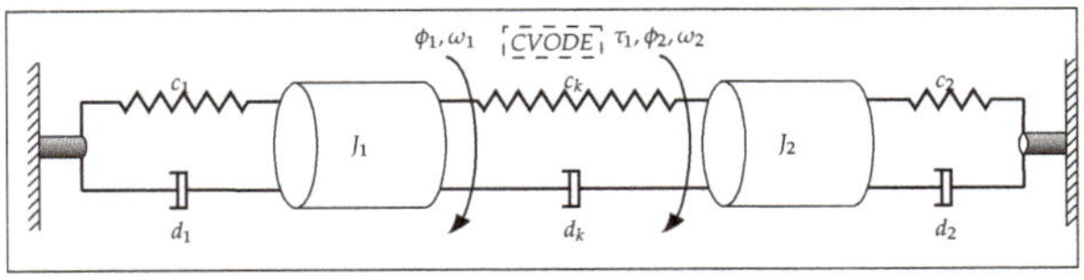

(**a**)

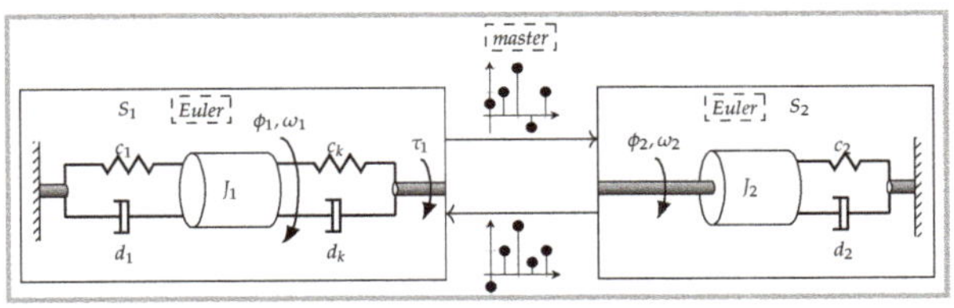

(**b**)

Figure 3. During co-simulation, a co-simulation master orchestrates co-simulation slaves. In the case of the monolithic simulation, a solver solves the entire system of equations: (**a**) Monolithic simulation; (**b**) Co-simulation.

The example system consists of two slaves $i \in \{1,2\}$ that solve the following system of equations

$$\dot{\mathbf{x}}_i(t) = \mathbf{f}_i(\mathbf{x}_{i(t)}, \mathbf{u}_{i(t)}) = \mathbf{A}_i\mathbf{x}_1(t) + \mathbf{B}_1\mathbf{u}_1(t), \tag{40a}$$

$$\mathbf{y}_i(t) = \mathbf{g}_i(\mathbf{x}_{i(t)}, \mathbf{u}_{i(t)}) = \mathbf{C}_i\mathbf{x}_i(t) + \mathbf{D}_i\mathbf{u}_i(t), \tag{40b}$$

$$\mathbf{x}_i(0) = \mathbf{x}_{i0} \tag{40c}$$

connected by

$$\mathbf{u}_1(t) = \mathbf{y}_2(t), \qquad \mathbf{u}_2(t) = \mathbf{y}_1(t) \tag{41}$$

where

$$\begin{aligned}
&\mathbf{y}_1(t) = \left[\tau_1(t)\right], \quad \mathbf{u}_1(t) = \left[\omega_2(t)\right], \\
&\mathbf{x}_1(t) = \left[\phi_1(t) \quad \omega_1(t) \quad \phi_2(t)\right]^T, \quad \mathbf{x}_{10} = \left[\phi_{10} \quad \omega_{10} \quad \phi_{20}\right]^T, \\
&\mathbf{A}_1 = \begin{bmatrix} 0 & 1 & 0 \\ -\frac{c_1+c_k}{J_1} & -\frac{d_1+d_k}{J_1} & \frac{c_k}{J_1} \\ 0 & 0 & 0 \end{bmatrix}, \quad \mathbf{B}_1 = \begin{bmatrix} 0 \\ \frac{d_k}{J_1} \\ 1 \end{bmatrix}, \\
&\mathbf{C}_1 = \left[c_k \quad d_k \quad -c_k\right], \quad \mathbf{D}_1 = \left[-d_k\right]
\end{aligned} \tag{42}$$

and

$$\begin{aligned}
&\mathbf{y}_2(t) = \left[\omega_2(t)\right], \quad \mathbf{u}_2(t) = \left[\tau_1(t)\right], \\
&\mathbf{x}_2(t) = \left[\phi_2(t) \quad \omega_2(t)\right]^T, \quad \mathbf{x}_{20} = \left[\phi_{20} \quad \omega_{20}\right]^T, \\
&\mathbf{A}_2 = \begin{bmatrix} 0 & 1 \\ -\frac{c_2}{J_2} & -\frac{d_2}{J_2} \end{bmatrix}, \quad \mathbf{B}_2 = \begin{bmatrix} 0 \\ \frac{1}{J_2} \end{bmatrix}, \\
&\mathbf{C}_2 = \begin{bmatrix} 0 & 1 \end{bmatrix}, \quad \mathbf{D}_2 = \begin{bmatrix} 0 \end{bmatrix}
\end{aligned} \tag{43}$$

Model parameters are set to

$$\begin{aligned}
&J_1 = 10\ \mathrm{kg\,m^2}, \quad c_1 = 1\ \tfrac{\mathrm{N\,m}}{\mathrm{rad}}, \quad d_1 = 1\ \tfrac{\mathrm{N\,m\,s}}{\mathrm{rad}}, \quad c_k = 1\ \tfrac{\mathrm{N\,m}}{\mathrm{rad}}, \\
&d_k = 2\ \tfrac{\mathrm{N\,m\,s}}{\mathrm{rad}}, \quad \phi_{10} = 0.1\ \mathrm{rad}, \quad \omega_{10} = 0.1\ \tfrac{\mathrm{rad}}{\mathrm{s}}, \quad J_2 = 10\ \mathrm{kg\,m^2}, \\
&c_2 = 1\ \tfrac{\mathrm{N\,m}}{\mathrm{rad}}, \quad d_2 = 2\ \tfrac{\mathrm{N\,m\,s}}{\mathrm{rad}}, \quad \phi_{20} = 0.2\ \mathrm{rad}, \quad \omega_{20} = 0.1\ \tfrac{\mathrm{rad}}{\mathrm{s}}
\end{aligned} \tag{44}$$

The analytic solution is approximated by a monolithic solution of the system (Figure 3a) solved using the CVODE solver [27] with a tight tolerance bound. The absolute tolerance limit for the solver used is set to 10^{-8}. This solution is used to give a reference solution for the co-simulation and to approximate the numerical error.

The internal equations of co-simulation slaves are solved using the forward Euler method. The forward Euler method is a first-order numerical solver for the same equations

$$\begin{aligned}
\widetilde{\mathbf{x}}_i^{(T[k-1],T[k]]}(\mathrm{t}) =& \widetilde{\mathbf{x}}_i^{(T[k-2],T[k-1]]}(T[\mathrm{k}-1]) \\
&+ (t - T[\mathrm{k}-1])\ \mathbf{f}_i\left(\widetilde{\mathbf{x}}_i^{(T[k-2],T[k-1]]}(T[\mathrm{k}-1]), \widetilde{\mathbf{u}}_i^{(T[k-1],T[k]]}(T[\mathrm{k}-1])\right)
\end{aligned} \tag{45}$$

The state derivative values of the Euler solver are equal to

$$\frac{\mathrm{d}^n \widetilde{\mathbf{x}}_i^{(T[k-1],T[k]]}}{\mathrm{d}t^n}(T[k]) = \begin{cases} \mathbf{A}_i \widetilde{\mathbf{x}}_i^{(T[k-2],T[k-1]]}(T[\mathrm{k}-1]) + \mathbf{B}_i \widetilde{\mathbf{u}}_i^{(T[k-1],T[k]]}(T[\mathrm{k}-1]), & n = 1 \\ 0, & n > 1 \end{cases} \tag{46}$$

Output polynomials are Taylor polynomials (12) with output derivative values calculated using (18) and

$$\frac{\mathrm{d}^n \widetilde{\mathbf{y}}_i^{(T[k-1],T[k]]}}{\mathrm{d}t^n}(T[k]) = \mathbf{C}_i \frac{\mathrm{d}^n \widetilde{\mathbf{x}}_i^{(T[k-1],T[k]]}}{\mathrm{d}t^n}(T[k]) + \mathbf{D}_i \frac{\mathrm{d}^n \widetilde{\mathbf{u}}_i^{(T[k-1],T[k]]}}{\mathrm{d}t^n}(T[k]), n = 1, \ldots, n_i \tag{47}$$

Input polynomials are Taylor polynomials (14) with input derivative values calculated using (15).

Figure 4a,b shows the piecewise response for both fixed and variable-step co-simulation using Algorithm 1. Figure 4a shows the responses obtained by fixed-step co-simulation with the step size

$$H = H[k] = H[k-1] = H_1 = 1 \tag{48}$$

Figure 4b shows the responses obtained by variable-step co-simulation with the initial step size and tolerance

$$H_1 = 1, \quad tol = 0.005 \tag{49}$$

The step size is controlled by the step controller (39) with the control parameters set to

$$K_P = 0.13, \quad K_I = \frac{1}{15}, \quad \theta_{max} = 2 \tag{50}$$

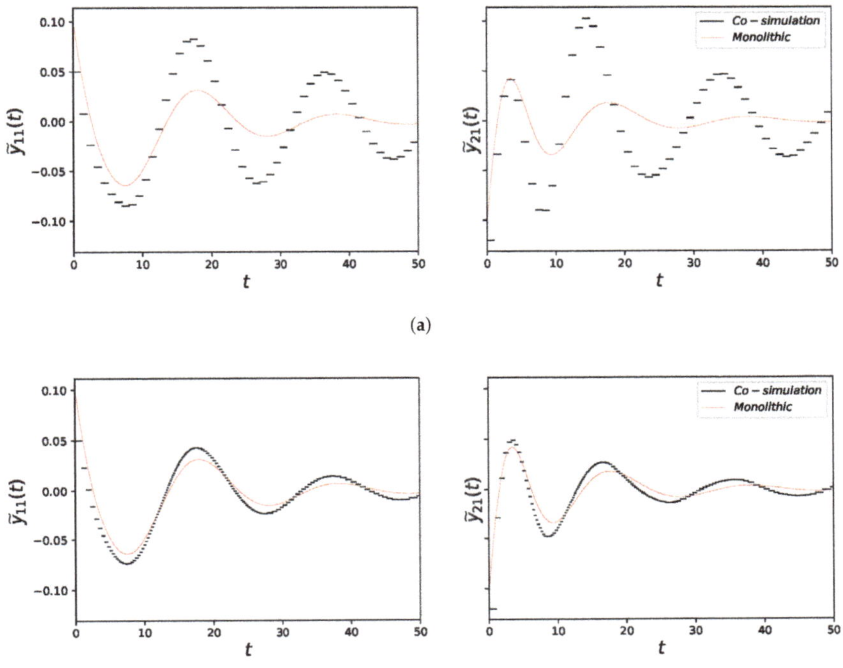

(a)

(b)

Figure 4. The diagrams show numerical solutions that were calculated with the Jacobi co-simulation method (Algorithm 1). The numerical solutions are compared with the monolithic solution: (**a**) Fixed step; (**b**) Variable step.

The comparison of figures shows how the step size controller reduces the step size during the co-simulation. In Figure 4a,b

- orders of output (12) and input (14) polynomials are fixed to 0,
- and compared to the monolithic system (Figure 3a) solution found using CVODE (tolerance 10^{-8}, [27]).

Theorems 2 and 3 show that the connection and the output defect can be limited by reducing the communication step size. In order to verify this statement, the root mean square value of the connection

$$RMS(\delta\widetilde{u}_{i1}) = \sum_{0<kH\leqslant t_{end}} \int_{T[k-1]}^{T[k]} \delta\widetilde{u}_{i1}(\tau)\mathrm{d}\tau \tag{51}$$

and output defect

$$RMS(\delta\widetilde{y}_{i1}) = \sum_{0<kH\leqslant t_{end}} \int_{T[k-1]}^{T[k]} \delta\widetilde{y}_{i1}(\tau)\mathrm{d}\tau \tag{52}$$

is calculated for fixed-step co-simulations with different step sizes

$$H = H_{[k]} = H_{[k-1]} = H_1 \in \{10^{-3}, 10^{-2.8}, \ldots, 10^{0}\} \tag{53}$$

The results are shown in Figure 5a,b.

The output defect (2b) is estimated using (32). The order of convergence of the output defect is given with Theorem 3. Figure 5a confirms this theorem. It is interesting to observe the output defect of the Euler solver (45) in Figure 5a. From (12), (40b), (45), (46) and (47) it follows that

$$\widetilde{y}_{i1}^{(T[k-1],T[k])}(t) = 0.5\,\widetilde{x}_{i1}^{(T[k-1],T[k])}(t), \quad n_i > 0 \tag{54}$$

and

$$\delta\widetilde{y}_{i1}(t) = 0, \quad n_i > 0 \tag{55}$$

for the Euler solver. This result agrees with the asymptotic upper limit from Theorem 3. This is interesting because it shows that the output defect for such a solver setup is zero for any output interpolation order greater than 0. However, the numerical error is larger than that of an analytic solver (Figure 6).

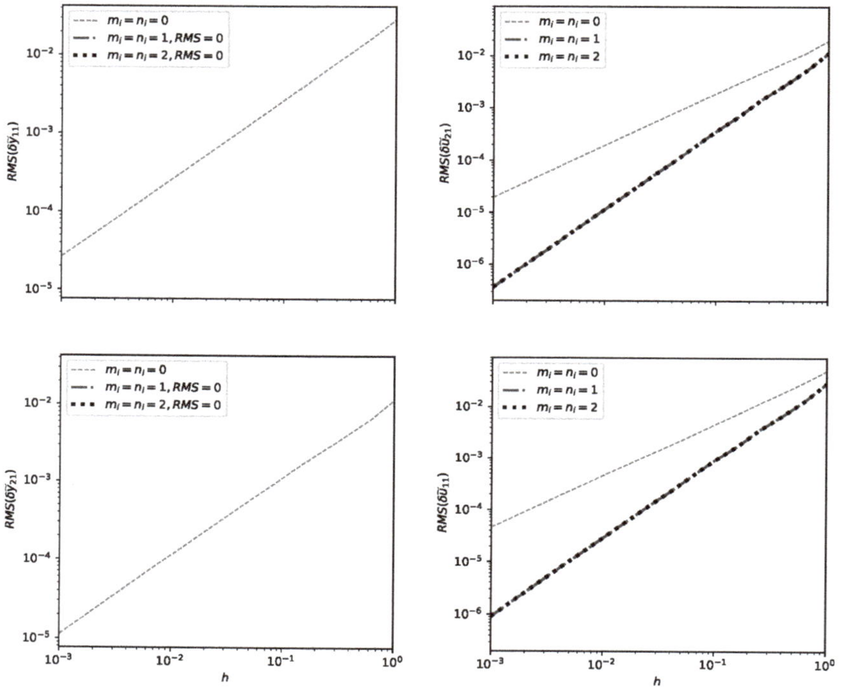

(a) (b)

Figure 5. The diagrams show the defects of the fixed-step Jacobi co-simulation method (Algorithm 1, $H_{[k]} = H_{[k-1]} = H_1$) and different orders of interpolation polynomials $m_i = n_i$: (**a**) Output defects; (**b**) Connection defects.

Theorem 2 shows that the connection defect converges (by assuming that the output equations are independent of the input signal) , but does not show the order of convergence. The input assignment (15) suggests that the input signal depends on the order of the input polynomial as well as the connected output polynomial. However, Figure 5b shows a relationship between connection defects and an internal solver. The connection defect when using the analytic solver seems to correlate with the interpolation order and appears to be $\mathcal{O}(H^{\min(m_i,n_i)+1})$. In the case of the Euler solver, the connection defect seems to be limited to $\mathcal{O}(H^2)$. The latter seems to be a consequence of (46).

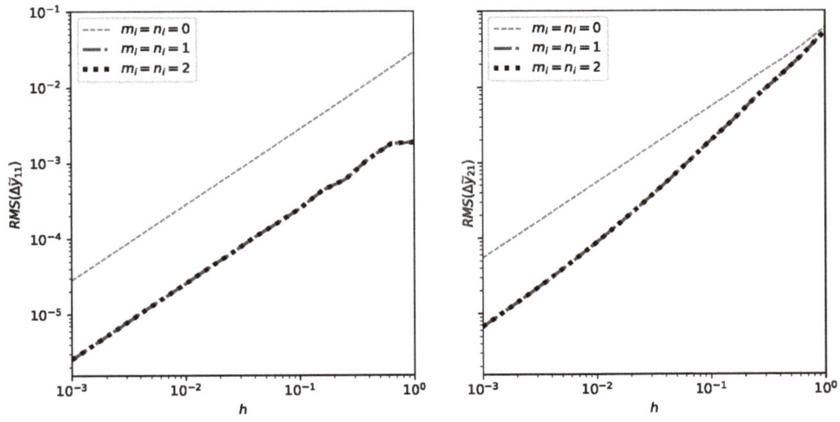

Figure 6. The diagrams show the numerical errors of the fixed-step Jacobi co-simulation method (Algorithm 1, $H_{[k]} = H_{[k-1]} = H_1$), different orders of interpolation polynomials and different internal subsystem solvers.

The focus of future work will be on the investigation of the order of convergence of connection defects. Theorem 2 uses a simplification to avoid the analysis of direct influences of input signals on output signals. This simplification prevents the analysis of algebraic loops, which could make the system unstable. Direct influences of input signals on output signals have an effect on the local co-simulation error shown in [24]. This indicates that a direct output input dependency could affect the order of the connection defect. This will be a topic for future work, along with the analysis of the influence of the solver on connection defects.

Theorem 1 suggests that by limiting the overall co-simulation defect, the global co-simulation error should be limited. Theorems 2 and 3 show that by limiting the step size, connection and output defects can be limited. Figure 5 confirms this. The three theorems suggest that by limiting the step size, the global co-simulation error can be limited. This is confirmed by Figure 6. It is worth noting that the conclusions given apply to a coupled ordinary differential system 1.

Reducing the step size limit is not the only way to reduce connection and output defects. The order of the polynomials used to transmit input and output signals also has an effect. This effect can be observed in Figure 6. Theorem 1 shows that the co-simulation error is bounded by connection, output, and integration defects. If defects are

$$\delta\tilde{\mathbf{u}}(t) = \mathcal{O}(H^{p_i}), \quad \delta\tilde{\mathbf{y}}(t) = \mathcal{O}(H^{q_i}), \quad \delta\tilde{\mathbf{x}}(t) = \mathcal{O}(H^{r_i})) \tag{56}$$

then the errors are

$$\Delta\tilde{\mathbf{u}}(t) = \mathcal{O}\big(H^{\min(p_i,q_i,r_i+1)}\big), \quad \Delta\tilde{\mathbf{y}}(t) = \mathcal{O}\big(H^{\min(p_i,q_i,r_i+1)}\big), \quad \Delta\tilde{\mathbf{x}}(t) = \mathcal{O}\big(H^{\min(p_i,q_i,r_i+1)}\big) \tag{57}$$

All co-simulation errors are limited by the worst co-simulation defect. Figure 6 shows how the integration defect of the Euler solver limits the co-simulation error to $\mathcal{O}(H)$.

Co-simulation errors can be limited by limiting the co-simulation defects. The rate of convergence of the output defect is given by Theorem 3. It is important to note that the order of convergence for the output defect estimate is influenced by the Euler solver. The Euler solver brakes the assumption (33). This is an example where an integration defect can affect the output error estimate.

It is interesting to observe the effect of the internal solver on the connection defect. In Figure 5b, it can be seen that for the Euler solver and larger orders of extrapolation for input and output signals the connection defect is $\mathcal{O}(H)$. The connection defect (17) in the explicit co-simulation is influenced by the difference of the state signal at different co-simulation steps (26). This observation suggests that a connection defect can be used to detect numerical errors introduced by solving state, output, and connection equations. The authors plan future work to rigorously analyze whether there are conditions under which this hypothesis is true.

The previous experiments use fixed-step co-simulation to confirm Theorems 1, 2 and 3. Theorem 1 shows that defect control can be used to limit the co-simulation error. Theorems 2 and 3 show that output and connection defects can be limited by limiting the step size. The previous experiments and theorems justify the use of variable step size co-simulation using defect control. The next experiments show the results of applying the variable-step Jacobi co-simulation method to the system (40) and (41). The method is presented in Algorithm 1 and the step size is calculated with (39). The numerical experiment was performed with the reference $tol = 0.1$, controller parameters (50) and the initial step size $H_1 = 0.001$. The comparison of the obtained output signals with the monolithic solution (Figure 3a) is shown in Figure 4b.

Next, the tolerance was varied

$$tol \in \{10^{-3}, 10^{-2.8}, \dots, 10^{0}\} \tag{58}$$

to demonstrate that such a controller can limit output and connection defects. Figure 7 shows that the output defect is limited by the tolerance. Figure 8 shows that the connection defect is limited by the tolerance. This may not always be the case for explicit co-simulation. In the presented experiments, the initial step size was set to small $H_1 = 0.001$ to ensure that the numerical defect produced in the initial step stays within tolerance. The experiment shows that by controlling (38) both connection and output defects can be controlled.

Furthermore, Figure 9 shows that by reducing the tolerance, the co-simulation error can be reduced. It is interesting to observe that plots of the output defect (Figure 7) and connection defect (Figure 8) are similar shapes to the error plot (Figure 9). This comparison suggests that there are cases where such variable step co-simulation can be used successfully.

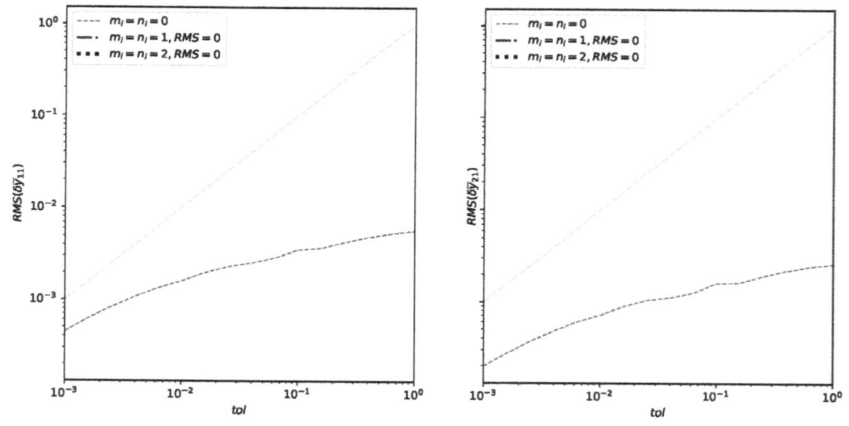

Figure 7. The diagrams show the output defects of the variable-step Jacobi co-simulation method (Algorithm 1, (39) and (50), $H_1 = 10^{-4}$) and different orders of interpolation polynomials.

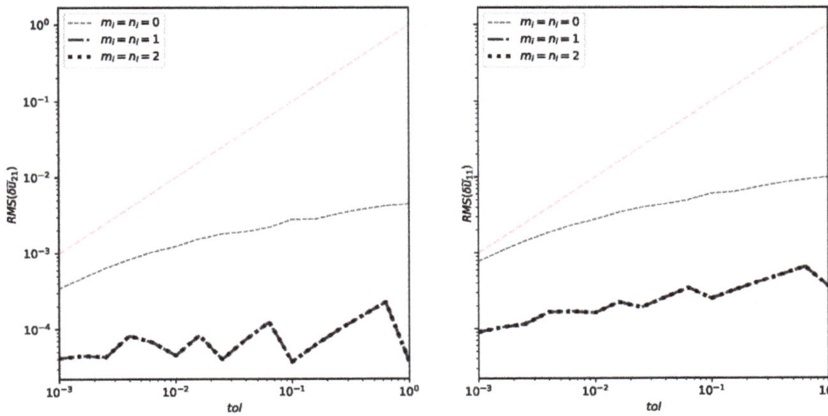

Figure 8. The diagrams show the connection defects of the variable-step Jacobi co-simulation method (Algorithm 1, (39) and (50), $H_1 = 10^{-4}$), different orders of interpolation polynomials and different internal subsystem solvers.

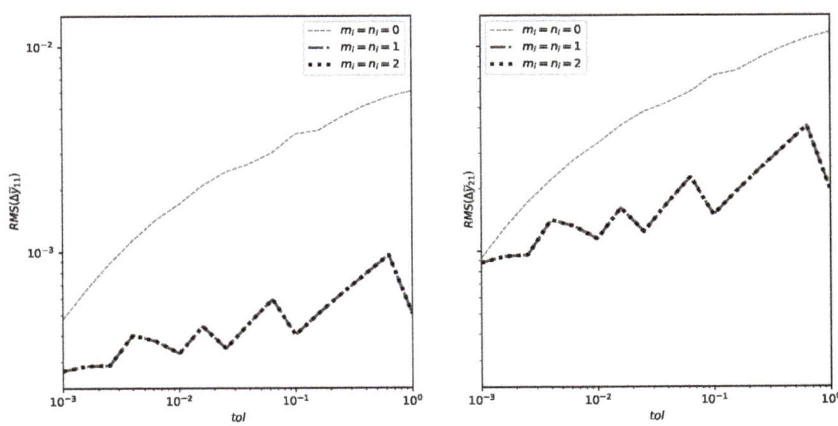

Figure 9. The diagrams show the numerical errors of the variable-step Jacobi co-simulation method (Algorithm 1, (39) and (50), $H_1 = 10^{-4}$), different orders of interpolation polynomials and different internal subsystem solvers.

It should be noted that the integration defect (2a) is not directly controlled in this example. In the case of the analytic solver, the defect is completely eliminated. In the case of the Euler solver (45), the integration defect is $\mathcal{O}(H)$. In practice, co-simulation slaves are black boxes without the ability to monitor the integration. This is why the integration defect is not included in this analysis.

In Figure 9, it can be seen that co-simulation errors are similar in order of magnitude for different extrapolation orders. Figure 10 shows the benefit of increasing the extrapolation order. It shows how an average step size during co-simulation depends on the requested tolerance. The step size controller takes smaller steps to achieve the same tolerance if higher extrapolation order is used. This conclusion may not be generalized to more complex subsystems. It shows the idea that an extrapolation order could be used to decrease the CPU and communication network load during co-simulation.

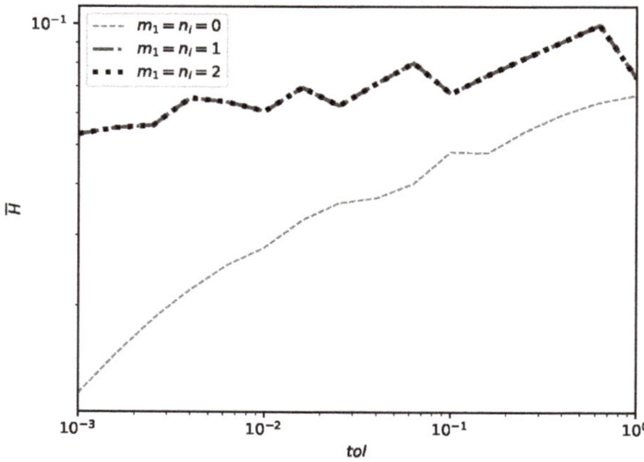

Figure 10. The diagrams show the average step sizes of the variable-step Jacobi co-simulation method (Algorithm 1, (39) and (50), $H_1 = 10^{-4}$), different orders of interpolation polynomials and different internal subsystem solvers.

5. Conclusions and Future Work

This article presents an analysis of the co-simulation defect for a system of coupled ordinary differential equations. The analysis is motivated to deepen the understanding of the co-simulation configuration. In practice, co-simulation slaves are black boxes coupled with connection equations (Figure 1). A quality measure that does not require knowledge of the slave's internal equations can facilitate the co-simulation configuration. The defect analysis was only applied to the co-simulation in [15]. This article continues the application of defect analysis and applies it to variable-step co-simulation with different orders of interpolation polynomials.

The main contribution of this article is a non-iterative co-simulation method with variable communication step size (Figure 2, Algorithm 1). Theorem 1 states that the co-simulation error is bounded if the co-simulation defect is bounded. Theorem 2 and Theorem 3 show that the connection and the output defect can be limited by reducing the communication step size. These theorems justify the use of variable step co-simulation based on defect control. Section 4 shows an application of the proposed method to an example of a two-mass oscillator and gives a verification of the above statements.

Such a method is valuable in practice because it requires little configuration. The parameters for the procedure are the initial communication step size H_1 and the required tolerance *tol*. The method does not require a co-simulation slave to repeat a communication step. This relaxes the implementation requirements for co-simulation slaves. In addition, like any variable step method, it can save computation time by calculating the step size for the results of the desired quality.

One goal of future work would be to see if there is a way to eliminate the need to perform additional sampling of the communication points to estimate output defects. It is worth considering under what conditions the calculations of the connection defect are sufficient to assess the quality of the co-simulation.

Another goal of future work would be to focus on the properties of a model and try to estimate the correct initial step size H_1 for co-simulation. This would reduce the configuration effort even further and achieve an almost ideal configuration. In this case, only the required quality of the co-simulation is requested by a user *tol*.

Author Contributions: Conceptualization, S.G. and Z.K.; Formal analysis, S.G.; Investigation, S.G.; Software, S.G; Supervision, Z.K.; Visualization, S.G.; Writing—review & editing, S.G. and Z.K. All authors have read and agreed to the published version of the manuscript.

Funding: This research received no external funding.

Institutional Review Board Statement: Not applicable.

Informed Consent Statement: Not applicable.

Data Availability Statement: Not applicable.

Conflicts of Interest: The authors declare no conflict of interest.

References

1. Kübler, R.; Schiehlen, W. Two Methods of Simulator Coupling. *Math. Comput. Model. Dyn. Syst.* **2000**, *6*, 93–113. [CrossRef]
2. Gomes, C.; Thule, C.; Broman, D.; Larsen, P.G.; Vangheluwe, H. Co-Simulation: A Survey. *ACM Comput. Surv.* **2018**, *51*, 49:1–49:33. [CrossRef]
3. Functional Mock-Up Interface for Model Exchange and Co-Simulation, Version 2.0. 2014. Available online: https://svn.modelica.org/fmi/branches/public/specifications/v2.0/FMI_for_ModelExchange_and_CoSimulation_v2.0.pdf (accessed on 26 October 2018).
4. Blochwitz, T.; Otter, M.; Akesson, J.; Arnold, M.; Clauss, C.; Elmqvist, H.; Friedrich, M.; Junghanns, A.; Mauss, J.; Neumerkel, D.; et al. Functional mockup interface 2.0: The standard for tool independent exchange of simulation models. In Proceedings of the 9th International MODELICA Conference, Munich, Germany, 3–5 September 2012; Linköping University Electronic Press: Linköping, Sweden, 2012; pp. 173–184. [CrossRef]
5. Tools | Functional Mock-Up Interface. Available online: https://fmi-standard.org/tools/ (accessed on 1 May 2021).
6. Schweizer, B.; Li, P.; Lu, D. Explicit and implicit cosimulation methods: Stability and convergence analysis for different solver coupling approaches. *J. Comput. Nonlinear Dyn.* **2015**, *10*, 051007. [CrossRef]
7. Hairer, E.; Nørsett, S.P.; Wanner, G. *Solving Ordinary Differential Equations. 1, Nonstiff Problems*; Springer: Berlin/Heidelberg, Germany, 1991.
8. Isermann, R.; Schaffnit, J.; Sinsel, S. Hardware-in-the-loop simulation for the design and testing of engine-control systems. *Control. Eng. Pract.* **1999**, *7*, 643–653. [CrossRef]
9. Fathy, H.K.; Filipi, Z.S.; Hagena, J.; Stein, J.L. Review of hardware-in-the-loop simulation and its prospects in the automotive area. In Proceedings of the Modeling and Simulation for Military Applications. International Society for Optics and Photonics, Kissimmee, FL, USA, 18–21 April 2006; Volume 6228, p. 62280E. [CrossRef]
10. Glumac, S.; Varga, N.; Raos, F.; Kovačić, Z. Co-simulation perspective on evaluating the simulation with the engine test bench in the loop. *Automatika* **2022**, *63*, 275–287. [CrossRef]
11. Borutzky, W. *Bond Graph Modelling of Engineering Systems*; Springer: Berlin/Heidelberg, Germany, 2011; Volume 103.
12. Siciliano, B.; Khatib, O.; Kröger, T. *Springer Handbook of Robotics*; Springer: Berlin/Heidelberg, Germany, 2008; Volume 200.
13. Shampine, L.F. Error estimation and control for ODEs. *J. Sci. Comput.* **2005**, *25*, 3–16. [CrossRef]
14. Arnold, M.; Clauß, C.; Schierz, T. Error analysis and error estimates for co-simulation in FMI for model exchange and co-simulation V2.0. In *Progress in Differential-Algebraic Equations*; Springer: Berlin/Heidelberg, Germany, 2014; pp. 107–125.
15. Glumac, S. Automated Configuring of Non-Iterative Co-Simulation Modeled by Synchronous Data Flow. Ph.D. Thesis, Faculty of Electrical Engineering and Computing, University of Zagreb, Zagreb, Croatia, 2022.
16. Enright, W. Continuous numerical methods for ODEs with defect control. *J. Comput. Appl. Math.* **2000**, *125*, 159–170. [CrossRef]
17. Shampine, L.F. Solving ODEs and DDEs with residual control. *Appl. Numer. Math.* **2005**, *52*, 113–127. . [CrossRef]
18. Gustafsson, K.; Lundh, M.; Söderlind, G. A PI stepsize control for the numerical solution of ordinary differential equations. *BIT Numer. Math.* **1988**, *28*, 270–287. [CrossRef]
19. Nguyen, P.H. *Interpolation and Error Control Schemes for Algebraic Differential Equations Using Continuous Implicit Runge-Kutta Methods*; Department of Computer Science, University of Toronto: Toronto, ON, USA, 1995.
20. Spitzbart, A. A Generalization of Hermite's Interpolation Formula. *Am. Math. Mon.* **1960**, *67*, 42–46. . [CrossRef]
21. Busch, M.; Schweizer, B. An explicit approach for controlling the macro-step size of co-simulation methods. In Proceedings of the 7th European Nonlinear Dynamics Conference (ENOC 2011), Rome, Italy, 24–29 July 2011; pp. 1–6.
22. Benedikt, M.; Watzenig, D.; Hofer, A. Modelling and analysis of the non-iterative coupling process for co-simulation. *Math. Comput. Model. Dyn. Syst.* **2013**, *19*, 451–470. [CrossRef]
23. Schweizer, B.; Lu, D. Predictor/corrector co-simulation approaches for solver coupling with algebraic constraints. *ZAMM J. Appl. Math. Mech. Z. Für Angew. Math. Und Mech.* **2015**, *95*, 911–938. [CrossRef]
24. Busch, M. Continuous approximation techniques for co-simulation methods: Analysis of numerical stability and local error. *ZAMM J. Appl. Math. Mech.* **2016**, *96*, 1061–1081. [CrossRef]

25. Glumac, S.; Kovacic, Z. Relative consistency and robust stability measures for sequential co-simulation. In Proceedings of the 13th International Modelica Conference, Regensburg, Germany, 4–6 March 2019; Linköping University Electronic Press: Linköping, Sweden, 2019; p. 157. [CrossRef]
26. Sglumac/DefectAnalysisArticle. 2023. Available online: https://github.com/sglumac/DefectAnalysisArticle (accessed on 25 February 2023).
27. Hindmarsh, A.C.; Brown, P.N.; Grant, K.E.; Lee, S.L.; Serban, R.; Shumaker, D.E.; Woodward, C.S. SUNDIALS: Suite of nonlinear and differential/algebraic equation solvers. *ACM Trans. Math. Softw. (TOMS)* **2005**, *31*, 363–396. [CrossRef]

mathematics

Article

A Novel Coupled Meshless Model for Simulation of Acoustic Wave Propagation in Infinite Domain Containing Multiple Heterogeneous Media

Cheng Chi [1], Fajie Wang [2,*] and Lin Qiu [2]

[1] Institute of Remote Sensing, Navy Submarine Academy, Qingdao 266000, China
[2] College of Mechanical and Electrical Engineering, National Engineering Research Center for Intelligent Electrical Vehicle Power System, Qingdao University, Qingdao 266071, China
* Correspondence: wfj88@qdu.edu.cn

Abstract: This study presents a novel coupled meshless model for simulating acoustic wave propagation in heterogeneous media, based on the singular boundary method (SBM) and Kansa's method (KS). In the proposed approach, the SBM was used to model the homogeneous part of the propagation domain, while KS was employed to model a heterogeneity. The interface compatibility conditions associated with velocities and pressures were imposed to couple the two methods. The proposed SBM–KS coupled approach combines the respective advantages of the SBM and KS. The SBM is especially suitable for solving external sound field problems, while KS is attractive for nonlinear problems in bounded non-homogeneous media. Moreover, the new methodology completely avoids grid generation and numerical integration compared with the finite element method and boundary element method. Numerical experiments verified the accuracy and effectiveness of the proposed scheme.

Keywords: singular boundary method; Kansa's method; heterogeneous media; acoustic wave; meshless method

MSC: 35J05; 65N35; 65D12

Citation: Chi, C.; Wang, F.; Qiu, L. A Novel Coupled Meshless Model for Simulation of Acoustic Wave Propagation in Infinite Domain Containing Multiple Heterogeneous Media. *Mathematics* **2023**, *11*, 1841. https://doi.org/10.3390/math11081841

Academic Editor: Nikolaos L. Tsitsas

Received: 15 March 2023
Revised: 31 March 2023
Accepted: 11 April 2023
Published: 12 April 2023

1. Introduction

The propagation of sound waves in fluids and solids is an important issue in science and engineering. In the past few decades, the boundary element method (BEM) has become established as an effective tool for sound propagation analysis, especially for the infinite and semi-infinite domains [1–4], due to the used fundamental solution automatically satisfying the far-field radiation condition. Compared with other well-established mesh-based methods, such as the finite element method (FEM) [5–8] and the finite difference method (FDM) [9,10], the BEM can solve acoustic problems merely through boundary discretization. However, it involves a sophisticated mathematical formulation and a tedious estimation of singular and hyper-singular integrals [11,12]. Furthermore, these methods require the use of domain truncation techniques for infinite domain problems for the numerical solution of problems on unbounded domains.

In recent years, various meshless/meshfree methods [13–19] have been proposed to reduce or even eliminate the tasks of mesh generation and singular integration. Among these approaches, the singular boundary method (SBM) [20–23] is a boundary-only discretization meshless technique, which does not require mesh generation and numerical integration. This method is very simple and accurate for the analysis of sound fields in unbounded domains, since it also employs the fundamental solution satisfying the governing equation and the far-field radiation condition [24,25]. Another common meshless scheme is Kansa's method (KS) [26–29], which is based on the radial basis function (RBF). This method does not require the fundamental solution, and is suitable for solving arbitrary partial differential equations in bounded domains [30–33].

As can be inferred from above, the SBM and KS have their respective advantages in addressing unbounded homogeneous media and bounded non-homogeneous media. In order to avoid complex computational processes such as mesh generation and singular integral computation using traditional methods such as the FEM and the BEM, this research made a first attempt to couple these two methods (named SBM–KS) for simulating acoustic wave propagation in heterogeneous media. The SBM is adopted to model the homogeneous part of the propagation domain, while KS is employed to model a heterogeneity. A direct coupling strategy between the SBM and KS is presented based on the continuity conditions of velocities and pressures on the interface. The coupling method shows unique advantages in solving such problems compared to existing methods, such as simplicity, accuracy, and being free of mesh and integration.

The organization of this manuscript is as follows: Section 2 briefly describes acoustic wave propagation problems of heterogeneous media. Section 3 introduces the SBM for an unbounded acoustic medium, KS for a heterogeneous acoustic medium, and the coupling strategy of these two methods. In Section 4, two classical numerical examples are provided to verify the accuracy and effectiveness of the proposed methodology. Finally, Section 5 provides some conclusions and remarks.

2. Problem Statement

Consider an unbounded homogeneous medium Ω_1, containing a subdomain Ω_2 in which the sound velocity is variable (see Figure 1a), and the sound field is excited by a harmonic pressure source at position $s = (x_0, y_0)$. In this regard, the sound waves travel at a constant speed $v_1(x) = v_1$ in Ω_1 and a variable speed $v_1(x)$ in Ω_2 at $x = (x, y)$. Then, the acoustic pressure fields $p_1(x)$ and $p_2(x)$ within homogeneous and heterogeneous media can be described by the following Helmholtz equations:

$$\nabla^2 p_1(x) + \left[\frac{\omega}{v_1}\right]^2 p_1(x) = 0, \ \ x \in \Omega_1, \tag{1}$$

$$\nabla^2 p_2(x) + \left[\frac{\omega}{v_2(x)}\right]^2 p_2(x) = 0, \ \ x \in \Omega_2, \tag{2}$$

where ∇^2 is the Laplace operator, and ω is the angular frequency.

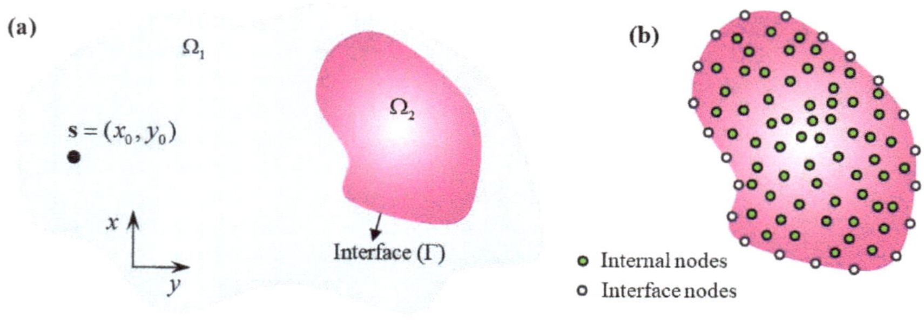

Figure 1. Schematic diagrams of (**a**) acoustic wave propagation in heterogeneous media and (**b**) nodal distribution for the coupled method.

Notice that the governing equations are the PDEs with constant and variable coefficients in domains Ω_1 and Ω_2, respectively. The conventional boundary-type methods, such as the BEM, the SBM, and the fundamental solution method, cannot be directly applied to solve variable-coefficient PDEs. Meanwhile, domain-type methods, such as the FEM, the meshless local Petrov–Galerkin (MLPG) method and Kansa's method, require the truncation of boundaries and the division of grids, which is extremely troublesome when dealing with problems in infinite homogeneous media. It should be noticed that the fundamental solution employed in the SBM automatically satisfies the Sommerfeld radiation condition at infinity:

$$\lim_{r\to\infty} r^{\frac{1}{2}(d-1)}\left(\frac{\partial p(x)}{\partial r} - \mathrm{i}kp(x)\right) = 0 \tag{3}$$

where d is the spatial dimension, $\mathrm{i} = \sqrt{-1}$ is the imaginary unit, k is the wave number, and r is the distance between point x and the sound field's center.

In the present study, the above-mentioned problem was solved by coupling the SBM and KS to overcome the limitations posed separately by each method. The SBM was employed to model the unbounded acoustic medium, while KS was used to model the heterogeneous medium. The coupling between the two approaches was accomplished by utilizing continuity conditions of pressures and velocities on the boundary of the heterogeneous medium. Figure 1b illustrates the schematic diagram of the nodal distribution for the coupled meshless model. The two methods used the same nodes on the interface.

3. Methodology

3.1. *SBM for Unbounded Acoustic Medium*

Assuming the total number of nodes on the interface is M, the sound pressure at point $x \in \Omega_1 \cup \Gamma$ can be calculated by the following SBM formula:

$$\hat{p}_1(x) = \sum_{j=1}^{M} \alpha_j G(x, x_j) + p_{inc}(x_i, \mathbf{s}),\ \ x_j \in \Gamma \tag{4}$$

where α_j is the unknown coefficient, x_j is the boundary node shown in Figure 1b, $p_{inc}(x_i, \mathbf{s}) = H_0^{(2)}(\frac{\omega}{v_1}\|x_i - \mathbf{s}\|_2)$ represents the incident pressure field generated by a harmonic pressure source at position $s = (x_0, y_0)$ in the domain Ω_1, and $G(x, x_j)$ is the fundamental solution of the Helmholtz equation, which is given by the following:

$$G(x, x_j) = -\frac{\mathrm{i}}{4} H_0^{(2)}\left(\frac{\omega}{v_1}\|x - x_j\|_2\right) \tag{5}$$

where $H_0^{(2)}$ is the zeroth-order Hankel function of the second kind.

To solve the unknown coefficients $\{\alpha_j\}_{j=1}^{M}$, let x in Equation (4) be the boundary node x_j; we have the following equations for the Dirichlet boundary condition:

$$\hat{p}_1(x_i) = \sum_{\substack{j=1 \\ i\neq j}}^{M} \alpha_j G(x_i, x_j) + \alpha_i p_{ii} + p_{inc}(x_i, \mathbf{s}),\ \ i = 1, 2, \ldots, M, \tag{6}$$

and for the Neumann boundary condition, we have the following:

$$\frac{\partial \hat{p}_1(x_i)}{\partial n_{x_i}} = \sum_{\substack{j=1 \\ i\neq j}}^{M} \alpha_j \frac{\partial G(x_i, x_j)}{\partial n_{x_i}} + \alpha_i q_{ii} + \frac{\partial p_{inc}(x_i, \mathbf{s})}{\partial n_{x_i}},\ \ i = 1, 2, \ldots, M, \tag{7}$$

where x_i and x_j denote the ith and jth boundary nodes, p_{ii} and q_{ii} are the origin intensity factors when the source point and the field point coincide (i.e., $i = j$), which can be computed using the following formulas in references [34,35]:

$$u_{ii} = \frac{\mathrm{i}}{4} - \frac{1}{2\pi}\left(\ln\left(\frac{L_i}{2\pi}\right) + \ln\left(\frac{k}{2}\right) + \gamma\right), \tag{8}$$

$$q_{ii} = \frac{1}{L_i} - \sum_{\substack{j=1 \\ j \neq i}}^{N} \zeta_{ji} \frac{\partial G_0(\boldsymbol{x}_i, \boldsymbol{s}_j)}{\partial \boldsymbol{n}_s}, \tag{9}$$

where L_i is the influence range of the boundary point x_i (see Figure 2), γ is the Euler constant, $G_0(\boldsymbol{x}_i, \boldsymbol{x}_j)$ the fundamental solution of the Laplace equation, as follows:

$$G_0(\boldsymbol{x}_i, \boldsymbol{x}_j) = -\frac{1}{2\pi} \ln \|\boldsymbol{x}_i - \boldsymbol{x}_j\|_2. \tag{10}$$

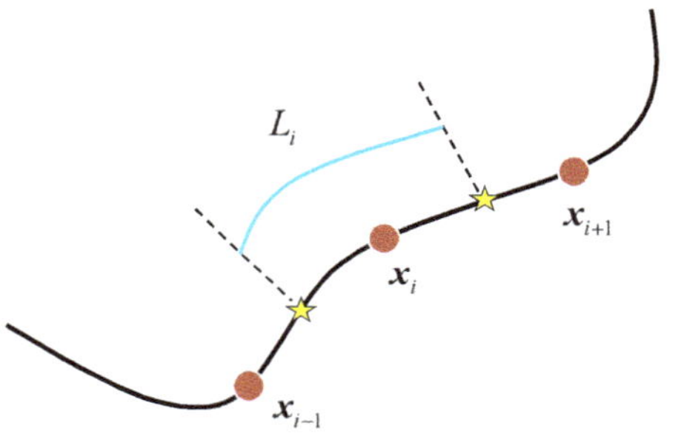

Figure 2. Diagram of the influence range for a source point.

For the convenience of coupling calculations, Equations (6) and (7) can be written in the following matrix forms:

$$\hat{\mathbf{p}}_1 = \mathbf{G}\boldsymbol{\alpha} + \mathbf{p}_{\text{in}}, \tag{11}$$

$$\hat{\mathbf{q}}_1 = \mathbf{H}\boldsymbol{\alpha} + \mathbf{q}_{\text{in}}. \tag{12}$$

3.2. *Kansa's Method for Inhomogeneous Acoustic Medium*

For the closed domain Ω_2 with the boundary Γ, we chose a set of N collocation points, including Ni internal points and M boundary points, as shown in Figure 1b. According to the basic idea of KS, the sound pressure in subdomain Ω_2 can be approximated using a linear combination of RBFs, as follows:

$$\hat{p}_2(\boldsymbol{x}) = \sum_{k=1}^{N} \beta_k \varphi_k(\boldsymbol{x}), \tag{13}$$

where β_k is the unknown coefficient to be determined, and $\varphi_k(\boldsymbol{x})$ is the multiquadric (MQ) RBF function, which is defined as the following:

$$\varphi_k(\boldsymbol{x}) = \sqrt{r_k^2 + c^2}, \tag{14}$$

where $r_k = \|\boldsymbol{x} - \boldsymbol{x}_k\|_2$ is the distance between nodes $\boldsymbol{x}$ and $\boldsymbol{x}_k$, and c is the shape parameter, which is fixed at 0.5 in this study. The MQ-RBF is a highly sought-after function due to its numerous advantages for various applications. Its main advantages include the following:

(1) Smoothness: it is a smooth function with continuous derivatives of all orders, which is a crucial requirement for many applications. (2) Accuracy: it offers exceptional approximation accuracy for a wide range of functions and can converge faster than other RBFs for some problems, making it an excellent choice for large-scale applications. (3) Scalability: it is computationally efficient, making it a perfect fit for large-scale problems. It has a low computational cost for interpolation and can be easily parallelized. (4) Robustness: it is less sensitive to data outliers than other RBFs, making it a robust choice for applications where data may contain noise or outliers. (5) Universality: it is a universal approximator, meaning it can approximate any continuous function to any desired accuracy, given sufficient data points.

Substituting Equation (13) into Equation (1) for internal nodes, one obtains the following:

$$\nabla^2 \sum_{k=1}^{N} \beta_k \varphi_k(\boldsymbol{x}_i) + \left[\frac{\omega}{v_2(\boldsymbol{x}_i)}\right]^2 \sum_{k=1}^{N} \beta_k \varphi_k(\boldsymbol{x}_i) = 0, \;\; \boldsymbol{x}_i \in \Omega_2 \tag{15}$$

In addition, the sound pressure and its normal derivative at the boundary nodes satisfy the following equations:

$$\hat{p}_2(\boldsymbol{x}_i) = \sum_{k=1}^{N} \beta_k \varphi_k(\boldsymbol{x}_i), \;\; \boldsymbol{x}_i \in \Gamma, \tag{16}$$

$$\frac{\partial \hat{p}_2(\boldsymbol{x}_i)}{\partial n_{x_i}} = \sum_{k=1}^{N} \beta_k \frac{\partial \varphi_k(\boldsymbol{x}_i)}{\partial n_{x_i}}, \;\; \boldsymbol{x}_i \in \Gamma. \tag{17}$$

Equations (15)–(17) can be rewritten in the following matrix forms:

$$\mathbf{R}\boldsymbol{\beta} = \mathbf{0}, \tag{18}$$

$$\hat{\mathbf{p}}_2 = \mathbf{B}\boldsymbol{\beta}, \tag{19}$$

$$\hat{\mathbf{q}}_2 = \mathbf{F}\boldsymbol{\beta}. \tag{20}$$

3.3. Coupled Model Dymamic System

This study proposed a direct coupling strategy between the two methods, under the condition that the nodes used in the SBM model matched the boundary nodes used in KS. Note the following:

$$\frac{\partial p(x)}{\partial n_x} = -\mathrm{i}\rho\omega v(x), \tag{21}$$

where the coupled system can be established by employing the continuity of pressure and velocity on the interface between the two media, which can be expressed as follows:

$$p_1(\boldsymbol{x}) = p_2(\boldsymbol{x}) \quad \text{or} \quad \mathbf{p}_1 = \mathbf{p}_2, \qquad \boldsymbol{x} \in \Gamma, \tag{22}$$

$$\frac{\partial p_1(\boldsymbol{x})}{\partial n_x} = -\frac{\partial p_2(\boldsymbol{x})}{\partial n_x} \qquad \text{or} \quad \mathbf{q}_1 = \mathbf{q}_2, \qquad \boldsymbol{x} \in \Gamma. \tag{23}$$

Considering all the nodes within the domain Ω_2, and using the above continuity conditions, Equations (11), (12), and (18)–(20) can be combined to form a total linear system, namely, the following:

$$\begin{bmatrix} \mathbf{G} & -\mathbf{B} \\ \mathbf{H} & \mathbf{F} \\ \mathbf{0} & \mathbf{R} \end{bmatrix} \begin{bmatrix} \boldsymbol{\alpha} \\ \boldsymbol{\beta} \end{bmatrix} = \begin{bmatrix} -\mathbf{p}_{\text{in}} \\ -\mathbf{q}_{\text{in}} \\ \mathbf{0} \end{bmatrix} \tag{24}$$

After solving Equation (24), unknown coefficient vectors $\boldsymbol{\alpha}$ and $\boldsymbol{\beta}$ can be determined. Then, the sound pressures at any position in medium Ω_1 and Ω_2 can be easily obtained by employing Equations (4) and (13).

4. Numerical Results and Discussion

In this section, we examine the proposed SBM–KS by three numerical examples, including single and multiple heterogeneous inclusion materials. To assess the numerical errors, the following absolute error was employed:

$$Absolute\ error = |p_{num}(\boldsymbol{x}) - p_{ana}(\boldsymbol{x})|, \tag{25}$$

where $p_{num}(\boldsymbol{x})$ and $p_{ana}(\boldsymbol{x})$ represent the numerical and analytical solutions at point $\boldsymbol{x}$, respectively. Note that $\boldsymbol{p}$ can be a real part or an imaginary part of the sound pressure.

Example 1. *We consider an infinite homogenous fluid medium with a circular inclusion of radius 1.0 m [36]. The sound velocities are 1500 m/s and 2500 m/s in the infinite fluid medium and the circular inclusion, respectively. Both media have a same density of 1000 kg/m^3. The pressure source is placed at ($x_0 = -5\ m$, $y_0 = 0\ m$).*

To numerically solve this problem, the SBM–KS chose 100 interface nodes and 688 internal nodes. Figure 3 shows the comparison of the analytical solution [37], and numerical results obtained by the proposed SBM–KS and COMSOL software under a frequency of 1000 Hz. Absolute errors of these two methods are also provided in Figure 4. In the simulation, the finite element method with 7780 elements used the perfectly matched layer. We can see from Figure 3 that the numerical results obtained from the SBM–KS and the COMSOL FEM are in good agreement with the analytical solutions. It can also be clearly observed that the curve of our method completely coincides with the curve of the analytical solution, while the FEM has certain errors. Moreover, it can be noted that the calculation accuracy of the proposed method is at least two orders higher than that of the FEM. In this example, the condition number of the proposed approach is 1.426×10^{11}. The SBM has a small condition number, but KS has a large condition number [38], which leads to a large value of the condition number for the final coefficient matrix. However, the method can still obtain accurate numerical results.

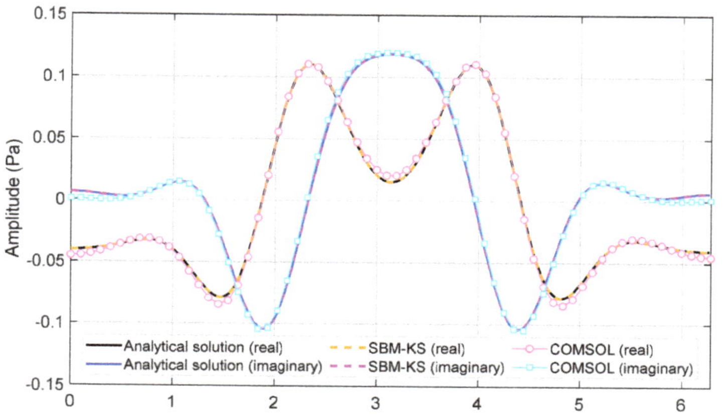

Figure 3. Comparison of the numerical and analytical solutions for hydrodynamic pressures along the common interface under a frequency of 1000 Hz.

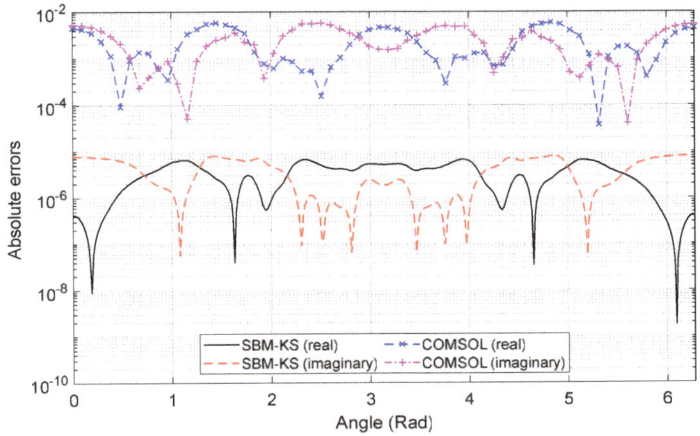

Figure 4. Absolute errors of the SBM–KS and the COMSOL Multiphysics finite element methods.

Example 2. *This example considers a non-homogeneous circular region of radius 1 m centered at point (0, 0), which is embedded in an unbounded fluid medium. The pressure source with a frequency of 1000 Hz is placed at ($x_0 = -2.5$ m, $y_0 = 0$ m). Both media have a same density of 1000 kg/m^3. The outer fluid medium allows sound waves to travel at 1500 m/s, while the non-homogeneous medium allows sound waves to travel at the following:*

$$v_2(x,y) = 1500 + 150\left[1 + \sin\left(\pi\sqrt{x^2+y^2} + \frac{\pi}{2}\right)\right], \tag{26}$$

which is illustrated in Figure 5.

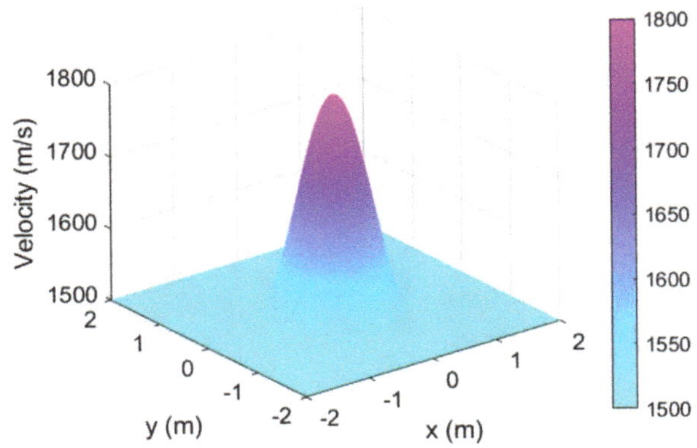

Figure 5. Velocity distribution in a heterogeneous domain for Example 2.

In practical problems, the node distribution may be scattered and uneven. As a meshless technique, the proposed SBM–KS can address the non-uniform node distribution in a leisurely manner. In order to test the effect of node distribution on the calculation accuracy, distributions of regular and irregular nodes were investigated in the calculation, as shown in Figure 6. It includes 100 interface nodes and 688 internal nodes.

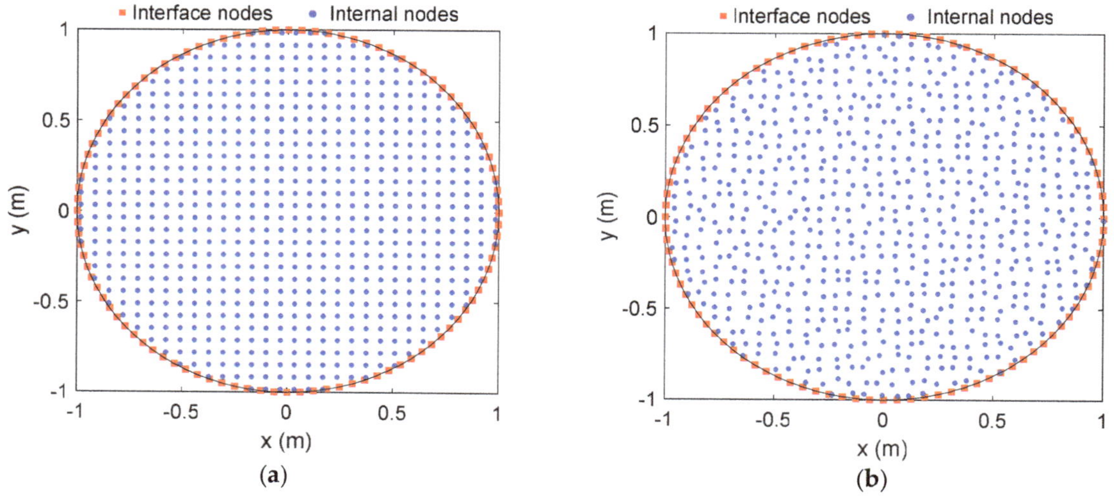

Figure 6. Nodal distributions: (**a**) regular nodes and (**b**) irregular nodes.

Figure 7 displays the profiles of the analytical response in the domain $[-2,2] \times [-2,2]$, and Figures 8 and 9 depict the absolute errors of the proposed method under regular and irregular nodes, respectively. It was noted that the numerical solutions are in good agreement with the analytical one for the regular and irregular distributions of nodes, and the numerical errors are small. In this example, the condition number of the proposed approach is 4.665×10^{11}.

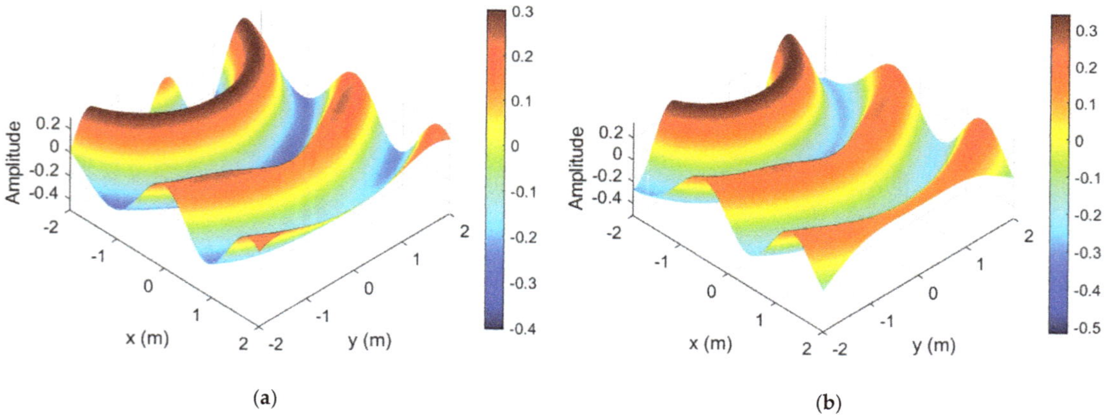

Figure 7. Analytical responses in the domain $[-2,2] \times [-2,2]$: (**a**) real part, (**b**) imaginary part.

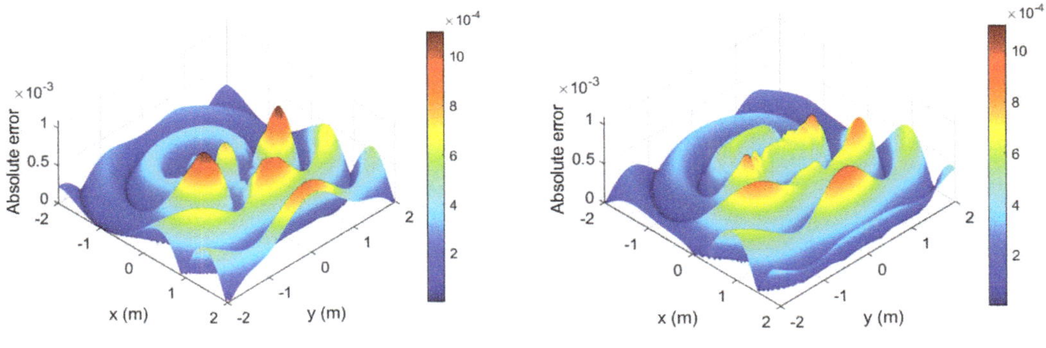

(**a**) Real part (**b**) Imaginary part

Figure 8. Distributions of absolute error in the domain $[-2, 2] \times [-2, 2]$ with regular nodes: (**a**) the real part with (**b**) the imaginary part.

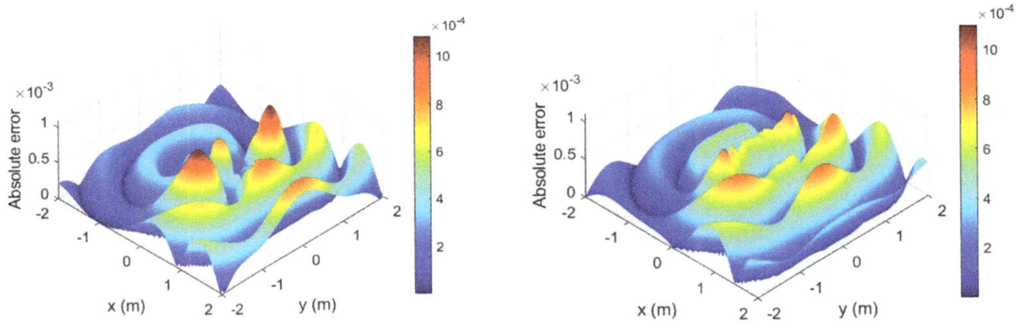

(**a**) Real part (**b**) Imaginary part

Figure 9. Distributions of absolute error in the domain $[-2, 2] \times [-2, 2]$ with irregular nodes: (**a**) the real part with (**b**) the imaginary part.

Example 3. *The last example considers a complex sound propagation problem in a heterogeneous medium, shown in Figure 10. The domain Ω_1 is an infinite domain, in which the speed of sound is $v_1 = 1500\ m/s$ and the density is $\rho_1 = 1000\ kg/m^3$. The pressure source is placed at $(x_0 = -5\ m,\ y_0 = 0\ m)$. The bounded domains Ω_2, Ω_3, and Ω_4 are all heterogeneous media, and their boundaries can be expressed as the following parameter forms:*

$$\Gamma_2 = \left\{ (x = r_2(\theta)\cos\theta, y = 2 + r_2(\theta)\sin\theta) \middle| r_2(\theta) = \sqrt[3]{\cos(3\theta) + \sqrt{2 - \sin^2(3\theta)}},\ 0 \le \theta \le 2\pi \right\}, \tag{27}$$

$$\Gamma_3 = \left\{ (x = r_3(\theta)\cos\theta, y = -2 + r_3(\theta)\sin\theta) \middle| r_3(\theta) = e^{\sin\theta}\sin^2\theta + e^{\cos\theta}\cos^2\theta,\ 0 \le \theta \le 2\pi \right\}, \tag{28}$$

$$\Gamma_3 = \{ (x = 4 + r_4(\theta)\cos\theta, y = r_4(\theta)\sin\theta) | r_4(\theta) = 1,\ 0 \le \theta \le 2\pi \}. \tag{29}$$

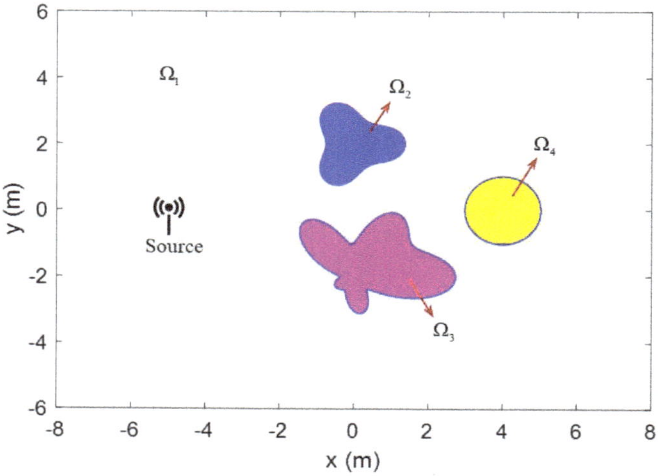

Figure 10. Geometry of the heterogeneous medium in Example 3.

In the present study, we assumed that the density of the three heterogeneous media is the same as that of the infinite medium, while these three media allow sound waves to travel at the following velocities:

$$v_2(x,y) = 1500 + 200\left[1 + \sin\left(\pi\sqrt{x^2 + (y-2)^2}/r_2(\overline{\theta}) + \frac{\pi}{2}\right)\right], \quad (x,y) \in \Omega_2, \tag{30}$$

$$v_3(x,y) = 1500 + 100\left[1 + \sin\left(\pi\sqrt{x^2 + (y+2)^2}/r_3(\overline{\theta}) + \frac{\pi}{2}\right)\right], \quad (x,y) \in \Omega_3, \tag{31}$$

$$v_4(x,y) = 1500 + 150\left[1 + \sin\left(\pi\sqrt{(x-4)^2 + y^2}/r_4(\overline{\theta}) + \frac{\pi}{2}\right)\right], \quad (x,y) \in \Omega_4, \tag{32}$$

where $\overline{\theta}$ denotes the azimuth angle of the point (x, y), functions r_2, r_3, and r_4 have are given in Equations (27)–(29). The velocity variations in the domain $[-8, 8] \times [-6, 6]$ are shown in Figure 11.

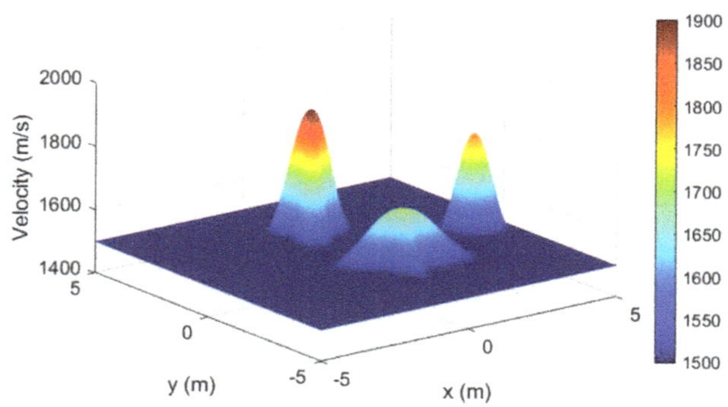

Figure 11. Velocity distribution in the heterogeneous domain for Example 3.

In this example, the proposed method was used to solve the problem of sound propagation in an infinite domain with three heterogeneous media. In the calculation, the SBM was employed to simulate the external sound field Ω_1, while KS was used to approximate the sound field in heterogeneous media Ω_2, Ω_3, and Ω_4. The two methods were coupled by employing the continuity conditions of pressure and velocity on the interfaces Γ_2, Γ_3, and Γ_4.

In order to obtain accurate and reliable numerical results, a total of 6422 nodes were used in the study. On each interface, 400 nodes were evenly arranged according to the angle. In domains Ω_2, Ω_3, and Ω_4, 1360, 2616, and 1246 nodes were configured, respectively. The node distribution is shown in Figure 12. The proposed SBM–KS was used to calculate the sound field with two different frequencies. The FEM results were also obtained using the COMSOL Multiphysics software to compare with our method. In the simulation, the FEM used 242,444 domain elements and 2846 boundary elements to achieve the reliable solutions.

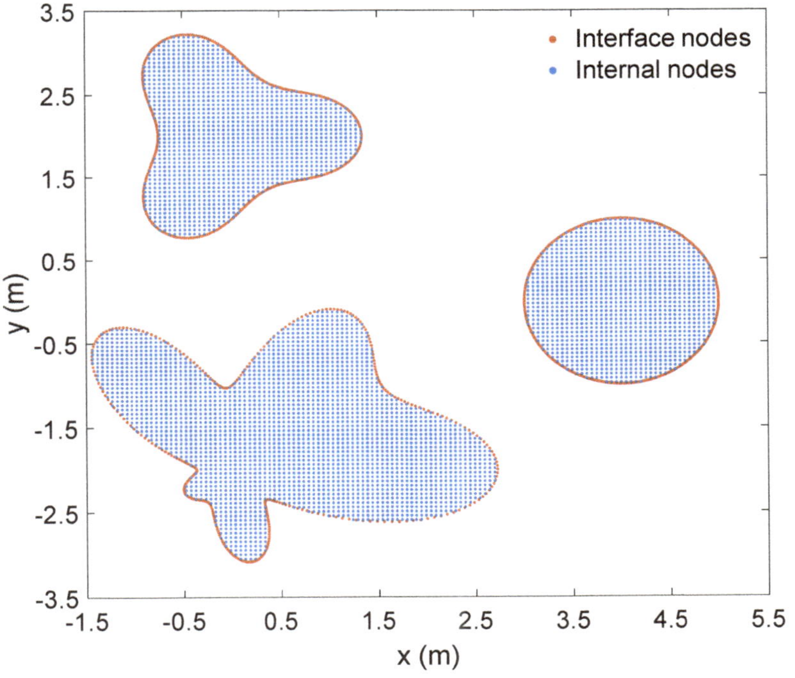

Figure 12. Node distribution of the coupling method.

Figures 13 and 14 give numerical results of sound pressure and sound pressure level at frequencies 1000 Hz and 1500 Hz. From these figures, it can be observed that the sound wave propagates regularly when it does not encounter heterogeneous materials. However, after passing through heterogeneous materials, the waveform changes. The higher the frequency, the more noticeable the impact effect. In addition, it can be observed from Figures 13 and 14 that the results of the two methods basically have the same trend from a global perspective, and can reveal the propagation law of sound waves. In terms of details, the numerical solutions of the two methods differed slightly. It should be clarified that this example did not have an analytical solution to verify the computational accuracy of the two methods, but the previous two examples indicated the reliability of the proposed SBM–KS approach.

In this example, the condition numbers of the proposed approach are 2.177×10^{19} and 4.408×10^{19} for 1000 Hz and 1500 Hz, respectively. Compared with the previous two examples, the geometry investigated in this example is more complex, including three heterogeneous media with irregular boundaries in an infinite domain. Note that the condition number increased sharply as the frequency increased, and the number of nodes increased.

The proposed method in this study successfully solved the problem of infinite domain acoustic wave propagation involving multiple heterogeneous media. It provides a new and simple mesh-free numerical technique for the efficient and accurate numerical simulation of such problems, and also serves as a reference for validating the numerical effectiveness of other methods.

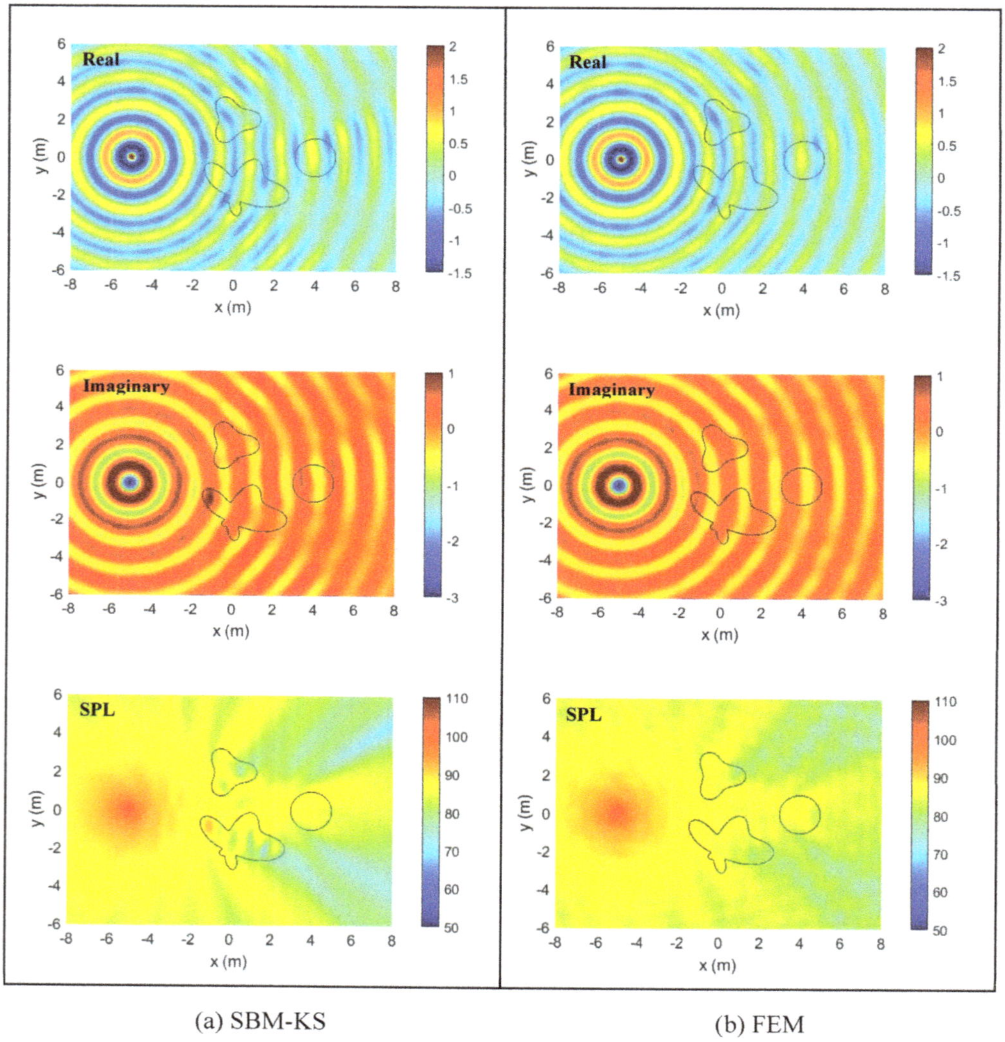

Figure 13. Profiles of sound pressure and sound pressure level obtained using the SBM–KS approach and COMSOL FEM at a frequency of 1000 Hz.

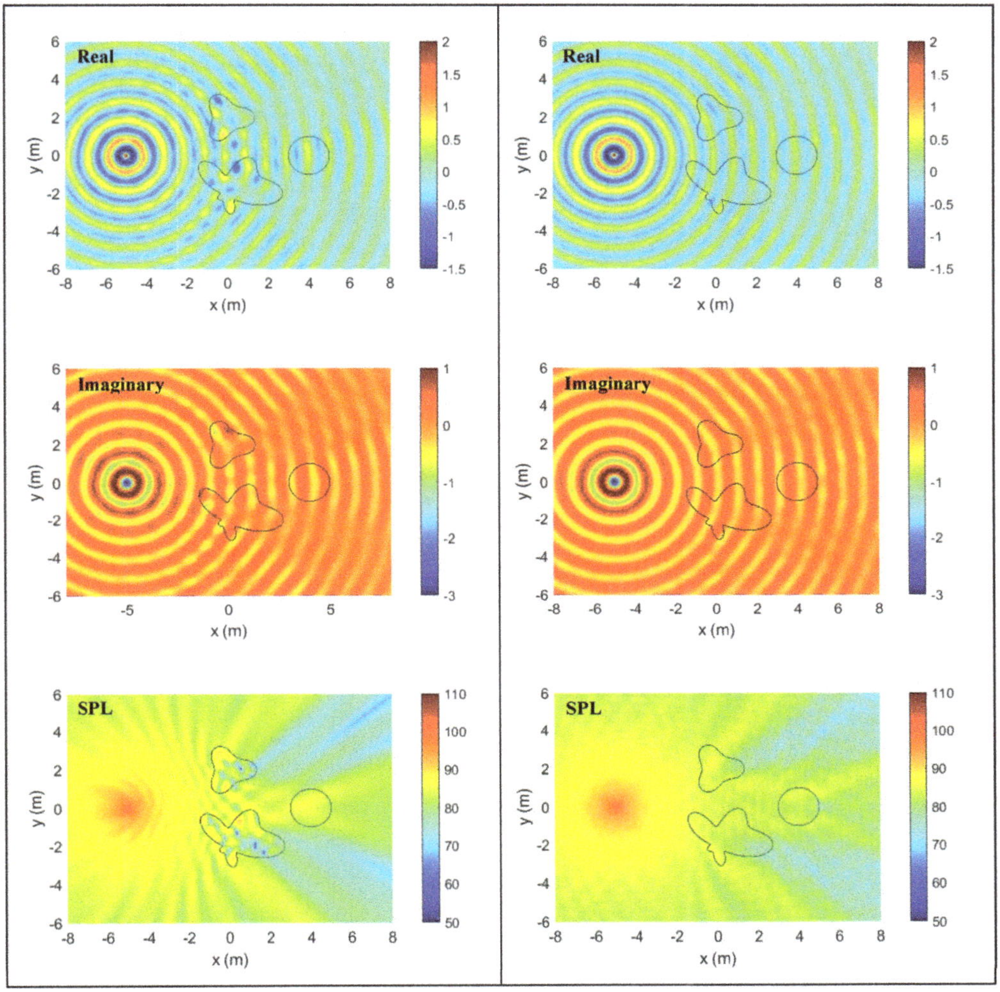

(a) SBM-KS (b) FEM

Figure 14. Profiles of sound pressure and sound pressure level obtained using the SBM–KS approach and COMSOL FEM at a frequency of 1500 Hz.

5. Conclusions

In this study, a novel coupled algorithm was presented for the analysis of acoustic wave propagation in heterogeneous media, based on the SBM and KS. The proposed model can accurately solve problems of heterogeneous media containing localized regions with varying medium parameters, for which the application of the SBM is not suitable. The new methodology completely avoids grid generation and numerical integration, and greatly exerts the respective advantages of the two methods.

Numerical examples investigated the sound propagation problems through single and multiple heterogeneous materials. Numerical results demonstrated that the proposed scheme is accurate and reliable for simulated acoustic wave propagation in heterogeneous media. On the one hand, the method eliminates the preprocessing process in the FEM, such as mesh division and perfect matching layer setting. On the other hand, it is superior to the traditional FEM in terms of accuracy and efficiency. In addition, compared with the BEM and MFS coupling methods, the calculation of singular integrals and the selection of fictitious boundaries are avoided completely. Therefore, the proposed methodology can be considered a competitive candidate for solving this type of problem.

Author Contributions: Conceptualization, F.W.; Methodology, C.C. and F.W.; Software, C.C. and L.Q.; Validation, L.Q.; Investigation, L.Q.; Writing—original draft, C.C.; Writing—review & editing, F.W. All authors have read and agreed to the published version of the manuscript.

Funding: This research received no external funding.

Data Availability Statement: Not applicable.

Conflicts of Interest: The authors declare no conflict of interest.

References

1. Premat, E.; Gabillet, Y. A new boundary-element method for predicting outdoor sound propagation and application to the case of a sound barrier in the presence of downward refraction. *J. Acoust. Soc. Am.* **2000**, *108*, 2775–2783. [CrossRef]
2. Liu, Y. On the BEM for acoustic wave problems. *Eng. Anal. Boundary Elem.* **2019**, *107*, 53–62. [CrossRef]
3. Chen, X.; He, Q.; Zheng, C.-J.; Wan, C.; Bi, C.-X.; Wang, B. A parameter study of the Burton-Miller formulation in the BEM analysis of acoustic resonances in exterior configurations. *J. Theor. Computat. Acous.* **2021**, *29*, 2050023. [CrossRef]
4. Aimi, A.; Boiardi, A.S. IGA-Energetic BEM: An effective tool for the numerical solution of wave propagation problems in space-time domain. *Mathematics* **2022**, *10*, 334. [CrossRef]
5. Ganesh, M.; Morgenstern, C. High-order FEM domain decomposition models for high-frequency wave propagation in heterogeneous media. *Comput. Math. Appl.* **2018**, *75*, 1961–1972. [CrossRef]
6. Li, W.; Zhang, Q.; Gui, Q.; Chai, Y. A coupled FE-Meshfree triangular element for acoustic radiation problems. *Int. J. Comp. Meth.* **2021**, *18*, 2041002. [CrossRef]
7. Chai, Y.; Li, W.; Liu, Z. Analysis of transient wave propagation dynamics using the enriched finite element method with interpolation cover functions. *Appl. Math. Comput.* **2022**, *412*, 126564. [CrossRef]
8. Sun, T.; Wang, P.; Zhang, G.; Chia, Y. Transient analyses of wave propagations in nonhomogeneous mediaemploying the novel finite element method with the appropriate enrichment function. *Comput. Math. Appl.* **2023**, *129*, 90–112.
9. Di Bartolo, L.; Dors, C.; Mansur, W.J. A new family of finite-difference schemes to solve the heterogeneous acoustic wave equation. *Geophysics* **2012**, *77*, T187–T199. [CrossRef]
10. Li, K.; Liao, W. An efficient and high accuracy finite-difference scheme for the acoustic wave equation in 3D heterogeneous media. *J. Comput. Sci.* **2020**, *40*, 101063. [CrossRef]
11. Tadeu, A.; Stanak, P.; Sladek, J.; Sladek, V. Coupled BEM-MLPG acoustic analysis for non-homogeneous media. *Eng. Anal. Boundary Elem.* **2014**, *44*, 161–169. [CrossRef]
12. Keuchel, S.; Hagelstein, N.C.; Zaleski, O.; von Estorff, O. Evaluation of hypersingular and nearly singular integrals in the Isogeometric Boundary Element Method for acoustics. *Comput. Methods Appl. Mech. Eng.* **2017**, *325*, 488–504. [CrossRef]
13. Wang, C.; Wang, F.; Gong, Y. Analysis of 2D heat conduction in nonlinear functionally graded materials using a local semi-analytical meshless method. *Aims Math.* **2021**, *6*, 12599–12618. [CrossRef]
14. Jiang, S.; Gu, Y.; Golub, M.V. An efficient meshless method for bimaterial interface cracks in 2D thin-layered coating structures. *Appl. Math. Lett.* **2022**, *131*, 108080. [CrossRef]
15. Li, P.W. The space-time generalized finite difference scheme for solving the nonlinear equal-width equation in the long-time simulation. *Appl. Math. Lett.* **2022**, *132*, 108181. [CrossRef]
16. Sun, L.; Fu, Z.; Chen, Z. A localized collocation solver based on fundamental solutions for 3D time harmonic elastic wave propagation analysis. *Appl. Math. Comput.* **2023**, *439*, 127600. [CrossRef]
17. Chen, Z.; Wang, F. Localized method of fundamental solutions for acoustic analysis inside a car cavity with sound-absorbing material. *Adv. Appl. Math. Mech.* **2023**, *15*, 182–201.
18. Li, Y.; Liu, C.; Li, W.; Chai, Y. Numerical investigation of the element-free Galerkin method (EFGM) with appropriate temporal discretization techniques for transient wave propagation problems. *Appl. Math. Comput.* **2023**, *442*, 127755. [CrossRef]
19. Ju, B.; Qu, W. Three-dimensional application of the meshless generalized finite difference method for solving the extended Fisher-Kolmogorov equation. *Appl. Math. Lett.* **2023**, *136*, 108458. [CrossRef]
20. Wei, X.; Luo, W. 2.5D singular boundary method for acoustic wave propagation. *Appl. Math. Lett.* **2021**, *112*, 106760. [CrossRef]
21. Cheng, S.; Wang, F.; Wu, G.; Zhang, C. A semi-analytical and boundary-type meshless method with adjoint variable formulation for acoustic design sensitivity analysis. *Appl. Math. Lett.* **2022**, *131*, 108068. [CrossRef]
22. Li, W.; Wang, F. Precorrected-FFT accelerated singular boundary method for high-frequency acoustic radiation and scattering. *Mathematics* **2022**, *10*, 238. [CrossRef]

23. Fu, Z.; Xi, Q.; Gu, Y.; Li, J.; Qu, W.; Sun, L.; Wei, X.; Wang, F.; Lin, J.; Li, W.; et al. Singular boundary method: A review and computer implementation aspects. *Eng. Anal. Boundary Elem.* **2023**, *147*, 231–266. [CrossRef]
24. Shojaei, A.; Hermann, A.; Seleson, P.; Silling, S.A.; Rabczuk, T.; Cyron, C.J. Peridynamic elastic waves in two-dimensional unbounded domains: Construction of nonlocal Dirichlet-type absorbing boundary conditions. *Comput. Methods Appl. Mech. Eng.* **2023**, *407*, 115948. [CrossRef]
25. Shojaei, A.; Galvanetto, U.; Rabczuk, T.; Jenabi, A.; Zaccariotto, M. A generalized finite difference method based on the Peridynamic differential operator for the solution of problems in bounded and unbounded domains. *Comput. Methods Appl. Mech. Eng.* **2019**, *343*, 100–126. [CrossRef]
26. Kansa, E. Multiquadrics-A scattered data approximation scheme with applications to computational fluid-dynamics-I: Surface approximations and partial derivative estimates. *Comput. Math. Appl.* **1990**, *19*, 127–145. [CrossRef]
27. Godinho, L.; Tadeu, A. Acoustic analysis of heterogeneous domains coupling the BEM with Kansa's method. *Eng. Anal. Boundary Elem.* **2012**, *36*, 1014–1026. [CrossRef]
28. Wang, F.; Chen, W.; Zhang, C.; Hua, Q. Kansa method based on the Hausdorff fractal distance for Hausdorff derivative Poisson equations. *Fractals* **2018**, *26*, 1850084. [CrossRef]
29. Popczyk, O.; Dziatkiewicz, G. Kansa method for solving initial-value problem of hyperbolic heat conduction in nonhomogeneous medium. *Int. J. Heat Mass Transf.* **2022**, *183*, 122088. [CrossRef]
30. Kumar, S.; Jiwari, R.; Mittal, R.C. Radial basis functions based meshfree schemes for the simulation of non-linear extended Fisher-Kolmogorov model. *Wave Motion* **2022**, *109*, 102863. [CrossRef]
31. Jiwari, R. Local radial basis function-finite difference based algorithms for singularly perturbed Burgers' model. *Math. Comput. Simulat.* **2022**, *198*, 106–126. [CrossRef]
32. Jiwari, R.; Kumar, S.; Mittal, R.C. Meshfree algorithms based on radial basis functions for numerical simulation and to capture shocks behavior of Burgers' type problems. *Eng. Comput.* **2019**, *36*, 1142–1168. [CrossRef]
33. Pandit, S. Local radial basis functions and scale-3 Haar wavelets operational matrices based numerical algorithms for generalized regularized long wave model. *Wave Motion* **2022**, *109*, 102846. [CrossRef]
34. Cheng, S.; Wang, F.; Li, P.-W.; Qu, W. Singular boundary method for 2D and 3D acoustic design sensitivity analysis. *Comput. Math. Appl.* **2022**, *119*, 371–386. [CrossRef]
35. Lan, L.; Cheng, S.; Sun, X.; Li, W.; Yang, C.; Wang, F. A fast singular boundary method for the acoustic design sensitivity analysis of arbitrary two-and three-dimensional structures. *Mathematics* **2022**, *10*, 3817. [CrossRef]
36. Soares, D.; Godinho, L.; Pereira, A.; Dors, C. Frequency domain analysis of acoustic wave propagation in heterogeneous media considering iterative coupling procedures between the method of fundamental solutions and Kansa's method. *Int. J. Numer. Methods Eng.* **2012**, *89*, 914–938. [CrossRef]
37. Tadeu, A.; Godinho, L.; António, J. Benchmark solution for 3D scattering from cylindrical inclusions. *J. Comput. Acoust.* **2001**, *9*, 1311–1328. [CrossRef]
38. Wei, X.; Chen, W.; Fu, Z.J. Solving inhomogeneous problems by singular boundary method. *J. Mar. Sci. Tech.* **2013**, *21*, 2.

mathematics

MDPI

Article

Lattice Boltzmann Numerical Study on Mesoscopic Seepage Characteristics of Soil–Rock Mixture Considering Size Effect

Peichen Cai, Xuesong Mao *, Ke Lou and Zhihui Yun

College of Highway, Chang'an University, Xi'an 710064, China; peichencai@chd.edu.cn (P.C.)
* Correspondence: xuesongmao@chd.edu.cn

Abstract: One of the hot topics in the study of rock and soil hydraulics is the size effect of a soil–rock mixture's (SRM) seepage characteristics. The seepage process of the SRM was simulated from the pore scale through the lattice Boltzmann method (LBM) in this paper to explore the internal influence mechanism of sample size effect on the SRM seepage characteristics. SRM samples were generated using the improved Monte Carlo method (IMCM), and through 342 simulation test conditions the influence of size feature parameters such as resolution (R), segmentation type, model feature size (S), feature length ratio (F), and soil/rock particle size feature ratio (P) was examined. The study demonstrated that as R increases, the permeability of the SRM gradually rises and tends to stabilize when R reaches 60 ppi. At the same S, the dispersion degree of model permeability obtained by the four segmentation types is in the order of center < random < equal < top. With an increase in S, the permeability (k) of the SRM gradually decreases, conforming to the dimensionless mathematical model, $k = a_0 \cdot S^{-b_0}$, and tends to stabilize at S = 80 mm. With an increase in F and an increase in S, the permeability of the SRM exhibits a linear "zonal" distribution that declines in order. When F is greater than 12, the dispersion of the permeability value distribution is especially small. With an increase in P, the permeability of the SRM decreases gradually before rising abruptly. P is crucial for the grading and structural makeup of the SRM. Overall, this paper concludes that the conditions of R = 60 ppi, center segmentation type, S = 80 mm, $F \geq 12$, and P set by demand can be used to select and generate the size of the SRM optimal representative elementary volume (REV) numerical calculation model. The SRM can serve as a general reference for test and engineering construction as a common geotechnical engineering material.

Keywords: soil–rock mixture; lattice Boltzmann method; size effect; permeability

MSC: 76M55

Citation: Cai, P.; Mao, X.; Lou, K.; Yun, Z. Lattice Boltzmann Numerical Study on Mesoscopic Seepage Characteristics of Soil–Rock Mixture Considering Size Effect. *Mathematics* **2023**, *11*, 1968. https://doi.org/10.3390/math11081968

Academic Editors: Fajie Wang and Ji Lin

Received: 22 March 2023
Revised: 18 April 2023
Accepted: 19 April 2023
Published: 21 April 2023

1. Introduction

A special type of geological material called a soil–rock mixture (SRM) exists between massive rock masses and fine-grained soil masses [1–3]. There is the existence of SRM and hydraulics involved from natural mountain landslides to artificial subgrade fill erosion [4,5]. According to the study's findings [6], the hydraulic properties of the SRM have clear structural and size effects, which undoubtedly make it more challenging to determine the permeability parameters of the SRM. Therefore, it is crucial to understand how the size of the SRM influences the characteristics of seepage.

Currently, the size effect of seepage characteristics of rock and soil masses is mainly manifested as follows: the permeability of rock and soil mass changes correspondingly with the change in sample size or research scope. Researchers have conducted many studies to address the issue of the size effect of rock and soil permeability. The size effect (including particle and model size effect) and boundary effect are the most significant influencing factors in seepage research, according to Lin et al. [7], who also made some evaluations on the size effect in subsequent research. Research on rock mass permeability characteristics and representative elementary volume (REV) analysis were conducted by Rong et al. [8]. According to the simulation results, the jointed rock mass group number and spacing are more sensitive to the effects of REV, while the crack opening has the biggest impact on its permeability characteristics. According to the analysis by Chen et al. [9] about the causes of the pore size effect in low permeability clay seepage, a microscale seepage theory model of the pore size effect was proposed. Wang [10] examined the statistical characteristics and size effect of the permeability coefficient of samples with different rock content and tested the ratio of sample side length to the maximum particle size of block stone (millimeter scale) to determine the effect of rock content on the permeability coefficient and its REV. A rock mass seepage test was performed by Liu et al. [11] by using the boundary element method after nine two-dimensional (2D) rock mass networks of various sizes were built using the Monte Carlo method. The findings demonstrated that the permeability is in a fluctuating state when the sample size is less than 12 m and that until the model size is greater than 12 m, the curve gradually tends to be stable. The REV of the rock and soil mass and the corresponding characterization size were determined in the aforementioned research from various angles and fields, but the characterization size was determined using various methods, resulting in different results. Additionally, most of the aforementioned studies concentrate on the size effect of the permeability for a single mass of soil or rock, and the study of the size effect of the permeability of the SRM with unique building materials is infrequently included. It is still unclear how many size factors affect the seepage characteristics of the SRM because of the various research scales and objectives.

The study of the numerical method for determining the permeability of rock and soil mass is currently fairly advanced, but some areas still require improvement. While it is well known that the SRM belongs to discrete particles of a discontinuous medium [12], the numerical simulation method typically adopts the continuous medium assumption.

In light of this, the lattice Boltzmann method (LBM) was created. In the field of porous media seepage, it was first proposed by McNamara et al. [13] and quickly developed due to its advantage of easy implementation and parallel computing [14–16]. Many researchers have used LBM with better success to simulate and study the mesoscopic seepage characteristics of porous media [17–20]. The premise of the SRM's permeability study is also the construction of the SRM model. At the moment, scanning electron microscopy (SEM) and random generation are the two techniques most frequently used. Additionally, by adjusting the pertinent key parameters, the random generation method can create the necessary SRM model. Its models have unique shapes that resemble the actual SRM [12]. To simulate the seepage process within the SRM, it can easily be combined with LBM.

Since different types of SRM samples are generated using the improved Monte Carlo method in this study, LBM is used to simulate the mesoscopic seepage process within the SRM from the pore scale. It is expected to reveal the internal influence mechanism of sample size effect on SRM seepage characteristics and provide a certain reference basis for further research. Finally, through 342 simulation test conditions, the influence of size characteristic parameters such as resolution (R), segmentation type, model feature size (S), feature length ratio (F), and soil/rock particle size feature ratio (P) on the seepage characteristics of SRMs is discussed in detail.

2. Materials and Methods

To verify the viability of the BGK-LBM model from flow velocity through the conventional theoretical value of the Poiseuille and the numerical value, the study first introduces the construction of the SRM model and the LBM numerical model. The influence of size effect on SRM seepage characteristics is then thoroughly discussed. The paper concludes by delving deeply into the selection of the SRM's optimal representative elementary volume model size.

2.1. Discrete Models of Soil–Rock Mixture

The overall porosity of the model, the physical characteristics of the rocks (rock content, rock particle size, etc.), and the soil/rock ratio are all strongly correlated with the physical and mechanical characteristics of the SRM [19]. Additionally, in reference to the research that was conducted by other researchers on SRM seepage characteristics [17,21,22], it has been observed that employing 2D models to simulate SRM seepage characteristics also possesses a particular representativeness. As a result, the classical Monte Carlo method [23] is used to investigate how the aforementioned variables affect the SRM's permeability. Considering this, the important parameter of the distance *dd* between particles is introduced, and the MATLAB program is put together to produce various kinds of 2D SRM models for further study. Following is the specific implementation procedure:

Step 1: Determine the SRM model with the size boundary $l \times b$, the initial porosity ($n_0 = 1.0$), particle size (the particle size here refers to the diameter, $D_m = [d_1, d_2, \ldots, d_m]$), and other important parameters.

Step 2: Using the primary parameters from Step 1, the MATLAB program's rand function is used to generate the particle distribution position (x_i, y_j) in the delivery area at random. The position is then given the particle size d_i ($i = 1, 2, \ldots, m$), meaning that a solid random particle m can be drawn from these parameters.

Step 3: The crucial parameter of the distance *dd* between particles is introduced to make it easier to adjust the position relationship between the particles. By repeating Step 2 based on this, a string of independent particles can be created. The generation of the SRM model is not complete until the porosity n satisfies Equation (1).

$$n = n_0 - \frac{\sum\limits_{i=m} \pi \left(\frac{D_m}{2}\right)^2}{l \cdot b} \tag{1}$$

Using the aforementioned technique, the porosity of the SRM is set within the range 0.36–0.51 and the particle size d_i is set to 4, 6, 10, 25, and 35 mm based on References [19,24] and combined with the focus of this study. Various types of SRM–1, SRM–2, and SRM–3 are generated at random (see Figure 1a–c), where the model's size is l = 100 mm by b = 100 mm and the black area represents soil/rock particles and the white area represents pores. Calculate the direction frequency of particle distribution for various models concurrently to reflect the change in the particle distribution rule generated randomly by the SRM, as shown in Figure 1d–f. Figure 1d–f show how the distribution of soil/rock particles vary among the three models and is disordered, which is consistent with the anisotropic properties of the SRM [12]. In conclusion, the SRM model created by the random method described in this paper has a good effect on the distribution of soil/rock particles. Based on this, it is quick and convenient to study the influence of many factors on its seepage characteristics, so other models are generated using this method in the future.

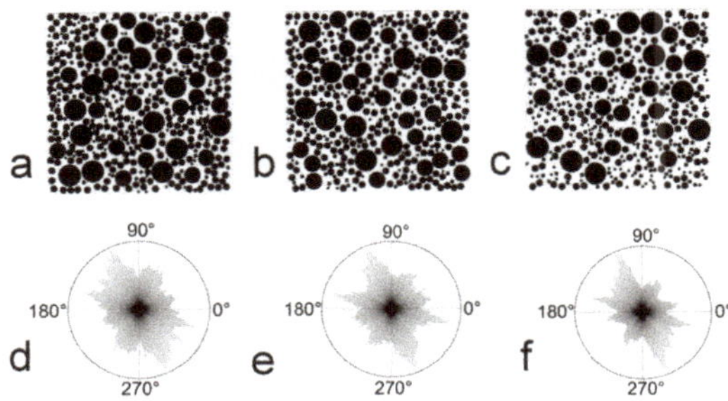

Figure 1. Soil–rock mixture model and particle distribution rose. (**a**) SRM–1, n = 0.3642; (**b**) SRM–2, n = 0.4008; (**c**) SRM–3, n = 0.5060; (**d**) SRM–1 particle rose diagram; (**e**) SRM–2 particle rose diagram; (**f**) SRM–3 particle rose diagram.

2.2. Theoretical Part

2.2.1. Lattice Boltzmann Theory and Boundary Conditions

In general, the discrete Boltzmann equation for $F(\omega,t)$ can be solved using the lattice Boltzmann method (LBM) to derive the Navier–Stokes (N–S) equation [16], which can then be used to simulate the laws of fluid flow from the mesoscale. The most commonly used BGK-LBM model [17–19], which can be represented by discrete LBE, is used in this paper:

$$F_\alpha(\boldsymbol{\omega} + \boldsymbol{e}_\alpha\delta_t, t + \delta_t) = F_\alpha(\boldsymbol{\omega}, t) - \frac{F_\alpha(\boldsymbol{\omega}, t) - F_\alpha^{\mathrm{eq}}(\boldsymbol{\omega}, t)}{\tau} \tag{2}$$

where $F(\omega,t)$ is the particle distribution function along α at lattice point ω at moment t; $\boldsymbol{e}_\alpha$ is the discrete velocity; δ_t is the discrete time; τ is the dimensionless relaxation time; $F_\alpha^{\mathrm{eq}}(\boldsymbol{\omega}, t)$ is the local equilibrium state distribution function in the discrete velocity space.

The classical D2Q9 model is used in the LBM discrete velocity model [17,18]. The model is depicted in Figure 2, and the following parameters describe its equilibrium distribution function:

$$F_\alpha^{\mathrm{eq}} = \rho\omega_\alpha[1 + \frac{\boldsymbol{e}_\alpha \cdot \boldsymbol{u}}{c_s^2} + \frac{(\boldsymbol{e}_\alpha \cdot \boldsymbol{u})^2}{2c_s^4} - \frac{\boldsymbol{u}^2}{2c_s^2}] \tag{3}$$

$$\omega_\alpha = \begin{cases} \frac{4}{9}, \ \alpha = 0 \\ \frac{1}{9}, \ \alpha = 1,2,3,4 \\ \frac{1}{36}, \ \alpha = 5,6,7,8 \end{cases} \tag{4}$$

where ρ is the density; ω_α is the weight coefficient; $\boldsymbol{u}$ is the macroscopic velocity; c_s is the sound velocities in lattice units, ${c_s}^2$ takes the value of $c^2/3$, and c is the lattice velocity.

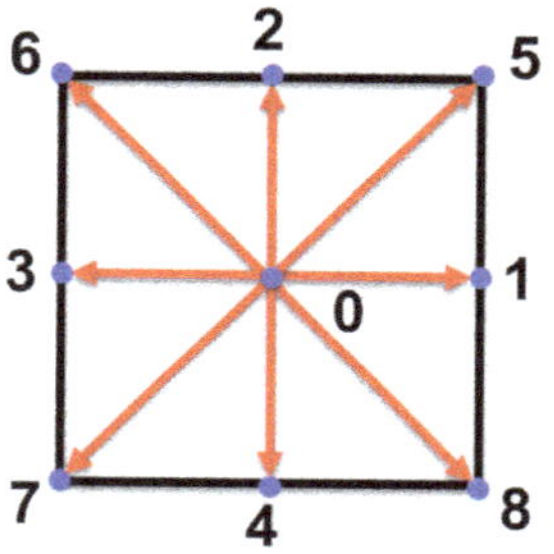

Figure 2. D2Q9 model.

The N–S equation in hydrodynamics that correspond to the fundamental LBE model was derived using the Chapman–Enskog expansion [16]. The relationship between the macroscopic density ρ, pressure p, velocity $\boldsymbol{u}$, and kinematic viscosity coefficient of fluid v and the dimensionless relaxation time τ of the model is given by:

$$\rho = \sum_{\alpha=0}^{8} F_\alpha \tag{5}$$

$$p = \rho c_s^2 \tag{6}$$

$$\boldsymbol{u} = \frac{1}{\rho}\sum_{\alpha=0}^{8} F_\alpha \boldsymbol{e}_\alpha \tag{7}$$

$$v = c_s^2(\tau - \frac{1}{2})\delta_t \tag{8}$$

The Mach number (M_a) of the fluid flow must be low enough [19,25] to guarantee that the numerical solution of the LBM converges to the N-S equation for an incompressible fluid, and it should typically satisfy $M_a < 0.1$, which is defined as:

$$M_a = \frac{u_{\max}}{c} \tag{9}$$

where $u_{\max}$ is the highest possible fluid flow rate.

In addition, LBM fluid flows along the Z-direction of the SRM in the study. The inlet and outlet pressure boundary and the fluid–solid boundary are addressed, respectively, using the Zou/He boundary [16] and standard rebound format [18]. In Figure 3, the precise settings are displayed. The model must be binarized (0–1) before boundary processing to identify and pinpoint the fluid and solid region (the region with pixel value 0 is the fluid domain, while the region with pixel value 1 is the solid domain).

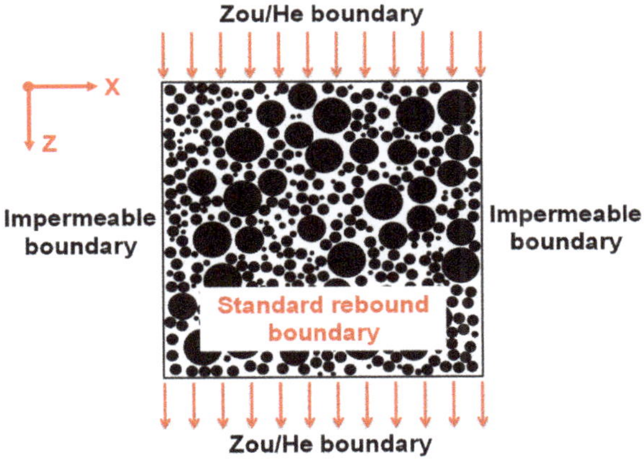

Figure 3. Model boundary conditions.

2.2.2. Conversion of Lattice Unit and Physical Unit

The LBM unit conversion part is described with reference to the method in Succi [26]. Basic parameters in the model (lattice unit) are length l, density ρ, time t, pressure p, and kinematic viscosity coefficient v. Corresponding parameters of the model (physical unit) are length l', density ρ', time t', pressure p' and kinematic viscosity coefficient is v'. In order to realize the conversion between the above two parameters, it is necessary to introduce some reference quantities [16]: reference length l_r, reference density ρ_r, and reference velocity u_r, which are defined as:

$$l_r = \frac{l'}{l} \tag{10}$$

$$\rho_r = \frac{\rho'}{\rho} \tag{11}$$

$$u_r = \frac{c'_s}{c_s} \tag{12}$$

where $c_s{}'$ and c_s are the sound velocities in physical units and lattice units, respectively.

For a specific problem, the l, ρ, c_s, and v are known. The actual physical quantity can also be obtained through the relevant equation. Therefore, ρ_r and u_r can be determined, but l' and l_r cannot. In view of this, the following relationship is added:

$$l_r u_r = \frac{v'}{v} \tag{13}$$

In addition, the conversion between t, p, and t', p' can be solved based on the following equations:

$$\frac{l_r}{u_r} = \frac{t'}{t} = t_r \tag{14}$$

$$p = \frac{p' {t_r}^2}{{l_r}^2 \rho_r} \tag{15}$$

So far, the conversion between the grid and the actual physical unit is completed [16]. Generally, the following equations are suitable: $\delta_x = \delta_y = 1$, $\delta_t = 1$, and ${c_s}^2 = 1/3$, and converted to physical units.

$$\delta'_x = \delta'_y = l_r \tag{16}$$

$$\delta'_t = \frac{l_r}{u_r} \tag{17}$$

$$c'_s = \frac{u_r}{\sqrt{3}} \tag{18}$$

2.2.3. Soil/Rock Particle Size Threshold

The soil/rock threshold can be comprehensively determined by using the following equation, which is in accordance with the research findings of Xu and Medley et al. [12,27] on the threshold of soil/rock particle size in the SRM, and combined with the particle generation and distribution characteristics of the SRM model in this paper.

$$D_{SRT} = 0.05 L_p \tag{19}$$

where D_{SRT} is the soil particle size threshold value, and L_p is the engineering feature size of the SRM, with the engineering feature size for the plane study area being equal to the arithmetic square root of the study area's dimensions. So, $L_p = \sqrt{100 \times 100} = 100$ mm.

In this study, SRM-1, SRM-2, and SRM-3 were used, and their respective rock contents were 67.69%, 61.07%, and 52.96%. Wherein the rock content C_r is determined by dividing the total area of soil and rock in the SRM model by the area of rock.

2.2.4. Size Feature Parameters

In order to study the influence of the size effect on the seepage characteristics in the SRM model, this paper sets four size feature parameters: model resolution R, model feature size S, feature length ratio F, and soil/rock particle size feature ratio P.

(1) Model resolution (R) is the term used to describe the amount of data stored in a model image, which is typically expressed as the pixel density per inch (ppi) [28]. The output quality of an image is determined by resolution. The size of the model is determined by the image resolution and image size combined. The more significant the value, the more precise the model and image are.

(2) Model feature size (S) is defined as the arithmetic square root of the product of the numerical model's length l and width b. S represents the average length of the numerical model size.

$$S = \sqrt{l \cdot b} \tag{20}$$

(3) The feature length ratio (F), which is defined as the ratio of the rock feature particle size ($D_r = \sqrt{D_{r1} D_{r2} \cdots D_{rm}}$, D_{rm} refers to the particle size of the m-th type of rock in the SRM) to S, characterizes the relationship between the rock particle size and the model size in the SRM model.

$$F = \frac{D_r}{S} \tag{21}$$

(4) The soil/rock particle size feature ratio (P), which is defined as the ratio of the soil feature particle size ($D_s = \sqrt{D_{s1} D_{s2} \cdots D_{sm}}$, D_{sm} refers to the particle size of the m-th type of soil in the SRM) to D_r, characterizes the relationship between the soil/rock particle size feature in the SRM model.

$$P = \frac{D_s}{D_r} \tag{22}$$

2.2.5. Permeability Calculation Theory

The penetrating quality of the SRM is generally described by the permeability, which can be calculated using Darcy's law (Equation (23)) and the LBM seepage field simulation. It should be noted that a laminar flow state is required for Darcy's law to hold. By examining whether the permeability of the SRM remains constant under a range of pressure differences, it can be determined whether the SRM is in a laminar flow state and can satisfy the requirements of $M_a < 0.1$ and laminar flow when the pressure difference Δp is less than 0.01 m.u.·l.u.$^{-1}$·t.s.$^{-2}$ (3.67×10^{-2} Pa).

$$k = \frac{\mu \overline{u}}{\Delta p} = \frac{\rho \upsilon \overline{u} l}{\Delta p} \tag{23}$$

where k is the permeability; μ is the dynamic viscosity coefficient of the fluid; $\overline{u}$ is the average flow velocity; Δp is the seepage pressure difference; l is the length of seepage path.

The LBM calculation stops when the fluid reaches a stable state. The criterion for determining the stable state is that the standard deviation of the kinetic energy in the entire calculation domain within a certain number of time steps is less than 0.01% of the average kinetic energy [19]. Following the convergence of the calculation, Darcy's law can be used to determine the model's permeability.

2.3. Model Size Segmentation

A number of small size model samples are taken directly from the large size samples to ensure consistency in sampling. In addition, taking into account the possibility of contingency in the selection of the SRM model, this paper uses four segmentation types, namely random, center, top, and equal segmentation, to segment the SRM model [9], as shown in Figure 4. Table 1 contains a list of the specific segmentation scheme for the various SRM models used in the research that follows. The segmented SRM sample's seepage field is then calculated to investigate the influence of sample size on the permeability of the SRM. The dispersion of permeability under various test conditions is reflected in this paper using the coefficient of variation (c_v). The c_v is equal to the ratio of the standard deviation to the average value, which better illustrates the dispersion of the data compared to the standard deviation.

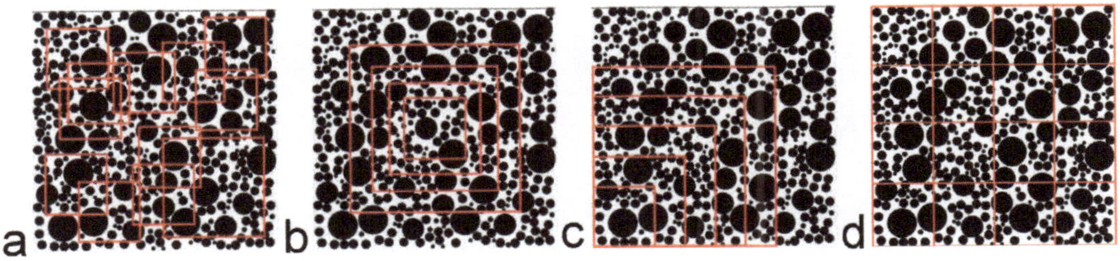

Figure 4. Segmentation type of model size. (**a**) random; (**b**) center, (**c**) top; (**d**) equal.

Table 1. Size segmentation scheme of different SRM models.

Projects	Model	Segmentation Type	Basic Information	S (mm)	Number of Test Conditions
Resolution	SRM–1/SRM–2/SRM–3	–	r–10, r–20, r–30, r–40, r–50 r–60, r–70, r–80, r–90, r–100	100	30
Segmentation type	SRM–1/SRM–2/SRM–3	Random/Center/Top/Equal	sj–25/jz–25/dd–25/df–25 sj–50/jz–50/dd–50/df–50 sj–75/jz–75/dd–75/df–75 sj–100/jz–100/dd–100/df–100	25 50 75 100	225
Model feature size	SRM–1/SRM–2/SRM–3	Center	jz–10, jz–20, jz–30, jz–40, jz–50, jz–60, jz–70, jz–80, jz–90, jz–100	10, 20, 30, 40, 50, 60, 70, 80, 90, 100	30
Feature length ratio	SRM–1/SRM–2/SRM–3 SRM–add	Center	F = 5, 6, 7, 8, 9, 10, 11, 12, 13, 14, 15, 16, 17, 18, 19, 20	50, 80, 100	48
Soil/rock particle size feature ratio	SRM–1/SRM–2/SRM–3 SRM–add	Center	P = 0.1, 0.2, 0.3, 0.4, 0.5, 0.6, 0.7, 0.8, 0.9	80	9

3. Results

3.1. Numerical Model Validation

The self-programmed LBM program is validated using the classical Poiseuille flow [17,18], and the validation computational model area is chosen as a grid of 50 × 25 mm (500 × 250 l.u.) with the same boundary treatment as described in Section 2.2.1. Table 2 displays the specific computational parameters, where l and b are the length and width of the computational model, and Δp is the pressure difference between the inlet and outlet of the fluid.

Table 2. Parameters of validation examples.

l (mm)	b (mm)	t (s)	μ (Pa·s)	ρ (kg·m^{-3})	T (°C)	Δp (Pa)
50	25	1.65×10^{-3}	1.01×10^{-3}	1000	20.0	3.67×10^{-2}

The surface cloud of the velocity field calculated by the Poiseuille flow model using the LBM program is shown in Figure 5, and it is clear that the velocity decreases gradually from the middle to the two ends. The comparison results of the velocity of each grid point in the middle cross–section with the Poiseuille flow analytical value are shown in Figure 6. The highest error is merely 4.33%, demonstrating the precision of the self-programmed technique.

Figure 5. Cloud chart of Poiseuille flow velocity field.

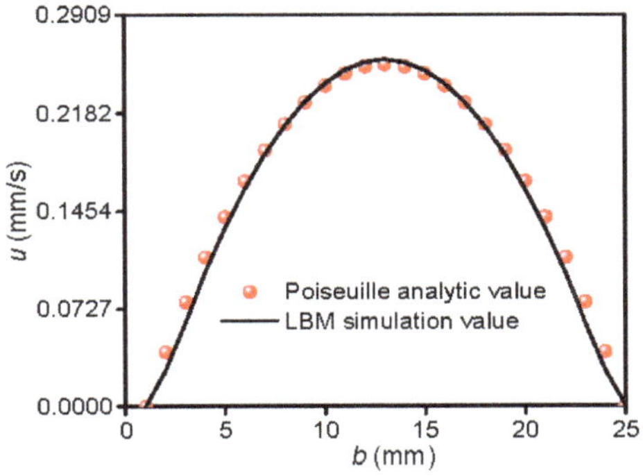

Figure 6. Comparison of Poiseuille flow analytical value and LBM simulation value.

3.2. Influence of Size Effect on Permeability

The seepage direction is set to follow the Z-direction of the SRM, and the flow is set to drive the model at a constant temperature (T = 20 °C) and pressure difference ($\Delta p = 3.67 \times 10^{-2}$ Pa) to make the seepage simulation results more realistic. The specific boundary conditions used in the calculation model are shown in Figure 3. The additional pertinent settings and calculation criteria for the validation example given above apply here as well (Table 2). Additionally, refer to Section 2.3 and choose the typical dimensions of models between 10 and 100 mm (grid unit: 100–1000 l.u.) to simulate various SRM models. There are 342 different simulation test conditions in total (Table 1).

3.2.1. Resolution R

Model resolution significantly affects the efficacy and accuracy of the results of the permeability calculation in the LBM seepage field simulation [28,29]. SRM–1, SRM–2, and SRM–3 models created in Section 2.1 are imported into LBM for calculation to examine the influence of model resolution on permeability. The permeability of SRM samples with various resolutions is simulated under the same boundary conditions and pressure difference, with a total of 30 simulation test conditions (Table 1). The simulation results are displayed in Figure 7.

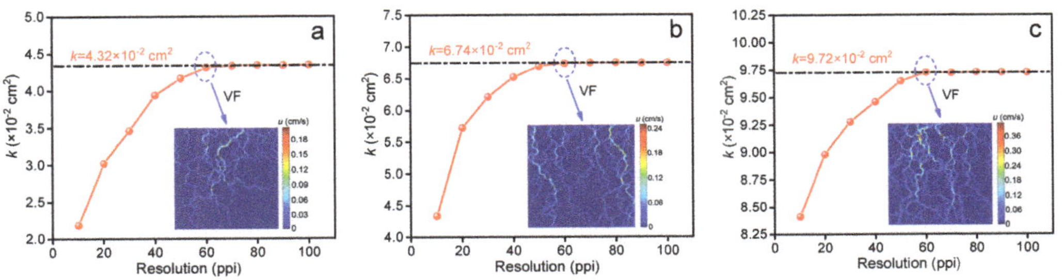

Figure 7. Relationship between resolution and permeability. (**a**) SRM−1; (**b**) SRM−2; (**c**) SRM−3.

The permeability of the three models exhibits a trend in gradual improvement with the resolution and tends to be stable when the resolution reaches 60 ppi, as can be seen in Figure 7. Permeability dispersion degree c_v values at this time are 0.00236, 0.00061, and 0.00028, respectively. Additionally, it is discovered that the porosity and rock content of the model has little bearing on the relationship between resolution and permeability (SRM–1, n = 0.3642, C_r = 67.69%; SRM–2, n = 0.4008, C_r = 61.07%; SRM–3, n = 0.5060, C_r = 52.96%) by comparing the velocity field cloud map (velocity field, VF) of the three models with a resolution of 60 ppi. The velocity field distribution in the models with various porosity and rock content exhibits a steady–state effect when the model resolution is 60 ppi. To guarantee the precision and effectiveness of the LBM permeability calculation, the resolution of the model sample is set to 60 ppi in the subsequent simulation reported in this paper.

3.2.2. Segmentation Type

The SRM models are created with feature sizes $S = 25, 50, 75$, and 100 mm using the four segmentation types described in Section 2.3 (random, center, top, and equal segmentation), with a total of 225 simulation test conditions (Table 1). The particular simulation test conditions of the model for each S are as follows. The number of random segmentation modes is 16, 8, 4, and 1. The number of center segmentation modes is 1, 1, 1, and 1. The number of top segmentation modes is 4, 4, 4, and 1. The number of equal segmentation modes is 16, 8, 4, and 1. Among them, "number" refers to obtaining simulated test models of S based on a certain segmentation type in SRM–1 for simulation, and selecting one of them as a typical representative model for display, as shown in Figure 8. Figures 9 and 10 show the distribution of the typical seepage velocity field under various segmentation types using SRM–1 as an example (the segmentation type is the same when the model feature size $S = 100$ mm, so it is not shown), and Figure 10 uses the average permeability value under the same S to show the dispersion degree under various segmentation types.

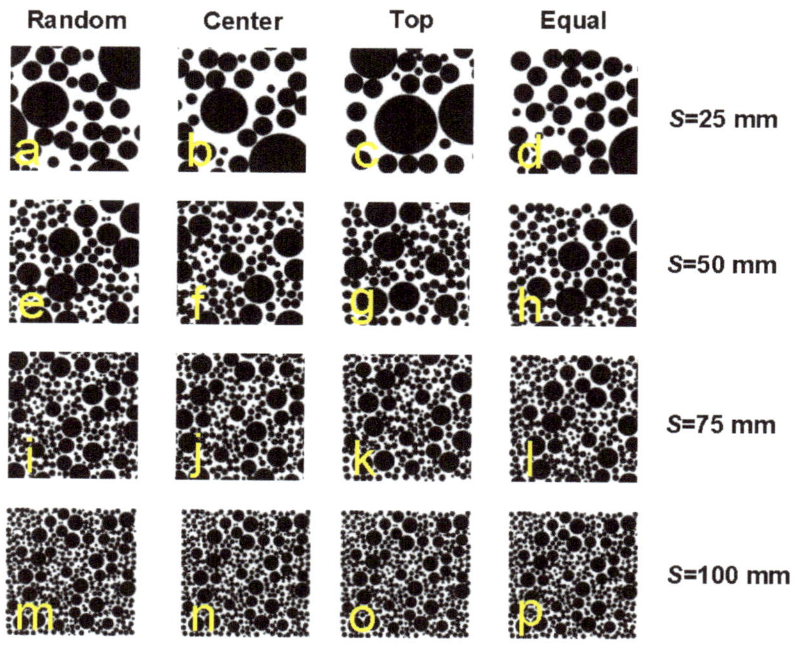

Figure 8. Typical model display under different simulation testing conditions in SRM–1. (**a–d**) $S = 25$ mm, (**e–h**) $S = 50$ mm, (**i–l**) $S = 75$ mm, (**m–p**) $S = 100$ mm; segmentation types are random, center, top, and equal.

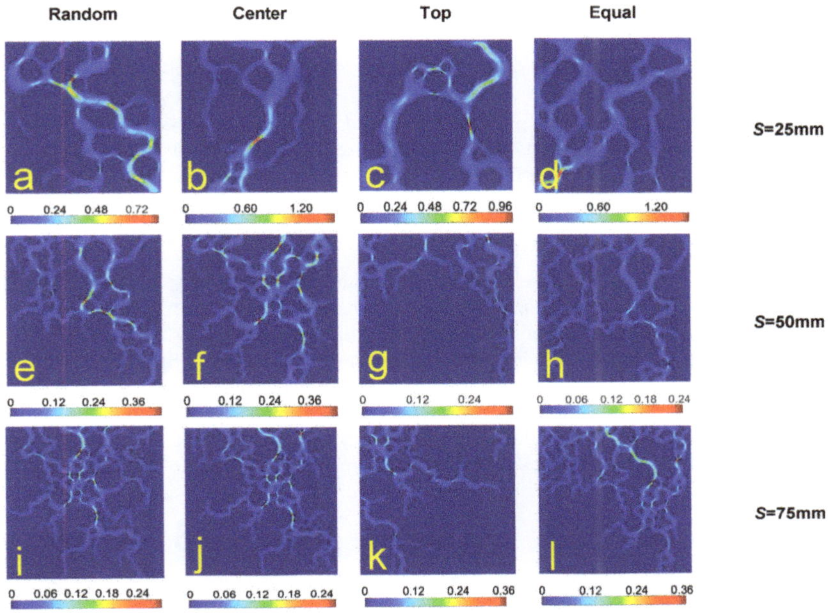

Figure 9. Seepage field velocity cloud map of different segmentation types in SRM–1 (unit: cm/s). (**a–d**) S = 25 mm, (**e–h**) S = 50 mm, (**i–l**) S = 75 mm; segmentation types are random, center, top, and equal.

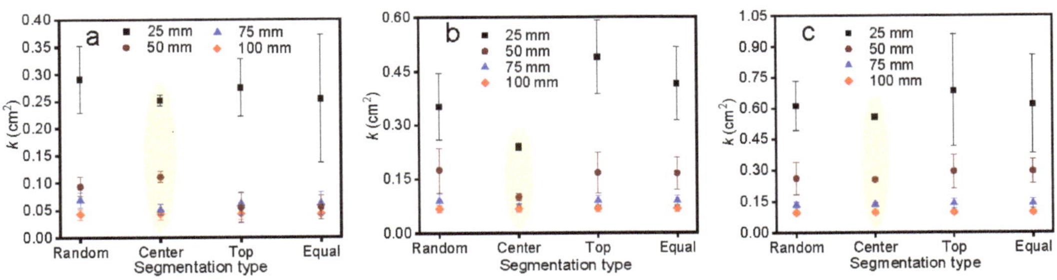

Figure 10. Relationship between segmentation types and average permeability. (**a**) SRM–1; (**b**) SRM–2; (**c**) SRM–3.

Figure 9 shows that the segmentation type has a greater impact on the permeability of the SRM with the same S. The random segmentation type and the center segmentation type have a more uniform seepage velocity field distribution than the top segmentation type and the equal segmentation type. The reason for this is that the models obtained by the top and equal segmentation type are mostly soil/rock particles in the SRM–1 model's corner area. The probability of disconnected channels appearing in the corresponding segmentation model is higher, which also leads to a large dispersion of the permeability of the model intercepted by the top segmentation and equal segmentation types. This can also be indicated by the flow velocity cloud map in Figure 9.

Furthermore, the dispersion degree of model permeability obtained by the four segmentation types under the same S is in order: center < random < equal < top (using SRM–1, S = 50 mm as an example, $c_{\text{v-R}} = 0.1684$, $c_{\text{v-C}} = 0$, $c_{\text{v-T}} = 0.4365$, and $c_{\text{v-E}} = 0.3729$), which is consistent with other relevant research conclusions [10]. Although the random segmentation type has good stability under certain conditions and is used by many researchers, it inevitably has great uncertainty and requires a large number of model data as support to produce the most stable and accurate permeability results. Additionally, when compared to the central segmentation type, it requires a significant amount of time and computing memory. According to Figures 9 and 10, the model's permeability exhibits a high degree of anisotropism as the model feature size increases under the same segmentation type, with the permeability results obtained by the top and equal segmentation types being particularly significant.

3.2.3. Model Feature Size *S*

To investigate the influence of the model's feature size S on the seepage characteristics of the SRM model, this section synthesizes the preceding research and obtains the model with the resolution $R = 60$ ppi, $S = 10, 20, 30, 40, 50, 60, 70, 80, 90$, and 100 mm, respectively, by using the center segmentation type for the SRM–1, SRM–2, and SRM–3 models. Then, numerical simulation tests were conducted on the seepage field combined with LBM, with a total of 30 simulation test conditions (Table 1). Figures 11 and 12 depict the simulated seepage velocity field and streamline distribution (limited to space, shown with SRM–1 as an example). Simultaneously, numerical fitting is used to examine the relationship between the permeability and the model feature size S, and the results are shown in Figure 13.

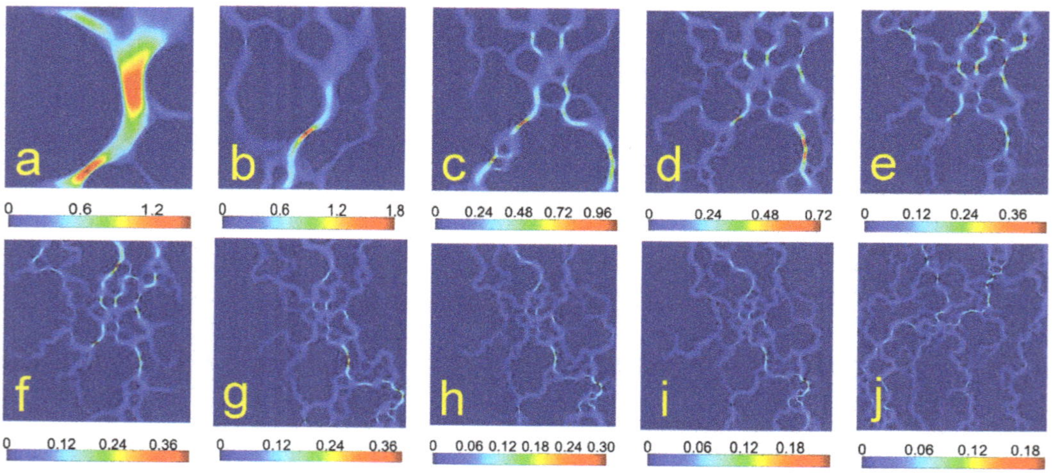

Figure 11. Seepage field velocity cloud map for different model feature sizes in SRM–1 (unit: cm/s). (**a**–**j**) $S = 10, 20, 30, 40, 50, 60, 70, 80, 90, 100$ mm.

Figure 11 shows that the seepage velocity generally decreases as the feature size of the model increases. With increasing feature size of the model, the distribution characteristics of the seepage fluid in the channel gradually change from scattered distribution of a single channel to interactive distribution of multiple channels, and the average seepage velocity of the models with different feature sizes is $u_{10} = 0.485$ cm/s, $u_{20} = 0.129$ cm/s, $u_{30} = 0.092$ cm/s, $u_{40} = 0.064$ cm/s, $u_{50} = 0.040$ cm/s, $u_{60} = 0.030$ cm/s, $u_{70} = 0.022$ cm/s, $u_{80} = 0.018$ cm/s, $u_{90} = 0.016$ cm/s, and $u_{100} = 0.015$ cm/s. According to the streamline distribution diagram (Figure 12), the distribution of streamlines in the model pores first appears sparse, thick, and wide, and then the streamline gradually becomes dense and narrow as the model's feature size increases. The reason for this is that the model's feature size is small, the number of soil and rock particles in the model area is small, and the distribution is single, which cannot represent the overall model's seepage characteristics. Simultaneously, when the velocity field and streamline distribution images of different feature sizes in SRM–1, SRM–2, and SRM–3 are combined, it can be seen that as the sample feature size *S* increases, the difference between the seepage velocity field and streamline distribution gradually decreases, indicating a relatively similar seepage trend. This demonstrates that selecting an appropriate model feature size has a significant impact on seepage characteristics. On the one hand, if the model feature size is too small, it is unable to represent the model's basic characteristics. On the other hand, if the model feature size is too large, it results in resource abuse. As a result, it is critical to investigate the appropriate model feature size to characterize the model's seepage characteristics.

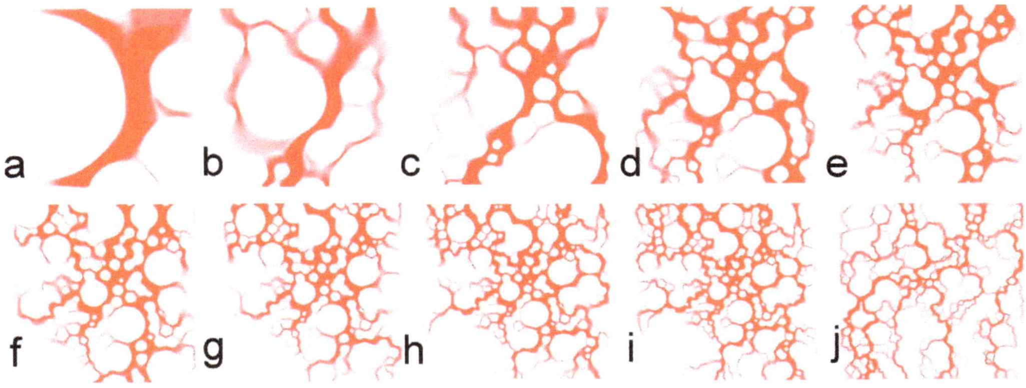

Figure 12. Streamline distribution of the velocity field for different model feature sizes in SRM–1. (**a**–**j**): S = 10, 20, 30, 40, 50, 60, 70, 80, 90, 100 mm.

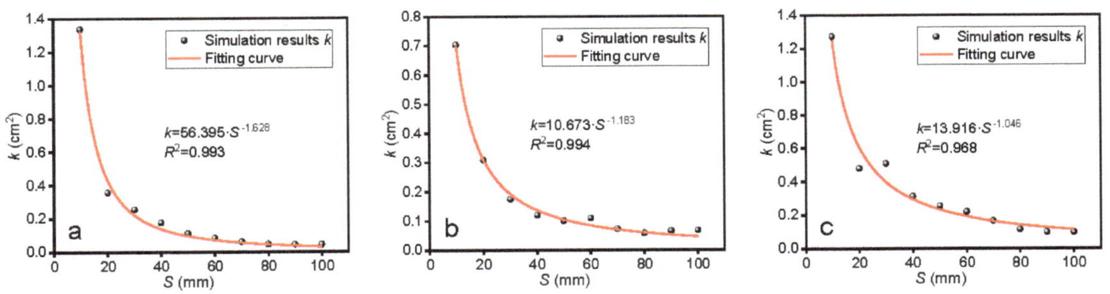

Figure 13. Relationship between model feature size and permeability. (**a**) SRM–1; (**b**) SRM–2; (**c**) SRM–3.

Additionally, the permeability of SRM models with various structures gradually decreases with an increase in the feature size of the model, as shown by the fitting curve in Figure 13. In addition, it satisfies the dimensionless mathematical model $k = a_0 \cdot S^{-b_0}$ (where a_0 and b_0 are numerical fitting parameters), and when S = 80 mm, it has a tendency to be nearly stable. With the increase of S (S = 80, 90, 100 mm), the degree of dispersion c_v for the permeability of the three models (SRM–1, SRM–2 and SRM–3) is only $c_{v\text{-}1}$ = 0.02281, $c_{v\text{-}2}$ = 0.06631, and $c_{v\text{-}3}$ = 0.07375. In conclusion, S = 80 mm can be regarded as the model for the representative numerical calculation unit of the SRM described in this paper.

3.2.4. Feature Length Ratio *F*

Based on the above study, various SRM models (F = 5–20) are created using the method in Section 2.1 with the model porosity set to n = 0.50 to ensure that it has no effect on the results. This is used to study the influence of feature length ratio (F) on the permeability of SRMs in more detail (many studies show that porosity has a significant impact on permeability). For further information on the specific scheme, see Table 1. A total of 48 simulation test conditions are used to model the permeability of SRM samples under various F under the same boundary conditions and pressure differential. Figure 14 displays the simulation outcomes.

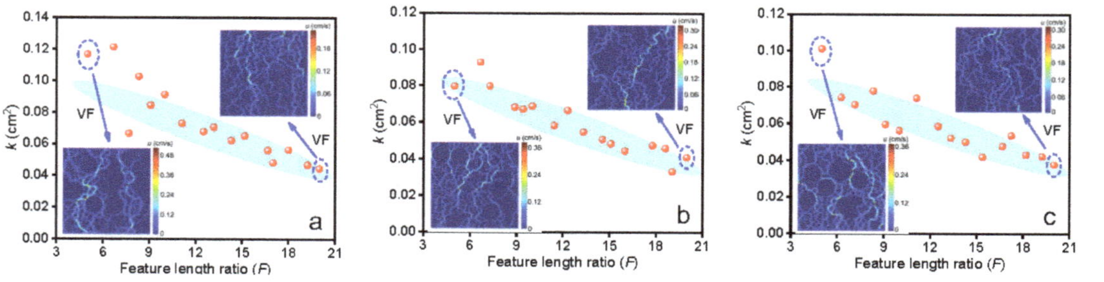

Figure 14. Relationship between feature length ratio and permeability. (**a**) S = 50 mm; (**b**) S = 80 mm; (**c**) S = 100 mm.

Figure 14 shows that the permeability of the SRM is roughly distributed along a linear "zonal" (blue area) with decreasing feature length ratio F and that as feature size S of the model increases, the dispersion of the permeability numerical distribution decreases. This finding is in line with the research findings in Section 3.2.3 regarding the relationship between feature size and permeability. In addition, it can be seen that the seepage channels of the F = 5 model are relatively wide but few in number, whereas the seepage channels of the F = 20 model are relatively narrow but numerous by comparing the seepage field velocity images of F = 5 and F = 20 under various model feature sizes. This is due to the fact that, given a constant feature size for the model, a larger feature length ratio results in a smaller maximum particle size for the rock and a smaller corresponding pore channel, which ultimately reduces the model's permeability. In addition, it is important to take into account that the permeability distribution dispersion of the model with a low feature length ratio is more pronounced than that of the model with a high feature length ratio, and the dispersion is significantly reduced when $F \geq 12$, which also suggests that the feature length ratio should not be too small when studying the permeability of the SRM model. Comprehensive comparison with other research or specific conclusions is more consistent [9,30]. The *Standard for Soil Test Methods* (GB/T 50123–2019) [30] states that when the sample size is 100 mm, the ratio of sample size to maximum particle size must be at least 10. The *American Society for Testing and Materials Standard Yearbook* [9] states that the diameter of the sample container must be 8–12 times the maximum particle size of the sample. Briefly describing the findings of relevant research, most of the time the sample size to particle size ratio is not less than 5 [31–33].

3.2.5. Soil/Rock Particle Size Feature Ratio *P*

The internal pore structure of the SRM is determined by its particle size distribution, which also affects its permeability. The soil/rock particle size feature ratio (P) can represent the composition of soil/rock particle size in the model sample of the SRM. Based on the previously mentioned study, this section utilizes samples of the SRM with various particle size feature ratios (P = 0.10–0.90) of S = 80 mm, R = 60 ppi, and n = 0.50 to explore the influence of P on the seepage characteristics of the SRM in more depth, with a total of nine simulation test conditions (Table 1). The simulation outcomes are displayed in Figures 15 and 16.

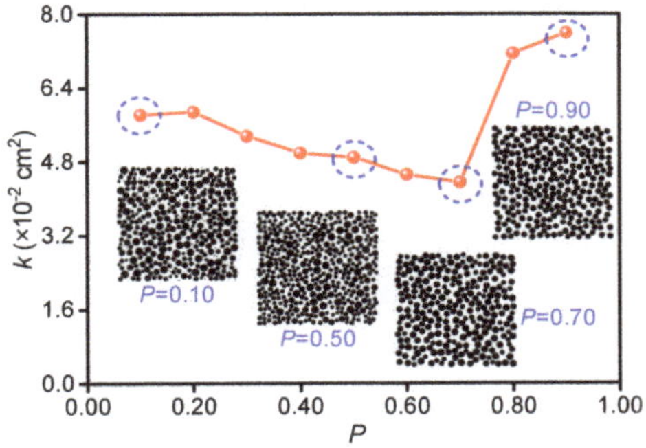

Figure 15. Relationship between soil/rock particle size feature ratio and permeability.

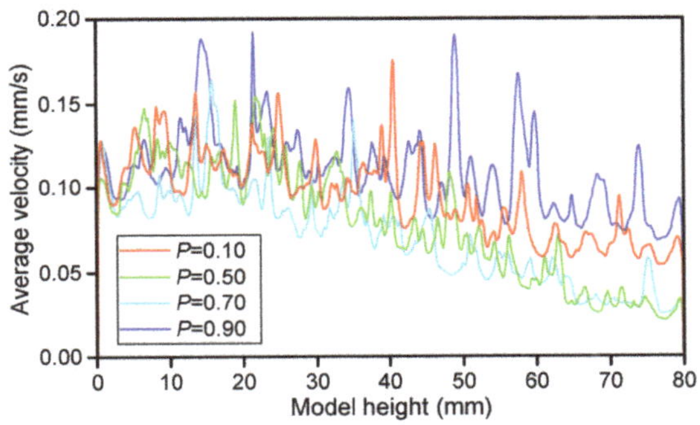

Figure 16. Seepage velocity distribution of different soil/rock particle size feature ratio models.

Figure 15 illustrates how significantly the feature ratio of soil/rock particle size affects the seepage characteristics of the SRM. Overall, the permeability of the SRM shows a characteristic of first slowly decreasing and then sharply increased with the increase in P. When compared to the model samples at the critical soil/rock particle size feature ratio ($P = 0.10$, $P = 0.20$, $P = 0.70$, and $P = 0.90$), it can be seen that as P increases, the difference in soil/rock particle size in the model sample decreases, changing the sample's pore structure from a multilevel distribution to almost a single–graded sample. At $P > 0.70$, the soil/rock particle size is nearly the same, almost becoming "rock", forming a skeleton structure together, so its permeability increases suddenly.

It can also be seen that the average seepage velocity of the model sample is typically higher when $P = 0.90$, while the average seepage velocity of the model sample is the lowest when $P = 0.70$, which corresponds to the permeability value shown in Figure 15. This is in comparison to the average velocity distribution curve of the seepage field in Figure 16. The average seepage velocity curve's shape also changes from multiple wave peaks and complex bending to a single wave peak and smooth characteristics with an increase in P value, which is closely related to the particle size distribution of soil and rock and also corresponds to the evolution characteristics. These findings come from examining the shapes of each average seepage velocity curve under various particle size feature ratios of soil and rock.

Compared with other researchers, it can be seen that References [22,34,35] focus on the influence of rock particle size on the SRM's simulated permeability, but had not considered the influence of the mutual relationship between soil and rock particle size on the SRM's simulated permeability. This study demonstrated that SRM's reproduced permeability is significantly influenced by the soil/rock particle size feature ratio (Figure 15). Additionally, Reference [34] showed that the presence of a critical value of rock content causes an unexpected shift in the pattern of the influence of rock particle size on permeability. The influence of particle size on permeability was clearly linked to rock content in the conclusion of Reference [35]. Compared with Reference [34], this study found that the soil/rock particle size feature ratio extent similarly has a particular threshold, which can cause an unforeseen increase in simulated permeability, and the two had explicit similarities in this regard.

3.3. Discussion

The detailed influences of resolution, segmentation type, model feature size, feature length ratio, and soil/rock particle size feature ratio on the seepage characteristics of SRMs were explored in Section 3.2 using 342 simulation test conditions. Differentiated and other specialists' preliminary focuses on the permeability of SRMs, it might be seen in References [12,36–38] that the permeability coefficient of SRMs obtained from the experiment has a large span (permeability and permeability coefficient can be converted from each other), ranging from 10^{-6} to 2.0 cm/s. This also indicates that the SRM's permeability is not uniform and varies depending on factors such as the type of soil, particle size, inside pore structure, experimental model size, etc. The pattern of permeability coefficient changes with the increase in rock content described in Reference [36] supports the reliability of the mimicked estimation of penetrability noted in this paper. In any case, it is important to note that the permeability values derived from this paper's mathematical calculations are significantly higher than those derived from experiments in References [22,36–38]. The reason is that the SRM used in the experiment has soil and rock particles that are mostly attached, whereas the SRM made by the mathematical model has sandy particles that do not have a bond, so the permeability is larger. Compared with the reenactment computation effects of SRM's penetrability described in Reference [34], it is consistent with the calculation data reported in this paper.

In addition, this section also provides an extensive discussion on the selection of the optimal unit volume model size of SRMs based on the findings of the research. Bear [39] made the initial suggestion for the representative elementary volume (REV). The REV scale, which represents the critical scale for the change from unstable to stable mechanical properties of rock and soil mass, is an objective reflection of the size effect of the mechanical properties of the rock and soil mass [40]. Larger-particle rock components and small soil particles comprise the SRM. Figure 16 of the research area of the research group illustrates how the internal structure of the model changes with continuous changes in the model's size [12]. Figure 17 shows that the REV–I region consists of single or partial block stones; the REV–II region has a certain amount of block stones and uses fine-grained soil as the filling material; the REV-III region contains a variety of block stones with different particle sizes in addition to the block stones that cannot be ignored in comparison to the REV–II region, which together forms a multilevel SRM. Additionally, the authors of References [41,42] used homogenization to create multiscale LBM models that successfully mimicked single–phase and two–phase flow simultaneously in pores of completely different length scales. This could be also applied to an SRM where the particle sizes and pores vary greatly. This demonstrates that the test and calculation results can only accurately reflect the pertinent properties of the SRM when the size range of the SRM studied is greater than or equal to its REV. The balance between numerical calculation accuracy and calculation efficiency should also be thoroughly taken into consideration on this basis for the numerical simulation of the size effect on SRM seepage characteristics.

Based on the aforementioned research, Section 3.2.1 first simulates 30 test conditions for SRM–1, SRM–2, and SRM–3 with various resolutions R = 0–100 ppi. It demonstrates that when the resolution reaches 60 ppi, c_v is 0.00236, 0.00061, and 0.00028, respectively, and R = 60 ppi can be thought of as the optimal resolution. Secondly, in Section 3.2.2, 225 kinds of seepage test simulations were carried out for the SRM model under the four segmentation types, and it was found that the model permeability obtained by the center segmentation type under the same model feature size was the least discrete, which was also consistent with other relevant research conclusions [10]. Thirdly, center segmentation type was used in Section 3.2.3 to create a model with resolutions of R = 60 ppi and S = 100 mm. Dimensionless $k = a_0 \cdot S^{-b_0}$ mathematical model fitting was used to analyze the results of 30 seepage test conditions. When S = 80 mm, it was discovered that the SRM's permeability tended to be almost stable. At this time, c_v was only $c_{v\text{-}1}$ = 0.02281, $c_{v\text{-}2}$ = 0.06631, and $c_{v\text{-}3}$ = 0.07375. Then, using n = 0.50 and F = 5, Section 3.2.4 simulates 48 seepage test conditions for various SRM models. It demonstrates that as F increases, the distribution of the SRM's permeability presents a decreasing "zonal" distribution, and that the dispersion of the permeability value distribution is significantly reduced when $F \geq 12$. The SRM samples with S = 80 mm, R = 60 ppi, n = 0.50, and P = 0.10–0.90 were studied under 10 different penetration test conditions in Section 3.2.5, showing that P plays a significant and decisive role in the grading and structural composition of the SRM, but that there is no clear distinction between good and bad for the selection of size effect.

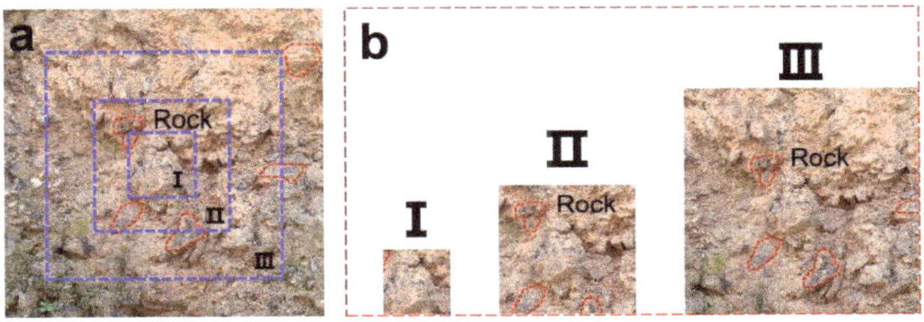

Figure 17. Relationship between soil–rock mixture structure and REV size. (**a**) Overall model of the soil–rock mixture; (**b**) REV model of the soil–rock mixture with different sizes.

As a result, the following guidelines can be used to determine the optimal size for the SRM's REV numerical calculation model reported in this paper: the center segmentation type is used, the model is R = 60 ppi, S = 80 mm, $F \geq 12$, and P determined by specific needs.

4. Conclusions

Based on the lattice Boltzmann method (LBM), the seepage process for the soil–rock mixture (SRM) is simulated from the pore scale. The following conclusions are drawn after a detailed discussion of the effects of size feature parameters on the seepage characteristics of SRMs under 342 simulation test conditions, including resolution (R), segmentation type, model feature size (S), feature length ratio (F), and soil/rock particle size feature ratio (P); the following conclusions are obtained:

(1) As R increases, the permeability of the SRM gradually rises and tends to stabilize when R reaches 60 ppi. The model's porosity and rock content also have only a minor impact on the correlation between resolution and permeability.

(2) The four segmentation types–center segmentation, random segmentation, equal segmentation, and top segmentation–are in order of decreasing dispersion in the permeability of the model obtained under the same S. The permeability of the model increases with S when using the same segmentation type, exhibiting a high degree of mutual anisotropy. The results for permeability obtained using the top and equal segmentation types are particularly noteworthy.

(3) The permeability of the SRM model decreases gradually as S increases, satisfying the dimensionless mathematical model $k = a_0 \cdot S^{-b_0}$ and tending to be stable at S = 80 mm. The permeability of the SRM increases in a linear "zonal" distribution as F increases, and as S increases, the dispersion in the permeability value distribution decreases, particularly when $F \geq 12$. The permeability of the SRM decreases gradually and then sharply as P increases, and it is important in the grading and structural composition of the SRM.

(4) In the current study, the conditions of $R = 60$ ppi, center segmentation type, $S = 80$ mm, $F \geq 12$, and P determined by specific need can be used to select and generate the optimal REV numerical calculation model size of the SRM.

Author Contributions: P.C.: analysis, writing—original draft, writing—review and editing; X.M.: supervision, resources, conventionalization, funding acquisition, writing—review and editing; K.L.: writing—review and editing, data curation; Z.Y.: analysis, data curation. All authors have read and agreed to the published version of the manuscript.

Funding: This research was funded by the National Natural Science Foundation of China (NSFC, Fund number: 51878064), the Grant Recipient is Xuesong Mao.

Data Availability Statement: The data that support the findings of this study are available upon request.

Acknowledgments: The authors gratefully acknowledge the support provided by the National Natural Science Foundation of China, fund number 51878064.

Conflicts of Interest: The authors had received research funding from National Natural Science Foundation of China.

References

1. Tao, M.; Ren, Q.; Bian, H.; Cao, M.; Jia, Y. Mechanical Properties of Soil-Rock Mixture Filling in Fault Zone Based on Mesostructure. *Comput. Model. Eng. Sci.* **2022**, *132*, 681–705. [CrossRef]
2. Gao, W.-W.; Gao, W.; Hu, R.-L.; Xu, P.-F.; Xia, J.-G. Microtremor survey and stability analysis of a soil-rock mixture landslide: A case study in Baidian town, China. *Landslides* **2018**, *15*, 1951–1961. [CrossRef]
3. Liu, L.; Mao, X.; Xiao, Y.; Wang, T.; Nie, M. Influence of water and rock particle contents on the shear behaviour of a SRM. *Transp. Saf. Environ.* **2020**, *2*, 29–43. [CrossRef]
4. Iqbal, J.; Thomasson, J.A.; Jenkins, J.N.; Owens, P.R.; Whisler, F.D. Spatial Variability Analysis of Soil Physical Properties of Alluvial Soils. *Soil. Sci. Soc. Am. J.* **2005**, *69*, 1338–1350. [CrossRef]
5. Wang, Y.; Mao, X.; Wu, Q.; Dai, Z. Study on the Influence of Seepage Conditions with Different Rainfall Intensities on the Structural Evolution of Soil-Rock Mixture Filler. *Geofluids* **2022**, *2022*, 7694663. [CrossRef]
6. Zhou, Y.; Sheng, G.; Qiao, S.; Zhou, L.; Cai, J.; Xu, H. A determination method for the shear strength of soil-rock mixture considering the size effect and its application. *Front. Mater.* **2022**, *9*, 1075310. [CrossRef]
7. Ke, L.; Takahashi, A. Strength reduction of cohesionless soil due to internal erosion induced by one-dimensional upward seepage flow. *Soils Found.* **2012**, *52*, 698–711. [CrossRef]
8. Rong, G.; Zhou, C.B.; Wang, E.Z. Preliminary study on permeability tensor calcution of fractured rock mass and its representative elementary volume. *J. Rock Mech. Eng.* **2007**, *26*, 740–746.
9. Chen, J.; Fang, Y.; Gu, R.; Shu, H.; Ba, L.; Li, W. Study on pore size effect of low permeability clay seepage. *Arab. J. Geosci.* **2019**, *12*, 238. [CrossRef]
10. Wang, L. Two-Dimensional Numerical Experiment Based on the Permeability of Soil-Rock Mixture Microstructure and Its Size Effect. Master's Thesis, China Three Gorges University, Sanxia, China, 2020. [CrossRef]
11. Liu, Q.; Li, H.; Zhang, Y.B. Scale effect in permeability characteristics of rock mass using boundary element method. *J. Univ. Jinan* **2015**, *29*, 210–215. [CrossRef]
12. Xu, W.J. Study on Meso-Structural Mechanics of Soil-Rock Mixture and Its Slope Stability. Ph.D. Thesis, Institute of Geology and Geophysics, Chinese Academy of Sciences, Beijing, China, 2008. Available online: http://ir.iggcas.ac.cn/handle/132A11/11061 (accessed on 5 January 2023).
13. McNamara, G.R.; Zanetti, G. Use of the Boltzmann Equation to Simulate Lattice-Gas Automata. *Phys. Rev. Lett.* **1988**, *61*, 2332–2335. [CrossRef] [PubMed]
14. Zhou, D.; Tan, Z. On the Application of the Lattice Boltzmann Method to Predict Soil Meso Seepage Characteristics. *Fluid. Dyn. Mater. Process.* **2020**, *16*, 903–917. [CrossRef]
15. Kim, P.; Kim, Y.G.; Paek, C.-H.; Ma, J. Lattice Boltzmann method for consolidation analysis of saturated clay. *J. Ocean. Eng. Sci.* **2019**, *4*, 193–202. [CrossRef]
16. He, Y.L.; Wang, Y.; Li, Q. *Lattice Boltzmann Method: Theory and Application*; Science Press: Beijing, China, 2009; Available online: https://onlinetoolsland.com/books/3352346 (accessed on 9 April 2023).
17. Li, J.J.; Jin, L.; Chen, T. Numerical Simulation of Mesoscopic Seepage Field of Soil-rock Mixture Based on Lattice Boltzmann Method. *Sci. Technol. Eng.* **2019**, *19*, 235–241.
18. Cai, P.C.; Que, Y.; Jiang, Z.L.; Yang, P.F. Lattice Boltzmann meso-seepage research of reconstructed soil based on the quartet structure generation set. *Hydrogeol. Eng. Geol.* **2022**, *49*, 33–42. [CrossRef]
19. Jin, L.; Zeng, Y.W.; Cheng, T.; Li, J.J. Seepage characteristics of soil-rock mixture based on lattice Boltzmann method. *Chin. J. Geotech. Eng.* **2022**, *44*, 669–677. [CrossRef]

20. Gao, J.; Xing, H.; Tian, Z.; Muhlhaus, H. Lattice Boltzmann modeling and evaluation of fluid flow in heterogeneous porous media involving multiple matrix constituents. *Comput. Geosci.* **2014**, *62*, 198–207. [CrossRef]
21. Chen, T.; Yang, Y.; Zheng, H.; Wu, Z. Numerical determination of the effective permeability coefficient of soil–rock mixtures using the numerical manifold method. *Int. J. Numer. Anal. Methods Géoméch.* **2018**, *43*, 381–414. [CrossRef]
22. Wang, T.; Yan, C.; Zheng, Y.; Jiao, Y.-Y.; Zou, J. Numerical study on the effect of meso-structure on hydraulic conductivity of soil-rock mixtures. *Comput. Geotech.* **2022**, *146*, 104726. [CrossRef]
23. You, X.H. Stochastic structural model of soil rock mixture and its application. *Chin. J. Rock Mech. Eng.* **2002**, *11*, 1748. Available online: https://www.cnki.com.cn/Article/CJFDTOTAL-YSLX200211040.htm (accessed on 7 January 2023).
24. Ding, X.; Shi, X.; Zhou, W.; Luan, B. Experimental Study on the Permeability of a Soil-Rock Mixture Based on the Threshold Control Method. *Adv. Civ. Eng.* **2019**, *2019*, 8987052. [CrossRef]
25. Feng, Y.T.; Han, K.; Owen, D.R.J. Coupled lattice Boltzmann method and discrete element modelling of particle transport in turbulent fluid flows: Computational issues. *Int. J. Numer. Methods Eng.* **2007**, *72*, 1111–1134. [CrossRef]
26. Succi, S. *Lattice Boltzmann Equation for Fluid Dynamics and Beyond*; Clarendon Press: Oxford, UK, 2001.
27. Medley, E. The Engineering Characterization of Melanges and Similar Block-In-Matrix Rocks (Bimrocks). Ph.D. Thesis, University of California at Berkeley, San Francisco, CA, USA, 1994. Available online: https://www.researchgate.net/publication/35292215 (accessed on 15 January 2023).
28. Yin, P.; Song, H.; Ma, H.; Yang, W.; He, Z.; Zhu, X. The modification of the Kozeny-Carman equation through the lattice Boltzmann simulation and experimental verification. *J. Hydrol.* **2022**, *609*, 127738. [CrossRef]
29. Hager, A.; Kloss, C.; Pirker, S.; Goniva, C. Parallel Resolved Open Source CFD-DEM: Method, Validation and Application. *J. Comput. Multiph. Flows* **2014**, *6*, 13–27. [CrossRef]
30. *GB/T 50123-2019*; Standard for Geotechnical Testing Method. Ministry of Water Resources of the People's Republic of China, Ministry of Housing and Urban-Rural Development of the People's Republic of China, State Administration of Market Supervision and Administration: Beijing, China, 2019. Available online: https://www.gb-gbt.cn/PDF.aspx/GBT50123-2019 (accessed on 25 January 2023).
31. Potyondy, D.O.; Cundall, P.A. A bonded-particle model for rock. *Int. J. Rock. Mech. Min. Sci.* **2004**, *41*, 1329–1364. [CrossRef]
32. Yang, B.; Jiao, Y.; Lei, S. A study on the effects of microparameters on macroproperties for specimens created by bonded particles. *Eng. Comput.* **2006**, *23*, 607–631. [CrossRef]
33. Schöpfer, M.P.; Abe, S.; Childs, C.; Walsh, J.J. The impact of porosity and crack density on the elasticity, strength and friction of cohesive granular materials: Insights from DEM modelling. *Int. J. Rock. Mech. Min. Sci.* **2008**, *46*, 250–261. [CrossRef]
34. Jin, L.; Cheng, T.; Zhang, Y.; Li, J. Three-dimensional lattice Boltzmann simulation of the permeability of soil-rock mixtures and comparison with other prediction models. *Int. J. Numer. Anal. Methods Géoméch.* **2021**, *45*, 1067–1090. [CrossRef]
35. Sheikh, B.; Pak, A. Numerical investigation of the effects of porosity and tortuosity on soil permeability using coupled three-dimensional discrete-element method and lattice Boltzmann method. *Phys. Rev. E* **2015**, *91*, 053301. [CrossRef]
36. Wang, P.F.; Li, C.H.; Ma, X.W.; Li, Z.J.; Liu, J.J.; Wu, Y.F. Experimental study of seepage characteristics of soil-rock mixture with different rock contents in fault zone. *Rock Soil Mech.* **2018**, *39*, 53–61. [CrossRef]
37. Chen, Z.H.; Chen, S.J.; Chen, J.; Sheng, Q.; Min, H.; Hu, W. In-situ Double-Ring Infiltration Test of Soil-Rock Mixture. *J. Yangtze River Sci. Res. Inst.* **2012**, *29*, 52–56. Available online: http://119.78.100.198/handle/2S6PX9GI/14025 (accessed on 8 April 2023).
38. Zhou, Z.; Fu, H.L.; Liu, B.C.; Tan, H.H.; Long, W.X. Orthogonal tests on permeability of soil-rock-mixture. *Chin. J. Geotech. Eng.* **2006**, *28*, 1134–1138.
39. Bear, J. *Dynamics of Fluids in Porous Media*; Elsevier: New York, NY, USA, 1972. [CrossRef]
40. Zhou, Z.; Sun, J.; Lai, Y.; Wei, C.; Hou, J.; Bai, S.; Huang, X.; Liu, H.; Xiong, K.; Cheng, S. Study on size effect of jointed rock mass and influencing factors of the REV size based on the SRM method. *Tunn. Undergr. Space Technol.* **2022**, *127*, 104613. [CrossRef]
41. Walsh, S.D.; Burwinkle, H.; Saar, M.O. A new partial-bounceback lattice-Boltzmann method for fluid flow through heterogeneous media. *Comput. Geosci.* **2009**, *35*, 1186–1193. [CrossRef]
42. Lautenschlaeger, M.P.; Weinmiller, J.; Kellers, B.; Danner, T.; Latz, A. Homogenized lattice Boltzmann model for simulating multi-phase flows in heterogeneous porous media. *Adv. Water Resour.* **2022**, *170*, 104320. [CrossRef]

mathematics MDPI

Article

Global–Local Non Intrusive Analysis with 1D to 3D Coupling: Application to Crack Propagation and Extension to Commercial Software

Matías Jaque-Zurita [1], Jorge Hinojosa [2] and Ignacio Fuenzalida-Henríquez [3,*]

[1] Master of Science in Mechanical Engineering, Faculty of Engineering, Universidad de Talca, Campus Curicó, Curico 3340000, Chile; matias.jaque@utalca.cl
[2] Industrial Technologies Department, Faculty of Engineering, University of Talca, Campus Curicó, Curico 3340000, Chile; jhinojosa@utalca.cl
[3] Building Management and Engineering Department, Faculty of Engineering, University of Talca, Campus Curicó, Curico 3340000, Chile
* Correspondence: ifuenzalida@utalca.cl

Abstract: Computational simulation is a highly reliable tool used to solve structural analysis problems. In recent times, several techniques have been developed in the field of computational mechanics in order to analyze non-linearities in less time, helping decision-making when structures suffer damage. The global–local analysis is a technique to increase the efficiency of computational simulations by using a global model to obtain boundary conditions in a coupling zone imposed on a local model. Coupling can be performed through the primal–dual method, which is used for crack propagation using 2D and 3D models with fine meshes, thus saving computational time. However, it has not been implemented at a commercial level to analyze large structures such as multi-story buildings with focused non-linearities. In this work, a global–local analysis with non-intrusive methodology and simplified models was implemented in a cracked framed structure, using a 1D (global) and 3D (local) coupling considering crack propagation with primal–dual interface conditions. Different lengths of the local model were analyzed, studying their influence on the convergence of the problem, and compared with a 3D monolithic model to check the reliability of the results. The results show that the proposed methodology solves the problem with an error less than 10%. Furthermore, it was determined that the dimensions of the local model affect the convergence of the problem. This work also provides an implementation of the method for large structures containing focused non-linearities and using commercial software, reducing computational time for the cracked structural analysis.

Keywords: global–local; non-intrusive; computational simulation; crack growth; frame elements; 3D solids; coupling

MSC: 74S05; 74R10

Citation: Jaque-Zurita, M.; Hinojosa, J.; Fuenzalida-Henríquez, I. Global–Local Non Intrusive Analysis with 1D to 3D Coupling: Application to Crack Propagation and Extension to Commercial Software. *Mathematics* **2023**, *11*, 2540. https://doi.org/10.3390/math11112540

Academic Editors: Fajie Wang and Ji Lin

Received: 22 April 2023
Revised: 13 May 2023
Accepted: 15 May 2023
Published: 1 June 2023

1. Introduction

The structures are designed to withstand different internal forces such as traction, compression, bending, cutting, torsion and combined forces. In addition, fatigue damage and seismic provisions must be considered in the design of structural steel buildings [1,2]. The performance of the structure is diminished under the effect of factors such as corrosion, maintenance and the nature of cyclic loads [3], producing increased stress, cracking and subsequent fracture of the material [4]. For these cases, numerical calculation methodologies based on finite elements have been developed to predict the behavior of structures with the presence of cracks, such as the extended finite element method (X-FEM) [5,6], which consists of discretizing a continuum using a mesh, and solving roughly at the nodes and then interpolate to the rest of the element. However, if a singularity occurs, it incorporates enriched shape functions to simulate this phenomenon, allowing the mesh to generate discontinuities and adapt as the problem changes, thus avoiding the remeshing of the problem [7].

However, for large structures subject to static and dynamic loads, these are calculated using beam elements (1D elements with 6 degrees of freedom per node) [8,9]. Even so, these types of elements do not account for crack propagation in their formulations, which means that to study this behavior, other types of complex modeling must be used at a higher computational cost. Therefore, to deal with large structures, multiscale methods have been developed, some of which are based on domain decomposition [10–15] that allow linking models to perform structural analysis of complex structures. Although these techniques have shown good performance in academic applications, they are rarely applied to practical industrial cases. Thus, in order for them to be useful in the industry, it is necessary to validate the simulations with these methods and ensure their computational efficiency and escalability [16]. The implementation of multiscale methods requires a high cost in time and computational resources, in addition to needing methods to link the different scales [16].

Based on domain decomposition methods, the global–local analysis [17] was developed, in order to improve the convergence of complex simulations. This technique uses an approximate global model with a coarse mesh and typically linear to obtain appropriate boundary conditions, which are imposed on the local model in the coupling zone, solving the latter independently.

In [18], is proposed a non-intrusive global–local coupling algorithm based on domain decomposition method, intended for large-scale non-linear analysis without the need to modify the solver base code global model [19]. In [20], the strategy is interpreted as an alternative decomposition method of optimized and non-overlapping Schwarz domains, improving the results. The non-intrusive global–local coupling is applied for complex non-linear behavior (plastic hardening, crack propagation, among others) in [21].

The non-intrusive method uses linear and non-linear solvers as a black box, which are optimized and already incorporated into commercial software to introduce these solutions in the form of displacements and/or forces in a linear model of the entire structure without modifying it (non-intrusive) [15].

An example of non-intrusivity is to use the tools provided by the free software Code_Aster [22] that uses XFEM to solve crack propagation problems and through a Python interface, linking it with its linear solver (FEM) or with other commercial software, such as SAP2000 which is used in this work. Other works where SAP 2000 software is used for different types of analysis can be reviewed in [23–26], among others. However, other commercial software has been used to analyze crack propagation and complex simulations, such as ANSYS [27–29] and Abaqus [30–34]. This methodology has been implemented in a two-dimensional domain with crack growth and mesh refinement in [19,35,36], as well as in analysis with plastic behavior with mesh refinement in [19,37], where the implementation for a three-dimensional domain was also studied. In addition, asynchronous global–local methods have been studied, allowing an improvement in execution times for complex structures [38,39].

In [21], Robin parameters or mixed coupling [15,35,40] was studied to improve the execution times. In these studies, a Robin parameter optimization was performed in 2D and 3D problems with crack growth and plastic hardening to improve the convergence of mixed global–local non-intrusive analysis.

In order to improve the performances of the mixed strategy, industrial problems have been analyzed by means of a two-scale approximation of Schur's complement as a Robin condition in the local model [41,42] being applied in models of an aircraft turbine blade, or other applications such as mechanical and hydraulic fracture modeling [35,43].

This work focuses on implementing a global–local non-intrusive analysis methodology using primal–dual coupling in a global model with 1D elements and a complex local model using 3D formulation, which presents crack growth. Specifically, the XFEM method is used to analyze the crack propagation without remeshing the model [5,6] implemented in different steel moment resisting frames, with a 250 Mpa yield strength.

The non-intrusive strategy is implemented in a frame structure that presents a localized crack. First, the software Code_Aster and the Python interface were used. Then, it is solved by linking Code_Aster and the commercial software SAP2000, obtaining a methodology that allows us to reduce the degrees of freedom analyzed, impacting the computational resolution time. The proposed methodology is validated by simulating a 3D monolithic model solved with the Code_Aster software.

The work is organized as follows. The methodology section presents the study case, software used and the formulation of the primal–dual coupling methodology for 1D and 3D models. In the results and analysis section, the validation of the methodology is shown, together with the convergence comparison of the study cases. Subsequently, the application of the methodology using the commercial software SAP 2000, the validation of the method using this software and the application in a large structure are analyzed. Finally, the discussion section summarizes the work conducted and also presents future studies regarding this topic.

2. Methodology

2.1. Primal–Dual Global–Local Analysis

Performing a global–local analysis on a structure with non-linearities (Figure 1) consists of separating the linear elastic global domain Ω_R of the structure (Figure 2) into two linear non-overlapping domains, the complementary domain Ω_C and auxiliary domain Ω_A. The auxiliary domain is duplicated on a 3D non-linear (with crack propagation) local domain Ω_L (Figure 3). The interfaces between subdomains are connected with linear Γ interfaces. The detailed formulation and mathematical background (functional spaces, Lagrangian definition, Lagrange multipliers among others) can be found in [21].

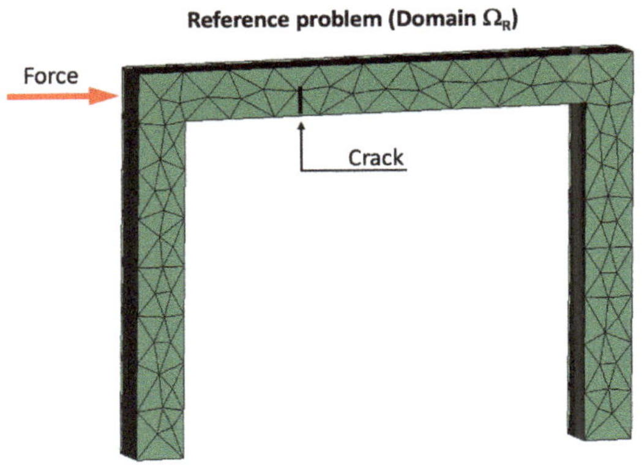

Figure 1. Reference mechanical problem (domain of the Ω_R structure).

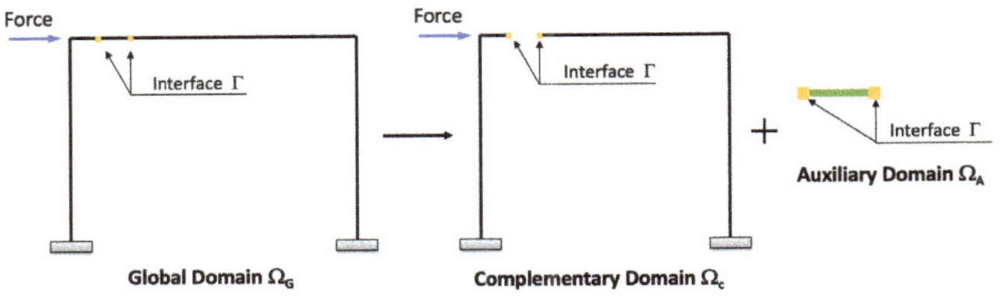

Figure 2. Global mechanical problem (domain of the Ω_G).

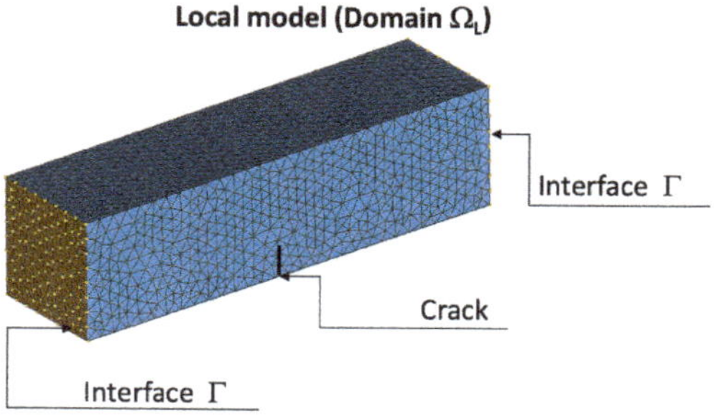

Figure 3. Local mechanical problem (local model domain Ω_L).

When implementing this methodology, the mechanical problem of each domain in which it was discretized (global, auxiliary and local models) must be solved for each iteration. Therefore, the problem to solve is the following:

- First, the global problem is solved by obtaining the displacements u_G^{n+1}:

$$K_G u_G^{n+1} = f_d^G + C_G^T P^n \tag{1}$$

  where K_G is the stiffness matrix of the global model, f_d^G is the external load vector in the domain Ω_G, C_G is a coupling operator of the global problem that relates the degrees of freedom of the interface with respect to the degrees of freedom of the complete domain, and P^n is the compensation force (vector) of the previous iteration. For the first iteration, P^n is a vector of zeros for a 3D frame global model with an interface of two nodes.
- Second, the auxiliary problem is solved by imposing the displacements $u_A^{n+1}|_\Gamma$ and solve for the reaction forces λ_A^{n+1} in the interface zone:

$$K_A u_A^{n+1}|_\Gamma - C_A^T \lambda_A^{n+1} = f_d^A \tag{2}$$

  where K_A is the stiffness matrix of the auxiliary model, f_d^A is the external load vector, and λ_A^{n+1} is the reaction force at the interface for the domain Ω_A.
  The λ_A^{n+1} can be obtained directly in some software, allowing the obtainment of the reaction forces from embedded structures within a global problem.
  The displacements $u_A^{n+1}|_\Gamma$ can be extracted from the solution of the global problem using the following relation:

$$u_A^{n+1}|_\Gamma = C_A u_A^{n+1} = C_G u_G^{n+1} \tag{3}$$

  where C_A is a coupling operator that relates the degrees of freedom of the interface with respect to the Auxiliary domain Ω_A and C_G was previously defined.
- Third, the local problem is solved by imposing the displacements $u_L^{n+1}|_\Gamma$ on the interface of the local model

$$u_L^{n+1}|_\Gamma = C_L u_L^{n+1} = \mathbf{Pr_{GL}}\{C_G u_G^{n+1}\} \tag{4}$$

  where C_L is an operator that relates the degrees of freedom of the interface with respect to the degrees of freedom of the local domain Ω_L, $u_L^{n+1}|_\Gamma$ are the displacement on the interface of the local model and $\mathbf{Pr_{GL}}$ is a projection operator, from the global 1D model to the local 3D domain. The formulation of this projector is presented in Section 2.3.

Hence, the reaction forces λ_L^{n+1} of the local model in the interface, solved by means of a nonlinear solver such as Arc Length Method [44] or Newthon–Raphson Method, is obtained from the following equation:

$$K_L u_L^{n+1}|_\Gamma - C_L^T \lambda_L^{n+1} = f_d^L \tag{5}$$

where K_L is the stiffness matrix of the local model, f_d^L is the external load vector in the domain Ω_L and λ_L^{n+1} is the reaction force at the interface.

- Fourth, the correction forces that will be applied to the global model P^n are calculated:

$$P^{n+1} = \lambda_A^{n+1} + \mathbf{Pr_{LG}}\{\lambda_L^{n+1}\} \tag{6}$$

where the projector operator $\mathbf{Pr_{LG}}$, from the local to the global domain, is also presented in Section 2.3 and is used with a Code_Aster built-in function.

- Fifth, the residual force r^{n+1} is calculated and the error η of the solution obtained in the iteration is estimated:

$$r^{n+1} = P^{n+1} - P^n \tag{7}$$

$$\eta = \| r^{n+1} \|_2 / \| r^0 \|_2 \tag{8}$$

- Finally, a relaxation scheme is considered, obtaining the following correction force:

$$P^{n+1} = \mu P^{n+1} + (1-\mu) P^n \tag{9}$$

This relaxation allows for better convergence, for example, when Aitken δ^2 relaxation method is used [19].

The compensation forces P_n assigned in the interface Γ of the global model (Figure 2) are applied to represent the local non-linear effects on the global model. These forces have 6 components for each node analyzed, as shown in Equation (10), since the force correction is performed in the global model.

$$P_n = [Fx \quad Fy \quad Fz \quad Mx \quad My \quad Mz]^T \tag{10}$$

It is important to mention that the coupling operators C_A, C_G, and C_L are sparse matrices, which relate the total degrees of freedom of each model to its interface.

2.2. Case Study

The steel frame used for the analysis is made up of a 3-meter-long beam and two two-meter-long columns, whose joints between them are considered rigid, as is the support of the columns. The section of the elements is a square section of two hundred millimeters on each side. The material used is a steel with a yield limit of 250 MPa, a modulus of elasticity equal to 200,000 MPa and a Poisson's ratio of 0.3.

The 1D model of the frame is discretized into six nodes and five elements (elements "a" to "e"), as can be seen in Figure 4, where the length of the element "c" is used to generate the local model and will be centered in the position x = 750 mm (crack location). Nodes 3 and 4 are the interface between domains to perform the non-intrusive coupling and at node 2 a horizontal force of 100 kN is applied. The global model of the considered frame has six degrees of freedom ($u_x, u_y, u_z, \theta_x, \theta_y, \theta_z$), while the local model, being modeled by 3D elements, only considers three degrees of freedom (u_x, u_y, u_z). Finally, nodes 1 and 6 correspond to fixed supports with restricted rotations.

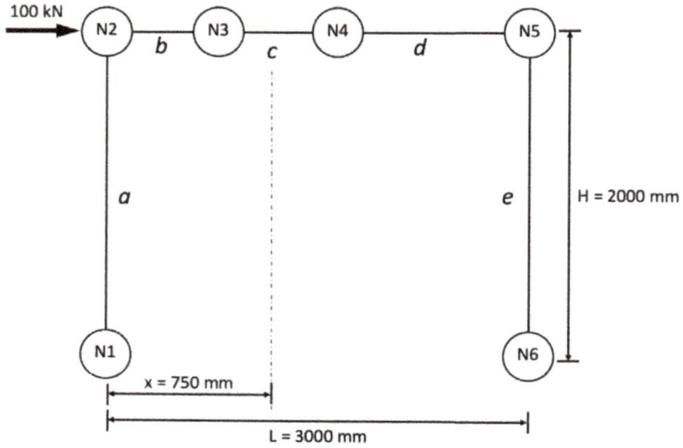

Figure 4. Representation and discretization of the 1D model of the analyzed frame.

The Code_Aster software was used for linear and non-linear analysis. Code_Aster has modules implemented to study crack growth using the XFEM methodology [5,6], without remeshing the local problem and allowing to analyze several propagation steps predefined by the user.

The global model is defined according to the Euler-Bernoulli beam theory and with linear behavior. The effects of the shear deformation energy are neglected in the stiffness matrix of the 1D frame elements, as presented in Equation (11), for the corresponding element shown in Figure 5.

$$K_{frame1D} = \begin{bmatrix} K_{11} & K_{12} \\ K_{21} & K_{22} \end{bmatrix} \tag{11}$$

where matrices K_{11}, K_{12}, K_{21} and K_{22} are defined in Equations (12), (13), (14) and (15), respectively:

$$K_{11} = \begin{bmatrix} EA/L & 0 & 0 & 0 & 0 & 0 \\ 0 & 12EI_z/L^3 & 0 & 0 & 0 & 6EI_z/L^2 \\ 0 & 0 & 12EI_y/L^3 & 0 & -6EI_y/L^2 & 0 \\ 0 & 0 & 0 & GJ/L & 0 & 0 \\ 0 & 0 & -6EI_y/L^2 & 0 & 4EI_y/L & 0 \\ 0 & 6EI_z/L^2 & 0 & 0 & 0 & 4EI_z/L \end{bmatrix} \tag{12}$$

$$K_{12} = \begin{bmatrix} -EA/L & 0 & 0 & 0 & 0 & 0 \\ 0 & -12EI_z/L^3 & 0 & 0 & 0 & 6EI_z/L^2 \\ 0 & 0 & -12EI_y/L^3 & 0 & -6EI_y/L^2 & 0 \\ 0 & 0 & 0 & -GJ/L & 0 & 0 \\ 0 & 0 & 6EI_y/L^2 & 0 & 2EI_y/L & 0 \\ 0 & -6EI_z/L^2 & 0 & 0 & 0 & 2EI_z/L \end{bmatrix} \tag{13}$$

$$K_{21} = K_{12} \tag{14}$$

$$K_{22} = \begin{bmatrix} EA/L & 0 & 0 & 0 & 0 & 0 \\ 0 & 12EI_z/L^3 & 0 & 0 & 0 & -6EI_z/L^2 \\ 0 & 0 & 12EI_y/L^3 & 0 & 6EI_y/L^2 & 0 \\ 0 & 0 & 0 & GJ/L & 0 & 0 \\ 0 & 0 & 6EI_y/L^2 & 0 & 4EI_y/L & 0 \\ 0 & -6EI_z/L^2 & 0 & 0 & 0 & 4EI_z/L \end{bmatrix} \tag{15}$$

where I_y and I_z corresponds to the second moment of area in the y and z axis, respectively, A is the section area, L is the length of the element and J is Saint Venant's or torsional constant of the section. The material constants are E and G corresponding to the Young modulus and shear modulus of the material, respectively.

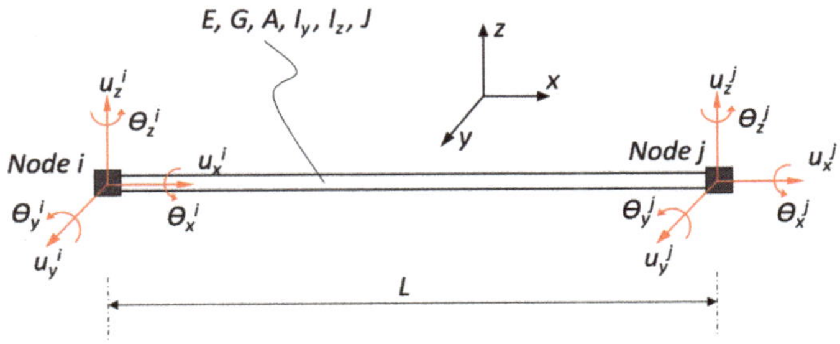

Figure 5. Representation of the degrees of freedom for a 1D frame element.

For the 3D tetrahedral element, the stiffness matrix is calculated using the constitutive matrix D presented in Equation (16) and the degrees of freedom are presented in Figure 6.

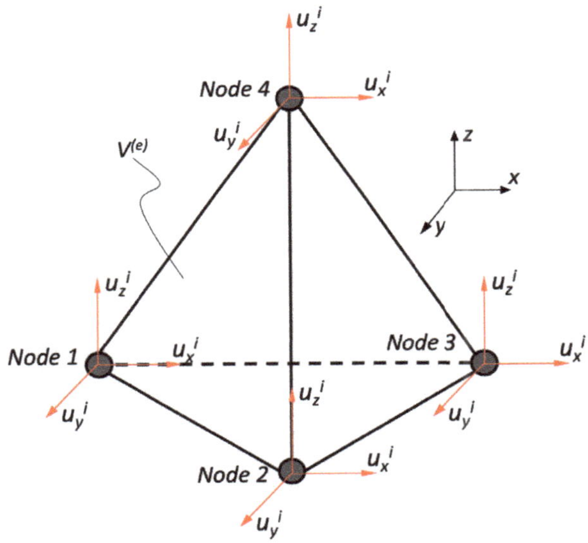

Figure 6. Representation of the degrees of freedom for a 3D tetrahedral element.

$$D = \frac{E(1-\nu)}{(1+\nu)(1-2\nu)} \begin{bmatrix} 1 & \frac{\nu}{1-\nu} & \frac{\nu}{1-\nu} & 0 & 0 & 0 \\ & 1 & \frac{\nu}{1-\nu} & 0 & 0 & 0 \\ & & 1 & 0 & 0 & 0 \\ & & & \frac{1-2\nu}{2(1-\nu)} & 0 & 0 \\ Symmetrical & & & & \frac{1-2\nu}{2(1-\nu)} & 0 \\ & & & & & \frac{1-2\nu}{2(1-\nu)} \end{bmatrix} \quad (16)$$

where ν and E correspond to the Poisson modulus and the Young Modulus of the material. Therefore, the stiffness matrix of a single element K^e is presented in Equation (17).

$$K^e = \begin{bmatrix} K^e_{11} & K^e_{12} & K^e_{13} & K^e_{14} \\ & K^e_{22} & K^e_{23} & K^e_{24} \\ & & K^e_{33} & K^e_{34} \\ Symmetrical & & & K^e_{44} \end{bmatrix} \tag{17}$$

where each term of the stiffness matrix can be calculated using the expression presented in Equation (18).

$$K^e_{ij} = \frac{1}{36V^{(e)}} \begin{bmatrix} (d_{11}b_ib_j + d_{44}c_ic_j + d_{55}d_id_j) & (d_{12}b_ic_j + d_{44}b_ic_j) & (d_{13}b_id_j + d_{55}b_ib_j) \\ (d_{21}c_ib_j + d_{44}b_ic_j) & (d_{22}c_ic_j + d_{44}b_ib_j + d_{66}d_id_j) & (d_{23}c_id_j + d_{66}d_ic_j) \\ (d_{31}d_ib_j + d_{55}b_id_j) & (d_{32}d_ic_j + d_{66}c_id_j) & (d_{33}d_id_j + d_{55}b_ib_j + d_{66}c_ic_j) \end{bmatrix} \tag{18}$$

where $d_{i,j}$ corresponds to the terms of the constitutive matrix D of Equation (16) and the terms c_i are the terms of the matrix B_i that presents the derivatives of the linear shape functions N_i for each node i, as presented in Equation (19).

$$B_i = \begin{bmatrix} \frac{\partial N_i}{\partial x} & 0 & 0 \\ 0 & \frac{\partial N_i}{\partial y} & 0 \\ & & \frac{\partial N_i}{\partial z} \\ \frac{\partial N_i}{\partial y} & \frac{\partial N_i}{\partial x} & 0 \\ \frac{\partial N_i}{\partial z} & 0 & \frac{\partial N_i}{\partial x} \\ 0 & \frac{\partial N_i}{\partial z} & \frac{\partial N_i}{\partial y} \end{bmatrix} = \frac{1}{6V^{(e)}} \begin{bmatrix} b_i & 0 & 0 \\ 0 & c_i & 0 \\ 0 & 0 & d_i \\ c_i & b_i & 0 \\ d_i & 0 & b_i \\ 0 & d_i & c_i \end{bmatrix} \tag{19}$$

The shape functions N_i are linear functions that interpolates the displacement field from the nodes into the element V^e, as presented in the classical Finite Element Methods [45].

In the case of the non-linear problem, 3D tetrahedral finite elements with linear shape functions are considered and XFEM is used for the calculation of crack growth (with 3 propagation steps). To analyze the convergence of the problem, three crack lengths (25 mm, 50 mm, and 75 mm) are considered, analyzing each one with three different local mesh lengths, as presented in Figure 7. Each mesh length will be named as follows:

- Local Mesh 1 (L.M. 1): Length 500 mm
- Local Mesh 2 (L.M. 2): Length 750 mm
- Local Mesh 3 (L.M. 3): Length 1000 mm

For the crack propagation of the local model, the crack is initialized and the location is defined (as described before in Figure 7). Code_Aster also required the following inputs for the crack propagation procedure:

- The direction of propagation is taken into account, with a tangent vector (0,0,1) and normal vector (1,0,0) with the function *DEFI_FISS_XFEM* of Code_Aster.
- The propagation is calculated internally, calculating the energy release rate using the intensity factors with the function *CALC_K_G* of Code_Aster for a predefined number of propagation steps (function *PROPA_FISS*).

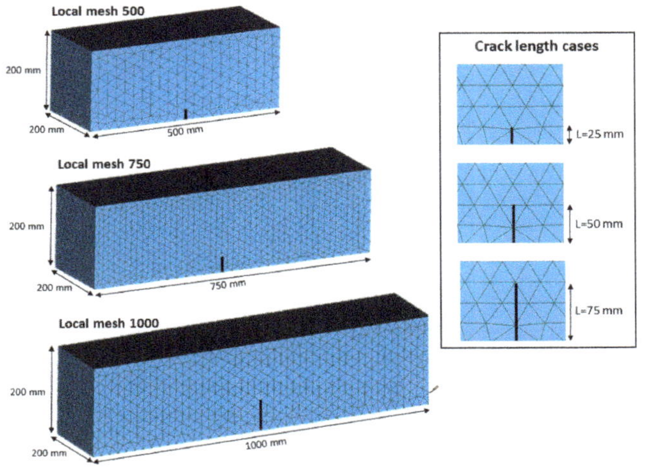

Figure 7. Representation of local mesh and crack length.

2.3. Projection of Displacements from the Global 1D Model to the Local 3D Model

When using 1D and 3D models for the implementation of a primal–dual analysis, there is no coincidence in the nodes of the different meshes. Hence, the projection of the results of one model to another must be carried out. Solving a 1D model subject to bending, torsion, and displacement in all 3 axes results in displacements and rotations that must be accounted for when projecting displacements.

The projection of the displacements and rotations was implemented using a Python function that takes as input parameters the displacements obtained in the global 1D model analysis ($u_x, u_y, u_z, \theta_x, \theta_y, \theta_z$) and the data of the local mesh. As output returns the displacements of all nodes (u_x, u_y and u_z) of the local model. This procedure is used to built the operator $\mathbf{Pr}_{\mathbf{GL}}\{\square\}$, as presented in Equation (4).

Thus, the procedure for projecting nodal displacements of the 1D global model (degrees of freedom u_x, u_y, u_z and rotations θ_x, θ_y and θ_z) are presented below. Specifically, for the rotation in the y direction θ_y the steps are:

1. To calculate the displacement generated from the rotation resulting from bending θ_y, kinematic compatibility is considered, using a non-deformable finite element (solid face with no warping) and rotating with respect to the centroid. The face of the 3D element analyzed has a maximum distance η_z from the centroid and when rotated it is maintained, producing a displacement Δ, as shown in Figure 8.

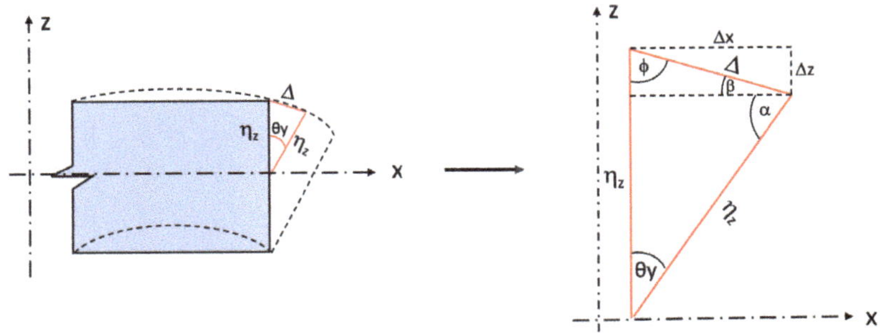

Figure 8. Displacements produced by the θ_y rotation of the bending moment in a finite element.

2. Then, the displacement components are determined geometrically, i.e., the angles of the figure and considering them as a function of θ_y, thus solving the value of Δ based on known parameters (η_z and θ_y). The final expressions are shown in Equations (20) and (21).

$$\frac{\sin\theta_y}{\Delta} = \frac{\sin(90 - \frac{\theta_y}{2})}{\eta_z} \tag{20}$$

$$\Delta = \frac{\eta_z \sin\theta_y}{\sin(90 - \frac{\theta_y}{2})} \tag{21}$$

3. Finally, the values of Δ_x and Δ_z are found, which would be the effects that must be considered due the bending rotations, leading to the following expressions:

$$\Delta_x = \Delta\cos(\frac{\theta_y}{2}) \tag{22}$$

$$\Delta_z = \Delta\sin(\frac{\theta_y}{2}) \tag{23}$$

Thus, the total displacement that is imposed on each node for the rotation θ_y is $u_x + \Delta_x$ and $u_z + \Delta_z$.

For the θ_z rotation due to bending, as shown in Figure 9, the equations are obtained using the same methodology presented above, obtaining the Equations (24)–(27).

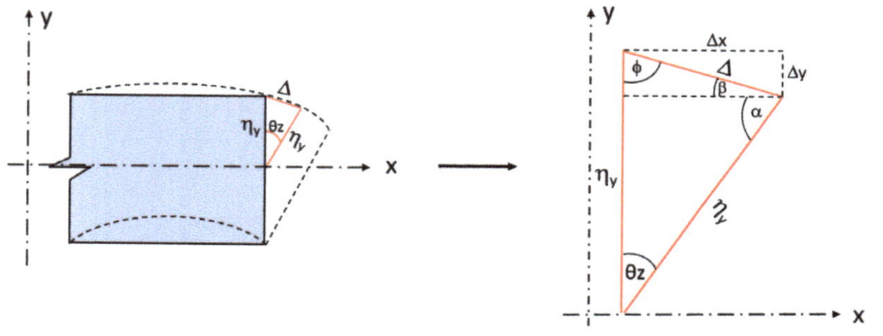

Figure 9. Displacements produced by the θ_z rotation of the bending moment in a finite element.

$$\frac{\sin\theta_z}{\Delta} = \frac{\sin(90 - \frac{\theta_z}{2})}{\eta_y} \tag{24}$$

$$\Delta = \frac{\eta_y \sin\theta_z}{\sin(90 - \frac{\theta_z}{2})} \tag{25}$$

$$\Delta_x = \Delta\cos(\frac{\theta_z}{2}) \tag{26}$$

$$\Delta_y = \Delta\sin(\frac{\theta_z}{2}) \tag{27}$$

where θ_z is the bending rotation along the Z axis and η_y is the distance from the centroid in the Y direction.

In the event that the structure is subjected to torsional moment, this effect must be considered in the local model imposed displacements.

Figure 10 will be used to determine the displacements imposed due to torsion (rotation in the "x" axis). Lets consider that the point a' represents a node of the element that will be rotated to a position a given an angle θ_x, generating a displacement Δ whose components will represent the mentioned effects.

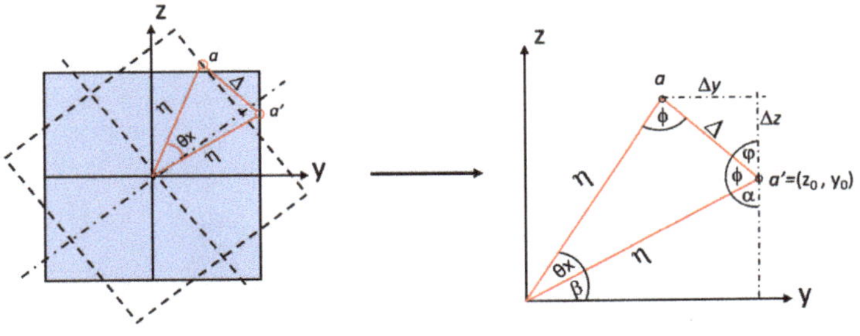

Figure 10. Displacements produced by the rotation of the torsional moment in a finite element.

The procedure to analyze the effects of the torsional rotation θ_x is presented below:

1. The first thing will be to determine the value of the angles based on θ_x and β, where the latter represents the initial angle of the node with respect to the origin. Then, the value of η must be calculated, obtaining the expressions shown in Equations (28) and (29) are obtained.

$$\eta = \sqrt{y_0^2 + z_0^2} \tag{28}$$

$$\Delta = \frac{(\sqrt{y_0^2 + z_0^2}) \sin\theta_x}{\sin(90 - \frac{\theta_x}{2})} \tag{29}$$

2. Then, the values of Δ_y and Δ_z are found, which would be the effects on the displacement due to torsional moment, leading to:

$$\Delta_z = \frac{(\sqrt{y_0^2 + z_0^2}) \sin\theta_x}{\sin(90 - \frac{\theta_x}{2})} \cos(\frac{\theta_x}{2}) \tag{30}$$

$$\Delta_y = \frac{(\sqrt{y_0^2 + z_0^2}) \sin\theta_x}{\sin(90 - \frac{\theta_x}{2})} \sin(\frac{\theta_x}{2}) \tag{31}$$

In addition to the displacements from 1D to 3D, the nodal forces of the local model must be transferred to resultant forces and moments to calculate the compensation forces that are imposed on the global 1D model. To that end, the sum of the nodal forces in each direction is performed and the resulting moment with respect to the centroid is calculated, through the function of Code_Aster *POST_RELEVE_T*, integrating the stresses and returning 3 forces and 3 moments (one for each axis, respectively) and used in Equation (6) of the iterative analysis procedure in the operator $\mathbf{Pr}_{\mathbf{LG}}\{\square\}$.

3. Implementation of the Methodology in Code_Aster

3.1. Validation of the Implementation in Code_Aster

In order to validate the procedure, the results of the non-intrusive global–local implementation are compared to a monolithic 3D solution of the problem, which considers the same properties of the crack location, number of propagation steps and also solved by means of the XFEM methodology. This analysis of the monolithic XFEM model allows us to do two things: to propagate the initialized crack in a model with a large number of degrees of freedom and also to compare the global–local methodology with a corresponding control model, obtaining displacement measurements and calculating errors between the mentioned methods. Figure 11 shows the graphical solution to the displacements obtained by the non-intrusive using a 1000 mm width local model, while Figure 12 presents the solution of the 3D monolithic problem, both with the same 50 mm crack.

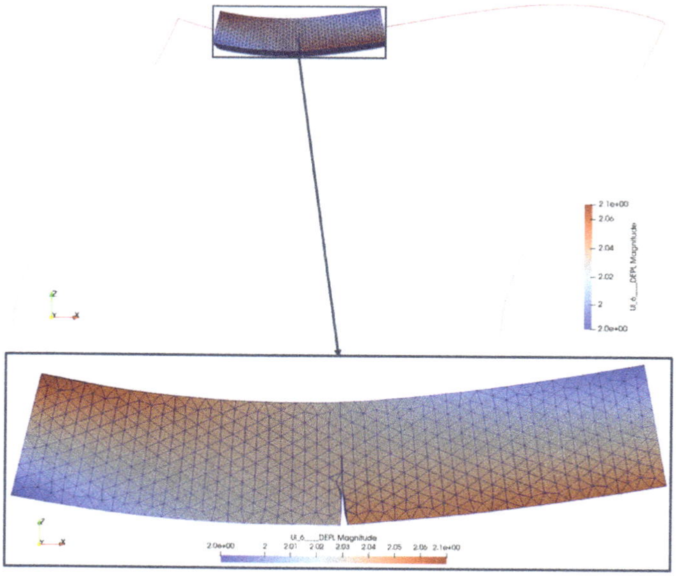

Figure 11. Deformed shape analysis of the global–local method with local model of 1000 mm.

Figure 12. Deformed shape analysis of the 3D monolithic model.

Figure 13 shows the displacements for the 3D monolithic model (upper figure) and for the non-intrusive global–local methodology (lower figures) for the case of linear behavior and in Figure 14 the results are presented for the 50 mm crack, where the differences in the magnitude of the displacements in the 3 directions are relatively small respect to the size of the structure (3000 mm in wide and 2000 mm in height). In Table 1, the error with respect to the norm of the displacement of the monolithic model is presented for all models, being less than 6.7% for all converged cases.

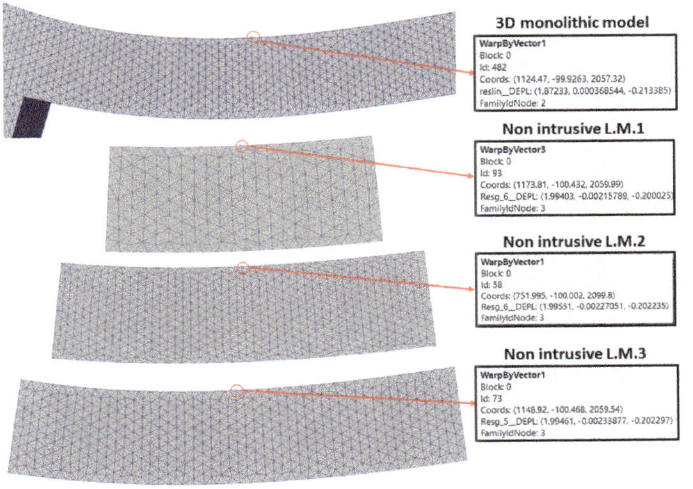

Figure 13. Comparison of displacement results between the linear solution of the 3D monolithic problem and the non-intrusive global–local problem.

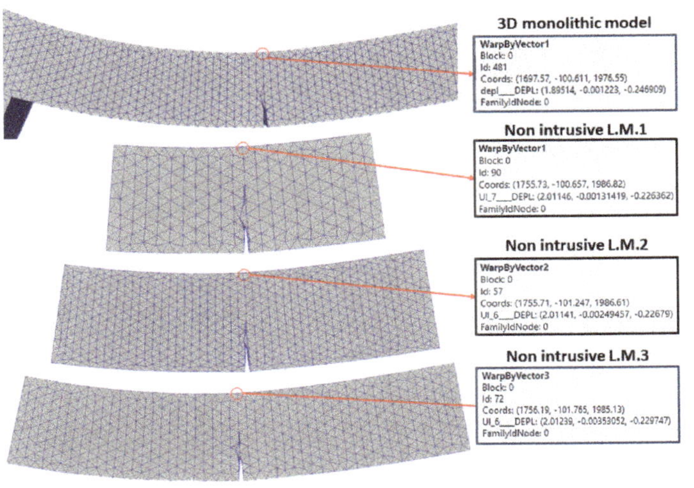

Figure 14. Comparison of displacement results between the cracked solution of the 3D monolithic problem and the non-intrusive global–local problem.

Table 1. Non-intrusive norm displacement error analysis *Code_Aster* for different meshes and crack initial lengths.

Local Mesh Model		Initial Crack Length in the Local Model			
		Linear	**25 mm**	**50 mm**	**75 mm**
Local Mesh 1	% disp. error	6.35%	5.96%	5.91%	non conv.
Local Mesh 2	% disp. error	6.44%	5.93%	5.91%	6.62%
Local Mesh 3	% disp. error	6.39%	5.95%	5.98%	6.44%

It can be concluded that the error is independent of the crack propagation, i.e., the nonlinear behavior does not affect in terms of the error but is intrinsic to the global–local methodology and the transformation of displacements and forces between 1D and 3D models.

3.2. *Effect of the Local Model Size*

For the first analysis, no crack was considered on the model, in order to make it linear. Figure 15 shows the evolution of the error with respect to the number of iterations obtained for the different local models. It can be seen that as the size of the local problem increases, the convergence rate improves from seven iterations for the L.M.1 to five iterations for the L.M.3. It can be said that the length of the local model affects the convergence of the problem.

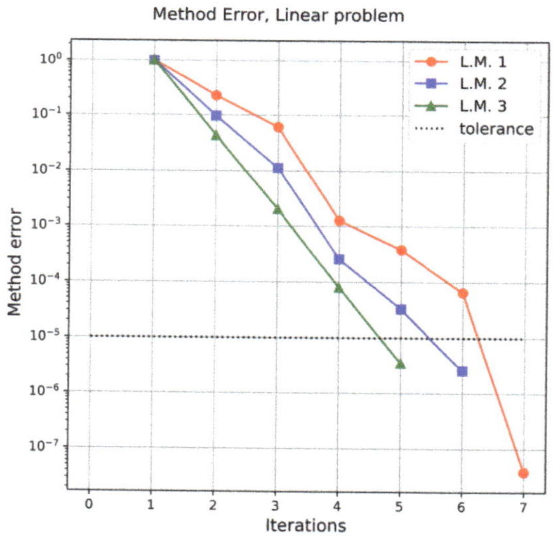

Figure 15. Comparison of the linear problem convergence with different local models.

To analyze the effect of the size of the local model for non-linear cases, 3 crack lengths were considered: 25 mm, 50 mm and 75 mm. Figures 16–18 shows the evolution of the error with respect to the number of iterations for the case of the crack of 25 mm, 50 mm and 75 mm, respectively.

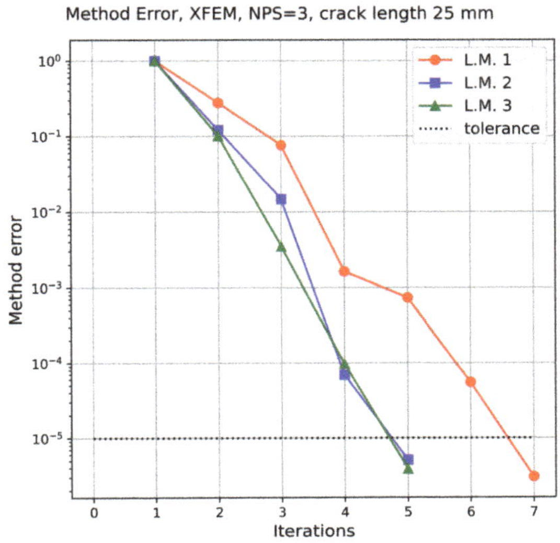

Figure 16. Primal–dual convergence comparison with an initial crack length of 25 mm and different local models.

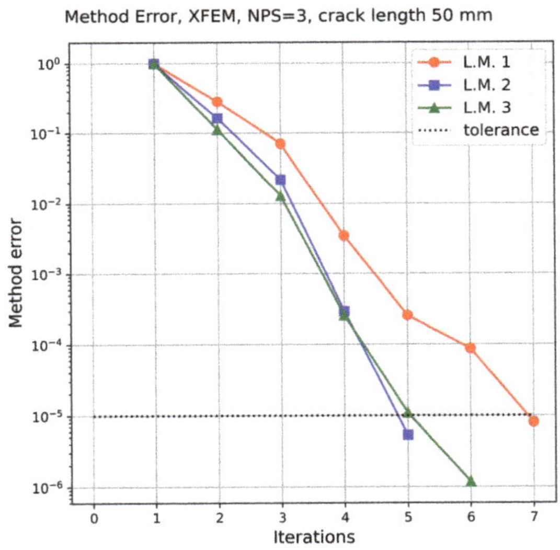

Figure 17. Primal–dual convergence comparison with an initial crack length of 50 mm and different local models.

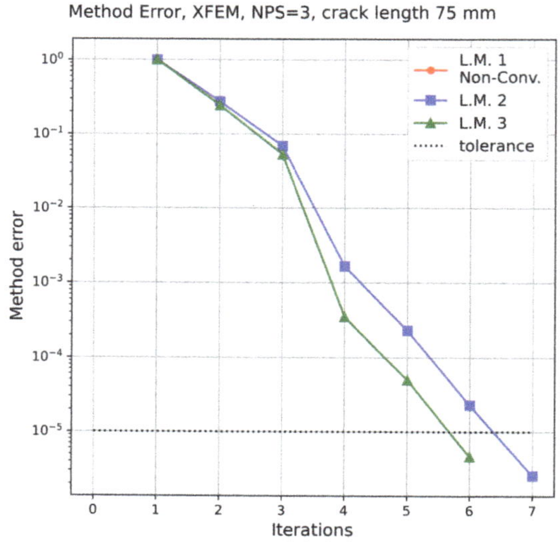

Figure 18. Primal–dual convergence comparison with an initial crack length of 75 mm and different local models.

It can be seen that L.M.2 and L.M.3 converge in a similar number of iterations giving a faster convergence rate than L.M.1, which required two more iterations on average or fails to converge (Figure 17).

With respect to the non-convergence of the L.M.1 analysis with 75 mm initial crack, there are two ways that the presented methodology considers this failed state:

- Stagnation of the solution: If the iterative analysis presents a divergent error (increasing with each iteration), jumps between an error greater than the tolerance, or does not converge within a maximum number of iterations, i.e., 50 iterations in the present study.
- Failed crack propagation analysis (XFEM internal procedure): Crack propagation in Code_Aster is calculated using the rate of energy release (G) method, using the built-in function $CALC\_K\_G$. This method calculates the intensity stress factors (K) evaluating the bilinear form of G with the asymptotic solution of Westergaard. In addition, an error indicator is obtained by comparing the difference between G and Irwin's energy release rate (G_{Irwin}), as shown in Equation (32) [46].

$$error_{XFEM} = \frac{|G - G_{Irwin}|}{|G|} \tag{32}$$

If the error calculated using the Equation (32) is greater than 50%, the analysis stops and displays an alert message as presented in [46]. This is the case for the L.M.1 local mesh with the 75 mm initial crack length, affecting the convergence of XFEM method and, therefore, the overall convergence of the global–local analysis. More information with respect to the convergence of the XFEM crack propagation method can be found in [47,48].

Therefore, it is possible to conclude that for small local domains, the non-linearity effect does not fully develop before the interface, as postulated in St. Venant's principle, generating problems in the coupling between the models.

4. Implementation with a Commercial Software

The selected software to test the non-intrusive strategy is SAP2000 [49], which is widely used for the analysis of reinforced concrete and steel structures. However, SAP 2000 does not have the capabilities to perform crack propagation, so it is proposed to couple the software with Code_Aster, using Python as an interface.

SAP2000 is a finite element program with an object-oriented 3D graphical interface, allowing to perform the modeling, analysis, and sizing of structural engineering problems. This software is used by engineers due to its versatility to model structures allowing to design of bridges, buildings, stadiums, dams, industrial structures, maritime structures, and generally all types of infrastructure that need to be analyzed and sized [49]. An important feature is that it solves simple static models that can be enriched with the non-intrusive methodology.

4.1. Validation of the Implementation in SAP 2000

The same structure analyzed in Section 3.1 is reviewed, with the same applied loads, sections and profiles to be analyzed. The SAP2000 model is shown in Figure 19.

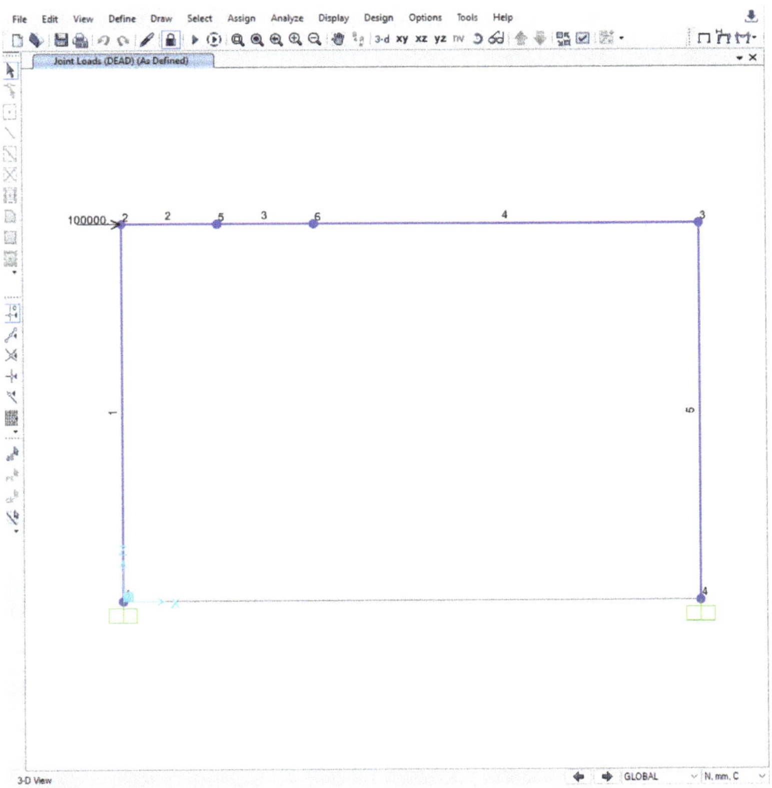

Figure 19. Frame model analyzed in SAP2000.

To communicate SAP2000 with Code_Aster, the library *comtypes* is used, which allows information such as displacements and forces to be sent between different software using Python as an interpreter. The same cases and crack positions as the model analyzed in Code_Aster are analyzed to validate the methodology but using the commercial software for 1D linear calculation.

The results for the crack length of 25 mm, 50 mm and 75 mm are shown in Figures 20–22, respectively. Solid lines correspond to the results of Section 3.1, while the dashed lines correspond to the implementation with SAP2000.

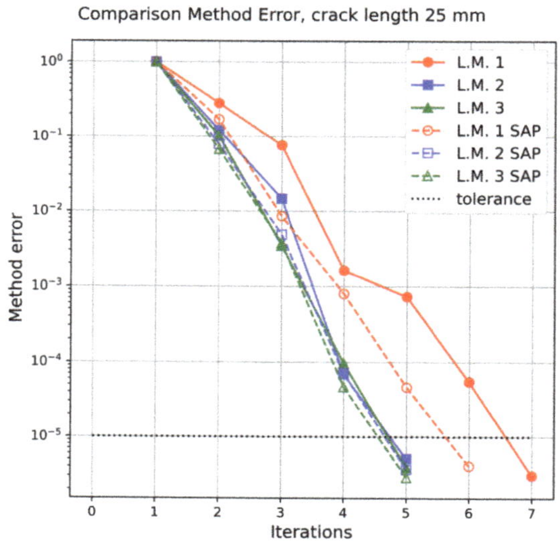

Figure 20. Comparison of SAP2000 and Code_Aster results and an initial crack length of 25 mm.

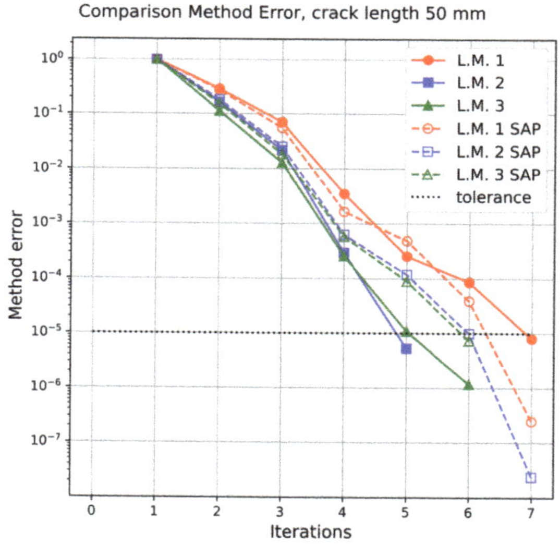

Figure 21. Comparison of SAP2000 and Code_Aster results and an initial crack length of 50 mm.

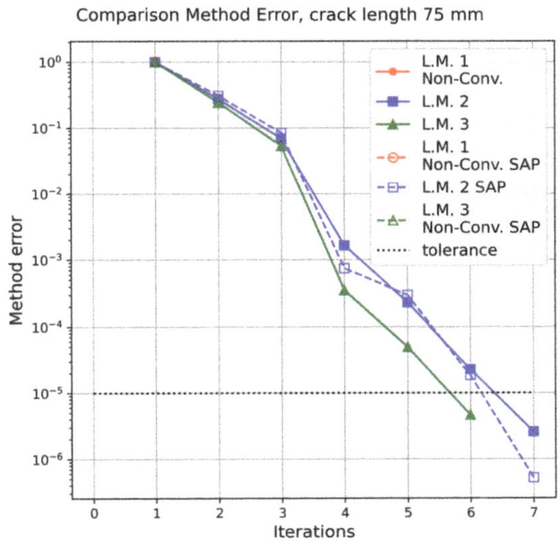

Figure 22. Comparison of SAP2000 and Code_Aster results and an initial crack length of 75 mm.

The error with respect to the norm of the displacement of the monolithic model is presented in Table 2, presenting an error lower than 9.2% for all converged cases. The magnitude of the displacements in the X and Z direction for both models are considered similar and the displacements in the Y direction are lower than 0.003 mm, and therefore are considered negligible.

Table 2. Non-intrusive norm displacement error analysis coupling with SAP 2000, different meshes and crack initial lengths.

Local Mesh Model		Initial Crack Length in the Local Model			
		Linear	25 mm	50 mm	75 mm
Local Mesh 1	% error disp.	8.94%	8.41%	8.32%	non conv.
Local Mesh 2	% error disp.	8.87%	8.33%	8.32%	9.11%
Local Mesh 3	% error disp.	8.79%	8.32%	8.37%	non conv.

As shown, the analysis with SAP 2000 for the case with L.M.1 and L.M.3 (for the initial crack of 75 mm) does not converge. As was presented in the previous section, these models failed to achieve a correct crack propagation analysis, and therefore, the XFEM stopped the global–local iterative procedure. Finally, the error is also independent of the nonlinear behavior analyzed and can be considered inherent to the global–local methodology.

4.2. Methodology Extension to 3-Story Building

The building corresponds to a three-story steel structure with a height between floors of 3 m. The length of the span is 10 m in the X and Y directions. Forces of 10,000 N are applied to each corner of the building in the X direction considering rigid supports, where the local model is shown in red in Figure 23. The global 1D model consists of 18 nodes and 108 degrees of freedom.

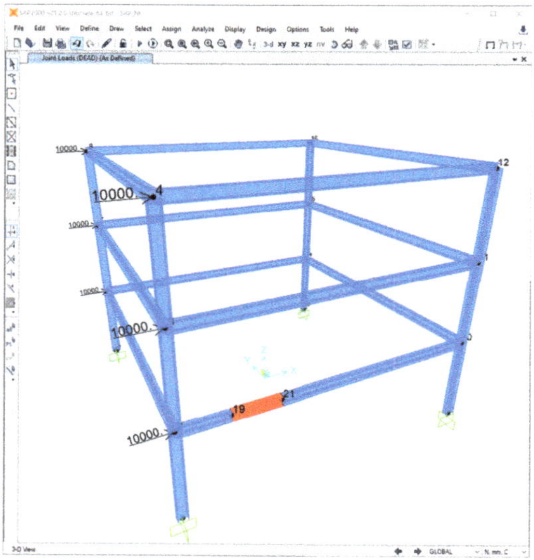

Figure 23. 3-story steel frame building model with SAP 2000.

The beams and columns correspond to Wide Flange profiles. The dimensions of the section are as follows:

- Total height: H = 300 mm.
- Flange width: B = 200 mm.
- Flange thickness: tf = 10 mm.
- Web thickness: tw = 6 mm.
- Material: Grade 50 quality steel.

The local problem, shown in Figure 24, is 1500 mm long, an initial crack length of 50 mm (centered on the local model), and three propagation steps.

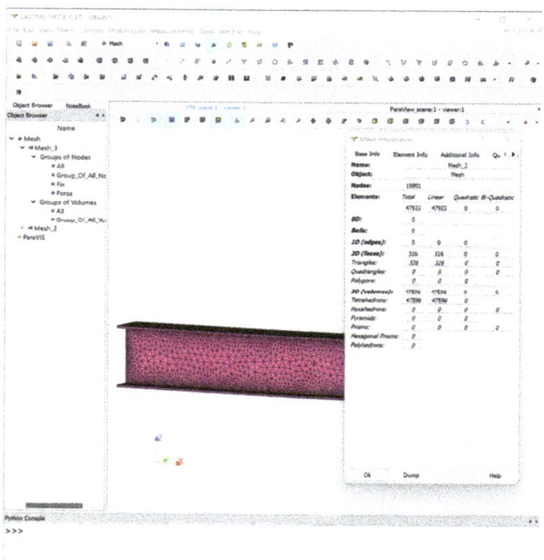

Figure 24. Local model in Code_Aster, length 1500 mm.

The local model consists of 15,900 nodes and 47,703 degrees of freedom, modeled using tetrahedral elements. As a reference, a complete 3D modeling of the building in Salome Meca (Code_Aster Visual Interface) is considered, shown in Figure 25. This model has approximately 1,459,000 nodes, which implies 4,377,000 degrees of freedom.

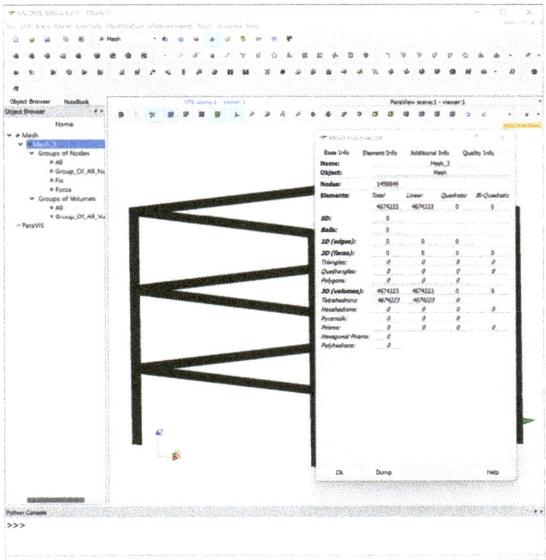

Figure 25. 3-story building modeled with Salome-Meca.

Figure 26 shows in overlapping the displacements of the monolithic model (Code_Aster) and the local model (SAP2000).

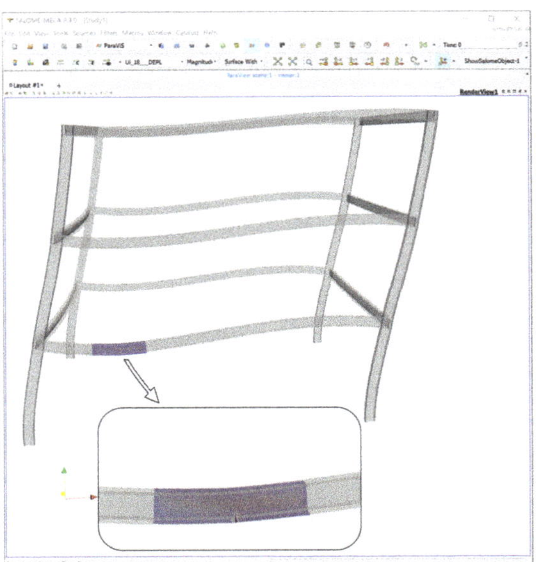

Figure 26. Comparison of the deformed shapes of the monolithic and local model amplified by a factor of 100.

The evolution of the error is presented in Figure 27.

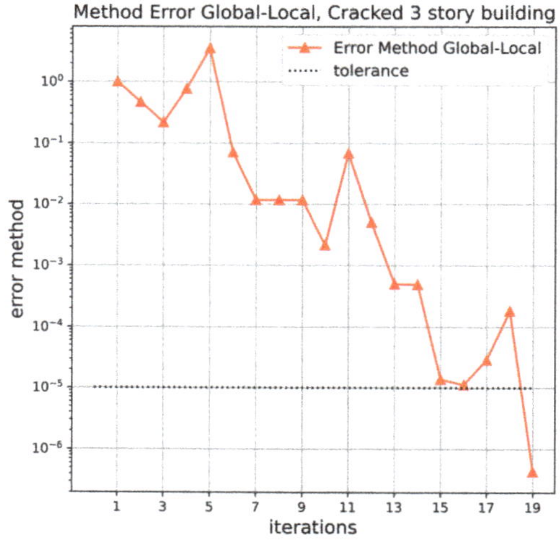

Figure 27. Global–local method convergence for the 3-story building and SAP2000.

Table 3 shows the magnitude in which the crack grows and the calculation time for each implementation. In addition, it indicates the percentage difference between the model in SAP2000 and Code_Aster. The results show that the growth of the crack, for both cases, is similar (difference of 1.6%). On the contrary, the calculation time is reduced by 82% for the non-intrusive case with SAP2000.

Table 3. Results for 3D monolithic model and SAP 2000 global–local model.

Model	Crack Tip Displ. (mm)	Execution Time (s)
3D Monolithic	6.01	2231
GL w/SAP 2000	5.89	391
Diff. r/Monolithic	1.6%	82%

It is expected that for the analysis of much larger structures (multiple-story buildings) the size of the local problem does not vary, but the global problem does. Being the global problem the one with the least number of nodes and d.o.f., this should not have a significant influence on the computation times for the non-intrusive problem, but it would mean a significant increase for the monolithic case.

5. Discussion

Non-intrusive global–local analysis with 1D to 3D coupling is a technique that allows a localized analysis of a problem which, in the framework of this work, was crack propagation, but can also be used regarding plasticity, crystalline plasticity, stress concentrations, etc.

The implementation that was developed allows us to consider the displacements in the six degrees of freedom of the global model and the three degrees of freedom of the local model, having a kinematic compatibility in the transfer of the displacements and subsequent compensation of forces.

The dimensions of the local model and the crack location affect the number of iterations required to obtain convergence. Despite this, it was possible to verify displacements obtained using the methodology through the displacements, resulting in low errors relative to the monolithic model.

This methodology was implemented in a test model and was the first step in the analysis of large civil structures (buildings, bridges, etc.) that present non-linearities. The correct implementation in larger cases would save costs without losing accuracy in the computational solution, since the degrees of freedom to be studied are significantly reduced considering that in the case study, the discretization of the structure was reduced from 3500 elements to about 250.

The non-intrusive global–local analysis with 1D to 3D coupling presented a displacement error of 10% according to the tolerance used, showing good primal–dual compatibility. However, there may also be cases of higher stiffness structures, so mixed coupling can be used to improve compatibility. In addition, the ideal dimensions of the local model can be determined according to the crack location and thus verify the methodology obtaining the energy release rate.

The methodology used was verified through the commercial software SAP 2000, obtaining a similar number of iterations to convergence with respect to those obtained using Code_Aster applying it to a 3-story building, significantly reducing the execution time with an acceptable error. This result opens up the possibility to extend this methodology to the industry and use it in practical applications.

This work is limited to monotonic loads in order to study the effect of the non-intrusive methodology for crack propagation in 1D global models to 3D local models. As shown in the results presented of the different problems analyzed, the error is low and maintained for the different cases investigated. Therefore, for future research, the study of sequential loading for crack propagation could be studied in order to verify the effect of nonlinear 1D structures with localized cracks and also to study the effect on the development of the crack for this type of loads. Another topic to consider is to analyze more section types, lengths of the local model, and crack location, in order to present in future studies a criterion to decide the length of the local model that optimizes the global–local non-intrusive analysis, given the properties of the problem. Finally, as was presented in this study, the crack propagation was analyzed considering only steel frame elements. Nevertheless, other materials and specific nonlinear behavior could be studied, such as the total crack strain model for reinforced concrete local models.

Author Contributions: Conceptualization, I.F.-H. and M.J.-Z.; methodology, I.F.-H. and M.J.-Z.; software, I.F.-H. and M.J.-Z.; validation, I.F.-H., M.J.-Z. and J.H.; formal analysis, M.J.-Z. and J.H.; investigation, I.F.-H., M.J.-Z. and J.H.; resources, M.J.-Z. and I.F.-H.; data curation, M.J.-Z. and I.F.-H.; writing—original draft preparation, M.J.-Z. and I.F.-H.; writing—review and editing, J.H.; visualization, M.J.-Z. and I.F.-H.; supervision, I.F.-H.; project administration, J.H.; funding acquisition, I.F.-H. and J.H. All authors have read and agreed to the published version of the manuscript.

Funding: This research received no external funding. The APC was funded by the Faculty of Engineering, Campus Curicó, University of Talca.

Institutional Review Board Statement: Not applicable.

Informed Consent Statement: Not applicable.

Data Availability Statement: Code_Aster files for the global–local 1D to 3D method can be downloaded from the following link: https://github.com/igfuenzalida/global_local_1D_3D (accessed on 14 May 2023).

Conflicts of Interest: The authors declare no conflict of interest.

References

1. AISC Committee. *Specification for Structural Steel Buildings (ANSI/AISC 360-10)*; American Institute of Steel Construction: Chicago, IL, USA, 2010.
2. AISC Committee. *Seismic Provision for Structural Steel Buildings (ANSI/AISC 341-16)*; American Institute of Steel Construction: Chicago, IL, USA, 2016.
3. Frangopol, D.M.; Soliman, M. Life-cycle of structural systems: Recent achievements and future directions. *Struct. Infrastruct. Eng.* **2019**, *12*, 46–65.
4. Cui, W. A state-of-the-art review on fatigue life prediction methods for metal structures. *J. Mar. Sci. Technol.* **2002**, *7*, 43–56. [CrossRef]

5. Moës, N.; Dolbow, J.; Belytschko, T. A finite element method for crack growth without remeshing. *Int. J. Numer. Methods Eng.* **1999**, *46*, 131–150. [CrossRef]
6. Belytschko, T.; Black, T. Elastic crack growth in finite elements with minimal remeshing. *Int. J. Numer. Methods Eng.* **1999**, *45*, 601–620. [CrossRef]
7. Khoei, A.R. *Extended Finite Element Method: Theory and Applications*; John Wiley & Sons: New York, NY, USA, 2014.
8. Erkmen, R.E.; Saleh, A.; Afnani, A. Incorporating local effects in the predictor step of the iterative global-local analysis of beams. *Int. J. Multiscale Comput. Eng.* **2016**, *14*, 455–477. [CrossRef]
9. Valipour, H.R.; Foster, S.J. Nonlocal Damage Formulation for a Flexibility-Based Frame Element. *J. Struct. Eng.* **2009**, *135*, 1213–1221. [CrossRef]
10. Roux, F.X. Method of finite element tearing and interconnecting and its parallel solution algorithm. *Int. J. Numer. Methods Eng.* **1991**, *32*, 1205–1227.
11. Pebrel, J.; Rey, C.; Gosselet, P. A Nonlinear Dual-Domain Decomposition Method: Application to Structural Problems with Damage. *Int. J. Multiscale Comput. Eng.* **2008**, *6*, 251–262. [CrossRef]
12. Hinojosa, J.; Allix, O.; Guidault, P.A.; Cresta, P. Domain decomposition methods with nonlinear localization for the buckling and post-buckling analyses of large structures. *Adv. Eng. Softw.* **2014**, *70*, 13–24. [CrossRef]
13. Guidault, P.A. Une Stratégie de Calcul pour les Structures Fissurées: Analyse Locale-Globale et Approche Multiéchelle Pour la Fissuration. Ph.D. Thesis, École Normale Supérieure de Cachan-ENS Cachan, Gif-sur-Yvette, France, 2007.
14. Kerfriden, P.; Allix, O.; Gosselet, P. A three-scale domain decomposition method for the 3D analysis of debonding in laminates. *Comput. Mech.* **2009**, *44*, 343–362. [CrossRef]
15. Oumaziz, P.; Gosselet, P.; Boucard, P.A.; Guinard, S. A non-invasive implementation of a mixed domain decomposition method for frictional contact problems. *Comput. Mech.* **2017**, *60*, 797–812. [CrossRef]
16. Allix, O.; Gosselet, P. Non intrusive global/local coupling techniques in solid mechanics: An introduction to different coupling strategies and acceleration techniques. In *Modeling in Engineering Using Innovative Numerical Methods for Solids and Fluids*; Springer: Berlin/Heidelberg, Germany, 2020; pp. 203–220.
17. Whitcomb, J.D. Iterative global/local finite element analysis. *Comput. Struct.* **1991**, *40*, 1027–1031. [CrossRef]
18. Gendre, L.; Allix, O.; Gosselet, P.; Comte, F. Non-intrusive and exact global/local techniques for structural problems with local plasticity. *Comput. Mech.* **2009**, *44*, 233–245. [CrossRef]
19. Duval, M.; Passieux, J.C.; Salaün, M.; Guinard, S. Non-intrusive Coupling: Recent Advances and Scalable Nonlinear Domain Decomposition. *Arch. Comput. Methods Eng.* **2016**, *23*, 17–38. [CrossRef]
20. Gosselet, P.; Blanchard, M.; Allix, O.; Guguin, G. Non-invasive global–local coupling as a Schwarz domain decomposition method: Acceleration and generalization. *Adv. Model. Simul. Eng. Sci.* **2018**, *5*, 4. [CrossRef]
21. Fuenzalida-Henriquez, I.; Oumaziz, P.; Castillo-Ibarra, E.; Hinojosa, J. Global-Local non intrusive analysis with robin parameters: Application to plastic hardening behavior and crack propagation in 2D and 3D structures. *Comput. Mech.* **2022**, *69*, 965–978. [CrossRef]
22. EDF. *Code Aster, Analysis of Structures and Thermomechanics for Studies and Research*; Électricité de France: Paris, France, 2019.
23. Nayak, C.B.; Thakare, S.B. Seismic performance of existing water tank after condition ranking using non-destructive testing. *Int. J. Adv. Struct. Eng.* **2019**, *11*, 395–410. [CrossRef]
24. dos Santos, R.B.; Tamayo, J.L.P. Coupling SAP 2000 with ABC algorithm for truss optimization. *DYNA* **2020**, *87*, 102–111. [CrossRef]
25. Zandi, N.; Adlparvar, M.R.; Javan, A.L. Evaluation on Seismic Performance of Dual Steel Moment-Resisting Frame with Zipper Bracing System Compared to Chevron Bracing System Against Near-Fault Earthquakes. *J. Rehabil. Civ. Eng.* **2021**, *9*, 1–25. [CrossRef]
26. Tampubolon, S.P.; Mulyani, A.S. Analysis and calculation of wooden framework structure by using Structural Analysis Program (SAP)-2000 and method of joint. *IOP Conf. Ser. Earth Environ. Sci.* **2021**, *878*, 012042. [CrossRef]
27. Zhang, Y.; Madenci, E.; Zhang, Q. ANSYS implementation of a coupled 3D peridynamic and finite element analysis for crack propagation under quasi-static loading. *Eng. Fract. Mech.* **2022**, *260*, 108179. [CrossRef]
28. Fageehi, Y.A. Fatigue Crack Growth Analysis with Extended Finite Element for 3D Linear Elastic Material. *Metals* **2021**, *11*, 397. [CrossRef]
29. Alshoaibi, A.M.; Fageehi, Y.A. 3D modelling of fatigue crack growth and life predictions using ANSYS. *Ain Shams Eng. J.* **2022**, *13*, 101636. [CrossRef]
30. Su, X.; Yang, Z.; Liu, G. Finite Element Modelling of Complex 3D Static and Dynamic Crack Propagation by Embedding Cohesive Elements in Abaqus. *Acta Mech. Solida Sin.* **2010**, *23*, 271–282. [CrossRef]
31. Molnár, G.; Gravouil, A.; Seghir, R.; Réthoré, J. An open-source Abaqus implementation of the phase-field method to study the effect of plasticity on the instantaneous fracture toughness in dynamic crack propagation. *Comput. Methods Appl. Mech. Eng.* **2020**, *365*, 113004. [CrossRef]
32. Távara, L.; Moreno, L.; Paloma, E.; Mantič, V. Accurate modelling of instabilities caused by multi-site interface-crack onset and propagation in composites using the sequentially linear analysis and Abaqus. *Compos. Struct.* **2019**, *225*, 110993. [CrossRef]
33. Gontarz, J.; Podgórski, J. Comparison of Various Criteria Determining the Direction of Crack Propagation Using the UDMGINI User Procedure Implemented in Abaqus. *Materials* **2021**, *14*, 3382. [CrossRef]

34. Navidtehrani, Y.; Betegón, C.; Martínez-Pañeda, E. A simple and robust Abaqus implementation of the phase field fracture method. *Appl. Eng. Sci.* **2021**, *6*, 100050. [CrossRef]
35. Noii, N.; Aldakheel, F.; Wick, T.; Wriggers, P. An adaptive global–local approach for phase-field modeling of anisotropic brittle fracture. *Comput. Methods Appl. Mech. Eng.* **2020**, *361*, 112744. [CrossRef]
36. Passieux, J.C.; Réthoré, J.; Gravouil, A.; Baietto, M.C. Local / global non-intrusive crack propagation simulation using a multigrid X-FEM solver. *Comput. Mech.* **2013**, *52*, 1381–1393. [CrossRef]
37. Blanchard, M.; Allix, O.; Gosselet, P.; Desmeure, G. Space/time global/local noninvasive coupling strategy: Application to viscoplastic structures. *Finite Elem. Anal. Des.* **2019**, *156*, 1–12. [CrossRef]
38. El Kerim, A.; Gosselet, P.; Magoulès, F. Asynchronous global–local non-invasive coupling for linear elliptic problems. *Comput. Methods Appl. Mech. Eng.* **2023**, *406*, 115910. [CrossRef]
39. Magoulès, F.; Gbikpi-Benissan, G. JACK: An asynchronous communication kernel library for iterative algorithms. *J. Supercomput.* **2017**, *73*, 3468–3487. [CrossRef]
40. Negrello, C.; Gosselet, P.; Rey, C. A new impedance accounting for short- and long-range effects in mixed substructured formulations of nonlinear problems. *Int. J. Numer. Methods Eng.* **2018**, *114*, 675–693. [CrossRef]
41. Gendre, L.; Allix, O.; Gosselet, P. A two-scale approximation of the Schur complement and its use for non-intrusive coupling. *Int. J. Numer. Methods Eng.* **2011**, *87*, 889–905. [CrossRef]
42. Peña, L.; Hinojosa, J. Implementation of a new expression for the search direction in simulations of structures with buckling and post-buckling: "Two-Scale Impedance". *J. Comput. Appl. Math.* **2022**, *403*, 113799. [CrossRef]
43. Aldakheel, F.; Noii, N.; Wick, T.; Wriggers, P. A global–local approach for hydraulic phase-field fracture in poroelastic media. *Comput. Math. Appl.* **2021**, *91*, 99–121. [CrossRef]
44. Crisfield, M.A. *A Fast Incremental/Iterative Solution Procedure That Handles "Snap-Through"*; Computers and Structures: Walnut Creek, CA, USA, 1981. [CrossRef]
45. Oñate, E. *Structural Analysis with the Finite Element Method Linear Statics*; Lecture Notes on Numerical Methods in Engineering and Sciences; Springer: Dordrecht, The Netherlands, 2013. [CrossRef]
46. EDF. *Code Aster, Manuel d'Utilisation Opérateur CALC G*; Électricité de France: Paris, France, 2019.
47. Lan, M.; Waisman, H.; Harari, I. A direct analytical method to extract mixed-mode components of strain energy release rates from Irwin's integral using extended finite element method. *Int. J. Numer. Methods Eng.* **2013**, *95*, 1033–1052. [CrossRef]
48. Sun, C.T.; Wang, C.Y. A new look at energy release rate in fracture mechanics. *Int. J. Fract.* **2002**, *113*, 295–307. [CrossRef]
49. Computers & Structures, Inc. *SAP2000, Modelado y Calculo de Estructuras a Traves de Elementos Finitos*; Computers & Structures, Inc.: Walnut Creek, CA, USA, 2022.

MDPI
St. Alban-Anlage 66
4052 Basel
Switzerland
Tel. +41 61 683 77 34
Fax +41 61 302 89 18
www.mdpi.com

Mathematics Editorial Office
E-mail: mathematics@mdpi.com
www.mdpi.com/journal/mathematics

www.ingramcontent.com/pod-product-compliance
Lightning Source LLC
Chambersburg PA
CBHW061544220926
51850CB00005B/249
* 9 7 8 3 0 3 6 5 8 2 8 4 9 *